PROPERTY ON TRIAL
Canadian Cases in Context

PATRONS OF THE SOCIETY

Blake, Cassels & Graydon LLP

Gowlings

Lax O'Sullivan Scott Lisus LLP

McCarthy Tétrault LLP

Osler, Hoskin & Harcourt LLP

Paliare Roland Rosenberg Rothstein LLP

Torkin Manes LLP

Torys LLP

WeirFoulds LLP

The Osgoode Society is supported by a grant from
The Law Foundation of Ontario.

THE LAW
FOUNDATION
OF ONTARIO

The Society also thanks The Law Society of Upper Canada
for its continuing support.

PROPERTY ON TRIAL

Canadian Cases in Context

edited by

ERIC TUCKER, JAMES MUIR, & BRUCE ZIFF

Published for The Osgoode Society for Canadian Legal History
by Irwin Law

Toronto

Printed and bound by CPI Group (UK) Ltd, Croydon, CR0 4YY

ISBN 978-1-55221-296-7

Library and Archives Canada Cataloguing in Publication

Property on trial : Canadian cases in context / edited by Eric Tucker, James Muir, & Bruce Ziff.

Includes bibliographical references and index.

ISBN 978-1-55221-296-7

1. Property – Canada – Cases. 2. Right of property – Canada – Cases.

I. Tucker, Eric II. Muir, James, 1971– III. Ziff, Bruce H
IV. Osgoode Society for Canadian Legal History

KE618.P74 2012 346.7104 C2012-906131-X
KF561.P76 2012

The publisher acknowledges the financial support of the Government of Canada through the Book Publishing Industry Development Program (BPIDP) for its publishing activities.

We acknowledge the assistance of the OMDC Book Fund, an initiative of Ontario Media Development Corporation.

1 2 3 4 5 14 13 12

Contents

Foreword

DESPITE THE HUGE STRIDES made by Canadian legal history in recent decades, we do not know as much as we should about the law of property, a crucial aspect of most peoples' engagement with the law, past and present. The Osgoode Society is thus especially pleased to publish this volume, which deals with topics as varied as the Newfoundland seal hunt in the nineteenth century to the modern Vancouver planning process. Some cases are well known, such as the Murdoch family property controversy, others less so, but the overall scope is very broad—Quebec nuisance law, restrictive covenants, pollution control, rental housing and human rights, picketing, taking by economic regulation, the theft of information, and land use regulation. The authors employ the detailed case study approach, allowing them to investigate not only the development of legal doctrine in particular contexts, but also to show the effect on the legal process of litigants' determination, lawyering skills, the broader political and social environment, and judicial attitudes.

The purpose of the Osgoode Society for Canadian Legal History is to encourage research and writing in the history of Canadian law. The Society, which was incorporated in 1979 and is registered as a charity, was founded at the initiative of the Honourable R. Roy McMurtry, formerly attorney general for Ontario and chief justice of the province, and officials of the Law Society of Upper Canada. The Society seeks to stimulate the study of legal history in Canada by supporting researchers, collecting oral histories, and publishing volumes that contribute to legal-historical scholarship in Canada.

It has published 88 books on the courts, the judiciary, and the legal profession, as well as on the history of crime and punishment, women and law, law and economy, the legal treatment of ethnic minorities, and famous cases and significant trials in all areas of the law.

The annual report and information about membership may be obtained by writing to the Osgoode Society for Canadian Legal History, Osgoode Hall, 130 Queen Street West, Toronto, Ontario. M5H 2N6. Telephone: 416-947-3321. E-mail: mmacfarl@lsuc.on.ca. Website: Osgoodesociety.ca

R. Roy McMurtry
PRESIDENT

Jim Phillips
EDITOR-IN-CHIEF

Preface

THIS ANTHOLOGY HAS BEEN years in the making and over the course of that period we have accumulated many debts of gratitude.

This project was modelled on an earlier Osgoode Society collection, *Work on Trial: Canadian Labour Law Struggles*, which in turn was inspired by an American series of works devoted to the underlying history of leading cases in various fields. Assembling a collection of Canadian property law micro-histories was the brain-child of Eric Tucker, who co-edited the labour law collection (along with Judy Fudge). The lessons from that endeavour were of great benefit in the conceptualization, development, and completion of this book.

This was both an individual and collective project. The editors compiled a list of potential case studies, but the authors were given considerable scope in the selection of cases and the manner of inquiry. In June 2010, contributors to the volume met at the University of Alberta in Edmonton for a two-day intensive workshop. Major funding for this event was provided by a grant awarded by the Social Sciences and Humanities Research Council of Canada. The Faculty of Law at the University of Alberta provided additional financial support, as did the Osgoode Society, and Osgoode Hall Law School.

During the workshop sessions, draft chapters were circulated, presented, and critiqued, and plans for the project as a whole were discussed. The papers were presented not by the authors, but rather by commentators. Most were graduate students in law or history; several were undergraduates; some members of law faculties. We are grateful to all of those who assumed this role: Sean Atkins, Michael Begg, Erin Black, David Hayman, Sarah Hamill, Felix Hoehn, Alex Kennedy, Kim Korven, Pooja Parmar, Steven Penney, Katie Pollock, Mary Stokes, and Maxwell Zhira. Mary Jane Mossman served as a general discussant during the seminars. We are grateful that she was willing to memorialize her commentary, which appears as an afterword in this volume.

Alex Kennedy, Suzette Golden, and Catherine Healy Varley did a preliminary edit of all of the papers. Administrative support for the workshop and the other aspects of this project was provided by Kim Cordeiro, Melissa Hartley, Racqel Kokaram, Merle Metke, Yolanda Poffenroth, Sandra Teves, and Tim Young at the University of Alberta.

We are also grateful for the support, in many and varied forms, received by Irwin Law, and in particular for the assistance provided by Jeffrey Miller; designer, Carmen Siu; and copy editor, Melissa Wilson. Two anonymous readers reviewed the essays. Their extensive comments greatly enhanced the overall quality of the finished product.

A special note of thanks is due to the Osgoode Society for Canadian Legal History and to Jim Phillips, the Society's editor-in-chief. In addition to co-authoring a chapter, Professor Phillips assisted at every stage of the process. He read the papers, often more than once, and provided detailed suggestions for each one. His enthusiastic support and sage counsel, on matters large and small, proved invaluable.

Finally, James Muir would like to thank Karine De Champlain, Cameron (who was there from the start), Katherine and Holden (who appeared by the end); Eric Tucker would like to thank Lisa Brand for all her good properties, not the least of which is her tolerance of his bouts of distraction; and Bruce Ziff wishes to acknowledge the support, and ultimately the forgiveness of, his family, Hannah, Eli, and Barb.

Eric Tucker
James Muir
Bruce Ziff

16 May 2012

Introduction

James Muir

You are currently reading a piece of property. If you bought this book, you can do what you want to with it: write notes in the margins, tear out pages, lend it to someone, gift it to someone else, or sell it online or to a used bookstore. But there are limits: Even though you may have bought the book, you do not own the content. At least as it is expressed in the work, that remains the property of the authors (and their heirs) or the publishers for some time. You cannot reprint the material and sell it to others without receiving permission to do so. You probably know all of this already. That you know these things intuitively is a sign of the ubiquity of property and property law principles in modern life.

The principles and rules of property law in Canada find their origins in the common law, statutes, and legal codes. In each case, the principles and rules are often drawn from court cases or are given full meaning only when interpreted by judges. This is a book of stories about historic property law cases and about disputes that ultimately led to or reflect upon some of the basic principles and rules of property law in Canada today. The authors of the chapters that follow each trace one or more cases, explaining the background incidents and personalities that led it to becoming a legal conflict in the first place, describing the events at court(s) or hearing(s) and reflecting on the long-term effects of the cases. Many of the chapters that follow deal with "leading cases": cases already taught in Canadian law schools and regularly referred to by lawyers and judges in making legal arguments and rendering decisions.[1] Others were before now more obscure but provide a valuable window onto the law, helping to show missed opportunities for legal change or simply the law in action.

Whether you encounter law through popular culture, law school, or legal practice, you are likely to see the law through the prism of cases. In books, movies, and television, cases are used because they make for coherent narratives.[2] Verdicts may be important, but legal reasoning almost never is.[3] In law school, students learn the law by reading and discussing the rulings judges make in specific cases.[4] In practice, common law litigators argue cases relying, in part, on rulings from previous cases. For lawyers in training or practice, the story behind the case is almost always irrelevant — what matters are only the facts and reasoning the judges memorialize in their decisions, and more specifically, those parts of the decision that can be applied generally in similar instances and thus that make a rule. In historical case studies like those in this volume, both the story of the dispute and the decision are important.

The case as understood in popular culture or the law school is mythical. Cases are part of many events and seldom comprise coherent or complete narratives without the application of an author's hand. Most decisions are of little interest, and even those that are referred to in the future often only partially resolve the issues that led to the case in the first place. But there is an element of truth to the myth: some cases are interesting as part of a larger story or because the decisions may be interesting, instructive, or generally important. The cases in this volume are unique and represent innovation in the law. They were chosen often for their historical and contemporary importance to a broad understanding of property law. The cases may stand for legal principles that remain applicable today, but none are typical, none can be said to represent the general practice of law, and many do not necessarily reflect intellectual or legal trends of their time or today.

Case studies like the ones here are one of the most popular methods of presenting legal history research in Canada,[5] and this is the second volume in a series of case studies on specific areas of Canadian law.[6] The value of such studies as these is twofold. First, these studies provide some explanation of particular legal developments within their historical context. The underlying theory behind the chapters in this book is that the law is contingent on the circumstances of litigants, the skills of lawyers, the philosophies of judges, and the social, political, and economic conditions of the time and place. This does not mean that there is no law there or that every legal act is capricious. Rather, these studies show that law works and changes within a context and that understanding the case (if not a proposition in a judgment) can best be done by seeing the case within its context.

Second, these cases constitute a history of property law doctrines in Canada. To date, historical study of Canadian property law has focused primarily on real property (i.e., land) and the nineteenth and early twentieth centuries. The book-length studies have been about real property legal regimes,[7] as part of a growing British Commonwealth literature on colonization,[8] or in relation to women's,[9] religious,[10] and First Nations' history.[11] This literature, however, does not begin to cover the range of issues faced in property law and regulation. The legal history of hunting, copyright, commons, or zoning, for example, have been approached in articles dispersed through academic journals and essay collections or contained as parts of some monographs,[12] but there has been no concerted attempt to address the history of these areas in law in conjunction with each other to map out Canadian property law as a whole. There have been attempts at general histories of property law in other parts of the common law world, but these have, overwhelmingly, been devoted to a single aspect of property, most often real property or land.[13] While this collection is not a thorough history of property law in Canada, the variety of cases studied gives it a broader sweep than the work that has come before.

One of the themes that runs through the historiography is the relationship between private and public interests in property and the role of the state. Almost all of the chapters here are concerned with private property, but the state and the public interest is a presence throughout. In some chapters, the state, be it federal (Phillips and Martin), provincial (McCallum), or municipal (Blomley, Harris, Kaplinsky), is engaged directly as a litigant. Through their actions, governments can alter the rights property owners have to their property (Phillips and Martin, Harris), prevent would-be owners from acquiring property (Kaplinsky, McCallum), or limit how people can use public (Blomley) or private (Kyer) property. Investigating the direct role of government in property law and litigation is important in understanding how property rights are acquired and can be limited in a liberal democratic society. Other chapters here, however, show that even in cases ostensibly between private parties, the state may play a key role by establishing some of the rules that lead to litigation. In the sealing capture cases discussed by Ziff, the parties are private and the property in question was created by them out of the wild, but the state looms as regulator of the industry. The role of statutes in creating and regulating property rights is evident in the property stories told by Tucker and Farnese. In still others, the cases lived on in the political arena long after the litigation was done. Jamie Benedickson shows how a handful of small businessmen facing serious economic loss could launch a suit against the paper company KVP that would eventually force the company to defend itself in court, in public, and finally in the provincial legislature. In *Murdoch v Murdoch*, justice for women like Irene Murdoch only came due to the country-wide organizing by feminists to seek a political reversal of the law as expressed by the Supreme Court. Overall, the cases here illustrate that even where the state is not a party, property law disputes are often cases in the shadow of the state.

A problem with any case study–based approach, however, is that legal cases arise out of those unusual disputes between people, businesses, or governments where one party decides that a legal resolution is necessary. The overwhelming majority of disputes are settled or abandoned without either party seriously considering litigation or, having solicited legal advice, before ever getting to trial and producing a judgment. This may happen in the shadow of the law, but legal rules may not be as important as the customs of those involved.[14] When a potential case is dropped before a ruling is made, as in one of the Eaton Centre cases Eric Tucker discusses in this volume, appeals or challenges to legal orthodoxy are not made.

Only a minority of individuals have the capacity and perseverance to spend emotional, intellectual, financial, and time resources to fight a case, especially if it involves a novel claim that will likely go through appeals to the highest levels of the judicial system. The case ends when the legal options or resources (fiscal, emotional, or otherwise) for one or more of the parties are exhausted. In his chapter, Philip Girard shows that *Galbraith v Madawaska Club* arose because of a particularly obstinate plaintiff in a long standing battle with the club and others. In *Regina v Stewart*, Ian Kyer argues that the prosecution was pursued primarily as a test case against an easier opponent than the primary object of concern (the Church of Scientology); neither the Crown nor anyone else involved had much interest in the fate of Wayne John Stewart. The stories are thus not simply stories of serious wrongs that are righted (or attempted to be); rather, they are the stories of peculiar circumstances and tenacious litigants whose fights over mundane or unusual disputes brought them broader legal or historical attention.

Each chapter in the book that follows can be read on its own, and the chapters can be read in any order. As editors, we have chosen to place the chapters chronologically. In doing so, we are not making an argument about the progressive development of the law over time. Rather, we wish to show how cases are contingent to their specific times and otherwise let readers draw their own links between cases and stories.

The book begins with Bruce Ziff's discussion of how private property rights in wild seals were created and secured in the Newfoundland sealing industry. The dispute here deals with the most elemental of private property issues: How, in law, can someone clearly establish ownership of something that in nature was not private property?

Having established where at least some private property comes from, the next several chapters are about the limits of private property owners' rights in relation to others, particularly neighbours and family. The chapters by Eric H. Reiter and Jamie Benedickson explore the limits of a property owner's rights vis-à-vis one's neighbours. Philip Girard's chapter involves a case testing the strength of the limits a property owner and neighbours can impose on the owner's inheritors and descendents. Vanessa Gruben, Angela Cameron, and Angela Chaisson pick up the discussion by looking at property within the family by interrogating the very idea of individual ownership within a family, especially in the context of family breakdown.

The public interest is invoked in these early chapters, but in the next five chapters it becomes much more important, often through the direct engagement of the state. Frank Luce and Karen Schucher describe an early Ontario Human Rights case that tested the state's ability to limit a property owner's power to discriminate in finding tenants. Eran Kaplinsky's chapter, on the zoning battle over the creation of a Zoroastrian temple in North York, details how different groups of property owners engaged with government officials to try to shape their neighbourhood. The *Manitoba Fisheries* case discussed by Phillips and Martin established limits on the state's ability to freely interfere in private property to advance a government's presumption of the public interest. The cases Tucker traces regarding Toronto's Eaton Centre offer a contrast to the other cases in this section, as they test whether there are public interest limits on private property owners absent direct state interference. McCallum's discussion of *Morgan and Jacobson* returns the reader to state action in a public's interest, in this case the legality of provincial government law and policy defining who could own how much real property in Prince Edward Island. In each case, public interest in using or acquiring property was asserted. As a whole, these chapters show how much power the Canadian state has in interfering with private property rights and how that power is constrained through expectations of good behaviour or requirements to compensate.

To this point, the chapters have traced the creation of private property, the legal controls imposed on property owners, and the limits of their rights against the state. The next three chapters, in different ways, investigate claims about misappropriations of property. Ian Kyer's chapter on *R. v Stewart* uses a case of alleged theft to question the limits of what could in fact be considered private property for the purpose of the criminal law. Nicholas Blomley shows how the City of Vancouver came to be able to legally limit the capacity of people to beg on public property through defining certain activities as misuses. In *Monsanto Canada Inc. v Schmeiser,* the dispute involved Percy Schmeiser's alleged misuse of a Monsanto patented canola seed. Property is often defined as the capacity to exclude or limit use by others; these three chapters deal with tests of that capacity.

All of the chapters in the book deal with Canadian cases, and as will be clear, all of the cases owe a great deal to their Canadian contexts. The final case, however, is Canadian in a different way. The doctrine of *de facto* expropriation described in *Manitoba Fisheries* owed a great deal to the American legal doctrine of regulatory takings. Douglas Harris' chapter on *C.P.R. v The City of Vancouver* returns to that doctrine and the limits the Supreme Court of Canada placed on it. As both Harris in his chapter, and Mary Jane Mossman in her afterword note, the case makes for a clear distinction between Canadian law and that of at least one other common law country.

As a whole the chapters canvass many of the core issues in private property law as it changed over the last 150 years. The cases are drawn from across Canada and from many different levels and sorts of courts and tribunals. Inevitably, however, there are a great many important topics in Canadian property law that are left out. The biggest absence concerns Aboriginal property rights. After much discussion, the editors decided that the distinct issues involved in Aboriginal property could not be effectively addressed in the space possible in this sort of collection. Moreover, Aboriginal property, like communal property (which is also ignored) is distinct from the private property that is at the core of the cases discussed here. Finally, the major questions of property law from the nineteenth century and earlier have been left out of this book. Like any piece of property, this book must be delimited. Within its borders, however, there are many places to go and stories to hear.

Notes

1 The standard for these sorts of studies was set by Brian Simpson in a series of essays beginning with "Legal liability for bursting reservoirs: the historical context of *Rylands v. Fletcher* (1868) LR 3 HL 330," *The Journal of Legal Studies* vol 13 (June 1984) at 209-64, and culminating in his *Leading Cases in the Common Law* (Oxford: Clarendon, 1995): rather than just collecting the case reports, or analyzing them based on their legal ruling or the facts as reported, Simpson dug into the backgrounds of the nine cases he studied to explain the litigation and the rulings in their historical context.

2 See, for example, the movies *Rashomon* (1950), *Witness for the Prosecution* (1957), *To Kill a Mockingbird* (1962), *The Verdict* (1982), or *Erin Brockovich* (2000), or the television shows *Perry Mason* (1957–1966), *The People's Court* (1981–present) or *Law & Order* (1990-2010)

3 One exception to this is William Gaddis' *A Frolic of His Own: A Novel* (New York: Simon & Schuster, 1994), which includes several complete judicial decisions.

4 The importance of the individual case is central to the popular culture of law regardless of jurisdiction. The law school focus on cases is generally peculiar to the common law world: England and many (although not all) of Britain's current and former colonies.

5 For example, see Constance Backhouse's books *Petticoats and Prejudice* (Toronto: The Osgoode Society and the Woman's Press, 1991), *Colour-Coded* (Toronto: The Osgoode Society and the University of Toronto Press, 1999), *The Heiress versus the Establishment: Mrs. Campbell's Campaign for Legal Justice*, with Nancy Backhouse (Vancouver: The Osgoode Society and University of British Columbia Press, 2004), and *Carnal Crimes* (Toronto: The Osgoode Society and Irwin Law, 2008) as well as James W St G Walker, *"Race," Rights and the Law in the Supreme Court of Canada: Historical Case Studies* (Waterloo: The Osgoode Society and Wilfred Laurier Press, 1997), Robert Sharpe's historical books *The Last Day, the Last Hour: The Currie Libel Trial* (Toronto: The Osgoode Society and University of Toronto Press, 1988 and 2009), *The Persons Case: The Origins and Legacy of the Fight For Legal Personhood*, with Patricia McMahon, (Toronto: The Osgoode Society and University of Toronto Press, 2007), *The Lazier Murder: Prince Edward County, 1884* (Toronto: The Osgoode Society and University of Toronto Press, 2011), or the *Canadian State Trials* series, edited by Murray Greenwood (vol 1-2), Barry Wright (vol 1-3), and Susan Binnie (vol 3) (all Toronto: University of Toronto Press, 1996, 2002, 2009).

6 The first volume is Judy Fudge and Eric Tucker, eds, *Work on Trial: Canadian Labour Law Struggles* (Toronto: The Osgoode Society and Irwin Law, 2010). These volumes are in part inspired by the "Law Stories" series from the US that began with Michael C. Dorf, ed, *Constitutional Law Stories* (New York: Foundation Press, 2004).

7 See, for a recent example, Greg Taylor, *The Law of the Land: The Advent of the Torrens System in Canada* (Toronto: Osgoode Society for Canadian Legal History and University of Toronto Press, 2008).

8 See, for example, and John C Weaver, *The Great Land Rush and the Making of the Modern World, 1650-1900* (Montreal: McGill-Queen's University Press, 2003) or the

collection AR Buck, John PS McLaren, and Nancy E Wright, *Despotic Dominion: Property Rights in British Settler Societies* (Vancouver: University of British Columbia Press, 2005).

9 See, for example, Lori Chambers, *Married women and property law in Victorian Ontario,* (Toronto: the Osgoode Society for Canadian Legal History, 1997) or Bettina Bradbury, *Wife to widow: lives, laws, and politics in nineteenth-century Montreal,* (Vancouver: University of British Columbia Press, 2011).

10 Alvin Esau, *The Courts and the Colonies: The Litigation of Hutterite Church Disputes* (Vancouver: University of British Columbia Press, 2004).

11 Some recent examples include Douglas C Harris, *Landing Native Fisheries: Indian Reserves and Fishing Rights in British Columbia, 1849-1925* (Vancouver: University of British Columbia Press, 2008) and Hamar Foster, Heather Raven, and Jeremy Webber, eds, *Let Right Be Done: Aboriginal Title, the Calder Case, and the Future of Indigenous Rights,* (Vancouver: University of British Columbia Press, 2007).

12 See the bibliography by Ziff at the conclusion of this volume.

13 See, for example, AWB Simpson, *A History of the Land Law,* Second Edition (Oxford: Oxford University Press, 1986) on England/Great Britain; AR Buck, *The Making of Australian Property Law,* (Sydney: Federation Press, 2006) on Australia. The focus on real property has been less strong in US legal history, in part because of the looming presence of slavery, and thus property in people, the presence of property rights in the US Bill of Rights and an intellectual history tradition concerned with the ideas of the revolutionaries and early republicans. See, for example, Stephen Michael Best, *The Fugitive's Properties: Law and the Poetics of Possession,* (Chicago: University of Chicago Press, 2004), James W Ely, *The Guardian of Every Other Right: A Constitutional History of Property Rights,* (New York: Oxford University Press, 1992), and Jennifer Nedelsky, *Private Property and the Limits of American Constitutionalism: the Madisonian Framework and its Legacy,* (Chicago: University of Chicago Press, 1990). A recent exception to these trends in the common law world or the United States in particular is Stuart Banner, *American Property: A History of How, Why, and What We Own,* (Cambridge, Mass: Harvard University Press, 2011), which considers a very broad range of property from real to intellectual.

14 The classic investigation of this phenomenon from a legal studies perspective is Stuart Macauley, "Non-Contractual Relations in Business: a preliminary study," *American Sociological Review* 28:1 (Feb. 1963), 55–67.

The Law of Property in Animals, Newfoundland-Style

Bruce Ziff[1]

Two men of some other sealer's crew frozen to death were always two men less in the power of a rival ship. Even so slight a factor was something in the incredibly tense rivalry of the seal-hunt. Azariah Stabb was not hard-hearted . . . But if it were God's will that any rival of his should lose two men, who was he to question the inscrutable ways of Providence.[2]

Introduction

IT WAS 17 APRIL 1869, in Green Bay, just off the northern coast of Newfoundland. A schooner called the *Brothers* lay jammed in the ice some distance from an ice pan containing a large number of seal pelts that had been gathered by its crew several days earlier. As the floes migrated, this pan moved within close proximity to a second schooner, the *Barbara*. Its crew hauled and stowed the pelts. Given the prevailing weather and sailing conditions, had the *Barbara*'s crew not done so, this catch might well have been lost for good. Not long after the ships returned to port, a lawsuit sparked by these events was launched. In essence, the Newfoundland Supreme Court was called upon to determine whether the second schooner was entitled to claim the pelts if the first had been rendered unable to do so.

The ruling, found in *Clift v Kane*,[3] is a central authority among a cluster of Newfoundland cases heard over about a twenty-six-year span (1858 to 1884)

SS *Nimrod*, one of the ships involved in the case of *Doyle v Bartlett* (1872).

that addressed that question. These decisions engage fundamental property law principles and values, and are as rich and edifying as any of the classic authorities on possession in law. Despite this, they have languished in obscurity for well over a century.[4] My aim in the chapter is to bring them to the light of day and to explore some well-known doctrines and the ways in which these rules were adapted to local circumstances. More specifically, this paper examines how the generic principles governing the laws of capture and first occupancy were shaped by the courts to meet the needs of the Newfoundland sealers.

A Brief History of the Seal "Fishery"

THE SEAL HUNT HAS a long history. Centuries ago, the indigenous peoples of present-day Newfoundland captured seals; the skins and fat were used for sustenance, clothing, heat, and light.[5] European interest in the seal stocks began in the late sixteenth century, and a commercial fishery undertaken by English and French settlers is known to have existed since the beginning of the eighteenth century. The skins were used for such things as shoes, boots, harnesses, and portmanteaus. (There is no indication on the early literature that pelts were used for fur coats.) The fat was rendered into oil and was used in places such as Great Britain for lighting in mines and lighthouses, for lubricating machinery, and in the manufacturing of fine soap. The processed residue was used locally for fertilizer. Seal meat was a staple of the local diet.

As will be explained below,[6] the methods employed in the hunt have varied considerably over time. In the period under study (generally, the last half of the nineteenth century), gaffs and guns were used. Commonly, carcasses were "sculped" — cleaned — on the spot and then collected in pans (i.e., piles or groupings on the floes). Seals that were not sculped were said to be left "round." The pans were marked, usually with flags on long poles bearing an insignia. Often, the panned seals would be collected days after the killing.

The hunt is held in early spring to coincide with the migration of the harp seals from the Grand Banks to the Arctic, along a route that traverses the ice floes off northern Newfoundland. At that time of the year, the ice is fugacious and is in virtually continuous motion, typically shifting to the south or south-east at a speed of one or two knots.[7] Ocean currents, temperature fluctuations, and especially prevailing winds can affect the movement of the ice. These migrations can cause the floes to collide, fracture, or become compacted. When the floes coalesce, ships can be trapped for extended periods, and even crushed.[8] It is a very treacherous undertaking for sealers, and many lives have been lost in the process.

The current public outcry against the seal hunt can be traced back to the period following World War II. In fact, concern over the hunt dates from at least the nineteenth century. Consider this commentary from 1874:

> The fearful cruelties perpetrated year after year, and the enormous waste of life entailed by the reckless manner in which the seal fishery is prosecuted, are well known ... The accounts of the cruelties practised in sealing are sickening in the extreme, the only thing considered being how to deprive as great a number of their skin and blubber in as short a time as possible.[9]

Hence, even in the period under study, the hunt was conducted somewhat under a cloud of disapproval.

Possession and the Law of Animals

Lord Mansfield's famous pronouncement that possession is nine-tenths of the law[10] may (or may not) be empirically flawed, but it stressed the centrality of the concept within Anglo-Canadian property law. Possession serves several functions, and principal among these is its use as a means to identify and order ownership rights. As a legal construct, possession can be dissected into two parts: intention (or *animus*) and the requisite dominion or control (sometimes called *corpus* or *factum*). In its paradigmatic form, both of these elements are manifestly present; to knowingly hold an article firmly in one's hand amounts to possession in its highest form. But that degree of control is not always demanded. Possession of land, for example, is not accomplished through manucaption (manual holding) at all. In general, in a variety of factual and legal contexts, the elements of *animus* and *factum* are diluted, modified, and even fictionalized.[11]

The flexibility in the stated requirements of possession is apparent even in the relatively narrow setting of the law governing the ownership of wild animals. The starting points are straightforward. Title in wild animals was secured through capture; that is, by taking possession. And that title subsisted only so long as possession of the animal was retained.[12] Put another way: should the animal escape, the claim based on capture evaporated. As Beamish Murdoch explained: "If an animal naturally wild, has been partly tamed, or has been restrained or imprisoned, and regain[s] its natural liberty and habits, the right of property in it ceases."[13] Conversely, if the animal was killed, title is perfected; at that point it was, strictly, neither wild nor an animal.

The minimum level of control needed to count as capture generated a substantial body of case law. In the much-celebrated and oft-studied American case of *Pierson v Post* (circa 1805)[14] a dispute arose as to the ownership of a fox, hunted relentlessly by Post, but caught first by Pierson. It was Pierson (referred to by the dissenting judge as a "saucy intruder") who prevailed. The majority holding adopted a bright-line rule of capture in the name of certainty. The fact that Post had laboriously tracked down the animal and was at its heels (at least figuratively) was not enough to vest him with a property right. However, it was also acknowledged that a hard-and-fast rule of manucaption was not always demanded: the snaring an animal in a trap or net so as to deprive it of its natural liberty would normally suffice.[15] Moreover, the mortal wounding of an animal by a person who maintains hot pursuit was said to vest title in that hunter.[16]

The pliability of the law of capture is perhaps best illustrated for present purposes by reference to the rules that emerged to govern whaling. Robert Ellickson's study of whaling law identifies the variety of customary norms that operated.[17] Three fairly distinct approaches can be seen, which Ellickson demonstrated emerged in part owing to the nature and propensities of the whales being hunted,[18] and the kinds of technologies that were employed.

First, under the fast-fish, loose-fish rule, a whale was treated as the property of the whaler who had secured the animal by a line or other device to the vessel (or, one would assume, to a dock or other land-based location); that whale was said to be held "fast." However, if the connection was broken, the whale, whether alive or not, was now considered "loose" and was once again available for the taking.[19] A second rule declared that the iron holds the whale. Therefore, title could be acquired by successfully harpooning a whale provided that the fresh pursuit was maintained. Some cases held that if the whale was not marked by a waif (a flag) or with some similar device, it was necessary to secure the animal before a second party had begun to strip the blubber from the carcass.[20] In essence, the iron-holds-the-whale approach is a rendition of the hot pursuit exception described in *Pierson v Post*. One might even understand the first-cut rule as a means of determining whether the first party was close enough to the prey to be entitled to assert priority.

A third type of rule provided for some measure of sharing. That approach might be adopted, for example, when a whale is disabled by virtue of an attack by *A*, although it is ultimately captured by *B*.[21] For instance, in the leading case of *Ghen v Rich*,[22] *A* had killed a finback whale with a lance-bomb. The carcass, which had been washed ashore, was later found by *B*. There was nothing exceptional in all of this, for this form of hunting assumed that the whale would sink on being killed, later to surface bloated, at which point it could be apprehended. It was the local custom that the finder would receive a salvage fee. (Salvage is an admiralty law concept under which a party rescuing a ship or its cargo is entitled to a reward.) In the *Ghen* case, the custom of awarding a salvage payment for the recovery of the whale was endorsed by the Massachusetts court.[23]

The whaling cases, and the varied rules that emerged from them, demonstrate that possession when used as a shorthand method for determining entitlements is to be deployed purposively, not mechanically. Possession provided a clear rule of ownership in the name of efficiency. That value and other policy factors affect the construction of the legal definition of possession and the juridical uses to which it is put. In the context of whaling, Ellickson argued that these homemade rules, devised as they were within a relatively close-knit community, and later affirmed by the courts, were selected because they made economic sense. His thesis is that those involved in the industry embraced wealth-maximizing principles, and the courts, motivated by similar concerns, appreciated and therefore affirmed these longstanding tried and true commercial practices.[24]

One final element needs to be set out before attention can turn to the Newfoundland cases — the conventional meaning of the term "abandonment." Abandonment refers to the intentional divesting of a property interest. Its elements are, in substance, the obverse of those required for possession-taking.[25] The *factum* of abandonment is constituted by the loss or surrender of control. The *animus* is defined as an indifference to the fate of the object in question. This is a subjective state of mind. Both the *animus* and *factum* of abandonment must exist for at least one moment in time. Therefore, to decide resolutely that one's shoes are to be thrown out and replaced with a new pair does not produce abandonment as long as they remain stashed in the back of the closet. Likewise, if one loses a valuable piece of jewellery while hiking in the woods, it cannot be said to be abandoned even if the chance of recovery is extremely remote, and even if the owner walks away in despair expecting never to see it again. The search may have been abandoned, but not necessarily the item.

The Seal Disputes

THE FIRST REPORTED NEWFOUNDLAND decision in which a rule of capture is described is *Power v Jackman* (1859).[26] There, it was alleged that seals that had been killed, sculped, piled, and marked by the crew of the *Iris* had been wrongfully taken by members of the schooner *Roxanna*. In charging the (civil) jury, Judge Philip Francis Little[27] advanced the general proposition that the law governing ownership was the same whether on land or sea: taking possession and killing a wild animal gives rise to a perfected property interest. In the trial it had been suggested (apparently in oral testimony) that seals left on the floes were fair game for the first taker. That position was tersely dismissed as a doctrine likely to prompt confrontation and perhaps even bloodshed.

However, the charge details the circumstances under which the plaintiffs' claim could fail. If, owing to the weather, the movement of the ice and so forth, the chances that the plaintiff would be able to retrieve the seals were "so slender as to amount to an almost downcast and a hopeless pursuit,"[28] then the claimant's property rights would cease to exist. The jury must have felt that this test had not been met, for a verdict was returned awarding damages against the defendants. Two years later, in *Noel v Warren* (1861),[29] Little J instructed the jury in the same manner and again the plaintiff prevailed.

Pausing here, one can see that the principle described in these cases differs from what I will call the "generic rule of capture." Under that rule, the killing of a wild animal in one's possession renders title absolute. Continued possession is not necessary, as would be the case prior to the animal's death. As a corollary, we have seen that the loss of possession of an object is not, on its own, to be regarded as an abandonment. A subjective intention to abandon must also be shown. Hence, I will call the rule being described in these two early cases as one of "deemed abandonment."

In *Clift v Kane* (1870),[30] a sealing dispute was heard for the first time by the Supreme Court of Newfoundland sitting *en banc* (the entire court presiding as a court of appeal). The facts of this case were briefly set out at the beginning of this paper; a more detailed account is now needed. At issue was the ownership of about a thousand seals. Most of these had been sculped, piled, and flagged, while others had been cut open or simply left round. The sealers were from a schooner called the *Brothers,* and at the relevant time the ship was jammed in the ice in Green Bay, off northern Newfoundland. The crew headed out on foot over the ice, killing some 3,000 seals. Over the next several days, carcasses were hauled back to the ship.

All the while the defendant's schooner, the *Barbara,* was in the vicinity, and when the shifting of the floes put the defendants significantly closer to the seal pans than were the plaintiffs, the crew of the *Barbara* began hauling the seals on board. The plaintiff's crew did as well, but conditions limited the extent to which they could tow across the ice. Although ice shifted again shortly afterwards making the seals more accessible to the plaintiff's crew, it was assumed that the pelts had all been appropriated by that time and so no attempt was made to return to the pans.

The jury was directed to determine whether the plaintiff had taken sufficient possession of the carcasses following the killing, by piling, sculping, and marking. The jurors were also asked to consider whether the taking by the defendants (if proven) was done out of necessity to prevent the total loss of the pelts. If so, the defendant would be entitled to a set-off to reflect this act of salvage. The jury found for the plaintiff, but the quantum of the award did reflect an allowance for salvage. Put another way, they found that the plaintiffs "had not the power of recovering the seals at the ice."[31]

On appeal, the Full Court was divided as to the governing ownership principle. Chief Justice Sir Hugh W Hoyles,[32] with whom Justice John Hayward agreed, applied the generic rule of capture. The seals having being killed and marked, were to be treated as property in precisely the same manner as any other kind of inanimate personalty. In brief, the longstanding English authorities governed. If, once killed and taken into possession, the pelts were not later intentionally abandoned, title continued; so stated Blackstone and other learned authors.

The rule of deemed abandonment was said to be unsupported by authority, and unsound in principle. As to authority, the Chief Justice addressed the earlier Newfoundland decisions of *Power v Jackman* and *Noel v Warren*, which were outlined briefly above.[33] These were neither binding on the Full Court, nor had their resolutions turned on a defense of deemed abandonment; in both, the plaintiffs had succeeded fully. The instant case was thus treated as a matter of first impression.[34] It was added that had the Full Court previously adopted such a doctrine, the best course would be to overrule it rather than to perpetuate an error.

As to principle, it was essential to establish a rule that sufficiently recognized the time, labour, and risk associated with the actions of the first taker. To visit upon them a loss of entitlement owing to circumstances beyond their control seemed unjust. Likewise, it was opined that a liberal salvage payment would provide a sufficient inducement to crews that chanced upon another's pan. Furthermore, an entitlement based on the probable ability of the first ship to regain possession would render rights precarious and uncertain. This in turn might prompt some — out of a "desire for the fruits of another's industry"[35] — to seek to take advantage of a rule based on a conjecture about whether recapture was possible. Crews might in fact be tempted to raid pans and take their chances in court. While it was acknowledged that the salvage rule created comparable uncertainty, it was maintained that it would be less likely to tempt plundering.

Justice John Hayward agreed: the generic rule found in the ancient authorities should govern. A crew member who happened to lose a watch or ring in the course of seal hunting was not thereby deprived of title. Likewise, when property is jettisoned from a ship out of a concern for safety, the goods may be later recovered by legal action. In the context of the seal hunt, it was both just and reasonable that the labours of the hunters be rewarded, and, in turn, that those who rescue the collected pelts be entitled to compensation for salvage. Hayward J acknowledged that there was a widespread support among those involved in the seal fishery for the deemed abandonment rule. But that approach would entail a departure from the current law, which was a matter solely within the competence of the legislature.

Justice Sir Bryan Robinson dissented.[36] He regarded the two earlier decisions as having settled the law. These authorities established that to perfect title, the animals not only had to be killed and taken into possession, but also that the claimant must intend to return to collect the pelts and — of critical importance — retained a reasonable prospect of being able to recover them. Furthermore, he claimed that many similar disputes had been resolved by reference to deemed abandonment over the previous forty years. Whether the courts adopted custom or the law guided practice was not certain in his mind, only that the rule he would have applied had been accepted for four decades.[37]

Robinson J also accepted the fundamental idea that the law should reward labour, but not so long as the job remained half-complete. And while the generic rule described by Blackstone and others was appropriate for hunting on land, it was ill-suited to the conditions that exist for the seal hunt, where a carcass could, in a functional sense at least, still "escape"[38]:

> [I]n the seal-fishery of Newfoundland every one knows that killing the seal is only one of several steps in the process of reducing the pelt into possession, no doubt it is the first, then follows sculping, then hauling over the ice (in which act the pelt is often lost) and finally securing it on board ship; but so long as the seal remains unshipped it is exposed to various casualties, which may remove it beyond the power and possession of the killer as completely as if it were live in the water, and may prevent him effectuating the object of his enterprise.[39]

The compromise position of allowing the defendants a right of salvage was rejected as unavailable in actions based on trover. It was also unprecedented. Newfoundland courts were bound, it was stressed, to administer justice on the same principles that prevail in English law. In addition, Robinson J doubted that the majority's approach would actually produce rough justice:

> I am unable to discover any equity in making one sealer — who secures animals *ferae naturae* found adrift upon the ocean abandoned by the killer, and lost to all the world — pay any portion of their value — to another sealer who, although he killed them, had failed through the ordinary casualties of the fishery, to secure possession of them, and was obliged, however involuntarily, to abandon the pursuit of them.[40]

Two hypothetical scenarios were designed to underline the adverse consequences that would result from the adoption of the majority holding, which Robinson J regarded as a new doctrine. In one, he reasoned that a ship wrecked at sea could still claim title to the seals that had been taken aboard. Likewise, panned seals lost on the floes remained the property of a first ship even if its cargo holds were later filled to capacity with other pelts.

The dissent relied, as had the Chief Justice, on an argument based on certainty: discarding a well-established rule laid down through a long and uninterrupted series of cases was likely to promote litigation. It might also generate confusion within a commercial sphere that now involved vessels not only from Newfoundland but also the United States and Great Britain.[41] It was better "to stand upon ancient ways,"[42] leaving it to the legislature to intervene if reform was sought.

So the law stood — the generic rule applied, though it was complemented by a set-off for salvage. Two years later, *Doyle v Bartlett*[43] was heard before the Full Court. There, a schooner called the *Native Lass* was engaged in the seal hunt off Fogo Island (off the north-east coast of Newfoundland). Its captain, Doyle, spotted a flag flying some five or six kilometres off, and dispatched a crew of men to see what was there. He anticipated, no doubt, that the flag marked a pan full of seals lying dead on the ice floes.

The crew sent on this reconnaissance was at first unable to see other vessels in the vicinity, the fog being thick. However, as they approached the flags, they were able to discern two steamships, both spotted the day before, cutting through the ice under sail and steam power. One was the SS *Nimrod*, under the command of White; the other, the SS *Panther*, captained by Bartlett. There were about 800 panned seals marked by flags and canvas badges bearing the name *Nimrod*. The crew of the *Native Lass* then resolved that, as there was no one left to watch the seals, they were a "lawful prize" available for taking. Some of the men returned to the ship with seals in tow, while two remained on the site.

As the pelts were being taken by the men of the *Native Lass*, the *Panther* arrived in the vicinity, and claimed title to the marked pelts by virtue of the authority of White (captain of the *Nimrod*). As the markings suggested, the seals had been collected initially by the *Nimrod*. The seals had been hunted prior to 23 March 1870, as part of sealing operations that had spanned an area about 11 or 12 kilometres in circumference. Collection of the pans occurred between 28 March and 8 April. The crew of the *Panther*, much larger in number than that of the *Native Lass*, took control at the scene and began loading the pelts onto the *Panther*. Doyle, on behalf of the outfitters of the *Native Lass*, sued Bartlett, captain of the *Panther*.

At a jury trial held in Harbour Grace, the plaintiffs obtained a verdict for the value of 800 seal pelts. On appeal, Chief Justice Hoyles, who had presided over the trial, held that the verdict should be set aside except for 200 pelts. The judgment does not fully spell out his line of reasoning, but it must have run as follows: the *Panther*'s crew interfered with the actual possession of Doyle's crew as to 200 pelts. That possession, however obtained, was good against a subsequent wrongdoer. Hence, it was the jury's task to determine if the *Panther*'s crew had authority from the *Nimrod* to take the pelts. If so, the *Native Lass* claim was trumped by the *Panther*'s superior right (derived from the *Nimrod*'s superior right). The jury must have concluded that there was no such authority.

The Chief Justice disagreed with the jury's finding. He was of the view that White et al. (of the *Nimrod*) were the absolute owners of the pelts (citing *Clift v Kane*), and that they had gifted them to Bartlett (of the *Panther*). Nevertheless, the Chief Justice deferred to the jury's conclusion that Bartlett had no valid authority to take the pelts. Absent such authority, the pelts were up for grabs. As the crew of the plaintiff (the *Native Lass*) had managed to take actual possession of 200 of the 800 seal pelts before these were seized by the crew of the *Panther*, the plaintiff was entitled to recover for the value of 200 pelts.

Justice Robinson arrived at a similar result, but through a different line of analysis. His reasons for judgment contain an unapologetic reaffirmation of his minority opinion in *Clift v Kane*.[44] Indeed, Robinson J took the circumstances of the instant case as evidence of the appropriateness of his earlier position. The nature of the seal hunt, conducted on floes that partake somewhat of land but also have the mobility of water, create a unique setting requiring peculiar rules. A party could not retain property in seals left on the ice if there was no demonstrated ability to reclaim them:

> [S]o long as the killer of seal has the "*animus revertendi*" combined with the *potentia recuperandi,* no one has a legal right to interfere with him, but the moment he abandons the pursuit of the dead animals, either from inability to reach them or incapacity to stow them, that moment they revert to the common stock and again become the prize of the first finder who can secure them.[45]

Applying this reasoning to the present case, Robinson J held that White of the *Nimrod* had indeed lost title to the pan. Therefore, the purported gift from White to Doyle was ineffective. Instead, the crews of the two ships at the site of the pan were engaged in a race to take manual possession of the pelts. As Bartlett's crew had retrieved 200 pelts that Doyle's ship had already taken into possession, Bartlett was liable to that extent.

Justice Hayward took a different approach. His judgment appears to have been based on a finding of subjective abandonment by Captain White of the *Nimrod.* He took the view that White had decided that it was not sensible to return to the pans, owing either to the number of pelts already on board, or to the existing sailing conditions. It was only then that the pelts were offered to the *Panther.* But by virtue of the intentional abandonment, the pelts were available to any first taker. As the crew of the *Native Lass* retained sufficient possession, manual or constructive, of all 800 pelts, it was entitled to recover for their value.

However, Hayward J's language is somewhat ambiguous. In a concluding passage he held that the transaction between the *Nimrod* and *Panther* was not a valid gift. In addition — and this is critical — he offered as an alternative "that it was not in the power of Capt. White [of the *Nimrod*] to transfer to the defendant that property floating on the sea *which he had not in himself the power to secure.*"[46] That reasoning suggests that the ability to recover the pelts is essential to retain title. This is the language of deemed abandonment.

In the result, then, the award was reduced in accordance with the views of Chief Justice Hoyles and Justice Robinson: only 200 pelts had been wrongfully taken. The generic rule remained good law in the eyes of Hoyles CJ, while Robinson J remained committed to the deemed abandonment rule. Hayward J's position is arguably unclear.

The last case is *Power v Kennedy* (1884).[47] The contestants were two steamers, the SS *Narwhal* and the SS *Vanguard.* The dispute involved round seals. The facts of the case are not reported in significant detail, but it would appear that the conflict concerned the large-scale slaughter of seals over a wide area. The carcasses were not marked and were left strewn over the floes for many miles. There was no suggestion that the seals had been intentionally abandoned.

Justice Robert J. Pinsent[48] treated the matter as not subject to binding authority. As to round seals, he wrote, there was no understood or generally accepted statement of the law. None of the earlier decisions were cited, though Pinsent J was undoubtedly mindful of them: he had acted as counsel in all of the earlier reported cases.

A simple rule of capture, perfected by killing, was rejected for three reasons. The first concerned fair competition. It was asserted that it would be "monstrous"[49] to support a rule that would allow the first sealers to pre-empt others, to the extent perhaps of killing all accessible seals, leaving them unmarked, on the ice at the spot where they were caught. Second, confusion as to what belonged to whom might arise whenever more than one crew was engaged in this reprehensible practice.[50] Third, seals deteriorate more rapidly if left round. Given these considerations, Pinsent J set out the governing principles:

> I admit the general proposition that property may be acquired and retained in "round seals," as well as in "sculped seals," and by similar means; but I hold that the killing must be accompanied by possession, and that when the next comer finds the body of a seal or the bodies of seals on the ice without any accompanying *indicia* of property, the man who claims as of right against him must be in a position then and there to assert his right of property, to point to the specific seals as his own or those of his fellows, and to exercise corporal control over them, unless he is resisted by force or deterred by threats of violence.
>
> Except under such circumstances I am of opinion that the killer must be held to have left or abandoned the dead round seals to the next finder who shall possess himself of them.[51]

It may be that this ruling is, despite first appearances, only designed to apply to round seals. If so, it is not inconsistent with the earlier cases. Otherwise, it can be taken as creating a curious hybrid. If we take this language literally, a stern rule of deemed abandonment is being described, one that demands close proximity, unless the pelts are marked, in which case something more akin to the generic rule of capture would apply.

The Socio-Economic Context

THESE SEALING CASES REPRESENT the extant jurisprudence. There have been no reported cases since. However, it may be telling that the cases emerged at a rather advanced stage in the history of the non-indigenous seal fishery. As noted at the outset, commercial sealing had existed in and around Newfoundland for about 300 years or so before these disputes emerged. On one reading of the decisions, there existed an established custom (that of deemed abandonment), which was discarded by the Supreme Court. From another point of view, prior to the spate of cases discussed in this article, the correct legal response had not been resolved in Newfoundland. Either way, one is prompted to ask: why did these conflicts emerge when they did?

Two major developments occurred during the period under review. One concerns radical changes in the mode of seal hunting that profoundly affected the functioning of the industry from top to bottom. I am referring to the introduction of wooden-hulled steamships, known simply as wooden walls. However, as will be argued below, technological advances taken on their own tell only part of the story of the transformation. A second aspect, tied closely to the first, concerns the depletion of the seal stocks.

Technological development has been a constant feature of the Newfoundland seal fishery.[52] Initially, seals were hunted on or close to the shore. The early Aboriginal hunters used nets and barbed harpoons. Traps, nets, and boats (called shallops) were often used by the first Europeans to engage in the hunt. As a rule, the shallops did not venture far beyond the major bays or the shore. The first sailing ships made their appearance near the end of the eighteenth century, and by the early part of the nineteenth century a substantial offshore seal industry had developed using large schooners.

Wooden wall steamships made their first appearance as part of the seal hunt in 1862. The impetus was the decision by Scottish whaling and sealing ventures operating mainly out of Dundee to seek out additional income streams in the face of declining stocks off Greenland and other northerly grounds.[53] These initial forays met with limited success, much to the relief, it would appear, of some Newfoundlanders. Yet in time, the use of steamships proved highly profitable and became an entrenched feature of the Newfoundland seal fishery. It took about a decade for the steamers to demonstrate their effectiveness.

It is the common wisdom that the introduction of steamships drastically altered the economic landscape.[54] A complex set of dynamics was triggered. Some within Newfoundland were apprehensive about the prospect of using steam-powered ships. In 1895, Daniel Prowse lamented that the day that steamships first took part in the seal fishery "was a poor day for Newfoundland."[55] In the first years, tensions sometimes flared between Scottish and Newfoundland crews when they hunted in close quarters. However, the Scottish firms came to appreciate the acumen and skill of the local crews, who were increasingly being recruited in place of Scottish whalers. Similarly, the economic advantages of establishing operations based in St. John's were appreciated. In other words, key sectors of the local community were being co-opted. In time the Scottish firms began to differ only slightly in the public eye from the so-called local enterprises, many of which were, in fact, controlled by head offices in Britain.[56]

It was becoming apparent to all concerned that steamers represented the future, and the industry was being readjusted accordingly. Sailing ships continued to participate in the seal fishery, though their numbers steadily dwindled; by the beginning of the twentieth century, their share of the industry was barely noticeable.[57] The movement from schooners to steamships is reflected in the five cases under study.

Table 1

Kinds of Vessels Involved in the Sealing Litigation

Power v Jackman (1859): schooner v schooner
Noel v Warren (1861): schooner v schooner
Clift v Kane (1870): schooner v schooner
Doyle v Bartlett (1872): two steamers v schooner
Power v Kennedy (1884): steamer v steamer

The number of men required for the hunt declined considerably. Steamers could carry larger crews, but overall it took about half as many sealers to collect an equivalent number of pelts. In 1860, 292 sailing ships carried 14,121 men.[58] There were 27 steamers used in 1881, employing some 5,815 men. By the turn of the century that number had dropped to around 4,500.[59] Moreover, the costs associated with the use of steamers meant that only the strong could survive low-yield seasons, of which there were plenty. A centralized oligopoly began to form. Moreover, St. John's replaced Conception Bay as the epicentre of the sealing industry.[60]

Of course, changes in the ways the actual hunt was carried out lay at the bottom of all of these developments. With the use of steam, and sail when needed, a steamer was able to navigate more effectively through the floes than a schooner, and it could cover a far greater range and carry more catch. Two and sometimes three trips to the floes were now possible. Importantly, seal pans were larger, more numerous, and spread over a wider area.[61]

However, panning came at a cost. There was a distinct danger not only of poaching, but also of loss due to the forces of nature. For instance, in *Doyle v Bartlett* it was noted in passing that, apart from the 800 pelts in dispute, the crew of the SS *Nimrod* had left behind some 3,000 pelts on the ice during that one voyage.[62] Owing to the heightened chance of loss, it has been argued that panning was wasteful in the extreme, and contributed to the depletion of the seal population.[63]

Indeed, whether or not accentuated by large-scale panning, seal stocks and annual yields were declining during this period. Export numbers varied wildly from year to year, but the apex of production was reached in the late 1840s and mid-1850s. By the time of the first cases under study, yields were beginning to fall. Newfoundland's second largest industry (after the cod fishery) was in a slow decline. If we examine the average over five year spans, a downward trend can be discerned.

Table 2

Total Number of Seal Skins Exported from Newfoundland By Year (1840 to 1884)[64]

1840 to 1844	422,622
1845 to 1849	429,419
1850 to 1854	481,498
1855 to 1859	394,264
1860 to 1864	299,842
1865 to 1869	255,979
1870 to 1874	294,429
1875 to 1879	386,084
1880 to 1884	287,538

The concern over the dissipation of the seal population and the movement from sail to steam were both reflected in the first Newfoundland statute directly related to the seal fishery. In 1873, the General Assembly introduced legislation[65] that set 12 March as the annual starting date for the hunt. No seals could be taken before then on penalty of fine. The purpose of the date was to prevent a premature exploitation of the resource that might impede its regeneration. The act also provided that steamers were not permitted to leave port before 10 March in any given year. For schooners the date was 5 March. The difference is an acknowledgment of the varying nautical capabilities of these two kinds of vessels.

Conclusion

It might be tempting to suppose that the two competing ownership rules signal certain biases held by the judges engaged in these five cases, such as a concern for the stability of local firms. The steamer, introduced by Scottish enterprises, eventually proved to be superior to the schooner, hitherto the vessel of choice both in St. John's and the outports. However, the outcomes of the reported cases reveal little to support such a theory. For one thing, there are too few known cases to be able to detect such preferences. Moreover, except in the very early years of the offshore steamers, the crews were predominantly comprised of Newfoundlanders. Conversely, many of the so-called local companies were branch plant operations with headquarters in England. In short, the line between foreign and local interests was blurred. In any event, both of the proffered rules discussed above are thoroughly reversible: their impact is contingent on the events as they unfold on the floes, and whether Scottish or local firms were involved was a matter of sheer circumstance, particularly since steamers were being widely adopted within the industry.

These cases draw one's attention to the competing legal players. A small cadre of respected, successful, and prominent Newfoundland lawyers and judges were involved. Philip Francis Little, who decided the early cases had been premier, as had Sir Hugh Hoyles. Sir Bryan Robinson and Sir Robert Pinsent had also held political office. Moreover, Hoyles, Robinson, and Pinsent had served as counsel in some of the seal cases. Pinsent (who had received his legal training from Robinson) served as either lawyer or judge in all of the seal cases discussed in this paper.[66]

These men held common views about the role of the courts. The judgments share quite similar attitudes about precedent, the elusive divide between judicial and legislative roles, and the kinds of policy factors that can be properly considered. Both sides were willing to draw on custom, an approach not unknown to Newfoundland jurisprudence. During the first part of the nineteenth century, deviations in English common law doctrines were occasionally reconfigured so as to reflect what was sometimes termed the custom of the island.[67]

The judges in the seal cases were engaged in an intuitive instrumental analysis, the goal of which was to construct a resolution that, at the very least, would not hamper the sealing industry. Morton Horwitz identified a comparable mode of analysis in the American case law of the same period.

He observed that by the 1870s "[t]he process of economic growth had drawn common law judges into openly instrumental uses of private law, thereby undermining their claim to political neutrality."[68] We see much the same mode of reasoning here (perhaps with the same implications). A changing commercial environment prompted the courts to reconsider the rules. Ships were operating on a larger scale than before, with pans assembled over greater regions, while at the same time the stocks as a whole were beginning to shrink. The importance of sustaining an industry so important to the economy of Newfoundland must have been a critical consideration. Just how the law could advance that aim is a matter on which views might legitimately differ.

Which of the competing approaches best advanced the business interests of the sealing firms is an open question. But looking back, there is certainly something to be said for applying the rule of deemed abandonment and not the generic rule of capture. If the generic rule is applied, Ship A has some incentive to overkill. By doing so, they hedge against a percentage of the pelts being lost at sea; they minimize the stock of unclaimed seals available to other crews; and if the pelts are later recovered by a second crew, Ship A nevertheless reaps some profit from pelts that they had left behind (after having paid the salvage fee to Ship B). Moreover, the salvage payment to Ship B may not induce that ship to collect the panned seals, for Ship B may calculate that its limited hull storage should be filled with pelts for which it is entitled to a 100 percent return. By contrast, the rule of deemed abandonment induces Ship A to be prudent, since any overkill may become a full windfall to Ship B.

There *may* be evidence to be drawn from the floes as to which approach might have been thought to work best in practice: on one view of the history of the seal fishery, the deemed abandonment rule was an established custom or legal principle by the time the full court of the Supreme Court of Newfoundland heard the first case on point, *Clift v Kane* (1870).[69] It will be recalled that in his dissenting opinion in that case, Robinson J claimed that there had been an established convention for at least forty years prior to *Clift v Kane*, quite possibly derived from sealing practice:

> Actions similar to the present have been common in our Courts. I have been engaged in the trial of many both as counsel and as judge, and up to the present, I do not remember and cannot find a report of a single one in which it was not the ruling of the Court that to vest in the plaintiffs such property

> and possession as would enable him to recover he must satisfy the jury not only that he killed the seals, but that they continued under his control, that he had not abandoned the intention to return, and the hope to recover them, and that he had a reasonable prospect of being enabled to take them into his complete possession . . .
>
> Whether such direction was coeval with the seal fishery, or whether it arose after the usage thereat had been proved and established and therefore had become settled law which judges are bound to notice judicially, or when and how it arose I cannot say; this much I can assert, that during my experience at the bar and on the bench such was the law inevitably laid down by the Court.[70]

Robert Ellickson's study of whaling norms, mentioned earlier,[71] can serve to underscore the significance of identifying the *source* of the rule of deemed abandonment. Ellickson argued that those engaged in the whaling industry sought to develop informal norms that were wealth-maximizing. Robert Deal, while questioning the extent to which the judiciary faithfully described and affirmed those norms, has said that "[t]he single rule of whaling universally recognized in all fisheries in every period was, of course, that not a drop of oil or a pound of bone should go to waste."[72] It is entirely possible that the sealing putative convention studied here (deemed abandonment) was influenced in the same way. At core, all of the justices seemed concerned with rewarding labour and avoiding waste. And just as whaling norms — recall that there were several — were adapted to conform to subtle variables in the nature of the whaling enterprise, it is entirely predictable that a sealing custom that emerged in Newfoundland would be *sui generis*.

However, one must tread lightly here before concluding that the rule of deemed abandonment had been regularly invoked by sealers and applied by earlier courts, for there is an evidentiary problem. The judges who endorsed the generic rule of capture doubted the existence of a sealing custom or rule of deemed abandonment. Chief Justice Hoyles wrote:

> [T]he evidence of custom, except so much as established what was not disputed, that a seal abandoned on the ice might be take possession by the finder, only went to show the illegal and conflicting practice of two or three sealing masters.[73]

Even if it is likely that those engaged in sealing hammered out some set of norms that were most workable to the needs of the industry, little material exists to substantiate or refute Justice Robinson's assertion that the rule of deemed abandonment was consistently applied over a forty-year period, apart from the two reported decisions mentioned previously.[74] The Newfoundland archives contain no records capable of shedding any light whatsoever on the matter, and the local newspapers of the time carry no accounts of such disputes. By contrast, there was an extensive jurisprudence as to whaling rights both in Britain and the United States. Those bodies of case law concern disputes occurring along the eastern seaboard of the United States, Greenland, and the South Pacific. In many instances there are extensive collections of unpublished court records still available for study. Not so for the law of sealing. The surviving Newfoundland court records of all civil actions launched during the relevant period consist almost entirely of ledgers listing the parties to the actions and the amounts at issue; nothing more. Hence, even if one might wish to follow Ellickson's lead and rely on the practice of the industry as a proxy for, or guide to, economic efficiency, the dearth of reliable information in relation to the Newfoundland seal fishery casts a fog over its history on this important issue.

Notes

1 This paper was first presented at the annual meeting of the British Association of Canadian Studies (Legal Studies Group) conference, held in London on 22 June 2007. Thanks are due to Tracie Scott for the initial research into the cases under study, and to Jeanette Browne for her assistance at the later stages. A research grant from the Joseph Smallwood Foundation enabled archival work to be undertaken in St. John's, Newfoundland. I benefited from comments provided by Jim Phillips, Eric Adams, Eran Kaplisnsky, Moe Litman, Russ Brown, the participants at the authors' workshop held at the University of Alberta in June 2009, and by two anonymous reviewers.

2 GA England, *The White Wilderness* (London: Cassell & Co, 1924) at 33.

3 (1870) 5 Nfld L R 327 (SC, *en banc*).

4 I was able to locate only a single reference in the literature to any of the cases: see JH Ingham, *The Law of Animals: A Treatise on Property in Animals, Wild and Domestic, and the Rights and Responsibilities Arising Therefrom* (Philadelphia: T & JW Johnson & Co, 1900) at 27-28 quoting, without analysis, from *Power v Kennedy*, below note 47. Also, the decision in *Clift v Kane*, below note 30, is referred to in *M.V. "Polar Star" v Arsenault* (1964) 43 DLR (2d) 354 (PEISC), a case involving the intermixture of seal pelts.

5 JE Candow, *Of Men and Seals: A History of the Newfoundland Seal Hunt* (Ottawa: Environment Canada, 1989) at 19-22. See also M Harvey, *A Short History of Newfoundland: England's Oldest Colony* (London: William Collins, Sons & Co., 1890) at 134-36.

6 See Socio-Economic Context below.

7 Candow, above note 5 at 15.

8 See further WH Greene, *The Wooden Walls Among the Ice Floes* (London: Hutchinson & Co, 1933).

9 T Southwell, "The Seal Fishery," (1874) 10 Nature 85 at 85-86. See also WT Grenfell, "The Seal Hunters of Newfoundland," (1897-8) Leisure Hour 284 at 290. On animal rights generally, see HS Salt, *Animals' Rights: Considered in Relation to Social Progress* (London: Macmillan, 1894), which refers in passing (at 83-84) to the use of seal fur for garments.

10 "Possession is very strong; rather more than nine points of the law": *Corp. of Kingston Upon Hull v Horner* (1774) Lofft. 576, at 591, 98 ER 807 at 815.

11 See further B Ziff, *Principles of Property Law*, 5th ed (Toronto: Thomson Carswell, 2010) at 132*ff*, and the references cited there.

12 See further Ingham, above note 4 at 1-2.

13 B Murdoch, *Epitome of the Laws of Nova Scotia* (Halifax: Joseph Howe, 1832-33) vol 3 at 3. Note that a wild animal possessing what is termed *animus revertendi*, literally translated as an intention to return, is not lost to its captor. I regard this sub-rule as recognition of the retained control over the animal; it is a kind of metaphysical leash through which continuing possession is maintained. See also B Welling, *Property in Things: In the Common Law System* (Gold Coast, Qld: Scribblers, 1996) at 77.

14 3 Cai R 175, 2 Am. Dec 264 (NYSC, 1805). For some recent literature on the case, see the forum on this famous case in 27 Law & Hist Rev 145-94 (2009); and A McDowell, "Legal Fictions in *Pierson v Post*," 105 Mich L Rev 735 (2007) D Dharmapala &

R Pitchford, "An Economic Analysis of 'Riding to Hounds': *Pierson v Post* Revisited," 18 JL Econ & Org 39 (2002); BR Berger, "It's Not About the Fox: The Untold History of *Pierson v Post*," 55 Duke LJ 1089 (2006); J Blackman, "Outfoxed: *Pierson v Post* and the Natural Law", online: http://ssrn.com/abstract=1403932; DR Ernst, "*Pierson v Post*: The New Learning," online: http://ssrn.com/abstract=1428874.

15 That standard was not met in *Young v Hichens* (1844) 6 QB 606. See also *"The Frederick Gerring Jr." v The Queen* (1897) 27 SCR 271.

16 See also *Buster v Newkirk*, 20 Johns. 75 (NYSC, 1822) (finding that title was lost when the hunter gave up pursuit of his wounded prey in the evening and set out again the next morning). See *Charlebois v Raymond* (1867) 12 Lower Canada Jur. 55 (Dist Ct).

17 RC Ellickson, *Order Without Law* (Cambridge, MA: Harvard University Press, 1991) at 191*ff*. Compare the analysis in RC Deal, *Laws of Honour: The Laws and Customs of Anglo-American Whaling, 1780-1880*, PhD Thesis, Temple University, 2010.

18 See Deal, above note 17 at 99*ff*.

19 *Hogarth v Jackson* (1827) 2 Car & P 595, 172 ER 271; *Aberdeen Arctic Co. v Sutter*, 4 Macq 355, 3 Eng Rul Cas. 93 (1862); *Littledale v Scaith* (1788) 1 Taunt. 244, 127 ER 826 (concerning the law in Greenland).

20 *Swift v Gifford*, 23 F 558 (Mass Dist Ct., 1872). See also *Bartlett v Budd*, 2 F. 966 (Mass Dist Ct., 1868); *Taber v Jenny*, 23 F. 605 (Mass Dist Ct, 1856).

21 *Heppingstone v Mammen*, 1863 WL 2538 (Hawai'i SC).

22 8 F. 159 (Mass Dist Ct, 1881).

23 See also *Fennings v Lord Grenville* (1808) 1 Taunt 241, 127 ER 825 (concerning the law applicable in the Galapagos Islands).

24 Robert Deal offers a more nuanced assessment. He has argued that the courts treated the customs as far more established than was the case, and that the role of honour as a factor influencing whaling disputes was not appreciated. Indeed, he goes so far as to maintain that "[c]ourts in seeking settled whaling customs and universal adherence largely invented what they were looking for" (Deal, above note 17 at ix), such that the legal doctrines that emerged were a combination of ill-defined customs and judicial edict: *ibid* at 55-56. By the same token, Deal has acknowledged that whalers shared a commitment to optimizing yields: *ibid* at 121. Whether the customs were efficient is, for Deal, an open question. See also RB Walton, "Ellickson's Paradox: It's Suicide to Maximize Welfare," 7 NYU Env'l L J 153 (1999), where the efficiency of the whaling customs is doubted.

25 See further *Stewart v Gustafson*, [1999] 4 WWR 695, 1998 CarswellSask 581 (QB), where English law (arguably different in ways that are not germane to this paper) is discussed.

26 (1859) 4 Nfld L R 333 (SC). In an earlier reported decision involving the appropriation of seal pelts, no rule of capture was discussed: see *White v McBride* (1857) 4 Nfld L R 178 (SC).

27 Philip Francis Little (1824–1897) born in Charlottetown of Irish parents, received his legal training in Prince Edward Island, but practised in Newfoundland. He was elected to the House of Assembly in a by-election in 1850, and two years later became the leader of the Liberal Party. He was prominent in the campaign for re-

sponsible government. He became premier and three years later accepted a judicial appointment in 1858: *Dictionary of Canadian Biography*, vol XII, online: www.biographi.ca/index-e.html.

28 Above note 26 at 335.

29 (1861) 4 Nfld L R 557 (SC).

30 (1870) 5 Nfld L R 327 (SC, *en banc*).

31 *Ibid* at 329, Hoyles CJ

32 Sir Hugh William Hoyles (1814–1888), a native-born Newfoundlander, was called to the bar in Nova Scotia in 1837, returning to Newfoundland in 1842, where he quickly earned a reputation as an able lawyer. He was elected to the House of Assembly in 1848, became the leader of the opposition in 1855, and premier in 1861. He left the Assembly in 1865 to become Chief Justice: *Dictionary of Canadian Biography*, vol XI, online: www.biographi.ca/index-e.html.

33 See text accompanying notes 26 to 29, above.

34 Above note 30 at 336. The Chief Justice also briefly discussed two unreported cases decided in 1858, which were referred to only as *Stone* and *Dwyer*. Passing mention is also made to *White v McBride*, above note 26.

35 *Ibid.*

36 Sir Bryan Robinson (1808-1887) was called to the bar in Nova Scotia in 1831 but shortly afterwards moved to Newfoundland, where he enjoyed a lengthy and celebrated legal career. He served as a member of the House of Assembly, as a justice of the peace, and was for a short time the acting solicitor and attorney general. He was appointed to the bench in 1858: *Dictionary of Canadian Biography*, vol XI, online: www.biographi.ca/index-e.html.

37 Above note 30 at 339.

38 *Ibid* at 346.

39 *Ibid* at 344.

40 *Ibid* at 341-42.

41 *Ibid* at 340, 342, and 346.

42 *Ibid* at 346.

43 (1872) 5 Nfld L R 445 (SC, *en banc*).

44 Above note 30.

45 Above note 43 at 451-52.

46 *Ibid* at 455 (emphasis added).

47 (1884) 7 Nfld L R 34 (SC).

48 Sir Robert John Pinsent (1834–1893), studied law under Sir Bryan Robinson in the mid-1850s. He served on the Legislative Council and the House of Assembly, and was appointed to the Supreme Court of Newfoundland in 1880: *Dictionary of Canadian Biography*, vol XII, online: www.biographi.ca/index-e.html.

49 *Ibid* at 35.

50 *Ibid.*

51 *Ibid* at 36.

52 "No other industry I know of in the world has been subject to so many changes in the short span of 141 years": A Kean, "Commentary on the Seal Hunt" in JR Smallwood,

ed, *The Book of Newfoundland* (St. John's: Newfoundland Book Publishers, 1937) vol 1, 73, at 74.

53 A detailed account of this development can be found in CW Sanger, "The 19th Century Newfoundland Seal Fishery and the Influence of Scottish Whalemen" (1980) 20 Polar Record 231.

54 See, e.g., J Feltham, *Sealing Steamers* (St. John's: Harry Cuff Pub Ltd, 1995) at 14; Candow, above note 5 at 41*ff*; EC Coish, *Season of the Seal* (St John's: Breakwater, 1979) at 24-25; G Hogan, *Harbour Grace in the 1860s*, BA Honours Dissertation, Dept. of History, Memorial University, 1983, at 25.

55 DW Prowse, *A History of Newfoundland* (London: Macmillan & Co., 1895) at 453.

56 See further Sanger, above note 53. And Prowse, above note 55 at 453, allowed that "[t]he only consolation we can lay to our hearts is that steam was inevitable."

57 S Ryan, *The Ice Hunters: A History of Newfoundland Sealing to 1914* (St John's Breakwater, 1994) at 168. See also J Hatton & M Harvey, *Newfoundland: Its History, Its Present Condition, and Its Prospects in the Future* (Boston: Doyle & Whittle, 1883) at 251.

58 Candow, above note 5 at 43.

59 Grenfell, above note 9 at 285.

60 In *Power v Kennedy*, above note 47, the real protagonists in that case were the Dundee Sealing and Whaling Company, owners of the SS *Narwhal*, and Messrs John Munn & Co, owners of the SS *Vanguard*. The Dundee Sealing and Whaling was among the very first Scotland-based companies to try its hand at the seal hunt through the operation of steamers. John Munn's firm epitomized the local element in two ways: not only was it a (successful) Newfoundland business of longstanding (est. 1833), but its headquarters were in Harbour Grace, not St John's.

61 As to other changes in the manner of carrying out the hunt, see BC Busch, *The War Against the Seals: A History of the North American Seal Fishery* (Kingston & Montreal: McGill-Queen's University Press, 1985).

62 Above note 43 at 454.

63 Candow, above note 5 at 69.

64 Kean, above note 52 at 75. The average for the period from 1870 to 1874 includes a meager yield of 39,228 in 1874. If that year is excluded altogether the average for that period rises to 358,105, which is still below the averages for the 1840s and 1850s.

65 *An Act to Regulate the Prosecution of the Seal Fishery*, SN 1873, c. 9.

66 See also above notes 27, 32, 36, and 48.

67 See, for example, *Coleman v Kennedy* (1817) 1 Nfld. LR 8 (SC). See further B Ziff, "Warm Reception in a Cold Climate: English Property Law and the Suppression of the Canadian Legal Identity" in J McLaren et al, eds, *Despotic Dominion: Property Rights in British Settler Societies* (Vancouver: University of British Columbia Press, 2005) 103, at 105-06.

68 M J Horwitz, *The Transformation of American Law, 1870-1960* (Oxford: Oxford University Press, 1992) at 112.

69 *Clift v Kane*, above note 30.

70 *Ibid* at 339.

71 Ellickson, above note 17.

72 Deal, above note 17 at 121.

73 *Clift v Kane*, above note 30 at 329.

74 *Power v Jackman* (1859), above note 26; *Noel v Warren* (1861), above note 29.

Nuisance and Neighbourhood in Late Nineteenth-Century Montreal: *Drysdale v Dugas* in its Contexts

Eric H. Reiter[1]

Introduction

Nuisance cases have a personal dimension that can belie the often relatively modest legal stakes involved. Pitting neighbour against neighbour, and involving perceived invasion of the homes, workplaces, or senses of the parties, nuisance complaints tend to elicit vehement reactions on both sides. One such affair is *Drysdale v Dugas*, which reached the Supreme Court of Canada in 1896.[2] Centring on a dispute between neighbours in Montreal, the case pits Drysdale, who built and ran a stable in a residential neighbourhood, against Dugas, who complained of the horses' unpleasant odours, foul liquids, and incessant noise. It also highlights difficult issues of property powers and duties, fault and liability, precedent and public policy, and remedies. Moreover, as the Supreme Court's first major pronouncement on nuisance in Canada, *Drysdale*'s influence has extended beyond its origins in the civil law of Quebec. Recently, its relevance was reaffirmed when the Supreme Court endorsed its view of liability for nuisance in *St Lawrence Cement v Barrette* of 2008.[3]

Like all nuisance cases, *Drysdale* sits at the intersection of the law of property and civil liability, and it reveals lawyers and judges alike seeking coherent — or at least workable — rules and concepts in a murky field of law. Like all Quebec nuisance cases, *Drysdale* also straddles the civil law and the common law, with French and English principles and precedents mingling sometimes in concert, sometimes in tension. Finally, like all legal cases of whatever kind, *Drysdale* has a story behind it, one that both fills out and at times challenges the rather lifeless published reports of the case.[4] In this article, I use *Drysdale* and its stories to explore the intersections of doctrinal legal principles and lived social ordering in a time of changing urban landscapes and neighbourly relationships.

Dramatis Personae: Dugas and Drysdale

Nuisance is a social concept. The smells, noises, smoke, vibrations, and other physical irritants behind the legal idea of nuisance become problematic when individuals live in close proximity to one another, and differences in personalities, sensibilities, and levels of tolerance give rise to conflict over the irritants. It is also, of course, a legal concept, and the principles, interpretations, and precedents of the legal system affect the social aspects of nuisance, as the social aspects affect the legal. Behind both are people — neighbours, lawyers, and judges — who come to litigation with previous histories, which provide another level of influence on the course of the case.

Calixte-Aimé Dugas, the plaintiff in *Drysdale*, was a prominent and well-connected member of the Montreal legal community.[5] Though it was no secret at the time,[6] it appears nowhere in the reported judgments that Dugas was himself a judge of the Montreal Court of Sessions, the lower criminal court. Born in 1845 in St. Rémi, near Montreal, Dugas studied law with both a future Quebec chief justice (A-A Dorion) and a future prime minister of Canada (JJC Abbott). After admission to the bar in 1868 his fortunate connections continued: he practised law with a future Supreme Court justice (Désiré Girouard), and in 1869 married Suzanne Harkin, a cousin of Lewis Drummond, justice of the Quebec Court of Queen's Bench. Dugas served briefly in municipal government, and in 1878 ran unsuccessfully for the provincial Liberals. Soon after his defeat he was rewarded with an appointment as judge of the Court of General Sessions of the Peace, serving also as extradition commissioner.[7] A proponent of military training, Dugas belonged to the 65th Battalion, Mount Royal Rifles, and saw active duty as a Major (later promoted to Lieutenant-Colonel) during the North-West Rebellion of 1885.[8] Dugas was also a member of several prestigious Montreal clubs, mingling with the francophone elite at the Club Canadien and the anglophone elite at the Metropolitan Club.[9]

"Judge Dugas, Montreal, QC, 1882" by William Notman & Son, 27 December 1882. This photograph of Dugas, like the photo of Drysdale below, is by Montreal's premier society photographer, William Notman. McCord Museum, II-67847.1. Reproduced with permission.

Besides his position as judge and his general knowledge of the law,[10] two other aspects of Dugas's personal history factor into this litigation: his litigiousness and a speculative streak. Like many legal professionals with knowledge of their rights and a drive to vindicate them, Dugas was involved in a number of legal actions over the years. Already in the 1870s as a young lawyer, he participated in a well-publicized fracas over his having hitched his horse to a gatepost, as a result of which he was arrested for allegedly assaulting a constable. Tellingly, he not only defended himself against the charge, but launched a $5,000 suit against the constable and the City of Montreal for false arrest and violation of his rights.[11] In 1885, in another *cause célèbre,* Dugas successfully brought private criminal libel charges against Edmund Sheppard, owner of the sensationalist and anti-French *Toronto Evening News,* over articles alleging cowardice, looting, and desertion by Dugas's regiment during the Rebellion.[12] Dugas also appears in various cases connected to his business dealings, such as a breach of contract suit arising from plans to form a company to exploit an invention to turn garbage into fuel.[13]

This business venture also illustrates Dugas's speculative streak. Besides his real estate investment at the heart of the case (discussed below), Dugas was also involved in various mining ventures that continued to the end of his life. In 1889 public notice was given that Dugas was one of the directors of an exploratory mining company,[14] and in 1891, possibly as part of the activities of this company, Dugas's name was on a mica mine in Gatineau.[15] As we will see below, Dugas's interest in mining continued during his second career in the Yukon.

Dugas's opponent was William Drysdale, a Scottish immigrant who since arriving in Montreal in the 1850s had held a succession of jobs involving the care of horses.[16] He first turns up as a coachman at the mansion of brewing magnate John HR Molson in 1861–62, and in the years following he appears variously as coachman and groom in different locations around the city. Before this, however, and immediately after his arrival, Drysdale had begun working for the prestigious Montreal Hunt Club as whipper-in, which involved supervising the dogs and bringing up the rear at the club's frequent fox hunts. In 1866 he was promoted to full-time huntsman, responsible for the hunts themselves and the workings of the club's stables and kennels.[17] He held this position until his retirement in 1889 at about the age of 60.[18] After leaving the Hunt, and after a year working at another stable, Drysdale opened his "Boulevard Boarding and Training Stable," newly built in a vacant double lot on St. Denis Street, a major north-south artery in east-end Montreal.[19]

If Dugas was highly knowledgeable in law and unafraid to assert his rights, nothing suggests Drysdale had had any previous experience before the courts. Though not himself expert in law, Drysdale's connections with the Montreal Hunt did give him access to advice at least, and perhaps more tangible assistance. The Club was the favoured haunt of Montreal's sporting classes, and more particularly its anglophone elite. As huntsman, Drysdale was not a member of the Hunt — he was its chief employee, and as such was not invited to its formal dinners and fancy balls — but he was on good enough terms after his departure for four members of the Club to testify on his behalf, including Robert Craik, Dean of the McGill Faculty of Medicine, and Duncan McEachran, first Dean of the McGill Faculty of Comparative Medicine and Veterinary Science.

"W.D. Drysdale and friends, Montreal, QC, 1882" by William Notman & Son, 1 December 1882. Drysdale, on the left, is in his huntsman regalia for the Montreal Hunt Club with unidentified fellow employees of the Hunt. McCord Museum, II-67592.1. Reproduced with permission.

The Physical and Social Environment

THE CONFLICT BETWEEN THESE two very different men, with different linguistic and educational backgrounds and connected to different elements of Montreal society, took place in a specific time and place. Just as the histories of the parties themselves affected the course of the conflict, so too did the particulars of the St. Denis Street neighbourhood in early 1890s Montreal. *Drysdale* arose in the sort of rapidly changing — in fact, declining — and ultimately mixed neighbourhood that bred nuisance-based conflicts. These changes and the disillusionment they caused created ample space for social contestation carried out through legal norms that, depending on point of view, either promoted or limited laissez-faire property use.

Drysdale built his stable on two adjoining vacant building lots in what was in 1890 a rapidly growing part of Montreal, as urban development spread north and east from the traditional centre of the city.[20] The area, until then

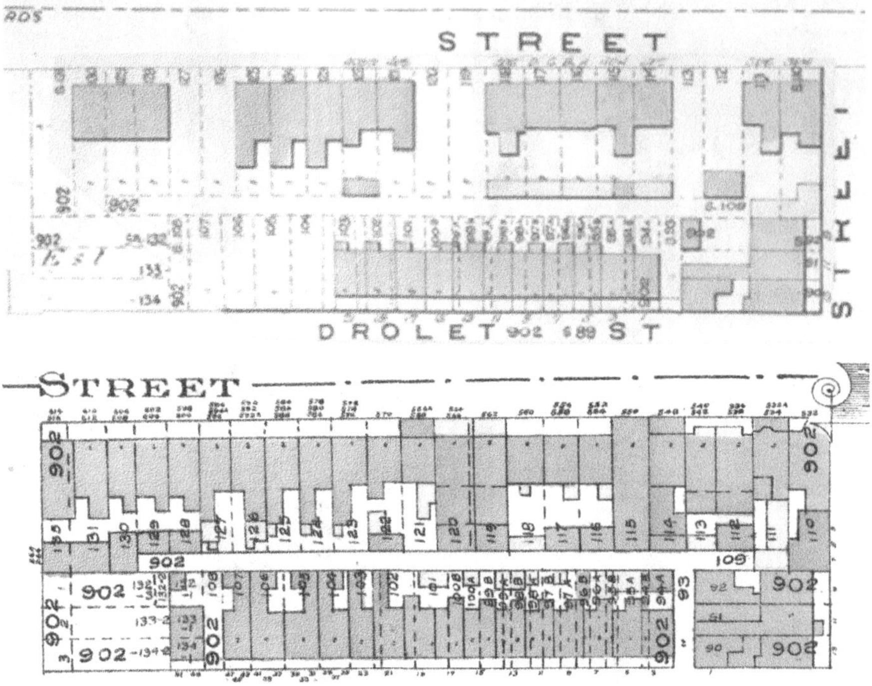

These details from Charles Goad fire insurance plans show the neighbourhood in 1890 just before Drysdale built the stable (top) and in 1912 after he had moved out. St. Denis Street is at the top margin on both plans. On the 1890 plan, the vacant double lot where the stable would be built is at the centre of the top row of houses. Dugas's residence is two houses to the left, the rental property is immediately to the right. The 1912 plan shows the extent of the stable building, which completely fills the double lot. Bibliothèque et archives nationales du Québec, 174398_31 (1890 plan) and 174399_031 (1912 plan). Reproduced with permission.

largely vacant, had been added to the city's cadastral plan in 1880, and by 1881 had been subdivided into building lots. Development followed quickly, and by 1890 about half of the lots had been built upon, mostly by residential row houses, many of which still stand.

Immediately to the south was St. Louis Square, then as now a well-to-do enclave. Further to the south on St. Denis Street was what had been the traditional home to Montreal's francophone elite, but by the 1890s that elite had mostly moved elsewhere.[21] The block in question was a row of attractive three-storey stone-fronted row houses, with a major institution across the broad street, the Deaf and Dumb Institute for Women. In the 1890s the houses were inhabited mostly by professionals and businessmen, but mixed among these more well-off residents were some tradesmen and a few retail shops. More ominously, during the course of the 1890s several of the buildings were subdivided into rooming houses for a more itinerant population, a fate shared by many residential blocks on major streets in the city. In the absence of zoning regulations — Montreal did not enact comprehensive urban planning legislation until almost a century later — the market, limited by informal social pressure bolstered by private legal actions like Dugas's, determined the character of the neighbourhood.

Still, the neighbourhood's decline was slow and not uniform. When Dugas moved out, his residence was taken over by a fellow judge on the Court of Sessions, and physicians and lawyers continued to be in evidence. The important point is that the location met various needs for each of the parties, but conflicting needs, and this conflict of expectations between the parties, helped drive the conflict behind the litigation.

For Drysdale, St. Denis Street was a major thoroughfare, served by a line of the street railway system. It was a decent neighbourhood, filled with relatively affluent horse owners who would be looking for a place to board their animals, and there were no other commercial stables nearby. Drysdale's stable was three storeys tall, with a stone front in keeping with the surrounding buildings; it completely filled the double building lot.[22] The front part, bordering the neighbouring houses, consisted of offices and vehicle storage, with apartments above. The back part, the stable proper where the horses were kept, extended to the rear property line, and bordered the backyards of the neighbouring houses. As witnesses for both sides acknowledged, the stable was constructed with modern drains and ventilation systems, with a wooden floor (essential to prevent foot problems in the horses), and with a manure box that was emptied most days. Drysdale's chosen name for his business — Boulevard Boarding and Training Stables — indicates that he was aiming higher than a livery stable (which hired out horses), and was targeting instead horse owners unable to bear the considerable expense of a private stable.[23] Drysdale had a veterinarian and other employees on staff, and he seems to have boarded about thirty horses. Despite the name, in his suit Dugas took pains to characterize it as a livery stable, which typically had much more coming-and-going and hence more noise and inconvenience for its neighbours, and the judges agreed. The stable seems in fact to have been primarily a livery stable, in which some boarding and training of horses was done. Compared to other such stables elsewhere in the city, it was of medium size. It was also the main anglophone presence on a primarily francophone block, though Montreal's other livery stables seem to have been run by anglophones as well.[24]

The neighbourhood also had specific attractions for Dugas. When he moved in, it had been a relatively prestigious corner of the city, befitting a judge. The stable was clearly an unwelcome inconvenience as far as his residence was concerned, and even though he lived two doors away, his complaints about the smells and the noise indicate his frustration with the direction his neighbourhood was taking. Personal discomfort did not, however, prevent Dugas the speculator from seizing the opportunity afforded by Drysdale's arrival to buy the rental property next to the stable at a steep discount. Knowing the ins and outs of Quebec nuisance law — particularly that judges tended to be pro-plaintiff, though not invariably so — Dugas may well have taken the calculated risk of "coming to the nuisance" by buying first, then chasing away the stable with a lawsuit. If he won, both of his properties would benefit.

Dugas's lawsuit involved more than simple self-interest, however. Stables presented a dual aspect in urban centres. On the one hand, they were absolutely essential to the functioning of nineteenth-century cities, where virtually all land transport of people and goods was by horse power. On the other hand, stables were dangerous neighbours, and raised genuine fears that they were health risks for harbouring disease and fire risks for containing combustible materials — straw, wood, varnish for carriages, oil for harnesses.[25] These fears lay behind the incipient urban regulation of such risks, though actions like Dugas's reflect the unsatisfactory nature of public solutions at the time.[26] Unlike Toronto, which had begun regulating stables in the 1840s and which had enacted a comprehensive regulatory regime for urban stables in 1886, Montreal dealt with them after the fact through general application bylaws against health risks (stables and other "unwholesome or nauseous" places had to be cleaned as often as required by the Board of Health) and fire-prone wooden structures (if deemed a nuisance, such structures could be ordered torn down by the building inspector).[27] Neither of these approaches really addressed the problem at issue here, namely smells that offended the sensibilities of the urban middle class and thus reduced their property values. Though stables were certainly inspected and shut down as nuisances in this period,[28] a private court challenge like Dugas's of a well-run stable allowed the debate to be pushed more decisively in the direction of propriety with its subtle but unmistakeable undertones of class.

The Legal Environment

IN BRINGING THE CONFLICT to court, Dugas and Drysdale had to work within a legal context that circumscribed how they framed their arguments. Precedents were few: aside from a few earlier antecedents,[29] nuisance cases in Quebec were first reported only in the later nineteenth century, and even then were never numerous. The lawyers on both sides of *Drysdale* were thus forced mainly to build their case on doctrinal principles, supplemented by the occasional Quebec and British precedents.

The overarching principle was the theoretically absolute nature of ownership in the civil law tradition, codified by article 406 of the *Civil Code of Lower Canada*: "Ownership is the right of enjoying and of disposing of things in the most absolute manner, provided that no use be made of them which is prohibited by law or by regulations."[30] Clearly such a virtually unlimited conception of property rights was unworkable in practice without some degree of tempering, and jurists had long recognized that owners' rights were necessarily limited by the requirements of living in society. The rights of *voisinage* (neighbourhood) so admitted provided that owners might use their property as they wished, subject to the associated duty of not thereby injuring their neighbours. Robert-Joseph Pothier described the principle as follows:

> Neighbourhood obliges neighbours each to use his land in a manner so as not to injure his neighbour . . .
>
> This rule should be understood as meaning that whatever the liberty one might have to do whatever seems good on one's land, one cannot do anything there which might send something over to the neighbouring land, which would be injurious to it . . .[31]

Conceptualizing these limits on ownership was difficult, however, as the Quebec law of nuisance was complicated by its falling between two different conceptions of liability for injury to one's neighbour: the property-based regime of neighbourhood obligations, a form of strict liability, and the general civil liability regime of article 1053 of the *Civil Code of Lower Canada*, based on fault.[32] The terms of the interplay between these two regimes were still far from settled in late nineteenth-century Quebec.

Nuisance actions tended to boil down to arguments resting on one of two competing Latin maxims, each with venerable Roman-law roots, but neither definitive in itself. The maxims, moreover, reflected the opposing pulls of the two liability regimes just mentioned. Plaintiffs relied on *sic utere tuo ut alienum non laedas* (use your own, but so as not to injure another), which suggested proximity-based limits on the right of ownership. In one of Quebec's first reported nuisance cases, Justice Thomas Aylwin elevated this principle almost to the level of natural law: "The pure morality of this beautiful rule would secure its introduction into the law of every Christian land, and it is not less English than it is Roman. Its application to nuisance is direct and manifest."[33] Most Quebec judges agreed.

Defendants had an opposing maxim, variously rendered as *neminem laedit qui suo jure utitur* (he who exercises his right injures no one) or *nullus videtur dolo facere, qui suo jure utitur* (no one commits a fault who exercises his right). In contrast to *sic utere tuo,* the maxim *qui suo jure* suggested that the existence of a right rendered licit any actions taken under it. Since doing what one was permitted to do could not be a fault, the argument went, there could be no liability. The idea of abuse of right would later challenge the basis of this maxim, but in the late nineteenth century it seemed to provide a time-honoured expression of the fault principle within property law.

The situation was further complicated because neither regime — *voisinage* nor fault — was free of the influence of the other. On the one hand, obligations of *voisinage* had no particular action associated with them, and so claims had to be brought under the general regime of civil liability in article 1053, which was explicitly based on fault.[34] Though actions for nuisance were regularly won by plaintiffs without proof of fault, as we will see, fault was clearly textually mandated and so purity of principle, one could argue, suggested that fault must play some role in nuisance liability, even if in practice judges tended to think otherwise.

On the other hand, the neighbourhood standards central to determining the scope of the obligations of *voisinage* also looked both ways. These obligations tended to be cast in terms of effects — trifling inconveniences producing little or no lasting or serious effect on neighbours had to be borne, while "excessive" or "unreasonable" ones were actionable.[35] Still, more than a hint of fault entered naturally into the calculation of whether a particular situation crossed the line between trifling and excessive. *Un bon père de famille* does not unreasonably cause serious injury to his neighbours by creating "excessive" neighbourhood inconveniences, and so the effect of injuring one's neighbour was easily attributable to the cause of fault. This came out especially in some of the defences invoked against claimed violations of neighbourhood obligations, which looked to the nature of the use as well as its effects. This elision is especially clear in the defence of character of the neighbourhood, where defendants argued that given the nature of the neighbourhood (already polluted, impoverished, or the like), their polluting behaviour caused no damage (effect), but at the same time could not be considered unreasonable or excessive (nature of the use). Some judges accepted this reasoning, such as Loranger J in an 1874 dissenting opinion: "Although in general refined persons do not like to live near this kind of establishment, for people of more vulgar tastes a meat processing plant might not raise the same objections, especially if there were other advantages present."[36]

In applying these principles, the Quebec courts — like the courts elsewhere in Canada — tended to be pro-plaintiff.[37] With two exceptions, the pre-*Drysdale* reported cases were either outright victories for the plaintiffs or dismissed because the plaintiffs had failed to prove damage or were found to have somehow brought the damage on themselves.[38] Defences like coming to the nuisance and public utility — which Drysdale himself invoked — were usually rejected by the courts, particularly for the smelly and dirty traditional nuisance industries.[39] A good example is an 1891 case, in which despite the plaintiff's having moved to the neighbourhood of the defendant's lime kilns, and despite the defendant's odd argument that the kilns increased the value of the plaintiff's property, the court awarded compensatory and future damages.[40]

The two exceptional defendant victories both dated from after *Drysdale* and the alleged nuisances were found not to violate neighbourhood standards. One involved stable odours, very similar to *Drysdale* but opposite in result.[41] The plaintiff had built a house on land adjoining the defendant's property, where the latter had for some years previous kept cows in a stable. Justice Louis Tellier found that the stable was kept in the best possible manner, and that the odours complained of did not violate the standards of the neighbourhood in question. The judge, however, was probably also swayed by the defendant's settlement offer and the fact that he no longer kept animals on his property. The other exception was more clearly a victory for the defendant. The neighbour of a major Montreal coal depot complained of noise and smoke created by steam-powered unloading towers. Justice CP Davidson, while acknowledging that the noise was such as to make conversation within the house impossible when the wind blew in certain directions, nevertheless held that the character of the neighbourhood — an almost entirely industrial district — precluded the plaintiff's suit. Moreover, the public value of the coal yard outweighed whatever countervailing rights the plaintiff claimed.[42]

More typically, however, judges invoked *sic utere tuo* to side with plaintiffs, taking a strict view of what constituted normal neighbourhood inconveniences and allowing little space for arguments that the defendant was not at fault. In this the Quebec courts contrasted with those in France, which by the end of the nineteenth century were moving to a fault standard.[43]

The Trial at the Superior Court

Dugas initiated his action on 6 July 1892 before the Superior Court.[44] On 18 October 1893 his motion to amend his initial demand was granted, resulting in an action for $4,500 in damages: $3,500 for loss of rent and decline in property value, plus an additional $1,000 for unspecified injuries to himself as owner and resident.[45] This was a fairly large sum, approximately half the estimated value of Dugas's residence. Whether there had been efforts to settle the matter before going to court is not mentioned in the surviving record. In any case, Dugas had instrumental reasons for undertaking his action. A successful suit — perhaps even the threat of one — would bring immediate benefits for him personally by driving Drysdale out of the neighbourhood so that Dugas might live in peace and his property investments prosper. Dugas's success, of course, would benefit the rest of the neighbourhood as well, and Drysdale's lawyers sought, unsuccessfully, to get one witness to admit that the case was a concerted action among some of the neighbours, with Dugas as spearhead.[46]

Both parties brought high-powered legal talent to bear on what was really a minor neighbourhood dispute. Dugas's lawyer at trial (he changed for the appeals) was Alfred Girard, of the staunchly Liberal firm Pelland and Girard. Younger than Dugas by about fifteen years, Girard had been in practice for about a decade, and by the time of the trial was a Liberal member of the Quebec Legislative Assembly.[47] Drysdale, fighting for his livelihood, retained the respected anglophone firm of Greenshields, Greenshields and Mallette, perhaps suggested to him through Montreal Hunt Club connections. The case was directed by the younger Greenshields, James Nasmith, who had been part of the defence team at Louis Riel's 1885 treason trial in Regina, and who had more recently successfully defended former Quebec Premier Honoré Mercier against criminal fraud charges.[48]

In framing their respective cases, each side was faced with a factual situation that had to be explained away. For Dugas's lawyers, there was a smelly but well-run stable, similar to or better than other stables in comparable sections of the city where people and stable coexisted apparently without complaint. Moreover, the nuisance seems to have been fairly tolerable, at least according to nineteenth-century sensibilities. Dugas's tenant, a physician whose demand for rent reduction prompted the lawsuit, was content to remain in the house despite the supposedly "intolerable" stable, as long as the price was right. For Drysdale's team, there was the decline in rents and property values, which had begun at the precise moment the stable appeared. In other words, the conflict mirrored the two sides of Quebec nuisance law: from one point of view Drysdale had done nothing wrong, and was merely using his property in a lawful way; from the other point of view, Dugas's property had suffered damage through the appearance of Drysdale's stable. As in all nuisance cases, negotiating this opposition was the challenge the lawyers faced.

The case was heard on 12 and 13 October 1893 before Charles-Ignace Gill J of the Superior Court, a francophone who had been named to the bench in 1879 at the age of thirty-five, following a brief political career with both the provincial and federal Conservatives.[49] In an irony that may have had a bearing on the case, Justice Gill also lived on St. Denis Street, in a similar neighbourhood three blocks north of Dugas and Drysdale.[50]

The parties' cases as framed for trial remained more or less consistent through the Supreme Court. In general terms, Dugas insisted from the beginning that this was a matter of *voisinage*, of the limits of the inconveniences neighbours are expected to bear. The odours and noises coming from Drysdale's stable exceeded normal neighbourly tolerance, and therefore constituted a nuisance to be abated or at least compensated. Drysdale, for his part, mostly put his eggs in the fault basket, arguing that the stable was the best possible in design, construction, maintenance, and management, and that he had violated no laws or regulations in operating it, even in a residential neighbourhood.

Dugas's argument required first of all establishing the character of the neighbourhood. In his amended declaration, he notes that

> the said property offers, besides the advantages of nature generally, all the benefits of pure and healthy air, much appreciated by those who make their

> private residence there, and which gives the buildings of the area a high value which has been going steadily up.[51]

This rather idyllic view of the area was of course dictated by the needs of the litigation, but at the same time suggests Dugas's idea of what his neighbourhood should be like was somewhat at odds with its current character. From there, he seeks to establish that Drysdale's use of the property goes beyond what one would normally expect in such an environment. His complaint specifies foul odours, which endanger public health and render nearby houses uninhabitable; noises; vehicles left in the street or on the sidewalk in front of the stable; and specific violations of provincial and municipal law. As to the measure of damages, he presents evidence that the value of his property had gone down, and that the rents it produces are lower than when he bought.

Drysdale's defence moves in several directions at once.[52] He begins by mentioning (without much development) that Dugas came to the nuisance in buying the rental property, and so could not complain. Drysdale also suggests that Dugas's injuries were due to some other unspecified cause. He devotes most of his effort, however, to arguing that he was in no way at fault: the stable was the best possible in design, construction, and management; it conforms to the law; and it is in no way a danger to public health. At this early point in developing the case, Drysdale's lawyers pay little attention to Dugas's *voisinage* arguments, but they do attempt to establish the stable as a necessary service which must therefore be tolerated:

> That public stables are maintained and carried on in all parts of the City of Montreal, and the same is an essential trade and calling, and necessary to the convenience of the public and to the due carrying on of all business in the City of Montreal.[53]

The examination of the witnesses closely reflects the parties' positions. Dugas called nineteen witnesses, all francophones. His lawyers sought to create a before and after contrast of the character of the neighbourhood. Auguste Laforce, for example, who sold Dugas the rental property, testified about the state of the area before the stable arrived:

> Q. It's a neighbourhood were there's not much commerce, the neighbourhood where this house is built?
>
> A. At the time it wasn't a commercial street, but it can come to that, one doesn't know, someone built a grocery which is occupied.

Q. It's a good area?

A. Yes, sir.

Q. Where a well-to-do class of the population lives?

A. Yes, sir.[54]

To contrast with this, several neighbours testified to establish that once the stable opened, the surrounding houses were beset with odours, foul liquids, and noises, and were generally unhealthy.[55] They paint a bleak picture of summers spent with all the windows closed, guests who refused to stay more than a few minutes, and headaches and other ailments. Four physicians were examined, only one of whom would admit that the odours were dangerous in themselves, but all agreed that being forced to live with the windows closed made the houses unhealthy.[56] Building on this, other witnesses — real estate agents, prospective tenants — were called to demonstrate the injury this caused Dugas, specifically the ever lower rents he was able to charge and the general decline in his property values.[57] Dugas's team brought little evidence about the state of the stable itself, that is, about fault, with the exception of allegations that the stable's design and construction violated municipal bylaws and the civil law regarding common walls.[58]

In cross-examining Dugas's witnesses, Drysdale's lawyers tried to make several points at once, crucial given the fluid nature of nuisance liability. First, they tried to deny Drysdale's fault by pushing witnesses to admit that the stable was well-constructed and well-maintained. In this they had partial success: Dugas's witnesses generally admitted that the stable was no worse than others, though some faulted Drysdale for not doing everything possible to minimize the odours.[59] Second, they attempted to break the link between the damage Dugas suffered and Drysdale's stable by exploring other sources of damage: rats burrowing under the wall of the rental property might have caused the infiltration of liquids; a stand of carters and teamsters with horses directly across St. Denis Street from the properties might have been the source of the odours.[60] In this — a defence against strict liability — their success was more mixed. Dugas eventually ceased pursuing the issue of liquid infiltration, but the court — logically enough — refused to accept that the smell came from teamsters across a wide avenue when a large livery stable was operating next door. Third, Drysdale's lawyers sought to get Dugas's witnesses to admit that livery stables were necessary to the functioning of a major city. Cross-examining Auguste Laforce on this point, the lawyers had their hands full:

Q. It's a necessity in the city of Montreal to have livery stables?
A. For people who need them, but not for me.
Q. You know that it's a public necessity, don't you?
A. Could be.
Q. You have no doubt about that?
A. For me, I don't know.
Q. For the public?
A. I know there are some.
Q. For the public you know that a livery stable is a necessity?
A. Could be, yes.
Q. You have no doubt about that?
A. Well, that's a question I can't answer, it's not my business, I don't deal in horses, I deal in pianos, and they're completely different things.[61]

Finally, they challenged Dugas's characterization of the norms of *voisinage* and the bounds of "normal" neighbourhood inconveniences, by pushing witnesses to admit that the odours were normal stable smells,[62] or that even in finer neighbourhoods than this horses and their associated noises and smells were present,[63] or that the character of the neighbourhood was changing and already included other smell-producing residents.[64] Here again they had some success, though in the end Gill J seems to have taken the no-nonsense position that obviously the stable stank and no one should have to tolerate such an enterprise adjoining their residence.

The defence called sixteen witnesses, all anglophones, including several prominent professionals, connections from Drysdale's days with the Hunt Club. Drysdale's lawyers were perhaps trying to counter any classist inclinations the judge might have had by bringing the full weight of Drysdale's aristocratic connections to bear on the case. All the witnesses testified to the quality of the stable and the skill and care with which Drysdale ran it. A local farmer testified that he removed manure from the premises every day.[65] Several physicians testified that a clean and well-kept stable was not a source of disease, and that the typical ammonia smell would in fact have disinfectant qualities.[66] Other Montreal livery stable operators and several horse owners who boarded their animals with Drysdale asserted the quality of the stable and Drysdale's expertise.[67] Alongside this defence against fault, however, was a more subtle line of evidence. Several of the witnesses pointed out that other livery stables existed in posh neighbourhoods in Montreal without complaint, even when neighbours' fancy residences backed right up against dung pits.[68] The implication was clear: if Montreal's rich and cultured found a stable within the "normal" bounds of tolerance, what right did Dugas have to complain on busy St. Denis Street? More generally, by arguing that Drysdale's stable was cleaner than most, his lawyers were trying to place the stable firmly within the realm of "normal" stable smells and noises. This would make it difficult to argue that a "normal" stable exceeded the "normal" standards of tolerance owed between neighbours, given the necessity and ubiquity of horses and stables in the city.

Dugas's lawyers for the most part subjected the defence witnesses to only cursory cross-examination, particularly on any testimony related to fault. A typical example is the following exchange from the testimony of Colin Campbell, a member of the Montreal Hunt who boarded horses with Drysdale:

> Q. And how about the cleanliness of the stables?
> A. They were remarkably clean.
> Q. You know the general run of livery stables in the City of Montreal?
> A. Yes, sir.
> Q. How would it compare with other livery stables?
> A. It is far ahead of them.
>
> . . .
>
> *Cross-Examined by Mr. Robidoux, Q. C. of Counsel for Plaintiff.*
>
> Q. There was always, Mr. Campbell, a certain smell of amonia [*sic*] and manure, it is unavoidable, I suppose?
> A. Of course it is very hard to be in a stable and not have what we call a stable smell.[69]

Dugas's team is here content to make the small point that the stable smelled, without pursuing things further; with other witnesses they did not even do that, leaving testimony about the exemplary cleanliness of the stable unchallenged. This is interesting, since this was Drysdale's major line of defence. On the one hand, these points were perhaps invulnerable to attack – Dugas's own witnesses admitted that the stable was as well or better run than any.[70] On the other hand, however, Dugas's lawyers certainly knew that in the tradition of the civil law, fault was not an issue in liability for nuisance, and they were perhaps content to let Drysdale dilute his case with arguments about fault, as long as they took care to establish that the stable in fact smelled.

Implicit behind the parties' cases even at this early stage are the conflicting — in fact, irreconcilable — views of the same basic principle: that owners have the right to use their property as they see fit. Dugas sees the powers of ownership in a negative sense, as granting a veto on the activities of neighbouring proprietors. In this view, since owners have the right to enjoy their property fully, the mere fact that another has violated the standards of the neighbourhood — by crossing the line between a trifling inconvenience and a nuisance — gives rise to liability and compensation. For Drysdale, ownership is a positive power, which grants him licence to use his property as he sees fit. By this reading, only fault — and not the simple fact of injury to another — creates liability. As long as Drysdale has not used his property maliciously, or in an excessive manner, or in violation of applicable laws, he is within his rights as owner and insulated from the claims of his neighbours. Though the principle was just on the verge of being articulated in France, and would not be imported into Quebec for decades, Drysdale's position hints at the idea of abuse of right, that one cannot exercise one's rights — especially the right of ownership — maliciously or even negligently so as to injure another.[71]

Justice Gill rendered judgment in favour of Dugas on 9 March 1894. He issued brief reasons with no indication of the legal basis for his decision; he simply stated that it had been proved that Drysdale's stable depreciated the value of Dugas's property, lowered his rents, and caused general inconvenience.[72] He rejected Drysdale's arguments without comment. In the end, Dugas was awarded damages of $398: $248 for loss of rent and an arbitrary amount of $150 for inconveniences connected to his residence. Justice Gill also added $4,000 future damages for the depreciation in value of the two properties ($2,000 each), to become executable should Drysdale continue to run the stable after 1 May.[73] This amounted to a *de facto* injunction (the writ itself would not be available in Quebec in cases like this until 1897), since $4,000 was far more than a modest business like Drysdale's could absorb.[74]

Appeal to the Court of Queen's Bench

Drysdale filed an appeal the next week, with his son-in-law and two others standing surety for the appeal.[75] The parties' basic arguments remained unchanged, though refined and focused. Having seen the main direction of Dugas's case — and the positive reception it received at trial — Drysdale's lawyers now attempted to address Dugas's *voisinage* claims more explicitly. They began with the physical structure itself, noting that it was built in line with the other buildings and fit in stylistically.[76] They went on to try to challenge Dugas's image of the neighbourhood as primarily residential by emphasizing the testimony regarding commercial activity in the area: "as for this street, today commerce invades it; there are grocery shops and a butcher's stall nearby."[77]

More subtly, they tried to challenge the protection of *voisinage* by marshalling the argument of the need for industry in cities. Not only is Drysdale's stable properly run, they argued, but it is also a necessary industry in the urban context. Shutting it would open the floodgates to similar actions against other stables elsewhere in Montreal, with dire consequences for the city's commercial life.[78] The courts must take progress into account, and the law must progress as well:

> The very application of legal principles must change with the times, circumstances, and need. Modern progress has discovered and changed many things. In a manufacturing and commercial city like Montreal, neighbourhood obligations are subject to modern needs, circumstances, and progress. One cannot judge today as one judged a century ago.[79]

This was an attempt to defuse the *voisinage* argument by characterizing it as the anti-progressive protection of property owners in the face of the interests of industry and commerce. This was asking a lot of judges in the 1890s,[80] but as the lawyers pointed out, there was recent precedent for just this position in the 1888 case *Claude v Weir*, where the Court of Queen's Bench protected the tanneries of Côte-des-Neiges against a neighbour who had come to the nuisance, since to do otherwise "would have the effect of destroying this industry which adds to the prosperity of the inhabitants of this village and increases the value of their property."[81]

As at trial, however, Drysdale's lawyers focused most of their energies on proving he was not at fault. They pinned this argument on article 406 of the code and the unlimited right owners have to use their property, subject only to law and regulation. Since a livery stable is a lawful business if operated in keeping with the best practices and if all precautions are taken, there was no fault and consequently no liability for any inconveniences suffered by his neighbours.[82] In short, given the all-but-absolute nature of the right of ownership as set out in the code, "the appellant is within the limits of his right."[83]

Dugas changed legal teams for the appeal, to another francophone firm, Robidoux, Geoffrion & Chènevert, with Joseph-Emery Robidoux, who had already been involved in the case at trial, taking the lead on the appeal.[84] Curiously, they submitted no factum, relying on oral arguments to make their points. As summarized in the judgment,[85] Dugas's arguments remained largely unchanged: Drysdale was abusing his own property rights and infringing on those of his neighbours. Dugas made one interesting addition, however: he now explicitly made the point that Drysdale was making wrongful use of his property, in other words, that he was at fault. This was however mainly argued on the basis of alleged violations of municipal bylaws, and in any case the argument does not seem to have been pursued very vigorously.

The unanimous decision of the Court was delivered orally by Justice Jonathan Wurtele on 24 January 1895, and followed some time later by written reasons. Wurtele J, in another coincidence that reveals how small the Montreal legal community was, had practised law with JJC Abbott when Dugas was a student in the office.[86] The judgment fleshes out the details and analysis of the case, but stays close to the reasoning underlying the trial decision. The result was mixed. The court upheld Drysdale's liability and the damages of $398, but it reversed the award of future damages, holding that since it was impossible to assess the extent of depreciation of the property until it was actually sold (and Drysdale might have closed the stable or otherwise abated the nuisance in the meantime), such an award was necessarily speculative.[87]

Justice Wurtele begins by restating the absolute nature of ownership, but moves quickly to consider its social limitations, hinting at what would later be termed abuse of rights:

> However full the right of ownership may be, it must give way to certain limitations which are rendered indispensible by our social state. Living together, we have to respect the rights of others as others have to respect our rights, and we therefore have no right on our land, to do anything which might infringe upon the rights belonging to a neighbouring proprietor. There must necessarily be a mutual yielding of rights in the common interest.[88]

Though by the letter of the code ownership was an absolute right limited only by "law or regulations," a long customary tradition placed certain social limits on the powers of owners. The rule was that any "injury . . . must result, not from the deprivation of an advantage, but from the infringement of a right to which the other is entitled by reason of his ownership."[89] This might include a right to support if a neighbour is excavating, but does not include for example a pleasant view that the neighbour previously enjoyed.

In Dugas's case, since the right of ownership embraces the air above and the earth below (as stated in article 414 of the code), "[t]he owner of a piece of ground has the right to enjoy a pure and undefiled air and also to live on it without being disturbed by immoderate noises."[90] Justice Wurtele goes further: This right is violated not by just any smells or noises, but by "abusive use": the "smoke, offensive odours or noise must exceed that which arises in the ordinary usages of life or from necessity . . . ."[91] Drawing the line between the ordinary and the excessive or abusive, however, is a subjective assessment by the courts. In the end, Wurtele J took this subjectivity to heart, and simply asserted — contrary to much of the evidence presented at trial, as we have seen — that

> [t]here is no doubt that the disagreeable odours and the noise coming from the appellant's livery stable exceeded the measure or degree of inconvenience which would result from an ordinary use of the appellant's property, that they were intolerable and constituted a nuisance for which the respondent has a right of action to recover the damages which he suffered by reason of it.[92]

Having found that Drysdale's stable constituted an "abusive use" of his property, the rest of Drysdale's arguments fell as a necessary consequence. It was irrelevant that the stable was necessary for commerce or that Dugas came to the nuisance: the stable factually constituted a nuisance and Dugas, as the successor to the rights of his predecessor in title, has a right of action for the rental property even for depreciation suffered before he purchased.[93] Likewise, it was irrelevant that the city's commercial needs required stables and horses. It was not within the power of the court to order the stable shut down, but abusive use must be compensated. The result was the imposition of a kind of perpetual tax or surcharge on Drysdale's use of his property: yes he may keep the stable, but unless he abates the nuisance, he remained at the mercy of periodic lawsuits by his neighbours.

The decision rests entirely on the idea of abusive exercise of the right of ownership and what constitutes excessive use of property, and is supported by French authorities.[94] Justice Wurtele makes no mention of English nuisance law, nor does he explicitly address the character of the neighbourhood, a point argued by both parties. As such, the decision is an early expression in Quebec of the idea of abuse of rights, a characterization that would be picked up at the Supreme Court.

Appeal to the Supreme Court of Canada

PERHAPS EMBOLDENED BY THIS partial success, Drysdale appealed again to the Supreme Court of Canada. His petition for permission was granted by the Court of Queen's Bench on 11 March 1895, and two days later the same three sureties came forward to offer security of $500 for the appeal.[95]

Drysdale's lawyers sharpened his case still further for the Supreme Court, focusing mainly on the key aspect of the previous decision: that only interference with a right constitutes excessive use of property. They introduced a new distinction to address this point, between what is simply "disagreeable" and what is "unhealthy."[96] Bringing in progress and the needs of commerce again, they waxed poetic in arguing that scrupulous sensitivity could not be the standard:

> We are living in modern times, in the midst of a civilised society; Montreal is a large commercial community, and it were ridiculous to impose upon its citizens any of those precautions by which the peaceful slumber of the Sybarites of old was prevented from being disturbed.[97]

Their point was both broader and more technical than the appeal to the needs of commerce they had already argued in the lower courts, however. Basing their argument on French authorities as well as on the Quebec case *St Charles v Doutre*, they argued that simple injury was not enough — the injury must be *réel*, that is, an injury to the neighbour's right.[98] A merely disagreeable odour affects enjoyment of one's property in the same way that blocking a pleasant view does, whereas an unhealthy odour undermines the very nature of the right of ownership. The evidence clearly showed, moreover, that Drysdale's stable was not a danger to health. This same distinction was behind the holding of the House of Lords in *St Helen's Smelting v Tipping*, a point Drysdale's lawyers made at the very end of their factum in a nod to the common-law justices on the Supreme Court. The meat of their argument, however, rested entirely on French authorities and Quebec cases.[99]

This was a promising way to frame the argument, and it led finally (one might wonder why it took so long) to their final point, a consideration of the main focus of Dugas's case, the violation of neighbourhood standards: "We think the question could easily be solved by finding whether or not the inconvenience caused to the Respondent exceeds the ordinary inconvenience which neighbors are expected and are mutually bound to support without any recourse."[100] Again citing French authorities, they argue that smoke, odours, and the like, unless "*excessive, violent* and *continuous,*" must be tolerated by neighbours.[101] A merely disagreeable odour, they argue, does not meet the standard set in the authorities.

Dugas's lawyers lay out their arguments in a brief factum, almost half of which consists of excerpts from witness testimony. Their focus, as from the beginning, was on standards of *voisinage* and the maxim *sic utere tuo.* The absolute nature of ownership means Dugas may recover damages for any interference with his property. The rigour of this rule is tempered by the idea of normal neighbourhood inconveniences — slight inconveniences must be tolerated, "but the moment they attain to such proportions as would cause injury to a neighbour, either as to his health or as to his property, then such annoyances constitute nuisances, which the law must abate."[102] The evidence, they argue, is clear: "Appellant has exceeded his rights . . . ."[103]

In a relatively brief judgment, the Supreme Court dismissed Drysdale's appeal by a five to one majority.[104] In what was effectively a concurring opinion, Samuel Henry Strong CJ reviews the English authorities as a complement to Henri-Elzéar Taschereau J's review of the French principles. He focuses on the character of the neighbourhood, since a nuisance in a residential section would not necessarily be one in a different sort of environment.[105] In this case, since the neighbourhood is "a street occupied almost exclusively by private residences," the character of the neighbourhood is clear.[106]

Though the Chief Justice's opinion rests on the idea of neighbourhood standards, it also contains a curious ambiguity about the place of fault within the Quebec law of nuisance. He notes first that actions against "all abuses of proprietary rights" are based on article 1053 of the code, which involves injuries caused by one's fault.[107] Later, however, after having discussed the issue of neighbourhood standards, he returns to the idea of fault, dismissing the arguments that Drysdale had "acted with extreme care and caution in carrying on his business" with a casual invocation of the authority of the English case of *Bamford v Turnley.*[108] How liability under article 1053 might follow even though Drysdale had run his stable as *un bon père de famille,* the Chief Justice does not explain. This ambiguity about the role of fault in liability for property use would remain a central conceptual problem throughout the twentieth century.[109]

Justice Taschereau, basing his opinion on the French and Quebec authorities, holds that the case is effectively one of fact, not law: with damage having been proved, Drysdale is strictly liable for having violated the standards of *voisinage*. While Drysdale has a right to run a stable, his right ends when he seriously inconveniences his neighbours by "spreading (*emittere*) odours in the respondent's living and dining rooms, or corrupting his atmosphere."[110] Spelling out the implications, this means that Drysdale's right to run a stable is conditional on continual compensation of any serious damage he causes to his neighbours.

Finally, in a one-paragraph dissent that was doubtless of small consolation to Drysdale, John Gwynne J would have allowed the appeal, since the effect of the lower court decisions was to make it illegal to have a stable anywhere in Montreal, a conclusion beyond the power of the courts to declare. He hints at a fault standard: since no stable could be more perfect than Drysdale's, no stable could possibly reach the standards imposed by the judgment below.[111]

Outcomes

With the judgment of the Supreme Court, Drysdale had apparently had enough — nothing suggests that he contemplated a further appeal to the Privy Council, and he seems to have shut down the stable rather than face a yearly succession of damages suits from his neighbours.[112] After losing his stable, Drysdale worked for several years as a toll-booth keeper in Outremont, an affluent francophone suburb of Montreal. The stable building remained in the family, occupied for some years after by Drysdale's son and son-in-law. The space remained commercial amidst the residential properties: a bicycle livery business ran out of it for a year, followed by a grocer and butcher sharing the space. Drysdale died on 8 February 1908.[113]

Even before the litigation with Drysdale was over, Dugas had moved out of the neighbourhood, to another primarily residential, relatively affluent, mostly francophone neighbourhood a few blocks away. In 1898, he left Quebec for the Yukon, first as one of the royal commissioners charged with inquiring into the Canadian Pacific Railway's treatment of its workers during the construction of the Crow's Nest Pass,[114] and soon after as one of the first territorial judges in Dawson City.[115] Gold fever might have been an added motivation, since Dugas, ever the speculator, staked some mining claims after his arrival.[116] He became a prominent and somewhat controversial member of Dawson City society, accused by some of using his influence to help turn the Yukon "into a preserve for the aristocracy of French-Canadian office-seekers," among them his own son.[117] Dugas's health began failing in 1907, and he travelled to Paris, California, and Bermuda to seek medical attention and recuperation. He died in Quebec on 25 August 1914, after a fishing trip in the Laurentians.

As for *Drysdale v Dugas*, the case may have helped bring about a tightening of the regulation of traditional nuisance industries within Montreal. Five years after the Supreme Court's decision, the Montreal Building Bylaw of 1901, the first major revision of building controls since 1877, subjected stables to strict limits. This included the requirement of public notice before construction permits would be granted, "so that neighbouring owners and those who reside in the area as well as other interested parties may have the opportunity to oppose the granting of such permit."[118] There followed other bylaws prohibiting new stables altogether in certain parts of the city.[119] Existing stables were increasingly closely monitored as part of the developing public health system.[120] The effect was to begin to replace the subjective appreciation of nuisance that drove private litigation with objective regulatory criteria like fire risk and hygiene, as interpreted and applied by public inspectors. It meant, moreover, that the policing of class boundaries that lay behind many nuisance cases would now be publicly facilitated, rather than left to the vagaries of private litigation.

As a precedent, the Supreme Court's judgment in *Drysdale v Dugas* became a standard citation in Quebec nuisance cases, and occasionally elsewhere as well.[121] It came to stand for a strong version of neighbourhood liability, whereby "the owner of an objectionable establishment was obliged to indemnify his neighbour for damages suffered by the escape of noxious odors and exhalations where these constitute a grave inconvenience to the neighbour."[122] In the long run, tension continued in Quebec nuisance law between fault-based and no-fault conceptions of liability. The new *Civil Code of Québec*, which entered force in 1994, includes an explicit statement of the neighbourhood principle in article 976, and thus brings aspects of nuisance clearly within the property regime.[123] Though this change was explicit, controversy remained over whether the new article was to work in tandem with the general fault-based regime of civil liability or whether it created a distinct form of liability. The Supreme Court ended debate in *St Lawrence Cement* in 2008, unanimously affirming the existence in Quebec of a no-fault regime of liability for property damage, and recognizing *Drysdale*'s continuing relevance in the process.[124]

As is always the case with precedents, the story of Drysdale, Dugas, and their neighbourhood has been stripped away, and the case boiled down to a principle, with only the bare minimum of legally meaningful factual detail remaining to support the applicability of that principle. Nuisance law, however, in which liability traces the boundaries of interpersonal tolerance through analysis of unwritten but socially meaningful codes of neighbourliness, acceptable proximity, cleanliness, and propriety, needs such stories.

Notes

1 Associate Professor, Department of History, Concordia University; of the Quebec Bar. I would like to thank for their help and comments Raphaël Fischler, Shannon McSheffrey, the various audiences to whom this project was presented as a work in progress, and the editors of this collection. Donna Drysdale and Victoria Drysdale, both descendants of William Drysdale, provided useful information about their ancestor. Julie Perrone's research assistance was invaluable, and a Concordia University start-up grant for new faculty provided research funding. Special thanks to Nicholas Kasirer and Shauna Van Praagh, in whose 1999–2000 course at McGill on extracontractual obligations and torts I first encountered *Drysdale v Dugas* and the puzzles it raises.

2 (1896) 26 SCR 20, Strong CJC, Taschereau, Gwynne, Sedgewick, King, Girouard JJ [*Drysdale* (SCC)]. The lower court decisions are reported in (1894) RJQ 5 CS 418, Gill J [*Drysdale* (Sup Ct)] and (1895) RJQ 6 BR 278, Lacoste CJ, Baby, Bossé, Blanchet, Wurtele JJ [*Drysdale* (QB)].

3 [2008] 3 SCR 392, 2008 SCC 64. See Pierre-Claude Lafond, "L'heureuse alliance des troubles de voisinage et du recours collectif: portée et effets de l'arrêt *Ciment du Saint-Laurent*" (2009) 68 R du B 385-448. Though the case has been most influential in Quebec, it continues to be discussed elsewhere in various contexts. See e.g., GHL Fridman, *The Law of Torts in Canada*, 2d ed (Toronto: Carswell, 2002) at 213; Elizabeth Brubaker, "The Common Law and the Environment: The Canadian Experience" in Peter J. Hill & Roger E. Meiners, eds, *Who Owns the Environment?* (Lanham, Md.: Rowman & Littlefield, 1989) 87-118 at 97.

4 Exemplary contextual studies of historic cases include AWB Simpson, *Leading Cases in the Common Law* (Oxford: Clarendon Press, 1995) and Constance Backhouse, *Colour-Coded: A Legal History of Racism in Canada, 1900-1950* (Toronto: University of Toronto Press for Osgoode Society for Canadian Legal History, 1999). Few such studies have been done of Quebec cases, perhaps because the more principle-oriented nature of the civil law leads to a focus on doctrinal development rather than on the facts behind litigation. An exception is Sylvio Normand, "L'affaire Plamondon: un cas d'antisémitisme à Québec au début du XXe siècle" (2007) 48 C de D 477-504.

5 See William Cochrane, *The Canadian Album: Men of Canada . . .*, vol 2 (Brantford, Ont: Bradley, Garretson, 1893) at 355; Henry James Morgan, ed, *The Canadian Men and Women of the Time: A Hand-book of Canadian Biography* (Toronto: William Briggs, 1898) at 292; Charles Robillard, "Le juge Calixte-Aimé Dugas" in a scrapbook of newspaper clippings (dating from 1941-43) in Bibliothèque et Archives nationales du Québec [BANQ], Montreal Centre, P1000, S3, D2383 at 95-96; and a brief anonymous obituary of Dugas in (1914) 34 Can L Times 809.

6 After the trial, for example, the *Montreal Daily Star* reported on the case under the headline "Judge Dugas Wins" (9 March 1894) 6.

7 Dugas's appointment appears to have been a political *quid pro quo*, as the Liberals formed a minority government after the provincial election of 1 May 1878.

8 See generally Charles R Daoust, *Cent-vingt jours de service actif: récit historique très complet de la campagne du 65ème au Nord-Ouest* (Montreal: Eusèbe Senécal & Fils, 1886).

9 *Acte d'incorporation, constitution et règlements du Club canadien, avec les noms des membres. 296 rue Lagauchetière* (Montreal: Louis Perrault, 1880) at 23; *Act of Incorporation, Constitution, By-laws, Executive Committee and List of Members of the Metropolitan Club, Montreal: Revised to 1st January, 1894* (Montreal: [Metropolitan Club], 1894) at 30. Drysdale's counsel in the case, JN Greenshields, was also a member of the latter.

10 In 1889 Dugas was mentioned as writing a *Guide des juges de paix*, but this was apparently never published: Edmond Lareau, *Histoire du droit canadien: depuis les origines de la colonie jusqu'à nos jours*, vol 2 (Montreal: A. Périard, 1889) at 307.

11 Dugas was ultimately awarded $50 for malicious and false arrest. See "A Disputed Gateway," *Daily Witness* (Montreal) (22 September 1875) 3; *Montreal Herald and Daily Commercial Gazette* (23 September 1875) 4; "The Disputed Gateway Case: Judgment by the Recorder," *Daily Witness* (Montreal) (7 October 1875) 3; *Daily Witness* (Montreal) (13 October 1875) 3. The case file is BANQ Montreal, TP11, S2, SS2, SSS1, cont. 1987-05-007/3477 (no 957 of 1876).

12 The Court of Queen's Bench trial occupied the press in September 1885: "On Trial For Libel," *Daily Witness* (Montreal) (22 September 1885) 8; "The Sheppard Libel Case," *Daily Witness* (23 September 1885) 4; "Declared to Be Guilty," *ibid* at 8. The case file has not survived. On Sheppard, see Ramsay Cook, "Sheppard, Edmund Ernest" in GW Brown et al, ed, *Dictionary of Canadian Biography*, 15 vols to date (Toronto: University of Toronto Press, 1966-), 15: 932-34.

13 *Oligny v Brault* (1895), RJQ 8 CS 506 (in which Dugas was one of the plaintiffs).

14 *The Canadian Mining Review*, vol 8, no 2 (Ottawa: BTA Bell, 1889) at 23.

15 RW Ells for Geological Survey of Canada, *Mineral Resources of Canada: Bulletin on Mica* (Ottawa: SE Dawson, 1904) at 20.

16 Drysdale's life is less well documented than that of the public figure Dugas. His family situation (wife Mary, at least eight children) can be traced in the censuses of 1881, 1891, and 1901. Some of his positions are mentioned in his entries in the Lovell Montreal city directories for the years 1861 to 1907: see BANQ Montreal, Annuaires *Lovell* de Montréal et sa banlieue (1842-1999), online: http://bibnum2.banq.qc.ca/bna/lovell/. More detailed information can be found in the literature on fox hunting in Montreal: see below note 17. Two William Drysdales were active in Montreal around the time of the litigation; the other, a bookseller and publisher, was a slightly younger man.

17 See generally "The Montreal Hunt: William Drysdale, the Veteran Huntsman, Tenders his Resignation," *The Gazette* (Montreal) (31 July 1889) 8; John Irwin Cooper, *The History of the Montreal Hunt* ([Montreal]: Montreal Hunt, [1953?]). Cooper reproduces Drysdale's 1872 contract (between pages 86-87), which gives an indication of his responsibilities. See also A Henry Higginson & Julian Ingersoll Chamberlain, *The Hunts of the United States and Canada: Their Masters, Hounds and Histories* (Boston: Frank L. Wiles, 1908) at 107-8.

18 Cooper, *ibid* at 25.

19 The name of the stable is not mentioned in the surviving case files, but appears in Drysdale's entries in the Lovell city directories from 1891-92 to 1895-96.

20 What follows is based on contemporary maps and fire insurance plans, available at the BANQ, online: http://services.banq.qc.ca/sdx/cep/accueil.xsp. These include *Atlas of the City of Montreal* (Montreal: Charles E. Goad, 1879), plate E; *Cadastral Plans, City of Montreal* ([Montreal: n.p.], 1880), sheet 2; *Atlas of the City of Montreal* (Montreal: Charles E Goad, 1881), plate XXXI; *Atlas of the City of Montreal* (Montreal: Charles E Goad, 1890), plate XXXI; *Atlas of the City of Montreal and Vicinity* (Montreal: Charles E Goad, 1912), plate 31. The block in question is today bounded by rue St-Denis to the east, rue Drolet to the west, Avenue des Pins to the north, and Carré St-Louis to the south.

21 See *Les rues de Montréal: répertoire historique* (Montreal: Éditions du Méridien, 1995) at 423.

22 Described in deposition of Eugène Lafontaine (12 October 1893) at 47. Plans were submitted as exhibits at trial, but the trial file has not survived, and the plans were not reproduced in the appellate factums. Witness depositions from the trial were reprinted for the Supreme Court and are found in the Supreme Court case file (no 1496 of 1895), Library and Archives Canada, R125, vol 136, file 1496 (Supreme Court of Canada fonds, Series A — Case Files, *Drysdale v Dugas*) [SCC Case File]. The main depositions, taken 12-13 October 1893, are included in the printed case prepared for the Supreme Court. A further four depositions, dated 18 October 1893, were not reprinted, but appear as an appendix to Drysdale's factum from the Court of Queen's Bench, itself sent to the Supreme Court and included in the case file.

23 See generally Clay McShane & Joel A. Tarr, *The Horse in the City: Living Machines in the Nineteenth Century* (Baltimore: Johns Hopkins University Press, 2007) esp. 102-26 on stables. Livery stables in Montreal were subject to a lower water-use charge than boarding stables, so it seems likely Drysdale had prestige rather than economy in mind in naming the stable. See Montreal bylaw no 51, "By-law to provide for the Care and Management of the Montreal Water Works, and to establish a Tariff of Water Rates" (passed 15 March 1870) in Charles Glackmeyer, ed, *Appendix to the Charter and By-Laws of the City of Montreal Containing Amendments to the Charter and By-Laws Passed Since the Last Publication of the Municipal Laws in 1865* (Montreal: La Minerve Steam Press, 1870) at 234-35.

24 The three largest were McVey's, Osborne's, and Starr's. See deposition of Doctor Patterson (13 October 1893) at 82; deposition of Dr. Charles McEachran (13 October 1893) at 102.

25 McShane & Tarr, above note 23 at 120-22.

26 See generally Joel Franklin Brenner, "Nuisance Law and the Industrial Revolution" (1974) 3 J Legal Stud 403-33 at 414.

27 On health risks, bylaw No 105, *By-Law concerning Health* (adopted 21 December 1876), quotation from s 25. On fire, bylaw no 107, *Règlement pour régler la construction des bâtiments et pour prévenir les accidents par le feu* (adopted 6 April 1877), s 48. On the regulatory landscape generally, see Raphaël Fischler, "Development Controls in Toronto in the Nineteenth Century" (2007) 36 Urban Hist Rev 16-31.

28 See Louis Laberge, *Report on the Sanitary State of the City of Montreal, Also an Account of the Operations of the Board of Health and the Vital Statistics for the Year 1888* (Montreal: Eusèbe Senécal & Fils, 1889) (with subsequent reports for the years 1889, 1890, and 1891), which reports on stables inspected and found to be nuisances.

29 Especially *Côté v Measam* (LC KB, 1819), where the defendant's latrines fouled a stream running through the plaintiff's property. The case file is BANQ Quebec City, TL18, S2, SS1, cont 1960-01-587/1 (no 2 of 1818).

30 In its French version this was drawn virtually word-for-word from article 544 of the French *Code Civil*, which codified a long tradition of customary principles.

31 Robert-Joseph Pothier, *Contrat de société*, in M. Siffrein, ed, Œuvres de Pothier, nouvelle édition, vol 5 (Paris: Siffrein, 1821) at 245 (translation).

32 Article 1053 reads: "Every person capable of discerning right from wrong is responsible for the damage caused by his fault to another, whether by positive act, imprudence, neglect or want of skill."

33 *R v Bruce* (1860), 10 LCR 117 at 120 (QB, Crown Side).

34 Ronald I. Cohen, "Nuisance: A Proprietary Delict" (1968) 14 McGill LJ 124 at 136-37.

35 E.g., Charles Aubry & Charles Rau, *Cours de droit civil français d'après la méthode de Zachariæ*, 4th ed, vol 2 (Paris: Cosse, Marchal, 1869) at 195. See generally Anne-Marie Patault, *Introduction historique au droit des biens* (Paris: Presses universitaires de France, 1989) at 153-55, 222-23.

36 *St. Charles v Doutre* (1874), 18 LCJ 253 at 256 (QB) (translation).

37 Peter Karsten, *Between Law and Custom: "High" and "Low" Legal Cultures in the Lands of the British Diaspora — The United States, Canada, Australia, and New Zealand, 1600-1900* (New York: Cambridge University Press, 2002) at 215. On the situation elsewhere in Canada, see Jennifer Nedelsky, "Judicial Conservatism in an Age of Innovation: Comparative Perspectives on Canadian Nuisance Law 1880-1930" in David H. Flaherty, ed, *Essays in the History of Canadian Law, Volume I* (Toronto: Osgoode Society, 1981) 281-322. This contrasts with England and parts of the United States by the end of the nineteenth century, both more industry-friendly. See Brenner, above note 26; John PS McLaren, "Nuisance Law and the Industrial Revolution: Some Lessons from Social History" (1983) 3 Oxford J Legal Stud 155-221; Christine Rosen, "Differing Perceptions of the Value of Pollution Abatement Across Time and Place: Balancing Doctrine in Pollution Nuisance Law, 1840-1906" (1993) 11 Law & Hist Rev 303-81.

38 For example, in *Claude v Weir* (1888), MLR 4 QB 197, the court dismissed an action against a tannery that had allegedly fouled a stream running through the plaintiff's land because the plaintiff had failed to prove that the pollution originated specifically with the defendant, and not with one of the other tanneries upstream. In *McGibbon v Bédard* (1886), 30 LCJ 282 (QB, appeal side), another tannery case, the action was dismissed because the court found that the plaintiff had moved to the nuisance and had aggravated the odours by covering over a drain.

39 This reflects the situation earlier in the United States, where "traditional" and "new" industries were often treated differently: see Christine Meisner Rosen,

"'Knowing' Industrial Pollution: Nuisance Law and the Power of Tradition in a Time of Rapid Economic Change, 1840-1864" (2003) 8 Environmental Hist 565-97.

40 *Gravel v Gervais* (1891), MLR 7 CS 326.

41 *Forget v Laverdure* (1896), RJQ 9 CS 98. This decision was handed down nine days after the Supreme Court ruled in *Drysdale*, but makes no reference it.

42 *Robins v Dominion Coal Co.* (1899), RJQ 16 CS 195.

43 Patault, above note 35 at 222-23.

44 The Superior Court case file has not survived. A brief chronological summary of proceedings can be found in the court's *plumitif*, BANQ Montreal, TP11, S2, SS2, SSS7, cont 1987-05-007/5594 (vol 4 of 1892), . . . /5587 (vol 4 of 1893), and . . . /5569 (vol 3 of 1894), case number 961 in each [Sup Ct *Plumitif*]. Certain key procedural documents (Dugas's amended declaration, Drysdale's defence) as well as the witness depositions are reproduced in SCC Case File.

45 Amended Declaration (5 July 1893), SCC Case File at 3.

46 Deposition of Hilduard Perron, resident of the house three doors south of the stable (12 October 1893) at 68 (translation): "Q. — Are you one of those who instructed Mr. Justice Dugas to undertake this action, in order to have the stable demolished? A. — No sir."

47 Pelland and Girard were solicitors of record for the trial and were awarded subtraction of costs in the trial judgment, but the examination of witnesses in October 1893 was handled by Joseph-Emery Robidoux, QC, of the firm that would take over the case on appeal. Exactly how this arrangement worked is unclear in the absence of the Superior Court case file. On Girard, see Cochrane, above note 5 at 305.

48 Cochrane, *ibid* at 99; Morgan, above note 5 at 407.

49 J. Douglas Borthwick, *History and Biographical Gazetteer of Montreal to the Year 1892* (Montreal: John Lovell & Son, 1892) at 426.

50 Gill lived at number 642 St. Denis; the stable was at 354-356. See *Lovell's Montreal Directory for 1891-92* (Montreal: John Lovell & Son, [1891]) at 294.

51 Plaintiff's [Amended] Declaration (5 July 1893), SCC Case File at 2 (translation).

52 Defendant's Pleas (14 December 1892), *Ibid* at 4-6.

53 *Ibid* at 5-6.

54 Deposition of Auguste Laforce (12 October 1893) at 21 (translation). See also deposition of physician Joseph Beausoleil (12 October 1893) at 42 (translation): "Q. — St. Denis Street, doesn't it, with some others, forms the best part of the city, occupied by comfortable families? A. — Certainly."

55 Depositions (all 12 October 1893) of Arthur Desjardins (original lessee of the house next to the stable); Alphonse Letellier (current tenant of the rental house); Eugène Lafontaine (brother of Desjardins and frequent visitor to the rental house); Hilduard Perron (resident three doors down from the stable); George Martin (managed the house between Dugas's residence and the stable); and Arthur Desjardins, Jr. (lived in the rental house with his father).

56 Depositions (all 12 October 1893) of Paul Philippe, Azarie Brodeur, and Joseph Beausoleil. George Larin asserted that the odours made the houses unhealthy (deposition, 12 October 1893).

57 Depositions (all 12 October 1893) of Raymond Chartrand (contractor), Charles Berger (contractor), Raymond de Martigny (real estate agent), Joseph Lessard (prospective tenant).

58 Specifically, Dugas alleged that a rooftop wooden shed covering the elevator shaft made it a wooden structure over three stories, in violations of section 28 and 48 of bylaw 107 of 1877 (*Règlement pour régler la construction des bâtiments et pour prévenir les accidents par le feu*), which regulated construction standards to prevent fires. Also, he alleged that Drysdale and others lived in apartments on the upper floors, in violation of section 34 of bylaw 105 of 1876 (*By-Law concerning health*), which prohibited keeping "any horse, cow, calf, pig, sheep, goat or fowl" in any "house or tenement, or any portion thereof." On the law concerning common walls (*mitoyenneté*), see articles 510-519 of the *Civil Code of Lower Canada*.

59 See, for example, deposition of building inspector Pierre Lacroix (12 October 1893) at 51-52, who felt Drysdale had successfully minimized noise and odour. Other witnesses were more mixed in their assessment: see depositions (both 12 October 1893) of Arthur Desjardins at 31 and Pierre Lacroix at 52.

60 Deposition of Arthur Desjardins (12 October 1893) at 28 (rats) and 30-31 (teamsters).

61 Deposition of Auguste Laforce (12 October 1893) at 23 (translation).

62 See e.g., the deposition of Alphonse Letellier (12 October 1893) at 33, where he admits that the noises are normal stable noises, but asserts that the smells would be lessened if Drysdale took more precautions.

63 See especially the deposition of Raymond Chartrand (12 October 1893) at 58, where Drysdale's lawyer in cross-examination tried (mostly unsuccessfully) to get the witness to admit that stables were located in more affluent neighbourhoods elsewhere in Montreal.

64 Deposition of Auguste Laforce (12 October 1893) at 21; deposition of Joseph Beausoleil (12 October 1893) at 41-42.

65 Deposition of Thomas Irving (13 October 1893).

66 Deposition of Doctor Hingston (13 October 1893) at 79; Deposition of Robert Craik (October 18, 1893) at 35-36.

67 Depositions (all 13 October 1893) of James McVey, John H. Garth, S. Osborne, and Colin Campbell.

68 Deposition of livery stable owner S. Osborne (13 October 1893) at 92.

69 Deposition of Colin Campbell (13 October 1893) at 100-1.

70 See, for example, the deposition of Pierre Lacroix (12 October 1893) at 51-52.

71 For early discussion on the applicability of abuse of rights in Quebec, see Pierre-Basile Mignault, "The Modern Evolution of Civil Responsibility" (1927) 5 Can Bar Rev 1-18 at 10-14; George VV Nicholls, *The Responsibility for Offences and Quasi-Offences Under the Law of Quebec* (Toronto: Carswell, 1938) at 23-31.

72 *Drysdale* (Sup Ct) at 419. The case drew little attention from the press, though *La Minerve* provided brief coverage: "Jugement important," *La Minerve* (10 March 1894) 3.

73 The judgment reads "au 1er mai prochain" (*Drysdale* (Sup Ct) at 420), which the Court of Queen's Bench interpreted as 1 May 1895, or a year and two months later. See *Drysdale* (QB) at 282.

74 Before 1897, injunctions were available in Quebec only in specific circumstances provided for by statute, none of which applied to this case. See *An act to provide for the issue of the Writ of Injunction in certain cases, and to regulate the procedure in relation thereto*, SQ 1878 (41 Vic), c 14; Ivan Wotherspoon, *A Manual of the Practice and Procedure in the Several Courts Having Civil Jurisdiction in the Province of Quebec*, rev ed (Montreal: Dawson Brothers, 1880) at 166-69. The 1897 changes to the *Code of Civil Procedure* are outlined in Victor E. Mitchell & FL Snow, *A Manual of the Procedure in the Several Courts Having Jurisdiction in the Province of Quebec* (Montreal: John Lovell & Son, 1897) at liii.

75 Sup. Ct. *Plumitif* (1894). The case file from the Court of Queen's Bench includes only Drysdale's factum and filings regarding the subsequent Supreme Court appeal; Dugas appears not to have filed a factum. The file is BANQ Montreal, TP9, S2, SS5, SSS1, cont 2002-09-001/773 (no 116 of 1894) [QB Case File].

76 Factum de l'Appelant, QB Case File at 6-7. These arguments address two concerns that would eventually give rise to zoning protections: the "built line" of the street (all buildings should line up) and the desirability of consistent height and appearance.

77 *Ibid* at 7 (translation).

78 *Ibid* at 28. On nineteenth-century reliance on horse power, see McShane & Tarr, above note 23.

79 Factum de l'Appelant, QB Case File at 30 (translation).

80 See Nedelsky, above note 37.

81 *Claude v Weir*, above note 38 at 224 (translation). The Supreme Court affirmed the decision, with Justice Taschereau simply adopting the reasons of the Court of Queen's Bench: (1890), 16 SCR 575.

82 Factum de l'Appelant, QB Case File at 29-30.

83 *Ibid* at 33 (translation).

84 Robidoux had been professor of civil law at McGill and a Liberal member of the Legislative Assembly. He would later be the first president of the Canadian Bar Association, and later still a judge on the Superior Court. See Borthwick, above note 49 at 345.

85 *Drysdale* (QB) at 280.

86 See Borthwick, above note 49 at 449.

87 *Drysdale* (QB) at 286-87.

88 *Ibid* at 283.

89 *Ibid.*

90 *Ibid* at 284.

91 *Ibid.*

92 *Ibid* at 285.

93 *Ibid* at 286. This suggests that the Court viewed Dugas's right as a real (i.e., property) right, and not simply a personal (or contractual) right. This point was disputed (thought not particularly vigorously) at the Supreme Court. See Factum of the Appellant, SCC Case File at 11.

94 The decision mentions Aubry and Rau and François Laurent, authors of two influential commentaries on the French civil code, as well as Pothier, the principal authority for pre-Revolutionary French customary law.

95 Court of Queen's Bench, Registers (1895) at 99-100, BANQ Montreal, TP9, S2, SS5, SSS4, cont 2002-09-001/993.

96 Factum of the Appellant, SCC Case File at 10.

97 *Ibid* at 9.

98 *Ibid* at 13, citing Laurent (actually a Luxembourgeois, but writing on French law) (translation): "If the owner does not injure the right of his neighbour, he owes no reparation, even if he injures him."

99 *Ibid* at 12-17. The argument includes often lengthy quotations from Laurent, Charles Demolombe, and Armand and Désiré Dalloz, and brief citations of numerous other French authorities. The quotation from *St Helen's Smelting* is *ibid* at 17.

100 *Ibid* at 16.

101 *Ibid* (emphasis in original).

102 Respondent's Factum, SCC Case File at VII.

103 *Ibid* at VIII.

104 Justices Sedgewick, King, and Girouard concurred in dismissing the appeal, but filed no reasons.

105 He reviews the familiar English cases *Bamford v Turnley, St Helen's Smelting v Tipping, Brand v Hammersmith Railway*; *Drysdale* (SCC) at 24.

106 *Ibid* at 25.

107 *Ibid* at 22-23, quotation at 23.

108 *Ibid* at 25-26.

109 See *St. Lawrence Cement*, above note 3.

110 *Drysdale* (SCC) at 27 (translation; Latin in original).

111 *Ibid* at 28.

112 The stable disappears from the Lovell municipal directories beginning with the 1896-97 edition.

113 A brief obituary appears in W. Lefroy, *Canada: An Illustrated Weekly Journal for All Interested in the Dominion*, vol 9 (29 February 1908) at 217.

114 Canada, Parliament, "Commission to Inquire into Charges of Unjust Treatment of Persons Engaged in the Construction on the Crow's Nest Pass Railway" in *Sessional Papers*, No 90a (1898) (CA Dugas, F. Pedley, J. Appleton, commissioners).

115 See *Inventory to the Records of the Yukon Government, YRG 1, Series 11, Territorial Court Records, 1897-1950 Held at the Yukon Archives* (NP: Yukon Tourism and Culture, Yukon Archives, 2003), online: www.tc.gov.yk.ca/pdf/finding_aids/YRG_1_Series_11.pdf, which includes references to material on Dugas's judicial career in the Yukon, including his judicial notebooks.

116 His claims are listed in "Golden clean up edition," *Dawson Daily News* (1 January 1902); see Yukon Genealogy, online: www.yukongenealogy.com/content/database_cleanup.htm. Mineral fever seems to have run in the family: in 1849 Dugas's father temporarily left the family to join the California gold rush. See Robillard, above note 5 at 96.

117 "Conditions in the Yukon," *Victoria Daily Colonist* (18 May 1905) 3. On a happier note, there was extensive coverage of the wedding of Dugas's son: "Married at St. Mary's," *Yukon Sun* (Dawson City, 24 September 1903) 3.

118 *Règlement à l'effet de réglementer la construction, la modification, la réparation, l'enlèvement et l'inspection des bâtiments dans la cité de Montréal, et de prévenir les accidents par le feu*, no 260 (adopted 4 February 1901), ss 106-07 (translation; quotation at s 107).

119 E.g., *Règlement à l'effet de prohiber l'érection et le maintien d'écuries sur certaines rues dans le quartier St-Gabriel*, no 620 (adopted 16 April 1917); *Règlement au sujet de l'établissement de cours à bois, de garages publics et d'écuries*, no 630 (adopted 18 June 1917).

120 See generally Jay Cassel, "Public Health in Canada" in Dorothy Porter, ed, *The History of Public Health and the Modern State* (Amsterdam: Rodopi, 1994) esp. 291-92; Peter Keating & Othmar Keel, eds, *Santé et société au Québec: XIX*[e]*-XX*[e] *siècle* ([Montreal:] Boréal, 1995).

121 E.g., *Appleby v Erie Tobacco* (1910), 22 Ont R 533 at 538 (Dist Ct).

122 *Carpenter v Ville de Maisonneuve* (1897), RJQ 11 CS 242 at 247 (Sup Ct).

123 The article, in the chapter "Special Rules on the Ownership of Immovables" in the book on property, reads: "Neighbours shall suffer the normal neighbourhood annoyances that are not beyond the limit of tolerance they owe each other, according to the nature or location of their land or local custom." See Adrian Popovici, "La poule et l'homme: sur l'article 976 *C.c.Q.*" (1997) 99 R du N 214; Pierre-Claude Lafond, "L'exercice du droit de propriété et les troubles de voisinage: petit Code (civil) de conduite à l'intention des voisins" (1999) 33 RJT 225; Marie-Ève Arbour & Véronique Racine, "Itinéraires du trouble de voisinage dans l'espace normatif" (2009) 50 C de D 327.

124 *St Lawrence Cement*, above note 3 at para 86 (*Drysdale* discussed at paras 42-43).

KVP: Riparian Resurrection in 20th Century Ontario

Jamie Benidickson

Introduction

In 1946, when the Kalamazoo Vegetable and Parchment Company (KVP) re-opened a kraft paper mill that had been dormant for several years, the condition of the Spanish River deteriorated rapidly. The decline occurred despite an agreement between the Ontario government and KVP involving an undertaking not to deposit more refuse than necessary. KVP was soon discharging at least three and a half tons of chemical-laden fibrous materials from its sulphate process each day.[1]

The situation gave rise to a "celebrated and contentious" court battle[2] in which riparian property rights clashed with economic development. The KVP proceedings are of interest in and of themselves, but the case is equally noteworthy as a mid-twentieth-century landmark on the pathway leading from environmental protection as a by-product of privately enforced common law property rights to an elaborate regulatory regime intended to safeguard the public interest in water quality directly. For this reason it is helpful to consider in the second section the state of water quality law preceding KVP as a prelude to the trial decision by James Chalmers McRuer. This decision and the appeals are discussed in the third section together with a notorious legislative response, the KVP Act. Subsequent developments that were either inspired by or encouraged by the KVP experience are discussed in the final section.

Rhetoric and Reality Before KVP

"Pollution is always unlawful," Supreme Court Justice Thibodeau Rinfret boldly proclaimed in a 1928 decision, "and, in itself, constitutes a nuisance." Rinfret's dramatic assertion offered an encouraging rallying cry for the common law cause of clean rivers. But even in the memorable conflict between the Groat family and the City of Edmonton where this firmly worded utterance appeared, application of the proposition was not without difficulty.

En route to his broad condemnation of water pollution, Justice Rinfret had actually declared drains and sewers to be a necessity. Such facilities were generally constructed, he explained, pursuant to statutory powers and resulted in some respects from the exercise of common law rights enjoyed by local ratepayers, as represented through municipal governments. Though exercised for the benefit of all inhabitants, such collective rights were not without limitations. The judge specifically emphasized that statutory powers should not be construed as authorization to create a private nuisance — "unless the statute expressly so states."[3]

Rinfret's formulation of the principle governing drainage of riparian lands seemed unremarkable. The riparian proprietor, he observed, enjoys a common law right to drain his land into a natural stream, though such a right cannot be exercised so as to injure those downstream, because, to return to the boldly stated principle: pollution is always unlawful.

What exactly might constitute pollution was problematic. Would the judge's stark proclamation ensure that waterways were preserved in a natural state, or was some level of waste discharge, even accompanied by a degree of deterioration, to be tolerated in the name of competing principle? If the latter, how would that level be determined? Would this be accomplished in relation to conventional practices, social preference, or economic convenience, for example, or with regard to such environmental consequences as the actual condition of the waterways and their inhabitants?[4] Notwithstanding the rhetoric, a firm point of reference for an absence of pollution was not easily discerned.[5] If lines were to be drawn, public health rather than the natural environment tended to be the focus of concern,[6] and the advent of chlorination undermined further that rationale for safeguarding water quality in rivers, lakes and streams.[7]

On the basis of US experience during the first half of the twentieth century it could also be observed that courts were prepared to afford property holders only limited protection against pollution from municipal sources. To the Virginia Supreme Court of Appeals, for example, "one great natural office of the sea and of all running waters is to carry off and dissipate, by their perpetual motion and currents, the impurities and off-scourings of the land."[8] For his part, US Supreme Court Justice Oliver Wendell Holmes dismissed the efforts of oystermen to protect the source of their livelihood against risk of contamination. Surely no one would expect that the state, by issuing a lease had committed itself "against using its legislative power to sanction one of the very most important public uses of water already partly polluted, and in the vicinity of half a dozen cities and towns to which that water obviously furnished the natural place of discharge."[9] In other words: "Get used to it." Riparians protesting against effluent discharge found it increasingly difficult to establish that the practice was not a reasonable, and thus lawful, use of rivers and streams. In the words of a New Jersey appeals court, "it cannot be said that the discharge of treated sewage effluent into a running stream is *per se* an unreasonable riparian use in today's civilization."[10] In the United States, the proliferation of permits to treat and discharge sewage also seems to have deterred common law actions.[11] Even where litigants successfully pursued claims against polluters, American observers noted a general inclination on the part of the judiciary in the early decades of the twentieth century to offer damages and compensation rather than to award injunctions, as balancing the equities often highlighted economic and community benefits that would be lost if municipal or industrial polluters were compelled to cease operations or to incur the expense of protecting waterways.[12]

In Britain as well, riparian owners and others interested in preserving their beloved rivers also explored the legal options in the mid-twentieth century. John Eastwood, a Bow Street magistrate, concluded from a personal analysis of more than a dozen pieces of legislation ostensibly offering protection to the rivers of the United Kingdom that "none of them was any good." Yet Eastwood was convinced that the common law – and more particularly actions by anglers and riparian landowners to enforce their rights – would satisfactorily protect waterways from municipal and industrial pollution. "Is the industry entitled to destroy the pleasure of millions merely for the sake of cheaper production?" Clearly not, he reasoned, for as technology evolved, rights and duties were transformed by the possibility of avoiding environmental harm. Though industrial enterprises had responsibilities towards their shareholders, as local authorities had to their ratepayers, both were subject to a "wider duty . . . to the general public."[13] Eastwood set out to overcome the obstacles that had plagued such actions for decades; the daunting cost of the judicial process presented a formidable deterrent.

So, as deterioration of Ontario's Spanish River got underway in the mid-1940s, comparable conflicts between environmental protection and progress or economic development were evident elsewhere in the common law world. But given the procedural and attitudinal obstacles facing them, the likelihood that a handful of Spanish River property owners might successfully protest the operations of a valuable industry and significant employer would not have been rated high.

Litigating and Legislating KVP

Complaints to the Provincial Department of Lands and Forests about the impact of KVP operations on fishing and water quality brought government engineers to Espanola in 1947, but left fishermen and resort owners dissatisfied. Thus, Earl and Ted McKie, Jack Gifford, Russell and James Vance, and Dr. G. Downe considered their options. With the exception of Downe, a Sudbury dentist intent on establishing a commercial tourist resort, the complainants were fishermen and camp owners along the lower Spanish who experienced foul odours emanating from the water and found themselves unable to use ice from the river for their commercial and domestic purposes. Even after boiling, the water was unfit to drink. Nor would cattle drink river water, at least, the plaintiffs believed, not in sufficient quantities to maintain their normal milk supply. The plaintiffs judged the water unfit to bathe in; they observed that fish were either killed or driven elsewhere; and they lamented the destruction of wild rice beds which had formerly attracted wild ducks.

With DR Walkinshaw as counsel, the group launched five actions in May 1947. The claims, defended by JJ Robinette acting on behalf of the pulp mill, were eventually heard together by McRuer CJ of the High Court. The various allegations would have to be established and relevant law favourably ascertained if Walkinshaw hoped to secure a beneficial result for his clients. Ducks, cattle, and fish — certainly those said to have been killed or driven elsewhere by industrial effluent — were unavailable to advance evidence directly when the trial got underway in December.

With regard to fish, James Vance reported a substantial adverse impact on his year over year catch, with a decline from over 30,000 lbs in 1946 to around 23,000 the year after KVP revived the pulp facility. Vance believed the larger fish had moved out into the North Channel of Georgian Bay to avoid contamination, an opinion that Robinette sought to undermine with his own piscatorial ruminations. "There is nothing so elusive as fish," KVP's counsel remarked, adding in explanation that "for purely natural reasons fish move about."

The death of fish was equally contentious. Using mill effluent under test conditions, Walkinshaw's scientific experts had managed to kill fish in eleven hours, while Robinette's research team kept them alive for four days in a 50/50 mix of effluent and water. Indeed, he proclaimed triumphantly, fish survived successfully in an environment consisting of nine parts water to one part mill discharge. Unfortunately for Robinette, McRuer had formed the opinion that some of the defence witnesses were unable to distinguish their responsibilities as witness from the role of advocate. Walkinshaw may even have advanced his case on the fish question with evidence that never appeared in court: when he offered to produce "a very dead fish" as an exhibit, McRuer graciously declined. The judge's benchbooks nevertheless carefully record smells "like a lot of rotten cabbage," or an aroma that "nearly knocks you down." Anyone bold enough to dive in for a swim was "surrounded with a vile odour" and the prospect of a definite bad taste "when you get a mouthful."[14]

Robinette was no more fortunate in his attempts to undermine reports of lost milk production that plaintiffs attributed to deterioration in the quality of the river. He replied to complaints of declining milk yield by seizing on the fact that the cows apparently continued to drink from the river, incautiously adding, "I don't know whether you can ascribe rational behaviour to animals." Alas, the youthful farm-based experience of the man presiding over *KVP v McKie* was evidently unknown to counsel. Had he been aware of McRuer's background he might have been more circumspect. McRuer's biographer would later write that, "Jim's father put him in command of his own troop of white purebred Wyandotte chickens. The hens would nest anywhere, and it became a great game to find where they had laid their eggs."[15] It was also observed that, "His closest friends were four enormous Clydesdale draught horses, whose different personalities he came to love."[16] Despite his unfortunate misstep, Robinette got off lightly in the circumstances as the trial judge simply interjected, "You weren't brought up on a farm. If the water had a taste the animals wouldn't drink as much." McRuer's findings on this aspect of the evidence were in substantial agreement with the plaintiffs' allegations. Nor would it have helped the defendant's cause when the performance of one company official provoked McRuer to compose a marginal note: "This witness does not impress me as having tried to ascertain the causes of the complaints and making an effort to research them."[17]

Perhaps astutely observing that he had lost the judge's sympathy on certain crucial factual matters — notably fish being killed or driven from the Spanish River by his client's industrial discharges — Robinette, in closing argument, attacked the legal basis of the plaintiffs' concern with this matter. As the Spanish River was a navigable waterway, Robinette asserted that the riparian owners had no claim beyond the water's edge and therefore have "no proprietary right to fish in the waters."[18] He further back-stopped his efforts to eliminate or minimize claims relating to the Spanish fishery by denying the court's ability to award damages for "any conjecture or fanciful damages in the future."

McRuer accepted that latter element of the defence, describing much of the evidence on damages as "speculative." The compensation awarded for the plaintiffs' demonstrated losses was extremely modest by comparison with the amounts claimed. But if he had silenced the rifle fire of damages, Robinette remained exposed to the artillery: McRuer awarded an injunction to prevent KVP from further interfering with the property rights of the riparians. For that is how he viewed the claim, despite a valiant effort by defendants' counsel to present the conflict as a matter of nuisance law where the reasonableness of the industrial undertaking might become a factor. That hope was lost as the trial came to a close when McRuer firmly asserted: "After all, this is not a nuisance case. The issue is the right of the owner to have the water come to him as it did before. And if the water isn't good for making tea, because of alleged bad taste, for one person, it's not good for another."[19]

In awarding the injunction, McRuer specifically rejected the suggestion that KVP's economic significance was relevant to the determination of the dispute: ". . . if I were to consider and give effect to an argument based on the defendant's economic position in the community, or its financial interests, I would in effect be giving to it a veritable power of expropriation of the common law rights of the riparian owners, without compensation." The KVP origins of this dramatic and much-quoted insight are found in the evidence of Dr. Downe, who, when recalled to the stand, recounted a conversation with the plant manager:

> "I . . . told him I understood the plant was going to re-open. I asked him if he was going to dispose of the waste in the river. I told him it would ruin some

of the best fishing in North America. He said what are a few fish to what we are doing for the country. I suggested to him they could pipe the waste on over the sand flats. He said it was a matter of economics. They are spending money on the plant. I said are you going to put the effluent in the water. He said yes."[20]

With reference to the law, McRuer noted the classic *A.G. v Birmingham* decision, observing with regard to the injunction that "otherwise the court would be giving a license for a fee to invade a right."[21] KVP was certainly a significant financial contributor to the community — an employer of 1,500 people in Espanola, at a plant representing a capital investment over $13 million, with a monthly payroll of $430,000 .[22] If these numbers failed to alter McRuer's course in awarding the injunction, they at least seem to have influenced his views on its application.

To afford KVP an opportunity to make alternative arrangements for its effluent, McRuer suspended the operation of the injunction for six months, ample time, it must have appeared, for the company to introduce preventative or remedial measures along lines that were already in place at numerous similar facilities in the United States. In fact, the McRuer decision was appealed to the Ontario Court of Appeal, which handed down its decision dismissing the appeal on 22 November 1948[23] with a further appeal to the SCC launched shortly after. This was heard 13 and 14 June 1949 leading to a decision on 4 October 1949.[24]

Meanwhile, legislative action (later sharply denounced as a measure designed to "crush the property rights of those living downstream from pulp and paper mills"[25]) in the form of changes to the *Lakes and Rivers Improvements Act* was underway. As amended, the legislation authorized the court, when hearing an injunction claim against a mill in a water pollution case, to:

> refuse to grant an injunction if it is found that having regard to all the circumstances and taking into consideration the importance of the operation of the mill to the locality in which it operates and the benefit and advantage, direct and consequential, which the operation of the mill confers on the locality and the inhabitants of the locality, and within the same against the private injury, damage or interference complained of, it is on the whole proper and expedient not to grant the injunction.[26]

The invitation to moderate the potential rigour of an injunction award by weighing general industrial benefits against private injury could hardly have been clearer. Indeed, the measure was not without precedent in the annals of Ontario's pollution record.[27] But the amendment came into force 1 April 1949, too late to be of any significance in the Court of Appeal's deliberations and judgment handed down 22 November 1948. When the matter reached the top of the Canadian judicial pyramid in mid-June, the Supreme Court of Canada firmly declined to be influenced by parliamentary afterthought.

Justice Kerwin, writing for the Supreme Court of Canada, determined that the legislative effort had been in vain, for no provincial legislature could extend the Supreme Court's jurisdiction, and Kerwin found no other basis on which to exercise discretion to confine the plaintiffs' to damages. As if the matter might have escaped KVP's attention, he remarked that, "the rights of riparian owners have always been zealously guarded by the Courts." In mid-January 1950 the Judicial Committee of the Privy Council (JCPC) refused to hear KVP's appeal. The final judicial arbiter rejected the suggestion that the entire dispute should be reheard in light of the *Lakes and Rivers Improvement Act* amendments inviting courts to consider the importance of a pulp and paper mill to its local community. Lord Greene offered personal knowledge of mills in Britain that had drastically lessened river pollution during a stay of execution of an injunction. Their lordships were clearly sympathetic to Walkinshaw's insistence that KVP was "the kind of business which can be adapted so that river pollution is unnecessary."[28]

At what looked like the end of the line, KVP redirected its campaign from the courts to the forum of public opinion and legislative action. When company president Ralph Hayward forecast closure of the plant in April unless the injunction threat was removed, intense community pressure quickly mounted to safeguard the employment base.[29] KVP reportedly bought out several of the riparian claimants, while other successful plaintiffs assured their anxious neighbours that no attempt would be made to have the injunction judicially enforced, provided that steps were taken to prevent pollution on the Spanish and, more generally, that a royal commission on provincial water pollution was established. [30]

Meanwhile, petitions and municipal delegations seeking more certain guarantees for the protection of the local employment base arrived in Queen's Park. A citizens' emergency committee was established, which consisted of municipal representatives, business union leaders, members of the agricultural and teaching professions, and, for good measure, a medical man, a dentist, a Catholic priest, and an Indian chief. The dentist was perhaps intended to counteract the opinion of plaintiff Dr. Downe, while Chief Douglas

Sissenah of the Spanish River Indian Reserve provided assurances that the condition of the river was much improved following measures implemented in 1949. For his part Father Tourigny of Espanola expressed apprehension that his community might revert to ghost town status, and he was directly concerned with the spiritual well-being of his flock: "It is hard for people to be good when they have no work."[31]

Premier Leslie Frost, a former minister of mines, and a man whose own constituency contained several resource-based communities, was quick to provide reassurances to mill supporters, although what might be done on their behalf was not immediately apparent. Frost rose in the legislature on 24 February 1950 to state solemnly: "We do not regard lightly the matter of pollution of our streams. Indeed, we think it is a very serious matter . . . We do not hold lightly the rights of individuals to protect their interests in the courts or this land." The premier equally emphasized,

> We also regard as a matter of high importance the employment of our people and we do recognize that in these days industrialization and the expansion of industry and the increase of population in areas of the province that we are bound to get a certain amount of pollution in our lakes and streams. At the same time, we are determined to hold that to the least possible limit.

This was balance-beam work of Olympic calibre: observers might be forgiven for failing to appreciate how the premier proposed to resolve an apparent impasse between the water quality rights of riparians that McRuer had so forcefully defended and the tendency of industry and population growth to produce "a certain amount of pollution."

Premier Frost engaged the Ontario Research Council in the controversy, calling upon the agency to examine the situation with a view to ensuring "that every reasonable step, scientific and otherwise, is now taken, and will be taken in the future by the company so that pollution will be reduced consistent with reasonable practice." The premier offered his assurance that the Ontario Research Council would enjoy unlimited powers to investigate the Spanish River situation and to consult authorities in other countries about the general problems of pulp mill waste. Returning to the balance beam with a more pronounced list towards economic considerations, Premier Frost reiterated: "we have no intention of putting people of that community out of employment . . . . At the same time, we intend to protect to the fullest extent that we are able all the interests of the people of Ontario."[32] Within a month, an extraordinary bill appeared on the legislative agenda, and was soon passed into law.

The *KVP Company Limited Act* dissolved the injunction in favour of damages while it simultaneously entrenched the foundations of a substantial research programme.[33] The key provisions are as follows:

> 1 (1) Whether or not its operation is now stayed, every injunction heretofore granted against The KVP Company Limited, herein called "the Company," restraining the Company from polluting the waters of the Spanish River, is dissolved . . .
>
> 4 (1) The Research Council of Ontario shall endeavour to develop methods that, if applied by the Company, would abate or lessen the pollution of the waters of the Spanish River by the Company.

KVP v McKie, a landmark common law defence of riparian property rights to water quality, and the *KVP Act*, a forceful illustration of highly particularized legislative authority, are justly commemorated incidents in the saga of Canadian property and environmental law. These events have provided the foundations for courses on legal process, and even resulted in a musical tribute to the presiding judge.[34]

Unsurprisingly, the judicial decision has remained controversial. For rejecting "the all too common argument that the social benefits of an activity can justify pollution," McRuer has been praised by some[35] while the decision has also been cited for illustrating the most serious drawback of the judicial process, its single-minded "focus on the rights and obligations of the parties before the court." From this perspective, judicial action is poorly suited to pollution control, for it is "reactive, potentially discriminatory, and examines a relatively narrow set of issues."[36] KVP may also be regarded as an instructive example of dialogue between courts and legislatures, or, even as having initiated an extensive and ongoing conversation.

The Regulatory Aftermath and McRuer's Last Words

THE KVP DECISIONS DID not feature prominently in citation rankings, but the influence of the proceedings in three areas is noteworthy. KVP contributed to mid-twentieth century industrial pollution regulation across Ontario; it echoed, even if indirectly, in municipal sewage pollution claims; and, as a property rights case its presence cast a long shadow over debates about civil liberties, administrative process, and instrument choice for environmental protection.

KVP and Industrial Pollution

On 13 January 1950, one day after the JCPC dismissed KVP's petition for leave to appeal, the Deputy Minister of Natural Resources delivered his personal reflections on the legal drama and its implications to Premier Frost. Frank MacDougall argued that the pollution problem that had originated in the pulp mill sector had become "acute." Unimpressed by judicial treatment of such matters, MacDougall dismissed legislative amendment as a solution, due to the reasoning that such measures would only send the matter back to the courts once again. Instead, MacDougall urged the premier to consider a pollution board to address problems of this kind. If a situation similar to *KVP* arose in future, such an agency could "deal with it in all aspects, including employment and the public interest."[37] *KVP* thus provided Ontario with a strong impetus to explore a regulatory alternative to industrial water pollution control.

Clear statutory signals certainly appeared attractive, although the most extreme response to critics of deteriorating water quality was to pursue legislative measures to constrain their ability to take legal action against polluters. Indeed, legislatures and administrative authorities in Europe and North America took a variety of such steps to lessen the impact of common law claims against municipal and industrial polluters.[38]

On the other hand, legislative and administrative initiatives directed against water pollution were often modest or of limited effect, as evident in post-war Ontario. The post-war Division of Sanitary Engineering within the Department of Health oversaw municipal applications for waterworks and sewage system construction. At the Department of Lands and Forests, a chemical engineer with special training in sanitation, public health, and pollution was hired on a seasonal basis in 1946. In 1949 one chemical engineer was added to the permanent staff.[39] It's little wonder that the Spanish River riparians had been disappointed by the original departmental response.

Encouraged to do so by various naturalist and resource use organizations, the Ontario government provided for conservation authorities in 1946. These agencies were given powers to develop and implement schemes for the conservation, restoration, and development of natural resources (not including gas, oil, coal, and minerals). In addition, under the *Conservation*

Authorities Act, 1946, conservation authorities were empowered to engage in water control activity in order to prevent floods and pollution.[40] But to other governmental observers it appeared that conservation authorities showed little inclination to act in relation to pollution perhaps because "present legislation relating to pollution has been stated in such general and such severe terms."[41] The ineffectiveness of post-war pollution control in Ontario may have been among the factors that inspired efforts to remedy the situation at the federal level following an oil slick that contaminated the beaches of Lake Ontario in the summer of 1949.[42]

Representatives of the Lands and Forests Department met with counterparts in Health, Mines, Agriculture, and Planning and Development to develop an inventory of existing anti-pollution initiatives and to formulate a "co-ordinated and united effort" for pollution control. Despite evidence of progress, the inter-departmental discussions identified "rather loose co-ordination of the government administration related to air and water pollution" as a source of concern. A number of departments were responsible in some way for pollution control, each with "a limited authority."

"The control of pollution," officials explained in a submission to cabinet, "is both a research and administrative problem." From a research perspective, adequate laboratory facilities and trained personnel would be required to apply the knowledge gained locally as well as that derived from the extensive amount of related work being carried out in the United States and elsewhere. In administrative terms, the problem would be "co-ordinating efforts on the part of all departments of government and industry in which pollution is a concern."[43]

Having consolidated their views in early 1952 the officials recommended the creation of an inter-departmental coordinating body, the Pollution Control Board of Ontario (PCBO), to pursue legislative reform along the lines of recent measures in the US and the UK.[44]

Newspapers welcomed the formation of the PCBO as "an innovation of great potential value." At the same time they offered sharp criticism of the conditions the new body would have to address. *The Globe and Mail* noted longstanding prohibitions whose penalties in its view were "ridiculously small." Toronto and various suburban municipalities, the paper charged, had essentially disregarded the provisions and had never been prosecuted. On the other hand, in what may be a reference to the KVP experience, the *Globe* proclaimed: "Only where aroused citizens have taken action to enforce the pollution laws has there been a determined effort to stop this practice. It has been such action in one or two places, which has brought the Government to realize the need for the Pollution Board."[45]

The PCBO soon adopted guidelines or objectives for water quality control in Ontario in May 1953. Revised versions of water quality objectives, though not directly enforceable, continued to play a similar role for some time thereafter. This guidance was formulated in response to a broader understanding of water quality challenges across the province that had been developed alongside the wake-up call that KVP represented.

The PCBO shortly examined twenty-one pulp and paper plants across the province. Efforts to address the water quality impacts of this sector increased significantly in the aftermath of the KVP litigation and its statutory resolution. In the specific case of KVP, the Research Council of Ontario reported its findings in 1952.[46]

The Research Council report on KVP was prepared under the supervision of Dr. JR Dymond, a zoologist at the University of Toronto, and AV Delaporte of the Department of Health. Based on detailed studies of the pulp operation and the river (1950–1951), the researchers identified three types of waste — chemical plant wastes, fibrous materials, and sewage, the latter including municipal effluent from Espanola alongside discharges from the mill. Overall, the mill was responsible on a daily basis for 63 tons of solids consisting of 5.5 tons of inorganic suspended solids, 11.5 tons of volatile suspended solids, 26 tons of inorganic dissolved solids, and 20 tons of volatile dissolved solids. To put the impact in perspective, the researchers estimated that the biological oxygen demand (BOD) of these discharges was equivalent to the requirements of a population of 74,000 people. But these results represented a significant improvement over conditions in 1949 when KVP was discharging 129 tons of solid wastes with a population equivalent of BOD of 196,000 people. Of paramount concern, however, were the impacts of intermittent toxic "slugs" associated with discharges of the mill's storage tanks. As the researchers observed: "The toxic material appeared to travel as an entity at a speed somewhat less than one mile per hour. It was effectively killing the fish . . . fifteen hours after its release from the mill, and this was more than 16 miles downriver from the KVP outfall."[47]

Remedial measures identified by the researchers and recommended by an advisory committee were forwarded directly to Premier Frost by the Minister of Lands and Forests, to whom they did "not seem too technical or expensive." The Minister anticipated discussions with KVP officials "at the first opportunity."[48] The riparian litigators could anticipate some satisfaction in the form of water quality improvement along the lower Spanish.

The Ontario pulp and paper industry was moving to address water quality concerns more systematically, most notably those associated with the discharge of suspended matter that depleted oxygen supplies from North American waterways.[49] In addition, pulp and paper pollution figured prominently on the province's industrial pollution programme, highlighted, beginning in 1954, with an annual industrial waste conference.[50] Yet by 1961, with forty-one plants operating in Ontario, it was estimated that water consumption exceeded 400 million gallons per day. "Most of this is discharged to surface waters as process wastes with little or no treatment."[51]

KVP and Municipal Pollution

In its final recommendation, the Ontario Research Council report called for measures to ensure adequate treatment of sanitary sewage from the KVP mill and the town of Espanola, thereby underscoring the contribution of municipal wastes to the mid-century deterioration of Ontario waterways. This was a growing issue in the post-war era as a significant infrastructure deficit — the result of depression, wartime priorities, and accelerating expansion — called for attention. In 1950, a select committee of the Ontario Legislature on Conservation also directed its concerns on the water pollution front towards the problems of municipal sewage. Even efficient sewage plants, it was noted, continued to discharge liquid sewage. But a more striking observation was the widespread lack of treatment facilities.

The Conservation Council of Ontario was another organization pioneering a public interest sector attempt to channel the attention of legislators towards water pollution questions. On 27 May 1955, CCO president FH Kortright wrote candidates in the provincial election to ascertain their willingness to address pollution abatement and control as a "concern of extreme urgency." In setting out its inquiry, Kortright noted that " . . . there is today hardly a river or lake in the more settled parts of Ontario that is not in some degree being fouled by untreated domestic sewage, poisonous industrial wastes, or the silt from eroded farm lands."

Against this backdrop of limited and sporadic concern for the environment, the boldness of the Spanish River riparians' willingness to pit their property-based claims against KVP's contribution to post-war economic development is even more striking. But who would take up a similar challenge against municipal authorities discharging local effluent in furtherance of the interests of their communities? Eventually, Woodstock and Richmond Hill, using the Thames River and a branch of the Don River, respectively, to disperse wastes from municipal treatment plants ran afoul of downstream neighbours who were determined to protect their own property interests.

The deterioration in water quality came to public attention when Annie Stephens, a downstream resident on the Don, and a war veteran named Burgess with aspirations to farm along the Thames, invoked the judicial process in search of damages and an injunction to prevent the continued operation of offending facilities.[52]

In 1955, Ontario courts ruled in favour of both plaintiffs, awarding damages to compensate for injury or loss, and, emboldened by the KVP experience, imposing injunctions — whose effective date was in each case deferred — against the municipal sewage operations. Richmond Hill and Woodstock had been ably defended, in the latter case by JJ Robinette, increasingly experienced in pollution claims. One argument, advanced in both the Woodstock and Richmond Hill cases, suggested that the municipal operations were essentially immune from liability on the basis of the statutory authority under which they had been established.

Neither trial court had the slightest sympathy for such an assertion on the grounds that immunity could only extend to interference that was an inevitable consequence of the statutorily authorized undertaking. Since neither municipality conducted its sewage disposal operations with a facility adequate to the task nor in a fully satisfactory manner, the resulting pollution was hardly inevitable. Other measures, larger plants or sewage farms, for example, might have been employed.

Moreover, in a statement that sharply distinguished the judicial role from the responsibilities of government, the trial courts echoed McRuer's firmly expressed position in KVP that such costs were not their concern:

> [I]t is not for the judiciary to permit the doctrine of utilitarianism to be used as a make-weight in the scales of justice. In civil matters, the function of the Court is to determine rights between parties. It investigates facts by hearing "evidence" (as tested by long-settled rules) and it investigates the law by consulting precedents. Rights or liabilities as ascertained cannot, in theory, be refused recognition and enforcement, and no judicial tribunal claims the power of refusal.

> It is the duty of the state (and of statesmen) to seek the greatest good for the greatest number. To this end, all civilized nations have entrusted much individual independence to their Governments. But be it ever remembered that no one is above the law. Neither those who govern our affairs, their appointed advisers, nor those retained to build great works for society's benefit, may act so as to abrogate the slightest right of the individual, save within the law.

When Richmond Hill officials chose to pursue the defense of statutory authority on appeal, the village suffered a further rebuke.[53] Indeed, the judgment severely constrained the authority of the Department of Health to approve similar facilities elsewhere in the province. Justice Laidlaw determined Richmond Hill's failure to provide notice to its downstream neighbour, Markham Township, as required by the *Public Health Act*, rendered the commencement of construction unlawful. But, hypothesizing that the correct procedures might have been followed, Laidlaw went further to reflect upon the relationship between the Department's power to approve a sewage facility approval and an historic, though long-neglected, prohibition against contaminating the waterways:

> 103(1) No garbage, excreta, manure, vegetable or animal matter or filth shall be discharged into or be deposited in any of the lakes, rivers, streams or other waters in Ontario or on the shores or banks thereof, and no industrial or other wastes dangerous or liable to become dangerous to health or to become a nuisance or to impair the safety, palatability or potability of the water supply or any municipality or riparian owner, shall be discharged into or be deposited in any of the lakes, rivers, streams or other waters of Ontario, or on the shores or banks thereof.

Half a century after it came into effect in 1906, this particular legislative time bomb exploded around the agency responsible for its enforcement. As Laidlaw stated:

> ... the Department of Health cannot in any case disregard the express prohibition contained in that section . . . . It cannot be argued successfully that in the absence of power, expressed in the plainest possible terms, either the Department of Health or the Municipal Board could make lawful what the Legislature declared in express terms to be unlawful.

In the immediate aftermath of the Court of Appeal decision, Richmond Hill sought relief from the legislature. But the injunctions obtained by Stephens and Burgess — and the fact that as many as sixty municipalities were vulnerable to similar constraints — had already served to direct general attention to the overall statutory framework regulating Ontario water quality.[54] In legislation providing specifically — as in the earlier KVP context — for the dissolution of the injunctions against Richmond Hill and Woodstock, the province infused new life into the series of municipal defenses that the courts had swept aside. Amendments to section 106 of the *PHA* established that sewerage projects carried out in accordance with terms and conditions imposed under the *Act* "shall be deemed to be under construction, constructed, maintained or operated by statutory authority."[55] The right to seek compensation or damages was preserved, but jurisdiction over such claims was clearly conferred upon the Ontario Municipal Board.[56] Furthermore, sewerage projects operating in conformity with their approvals and applicable orders were exempted from the broadly crafted prohibition that Laidlaw had invoked.

KVP and Civil Rights

If municipal authorities were relieved by legislative salvation, not all observers welcomed the changes. On 2 April 1956, *The Globe and Mail* lamented the elimination of the injunction remedy in such situations, a result it foresaw "unless some private person assumes the onus which is now placed upon him to petition the courts for a declaration that such a law violates the Common Law rights of British subjects." The newspaper's indictment continued with an attack on the legislation as an "arbitrary" measure that "gives municipalities an apparent right to continue injuring, by stream pollution, the properties of citizens outside their borders, instead of requiring such municipalities to have as much care for public health beyond their borders as they are required to exercise on behalf of their own residents."

In *The Globe and Mail*'s view, the statutory response to the court decisions demonstrated that it was "a positive policy of the Ontario government to permit the pollution of streams contrary to the public interest." The paper went on to insist that, "the real gist of the whole matter is that existing sewage disposal legislation is inadequate, and that no denial of Common Law remedies can be considered as a remedy for laws which can be either evaded or ignored."

Building on the KVP legacy, the Richmond Hill and Woodstock cases accelerated legislative developments, and contributed to the creation of a new institution: the Ontario Water Resources Commission. Premier Frost, upon introducing legislation to establish the OWRC in 1956, declared its purpose to be in "ending the possibility of the water shortage in southwestern Ontario" and eliminating the province's pollution problem, an issue he rather curiously suggested was not even apparent one year earlier when a committee was established to examine water resources and supply.[57] The relationship of water supply to pollution was also clearly noted by the premier, although the origins of the general concern with water issues in industrial demand is evident: "The availability of water, and its freedom and protection from pollution which run hand in hand. They are inseparable."[58]

Little more than a year later the *Ontario Water Resources Commission Act* (1957) was introduced in order, it was said, to expand and clarify the powers of the commission in relation to financial matters, and in addition to transfer to the commission powers over sewage and sewage works then exercised by the Department of Health.[59]

One assessment of the KVP experience and the municipal aftershocks that it (to some degree) inspired, would suggest that Ontario courts moved themselves to the margins: By insisting so firmly on the rights of riparian proprietors, the courts encouraged legislative intervention. The legislature, for its part, expressed sympathy for economic and municipal development, subordinating property interests in a new administrative framework, largely immune from judicial interference.

But this was not to be. Two decades after his forceful resolution of the KVP litigation, McRuer J enjoyed an opportunity to consider the operation of Ontario's new water quality regime. As the 1957 legislative reforms to the OWRC appeared to the landmark Inquiry into Civil Rights (1964–1968), over which McRuer presided, "very extensive administrative and judicial powers were added to those formerly conferred on it. It was made the recipient of a conglomerate of powers of such a nature that the question arises as to whether such powers should be exercised by a body corporate that is engaged in the business of providing water supply and sewage disposal."

Citing a very familiar case — KVP — the McRuer report cautioned that, "riparian rights are very important rights to those who enjoy them and they are rights that the common law has jealously guarded."[60]

The OWRC's wide powers to confer "the permission to pollute" were singled out for special consideration.[61] The Royal Commission eventually acknowledged that an approval authority to exempt from the prohibition against discharges that may impair water quality "may well be necessary and unavoidable." However, the lack of procedural safeguards came in for severe criticism. "The least one would expect would be that a person who would be affected by the approval granted should have an opportunity to be heard before a decision is made."[62] The absence of standards applicable to decision-making or regulation was another source of profound concern.[63]

More broadly, the Inquiry into Civil Rights identified a potential conflict of interest in the Commission's simultaneous exercise of administrative or operational and judicial powers and expressed the view that administrative powers exercised by the OWRC were insufficiently subject to political control.[64] In addition to numerous recommendations intended to introduce procedural safeguards, the McRuer report presented two more substantive proposals regarding water. It called for a thorough review of provincial legislation respecting the use of water in order to determine "a coherent policy" and to address conflicts between statutory provisions. The inquiry also urged amendments to "particularize in greater detail the standards which should be applicable to approvals by the Commission of water works and sewage works" with relevant decisions subject to an appeal to the Minister.[65]

With respect to pulp and paper pollution, variants of the situation that initiated the KVP saga, official intervention followed a still more-extended course. In January 1965, the OWRC circulated a "Proposal for Pulp and Paper Waste Pollution Control" to the industry. With forty-four facilities then operating in the sector, ten were understood to "dispose of waste in a satisfactory manner," and while a number of operations had submitted proposals, many of the remaining plants had "unacceptable control."[66] Nearly three years later, in November 1967, officials authorized the first prosecution of a major pulp and paper company in northwestern Ontario.[67] Grounds of the alleged impairment of water quality closely echoed the damages that had brought Earl McKie and his Spanish River neighbours to McRuer J's court twenty years earlier. As for the river itself, the silent protagonist, its fate has intermittently returned to the courts in the aftermath of the official judgments of jurists and politicians detailed here.[68]

Notes

1 Patrick Boyer, *A Passion for Justice* (Toronto: Osgoode Society for Legal History, 1994).

2 *Ibid* at 228. For another extensive review of the proceedings, see E. Paul Emond, "Environmental Law and Policy: a retrospective examination of the Canadian experience," in Ivan Bernier and Andrée Lajoie, eds, *Consumer Protection, Environmental Law and Corporate Power* (Toronto: University of Toronto Press, 1985).

3 *Groat v City of Edmonton* [1928] SCR 522 at 532-33.

4 Keith Hawkins, *Environment and Enforcement: Regulation and the Social Definition of Pollution* (Oxford: Clarendon Press, 1982).

5 This issue presents continuing challenges. See, for example, *R v Inco Limited*, 2008 ONCJ 332 (CanLII).

6 *Campbell v Kingsville*, [1929] 4 DLR 772 (Ont. SC); *Costanza v Dominion Canners, Ltd.* (1921), 67 DLR 413 (Ont. SC); *McQueen v Owen Sound* (1927), 32 OWN 383 (Ont SC).

7 Jennifer Read, "'A Sort of Destiny': The multijurisdictional response to Great Lakes Pollution, 1900-1930," (1999) 55 *Scientia Canadensis*, 122.

8 *City of Hampton v Watson*, 89 SE (Virginia, 1916) 81-83, quoted in John Capper, Garrett Power & Frank Shivers, *Chesapeake Waters* (Centreville, MD: Tidewater Publishers, 1983) at 94-95.

9 *Darling v City of Newport News*, 249 U.S. 540-4 (1918), quoted in Capper, Power and Shivers, *Chesapeake Waters* at 95-96.

10 *Borough of Westville v Whitney Home Builders*, (1956) 40 N.J. Super. 62, 122 A. 2d 233.

11 Albert Reitze, "Wastes, Water, and Wishful Thinking: The Battle of Lake Erie" (1968) 20 *Case Western Reserve Law Review* at 65.

12 Warren H. Resh, "Court Decisions and Statutory Provisions in Water Pollution Control Law," (1956) 28 *Sewage and Industrial Wastes* at 211-220.

13 Roger Bate, "Saving Our Streams: The Role of the Anglers' Conservation Association in Protecting English and Welsh Rivers" (London: Institute of Economic Affairs, 2001) at 36.

14 Ontario Archives, (hereafter OA) JC McRuer Papers, Benchbooks (hereafter, McRuer Benchbooks) No 9 at 351, 352; No 10 at 13.

15 See Boyer, above note 1 at 13.

16 *Ibid* at 14.

17 McRuer Benchbooks No 10 at 61.

18 Northern Ontario outfitters and tourist operators were outraged by this suggestion and other seemingly disparaging comments from Robinette. See Bob Turnbull, "The Outdoor Trail," *The Globe and Mail* (10 January 1948).

19 *Toronto Star* (9 January 1948) 15.

20 McRuer Benchbooks No 10 at 73.

21 *Ibid* at 129.

22 *The Globe and Mail* (12 January 1950) 10.

23 [1949] 1 DLR 38.

24 *KVP v McKie*, [1949] SCR 698.

25 Elizabeth Brubaker, *Property Rights in the Defence of Nature* (New York: Earthscan, 1995).

26 SO 1949 c. 48 s 6 amending RSO 1937 c 45 s 30.

27 Jamie Benidickson, "Private Rights and Public Purposes in the Lakes, Rivers and Streams of Ontario" in David H. Flaherty, ed., *Essays in the History of Canadian Law, II* (Toronto: Osgoode Society, 1983) at 381.

28 "Spanish River Pollution Studied by Privy Council" *The Globe and Mail* (12 January 1950).

29 "May Close Pulp Mill as Ruling Result" *The Globe and Mail* (13 January 1950); "Espanola Problem Eyed by Experts; Petitions Pour In" *The Globe and Mail* (27 January 1950).

30 "Pulp Company Studies Offer On Spanish River Pollution" *The Globe and Mail* (1 February 1950); "Pollution and the Law" *The Globe and Mail* (16 February 1950).

31 "Unthinkable KVP Plant Be Permitted to Close, Frost Reassures Group" *The Globe and Mail* (7 February 1950).

32 Ontario Legislature, *Debates* 24 February 1950.

33 SO 1950, c 33.

34 See Boyer, above note 1 at 234.

35 See Brubaker, above note 25 at 73-74.

36 E. Paul Emond, "Environmental Law and Policy: a retrospective examination of the Canadian experience" in Ivan Bernier and Andrée Lajoie, eds., *Consumer Protection, Environmental Law and Corporate Power* (Toronto: University of Toronto Press, 1985) at 129.

37 OA, MacDougall Papers MU 1790, "Pollution, Espanola 1950."

38 See Bate, above note 13 at 15, 76, and 90.

39 OA, OWRC, "Sulphur Fumes Arbitration Records" "A Programme for Pollution Control in Ontario" 10 January 1952.

40 s 13 (a).

41 OA, Pollution Control Board of Ontario, 1952.

42 "Anti-Pollution Bill Defeated in Commons," *The Globe and Mail* (7 October 1949).

43 PCBO, 1952.

44 US *Water Pollution Control Act*, 1948 and UK *Rivers (Prevention of Pollution) Act*, 1951

45 *The Globe and Mail* (15 July 1952).

46 Ontario. Department of Lands and Forests, *Pollution of the Spanish River* (1952).

47 *Pollution of the Spanish River* at 75.

48 Hon HR Scott to Hon Leslie M Frost, 10 January 1952.

49 Russell L. Winget and Russell O. Blonsor, "The Pulp and Paper Industry Pollution Abatement Program in the United States," Ontario Water Resources Commission, Proceedings of the Fourth Industrial Waste Conference, (1957) at 105.

50 Pollution Control Board of Ontario, First Ontario Industrial Waste Conference, (1954); Ontario Water Resources Commission, Fourteenth Ontario Industrial Waste Conference, 1967.

51 RH Millest, "A Review of the Pulp and Paper Waste Problem in Ontario," Surveys and Evaluation of Waste Disposal Problems, Part II, (Ontario Water Resources Commission, 1961) at 42.

52 *Stephens v Richmond Hill* [1955] 4 DLR 572.

53 [1956] OR 88; [1956] 1 DLR 2nd 569.

54 In 1957 Richmond Hill, through their consulting engineers, Proctor and Redfern, requested the Ontario Water Resources Commission to provide sewage and water works estimated to cost $842,000. Given the existing gross debt/assessment ratio of 31 percent, a further obligation of this size would raise the financial obligation of Richmond Hill well above a level that the OMB would ordinarily regard as reasonable. However, following informal discussions with the Chairman of the OMB, at which the urgency of the extensions to the sewage treatment plant was emphasized, the Richmond Hill sewage works obtained the necessary approval. See OWRC Minutes, 26 September 1957; 27-28 November 1957.

55 *Public Health Amendment Act* SO 1956, c 71 s 6(1) re PHA 106 (22).

56 PHA s 106(13)(d), (19)-(22).

57 Ontario Legislature, *Debates* 23 February 1956, at 447.

58 *Debates*, 28 February 1956, at 557.

59 Ontario Legislature, *Debates*, 28 March 1957, at 1778.

60 Royal Commission Inquiry into Civil Rights, Report No 3, Volume 5 (Queen's Printer, 1971) at 2109

61 *Ibid* at 2112.

62 *Ibid* at 2113.

63 *Ibid* at 2114.

64 *Ibid* at 2106-07.

65 *Ibid* at 2124-25.

66 OA, Ontario Water Resources Commission, Division of Industrial Wastes, Status of Industrial Pollution Control in Ontario, June 1967, at 32.

67 OA, RG 12-29, Temp Box No. 27 – File: Liaison with Ontario-Minnesota Industries Pulp and Paper Plant, Kenora, 6/566 – 29/12/67 Vol 1.

68 "Many helped save the Spanish River," *Sudbury Star* (27 June 2000).

Cottages, Covenants, and the Cold War: *Galbraith v Madawaska Club*

Philip Girard

Introduction

MUCH OF THE LAW of real property is about attachment to place, and so it is with *Galbraith v Madawaska Club*. The dispute is set on a rugged, windswept shore of Georgian Bay that has inspired a national iconography of leaning pines, ancient granite, and wild water. Yet when AY Jackson first travelled to the area in 1910, he made these observations:

> I have done very little sketching, this country does not lend itself to it . . . . It is a great country to have a holiday in, but it's nothing but little islands covered with scrub and pine trees, and not quite paintable.[1]

As environmental historian Claire Campbell notes, three years later Jackson would render this "not quite paintable" landscape as *Terre Sauvage*, "one of his most famous paintings, . . . [one that] signalled a new era in Canadian art."[2]

I confess that at the outset of this assignment, my reaction to *Galbraith v Madawaska Club* was similar to Jackson's to Georgian Bay. Could a case on the law of restrictive covenants that has never been the subject of any extended academic commentary really be a leading case? Everyone would agree that *Noble and Wolf v Alley*, where the restrictive covenant was racially and religiously exclusive, is a leading case.[3] But the covenant in *Galbraith* purported to exclude only those who were not graduates of the University of Toronto — a possibly objectionable but hardly earth-shattering restriction; and its main point about the need for the dominant tenement to be easily ascertained in the deed creating the covenant was not exactly novel. Was my task perhaps the legal equivalent of "not quite paintable"?

Fortunately the archival record yielded the raw materials for a treatment of *Galbraith* that goes beyond the technical requirements for the running of covenants. It provided a little-known backstory of the state-supported colonization of a now-iconic part of northern Ontario by a highly self-conscious group of university scholars in the name of scientifically-informed conservation. The archival trail also suggested themes of enduring interest, including chivalry and family honour, the limits of free alienability, and that quintessential property law theme of belonging/not belonging, set against a backdrop of intense Cold War anxiety. And last but not least, the archives disclosed an interesting cast of characters, particularly in the person of our protagonist, John Stupart Galbraith.

So much for *Galbraith* itself. But what about its impact? Academic interpretation of *Galbraith* has run curiously parallel to academic interpretation of the Group of Seven's depiction of Georgian Bay: both are seen as manifestations of a nascent Canadian nationalism, in the legal and artistic spheres respectively. *Galbraith* confirmed a trend in Canadian law towards making the requirements for the running of restrictive covenants more precise and rigorous than those recognized in English law. This view fits nicely with a postwar trend of Anglo-Canadian legal nationalism, but I want to suggest another larger theme illustrated by the divergence between English and Canadian law evident in *Galbraith*.[4] That is the theme of liberalism, in particular what I have called elsewhere facilitative liberalism.[5] When confronted with the complex legacy of English real property law which permitted a wide variety of restraints to be imposed on the use and alienation of property, the Supreme Court of Canada has tended to whittle down the most intrusive ones, promoting freer alienability and a more autarkic, individualistic property law.[6]

A brief primer on restrictive covenants may be in order. A covenant is the name given to contractual promises contained in documents under seal, which deeds of land usually are. Typically such a promise benefits one party and burdens another, for example, where the purchaser of land agrees not to operate a certain kind of business on it in order not to compete with a similar business run by the vendor on land retained nearby. The common law said that the purchaser's promise could not "run with the land": i.e., the purchaser was bound to observe the covenant but if she sold the land, the new purchaser could break it with impunity, even if he bought with knowledge of the covenant. The doctrine of restrictive covenants, developed in England after 1848, was an important exception to this rule created by the court of chancery (or equity) which at that time was distinct from the courts of common law. It allowed the burden of a negative covenant to be enforced in equity by injunction against subsequent purchasers provided certain conditions were met. These conditions were that two parcels of land were involved, the "dominant tenement" (land to be benefited) and the "servient tenement" (land to be burdened); and the burden of the covenant had to be intended to run with the land, as opposed to being personal to the initial parties. Equity also imposed certain requirements for the benefit to run to a successor in title of the vendor: the covenant had to "touch and concern the land" to be benefited (i.e., be connected to its use or affect its value) and the benefit had to be annexed to the land in a recognized way. On these latter two points the law continued to be somewhat unsettled, as we shall see.[7] The larger point lurking behind the legal debate was the extent to which private parties would be allowed to use the restrictive covenant device to engage in privatized forms of land use planning.

The Founding and Early Years of the Madawaska Club 1898–1915

LATE IN THE NINETEENTH century a small group of well-connected scientists, scholars, and engineers in Toronto hit upon the idea of combining scientific research into the flora, fauna, and natural resources of northern Ontario with the founding of a summer vacation colony. Among them were John Galbraith, principal of the School of Practical Science in Toronto and future dean of engineering at the University of Toronto, Charles Wright, also of the School of Practical Science and later head of the architecture department at the University of Toronto, and WJ Loudon, professor of physics at the University of Toronto and nephew of its then president, James Loudon (1892–1905).[8]

From Loudon's first discussions with his university colleagues, he always had in mind a family-oriented summer colony, not the all-male sporting or fishing camp so popular at the time. By 1896 he found eighty people, mostly connected with the university, willing to contribute the not inconsiderable sum of $25 (over $500 today) to the cause. With this money, a club could be incorporated to purchase land suitable for the envisaged community. At first Loudon had in mind a site on Rock Lake at the headwaters of the Madawaska

River, just outside the newly created (1893) Algonquin Park. When he went to see Aubrey White, the assistant commissioner of Crown lands at Queen's Park, however, he was told that the timber was too valuable to allow vacationers with their attendant fire risk to settle nearby. The name for the Club stuck even though the location did not.[9] When Loudon learned that a large tract of land with little valuable timber near Go Home Bay on Georgian Bay might be available, White was more accommodating. As Loudon recalled years later, White advised that if the Club's members could guarantee that they "would build summer homes and improve the district which was nothing but a barren shore he was sure that a very small amount would purchase a great lot of land and a large number of islands."[10]

White was as good as his word, except for the islands: in 1898 the Madawaska Club was allotted 1084 acres in the Township of Gibson on the eastern shore of Georgian Bay at a price of twenty-five cents an acre, half the going rate. But White had some definite ideas about how the lands should be held. While he thought it "desirable to encourage as far as possible, the formation of places of summer resort by those connected with our educational and scientific institutions," he was also of the view that there should be a condition in the patent preventing the sale of the land.[11] John Gibson, the commissioner of Crown lands, was not quite so absolute but suggested to the Club's promoters "that their charter should provide that its shareholders should be limited to the original petitioners . . . and such professors or other gentlemen connected with the University of Toronto as may from time to time come into the Club" and that while Club members might transfer lots between themselves "no one not connected with the University in a manner . . . [to be] defined by the charter, shall have a right to acquire any interest in any of the lands." And "in order to make this condition effective, a provision for forfeiture" upon breach should be inserted in the charter.[12]

When the charter was issued in July 1898 it duly limited the right to hold shares in the corporation to the initial incorporators "and to any Graduate or Under-Graduate of The University of Toronto or of The School of Practical Science, or any official connected either with the said University . . . or . . . School" and provided that the shares "shall be deemed . . . incapable of being assigned" to anyone without those qualifications. Furthermore, inasmuch as the lands to be acquired were to be used "for summer-holidaying purposes as well as for experimental work in forestry, biology and other branches of Natural Sciences," they were, after being divided up by the Club pursuant to its bylaws, not to be "conveyed or leased" to anyone without the same qualifications, on pain of forfeiture of such lands, although there could be "transfers of particular portions of the said lands from one shareholder of the Club to another shareholder."[13] When the letters patent to the tract were issued in 1904 they were stated to be "subject to the limitations and conditions set out in the charter of the said Club," and particularly mentioned the forfeiture clause just noted. The Club began to divide up the sites informally among its members in 1898 so that cottage-building could begin, but duly formalized the process with a set of bylaws adopted in December 1904.

The entire grant from the province was on the mainland, but many nearby islands also afforded agreeable sites for cottages. These islands were owned by the Dominion government; in 1905 it leased a large collection of them to the Club with an option to purchase which the Club exercised in 1911. On island 122 the Rev WP Firth and his wife Ella Firth constructed a cottage which was eventually purchased by John S. Galbraith in 1947; it was this property that became the subject of the litigation, not the Galbraith family cottage property on the mainland which dated back to 1898. The crucial distinction with the island properties, of course, is that they were not subject to the restrictions contained in the grant from the Crown in right of Ontario. The Club would only allocate island sites to members, however, and in its deeds to them inserted covenants requiring the grantee to convey only to Club members with the U of T qualification and to exact similar covenants from any purchaser to whom they ultimately sold.

What Commissioner Gibson wanted to achieve from a policy perspective is relatively clear. In return for giving these eminent scholars and their families a good deal on some scrub land on Georgian Bay, he felt a need to protect the public interest by ensuring that they did not secure a speculative windfall at a time when demand for vacation spots in the "near north" was expanding rapidly. What Gibson wanted to achieve from a legal perspective was somewhat less clear, even though he was a lawyer and indeed became attorney general in October 1899 in the Liberal administration of GW Ross. Arguably the corporation was the key to the whole scheme. It was meant to function as a sort of lord of the manor with an ongoing responsibility for maintaining the exclusive nature of the community while the cottagers were more like copyholders, possessing something less than a freehold interest which they could transfer inter se but not to outsiders. Even if the cottagers were to have fee simple interests, the severely limited market would serve the government's purpose of preventing speculation.

Such restraints on alienation might seem *prima facie* invalid today, but in the late nineteenth century, as I have noted elsewhere, "an extensive array of conditions and restraints were consistently held immune from attack by Ontario courts, whether on the ground of certainty or for substantive reasons."[14] It was not until the 1903 decision of the Supreme Court of Canada in *Blackburn and Cox v McCallum* that clearer limits were put on the ability of landowners to fetter alienability by subsequent purchasers.[15]

Partly as a result of the restrictions imposed by the province, the Madawaska Club soon evolved into a highly self-conscious entity, one infused with an almost religious sense of purpose centred on the notion of stewardship. This was manifested early on by the presence of a Dominion-funded biological research station at Go Home Bay run by the Club members.[16] As WJ Loudon put it somewhat astringently in his memoir, the children of cottagers "would be much better employed doing some research work, however trivial or apparently useless, than running around in circles in Go Home Bay, storing up habits of idleness and incompetence for the future."[17] The cessation of Dominion funding in 1914 resulted in the station's closure but the sense of mission continued unabated. Every twenty-five years since its founding the Club has published a substantial retrospective, covering topics from ecological change to shifting social mores to cottagers' literary and scientific output.[18] The Club's strong sense of identity inevitably generated wry commentary by non-members, as in this 1958 account by an old Georgian Bay hand:

> Go Home Bay is sacred to the faculty of the University of Toronto. If you are fortunate enough to be a member of that august band you may own and occupy a cottage . . . . If you are a graduate . . . it is just possible that you may be able to rent a cottage there. If you are neither, the grass on the shore will wilt as you walk on it and the fish in the bay will turn up their noses at your hook. You will be welcome in the bay . . . just so long as the storm lasts, and just so long as you do not assume that the one considerable wharf in the bay is a public one. It isn't.[19]

By the time the first generation of Go Homers passed on, however, the restrictions on land ownership there were stimulating not just the envy of outsiders but also dissent within the community itself.

The Dispute Simmers and Erupts, 1915–1957

The plaintiff John Stupart Galbraith was the son of Club founder Professor John Galbraith, and the maternal nephew of Sir Frederic Stupart, director of the Meteorological Service of Canada (1894–1929) and one of the original incorporators. It is perhaps not surprising that he became so passionate about the restrictions contained in the Club's charter as Go Home Bay was virtually in his blood. According to family lore his father, who had explored various corners of the Ontario wilderness during his youth, picked out the spot for their cottage on the mainland in 1878.[20] John S. Galbraith was born in 1891 and remembered the building of their cottage during the first summer of the Go Home Bay colony, in 1898. By acquiring a degree in engineering from the University of Toronto in 1913, he qualified as a potential Club member and landowner in his own right. When Galbraith married his first wife shortly after the outbreak of the Great War they spent their honeymoon at Go Home Bay, adding another layer of memory to an already thick palette of emotional associations.

Galbraith's father died at Go Home Bay in July 1914, leaving the cottage to his widow for life with remainder to their three children. That soon led to the family's first run-in with the Club bylaws, as the widowed Mrs. Galbraith was not a graduate of the University of Toronto. Bylaw 21 stated that upon the death of a member, "his [sic] immediate family may continue to occupy the premises . . . for a period of two years, and thereafter from year to year, upon the annual permission of the Board of Directors." Bylaw 22 mandated a valuation of the deceased's interest and allowed the Club to purchase it from the estate within a certain period of time. According to Galbraith's testimony at trial, when his mother went to stay at the cottage in 1915:

> The Secretary and his wife called frequently on her and reminded her that By-laws 21 and 22 . . . applied to her. I was an engineer at [the military base at] Val Cartier, and she sent for me. I came up and saw The Hon. Wallace Nesbitt, and I said: "I will not go to the war," but he said: "Look, you go to the war and I will take care of your mother, and I will break that place wide open if she has any further trouble with them."[21]

With his mother under Nesbitt's protection, Galbraith entered the armed forces and fought in France, where he was gassed and invalided home; he was later decorated for bravery by King George V. His mother's death in 1919 removed a source of friction with the Club directors but their (in his view) arrogant and insensitive treatment of her rankled with him for many years, and nourished his determination to alter the terms on which cottages were held at Go Home Bay.

The U of T qualification also caused discord in other families over the years. As the statement of claim put it many years later, the effect of the distinction was

> to place those shareholders whose children and grandchildren are graduates of the University of Toronto in a preferred position, since such shareholders . . . can acquire the summer cottages of other shareholders whose estates are forced to sell. The division of children of shareholders into those who may and those who may not inherit their parents' property depending on the place and extent of their formal education is socially undesirable and can scarcely fail to have an injurious effect upon those children who are excluded and made to feel inferior.[22]

The fact that no corporate body could hold title to Madawaska Club land was also thought to preclude any mortgaging of the properties, which in more recent times has posed additional problems.

After the war Galbraith became a civil engineer and community planner; he laid out the Town of Mount Royal, Forest Hill Village in Toronto, and other towns across Canada. In 1944 he was appointed director of the community planning division of the National Housing Administration — a somewhat ironic move in light of his continuing conflictual relationship with the Go Home Bay community.[23] After his mother's death, Galbraith took no steps to have title to the family cottage transferred to himself; rather he left it in his father's estate for decades.[24] He acquired his own recreational property elsewhere and distanced himself from the Madawaska Club, although a motion proposed by him at a Club meeting in 1932 showed that he had not relaxed his opposition to the ownership restrictions. The motion, which attracted no support, would have authorized the directors to seek an amendment to the Crown grant "to permit children of members to be eligible to become shareholders after election to membership without further qualification."[25]

There matters rested until Galbraith decided to acquire a property in his own right at Go Home Bay, this time on island 122. The Dominion Crown grant of the islands, it will be recalled, did not contain the same restrictions as that of the mainland property, but the Club inserted similar restrictions in deeds of the island properties, requiring grantees to obtain identical covenants from their purchasers. Such covenants were thus part of the transaction

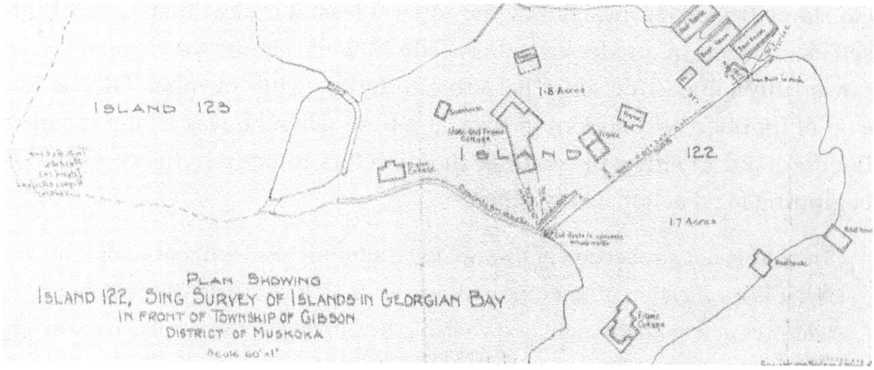

Plan of survey of island 122, Go Home Bay.

when the Club deeded the property in question to Mrs. Ella Firth in 1945.[26] There is no direct evidence as to why Mr. Galbraith chose to purchase the island lot from her in 1947, when he could easily have arranged to settle on his father's lot on the mainland. In his examination for discovery Galbraith portrayed himself as coming to the rescue of the recently widowed Mrs. Firth when she wished to sell and "could not get any person up there to take it."[27] He was familiar with the legal position on the islands, however, and it may be that purchase of the Firth property was the first step in his long-term plan to get rid of the restrictions on all the Madawaska Club sites.

Four years after the purchase, Galbraith conveyed title to himself and his wife Frances Howes Galbraith as joint tenants, in a deed containing none of the covenants he had obliged himself to insert in any such instrument. As his wife was not a graduate of the University of Toronto, he was clearly throwing down the gauntlet, but the Club directors did not rise to the occasion. In 1952 the Club commissioned a legal opinion by KG Morden, QC to the effect that a court might well disregard the restrictions on the islands, but still no action was forthcoming by the Club.[28] In 1956 Galbraith finally acquired the mainland property from his father's estate by buying out his sister, and upped the ante by registering a caution against the Club's lands; in January 1957 he filed his action in the High Court of Justice of Ontario.

One of the perennial fascinations about leading cases is the motivation of the principal actors. It usually takes very determined, ornery, or just plain obsessive individuals to stick to their goals through two or more levels of appeal with all the attendant commitment of money, time, and emotion. So far I have portrayed Mr. Galbraith as being motivated by a sense of chivalry and family honour in his attempts to remove the restrictions attached to the

Go Home Bay properties. But by the 1950s at least it is clear that he saw himself as engaged in an ideological crusade as well. These two elements were powerfully joined in a letter he wrote to fellow Club member TR Loudon (son of founder WJ Loudon) in 1952, at a time when he was trying to enlist Loudon's aid in either persuading the directors to address his concerns or beginning legal action against them.

> The MC is not a collection of by-laws to be administered without compromise; it is a collection of families with homes they love. To deny a widow or widower or a child the right of ownership because he or she is not a member of the "party" is communism at its very worst. To carry on the by-laws as presently constituted is the antithesis of the ideals for which two wars have been fought and for which a third is in the process of being fought.[29]

With such motivation, Mr. Galbraith's perseverance becomes more comprehensible. And although in the post-communist era he may seem like a paranoid crank, his worldview reminds us of the intense Cold War atmosphere pervading a number of key decisions around this time, such as *Noble and Wolf v Alley*.

In the end TR Loudon resisted Galbraith's invitation to join him in the legal struggle, and so did all the other Club members. However, one wonders whether some of them secretly supported his efforts. Loudon had written to his own lawyer early in 1952, asking him to provide an opinion as to whether the original restrictions in the charter also applied to the islands. He also asked for his opinion of bylaws 21 and 22, observing "[y]ou can see that these bylaws amount to confiscation of property of a deceased member if the wife or husband is not a graduate, an undergraduate, or an official at the U of T."[30] If Galbraith was the type to press ahead even if he had to do so alone, any benefits he obtained would be shared by all Club members; there was thus little incentive to join him and suffer the liability for costs if he lost. Perhaps more importantly, taking sides with the cantankerous Galbraith would likely result in strained relations with one's cottage neighbours, a not unimportant consideration in a small and intimate community such as that at Go Home Bay.

The Litigation

Galbraith hired Terence Sheard, QC, of Johnston, Sheard & Johnston, a well-known counsel in the field of property and probate law, while the Club hired RF Wilson, QC, of the firm Day, Wilson, Kelly, Martin & Campbell. Sheard launched a two-pronged attack: Galbraith was the plaintiff in a derivative action, suing on behalf of himself and all other shareholders of The Madawaska Club Limited in an attempt to have the restrictive provisions in the bylaws declared invalid, and he also sued in his own capacity, seeking a declaration of invalidity of the covenants contained in his deed from Mrs. Firth. While the two issues are to some extent interrelated, it will be primarily the discussion of the (in)validity of the restrictive covenants that interests us. Sheard argued that the Supreme Court of Canada's decision in *Noble and Wolf v Alley* was right on point: the restrictive covenants in the deed did not relate to the use of the land but merely to the identity of the owners. Such restrictions did not touch and concern the land and thus could not run with it to bind subsequent purchasers of the burdened land, even with notice. Thus while Mrs. Firth was bound by the covenants on a contractual basis with the Club, Galbraith was not liable to the Club because he had no contract with it.

Justice Ferguson accepted this argument with regard to the covenants restricting alienation to non-members, except for the one that most exercised Mr. Galbraith. That was bylaw 19, the very bylaw that Galbraith felt had been used to humiliate his mother many years before.[31] Without any real explanation, Ferguson J held that this bylaw dealt with the use of land and therefore ran with it. Nothing was said about the need for the Club to demonstrate that it had retained land capable of being benefited or that such land should be described in the deed creating the covenant, even though the Supreme Court of Canada had recently ruled in *Canadian Construction Co v Beaver (Alberta) Ltd* on this very topic.[32] Justice Ferguson went on to declare invalid those bylaws restricting transfer of shares to non-members as contravening a section of the Ontario *Companies Act*, but held that the provisions of the charter itself on this topic were beyond attack as the attorney general was not a party to the action.

Sheard had also maintained at trial that the covenants should be invalidated because they contravened public policy, but Justice Ferguson was highly resistant to this line of argument. In some brief observations dismissing it in his judgment, he revealed the Cold War shadow that hovered over many of the restrictive covenant decisions of the 1940s and 50s.

> To my mind, the desire to exclude from this association persons whose background and training or any other reason tends to make him uncongenial is not a matter of public policy [but] a private matter. If liberty to choose one's

> own companions and associates is to be denied to us, then the loss of liberty to pursue our own calling will shortly follow.[33]

Ferguson J's views also illustrate the double-edged nature of these liberty-based arguments: where Galbraith saw the restriction on alienability as a threat to his liberty to freely dispose of his property, Ferguson J saw attacks on the restriction as threats to one's liberty of association.

Mr. Galbraith had achieved much, but not the core of what he sought. The island properties had been liberated from the despised covenants, and freedom of disposition and testation restored. Transferees of island properties no longer needed to be members of the Club or graduates of the University of Toronto. The mainland properties, however, were not touched by the decision, and even on the islands, bylaw 19 had been upheld as a valid restrictive covenant. The effect of the decision could be summed up as follows. An island proprietor could transfer or will property to whomever he or she liked, but the *occupation* of that property would still require the consent of the directors if the occupant were not a member of the Club, and the qualifications for membership were beyond attack as they were entrenched in the charter. From Galbraith's point of view, this was almost worse than the status quo ante: now his widow could own island 122 but not occupy it without the consent of the directors. Galbraith decided to appeal solely on the point regarding the validity of bylaw 19, while the Club cross-appealed on all points decided against it.

These issues were argued on 9 June 1959 before a Court of Appeal consisting of Chief Justice Dana Porter, Justice Colin Gibson, and Justice Frederick George MacKay.[34] On the issue of the bylaws' validity, the Court pointed out that the trial judge had mistakenly assumed that they were enacted for the first time in 1932, when in fact they had been adopted in 1904. Only in 1912 had it been legislated that a company bylaw could not impose a restriction on the transfer of shares; such provisions were legal in 1904 and therefore they should stand. The bylaws in any case only implemented the charter and could not be attacked. On this point the judgment was upheld in the Supreme Court.

On the issue of the restrictive covenants, however, the Court went off on a totally unanticipated tack. The Court began to worry that on the wording of the bylaws there was a threshold issue as to the Club's power to convey fee simple estates to cottagers, and asked counsel for further argument on this point. Neither party had raised this issue and both were stunned that their fundamental assumption of the existence of fee simple estates was being questioned at this late date. And sure enough, when the judgment came down it denied that the Club had ever had the power to grant sites in fee simple. The intent of the bylaws, said the Court, was "that the Club should retain the fee simple in the lands and allot sites to members, subject to the conditions of the by-laws."[35] The Club directors "were empowered to give nothing more than leases, or occupational licences of a contractual nature"[36] which were "not inheritable," and had acted beyond their powers in purporting to grant Mrs. Firth a fee simple interest. The Club could thus burden these licences with whatever conditions it saw fit, making the law of restrictive covenants irrelevant as a licence to occupy cannot be a dominant or servient tenement.[37]

The closest analogy to the interests created under the bylaws, in the view of the Court of Appeal, would thus appear to be a ticket of occupation allocated by a band council under the *Indian Act* or, indeed, some Soviet land-holding practices. Something along these lines may indeed have been closer to the original intent of the provincial government in chartering the Club, as we have seen. But 1960 was the era of *Mad Men*, not Queen Victoria. That cottagers who had improved their lands and occupied them to the exclusion of all others for three generations should now be told that they had something far less than a fee simple, was simply beyond the pale. It remains a mystery why the Court of Appeal went out of its way to pursue a line of reasoning so far outside the arguments presented by the parties. Dana Porter, who wrote the decision, had been attorney general of Ontario from 1949 to 1955 and perhaps felt a special duty to uphold the intentions of his governmental predecessors as he understood them, but that is only speculation.

This result was definitely Galbraith's worst nightmare, though even the supposedly victorious Club was not happy about it. Galbraith retreated to his home at Peace Acre Farm, Kettleby Point, and circulated the following blast to his fellow Club members:

> It is the duty of every parent and veteran to protect his family and his community against the pitfalls of Communism. When the "fee simple" vests in the State, it is Communism, dictatorship and slavery for the individual. When the "fee" vests in the individual it is democracy, freedom and dignity for the human being. . . . I for one will not submit to the Communist type of set-up for Go Home and I do not believe any other freedom loving person will . . . .[38]

He had no choice at this point but to appeal to the Supreme Court of Canada. A bench of five, Kerwin CJ and Taschereau, Abbott, Judson and Ritchie JJ, heard the appeal on 28 February 1961 and rendered its decision four months later, on 26 June.[39]

The Court made short work of Porter CJO's interpretation of the bylaws, observing that he had given insufficient attention to bylaw 17, which clearly stated that anyone allotted a site "who desires to own the said site instead of leasing it from the Club may do so."[40] As to the effect of the restrictive covenants, including the one contained in bylaw 19, the Court unanimously agreed with Judson J's opinion that they were not enforceable for several reasons: first, as the trial judge had found, because of the *Noble v Alley* interpretation of the test for what touches and concerns the land; second, because at the time of the sale to Mrs. Firth, it was not clear whether the Club retained any land to be benefited (Sheard had argued this in his factum); and third, even if it did, the benefit had not been expressly annexed to those lands, nor had they been described in the deed to her in a way to make them "easily ascertainable."

Judson's judgment was short and to the point, as his usually were. He briefly cited two classic English authorities, *Rogers v Hosegood*[41] for the definition of "touch and concern" and *Zetland v Driver* for the proposition that "the deed itself must so define the land to be benefited as to make it easily ascertainable."[42] On the first point, Judson J observed that the impugned covenant "has nothing to do with the use to which the land may be put, but relates only to the kind of person who may be given occupation . . . . It calls into being the exercise of an unfettered personal discretion by the club management and its plain purpose is to preserve the amenities of the Club."[43] It was thus right on point with the Court's own decision in *Noble and Wolf v Alley*. On the second point, the Court could again rely on one of its own precedents, this time in the *Beaver Lumber* case,[44] where the failure to specify any dominant land was held to be fatal. In *Galbraith* the problem was the same — no dominant land at all was specified — such that the statement about the deed itself defining the land so "as to make it easily ascertainable" was strictly obiter. But it was this aspect of the decision that was subsequently seized upon and has come to be the principal proposition for which *Galbraith* is understood to stand.

The Supreme Court has sometimes been criticized for deciding *Galbraith* on technical grounds, rather than invoking the doctrine of public policy more forthrightly. I have done so with my own students, but I see now that

I was wrong because I did not understand the full context of the case. The peculiar nature of the Madawaska Club setup really left the Court no choice. The restrictions were hard-wired into the Club's mainland properties via its charter. They had not been sought by the Club and had been imposed on it precisely *to implement* public policy: the government wished to restrict the pool of purchasers in order to prevent the lands from becoming available for speculation. Any argument that these restrictions were themselves against public policy should have been a non-starter (though neither counsel for the Club nor Ferguson J at trial pursued this line of argument). And while the restrictions were not hard-wired into the island properties in the same way, surely it would have been a complete defence for the Club to say they were merely trying to extend the geographic range of restrictions which were themselves the very embodiment of public policy. How could a set of restrictions compatible with public policy on the mainland contravene it when imposed on the islands, even if it was the Club's, rather than the government's, decision to impose them?

Aftermath: Impact on the Club

The Supreme Court's decision in no way settled all the issues regarding the alienation of properties originally owned by the Club, and echoes of the decisions taken at Queen's Park in the summer of 1898 reverberate to this day at Go Home Bay. *Galbraith* did confirm that cottagers held ordinary fee simple ownership and not some exotic kind of licence of occupation. But in some ways it magnified the problems by entrenching the distinction between the island properties, which could now be sold and occupied by non-members and probably mortgaged, and the mainland properties, which could not. At first the Club tried to get the province to eliminate the offending restriction from the charter but the Minister of Lands and Forests, Kelso Roberts, advised that the department had obtained a legal opinion that this could not be done. He would not commit even to the issuance of new letters patent to the Club lands, without the restrictions.[45] In 1968 a new set of bylaws was approved setting up a share-trust scheme for those without the U of T qualification wishing to purchase lands on the mainland, whereby their shares in the Club would be held by persons having the U of T qualification; and for the issuing of site leases to Club members with the U of T qualification and licences to those without. This still left the island owners in a better position than mainlanders, and as Club member George Gale observed, "we cannot long survive half-slave and half-free."[46]

Finally a private members' bill was passed by the Ontario Legislature in 1989 reissuing the letters patent to the Club lands on the mainland without the U of T restriction.[47] Given that the Club's corporate charter itself still stands intact with the restriction and the forfeiture clause, however, it is not clear that owners of former Club lands possess absolute title even now.

Aftermath: Impact on the Law

Galbraith has been applied consistently across the country in the half-century since the case was decided. As explained in *Re Sekretov and City of Toronto,* to be discussed shortly, *Galbraith* has become the cornerstone of an exacting approach to the law of restrictive covenants, requiring both explicit annexation of benefit to the dominant tenement and a high degree of specificity in the description of the dominant lands. Outside of building schemes, where the rigorous approach to identification of the properties is a necessary corollary of the requirement of mutuality, restrictive covenants are regularly struck down in Canada because the dominant tenement is either not specified at all, or is inadequately described.

In *Re Sekretov and City of Toronto,* the village of Swansea (later amalgamated with the City of Toronto) had sold land to Sekretov's predecessor in title with a deeded restriction that "the Transferees, their executors, administrators, heirs and assigns, shall not use the lands herein for any other purpose than that provided by resolution of Council, . . . [and] shall not cut down any trees on said lands, or make any alterations" except with the consent of Council.[48] A parallel resolution of Council, however, not included in the deed, had said that no buildings were to be erected and the land was to be kept in its natural state. Through poor internal organization the building department was not aware of either the initial resolution or the deeded restrictions; Sekretov was granted a building permit and succeeded in completing 85 percent of his projected house before a stop-work order was issued. The Ontario Court of Appeal had no difficulty in striking down the deeded restriction as no lands to be benefited were mentioned. However, Schroeder JA went out of his way to declare that two English cases, to the effect that the dominant tenement could be inferred from "surrounding or attendant circumstances," were incompatible with the Supreme Court's decision in *Galbraith*: "The language used in the Madawaska Club case clearly excludes any notion of annexation to dominant land by implication.'[49] He then went on to provide what he saw as the rationale for this rule, a rationale not provided in *Galbraith* itself. If the purchaser has no indication in the deed as to what lands are to be benefited, said Schroeder, "[h]e would be placed in a most precarious position if he must first breach the covenant and then wait in fear and trembling to see if he is to be sued." In other words the reason for a strict rule is certainty and fairness to the purchaser.

Why should this be so? There was sufficient wiggle room in Judson's reference to an "easily ascertainable" description that later courts might have interpreted it more flexibly. And as we have seen, Judson's comment was obiter in any case and might been avoided. What was it that was attractive about a stricter interpretation of *Galbraith*?

Based on Schroeder's later elaboration of *Galbraith*, it appears that the lure of certainty and its close cousin, free alienability, in property law had some overriding appeal, more so than in England itself. But is this conception of certainty, as free alienability and absence from restraint, adequate for our largely urban, inter-connected society? According to English scholars Kevin Gray and Susan Francis Gray,

> a creative tension exists between the need to render land alienable and the need to allow private ordering by consensual arrangement. The stability and convenience of land use secured by durably binding covenants often ensures, in practice, that enforceable covenants, far from sterilizing title, operate to enhance the market value of both the benefited and the burdened land. Thus, while a sense of cautious concern still remains today at the core of the legal response, it is also apparent that in recent times the [English] courts have adopted a more sympathetic view of restrictive covenants. This relaxation of approach may in part reflect a general change in community attitudes towards the importance of preserving the integrity and attractiveness of local environments.[50]

These kinds of concerns, which ironically lay behind the creation of the Madawaska Club itself, are notably absent from judicial discussions in subsequent restrictive covenant cases in Canada. *Galbraith* is applied more or less mechanically, but not reluctantly. It seems to have acquired a common sense appeal.

Galbraith is, in short, an example of the facilitative liberalism I have spoken of elsewhere as being a growing theme in twentieth-century Canadian property law.[51] It is a vision of property law appropriate for a country with abundant land under a big sky, where the independent yeoman is seen to be the best judge of how his [sic] lands should be used and disposed of. This view was adopted most clearly by the Ontario Court of Appeal in *Re Nicholls*, where it was called upon to decide how far a testator could go in delegating the power to distribute estate assets to third parties. Krever JA observed that "the authorities . . . are in such a state of uncertainty that this appeal should be decided on the basis of principle or policy."[52] Justice Krever found the desired policy in an Ontario Law Reform Commission report on the law of wills: "The right of an individual to own and dispose of his assets is basic to our law. Any effort to restrict or circumscribe that right should only be permitted where the necessity for restriction clearly justifies interference with the basic freedom of the individual to dispose of his property."[53] It would be hard to get more "facilitative" than that.

There may be another factor accounting for the popularity of the *Galbraith-Sekretov* approach, however, related to facilitative liberalism but distinct from it. That is the registry factor. Canadians have long been accustomed to a system of publicity of title, whether under the older registry system or the newer land titles system pioneered in western Canada. Even under the registry system, which does not contain a statutory guarantee of registered title, lawyers expect to see all relevant charges and burdens registered on title with the exception of well-known overriding interests such as prescriptive easements and adverse possession. The more the law makes room for implicit burdens not clearly set out in registered instruments, the less effective the registry becomes as a tool for managing risk in conveyancing. This makes Canada quite distinct from England, where registration really did not take off until the later twentieth century, and where the notion of implicit burdens consequently did not represent the same threat to the registry.

The obvious solution to the problem would appear to be a statutory requirement, at least in land titles jurisdictions, for dominant lands to be identified according to the descriptive standards required for all other registered instruments whenever a restrictive covenant is sought to be registered. Some land titles acts purport to require this now, but it appears not to be enforced by the relevant officials, as various examples in the case law reveal the registration of soi-disant restrictive covenants without reference to any dominant tenement at all.[54] And courts have consistently said that the annexation of benefit to dominant lands is a question of law that cannot be conclusively decided by a master of titles, creating a potential inroad on the "mirror principle" contained in land titles legislation.[55]

The key role played by the register is recognized by recent proposals for reform in England, based on the long-mooted idea of a "land obligation" comprising both positive and negative obligations. The Law Commission has recommended that "all new covenanted arrangements respecting registered land should take effect as expressly labelled 'land obligations' appurtenant to the respective estates of the dominant and servient proprietor," and requiring all such obligations "to be completed by entry in the register of title of both dominant and servient tenements." Thus, benefits and burdens "would attach to the relevant tenements, being enforceable only as between the current owners of those tenements" with "the highly beneficial consequence of eliminating the extremely technical rules relating to the transmission of the benefits and burdens of both positive and negative covenants."[56] There is a nice irony in this from a Canadian point of view, in that Schroeder JA in *Sekretov* took comfort in his stringent approach to the identification of dominant lands by referring to the English Law Commission's 1967 report on restrictive covenants and the draft Land Obligations Bill that followed it, both of which adopted a similar approach.[57] The Commission's proposals long remained a dead letter, however, and the bill did not become law.

There is one caveat about the effect of *Galbraith*, and that relates to the use of extrinsic evidence. It might be thought that any ambiguity in the deed's description of the dominant tenement would be fatal. However, the courts have here permitted the general principles of contract law to play a role; i.e., as long as a dominant tenement is in fact identified, any ambiguity in the description opens the way to the admissibility of extrinsic evidence to satisfy the ambiguity. Lieff J stated this as far back as 1966 in his decision in *McGregor v Boyd Builders*, but this approach seemed to have been forgotten until recently.[58] In *Kirk v Distacom Ventures*, the BC Court of Appeal expressed discomfort with the extremely rigorous approach of some other courts to this question and admitted extrinsic evidence to try and discern the meaning of an ambiguous description.[59] Even with the extrinsic evidence, however, the description in the deed in question could not reach the required threshold of certainty. This approach is not inconsistent with the respect for the registry adverted to in the previous discussion. Where a dominant tenement is at least identified in a registered instrument, albeit ambiguously, arguably the burden shifts to the purchaser to satisfy herself as to the extent of the dominant lands if that is a matter of concern.

Conclusion

Is *Galbraith v Madawaska Club* a leading case in Canadian property law? Perhaps there are two kinds of leading cases. There are those almost mythical cases such as *Calder* or *Morgenthaler* or *Brown v Board of Education* that stand out like beacons on the plain of surrounding jurisprudence. *Galbraith* is not one of those. It is a case that leads by example, as it were, not shattering previous ideas or presenting novel approaches to familiar issues or deciding between two irreconcilable streams of authority. Rather, it sums up tendencies in the existing law and shunts the law on to a clearer, not a new, path.

Galbraith did not purport to make new law at all, but when read along with *Noble and Wolf v Alley* and *Sekretov*, it reveals some interesting tensions within the law of restrictive covenants and within Canadian property law generally. There is no doubt that restrictive covenants, properly drafted and deployed, can be powerfully effective in (re-)shaping the landscape of urban areas, for good or ill. Existing scholarship has identified a possible role for restrictive covenants in reducing potential locations for affordable housing, and, as a result of grocery retailers' policy of aiming for fewer, larger stores, in creating "food deserts" in Prairie cities.[60] Other, more positive, uses of covenants include maintaining green or non-commercial spaces in urban areas.[61] Both *Noble and Wolf* and *Galbraith* placed an important limit on the ambit of restrictive covenants: henceforth they could not be used to create "congenial communities" defined by the personal characteristics of the inhabitants. Freedom of association was thus redefined in an inclusive rather than exclusive manner. Indirectly, of course, by specifying the minimum value of homes within a particular development, restrictive covenants could validly use personal wealth as a criterion for inclusion/exclusion, but the courts may have reasoned that price will always exclude some buyers even without the existence of restrictive covenants. All of this is perfectly consistent with a liberal society, where a fierce defence of the abstract equality of citizens co-exists with a broad acceptance of economic inequality.

Galbraith and *Sekretov* threw another spanner into the restrictive covenant works. By imposing stringent requirements for the identification of the dominant tenement and the annexation of benefit to it, the courts added another layer of complexity to an already dense doctrine. This change in effect made it easier to render restrictive covenants ineffective, and took Canadian law in a direction opposite to that noted in English law by Gray and Gray. Whether this has any great empirical significance is hard to say, but at the level of ideas it suggests a skepticism about collective constraints and a faith in individual judgment and initiative that privileges development over stewardship. That a community planner should have been the person responsible for bringing this issue before the Supreme Court of Canada is thus one of the enduring ironies of *Galbraith v Madawaska Club.*

Notes

1 As cited by Claire Campbell, *Shaped by the West Wind: Nature and History in Georgian Bay* (Vancouver: University of British Columbia Press, 2005) at 139.

2 *Ibid.*

3 See the treatment by James W. St. G Walker in *"Race," Rights and the Law in the Supreme Court of Canada* (Waterloo, ON: Wilfrid Laurier University Press for the Osgoode Society for Canadian Legal History, 1997) at 182-245.

4 On Anglo-Canadian legal nationalism, see Philip Girard, "Who's Afraid of Canadian Legal History?" (2007) 57 U.T.L.J. 727.

5 "Land Law, Liberalism, and the Agrarian Ideal: British North America, 1750-1920" in John McLaren, AR Buck, and Nancy E. Wright, eds, *Despotic Dominion: Property Rights in British Settler Societies* (Vancouver: UBC Press, 2005).

6 Bruce Ziff argues in "Warm Reception in a Cold Climate: English Property Law and the Suppression of the Canadian Legal Identity" in *Despotic Dominion, ibid,* that Canadian judge-made law has tended to follow unreflectively English precedent, while Canadian legislators have been bolder in departing from the English model where local circumstances seemed to warrant it. At a general level it is hard to disagree with this proposition, reflecting as it does a longstanding assumption of Canadian judges that it was for legislators, not judges, to change the law. It does, however, assume an agreed-upon singular definition of what the common law of England was on any given point, when quite often it presented a plethora of possibilities, leaving room for creative interpretation by the judiciary.

7 Bruce Ziff, "Restrictive Covenants: The Basic Ingredients" in *Special Lectures 2002 Real Property Law: Conquering the Complexities* (Toronto: Law Society of Upper Canada, 2003) at 293, 298-99, 304. For more on the history of restrictive covenants, see his "Bumble Bees Cannot Fly: and Restrictive Covenants Cannot Run" (unpublished, 2010).

8 The School of Practical Science of which John Galbraith Sr. had been the founder and principal was a free-standing institution for the education of engineers; it became part of the University of Toronto in 1906 as the faculty of applied science and engineering, and Galbraith Sr. became its dean. See Richard White, "Professionals and Academics: Relations Between the School of Practical Science and the University of Toronto, 1878-1906" (2001) 13:2 Historical Studies in Education/Revue d'histoire de l'éducation 147.

9 The Rock Lake area initially desired by the Club was added to Algonquin Park in 1903.

10 WJ Loudon, *A short history of the founding of the Madawaska Club and its early settlement at Go Home Bay, 1898-1903* (privately published, 1938) at 28. This memoir was reprinted in 1982 and I am grateful to WJ Loudon's great-grandson Tom Clark for making a copy available to me. I also thank Sue Grundy of Blake Cassels Graydon LLP for discussing some of the legal issues relating to the charter of the Madawaska Club.

11 University of Toronto Archives, Madawaska Club fonds, B1975-016, box 3, memo from Assistant Commissioner of Crown Lands to Commissioner, 6 April 1898 [hereafter, Madawaska Club fonds].

12 *Ibid*, memo from Commissioner of Crown Lands to Assistant Provincial Secretary, 7 April 1898.

13 Provisions from the charter as quoted by Ferguson J at trial in *Galbraith v Madawaska Club* (1959), 18 D.L.R. (2d) 424 (Ont. H.C.J.) at 426-27.

14 "Land Law, Liberalism, and the Agrarian Ideal," above note 5 at 128.

15 (1903), 33 SCR 65.

16 Loudon had written to Sir Louis Davies, then Minister of Marine and Fisheries, in 1900 requesting federal funding for such a station. As he observed casually in his memoirs, he was "agreeably surprised to get a letter in reply, granting us a substantial sum, on condition that we obtain the services of a competent biologist as director" (*A short history* at 117). Significant research in fish biology in particular was carried out as part of this project. Although a physicist, Loudon published a short treatise based on his research at Go Home Bay: *The Small-Mouthed Bass* (Toronto: Hunter-Rose, 1910). The initial director of the station, Robert Russell Bensley, was an eminent biologist who left the University of Toronto for a brilliant career at the University of Chicago. He was succeeded by his brother Benjamin Arthur Bensley, a professor of zoology at the University of Toronto; one of his reports on "The Fishes of Georgian Bay" was published along with other studies conducted at Go Home Bay in *Contributions to Canadian Biology* (Toronto: Biological Board of Canada, 1915).

17 See Loudon, *A short history*, above note 10 at 116.

18 *The Madawaska Club: Go-Home Bay 1898-1923* (n.p., 1923?); *The Madawaska Club Go-Home Bay 1898-1948* (n.p., n.d.); *Madawaska Club 1898-1973 Go Home Bay* (n.p., Madawaska Club, 1973); the fourth instalment was published in 1998 but I have not been able to obtain a copy. Mary Barnett's account of "A Community of Scholars" in the 1973 volume provides a good overview of the scholars, writers, and scientists who have summered at Go Home Bay, from historian J. Bartlet Brebner to novelist Gwethalyn Graham to geologist J. Tuzo Wilson.

19 Kenneth M. Wells, *Cruising the Georgian Bay* (Toronto: Kingswood House, 1958) at 77.

20 *Galbraith v. Madawaska Club*, Case on Appeal in the Supreme Court of Canada, transcript of examination in chief of John S Galbraith, at 26 [Case on Appeal SCC].

21 Case on Appeal SCC at 38. Nesbitt was one of the best-known counsel of his day; he sat briefly on the Supreme Court of Canada (1903-05) before resigning to resume his career at the bar.

22 Madawaska Club fonds, box 4, file "Galbraith v Madawaska Club no. 4."

23 Biographical information on Galbraith is derived from University of Toronto Archives, graduate record file A73-0026/111/95, which also contains his obituary: *Globe and Mail*, 30 January 1968.

24 Galbraith's only brother had died without issue soon after their mother, leaving Galbraith and his sister Emily Beatrix Galbraith (later Jamieson) as sole heirs; it is unclear whether his sister was a graduate of the University of Toronto.

25 Madawaska Club fonds, box 3, extract from Club minutes, 21 March 1932.

26 The Firths had occupied this site for a long time but in accordance with Club practice no deed had been issued during the Rev. Mr. Firth's lifetime.

27 Copy of transcript in Madawaska Club fonds, box 4, file "Galbraith v. Madawaska Club no. 3" at 29.

28 *Ibid*, memo to Club members dated "June 1952."

29 University of Toronto Archives, Thomas Richardson Loudon fonds, B76-0003, box 7, file 12, Galbraith to Loudon, 10 January 1952.

30 *Ibid*, Loudon to Norman Keys, KC, 3 January 1952.

31 As a result of a 1947 revisions of the bylaws, the initial bylaws 21 and 22 containing these restrictions became bylaw 19.

32 [1955] SCR 682.

33 (1959), 18 DLR (2d) 424 at 441 (Ont HCJ).

34 (1960), 23 DLR (2d) 6 (Ont CA).

35 *Ibid* at 14.

36 *Ibid* at 18.

37 A leasehold interest can serve as a dominant or servient tenement: *Russo v Field*, [1973] SCR 466. The Court did not identify exactly what interest Galbraith had received from Ella Firth but found that in any case he was contractually bound to the Club itself as a shareholder to observe its bylaws and therefore no question of the running of covenants needed to be addressed.

38 Madawaska Club fonds, box 4, file "Galbraith v. Madawaska Club 4," "Notice" dated 14 July 1960.

39 [1961] SCR 639.

40 *Ibid* at 646. This, of course, begged the question of whether such a bylaw was authorized by the charter itself.

41 [1900] 2 Ch 388.

42 [1939] Ch 1.

43 [1961] SCR 639 at 652.

44 Above note 32.

45 Madawaska Club fonds, B83-0021, box 1, file 07, "Memorandum re The Madawaska Club meeting with Minister of Lands and Forests January 27, 1965" at 2.

46 *Ibid*, George Gale to Robert Harris, February 1966. Gale was Chief Justice of the high court and would become Chief Justice of Ontario the next year.

47 *An Act respecting The Madawaska Club Limited*, SO 1989, c. Pr16.

48 [1973] 2 OR 161 at 162-63 (CA).

49 *Ibid* at 166. The English cases were *Newton Abbott Co-operative Society Ltd. v Williamson & Treadgold Ltd.*, [1952] Ch 286 and *Marten v Flight Refuelling Ltd.*, [1962] Ch 115.

50 *Elements of Land Law*, 5th ed (Oxford: Oxford University Press, 2009) at 263. For an example of such community attitudes in the Canadian context, see *Save the Heritage Covenant Society v Kelowna (City)*, 2008 BCSC 1084, 296 DLR (4th) 419, where a heritage group tried to prevent the city from selling property deeded to the city in 1946 with a covenant that it be used for municipal purposes only and never sold for commercial or industrial purposes. The covenant was held unenforceable for lack of a

dominant tenement but the arrangement was upheld as a charitable trust binding on the city.

51 "Land Law, Liberalism, and the Agrarian Ideal," above note 6. To be clear, I am referring here to trends within the judge-made law, not legislation, which obviously began to impose more and more restrictions on land use and transfer in the twentieth century.

52 (1987), 57 OR (2d) 763 at 771 (CA).

53 As cited *ibid* at 772.

54 Since 1961 the Ontario *Land Titles Act* has contained a provision stating that "a covenant shall not be registered . . . unless . . . (c) the covenantee owns land to be benefited by the covenant and that land is mentioned in the covenant." However, a later sub-section states that "the entry on the register of a condition or covenant as running with or annexed to land does not make it run with the land, if . . . [it] would not otherwise be annexed to or run with the land." In spite of the first provision, *Piazza v Hopley*, [2001] OJ No. 4855, 46 RPR (3d) 133 (Sup Ct J) provides an example where a post-1961 restrictive covenant was registered with no reference to a dominant tenement. The Alberta *Land Titles Act* is to the same effect: *Kolias v Condominium Plan 309 CDC* (2008), 440 AR 389, 303 DLR (4th) 314 (CA).

55 See the *Piazza* and *Kolias* cases, above note 54.

56 Gray and Gray, *Elements of Land Law* at 253. Draft legislation based on the Commission's recommendations has been expected for some time but appears nowhere on the parliamentary horizon as of October 2011.

57 *Sekretov*, above note 48 at 167. See Law Commission of Great Britain, *Transfer of Land: Report on Restrictive Covenants* (London: HMSO, 1967).

58 [1966] 1 OR 424.

59 [1996] BCJ No. 1879, 4 RPR (3d) 240 (CA). The Court distanced itself from the tenor of the decisions in *Guaranty Trust v Campbelltown Shopping Centre* (1986), 44 Alta LR (2d) 270 (CA) and *Sawlor v Naugle* (1990), 101 NSR (2d) 160 (SCTD), where Justice Tidman stated at 166 that "there must be either a metes and bounds description of the lands, a reference to a plan identifying the lands or some other specific reference by which the lands to be benefitted may be readily identified or ascertained."

60 P. Filion, *The Impact of Restrictive Covenants on Affordable Housing and Non-Single Uses of Homes: A Waterloo Region Case Study* (Ottawa: CMHC, 1993). KE Smoyer-Tomic et al, "Food Deserts in the Prairies? Supermarket Accessibility and Neighborhood Need in Edmonton, Canada" (2006) 58 Professional Geographer 307. And see generally Bruce Ziff, "Bumble Bees Cannot Fly: and Restrictive Covenants Cannot Run" (unpublished, 2010).

61 As was attempted in *Save the Heritage Covenant Society v Kelowna (City)*, above note 50.

"The right to discriminate": Kenneth Bell versus Carl McKay and the Ontario Human Rights Commission[1]

Frank Luce and Karen Schucher

Introduction

HUMAN RIGHTS LEGISLATION OFTEN infringes on common law property rights in order to advance social justice. From the perspective of Ontario's Black population, such infringement was required to abolish the common law property rights of slaveholders in nineteenth century Ontario,[2] and was again required to ban racial discrimination in employment, services, and housing in the twentieth century. This conflict between human rights and property rights was considered by the Supreme Court of Canada when Ontario's legislative approach to discrimination met an early challenge in the common law courts. The case in question, cited as *Bell v McKay*, was decided on a point of law on which the Supreme Court recently reversed itself, although the social impact of its original decision cannot be so easily reversed.[3]

In *Bell v McKay*, a conflict between the human rights of Carl McKay, a prospective tenant, and the ownership rights of Kenneth Bell, a landlord, played out in the context of the statutory procedure set out in the Ontario *Human Rights Code* ("Code")[4] to process human rights complaints. Bell had advertised a flat for rent on the second and third floor of a house he owned, in which he and his wife occupied the main floor. When McKay, self-styled as "a Black man from Jamaica," appeared at his door as a potential tenant, Bell told him that the flat was no longer available, an untruth that prompted McKay to complain to the Ontario Human Rights Commission ("OHRC").

The complaint, alleging discrimination based on race, colour, and place of origin, proceeded through an internal investigation and on to a Board of Inquiry, chaired by Walter Tarnopolsky. However, the inquiry was halted when Bell's lawyer served a notice of application for prohibition and proceeded to challenge the jurisdiction of the Board of Inquiry in a common law court. The application was initially granted, then overturned by the Ontario Court of Appeal, and ultimately reinstated by the Supreme Court of Canada.

The legal context in which the case was argued involved the emerging field of administrative law in Canada. The emergence of an administrative law model for dispute resolution led to a jurisdictional conflict between the common law courts and a growing body of administrative tribunals, a conflict in which the courts were often depicted as the defender of individual rights against government intrusion. This new field of law gave rise to questions about the relationship between government as legislator and the courts, as well as the relationship between the government's administrative agencies and the courts. In this context the *Bell v McKay* case was significant because it consolidated the construction of the legal doctrine of "jurisdictional fact" at the level of the Supreme Court of Canada.[5] The Court's approach to this doctrine in turn reflected a jurisprudential conflict between legal formalism and the more contextual approach that generally characterizes the Court's current approach to statutory interpretation. In this context the case represents a high water mark for the formalist approach.

The "jurisdictional fact" at issue in *Bell v McKay* was whether the flat in question was "self-contained" within the meaning of the Code. The social context in which this issue arose involved a serious concern within racialized communities, including Black and Jewish communities, that discrimination in the housing market was preventing them from renting decent housing. It also involved a social movement that demanded compliance with the *Universal Declaration of Human Rights*' proclamation " . . . that human rights should be protected by the rule of law," to bring an end to the racial and religious discrimination that the common law tolerated.[6] Confronting this common law tradition, social activists demanded "affirmative legislative action" to promote human rights and combat discrimination.[7]

When the OHRC was established in 1961, the Conservative government of the day turned to one of the social movement activists, Dr. Daniel Grafton Hill III, to serve as its first director. As a human rights activist, Hill was aware of the relative strength of the movement's opponents who relied on the common law's traditional protection of their property rights. In designing the OHRC procedure for processing human rights complaints, Hill and his colleagues sought to avoid the interference of the common law courts, choosing instead an alternative dispute resolution mechanism that reflected the duality that they read into the OHRC's statutory mandate, that is, to conciliate if possible and to litigate only if necessary. Here the legal and social contexts intersected, as the conflict that played out in *Bell v McKay* was as much focused on Bell's procedural rights as it was on McKay's right to be free from discrimination. The competition between McKay's social rights and the property rights that the common law courts were designed to protect remained central to both the substantive and the procedural aspects of this legacy.

The chapter begins with a brief review of the legislative history of the Code and the process of enacting anti-discrimination statutes in response to the reform strategies of the social movement. This review pays particular attention to the evolution of statutory provisions that prohibited discrimination in housing up to the time of McKay's complaint and the evolution of the procedural response adopted by the OHRC. The chapter then follows the legal path taken by McKay's complaint as it proceeded, first through the OHRC's internal process and then through the courts, with particular attention to the legal actors, their arguments, and the social context in which they were operating. This case study examines a significant court challenge to Ontario's legislative approach to the issue of discrimination and the first instance in which the Supreme Court of Canada was called upon to interpret and apply a Canadian human rights statute. The article concludes with some reflections on the legacy of the case itself, the social movement, and the underlying competition between social and property rights.

The Ontario *Human Rights Code* and Protection Against Discrimination in Rental Housing

ONTARIO'S *HUMAN RIGHTS CODE* evolved from "fair practices" legislation that social activists fought for in the 1940s and 1950s to address discrimination against racial and religious minorities.[8] The social activists campaigned for affirmative legislative action in response to specific forms of discrimination, including anti-Semitic and racist[9] speeches, publications, advertisements, and signs; anti-Semitic and racist restrictive covenants on the sale of land; anti-Semitic and racist employment practices; and anti-Semitic and racist exclusions from public recreational facilities and from access to services, such as services provided by restaurants, barbershops, and hairdressers. Both the fair practices statutes, and the Code when it was first enacted, focused on racial and religious discrimination.[10] These new statutes posed a dual challenge to employers, service providers, and landlords. Substantively, the legislation challenged the common law's protection of freedom of contract, including the "right" to deny employment or services or rental housing to people because of their race or religion. Procedurally, the legislation placed disputes about discrimination in the hands of administrative law processes instead of in the hands of the courts.

Both substantive and procedural aspects of the Code were at play in *Bell v McKay*. The Code's preamble, like those of the predecessor fair practices statutes, incorporated the language of equal rights from the *Universal Declaration of Human Rights*, including reference to the "dignity and worth of *every person*" [emphasis added].[11] From the perspective of groups that had been subjected to unequal treatment, the purpose of human rights legislation was to prevent these forms of discriminatory and unequal treatment from continuing. However, the language of equal rights can also be one of "competing rights" when used to frame a competition between anti-discrimination social rights — developed by affirmative legislative action and enforced using the administrative law approach — and property rights — developed by the common law and enforced primarily by the courts.

Toronto's Jewish community was at the centre of the social movement that campaigned for affirmative legislative action against discrimination. The Canadian Jewish Congress and B'nai Brith established a "Joint Public Relations Committee" (JPRC), which allied with and helped finance the Jewish Labour Committee of Canada (JLC). The JLC acted through a series of Joint Labour Committees for Human Rights, which local unions and Labour Councils established in various urban centers, including Toronto ("the Toronto Joint Committee"). The JPRC and Toronto Joint Committee joined forces with the newly formed Association for Civil Liberties (later the Canadian Civil Liberties Association).[12] The Toronto Joint Committee also made common cause with various Black organizations and individuals, so the composition and character of the social movement could be best described as a coalition of Jewish, labour, and Black organizations and activists.

However, the social movement campaigns also faced strong opposition from social conservatives, judicial conservatives, and pure racists. The campaigns' opponents did not publicly support discrimination, since such a position would not have held sway in the post–World War II environment.

Instead, they unveiled a variety of oppositional tactics: couching their opposition in Cold War rhetoric, questioning claims that discrimination was in fact a real social problem, emphasizing the language of "competing rights," and opposing the use of affirmative legislative action. For some opponents, the objection to affirmative legislation action was framed as "support for traditional British rights and freedoms."[13] *The Globe and Mail* was often the public voice of this opposition, and its editorial board regularly published the opinion that affirmative legislative action was neither an appropriate nor an effective method of eliminating prejudice and achieving tolerance.[14]

One of the co-founders of the Association for Civil Liberties was Bora Laskin, who in 1965 became the first Jew appointed to the Ontario Court of Appeal and later the first Jew appointed to the Supreme Court of Canada. Laskin was a member of the legal committee of the JPRC, and as such was influential in constructing the legal strategy that led to the establishment of the OHRC. His early efforts with the JPRC were channeled through a legal challenge to restrictive covenants for the transfer of land to Jews and other minorities, culminating in the decision of the Supreme Court of Canada known as *Noble and Wolf*.[15] Laskin knew that anti-Semitism was also prevalent within the legal community and that Jews experienced discrimination in obtaining articling positions and employment with non-Jewish firms.[16] Toronto's Lawyers' Club, which met at the Law Society of Upper Canada, admitted only applicants who were "male, white and of the Christian religion" until 1963.[17] Because he was Jewish, Laskin was unable to join the University Club when he was appointed to the Ontario Court of Appeal, even though his brother judges frequented it often.[18]

The campaigns against racial and religious discrimination in Ontario paralleled the civil rights movement against racial segregation in the United States. In both places the campaigns coalesced around the demand for affirmative legislative action, so that human rights would be governed by the rule of law, as the *Universal Declaration of Human Rights* proclaimed to be essential. In Ontario, politicians and activists from both the Cooperative Commonwealth Federation (CCF) and the Communist Party of Canada (CPC) were active within the campaigns, and eventually support was also garnered from the Progressive Conservatives and the Liberals.[19]

One of the techniques used by the social activists was known as "testing." In a typical testing case, a Black patron would request service in a bar or restaurant, or request to rent an apartment; upon refusal, a white patron would follow up with the same request which, when granted, provided proof of racial discrimination. As a law professor, Laskin himself had used his students to test the degree to which Toronto's housing market was racially discriminatory, knowledge that no doubt served him well when the issue came before him later in the Court of Appeal.[20] The testing technique was used first to demonstrate that racial and religious discrimination were prevalent social problems, and later to gather evidence in support of enforcement of the new affirmative legislative provisions.

The first victory for the coalition campaign was the enactment of the *Fair Employment Practices Act* in 1951.[21] This was followed by campaigns for legislation to address racial and religious discrimination in access to services. The coalition activists found that local forms of racial segregation were commonplace in Southwestern Ontario, particularly in former Underground Railroad "terminals" such as Dresden, where one may have hoped for a climate of tolerance to prevail for historical reasons.[22] The Toronto Joint Committee Executive Secretary who initiated and coordinated the first phase of the Dresden campaign in 1953 was Donna Hill who, like her husband Dan Hill, was a veteran of the civil rights movement in the United States.[23] Donna and Dan were a mixed-race couple who experienced firsthand the effects of the segregated housing market when they moved to Toronto after their marriage in Washington, DC, in 1952 and experienced difficulty finding decent rental accommodation.[24]

The Dresden campaign led to the enactment of the *Fair Accommodation Practices* statute in 1954,[25] prohibiting discrimination in "accommodation, services or facilities . . . to which the public is customarily admitted" and discrimination in signs and publications, again, on the basis of race, religion, and nationality.[26] The statute did not expressly define "accommodation" to include "housing," but the social activists expected that rental housing would be covered. However when they tried to support a case of discrimination in rental housing, District Court Justice Douglas C. Thomas of Bracebridge ruled that the statute did not apply because rental housing was not a place to which the public was customarily admitted.[27] Justice Thomas' decision triggered a fresh campaign to bring rental housing under the protection of anti-discrimination legislation, either by way of an amendment to the fair accommodation practices statute or by way of a new statute.

Debate over the housing amendment went through several stages that focused on defining at what point privately owned rental housing should be subject to the limits on freedom to contract imposed by anti-discrimination legislation. The *Fair Accommodation Practices Act* was first amended in 1961 to prohibit discrimination in the occupancy of "*any dwelling unit* in any building that contains more than six self-contained dwelling units [emphasis added]."[28] When Premier Leslie Frost introduced the amending bill for first reading, he made reference to apartheid in South Africa as a "cause of deep concern" and noted that 1961 was the 100th anniversary of the beginning of the civil war in the United States.[29] He also linked the rental housing protection amendment with legislation previously enacted to prohibit restrictive covenants,[30] but with a focus on the need to achieve the right balance between people's personal lives and public policy.[31] Frost maintained that buildings with six dwelling units involved "public" rather than "private" accommodation:

> We should not interfere with the rights of people to choose their own friends and to operate their own homes as they see fit. Accordingly, we have confined this legislation, insofar as apartments are concerned, to the type of accommodation which can really be termed public accommodation. We intentionally omit the small accommodation, and that is why the limit is set at more than 6 apartments. This involves no interference with the life of an individual in his own home which is, after all, his castle. It involves no interference with the little person who rents rooms or flats in his own home.
>
> This legislation is directed, instead, toward the broad area of commerce and public accommodation. This general public policy is in line with the thinking which has been accepted so widely in the evolution of our human rights code to date.[32]

The debate on this bill focused on the government's decision to draw the line at six units rather than some lower number, and on an unsuccessful motion by the CCF (soon to become the New Democratic Party or NDP) to draw the line at two units rather than six.[33]

When the fair practices statutes were consolidated into the *Human Rights Code* in 1961, the new housing provision was slightly reworded to substitute the phrase "any apartment" for "any dwelling unit."[34] A further amendment was passed in 1965 in which the word apartment was maintained but the legislative boundaries were redefined to apply to buildings with more than three, rather than six, self-contained dwelling units.[35] The government's proposal to reduce the number of units was in itself not controversial, and this time the debate focused only on the issue of whether there ought to be any minimum number of units at all before the protection would apply.[36] While arguing for no minimum number of units, MPP Donald MacDonald, then the leader of the NDP, began his remarks by referring to an 1852 anti-slavery speech given by George Brown and to the civil rights march from Selma to Montgomery, Alabama. He then offered the following analysis of a "self-contained" dwelling, one that may well have excluded the flat at issue in *Bell v McKay* because it did not have a separate entrance:

> I want to suggest to you, Mr. Speaker, that the principle is very clear. If it is a self-contained unit, then there should be no discrimination at all in the renting of that property. We concede that if a dwelling is not self-contained – in other words, if it is without separate entrance and without separate facilities – an owner has the right to decide, in effect, with whom he is going to share his home. That is his basic right. But if there is a separate entrance and if there are separate facilities, then he does not have the right to discriminate against those who may seek to rent that property because he does not happen to like their race or their colour or their creed.[37]

Although a motion by the NDP to remove the minimum three apartment requirement was voted down in this instance,[38] the requirement for a minimum number was subsequently removed with yet another amendment, passed in 1967, which returned to the original language of "any dwelling unit" instead of "any apartment," and extended the protection to "any self-contained dwelling unit."[39] On its face, this legislative history reflects a progressive expansion of protection for human rights and concomitant narrowing of the boundaries of private property that would be exempt from protection against discrimination. Indeed, the third amendment, which created the statutory provision considered in our case study, fulfilled a commitment made in the Speech from the Throne and was passed without debate. As the case study will show, however, not all of the judges agreed with what appears to have been the government's affirmative legislative action agenda.

The strategy of excluding the common law judiciary from the legislation's dispute resolution process led to the establishment of the OHRC, drawing on a model that was prevalent in various northern states in the US. Dan Hill, the first director of the OHRC, was one of the chief architects of a dual approach in which "the velvet glove," which emphasized settlement and conciliation, was held by "the iron fist," that is, the threat of a Board of Inquiry and the consequences that flowed from either adverse publicity or an adverse finding or both.[40] Hill was an African American who moved to Toronto to study sociology at the University of Toronto. His doctoral dissertation was the first sociological study of Toronto's Black community.[41]

The OHRC's dual approach was within the developing field of administrative law, which gave primary enforcement responsibility to administrative agencies instead of courts. This administrative law path to dispute resolution under the Code grew out of the enforcement processes that were first introduced with the fair practices statutes, and which were similar to a labour relations model that favoured conciliation and enforcement by a specialized tribunal. According to Philip Girard, "Laskin's work in labour law cannot be dissociated from his human rights work," and he was "especially pleased" with the OHRC being established to enforce the Code.[42]

Having studied at Harvard in the 1930s, Laskin had learned from the New Deal experience that "the courts were identified with the philosophy of laissez-faire,"[43] and he learned a similar lesson from the Canadian judiciary, who used common law reasoning to enforce discriminatory contracts and to privilege property rights over human rights. His Court of Appeal colleague Walter Schroeder had been the trial judge in the case of *Noble and Wolf*, and upheld the covenant that restricted alienation of property to "any person of the Jewish, Hebrew, Semitic, Negro or coloured race or blood" on the basis that, as a matter of public policy, freedom of contract was more important than freedom from discrimination.

County Court Justice Henry Grosch was one of the neighbouring property owners at the Beach O'Pines development on Lake Huron at issue in *Noble and Wolf* who intervened in defense of the racist covenant. Later on, as an appeal judge in a racial segregation case coming out of the Dresden campaign, Grosch J struck down a finding at trial that an act of racial discrimination had occurred, despite overwhelming evidence in support of the trial judge's position.[44] Robert Sharpe writes that, for Laskin, " . . . equality rights required *affirmative legislative action* which would infringe individual contract rights, and he did not want the courts attacking legislation designed to promote equality" [emphasis added].[45]

Under the dual approach, complaints of discrimination were filed with the OHRC, which had the discretion to conduct an investigation and attempt to settle the matter. If the OHRC could not achieve a settlement, it could recommend that the Minister of Labour appoint a Board of Inquiry to conduct a hearing; however, the decision to appoint a Board of Inquiry was at the Minister's discretion. Boards of Inquiry were appointed on an ad hoc basis, and were independent of the government. Law professors and County Court judges were chosen as the appointees.

After giving the parties a "full opportunity" to present their case, if it found that the evidence supported the complaint the Board of Inquiry would recommend a course of action to the OHRC. Where the Board recommended a course of action, the OHRC would then make a recommendation to the Minister who had the discretion to issue any order deemed necessary to carry out the Board of Inquiry's recommendations. Persons who were found to have contravened the Code or to have contravened an order made by the Minister were guilty of an offence, but the Minister's consent was required to prosecute. Where a complaint went to a Board of Inquiry for a hearing, the OHRC acted as advocate for the complainant, through an OHRC staff member or a lawyer from the Civil Division of the Ministry of the Attorney General.

The discretionary nature of the Code's enforcement process was consistent with the OHRC's emphasis on conciliation and voluntary resolution, as described by Hill:

> In administering this legislation the commission places a distinct priority on persuasion and conciliation and uses sanctions only when the expressed desires of the public are purposely being thwarted. This dual approach is an acknowledgement of the fact that civil and criminal procedures, by themselves, do not change prejudiced individuals who would deny fundamental rights to their fellow man.[46]

However, the OHRC could also resort to the "iron fist" of Boards of Inquiry and Ministerial orders and had no interest in turning the process over to the courts as *The Globe and Mail* editors would have preferred.[47] From Hill's perspective, the Code's enforcement process provided enhanced procedural fairness to a respondent by providing two distinct opportunities to present a defence — one before the Board of Inquiry and the other before a court upon prosecution.[48] Arguably, however, this description of the process did not acknowledge concerns over the fact that there were no prescribed limits on what the Minister could order, or concerns over the fact that an individual could be prosecuted for violating either the statute or a ministerial order.

The administrative law model itself came under attack in Ontario as a threat to civil liberties, fueled by opposition to the Robarts government's introduction in 1964 of Bill 99, legislation designed to increase the powers of the Ontario Police Commission for the purpose of combating organized crime. Bill 99 gave rise to a storm of protest from both the left and the right, as advocates for individual freedom raised the spectre of the authoritarian state and arbitrary police power.[49] The government withdrew the legislation and turned to Chief Justice McRuer, who resigned to head a Royal Commission "for the purpose of determining how far there may be unjustified encroachments" on the freedom of individuals by administrative law. In general terms, McRuer emphasized the role of the courts as the protectors of individual rights from the arbitrary action of government.[50] However, his report reached different conclusions depending upon the role of a particular commission or tribunal and how it operated. In the case of the OHRC, McRuer found that the resolution path was generally appropriate, subject to some modifications, several of which, as we will see later, were eventually enacted to balance the "competing rights" in *Bell v McKay*, to which the chapter now turns.

The Case Study: *Bell v McKay* and the OHRC

When the OHRC's dual approach and its interpretation of what constituted a self-contained dwelling unit were challenged in the case of *Bell v McKay*, the result arrived at in court was quite different from what the social activists had hoped for, as the Supreme Court of Canada denied the protection that low-income Blacks such as McKay had expected. Issues of class and race intersected in Toronto's housing market in the 1960s, as Blacks like McKay were most in need of the type of low-cost rental housing that Bell had on offer and were also most in need of protection against discrimination.[51] McKay's claim that Bell had denied him access to housing on the prohibited grounds of "race, colour and place of origin" arose within this economic and racial context, in which Black tenants in Toronto occupied a specific segment within Toronto's rental housing market. At the same time, from the perspective of landlords within this segment, the case study serves to illustrate, as Laskin had cautioned, that "anti-discrimination measures were necessarily a limitation of freedom of contract and the enjoyment of property."[52]

Within the "upstairs flat" rental segment of the downtown Toronto housing market, landlords such as Bell were more often working class than wealthy landowners. Landlords rented an upstairs flat in their sub-divided private home, often with the property owner sacrificing half a house to the rental market, in order to meet their mortgage payments. In fact, Bell's economic circumstances were not entirely dissimilar to those of McKay. Bell worked as a shipper at the Christie Bakery plant on Lakeshore Boulevard. In 1957, he and his wife rented the main floor of the same three-story house, located nearby the plant at 30 Indian Road, while the owner and his family

30 Indian Road, Toronto, Ontario (Photo by Frank Luce).

lived in the upstairs flat. Bell and his wife were able to purchase the house in 1965 and remained living on the main floor while renting the upstairs flat to a series of three married couples, the last of whom moved out in December 1968, creating the vacancy that McKay sought to fill.

On 10 December 1968, Bell placed an ad in the *Toronto Daily Star* to which McKay responded, first by telephone that same day to make sure the flat was available, and then in person the next day, in the company of another young Black male, both of them appearing to be "20 or 22 years of age." Upon meeting McKay and his companion at his front door, Bell denied that the flat was available. McKay then tested the veracity of Bell's denial by sending Nancy Sharp, a woman he described as his girlfriend, to inquire later the same day, and to her Bell confirmed that the flat remained available.[53] Although McKay did not specify Sharp's race in his complaint, the case proceeded on the assumption that she was white.

McKay's written complaint, filed on 12 December 1968, seemed to establish a *prima facie* case of direct discrimination, at least to the extent that Bell's denial that the flat was available called out for an explanation. Upon receiving the complaint, the OHRC appointed Brett Mann as its investigator. As a human rights investigator, Mann's mandate was both to investigate and to attempt a settlement through an informal conciliation process. He began his investigation by meeting with both McKay and Bell on 13 December, although the meeting with Bell did not give rise to the explanation that Bell later provided for his conduct through counsel. Pursuant to his mandate to pursue settlement, Mann wrote to Bell on 2 January 1969; in this letter Mann created an issue that dogged the OHRC throughout the proceedings, through his use of an unfortunate turn of phrase:

> The Commission has conducted a thorough investigation into Mr. McKay's complaint and *has found sufficient evidence supporting Mr. McKay's allegations of discrimination to warrant further involvement of the Commission in this matter.* The Commission views this matter most seriously and I would seek to meet with you at your earliest convenience to discuss possible terms of settlement and conciliation.[54] [emphasis added]

The highlighted phrase seemed to suggest that the OHRC may have pre-judged Bell's "guilt" without having afforded Bell a reasonable opportunity to advance his explanation. As Laskin later commented, when writing for the Ontario Court of Appeal:

> [I]t would have been more prudent and more consistent with the spirit which animates the Commission's work if tentativeness had been expressed and respect shown for the principle of *audi alteram partem*.[55]

Whether or not Mann had pre-judged the case on behalf of the OHRC, Bell was concerned enough to retain legal counsel and thereafter he avoided any direct dealings with the OHRC, except through counsel.

Bell turned to William Charles Cuttell, QC, as his legal counsel, a high ranking Freemason of Scottish descent, born in Toronto in 1910 and called to the bar in 1935. He was a sole practitioner at the time he was retained by Bell and he seemed to take a personal interest in Bell's case, managing the file with unusual vigour, given the nature of the incident and the stakes involved for his client.

Cuttell's first intervention was to press Mann further on the possible terms of settlement. In responding, Mann reinforced the impression that he had pre-judged the case by claiming that his investigation "has produced sufficient evidence to justify Mr. McKay's complaint" and again requesting that Bell attend for a conciliation meeting. In the face of no further response from Bell or his lawyer, the OHRC file passed to Herbert Sohn, Hill's assistant director, who threatened to refer the complaint to a Board of Inquiry,

William Charles Cuttell, QC (reproduced with permission of the Law Society of Upper Canada).

"the iron fist" referred to earlier, if Bell refused to attend a conciliation meeting. Cuttell remained defiant, responding to Sohn that since the OHRC had already investigated the complaint and reached a conclusion, if the matter were to be pursued it ought to prosecute his client in provincial court, rather than refer the matter for another investigation before a Board of Inquiry.

Of course, a quasi-criminal prosecution in provincial court was precisely what Hill sought to avoid with his dual approach, one that privileged conciliation over both findings of guilt and quasi-criminal prosecutions. Within this dual approach, the OHRC used a Board of Inquiry as its "iron fist," but these inquiries were different from a prosecution because they were chaired by expert adjudicators who followed the more flexible evidentiary rules of administrative law rather than the rigid rules of the criminal process. Instead of prosecuting, therefore, Hill asked the Minister to appoint a Board of Inquiry. When informed of Hill's position, Cuttell complained to the Minster, Dalton Bales. In his letter to the Minister, Cuttell argued that as "a native born Canadian citizen and a human being who has rights and is entitled to enforce them," his client's "legal rights" were being violated by this referral to a Board of Inquiry and the proper procedure would be for the Minister to consent to a prosecution.

Despite Cuttell's plea for prosecution, Bales appointed Professor Walter Tarnopolsky, then Dean of University of Windsor Law School, as a Board of Inquiry. Although his credentials as a human rights expert were beyond reproach, the choice of Tarnopolsky was noteworthy because in an earlier case he had already decided in general terms that the type of flat in question was "self-contained" within the meaning of the Code. In the earlier case Tarnopolsky had written that " . . . the necessity of using a common entrance hall, or stairway, or bathroom, would not similarly take accommodation out of the category . . . ."[56] According to the administrative law doctrine of the time, the question of whether or not a flat was self-contained was an issue of "jurisdictional fact" or "collateral fact": that is, whether or not the OHRC had jurisdiction over the flat in question depended on whether or not it was found to be self-contained. As Peter Hogg put it: "A jurisdictional fact is one which must exist 'objectively' before a tribunal has jurisdiction."[57]

When Tarnopolsky convened his Board of Inquiry at 10 a.m. in Room 140 of the provincial parliament buildings on 21 April 1969, a "jurisdictional fact" argument was only one of several collateral issues that Cuttell advanced on behalf of his client. By the time the Board of Inquiry was convened, Cuttell had already found grounds to suspect that the OHRC's motives in proceeding to a Board of Inquiry were improper. According to Cuttell's sworn affidavit, the hearing was scheduled to begin at 9:30 but was moved to 10:00 and to a larger room to accommodate between twenty and thirty spectators and at least three journalists; Cuttell swore that he had not advised anyone other than his client as to the time and date of the hearing, leaving the implication that the OHRC had set out to publicize the proceedings. In fact, one of Cuttell's six arguments before Tarnopolsky was that the appointment of the Board of Inquiry was for an improper purpose, that is, to bring about the "moral condemnation of the community" concerning the conduct of his client. Tarnopolsky dismissed this argument, despite its consonance with the stated purpose of the "iron fist" component of the OHRC's dual approach; he also dismissed two even less cogent arguments that Cuttell advanced to attack the alleged impropriety of the proceedings, one based on the presumption of innocence set out in the Bill of Rights with respect to criminal proceedings and the other grounded in the investigator's suggestion that a cash payment could form part of a potential settlement.

As for Cuttell's "jurisdictional fact" argument, Tarnopolsky's response was more procedural than substantive. Cuttell put Tarnopolsky in an impossible position by arguing that "I cannot bring any evidence before you because that would be inconsistent with my position," thereby calling on Tarnopolsky to make a ruling without the benefit of having heard any evidence to provide a factual basis. Cuttell simply asserted that the flat in question was not self-contained within the meaning of the statute, presumably because the upstairs and the downstairs flats shared a common entrance, as Cuttell later revealed. Cuttell admitted that his client had denied housing accommodation to McKay, but not on any prohibited ground of discrimination, advising only that his client would state the basis for this denial "at the proper time." With only this to go on, Tarnopolsky found that the Board of Inquiry was properly constituted under the statute, for the very purpose of deciding the issues that Cuttell was raising, so the inquiry would proceed to hear evidence. Cuttell then served a Notice of Application for prohibition, to which Tarnopolsky responded by adjourning the hearing *sine die*, pending an outcome of the prohibition application.

As the complainant, McKay had been present at the Board of Inquiry, but with his interests represented by Robin A. Scott, a lawyer from the Civil Division of the Ministry of the Attorney General, acting both as counsel for the OHRC and on behalf of the complainant. Scott accepted service of the Notice of Application on behalf of the Chairman of the OHRC and thereafter McKay faded from the proceedings, leaving the litigation as a contest between Bell's lawyers and the lawyers from the Civil Division.

The litigation was assigned to Edward Marshall Pollock, the Civil Division lawyer who acted as general counsel to the OHRC and who had general carriage of human rights matters on behalf of the Civil Division. Pollock was born in Winnipeg in 1938 and graduated from law school at the University of Saskatchewan in 1962. While enrolled in a master's program at the University of Toronto's Faculty of Law, he followed the advice of his supervisor, Bora Laskin, and articled with Charles Dubin at one of the few firms in Toronto where Jews were accepted. At the time Dubin acted both for trade unions and for the OHRC, allowing Pollock to come to the attention of Frank Callaghan, who a few years earlier had also articled for Dubin. Callaghan had been appointed Senior Crown Counsel and Pollock's first job after his call to the bar was as one of the "whiz kids" that Callaghan assembled in the Civil Division. According to Pollock, Callaghan was "very, very keen to elevate the status of the Attorney General's office to one which he thought it should achieve which is to be a place where the best counsel anywhere came."[58] Pollock handled both labour and human rights matters, both considered to be important social issues that Callaghan now hoped to keep in house. According to Pollock: "It was offensive to guys like Frank who was in fact the senior law officer of the Crown to lose control over issues."[59]

Early in his career with the Attorney General, Pollock had been assigned to serve for a two-year period as counsel to the Rand Commission,[60] which heard complaints from the province's trade unions about the role of the judiciary in labour disputes. These complaints echoed those of the social movement about the role of the judiciary in human rights disputes. One of the labour-positive results of the Rand Commission was to limit the jurisdiction of the courts to issue injunctions in a labour dispute, constituting another legislative blow to the power of the province's judges. After the Rand Commission had reported, Pollock returned to the Civil Division, working closely with Hill, whom he later referred to as "my good friend."

To match the legal talent that Callaghan had available in the Civil Division, Cuttell handed the barrister's work in the prohibition application over to Russell Nelles Starr, QC, a seasoned Toronto litigator who was reputed to be a "a formidable and tenacious forensic foe."[61] Starr was born in Toronto in 1908, graduated from Osgoode Hall Law School in 1934, and, like Cuttell, practiced mainly as a sole practitioner. Cuttell was no doubt attracted by Starr's reputation for tenacity. For Starr, any administrative tribunal was a natural target. In an earlier case of some notoriety, involving the Toronto Board of Police Commissioners, Starr had submitted:

> We are not going to allow it [i.e. the justice system] to be destroyed by arrogant conduct on the part of boards and commissions. This is a deliberate and calculated attempt to strike at the foundations of the system in which we believe . . . The time has come to put an end to it. Let's not have in this country as they had in England in the case of Archer-Shee or the Winslow Boy.[62]

In the Ontario High Court, the prohibition application was assigned to Charles Stewart J, an unfortunate choice from Pollock's perspective. Stewart was born in Barrie in 1905. Like Cuttell he was of Scottish descent, a third-generation lawyer whose "family belonged to the upper elite in the highly stratified society of Barrie," a small city about an hour north of Toronto.[63] Prior to his appointment to the bench in 1953, Stewart ran for office as a Progressive Conservative politician. After his appointment to the bench, Stewart joined the University Club; because it was located across the street from the court houses, this club was popular with white judges and lawyers who were untroubled by the fact that it excluded women and Jews, among others, from membership. Stewart was a patron of the theatre and had a flair for the dramatic, which manifested both within and outside the courtroom in his pronouncements about discrimination, as we will see later.

Russell Nelles Starr, QC (reproduced with permission of the Law Society of Upper Canada).

Justice Charles Stewart (reproduced with permission of the Law Society of Upper Canada).

The prohibition application was heard by Stewart J on 9 May 1969, with Starr appearing as counsel for the applicant Bell. Starr advanced the "competing rights" argument, to the effect that Bell was equally entitled to the protection of his procedural rights and ownership rights as McKay was to his human rights. Filed in support of the application was Bell's affidavit in which he admitted to having misled McKay but swore that it was not on any prohibited ground. McKay and his male companion appeared to be young students, at a time when age was not yet a prohibited ground,[64] and Bell swore that his concern was with protecting his home and his wife, given that his flat and the upstairs flat shared a common entrance. It seems that Bell worked the night shift and often left his wife alone behind unlocked doors, raising the inference that the presence of young males in the upstairs flat would be undesirable no matter what their race or colour. To disprove any racial motive, Bell swore that the flat was later rented to a forty-five-year-old single male who was "of Egyptian origin and is Semitic."[65] Left unchallenged, Bell's affidavit served to undermine the testing evidence that McKay relied on in support of his complaint.

In essence, Bell's affidavit fairly set out the relevant facts to describe the flat in question, and the case proceeded on the basis that these facts were not controversial, with no cross-examination on Bell's affidavit and no further evidence submitted by the Civil Division. Having successfully argued the meaning of self-contained using similar facts in the earlier case before Tarnopolsky referred to above,[66] Pollock framed his argument around the availability of prohibition, at least at this initial stage of the proceedings.[67] His first position was that a Board of Inquiry was not a judicial body and was therefore not subject to judicial review; its function was merely to advise the Minister, through the OHRC, and in this capacity it was immune from judicial review.[68] This argument may seem overly protective of an administrative tribunal, but it carried the authority of a precedent written by Laskin for the Court of Appeal, in an appeal argued by Dubin on behalf of the Ontario Labour Relations Board.[69] Pollock also advanced the alternative argument that the application was premature because the Board of Inquiry had neither heard any evidence nor made any determination of the issues.

Perhaps Pollock underestimated the extent to which his first position would antagonize a judge such as Stewart. While ignoring Pollock's alternative argument, Stewart expressed outrage at the suggestion that the human rights administrative process was immune from judicial review: "[Pollock] said in effect that there was nothing that anyone could do about anything related to the Act except, I suppose, to do the Minister's bidding."[70]

Instead of protecting the OHRC process and allowing the Board of Inquiry to hear the evidence, Stewart J focused on the "competing rights" of Bell, as Starr had argued. Stewart made clear that in his mind the OHRC had pre-judged the issue of whether the flat was "self-contained" and in his mind the OHRC's conclusion on the issue was incorrect. In finding that the flat was indeed not self-contained, Stewart relied on the facts set out in Bell's affidavit and cited three dictionary definitions and a line of precedents from other common law jurisdictions, while distinguishing a 1923 English King's Bench decision to the contrary. Although both the case law and the dictionary definitions were entirely indeterminate of the issue in question, for Stewart they provided a sufficient basis to conclude that the Board of Inquiry had no jurisdiction. According to Stewart J, "the *Act* was never intended to limit an arbitrary choice of tenants in a man's house to whom he rented unseparated rooms."[71] This conclusion was enough to decide the application, but Stewart J was so outraged by the OHRC's conduct that he went on to critique the Minister's decision to refer the matter to a Board of Inquiry rather than to prosecute, as Cuttell had requested. Judge Stewart's preference for a quasi-criminal procedure made paramount the protection of the procedural rights which Bell would have had available in a court of law:

> If the matter were heard by a Provincial Judge it is obvious that the accused would be brought before a tribunal where some are not more equal than others, where the rule against self-incrimination is observed, where the presumption of innocence until proven guilty is recognized and where proof beyond a reasonable doubt is required.[72]

To underline his distaste for the OHRC's process, Stewart J concluded his reasons for judgment with a resounding endorsement of the "competing rights" argument:

> It is equally as important that the rights of a middle-aged white Canadian homeowner be protected as those of a young, black, Jamaican tenant. Neither more important or less important. Equally. And perhaps it is time that this was made clear.[sic][73]

Nor did Stewart J end the matter there. The hearing had attracted considerable attention from the local media, and a press report had quoted the judge's comments made during the course of the hearing as him saying "that this law was a law to protect coloured people and the white man did not get any protection under this law."[74] After issuing an oral decision to grant prohibition, Stewart J took the unusual step of pronouncing further on the issues directly to the press, outside the courtroom. This conduct led to a series of questions in the provincial parliament, during the course of which he earned a rebuke from the Attorney General, Arthur Wishart. A defiant Stewart J again spoke to the press the next day, with a rebuke of his own, suggesting Wishart ought to direct his criticism to Pollock, who had also spoken to the press. With respect to the litigation, in this second meeting with the press Stewart J asserted that "[O]ne of the rights to discriminate that surely must be maintained is the right to say who shall sit at your table and who shall sleep under your roof."[75]

The matter of Stewart J's dealings with the press was again raised in parliament the next day, this time as a question of privilege, on the grounds that it was improper for a member of the judiciary to use the press to attack a member of parliament (such as the Attorney General) and to attack legislation that had been passed unanimously by the House. McDonald, then the leader of the NDP, spoke in support of this point of privilege, alleging also that Stewart had heard the case with "a closed mind." When the point was supported by Robert Nixon, then the leader of the official opposition, the Premier himself rose to diffuse the issue by citing the need for further investigation.

For his part, Wishart attempted to depoliticize the issue and contain it within the juridical field. Wishart was no doubt sensitive to the procedural issues raised by Stewart since his appointment to the office of Attorney General had been made in the wake of the political controversy surrounding the infamous Bill 99, the proposed legislation that had led to the report of the McRuer Commission, appointed to inquire into the protection of procedural rights similar to those that Bell was asserting.[76] Despite all-party support for the creation of the OHRC, the traditional opponents of affirmative legislative action, with *The Globe and Mail* as their mouthpiece, were consistent in their position that human rights complaints should be left to the common law courts. The day after Stewart's decision, the *Globe* editors reacted with glee, heralding it as "a landmark judgment" and proclaiming, without a hint of irony, that "[h]uman rights were magnificently defended yesterday by Mr. Justice C.D. Stewart." [77] The editors agreed that racial discrimination is "wrong, and a legal offence. But those who are accused of practicing it should be brought before the courts." When Wishart announced that his office would file an appeal to the Ontario Court of Appeal, the *Globe* asserted that the matter was of such importance that it should be carried even further until the Supreme Court of Canada clarifies that those accused of racial discrimination should be brought "before a court where their civil rights would be protected."

Press opinion was, however, far from unanimous. The *Toronto Daily Star* was consistent in its support for the OHRC's "informal procedure based on persuasion, rather than by taking the alleged offender to court."[78] The editors of Toronto's third major daily, the *Telegram*, referred to the Code as "a good law maligned . . . [by the] opponents of Ontario's Human Rights Code . . . . Now the same opposing forces have rallied around Mr. Justice Stewart of the Supreme Court of Ontario."[79] And so it appeared that the battle lines from the first two decades of the post-war human rights campaigns were being redrawn.

The OHRC, of course, was concerned with protecting its procedure. Stewart's ruling challenged the fundamentals of Hill's dual approach, and now the social forces that had organized in opposition to any affirmative legislative action to promote human rights in the first place seemed to be regrouping. From Hill's perspective, the government's support for the OHRC was ambivalent, and he now experienced difficulty convincing the Minister to appoint a Board of Inquiry in other cases, since it now appeared to both Wishart and Bales that public opinion was against the OHRC. Against this ambivalence, Hill's constituency from the social movement rallied to the OHRC's support, with Alan Borovoy calling on Premier Robarts to show political leadership:

> . . . we respectfully request that the Prime Minister of Ontario make a clear and unequivocal statement which will express on behalf of all the citizens of this province the deep confidence which we feel in the achievements, policies, and practices of the Ontario Human Rights Commission.[80]

Despite the politicization of the legal proceedings, Wishart maintained his containment strategy and focused his attention on the appeal. During the parliamentary debate, McDonald had suggested that Callaghan's "whiz kids" bore some of the responsibility for having lost the prohibition application, asking, " . . . why did the Minister, his deputy, or some senior counsel not appear to defend this important legislation?" To his credit, Wishart had risen to Pollock's defense, describing him as "very capable and very eminent."[81] Indeed, while Pollock was only thirty-one at the time of the application, Wishart's endorsement of his experience and competence was well founded, and Pollock later went on to become the first Assistant Deputy Attorney General, head of the Policy Branch, in 1972. In any event, as Wishart noted, the Civil Division "could not anticipate this sort of decision in the case." Despite this expression of confidence, Callaghan inserted himself into the appeal proceedings and teamed up with Pollock as a co-counsel, dividing their efforts so that Callaghan would argue the administrative law issue of whether prohibition was available while Pollock would argue the interpretation issue of whether or not the flat was self-contained, although as the case unfolded the appeal judges were not concerned about the interpretation issue.

In the Court of Appeal, Gale CJ presided over a five-judge panel that heard argument on 27 and 28 October 1969. As lead counsel for the appellant, Callaghan received a more sympathetic hearing than Pollock had experienced before Stewart J. However, even Callaghan was unable to maintain the position that the entire OHRC process was immune from judicial review, conceding under coaxing from Laskin that Bell retained the right to seek judicial review at a later point in the process should Tarnopolsky rule that the flat was self-contained. The Attorney General was left, therefore, with its alternative argument that the prohibition application was premature, in accordance with

Laskin's perspective. For his part, Pollock was prepared to argue the interpretation issue but he apparently was not called upon to do so.[82]

Appearing as counsel for the respondent, Starr's reception was the opposite of what he had experienced before Stewart J. His approach reflected a deep antipathy towards the OHRC process, a legal strategy that was decidedly not designed to gain the sympathy of an appeal panel dominated by Laskin, one of the architects of the process under attack. As was his wont, Starr's rhetoric was overblown and did not sit well either with Laskin or his brother judges. He submitted that the practice of "establishing boards and commissions [was] dangerous,"[83] referring to the Board of Inquiry as a "kangaroo method" of resolving human rights disputes, a phrase to which both Laskin and Gale CJ took exception. In Starr's submission, Bell had the right at common law "to have the matter disposed of in police (provincial judge's) court,"[84] as Cuttell had demanded, and he went so far as to argue that the OHRC process was *ultra vires* or unconstitutional because Bell's common law rights, or "rights at law," could not be taken away by an administrative process.

Laskin's reasons for allowing the appeal were unanimously endorsed, in deference to his expertise in the emerging field of administrative law in Canada. He decided the case on procedural grounds, as Hill may have hoped, reinforcing the legitimacy of the OHRC's dual approach by ruling that the prohibition application was premature. Even Schroeder J, Laskin's nemesis in the *Noble and Wolf* case, endorsed Laskin's defense of the OHRC process, deferring to Laskin's interpretation of the language of the statute over his personal preference for quasi-criminal prosecution.[85]

Laskin was singularly unimpressed with Starr's constitutional argument, which he found was based on a "startling proposition":

> Bell's "rights at law," as his counsel used the phrase, are not rights to refuse obedience to an applicable law. Of course, the Code has drastically changed the common law position of owners of certain kinds of housing accommodation, as it has changed the position of employers and of operators of places to which the public is customarily admitted . . . [86]

Here Laskin clearly articulated the substance of Bell's case, that is, the conflict between individual property rights at common law and the social rights of historically disadvantaged groups, as protected by affirmative legislative action.

The effect of Laskin's ruling would have been to refer the matter back to Tarnopolsky to decide, in the first instance, if the flat was self-contained, an issue that Laskin's reasons barely touched on. However, in a concurring opinion Judge Gregory Evans critiqued Stewart J's finding on this point, writing that "[t]he learned Judge of first instance held that the premises were [not] a self-contained unit and with respect I am unable to ascertain from the evidence how he arrived at such a conclusion."[87] With a similar conclusion likely to be forthcoming from the Board of Inquiry, given Tarnopolsky's previous decision on the same point, the question remained whether the process would be subject to judicial review at a later stage. Laskin expressly left this issue open, despite Callaghan's concession on this point, with Evans stating his view that judicial review would be available at a later stage. While agreeing with Laskin that the application was premature, Justice Evans emphasized that the issue was one of mixed fact and law rather than one involving the existence of an "objective" fact as the jurisdictional fact doctrine seemed to pre-suppose, at least according to the definition suggested by Hogg.

The Court of Appeal decision was welcomed as a vindication for human rights activists and Hill himself reacted with a degree of triumphalism, sending copies of Laskin's reasons to human rights advocates across the country and throughout the common law world. Among the many congratulatory bouquets he received in return was a word of caution from Professor Douglas Schmeiser, a distinguished legal scholar from the University of Saskatchewan law school, Pollock's alma mater, pointing out that "the judgment deals only with a very limited matter, i.e., a question of timing" and was therefore only procedural in its repercussions.[88]

In contrast to Hill's triumphalism, however, the social forces opposed to the OHRC were encouraged by another *Globe* editorial headlined "Rights for the Accused":

> Public confidence in the fairness of the code as it has been applied to people accused of discrimination has been destroyed . . . . Provincial legislators should re-read the preamble to the code and realize that accused people are among those who should be "free and equal in dignity and rights."[89]

As the *Globe* editors had earlier prompted, the stage was now set for the matter to be finally determined by the Supreme Court of Canada. Apparently even the unanimous reasoning of a five-member panel of the Ontario Court of Appeal was not sufficient to outweigh the national significance of the issues leading a Supreme Court of Canada panel consisting of Judson J, Spence J, and Cartwright J to grant Starr's application for leave to appeal, on 27 January 1970.

Faced with this further set-back, Hill was of the view that the Attorney General should retain outside counsel to argue the Supreme Court appeal, suspecting even that the government's insistence on keeping the file in house reflected a lack of political will to defend the OHRC to the fullest extent possible.[90] Although we saw earlier that McDonald had raised a similar view in parliament, an equally probable explanation for keeping the file in house may be found in Callaghan's determination to maintain control over social litigation within the Civil Division, with Pollock as his co-counsel.

In his written argument on the Supreme Court of Canada appeal, Starr first addressed the interpretation issue of whether or not the flat was "self-contained." He then went on to address the issue of whether the Board of Inquiry was immune from judicial review or whether the application for prohibition was premature. With his usual flow of rhetoric, he described this issue as one which reflected "the struggle between the courts and legislative tribunals over a period of 300 years."

With reference to the statutory procedure that Laskin had upheld in the Court of Appeal, Starr argued that "[t]he powers granted by that section bear not even a nodding acquaintance with the rights of an individual at law and reaffirm that the powers of the board [i.e. a Board of Inquiry] constitute that tribunal as a law unto itself." In support of his argument he cited the Court's landmark decision in *Roncarelli v Duplessis*.[91] However, this authority cut both ways: while standing for the proposition that an administrative decision was never entirely immune from judicial review, it undermined the proposition that the courts could not protect Bell at a later stage in the proceedings if prohibition was found to be premature. In *Roncarelli v Duplessis*, Martland J, who wrote the majority decision in the present case, had expressed the view that a purely administrative decision could not be based on "reasons which are unrelated to the carrying into effect of the intent and purpose of the Act." Perhaps with this point in mind, Starr stressed his argument that, in referring the matter to a Board of Inquiry, the Minister had based his decision on an improper purpose. In constructing this rather oblique argument, Starr returned to the "rights at law" proposition that Laskin had found so startling. In view of his client's "rights at law," Starr argued, the only legitimate purpose for a Board of Inquiry would be for the OHRC to ask the Board to recommend prosecution; since the OHRC and the Minister had both made clear their opposition to the prosecution option, the referral to the Board of Inquiry could only have been, Starr argued, for some improper purpose.

The written argument submitted on behalf of the Civil Division was structured around the statutory procedure upheld by Laskin and around Laskin's conclusion that the prohibition application was premature. Callaghan retained responsibility for constructing this central argument, and in doing so he could not resist reiterating the immunity argument that he had effectively abandoned before Laskin in the Court of Appeal. He again emphasized the advisory capacity of a Board of Inquiry and argued that, since its function was merely to make recommendations, prohibition was not available, assuming that the Board was properly constituted. As he and Pollock had done throughout the proceedings, he relegated the prematurity of the prohibition application to the status of an alternative argument. The further alternative argument, that the flat in question was indeed self-contained, was thoroughly canvassed by Pollock.

The oral arguments were heard by a Supreme Court panel of seven judges on 3 and 4 November 1970, during the course of which Starr submitted that even the power contained in "[t]he War Measures Act isn't in the same league" as the powers of a Board of Inquiry.[92] Unlike Stewart J, however, the Supreme Court judges expressed little interest in Starr's "rights at law" argument and approached the issue more narrowly as a question of administrative law, thereby joining issue with the Court of Appeal. While joining issue with Laskin, however, the Supreme Court justices reached the opposite conclusion.

Perhaps ironically, the majority reasons were written by Mr. Justice Roland Martland, a corporate lawyer from Alberta who was appointed to the Court in 1958 as one of four appointments made by Prime Minister John Diefenbaker. The irony may be found in Martland's troubled professional relationship with Laskin, who had been appointed to the Supreme Court of Canada by Prime Minister Pierre Trudeau in March 1970, six months prior to the oral hearing, although he of course could not sit on an appeal from one of his own judgments. Laskin's appointment marked a shift in the Court's judicial philosophy, from the legal formalism of Martland to Laskin's contextual approach to interpretation, which came to dominate the Court a few years after Laskin became Chief Justice.[93] Indeed, Laskin's appointment as Chief Justice in 1973 was at the expense of Martland, who according to judicial tradition deserved the appointment as the Court's senior judge.

Bell v McKay was a high water mark for the legal formalist approach as Martland, the conservative corporate lawyer, writing in his "flatly mechanical" style, overturned Laskin, the liberal academic, within Laskin's own area of expertise, thereby consolidating the administrative law doctrine of jurisdictional fact. Apart from the doubtful merits of the jurisdictional fact doctrine itself, the weakest point of Martland's reasoning was his finding that "the premises leased by the appellant located in his upstairs floors, may well be 'dwelling units,' but they were not 'self-contained' dwelling units."[94] After quoting Stewart J and citing the same dictionaries and the same legal precedents he cited, both for and against, Martland turned to the legislative history of the housing provisions of the Code, outlined above, and concluded that to be self-contained the flat would have to be premises "similar to an apartment in an apartment house," despite the legislature's removal of the word "apartment" from the substantive enactment. After having leapt to his own conclusion on this issue of interpretation, and without providing any coherent rationale, Martland framed the administrative law issue in terms that suggested the result he was so obviously seeking:

> This brings me to the main issue in this appeal, which I would state as follows: If a complaint of alleged discrimination is made, which relates to a field which is not within the provisions of the Act, has the Supreme Court of Ontario the power, by an order of prohibition, to prevent proceedings for the investigation of the complaint under s. 13 of the Act?[95]

In deference to a more contextualized approach, Martland acknowledged that the purpose of the legislation was to obtain racial equality, but reasoned that the statute also contained limitations intended to protect the rights of "householders" and "homeowners" in these and other circumstances. Martland went on to describe the inconvenience that a homeowner would suffer if required to undergo a Board of Inquiry and questioned whether judicial review would be available at a later stage in the proceedings. When he quizzed Callaghan on this point, it seemed that Callaghan was unprepared to make a concession similar to the one he made before Laskin, now suggesting that only declaratory relief would be available, rather than *certiorari*, thus playing into Martland's hand. In responding directly to Laskin's line of reasoning on the prematurity of the application, Martland emphasized that since the case involved a question of law, with the facts not in dispute, Bell had the option of applying to the Court for a writ of prohibition or allowing the Board of Inquiry to decide the point as a preliminary issue. While conceding that Bell had the option of waiting to see what Tarnopolsky would decide, Martland avoided the corollary issue of whether the courts ought to wait before intervening — an option Laskin strongly favoured. As did Laskin, Martland left open the question of what access to the courts Bell would have enjoyed if Tarnopolsky's decision had gone against him.

In allowing the appeal and restoring the order of Stewart J, Martland was joined by Fauteux CJ, Spence J, and two of his fellow Diefenbaker appointees, Judson J and Ritchie J. The fourth Diefenbaker appointee, Mr. Justice Emmett Hall, dissented by simply endorsing the reasons of Laskin in the Court of Appeal. A more wordy dissent was issued by Mr. Justice Douglas Abbott who, while agreeing with the judgment of the Court of Appeal, also made a strong argument in favour of judicial deference, particularly since the role of the Board of Inquiry was merely to investigate and make recommendations. To underline his point in a subtle manner, Abbott referred at length to an earlier decision by McRuer J:

> It is not for the Courts to legislate. Under our form of government . . . it is for those duly elected members to decide what jurisdiction will be conferred on an administrative tribunal when an administrative tribunal is set up.[96]

Now that the competing rights of Bell and McKay had been finally determined, it was time for Starr to proclaim triumph as *The Globe and Mail* continued its campaign against the OHRC by publishing Starr's letter to the editor:

> The Human Rights Code is now firmly under the rule of law, but as it was drafted and originally interpreted by the Attorney General and the law officers of the Crown it was infinitely more destructive than Bill 99. I would think the matter is now a political issue and we should all, including the press, attempt to see to it that no such similar attempt at arbitrary legislation be perpetrated. Otherwise, we will allow the legislature to destroy the system which is the only basis upon which a democratic community can survive.[97]

Contrary to Starr, however, there emerged a stream of academic criticism that focused both on the reluctance of the judges to yield power to the administrative tribunals and on the ethnocentric bias inherent in the judges' interpretation of the statutory language. In defending the concept of judicial deference, Hogg described Martland's judgment as "wrong, and the judicial technique for reaching the result was deplorable."[98] While taking a position opposite to that of Hogg on the issue of judicial restraint, David Mullan conceded that Martland was wrong on the issue of whether or not the flat was self-contained.[99] For his part, Ian Hunter complained that both

Stewart and Martland "preferred the policy which favours the traditional common law rights of a property owner to unrestricted control over his property"[100] and described Martland's decision as "a short-sighted essentially ethno-centric result."[101] Of course, by 1970 the Supreme Court of Canada was a court of final resort, and there the matter stood as decided until the government again resorted to affirmative legislative action.

Conclusion

While Starr could trumpet his victory in an individual case, assessing the long-term socio-legal implications of *Bell v McKay* requires a more nuanced analysis. On the substantive issue of the application of the Code to the flat in Bell's house, Bell's personal victory was short-lived. Within two years of the Supreme Court of Canada's decision, the Ontario government passed yet another amendment, one that effectively overturned the Court's ruling.[102] The amending bill, passed without opposition, substituted the phrase "housing accommodation" for "self-contained dwelling unit," and defined housing accommodation as "any place of dwelling" other than one in a building in which the owner or the owner's family lived and in which the tenant shared a bathroom or kitchen with the owner or the owner's family. Bell's flat would most likely have been captured by this amendment since Bell and his tenant were not required to share a kitchen or bathroom.

The government's decision to overrule the Supreme Court of Canada on the substantive issue reflects a choice to give anti-discrimination rights precedence over property rights. However, the subsequent history of the Code's enforcement process suggests that Starr and Cuttell's challenge to the OHRC's dual approach had longer-term consequences. The essence of the OHRC's dual approach remained intact, with the McRuer Report's acceptance of the structure of the process and the Supreme Court of Canada's reluctance to join with Stewart J in its condemnation. In response to the McRuer Report, the government amended the Code's enforcement process as part of the *Civil Rights Law Amendment Act*, passed in 1971,[103] but these amendments were arguably designed to strengthen the process. The amendments maintained the dual approach, but provided a clearer division between the role of the OHRC and the role of a Board of Inquiry, as McRuer recommended; in a similar vein, the power to make orders was removed from the Minister and assigned to the Board of Inquiry.

The amendments created a right of appeal to the courts from Board of Inquiry decisions on questions of both law and fact, ensuring that the judiciary would maintain supervision over all aspects of the adjudication process. At the same time, however, the "jurisdictional fact" doctrine itself was sidestepped by providing a Board of Inquiry with the specific jurisdiction to determine all questions of fact and law or mixed fact and law. Moreover, since the appeal would be based on the record rather than by way of trial *de novo*, the litigating parties were effectively required to build a record at the Board of Inquiry level.

The Code's administrative law enforcement process ultimately received the seal of approval from the Supreme Court of Canada in 1981 when Laskin, in his capacity as Chief Justice of the Supreme Court of Canada, closed the door on access to the courts for discrimination claims:

> . . . I would hold that not only does the Code foreclose any civil action based directly upon a breach thereof but it also excludes any common law action based on an invocation of the public policy expressed in the Code. The Code itself has laid out the procedures for vindication of that public policy, procedures which the plaintiff respondent did not see fit to use.[104]

The following year, the same year the *Canadian Charter of Rights and Freedoms* came into effect, the Supreme Court of Canada expressed its support for the affirmative legislative action approach by declaring human rights legislation to be "fundamental" and quasi- constitutional.[105] Paradoxically, however, the courts rarely treated human rights tribunals themselves as having any special expertise.[106]

In practice, however, the Code's enforcement process became increasingly slower and relatively few complaints were referred to Boards of Inquiry,[107] giving credence to Philip Stenning's argument that the enforcement process underwent a change in direction because of "two very potent influences" — the McRuer Commission and *Bell v McKay*.[108] For some human rights advocates, the delays, backlogs, and limited number of formal hearings challenged the legitimacy of the dual approach,[109] and a new round of activism led to its demise in Ontario in 2006,[110] when the dual approach was replaced by a "direct access" system requiring claims to be filed with the Human Rights Tribunal of Ontario. Although the OHRC may participate as an intervener in tribunal hearings, it is no longer responsible for enforcing the Code or for referring complaints to a formal hearing. Its role now focuses more exclusively on public education, research, and policy development.

Very few housing discrimination complaints were filed in the years following *Bell v McKay*, although recent reports conclude that housing discrimination continues to be an issue of serious concern.[111] While prospective tenants seemed to be reluctant to pursue claims of discrimination under the dual approach, it remains to be seen whether the new enforcement process will lead to more housing cases being taken forward.

For McKay, Hill, and the OHRC, the Supreme Court of Canada's formalist approach to interpreting the Code highlighted the tendency of the courts to privilege common law property rights over legislated social rights. For Callaghan and Pollock, however, the Court's decision was merely a temporary setback, as both the forces of social change and judicial appointments, such as that of Laskin, were in their favour. The jurisdictional fact doctrine, as consolidated in *Bell v McKay*, also privileged the authority of the courts over administrative tribunals, but the Supreme Court of Canada soon abandoned the doctrine in favour of one which recognized tribunals as legitimate adjudicative bodies, with authority to have at least the first word on defining the boundaries of their jurisdiction.[112] As the Court's approach to judicial review of administrative tribunals evolved, *Bell v McKay*'s precedential influence waned, although the decision recently had a brief revival in a case challenging a board of inquiry referral decision made by the Halifax Human Rights Commission. Ultimately, however, this revival created an opportunity for the Supreme Court of Canada formally to lay to rest the jurisdictional fact doctrine, by ruling that *Bell v McKay* ". . . should no longer be followed in relation to its approach to preliminary jurisdictional questions or when judicial intervention is justified in an ongoing administrative process."[113] There continues to be debate about the role of the courts in reviewing the decisions of administrative tribunals, and the extent to which courts should defer to the tribunal, but this debate is more generally informed by a perspective in which administrative tribunals are clearly part of the formal legal process landscape.

When Pollock appeared before Stewart J, his legal talent was not recognized or respected by the judge because, as a government lawyer, he was not part of the legal establishment and his arguments carried little weight. Since then, the Attorney General's Civil Division has grown and flourished, as Callaghan had hoped, to the point that it soon came to be considered an equal player in the litigation arena. It is also interesting to reflect on how the litigation process in cases like *Bell v McKay* has evolved over time. In *Bell v McKay*, the government defended itself using only formal legal arguments: that is, it did not present any evidence, either of the social problem underlying the legislation or of the enforcement process, and it did not refer to the preceding Board of Inquiry decisions which interpreted the legislated provision in question. There may have been solid strategic reasons for these choices — the legislative history proved to be harmful to the OHRC's case, and referring to the earlier Board of Inquiry decisions, including Tarnopolsky's, may have served to reinforce Bell's argument that he would not receive a fair hearing. Today, however, in keeping with the contextual approach that Laskin introduced to the Supreme Court of Canada, cases involving social rights are rarely fought on formal grounds alone. Both attackers and defenders will present wide-ranging evidence and academic commentary, along with legal precedents, to support their positions. This litigation is part of a new social context, one in which social rights — regardless of what you think of them and their effectiveness — are in a much more competitive position vis à vis property rights than they were at the time of *Bell v McKay*.

Reprinted with permission of the Harriet Tubman Institute.

Notes

1 This chapter grew out of a symposium on the life and work of Daniel Grafton Hill III organized by The Harriet Tubman Institute of York University and the Ontario Black History Society held on 25 September 2010. The authors wish to acknowledge the insights and contributions of Marshall Pollock, Mary Jane Mossman, Eleanor Meslin, Marty Meslin, Jim Phillips, the editors of this collection, and two anonymous reviewers. The authors also wish to thank Ann-Marie Langlois of the Law Society of Upper Canada for her research assistance.

2 By 1793, the position of the common law seemed to disapprove of slavery within England while it tolerated slavery in the colonies, including what is now the province of Ontario. A statute proclaimed by Lord Simcoe banned the further importation of slaves and provided that "it is highly expedient to abolish slavery in this Province, so far as the same may be gradually done without violating private property": *An Act to prevent the further introduction of Slaves, and to limit the Term of Contracts for Servitude within this Province* 3 Statutes of Upper Canada, 3 George III, cap. 7, 1793

3 *Bell v Ontario (Human Rights Commission)*, [1971] SCR 756; rev'g *sub nom Regina v Tarnopolsky, Ex parte Bell*, [1970] 2 OR 672 (CA); rev'g [1969] 2 OR 709 (HCJ). Reversed by *Halifax (Regional Municipality) v Nova Scotia (Human Rights Commission)*, 2012 SCC 10. Our thanks to Philip Girard for this reference.

4 *Ontario Human Rights Code, 1961-62*, SO 1961-62, c 93.

5 For a discussion of the jurisdictional fact doctrine contemporary with *Bell v McKay*, see PW Hogg, "The Jurisdictional Fact Doctrine in the Supreme Court of Canada: Bell v. Ontario Human Rights Commission" (1971) 9 Osgoode Hall LJ 203 ("Jurisdictional Fact Doctrine"), and for a contrary view see David Mullen, "The Jurisdictional Fact Doctrine in the Supreme Court of Canada – A Mitigating Plea" (1972) 10 Osgoode Hall LJ 440.

6 James W St G Walker, "The 'Jewish Phase' in the Movement for Racial Equality in Canada" (2002) 34 Canadian Ethnic Studies 1 at 3-4. For an example of how the common law operated in this area, see *Christie v York Corp.* [1940] SCR 139

7 The phrase in quotation marks is taken from RJ Sharpe, "Bora Laskin and Civil Liberties" (1985) 35 U Toronto LJ 632 at 639 .

8 Our discussion of the Ontario social movement campaigns for anti-discrimination legislation draws on: Walker, "Jewish Phase," above note 5; Ben Kayfetz, "On Community Relations in Ontario in the 1940s" (1994), 2 Canadian Jewish Studies 57 at 57-58; Ross Lambertson, *Repression and Resistance: Canadian Human Rights Activists, 1930-1960* (Toronto, Buffalo, London: University of Toronto Press, 2005), Introduction, Chapters 5, 6, and 7; Ross Lambertson, "'The Dresden Story': Racism, Human Rights, and the Jewish Labour Committee of Canada" (2001) 47 *Labour/Le Travail* 41 at 64-65.

9 We name anti-Semitism as a specific form of discrimination because it combines both racial and religious discrimination.

10 The prohibited grounds of discrimination named in the early statutes were: race, creed, colour, nationality, ancestry, or place of origin. The only exception was a separate statute prohibiting sex discrimination in wages: *Fair Remuneration for Female Employees Act*, SO 1951, c 26; broader legislative protection against sex discrimination did not come until the early 1970s.

11 *Code*, Preamble.

12 The ACL, and later the CCLA, became closely associated with the leadership of Alan Borovoy.

13 See Walker, "'Jewish Phase,'" above note 6 at 6.

14 See Lambertson, *Repression*, above note 8 at 237, quoting the *The Globe and Mail* published on 22 November 1950; Walker, "'Jewish Phase'" *Ibid* at 6, referencing the *The Globe and Mail* published 13 March 1944. Bruce Ziff, *Unforeseen Legacies: Reuben Wells Leonard and the Leonard Foundation Trust* (Toronto: University of Toronto Press, 2000) at 114, referencing *The Globe and* Mail published on 11 June 1949.

15 *Noble v Alley*, [1951] SCR 64; rev'g [1949] OR 503 (CA); aff'g [1948] OR 579 (Wkly Ct). For a socio-legal history of *Noble and Wolfe*, see Chapter 4 of James W. St.G. Walker, *"Race," Rights and the Law in the Supreme Court of Canada* (Canada: The Osgoode Society for Canadian Legal History and Wilfrid Laurier University Press, 1997). During the course of this litigation, the Ontario government amended the *Conveyancing and Law of Property Act* to prospectively void any covenant "running with the land" that restricted the sale, ownership, occupation or use of land on the basis of race, creed, colour, nationality, ancestry of place of origin — SO 1950, c 11, s 1. The *Labour Relations Act* was also amended at the same time, to deem invalid a collective agreement

that discriminated on the basis of race or creed — *Labour Relations Act, 1950*, SO 1950, c 34, s 34(b).

16 Philip Girard, *Bora Laskin: Bringing Law to Life* (Toronto, Buffalo, London: University of Toronto Press, 2005) at 265.

17 In 1952 the club removed the offending clause from its constitution but this was without effect until Jews began to be admitted in 1963. Girard, *ibid* describes the circumstances of the 1952 vote at 265.

18 See Girard, *Law to Life*, above note 16 at 340. According to Girard, Laskin's colleagues were unfazed by the fact that they had to sign him in as a guest because as a Jew he could not be admitted to membership. The club did not admit women until 1988.

19 McLeod and Salzburg were active as members of the CPC, while the CCF was staunchly anti-Communist.

20 See Girard, *Life to Law*, above note 16 at 264.

21 *Fair Employment Practices Act*, SO 1951, c 24; the statute did not apply to domestic employees, employees of charitable, philanthropic or religious organizations, and employers with fewer than five employees – s 2. The *Fair Remuneration for Female Employees Act*, cited above, was passed that same year.

22 While the Mayor of Amherstburg, another terminal, chose the path of eliminating racial discrimination in his town, the white residents of the Town of Dresden chose to maintain their local version of "Jim Crow," to which the movement responded by making the integration of Dresden a *cause célèbre*.

23 See Walker, *The Jewish Phase*, above note 6.

24 A fictionalized account of the type of difficulty they encountered was told by their son Lawrence Hill in his novel *Any Known Blood* (Toronto, Harper Collins Publishers Inc., 1997).

25 SO 1954, c 28.

26 *Ibid*, sections 2 and 3.

27 Quoted in Ian Hunter, "The Development of the Ontario Human Rights Code: A Decade in Retrospect" (1972) 22 U Toronto LJ 237 at 251.

28 *The Fair Accommodation Practices Amendment Act*, 1960-61, SO 1960-61, c 28, s 2a.

29 Ontario, Legislative Assembly, *Official Report of Debates (Hansard)*, 2th Parl, 2nd Sess No 40 (14 February 1961) at 1099.

30 For a discussion of this legislation, see above note 15.

31 See *Hansard*, above note 29 at 1100.

32 *Ibid* at 1100.

33 Ontario, Legislative Assembly, *Official Report of Debates (Hansard)*, 26th Parl, 2nd Sess, No. 55 (1 March 1961) at 1619-1628; Ontario, Legislative Assembly, *Official Report of Debates (Hansard)*, 26th Parl, 2nd Sess, No. 68 (15 March 1961) at 2157-59.

34 The housing provisions were also modified to include protection against discrimination in terms and conditions of occupancy, in addition to protection against discrimination in providing occupancy: *Code*, above note 4, s 3(a),(b).

35 *The Ontario Human Rights Code Amendment Act, 1965*, SO 1965, c 85, s 2. This amendment also added protection against discrimination in commercial units.

36 Ontario, Legislative Assembly, *Official Report of Debates (Hansard)*, 27th Parl., 3rd Sess., No. 53 (22 March 1965) at 1487-91; Ontario, Legislative Assembly, *Official Report of Debates (Hansard)*, 27th Parl, 3rd Sess, No. 74 (13 April 1965) at 2207-08.

37 This analysis of the significance of a separate entrance is perhaps ironic in light of the legal position the Attorney General took on this issue in the *Bell v McKay* case, and the eventual legislative amendment which did away entirely with the requirement that there be a separate entrance.

38 Ontario, Legislative Assembly, *Official Report of Debates (Hansard)*, 27th Parl, 3rd Sess, No 53 (22 March 1965) at 1487.

39 *The Ontario Human Rights Code Amendment Act, 1967*, SO 1967, c 66, s 1. Ontario, Legislative Assembly, *Official Report of Debates (Hansard)*, 27th Parl, 5th Sess, No 58 (10 April 1967) at 1907.

40 Daniel G. Hill and E. Marshall Pollock, "Human Rights Legislation in Ontario" (1967) 9 Race & Class 193 at 196. Virtually the same article had been published several years earlier, but under the co-authorship of Tom Eberlee and Dan Hill: TM Eberlee and DG Hill, "The Ontario Human Rights Code" (1963-1964) 15 U Toronto LJ 448.

41 Daniel G. Hill, *Negroes in Toronto: A Sociological Study of a Minority Group* (Thesis: University of Toronto, 1960).

42 See Girard, *Law to Life*, above note 16 at 265-66. According to Philip Stenning, the *Human Rights Code* conciliation procedure "was imported directly from the *Labour Relations Act.*" — *From Conciliation to Judgement: The Role of Boards of Inquiry under the Ontario Human Rights Code, 1962-1974* (LL.M. Thesis, York University, 1977) at 33.

43 See Sharpe, "Laskin and Civil Liberties," above note 7 at 639.

44 For a critical analysis of Grosch's reasoning, see A. Alan Borovoy, "The Fair Accommodation Practices Act: The 'Dresden' Affair" (1956) 14 University of Toronto Fac L Rev 13.

45 See Sharpe, "Laskin and Civil Liberties," above note 7 at 636. See also Girard, *Law to Life*, above note 16 at 493.

46 See Hill and Pollock, "Human Rights Legislation," above note 40 at 203.

47 "Human Rights – at all costs" *The Globe and Mail* (20 June 1968).

48 Dan Hill, "Protecting Human Rights in Ontario, 1793-1968" (1968) 8 Human Relations 8-9, as quoted in Honourable JC McRuer, Commissioner, *Royal Commission Inquiry Into Civil Rights, Report Number Two* (Toronto: Queen's Printer, 1969) at 1556-58.

49 "Historicist: Kill Bill 99," online: torontoist.com/2010/07/historicist_kill_bill_99.php.

50 McRuer's critics responded that administrative bodies were often created for the social purpose of advancing collective (rather than individual) rights and that his remedy was premised on "the constant assumption that everyone (even trade unions apparently) thinks they get 'justice' from the judges." According to his chief critic, McRuer's answer was that administrative bodies should "imitate, as far as you can, the way we lawyers do things at the building in Toronto called Osgoode Hall." John Willis, "The McRuer Report: Lawyers' Values and Civil Servants' Values" (1968) 18 U Toronto LJ 351 at 352.

51 Paul Weiler, *In the Last Resort: A Critical Study of the Supreme Court of Canada* (Toronto: Carswell, Methuen, 1974) at 142. According to Weiler: "The people who really need the Code's protection are lower income blacks or other immigrant groups. They naturally prefer the kind of low-cost accommodation offered by Bell, a flat in a converted private home."

52 See Sharpe, "Laskin and Civil Liberties," above note 7 at 639.

53 These facts are taken from the reported decision of Stewart J, above note 3.

54 *Bell v McKay*, SCC, above note 3 at 762.

55 *Bell v McKay*, OCA, above note 3 at 680

56 *Mitchell v O'Brien* (11 July 1968), Ontario Board of Inquiry at 11.

57 Hogg, "Jurisdictional Fact Doctrine," above note 5 at page 209. *Bell v McKay* became the leading case on the jurisdictional fact doctrine, following the decision of the Supreme Court of Canada which is discussed below.

58 Marshall Pollock Osgoode Society Interview, Cynthia Smith (21 October 2004) at 9.

59 *Ibid* at 43.

60 For some insight into the origins of the Rand commission, see Joan Sangster, "'We No Longer Respect the Law': The Tilco Strike, Labour Injunctions, and the State" (2004) 53 Labour / Le Travail 47. The inside workings of the commission are described by William Kaplan in his recent biography of Rand: *Canadian Maverick: The Life and Times of Ivan C. Rand* (Toronto, Osgoode Society, 2009), 377*ff*.

61 George Finlayson, *John J. Robinette Peerless Mentor: An Appreciation* (Toronto, Osgoode Society, 2003) at 225. Finlayson wrote: "Starr has been described as 'a pure litigator and also an iconoclast ... [and] an enthusiastic critic of the judiciary and other legal institutions.'" In a post-mortem tribute published in the Law Society *Gazette*, William Anderson J described Starr in the following terms: "Among the more colourful characters at the Ontario Bar during my years in practice and my early years on the Bench was the late R. Nelles Starr, Q.C. He was a vigorous advocate and a dangerous opponent in a lawsuit . . . . By way of a significant avocation, he was an enthusiastic practicing iconoclast." William Anderson, "R. Nelles Starr, Q.C." (June 1993) XXVII No. 2 *Law Society of Upper Canada Gazette* at 117.

62 *Ross v Lamport*, [1956] SCR 366. Archer-Shee was a young boy from an upper class British family who was expelled from school on an allegation of petty theft that was later disproved in court. The case was fictionalized in the play entitled "The Winslow Boy."

63 "The 26 just men who rule Ontario's high court," *Toronto Star* (14 September 1968).

64 The province's first statute against age discrimination was the *Age Discrimination Act*, enacted in 1966, which protected workers between the ages of 40 to 65, but only in matters related to employment.

65 Bell's affidavit is set out in part in the decision of the Supreme Court of Canada.

66 See *Mitchell v O'Brien*, above note 56.

67 When Pollock was interviewed for this article he invoked a vivid memory of this file and particularly of the hearing before Stewart J.

68 The fact that this was the official position of the Attorney General was later made clear by the Attorney General himself, Arthur Wishart, when, in contemplation of an appeal of Stewart J's decision, he stated in Parliament on 12 May 1969:

> We will, no doubt, say in our appeal that prohibition does not lie here. This is a tribunal of inquiry assessing no penalties, making no judgments, furnishing a report from which the Minister of Labour would act.

Ontario, Legislative Assembly, *Official Report of Debates (Hansard)*, 28th Parl, 2nd Sess, No 113 (12 May 1969) at 4224.

69 *Regina v Ontario Labour Relations Board, Ex parte Kitchener Food Market Ltd.*, [1966] 2 OR 513 (CA).

70 See *Bell v McKay*, above note 3 at 714.

71 *Ibid* at 771.

72 *Ibid* at 714 and 718.

73 *Ibid* at 718-19.

74 Ontario, Legislative Assembly, *Official Report of Debates (Hansard)*, 28th Parl, 2nd Sess, No 113 (12 May 12 1969) at 4224.

75 Quoted in Ontario, Legislative Assembly, *Official Report of Debates (Hansard)*, 28th Parl, 2nd Sess, No on No 114 (13 May 1969) at 4229. In his written reasons, Stewart added the qualifier "not, of course, dealing with self-contained units."

76 "Historicist: Kill Bill 99," above note 49.

77 *The Globe and Mail* (14 May 1969). This is the source of the three phrases quoted in this paragraph.

78 *Toronto Daily Star* (14 May 1969)

79 "A good law maligned," *The Telegram* (15 May 1969).

80 Letter from A. Alan Borovoy to The Hon John P. Robarts dated 3 June 1969. See "OHRC Bell *v* McKay", RG 7-1, Archives of Ontario.

81 Ontario, Legislative Assembly, *Official Report of Debates (Hansard)*, 28th Parl, 2nd Sess, No 113 (12 May 1969) at 4223. Wishart's complete statement was the following:

> The counsel who appeared [i.e., Pollock] is a man who has worked for several years with the human rights commission. He is admirably qualified to deal with the case. He is as competent as any man in the department, I think, to argue the matter before the courts, or he would not have been given the brief. I think he is very capable and very eminent, and has had a lot of experience in this work. He has been on panels, he has written articles, he has worked with the Hon. Mr. McRuer [sic] for some two years in this field, and I think no more competent man could have been found. And, of course, we could not anticipate this sort of decision in the case.

Although Wishart's reference was to the McRuer Commission, it is obvious that the intention was to refer to the Rand Commission.

82 When interviewed for this article, Pollock indicated that he did not recall having been called on to make his argument.

83 "'Sky the limit,' lawyer says: Right Code inquiry is criticized," *The Globe and Mail* (29 October 1969).

84 "Lawyer asserts Code destroys client's rights," *The Globe and Mail* (28 October 1969).
85 *Ibid.*
86 *Bell v McKay*, OCA, above note 3 at 682.
87 For reasons unknown, Evans J's reasons were omitted from the reported decision in the Ontario Reports.
88 Letter dated 22 December 1969 from Douglas A. Schmeiser to Mr. Daniel G. Hill, Minister of Labour's general correspondence and subject files, "OHRC *Bell v McKay*," RG 7-1, Archives of Ontario.
89 "Rights for the accused," *The Globe and Mail* (24 November 1969).
90 It appears that Hill thought that John Sopinka was the only choice to argue the commission's case before the Supreme Court: see Dan Hill [Jr], *I Am My Father's Son: A Memoir of Love and Forgiveness* (Toronto: Harper Collins Canada, 2009) at 168.
91 *Roncarelli v Duplessis*, [1959] SCR 121. The passage quoted a few lines later is from Martland at 156.
92 Quoted in the *The Globe and Mail* (24 November 1969).
93 The comments on Martland's style and the relationship between him and Laskin are taken from Peter McCormick's study of the Supreme Court: *Supreme at Last: The Evolution of the Supreme Court of Canada* (Toronto: James Lorimer & Company Limited, 2000).
94 *Bell v McKay*, SCC at 768.
95 *Ibid.*
96 *Ibid* at 779, per Abbott J, quoting McRuer J in *Jackson v Ontario Labour Relations Board* (1955) 3 DLR 297 at 300.
97 *The Globe and Mail* (11 February 1971).
98 Hogg, "Jurisdictional Fact Doctrine," above note 5 at 217.
99 Mullan, "Jurisdictional Fact – Mitigating Plea," above note 5 at 440.
100 Ian A Hunter, "Judicial Review of Human Rights Legislation: *McKay v Bell*" (1972) 7 U Brit Colum L Rev 17 at 28.
101 *Ibid* at 31.
102 *The Civil Rights Law Amendment Act, 1971*, SO 1971, s 63.
103 McRuer, above note 48, vol 5 at 1975-84; recommendations at 1984.
104 *Seneca College of Applied Arts and Technology v Bhadauria*, [1981] 2 SCR 181 at 195.
105 This approach to human rights statutes was first stated by the Supreme Court of Canada in *Insurance Corp. of British Columbia v Heerspink*, [1982] 2 SCR 145 and has since been a staple ingredient of human rights doctrine.
106 Karen Schucher, "A Further Diminishing of the Role of Human Rights Tribunals" (Case Comment on *Cooper v Canada (Human Rights Commission); Bell v Canada (Human Rights Commission)* (1997) 5 Cdn Labour and Employment LJ 173.
107 The dual enforcement process developed in Ontario was adopted by all provinces and by the federal government for their human rights legislation. The issues of delays, backlogs, and few referrals to boards of inquiry were ones that developed in all jurisdictions.
108 Stenning, *Conciliation to Judgment*, above note 42 at 51.

109 Human rights advocates were sharply divided over whether the dual process should be eliminated or improved.

110 *Human Rights Code Amendment Act, 2006*, SO 2006, c 30 (Bill 107).

111 Ontario Human Rights Commission, *Policy on Rental Housing* (Toronto: Queen's Printer for Ontario, 2008), online: www.ohrc.on.ca/en/issues/housing/en/resources/Policies/housing. See also Centre for Equality Rights in Accommodation, *Sorry, It's Rented: Measuring Discrimination in Toronto's Rental Housing Market* (2009), online: www.equalityrights.org/cera/?page_id=179, and Centre for Equality Rights in Accommodation, *Women and Housing in Canada: Barriers to Equality* (2002), online: www.equalityrights.org/cera/?page_id=179.

112 As a result of Code amendments passed in 2006, decisions of the Human Rights Tribunal of Ontario (the successor administrative tribunal to the Board of Inquiry) are now subject to judicial review rather than appeal: *Human Rights Code*, RSO 1990, c 19, s 45.8.

113 *Halifax (Regional Municipality) v Nova Scotia (Human Rights Commission)*, above note 3 at para 38.

"The courts have turned women into slaves for the men of this world": Irene Murdoch's Quest for Justice[1]

Vanessa Gruben, Angela Cameron, and Angela Chaisson[2]

"If they hadn't abolished appeals to the Privy Council . . .
I would have gone all the way to the Privy Council."[3]
—Ernest Shymka

Introduction

In 1973 the Supreme Court of Canada issued a ruling in *Murdoch v Murdoch*,[4] denying Irene "Ginger"[5] Murdoch an interest in the cattle ranch that she and her husband, James Alexander "Alex" Murdoch, had built together over many years. Irene performed extensive manual labour on the farm, including driving, branding, vaccinating and de-horning cattle, haying, raking, and mowing. She often did this work alone due to long, off-ranch, work-related absences by Alex. When their marriage began to break down, Irene sought to receive her ownership interest in the ranch property.[6] However, the certificate of title to the property showed that the land belonged solely to Alex Murdoch. For Irene to receive an interest in the property it would be necessary for a court to declare that a portion of the title to the ranch was held by Alex Murdoch in trust for his wife.[7] The principal basis for finding such a trust, her lawyer argued, was her contribution through labour to the ranch operations. That argument was rejected at trial and ultimately also by the Supreme Court of Canada, which held that under existing Canadian law no property claim was available to Irene Murdoch in the circumstances of her case.

In one sense, the case was unremarkable. Irene Murdoch's circumstances reflected the socio-economic reality of many Albertan farm wives, in fact most married women in Canada, during the 1960s and 70s. Cultural and legal perceptions of farms had been profoundly shaped by the traditional belief that "men farm, women help" and remained an omnipresent example of the invisibility of women's work.[8] While husbands no longer subsumed their wives' legal and financial identities (as was the law in Alberta until 1915), anachronistic matrimonial law, as well as hierarchical farming and family structures subjugated wives, forced them into positions of dependency, and often trapped them in relationships.[9] Those who left their husbands often found themselves invisible under the law, and left their marriages with nothing.[10] The case reports were replete with decisions similar to that in *Murdoch*, almost all unsuccessful.[11] In these and other cases, women worked on family farms and in households held in their husbands' names and were left without proprietary interests at the relationship's dissolution. Behind these, there are likely unreported judgments to the same effect, as well as many instances in which no claim was advanced owing to the perceived futility of such a tack, the absence of the needed resources to take legal action, or myriad other personal factors.

What is exceptional is that the *Murdoch* case prompted outrage in Canada and undoubtedly contributed to law reform that sought to ameliorate the plight of women in the position of Irene Murdoch. Her circumstances provided an important narrative tool to feminists and other advocates for law reform. Canadian women identified with Irene, and became conscious of how easily they could find themselves in a similar situation. Women's groups mobilized around her experience, stood up to say "I am an Irene Murdoch," and successfully secured reforms to Canadian marital property law regimes.[12]

None of that would have been possible had it not been for Irene Murdoch's personal determination — and that of her lawyer, Ernest Shymka — to bring her case to court in the face of formidable obstacles.[13] Irene suffered extreme violence at the hands of her husband, had little money and even less desire for public fanfare, and faced an uphill legal battle. Yet she and Shymka pursued the case to the Supreme Court of Canada.

Much has been written about the political and legislative consequences of this decision.[14] This chapter looks at the *Murdoch* case through two lenses. The first is through the personal account of Ernest Shymka.[15] The second is by framing the case as part of a larger feminist movement for law reform, including reform to matrimonial property regimes. *Murdoch* was not only the product of personal struggle by Irene and her lawyer; it was also a pivotal event within the Canadian women's movement.

Irene as Rancher and Wife

In 1968, Irene and Alex Murdoch separated after twenty-five years of marriage. The trial transcript reveals that Irene worked tirelessly throughout her marriage, as a "wife," as a "ranch hand," and at "outside jobs to augment the farm income."[16] Shortly after they married, Irene worked with Alex on other ranches and they pooled their earnings.[17] In 1947, they used their $3,000 savings from this work, together with a $3,000 contribution from Irene's father, to acquire a guest ranch known as the Bragg Creek property, the title to which was taken in Alex's name alone. Throughout the marriage they bought and sold various properties to which both Alex and Irene contributed financially.[18] In 1957, they purchased the Ward property for $4,500 and in 1958, the Brockway property was purchased for $25,000. It was the Brockway property that was the subject of the case before the Supreme Court of Canada[19] These properties were purchased in part with the proceeds from Irene's father's life insurance policies. Upon his death, Irene's mother, Mrs. Nash, had deposited part of the proceeds in Irene's account and these monies were later used to acquire grazing rights and to purchase land.[20] Yet, in each instance title was held in Alex's name.[21]

For most of their marriage, Irene was almost exclusively responsible for the day-to-day running of the ranch, bearing the brunt of the physically demanding work, while Alex was employed with the stock association in the Forestry Service.[22] Her labour was back-breaking. At trial, Irene described her work as: "haying, raking, swathing, moving, driving trucks and tractors and teams, quieting horses, taking cattle back and forth to the reserve, dehorning, vaccinating, branding, anything that was to be done."[23] In her own words, she worked "like any other man."[24] In addition to her farm work and domestic labour as a wife and mother to their one child, William Frederick Murdoch, Irene frequently worked off the ranch, as a waitress or as a labourer.[25]

Throughout, Irene endured an unhappy and often abusive marriage. It seems she was a victim of domestic violence for much of her marriage. Irene indicated in her pleadings that Alex had "assaulted [her] on a number of occasions causing her grievous bodily harms."[26] Irene's mother confirmed this history of violence at trial. She testified that Irene had been the victim of other "physical skirmishes" in the past.[27] On at least two occasions, Nash witnessed Alex holding Irene by the back of the neck. She also testified that she saw Alex kick Irene in the knees with his riding boots on one or two occasions.[28] She recalled an incident in which Alex "threw a hot cup of cocoa in [Irene's] face."[29] Irene confirmed in later court proceedings against Alex, that their marriage was rife with physical abuse. In a recent interview, Alex's counsel, Les Duncan, also acknowledged the ongoing abuse.[30]

The Dower Caveat

In 1964, in the wake of Alex's violent behaviour, Irene decided to file a caveat against the title to the Brockway property, pursuant to the *Dower Act*.[31] Alberta's dower legislation severely limited the right of a spouse to sell the home without the consent of the other spouse. The caveat serves as a notice to potential buyers that such dower protections apply to the lands in issue. Four years later Alex demanded that the caveat be discharged. She refused. Alex was furious at Irene's stated intention to invoke her dower veto after he insisted that she release the caveat in order to facilitate sale of the Brockway property. Irene stood firm. It was a decision that had terrible consequences and that would change Irene's life forever.

In reaction to her refusal, Alex violently attacked both Irene and her mother. The vicious assault began on Nash, who was sixty-nine years old at the time and weighed a mere ninety-eight pounds.[32] Shymka described Nash as "a tiny lady; just skin and bones."[33] Nash recalled at trial that Alex "knocked me down and gave me a black eye and pulled my hair out."[34] When Irene came to her mother's aid, Alex turned on her. As Nash explained, "my daughter stepped in to help me and that is when he grabbed her and broke her jaw . . . he had both arms wrapped around her face like that [indicating] and was putting pressure on it." Alex broke Irene's jaw in three places. She was hospitalized for several days with her jaw wired shut. When she returned home from the hospital she found the locks to her home changed. Irene turned to the legal system for help.[35]

Irene's Decision to Litigate

Criminal assault charges were brought against Alex, and convictions were apparently entered.[36] Shortly afterwards, Irene launched two lawsuits against Alex, although she did not file for divorce.[37]

It may seem incredible, given the violence used against her, that Irene did not seek a divorce. There were both systemic and personal reasons for this. First, there was little or no assistance for women leaving abusive relationships at that time. Not only was abuse within intimate relationships seen as an exclusively "domestic" issue, but women who did leave their abusive spouses often had nowhere to go. As noted by Constance Backhouse,

> [o]ver the past several decades both Canada and the United States have witnessed the phenomenal growth of feminist-based rape crisis centres, battered women's shelters, and, incipiently, incest survivors' groups. The delivery of services to women and children who suffer from violence has been one of the prime goals of the women's movement.[38]

At the time, however, such resources simply did not exist. The first women's shelters in Canada did not open until in 1973 — five years after Irene was kicked out of her house. Once those resources did become available, very few served rural areas, such as the farmlands where Irene Murdoch lived. The only transition house in Alberta in the early 1970s appears to have been the Oasis House, now the Calgary Women's Emergency Shelter.[39]

Second, at a personal level, Irene hoped to reconcile with Alex. As Shymka explains, she hoped that legally securing an interest in the ranch would tempt her husband back into the relationship in order to keep the ranch together, returning their lives to normal and giving her access to her son.

> As I recall, she didn't want a divorce, that I think was clear, she was hoping that she could obtain a declaration from the court that said: "look I have . . . some interest in this property . . . in the land." And she felt that if she could obtain that naturally her husband would want to keep that ranch, keep things together and so they could keep the property together ... and in order for him to do that they would get back together.
>
> And she had great affection for her son, that was just tearing her up. The boy was at an age where he preferred to be with his father because he had the ranch and he liked riding horses and all of those things that a young boy would enjoy as opposed maybe to living in some basement suite with the mother.
>
> So she was trying to just return things to the way they were. It might have been farfetched on her part to do that, but that is what she wanted. She wanted to restore things back to the way they were if only her husband would acknowledge that she was entitled to something here.[40]

Irene's decision to seek justice in the legal system was made in the face of great physical and emotional adversity. It would take months for her jaw to begin to heal, and she never completely recovered her health. At trial, Irene explained:

> I had my jaws wired together, my teeth were wired and my jaws were wired and I was in and out several times to have them[41] removed. I had to have a bone graft because there was too much, the bone was broken in two places on the right side and the bone . . . was crushed completely, so it didn't heal and I had to go back in and have a bone graft from my hip into my jaw and have that wired. Now there is permanent paralysis and I go for therapy treatments to get try to get my jaw to move again so they will be able to eat again.[42]

Irene was a shadow of her former self. At the time of the trial in February 1971, nearly two and a half years after the attack, she was still subsisting mainly on a liquid diet. She had a great deal of trouble speaking, and at the trial was only able to talk out of the corner of her mouth because of the jaw paralysis.[43] The injury was so severe that she would wear a neck collar for two years.

Irene was likely suffering emotionally as well. Following the assault, Irene had been locked out of her matrimonial home "without even so much as a spoon," despite the fact that she had been the one to purchase most of the household items.[44] Alex would not allow Irene to collect most of her possessions. She only had the clothes she had worn to Holy Cross Hospital after the beating: her blouse, slacks, ankle socks, and slippers.[45] Irene was forced to live in a motel and it appears that she had little to no access to her only child, William. For months after the attack, she received only $20 per month from Alex.[46] Irene's primary support came from her elderly mother.[47]

Her weak state rendered Irene Murdoch virtually unemployable. Indeed, she was still unemployed at the time of trial in 1971 and in great debt. She owed at least $3,000 for medical expenses and she owed her mother roughly $800 for the motel bills. Irene could not even afford the dentures required due to the extensive damage to her jaw.[48] Being homeless and penniless must have been devastating, particularly for a woman who had spent most of her life doing the physical work of a ranch hand and always had been able to earn money and ensure her own financial security.

All of this made retaining a lawyer a daunting task. She had to find one who would take her case on a contingency or pro bono basis. Under these circumstances, most people might well accept any lawyer willing to represent them and accede to the litigation strategy recommended by that lawyer — in this case to seek a divorce together with a lump sum settlement.[49] This advice was likely prudent given the absence of any legislation requiring the sharing of matrimonial property and the reticence of courts to use trust law to remedy unfairness.[50] Provincial legislation and the *Divorce Act* did, however, provide for the payment of maintenance of the wife upon relationship breakdown. Spousal maintenance could take the form of monthly payments or a larger one-time payment, although lump-sum payments were exceedingly rare in 1968,[51] when Alex and Irene separated.

Despite these challenges, Irene was determined to find a lawyer who would argue that she was entitled to an ownership interest in the Brockway property. She felt that recognition of her property interest would allow her to keep ranching and ultimately lead to their hoped-for reconciliation.[52]

Irene needed a lawyer who would craft a novel and compelling legal argument. She initially retained Grosvenor Atchell, who drafted the statements of claim.[53] In addition, it appears that she was represented early on by two future judges: Jack Major, who was later appointed to the Supreme Court of Canada,[54] and John Wesley "Buzz" McClung, who would serve on the District Supreme and Appeal courts of Alberta.[55] There were likely other lawyers as well.[56] Ultimately, she retained Ernest Shymka, a Calgary-based lawyer with the firm of Shymka, Davis & Kay, to represent her at trial.

Ernest Skymka graduated from the Faculty of Law at the University of Alberta in 1957.[57] He became a lawyer in general practice at the firm of Shymka and Company with five or six lawyers in Calgary. He was a general litigator who also practiced property and personal injury law. It was "a privilege to have practiced in those years," according to Shymka.[58] "Practice is much more adversarial now, probably not as pleasant to practice law as it was in the golden years."[59]

Shymka was initially reluctant to take on the case, but after a thorough review of the documentary evidence Irene provided to him, he was convinced that she had suffered a great injustice. Shymka was also encouraged by his wife to take the Murdoch case:

> There was no monetary gain and at first I didn't think I was going to take the case, but my wife she got so upset. "You have to take case, you have to help this poor woman," she said. She was something of a feminist, her mother was a university chum of Charlotte Whitten, Mayor of Ottawa. She got pretty exercised about this and pushed me to do everything I could to help her (Irene).

According to Shymka, despite defeats at the trial and Court of Appeal levels, he persisted with Irene's case as a way of honouring another strong women in his life, his mother:

> My mother and dad ran a bunch of stores in northern Alberta. My mother ran the main store and I was brought up in the store. The thought that women had no place in the business world was foreign to me. She was a very good business woman. I have been blessed with great women in my life, yes, both my mother and my wife for sure.[60]

Like Irene, he believed that the courts would remedy this injustice through a property law claim. Not only was Shymka willing to vigorously pursue Irene's claim, he agreed to take the case on a contingency basis, meaning that his fee would be taken as a percentage of the court award, if any.[61] When asked to comment on taking the case on contingency, Shymka dismissed it as a noble gesture, claiming that it was common practice amongst his peers.

> A contingency sounds like "oooh wow" . . . today there are fewer contingency agreements . . . lawyers proceed on the basis of time spent and so on . . . Most lawyers at that time never kept track of time. You didn't do it like they do today . . . they keep track of every minute . . . You did what you had to do, if you needed to spend 100 hours more than you really should then you spent it . . . Here it went out the window because the amount of time spent was *enormous* . . . even on the hourly rates in those days which were lower.[62]

Shymka describes Irene as a very committed client, although in a fragile emotional state: "she was very distraught; 25 years of her life in this venture with her husband starting virtually with nothing." He noted that she would "often break into tears" and relied heavily on the support of her mother, who "stood very much behind her and encouraged her to do something." Nash also felt that she had personally suffered a grave injustice because she had given significant sums of money to Irene for Irene's benefit.[63] Shymka was determined to help them.

The Theory of Irene's Case

In the first of her two lawsuits, Irene sought an order for judicial separation. Once granted, the spouses would be released from the obligation to cohabit. This cause of action emerged at a time long before modern reform to the law of divorce, but even after the liberalizing of divorce in Canada in 1968, judicial separation was sometimes used in Alberta by spouses as a staging post on the road to divorce, although this was not Irene's intention at the time.[64]

An order of judicial separation triggers a right to seek ancillary relief, such as maintenance and custody. The Murdochs' son was then thirteen years of age, and both Irene and Alex sought custody over him. Importantly, an order for judicial separation did not, on its own, give rise to a court-ordered reallocation of matrimonial assets. As alluded to above, in 1968 there was no special regime for dividing marital property under either Alberta law or the federal *Divorce Act*. Apart from minor exceptions (such as dower), the rules of ownership then applicable to separating spouses were no different from the rules that governed property disputes generally. Thus, for Irene to receive a property interest in the ranch, she would have to turn to general property law principles.

Under general property law doctrine, the starting point is formal title. As already noted, the Brockway property was registered in the provincial land titles system in the name of James Alexander Murdoch. In appropriate circumstances, a court was entitled to look past formal title and award a share of the property to another person. For example, if the parties entered into a business partnership, a court may have allocated partnership assets on dissolution of the partnership relationship. Even where such a business partnership was not present, a share of property could be ordered to one party under the principles of equity. Where a party contributed financially to the purchase of property that was held in the name of another, it was presumed that the non-titled party intended to acquire an interest in that property. There is said to be a presumption of a resulting trust in favour of the party making the contribution. This presumption can be rebutted by showing that the contributor intended the party on title to have the property for their own benefit, in other words as a gift.

This general rule — presuming a resulting trust in favour of a contributing party — applied where a wife contributed financially to the acquisition of property and registered title in the name of the husband. It would be presumed that the wife intended to acquire an interest in that property.[65] Irene Murdoch's claim for an interest in the Brockway property was based on the operation of this presumption. Moreover, if an appropriate contribution could be found, it seemed unlikely that Alex could succeed in demonstrating that Irene actually intended to confer a gift of that contribution (and ergo the Brockway property) on him.[66]

Even in the absence of a direct financial contribution by the wife, the courts had indicated a willingness to expand the doctrine of resulting trust in two situations. First, was the "common intention" resulting trust. Where there was evidence of a common intention by the spouses that the property be regarded as co-owned, Canadian courts had (uniquely) recognized a resulting trust in favour of the non-titled owning spouse (most often the wife) even when the property was purchased by the very person in whose name the title was taken.[67]

Second, the Alberta Court of Appeal had concluded in the exceptional case of *Trueman v Trueman*, that *non*-pecuniary contributions made by a wife to the property such as working in the fields and building the home could support her claim for a resulting trust in the matrimonial home.[68] There is little question that the courts had expanded the resulting trust doctrine in these situations to address the unfairness generated by the unsatisfactory state of the law regarding the property rights of wives, who generally were not title holders, upon marriage breakdown.

In addition to these situations, it was possible for a court to recognize an interest in property by means of a constructive trust. At the time *Murdoch* was decided, these circumstances were carefully circumscribed. Generally speaking, the claim had to fall within a set of established categories before the court would impose a constructive trust. Because of such a strict categorical approach, these are sometimes referred to as institutional constructive trusts. For example, it was well established that when a person knowingly acquires property that is subject to a trust, a court will impose a constructive trust upon that recipient, in essence deeming the wrongful recipient to be a trustee for the party entitled to the benefit of the trust property. At the time of the *Murdoch* decision, no Canadian court had imposed a constructive trust simply on the basis that such action was appropriate to remedy unjust enrichment. In other words, there was at this moment in time no place in Canadian law for a more flexible approach, one that would support the imposition of what is sometimes called a remedial constructive trust as a remedy for unjust enrichment. Put simply, to find a constructive trust in the circumstances of the *Murdoch* case would require the Court to expand the reach of that doctrine dramatically. As will be seen below, the Supreme Court of Canada was not yet prepared to take that step.

Based on the facts and the existing jurisprudence, Shymka decided to advance Irene's case on the basis of the resulting trust doctrine. He sought a declaration that Irene and Alex were equal partners and that Alex was a trustee for Irene in a one-half interest in the "land, cattle brand, cattle, and other assets."[69] Shymka's theory of the case rested on two principal arguments.

The first was based on Irene's direct and indirect financial contributions to the various properties acquired by the couple during their marriage, which were nominally owned by Alex. Although Shymka relied on a number of transactions, the use of the life insurance monies was a key component of this argument. In Shymka's view, the life insurance monies that Nash deposited in Irene's account were intended to be a gift from Nash to Irene or, at the very least, to both Irene and Alex.[70] The use of Irene's share of that gift for the purchase of property would give rise to a presumption of resulting trust in her favour.

Shymka's second argument relied on the Alberta Court of Appeal's expanded view of the resulting trust in *Trueman v Trueman*. He sought to establish that Murdoch, like Mrs. Trueman, had made a "substantial" nonpecuniary contribution to the property through her extensive labour and accordingly was entitled to an equal ownership interest in that property.

In addition, Shymka planned to rely on evidence of the violence suffered by Irene at the hands of her husband to support her overall case. Shymka explained that he intended to use Alex's violent behaviour and explosive temper to undermine Alex's credibility and to bolster Nash and Irene's version of events.[71] This evidence arguably would have also provided important context and served to explain why Irene did not have title to any of the assets acquired during her marriage: she likely was fearful of asking Alex that she be recognized on title to the Brockway property despite her enormous contributions to its acquisition and maintenance.

At Trial and Appeal

The petition for judicial separation and the property claim were heard together before Justice Hugh John MacDonald. MacDonald J was a school teacher during the first years of the Great Depression, before going to the University of Alberta to train as a lawyer. Graduating in 1938, he was admitted to the bar on 1 September 1939, and shortly thereafter left for wartime service in the Royal Canadian Navy. When he returned, he began practising in Calgary, as well as serving as a Liberal member of the legislature for eleven years, from 1948 to 1959. Calgary at the time had a single electoral district that elected several seats in the legislature: with each of his three elections he ranked higher in the total vote. When he retired from the legislature he continued to practice in Calgary up to his appointment to the Calgary Trial Division of the Supreme Court of Alberta in 1968.[72] He had a tough personality and was not someone willing to suffer fools gladly, especially in his court. According to Shymka, it was common for the judiciary at that time to conduct themselves in a very imperious manner, but it did not affect their integrity.

> I'd had several previous cases with Mr. Justice MacDonald and I remember one in particular, I think it is even a reported decision, in the DLR . . . I recall he (laughing) showed a great deal of displeasure from the beginning and through that case but ultimately he sided with my client and (laughing) awarded us costs in double column five, which was very unusual . . . he was a tough judge but a fair judge. Fair. And what more can you ask of anyone?
>
> As of those judges, they called them as they saw them. Just like an umpire in a baseball game. If it is a strike it is a strike, if it is a ball it is a ball . . . in their view . . . they can be mistaken . . . but there is no question about their integrity.[73]

Shymka met significant resistance from MacDonald J from the outset of the trial. Shymka speculated that "they maybe started off on the wrong footing" when he requested an adjournment at the start of trial in the hopes of "making one last stab at trying to settle the matter because we didn't have to get a hold of our clients, they were there."[74] Shymka also requested that the pleadings be amended to include a claim that the two Murdochs had been in a partnership and that Alex was the trustee of Irene's equal ownership interest in the assets. Shymka speculated that these incidents left the impression with MacDonald J that the plaintiffs were not ready for trial.

Throughout the trial, MacDonald J frequently intervened. Notably, he refused to allow Irene to testify about the attack she suffered at the hands of Alex in October 1968 and the repercussions of that assault. Nash had described the attack in her testimony earlier on the same day Shymka examined Irene. When Shymka asked Irene to testify about the assault, MacDonald J stated "I don't think I need to go through that again . . . we don't have to pile the evidence up or repeat it." Instead, the court accepted the submission of Alex's lawyer that the issue of violence was not before the court on the basis that Alex was not defending the action for judicial separation. Each time Shymka sought to introduce evidence of the violence Irene had experienced, the court resisted. Although he was not able to get Irene's version of the attack or the prior abuse she had suffered at the hands of Alex on the record, Shymka did manage to elicit some information from her about the aftermath of the attack, including the medical expenses and the conditions of poverty she had endured as a result of her injuries.[75] However, MacDonald J's account of the marriage in his judgment renders all of the abuse invisible. He wrote in his decision: "[t]he relationship between the husband and wife in this instance I find to have been a normal husband and wife relationship until the parties separated."[76]

In regards to the court's resistance Shymka notes the "trial judge has discretion and I think what the trial judge felt was there was overemphasis on this, and there was a prejudicial aspect to this evidence that I was trying to cross examine him on . . . Time might have been better spent on other issues . . . I don't necessarily fault him on that."[77] Why then, did Shymka persist with introducing the evidence of abuse? According to Shymka he endured with this line of questioning for two reasons. First, he thought it related to Alex's credibility. "The question of getting at the particulars of the assault . . . I thought related to Alex's credibility and the trial judge felt that evidence was more prejudicial than probative . . . you don't always get a warm and cuddly reception." Secondly, Shymka wanted to rebut evidence given by Alex that Nash had started the physical altercation that lead to Irene's injury. "What I was trying to get at in the trial . . . Mrs. Nash was a tiny lady in her seventies — just skin and bones . . . To have told the court that Mrs. Nash had started the fight! She was very much a lady, prim and proper as was Irene Murdoch, but her mother in particular struck me as that way . . . And to say that she started the fight didn't make any sense!"[78]

Alex Murdoch did not defend the judicial separation petition, and the decree was issued accordingly. The court awarded custody of their son to Alex, despite the evidence of his abusive behaviour towards Irene. As part of the petition, Shymka also sought an order for exclusive possession of the home. That request was denied; the court stated that there was no legal basis for such an order. Alex was, however, ordered to pay $200 as monthly maintenance to his wife. A factor in setting the amount of support was the ability of Alex to pay. His capacity to do so, MacDonald J held, was due in part to success of the ranch:

> [F]rom the evidence that I have heard . . . I am satisfied that Mr. Murdoch has been a capable and a successful rancher, and has built up a substantial holding from a very small beginning, and that, directly or indirectly, the support

> that Mrs. Murdoch is entitled to has to come from his ability to farm and ranch this land and run the cattle successfully.[79]

The second action, the claim for a property interest, was entirely unsuccessful and ill-received. The reasons for judgment in relation to that dispute are short; no authority is cited. Macdonald J held that the evidence disclosed no partnership and no indication that the parties intended that the lands were to be co-owned. To find that there was a right to share assets under those circumstances would be to confer, in MacDonald J's view, a partnership interest to all ranch wives. He resisted that outcome because "I have read nothing and nothing has been referred to me that suggests that this is either public policy or the intention of any legislation that exists."[80]

No mention in the judgment was made of her non-pecuniary contributions to the ranching enterprise. In addition, MacDonald J found that money provided by Nash after the death of Irene's father was a loan subsequently repaid and was not a gift made to Alex for his and Irene's benefit (a factual finding which would ultimately play a pivotal role in the majority Supreme Court decision). Accordingly, MacDonald J concluded that there was no financial contribution to ground Irene's claim to a resulting trust.

Both Shymka and Irene were sorely disappointed by the loss at trial level. But Shymka reports that both he and Irene "had the utmost confidence" that the Alberta Court of Appeal would change that.[81] He assumed that they would have had a "good hearing" especially in light of the Court of Appeal's decision in *Trueman v Trueman*.[82]

Sadly, they were mistaken. "The Court of Appeal hearing lasted no more than ten, fifteen, twenty minutes"[83] and the court tersely dismissed Irene Murdoch's appeal.[84] The court did not purport to address the merits of the property claim. Rather, for them the fatal flaw in her appeal was that she had accepted the maintenance payments. The amount of those payments, which she was not challenging on appeal, was based in part on the fact that there was to be no property division. Hence, they held that she could not both accept the support and now seek a property award. Shymka now speculates that the court "preferred not to even get into this case." He explained that the *Trueman* decision had not been popular in Alberta as there had been quite a negative reaction to the Court of Appeal's expanded approach to the resulting trust. In Shymka's view "it was one thing to . . . give a wife an interest in a matrimonial home and another thing to . . . give her an interest in a quarter section of land with matrimonial home on it but it was quite another thing to extend and stretch the principles of *Trueman v Trueman*."[85]

However, the Court of Appeal's decision was not unanimous, as Justice Kane dissented, chiding his colleagues for failing to address the heart of the matter: "in the circumstances it may well be that whilst the notice of appeal purports to be an appeal from the whole of the judgment at trial, yet when it is read, it will be noted the complaint appears to be not in respect of the alimony awarded but as to the refusal to award to the appellant an interest in the property of the respondent."[86]

Pursuing the Case to the Supreme Court of Canada

The judgment at trial was disappointing. The decision of the Appellate Division was even more discouraging. It would have been completely understandable had Irene decided to forego a further appeal to the Supreme Court of Canada. The decision to press on to the Supreme Court despite these two losses was motivated first and foremost by the injustice of the lower court of decisions and the fact that the property issue was not squarely addressed by the Court of Appeal.[87] As Shymka recalls, "it just didn't strike me [as] fair that the husband would end up with all the assets."[88] Second, Shymka believed that there was a solid factual basis upon which to appeal. Shymka felt that MacDonald J's conclusion on the insurance monies, although somewhat ambiguous, supported Irene's claim for a resulting trust.[89] MacDonald J found that Nash had turned over the insurance monies to Irene, which she had deposited in her bank account. He also found that Nash considered the monies "to be her daughter's money to use as her daughter saw fit."[90] Shymka believed that this was sufficient evidence of Irene's direct financial contribution to the Brockway property. Even if the Court found that the money was a loan, rather than an outright gift, it was reasoned that at the very least it must have been a loan to both Alex and Irene since MacDonald J had concluded that it was in Irene's name and given to her for her own use.

Finally, Shymka was of the opinion that the timing of Murdoch's appeal was good. He believed that the doctrine of resulting trust in Canadian law was ripe for change. Shymka recalls spending many hours at the courthouse library reading about the expansion of the resulting trust in England and the law reform that was under way across Canada. Shymka concluded that these developments, together with the Court of Appeal's decision in *Trueman*, had pushed Canadian jurisprudence to a crossroads. Even if Shymka's argument on the financial contribution was not successful, he strongly believed their novel argument that a resulting trust could be founded on the basis of Irene's non-pecuniary contributions to the Brockway property would ultimately prevail. As he succinctly put it, "you didn't have to be a Philadelphia lawyer to figure that out."[91]

Irene also wished to pursue the appeal, despite her dire financial situation. She received $200 per month in alimony from Alex. (On the bottom left hand of each of her alimony cheques Alex wrote "Alimony- ha ha.") Shortly before the Supreme Court of Canada appeal, she found work as a cleaning woman, but she still had trouble making ends meet. Irene explained to a *Toronto Star* reporter at the time, "[i]t is bad enough just putting food on the table. My rented house is costing me $80 a month and with all the other bills I have to pay, I have less than $60 a month to live on." In addition, Irene still owed close to $2,000 in medical bills for her fractured jaw.[92] But this did not deter her. Shymka recalls that Irene was confident that the Supreme Court would find in her favour. He explained that Irene "knew what physical contribution she had made and the money that she and her parents had put into these various properties" and she strongly believed that she was entitled to an ownership interest in the Brockway property.[93] On 24 March 1972 Shymka filed a notice of appeal with the Supreme Court of Canada — complete with a $500 deposit for security. Because Irene's claim to the ranch was valued at more than $10,000, under the Supreme Court rules of the time Irene could appeal as of right — she would not have to seek leave to appeal.[94]

Irene's case was becoming important for women's groups even before the Supreme Court heard the case. The Calgary Local Council of Women took up Irene's case as one of "blatant discrimination," (in the words of one-time president and historian of the council, Lillian MacLennan). In late winter 1974, the Council began collecting money to help defray Irene's growing legal costs. Their campaign attracted a great deal of support from members, and the broader public. Kay Armstrong, president of the National Council of Women, acknowledged this work on Irene's behalf as actively helping women in general in Canada and called on other groups to take up the same or similar campaigns. Within the first month the Council had raised $1,226.[95]

Martland and the Majority

The sole issue before the Supreme Court of Canada was Irene's proprietary interest in the ranch. No claim based on a partnership per se was advanced at this level. The case was argued on the basis that a resulting trust existed in Irene Murdoch's favour. The majority judgment was written by Ronald Martland J, an appointee from Alberta. Throughout Martland J's twenty-four-year tenure on the Supreme Court he remained very conservative; he was a careful black-letter judge, not an innovator.[96]

The majority rejected Irene's claim for a resulting trust. Martland J, relying on the trial judge's finding that the money from Nash was a loan, concluded that Irene Murdoch made no financial contribution to the property necessary to ground a claim in resulting trust.[97] Martland J then turned to Irene's other claims for a resulting trust based on her physical contribution to the Brockway property. Martland J's judgment contains a lengthy review of the leading English and Canadian case law on resulting trusts, including the Alberta Court of Appeal judgment in *Trueman v Trueman*, where it was decided that non-pecuniary contributions made by a wife could support her claim for a resulting trust. But, Martland J argued, even if such contributions could count toward the recognition of resulting trust, that case could not assist Irene for two reasons. First, the *Trueman* claim was for an interest only in the matrimonial home; here the dispute pertained to the entire ranching operation. Second, in *Trueman*, the trial judge had found that the wife had made an extraordinary contribution to the acquisition of the farm home.[98] In the present case, "the trial Judge made no such finding, but was of the view that what [Irene Murdoch] had done, while living with [her husband] was the work done by any ranch wife."[99]

Much has been made of that statement, which, as can be seen, is attributed to the trial judge. However, MacDonald J did not explicitly say any such thing. At trial, Alex Murdoch had been asked to describe his wife's activities during the year. He replied: "Oh, just about what the ordinary rancher's wife does. Most of them can do anything."[100] One can only surmise that the trial judgment was based on such a view, because in fact MacDonald J provided virtually no explanation as to why he rejected the property claim.

However, Shymka did not begrudge the majority their decision, noting instead that although he did not agree with the principles themselves, the decision was rooted in consistently held philosophies:

> I think that maybe Mr. Justice Martland has got an unfavourable rap over this case. I think he was true to his principles. I certainly felt it a privilege to be even in the same room with him. I considered him a giant among men. He was certainly not only a lawyer's lawyer but a judge's judge. He was a

> very imposing figure and just to have been allowed to joust with him . . . and Mr. Justice Spence and some of the other judges . . . was an honour. I had the greatest admiration for him then, and I do now.
>
> He was true to his principles, and even in *Rathwell* again he didn't agree with the use of the constructive trust and showed judicial restraint . . . the Court has been criticised enough. I'll leave it at that. Many scholars still regard him as one of the greatest judges of the Court and I wouldn't argue with that.[101]

Laskin's Dissent

Justice Laskin's dissenting opinion strikes a markedly different tone. For Laskin J, Irene's financial and physical contributions to the ranch were significant and stated that the latter "can only be characterized as extraordinary."[102] Laskin J believed that Irene's contribution necessitated a proprietary remedy, but was unwilling to apply or expand resulting trust principles to the facts of the case. He did not feel able to conclude that Irene had made sufficient direct financial contributions to the acquisition of the property in dispute; nor was there sufficient evidence of a common intention to share the assets.

Instead, Laskin J was of the view that Alex could not in good faith retain a full beneficial interest in the property given his wife's extensive contributions. The appropriate remedy, he maintained, would be the imposition of a constructive trust based on unjust enrichment.[103] That line of reasoning was heavily influenced by American case law, some of which is cited by Laskin J. He also claimed, less convincingly, that such an approach was consonant with some English jurisprudence.[104] The recognition of such a remedial constructive trust imposed to respond to a situation of unjust enrichment — wherever found — would have radically altered Canadian law. It would have expanded the purview of the law of constructive trusts far beyond its existing contours. But Laskin J was prepared to go that far because, for him, the unjust enrichment analysis best resolved the critical issue in *Murdoch v Murdoch*. In applying that doctrine here, Irene Murdoch would be entitled to *some* share in the ranch properties, the precise calculation of which would be determined on a referral back to the trial court.

Summary

THIS ENDED THE LITIGATION on the ownership claim, but Irene's determination and courage in pursuing her case was not futile. Without her personal courage, her case would never have wound up before the Supreme Court of Canada, the dissenting opinion of Laskin J would never have been penned,[105] and women's demands for family law reform would not have resonated with such force nor provided "the grindstone [women's groups] needed to whet their lobbying efforts for the reform of matrimonial property law."[106]

Shymka praised Justice Laskin's dissent, characterizing it as marking a sea change in society and law relating to women's roles.

> Justice Bora Laskin certainly deserves a huge degree of credit for his judgement and taking the position he did. Based on how he considered the facts and the law that was available to him, that remedy that was available to him. The fact that he was ultimately proven right in *Rathwell* and *Rathwell*.
>
> We were at the crossroads in history that things were changing . . . some of the older judges were not quite aware . . . cause you know women were coming into the professions . . . into medicine and to business . . . the workforce and things were changing everywhere. And so my hat goes off to Bora Laskin he certainly distinguished himself in that case and I think that Mr. Justice Dickson in *Rathwell* at some point said that the one case that distinguished Mr. Justice Laskin more than any other was *Murdoch*.[107]

Personal Consequences

Irene Murdoch

WHAT WE KNOW ABOUT Irene Murdoch's personal circumstances following the Supreme Court of Canada ruling comes from the public record, which is surprisingly slim considering the substantial academic and media attention that the case generated. Much of that record is dedicated to negative opinions about the state of matrimonial property law and the Supreme Court decision, or accounts of feminist activism designed to stimulate legal reform in the area.[108]

Much of the reason for the lack of attention to Irene is that she did not seek the spotlight. According to Alberta author Nancy Millar, "[s]he just seemed to retreat in[to] the background . . . [S]he was very glad to get out of the public eye. You don't pick your heroines, they are created, and she never intended to be anybody's role model."[109]

The Calgary Counsel of Women lost track of her following the case. Irene appeared on the public record personally very few times. She gave an interview to Chris Dennett of the *Toronto Star* not long after the Supreme Court of Canada decision. She expressed outrage and disbelief, stating, "I hadn't realized women could be so badly treated . . . The courts have turned women into slaves for the men of this world."[110] This article recounted the facts of the case, painting the majority decision as egregiously unfair, and valourising Laskin J's dissent.

About a year later, in September 1974, *Chatelaine* magazine published an in-depth article on Irene Murdoch and Helen Rathwell, a woman who had also been engaged in matrimonial property litigation.[111] Irene was interviewed by reporter Eve Rockett, who noted that Irene had made previous public appearances because "she thought it would help other women." But during the period between her 1973 interview with the *Toronto Star* and this piece, Irene began to suffer in her role as a national public figure, and started to shrink from the spotlight. She also suffered personally, worrying that the publicity was hurting her estranged husband, and straining her relationships in the small town where she lived. [112]

The picture painted of Irene Murdoch in 1974 by Rockett is grim. Irene continued to live in poverty, compounded by the debts arising from the litigation, and she was permanently disabled by the abuse that left her with a partially paralysed jaw and a speech impediment. She was weary of the ongoing publicity, and according to friends, she had been "badly affected" by the media coverage, as had her estranged husband.[113] In fact, she reluctantly agreed to speak to Rockett, eventually accepting a call on a local payphone only once she knew that Alex had successfully survived a recent surgery. She feared more negative publicity would have a detrimental effect on his health. By that time Alex had filed for divorce, and she stated that she would not do any more public interviews until the divorce was finalized, which she believed would take from six months to a year. Irene Murdoch never gave another public interview.

Divorce Proceedings

Despite Irene's hope that she and Alex might one day reconcile, in November 1973, just weeks after the Supreme Court of Canada ruling, Alex filed for divorce based on three years of separation. Irene entered a counter-petition. The *Divorce Act* of 1968 introduced the concept of permanent marriage breakdown as a ground for divorce, while also retaining fault-based grounds, the most important of which were adultery and cruelty. Irene Murdoch alleged cruelty, with the assault supplying the main, but not only, factual basis for that allegation.[114]

About one year later, Alex transferred two quarter-sections of the Brockway property to his son for a nominal price. On the same date as those transfers, the son granted a lease of these properties back to the father for a term of fifteen years. A third quarter-section, the site of the matrimonial home and hence subject to the dower caveat, was not conveyed. Alex would later state that the purpose of the transfer was to begin the process of transferring the ranching operations to his son. Moreover, although the transfer occurred after the Supreme Court ruling, Alex also admitted that he remained concerned that his wife might ultimately get the land. He was aware of impending law reform that, he feared, might prevent him from transferring the land to his son.[115]

Alex's petition for divorce was heard on 10 October 1975, and a decree *nisi* was ordered. This decree awarded Irene $200 in monthly maintenance and adjourned her counter-petition. Alex then filed a decree *absolute* in his divorce petition in April 1976. The filing of the decree *absolute* dissolved the marriage.[116]

In that same month, Irene Murdoch brought an application seeking to set aside the transfers to their son and to have the titles to those lands restored to Alex Murdoch. She also sought a hearing on her adjourned counter-petition. If an order of support remained tenable under her counter-petition for divorce, the transfers could be struck down as fraudulent conveyances made for the purposes, as alluded to above, of reducing the amount of that support award. Irene Murdoch's counter-petition under the *Divorce Act* was again pursued.

At that hearing, Justice Bowen held that "under ordinary circumstances there is no doubt that a decree nisi can be granted both on a petition and a counter-petition but in the present instance in which the absolute has been entered on the petition, this cannot be done. I have therefore no power to deal with the wife's counter-petition as it pertains to an application for divorce."[117] The court still had jurisdiction to consider her claim for maintenance, however. It could also address the transfers to their son insofar as they were found to be fraudulent conveyances made for the purposes of reducing the amount of that support award.

This time Irene prevailed. Bowen J, unlike MacDonald J before him, was prepared to receive evidence of physical abuse. According to one account, Irene testified that "her health (was) poor, partly as a result of beatings administered by her husband." While she had already undergone one bone graft surgery on her broken jaw, she remained in need of another such surgery. Aside from her lasting jaw injuries, she had an arthritic condition resulting from a 1964 incident in which Alex dislocated her shoulder " . . . in a fit of temper over their son's bedtime."[118]

Bowen J acknowledged Irene Murdoch's suffering. Although he considered this evidence to be, at most, peripheral to the matter before him, the claims of cruelty received a considerable airing in this case. While Bowen J regarded both parties at fault in the marriage, he observed that Alex Murdoch's "actions after the altercation, in leaving his wife to fend for herself in the hospital and thereafter, certainly must offend one's sense of decent and acceptable behaviour."[119]

On the merits of the case, Bowen J held that that the decree absolute obtained by Alex Murdoch did not pre-empt Irene Murdoch's right to seek maintenance under her counter-petition. Moreover, it was held that the transfers to the son were void as an attempt to prejudice Irene's claim for spousal support. They were set aside.

After a detailed analysis of the value of the Murdoch lands, the Court concluded that their total value should be set at $127,000. That valuation, along with Alex's income, other assets, and a range of additional considerations, led Bowen J to conclude that Irene Murdoch should be awarded a lump-sum support payment of $65,000. One of the quarter-sections was to be charged as security for this obligation; in other words, if the money was not paid, that land could be sold. The order for monthly support of $200 was to be replaced by this new award. In the end, Irene Murdoch received a rare lump-sum award that was equal to about half of the value of the ranch properties.[120]

Legal Consequences

While Irene Murdoch was not successful in her property claim, her case — and the public's reaction to it — spurred matrimonial property law reform.

Mary Jane Mossman has argued that it was the outrageous unfairness of the majority Supreme Court of Canada decision that mobilized public — and then legislative — momentum to reform family law to better recognize equal partnership in marriage.[121] Newspaper editorials,[122] women's groups,[123] and federal and provincial law reform commissions[124] all decried the decision as antiquated and as failing to reflect the social reality of marriage in the 1970s in Canada.

Feminist and women's groups pushed publicly for legal reform to the matrimonial property regime, using Irene's case as the template. She became "viewed by women's organizations as a symbol of the inequities of Canadian property law." The Ontario Status of Women counsel held a special meeting with over fifty represented women's organizations to discuss the case, and to push for legislative reform. Feminist organizations were featured favourably in media coverage of the quest to change the law, and were able to meet and consult with legislators. Even before many provincial law reform commissions proposed changes, politicians of every stripe in Alberta and Ontario tabled resolutions asking the government to redraft the law.[125]

Curiously, the first legal reforms in the aftermath of the *Murdoch* case occurred in the Supreme Court of Canada, not the legislatures. Following *Murdoch*, a string of similar cases came before the Court. In the first of these, *Rathwell v Rathwell*,[126] a claim succeeded based on a resulting trust argument, but three of nine members of the Supreme Court accepted the view that a constructive trust over property could be tenable as a remedy for a claim based on unjust enrichment. In *Petkus v Becker* (1980),[127] a majority of the Court adopted that position. Laskin J's dissent in *Murdoch* had become the common law in Canada a mere seven years after the *Murdoch* case. Martland J continued to reject that analysis.

In the years since, the doctrine of unjust enrichment has flourished in a range of contexts, and has been refined. In 1993, the Supreme Court ruled that the doctrine of unjust enrichment was applicable not only when the efforts of a spouse were extraordinary (as they were in *Murdoch*), but also when conventional household work is undertaken.[128] Irene would very likely have received a substantial interest in the marital assets (probably a 50 percent entitlement) had her case been decided on the basis of the post-*Murdoch* case law. Although *Murdoch* has never been explicitly overruled, it is likely that the Supreme Court was affected by the adverse public reaction to its 1973 holding in that case.

During this same period, legislative reforms were enacted. Throughout the 1970s, all common law provinces brought in laws improving women's access to property upon dissolution of their marriages.[129] These reforms were a direct response to the *Murdoch* decision, and the subsequent public outcry. In fact the reforms surpassed even Laskin J's dissent,[130] and enabled women to presumptively receive an equal share of matrimonial property on the termination of marriage.[131]

Feminists remained critical of the reforms, claiming they did not go far enough. Laura Sabia, Chair of the Ontario Status of Women Counsel when Ontario was changing its legislation, called the final version of the new law "a small step in the right direction" and expressed displeasure that an automatic share of the matrimonial home was left out of the new law.[132] According to Lori Chambers, despite these and subsequent improvements to matrimonial property law regimes, most property law regimes in English Canada still explicitly exclude farms from presumptive division despite being inspired in part by *Murdoch*. As she states, "In essence, the farm wife in most provinces in English Canada still owes her labour to her husband on the farm as a labour of love and antiquated marital duty."[133]

Feminist Activism

While Irene's personal involvement in, and commitment to, the feminist movement[134] may have been ambivalent at best, there is little doubt that she and her story became key icons in Canada's 1970s women's movement. The palpable unfairness of the case itself, the physical abuse suffered at the hands of her husband, and her own self-effacing manner made her a feminist heroine that the broader public could support.[135] Irene's personal circumstances gave the feminist movement a public face for matrimonial law reform to which many average Canadians of both genders could relate.

The second-wave feminist movement emerged in English-speaking Canada in the 1960s. The movement was a response to the influx of women into the paid labour force, the peace movement, and the emergence of the women's liberation out of the civil rights movement. Three waves built on and influenced each other, creating a mass movement which would fundamentally challenge cultural definitions of masculinity and femininity by the 1970s.[136] The women's movement and women's groups gave women the tools to become aware of the structural nature of women's inequality.

The Royal Commission on the Status of Women (1967–70) was also instrumental in this regard. It is credited with bringing feminism to the mainstream Canadian consciousness, and an unprecedented public awareness of feminism, uniting individuals and women's organizations from every corner of the country.[137] Constance Backhouse noted that this garnered a great deal of media attention, movement, and 167 proposals for practical action. It brought to the forefront issues of reproductive rights, daycare, sex education, and gender-based wage gaps.[138] Women began to see themselves as part of their larger social context, and as linked in their oppression. They could relate to Irene Murdoch and her story; like Irene, women across Canada were challenging the unjust circumstances forces upon them.

Following the *Murdoch* decision, Shymka recalls seeing an increase in female lawyers: where once there had been few, it "crept up" and "leapt up." In Ontario for example, from Clara Brett Martin's admission in 1897 up to the 1970s, only 300 women had been called to the bar in the province. Upon graduation, many of them became the "only" woman practitioner in many communities outside Toronto.[139] This gender makeup changed precipitously from 1970 onwards, and by 1987 women comprised nearly half of law students in the province. The extent to which the feminist movement and decisions such as *Murdoch* incensed young women and motivated them to change the legal system from the inside is, of course, unknown. But the changes to the legal profession are indicative of changing notions of the role of women in the 1970s, and the movement of women from working inside the home to seeking admittance, and acceptance, into traditionally male workforces.

Irene was branded a "women's liberationist,"[140] and her case was compared in importance to the landmark Canadian "Person's Case."[141] Her name and her case became a rallying cry for women's groups interested in reforming matrimonial property.[142] The *Murdoch* decision and Irene's personal courage came to stand for systemic judicial unfairness against women.[143] The facts of the case even inspired a feminist performance piece entitled *The Balloon Lady* that was performed at women's conferences across Canada in the early 1970s, as a catalyst for legislative reform.[144]

Notes

1 Chris Dennett, "Ranch Wife: Court made me a slave" *Toronto Star* (18 October 1973) A1.

2 Special thanks to Mary Jane Mossman for generously sharing some of her primary research materials with us. Any mistakes or omissions in interpreting them are, of course, our own.

3 Interview of Ernest Shymka by Vanessa Gruben and Angela Cameron (29 October 2010) [Shymka Interview I].

4 [1975] 1 SCR 423 [*Murdoch* SCC].

5 Irene had red hair, and according to Ernest Shymka both her parents and Alex called her "Ginger." Interview of Ernest Shymka by Vanessa Gruben and Angela Cameron (5 November 2010) [Shymka Interview II Part I]. See also *Notice of Appeal Between Irene Florence Murdoch and James Alexander Murdoch* (21 March 1972), Ottawa, Supreme Court of Canada Archives (12624), at 122-23 [*Trial Transcript*].

6 See below for an exploration of Irene Murdoch's choice not to pursue a divorce in the first instance.

7 Irene ultimately did seek a divorce, but was at first reluctant to take so final a step in ending her marriage to Alex.

8 Barbara Heather et al, "Women's Gendered Identities and the Restructuring of Rural Alberta" (2005) 45 Sociologia Ruralis 86 at 89.

9 Lori Chambers, "Women's Labour, Relationship Breakdown and Ownership of the Family Farm" (2010) 25 CJLS 75 at 80. As Judge Rosalie Abella commented in her 1988 speech to the Canadian Club, "The family laws of property and support [had] created a systemic and generic dependency." Quoted in Sherrill MacLaren, *Invisible Power: The Women who Run Canada* (Toronto: Seal Books, 1991) at 258.

10 See Chambers, "Women's Labour," above note 9 at 76.

11 See, for example, *Thompson v Thompson*, [1961] SCR 3; *Klutz v Klutz*, [1968] SJ No. 146; *Rooney v Rooney*, [1969] SJ No. 73. For an exception, see the unusual Alberta case *Trueman v Trueman*, (1971) 18 DLR (3d) 109. The court found Mrs. Trueman's labour to be sufficiently extraordinary that she was granted the homestead — but not the farm into which her extraordinary labour was invested.

12 For an excellent summary of the feminist activism and subsequent property law reform resulting from *Murdoch v Murdoch*, see Mysty S. Clapton, "*Murdoch v. Murdoch*: The Organizing Narrative of Matrimonial Property Law Reform" (2008) 20 Can J Women & L 197 at 207.

13 *Ibid.*

14 See, for example, Clapton, "*Murdoch v. Murdoch*," above note 12, Mary Jane Mossman, *Families and the Law in Canada* (Toronto: Edmond Montgomery, 2004) [Mossman] and "Running Hard to Stand Still: The Paradox of Family law Reform" (1994) 17 Dalhousie Law Journal 5, Pamela Smith, "Murdoch's, Becker's and Sorochan's Challenge: Thinking Again about the Roles of Women in Primary Agriculture," in GS Basran & David Hay, eds, *The Political Economy of Agriculture in Western Canada* (Toronto: Garamond Press, 1988), Law Reform Commission of Canada, *Studies on Family Property Law* (Ottawa: Information Canada, 1975).

15 Two of the authors had the pleasure of interviewing Ernest Shymka by telephone twice in preparing this chapter. Despite insisting that " . . . the only caveat is that my recollection may not be what it was" (Shymka Interview I) the seventy-seven-year-old lawyer and businessman was eloquent, and displayed an uncanny recall of the events of over thirty years ago. Shymka spoke with animation and conviction about his role in the case, noting that it was ". . . a great honour and a privilege to have done it." (Interview I) He also expressed a profound sense of injustice regarding Irene Murdoch's personal circumstances.

16 *Trial Transcript,* above note 5 at 133. *Statement of Claim, 2nd action* (21 March 1972), Ottawa, Supreme Court of Canada Archives (12624) at para. 10(e) [Statement of Claim II].

17 See *Murdoch* SCC, above note 4 at 427.

18 Alex and Irene Murdoch kept account books, at least with respect to major transactions. These books were entered as exhibits at trial as evidence that Irene had contributed financially to the couple's properties through their marriage. With respect to more minor expenditures, however, little attention appears to have been paid to whose funds were being used for a given purchase, as is quite common in marriages.

19 Before the purchase of the Ward property, Irene and Alex rented the Sturrock property and bought the grazing rights to it. See *Murdoch* SCC, above note 4 at 427-28.

20 See *Murdoch* SCC, above note 4 at 427.

21 Irene did file a dower caveat against one of the quarter sections of the Brockway property (the North-East Quarter of Section 14, Township 19, Range 3, West of the 5th Meridian) in 1964.

22 Beginning in 1947 through to the time of their separation in 1968, Alex worked away from home during the day for approximately five months of the year. See *Trial Transcript* and *Murdoch* SCC, above notes 4 and 5 at 443. On Irene's work on the properties, see *Trial Transcript,* above note 5 at 136 and 146.

23 *Trial Transcript,* above note 5 at 139.

24 This was confirmed by Irene's mother, who testified that Irene was her father's "right hand man" on a property in Bragg Creek, which he co-owned with Alex Murdoch. Mr. Nash was not well and therefore Irene did most of the work: *Ibid* at 108-9.

25 Irene worked "in a trailer, a camper manufacturer's in Turner Valley and . . . in a restaurant." *Trial Transcript,* 133.

26 *Statement of Claim, 1st action* (21 March 1972), Ottawa, Supreme Court of Canada Archives (12624) at para. 7(a) [Statement of Claim I]. Notably this claim is separate and apart from the assault occurring on 14 October 1968 which resulted in Irene's broken jaw, described below.

27 *Trial Transcript,* above note 5 at 115.

28 *Ibid,* at 116.

29 *Ibid,* at 122.

30 Interview of Leslie Duncan, QC by David Mittelsadt (21 September 2006), Calgary Bench and Bar Oral History Program, Calgary, Legal Archives Society of Alberta (2008-019) [Duncan Interview] at 46.

31 Under Alberta law, a non-owning spouse, whether the husband or wife, holds various rights over the home, entitlements known as Dower. The *Dower Act* was enacted

in 1917 through the efforts of Emily Murphy J to protect married women's right to one-fourth of land held in their husband's name. It is an ancient doctrine that exists in modified form in Alberta to this day. Among other things, the province's dower legislation prohibits the disposition of the homestead by one spouse without written consent of the other, even when, as here, that other spouse has no title to the property. See *Dower Act*, RSA 2000, c. D-1. On the origins of the *Dower Act*, see Catherine Cavanaugh, "The limitations of the pioneering partnership: The Alberta campaign for Homestead Dower, 1909-25," (1993) 74:2 *Canadian Historical Review* at 198.

32 *Trial Transcript*, above note 5 at 115.

33 Shymka Interview I, above note 3.

34 *Trial Transcript*, above note 5 at 114.

35 *Trial Transcript*, above note 5 at 228. In a 1976 hearing, Alex offered another narrative of the events on that day. He alleged that Irene and her mother were pulling his hair at the dinner table. In an effort to free himself Irene was pushed away, fell against the refrigerator thereby breaking her jaw. *Murdoch v Murdoch* 1976 at para. 11. Alex had also offered another contradictory statement of the incident during the examinations for discovery.

36 During the cross-examination of witness Albert Nicoll Sandeman before the Supreme Court of Alberta, Shymka mentions that Mr. Sandeman also attended "police court" for a trial involving the assault, *Trial Transcript*, 193-94. Unfortunately, despite extensive searches, no materials on this action could be found.

37 The first lawsuit (Action No 94592) was for judicial separation together with ancillary relief and the second lawsuit (Action No 96500) was a claim for an ownership interest in the Brockway property.

38 Constance Backhouse, "The Contemporary Women's Movement in Canada and the United States: An introduction" in Constance Backhouse and David H. Flaherty, eds, *Challenging Times: the Women's Movement in Canada and the United States* (Montreal: McGill Queen's University Press, 1992), at 10.

39 YWCA Canada, *Effective Practices in Sheltering Women Leaving Violence in Intimate Relationships: Phase II Report* (2006), online: http://ywcacanada.ca/data/publications/00000013.pdf at 15.

40 Shymka Interview II, above note 5.

41 Later references to her inability to purchase dentures leads to the conclusion that it was her teeth, and not the wires, that were being removed. See note 53.

42 *Trial Transcript*, above note 5 at 151. It is unclear from the transcript whether Irene was referring to the removal of the wires or her teeth. We suspect she was referring to the removal of her teeth based on her earlier testimony (at 141) when she explained that she required dentures as a result of the injury to her jaw.

43 *Ibid*, at 152 and 126.

44 Including a "fridge, a washing machine, a sewing machine, bunk beds for our son, bedding, blankets, dishes, pots and pans." See *ibid*, 133 and 139.

45 Eve Rockett, "The Human Stories behind the Irene Murdoch/Helen Rathwell Cases" 1974 Chatelaine (September) 43 at 43 [Rockett].

46 *Trial Transcript*, above note 5 at 146. This is about $130 in 2012 dollars.

47 Shymka Interview II Part I, above note 5.
48 *Trial Transcript*, above note 5 at 141 and 147.
49 Interview of Ernest Shymka by Vanessa Gruben and Angela Cameron (5 November 2010) Personal Communication [Shymka Interview II Part II].
50 With the exception of *Trueman*, described in above note 11.
51 *Feldman v Feldman*, (1970) 14 DLR (3d) 222, *Krause v Krause* (1975) 64 DLR (3d) 352. The possibility of lump sum payments had only recently been added to the federal *Divorce Act*. It is now codified in s 15.2 of the act.
52 Shymka Interview II Part II, above note 49.
53 Statement of Claim I, Statement of Claim II, Shymka Interview I, above note 5.
54 See Duncan Interview, note 30 at 44.
55 Shymka Interview I, above note 5. McClung was grandson of Nellie McClung, who served on an Alberta government committee studying married women's property rights in the 1920s. See Cavanaugh, "Campaign for Homestead Dower," note 31 at 224.
56 It was rumoured that she was represented by as many as twelve different counsel over the years. See Duncan Interview, note 30 at 45.
57 He notes that Quicklaw was invented by his colleague Hugh Lawford who was from his hometown in Northern Alberta. "Two guys from corner gas Alberta have had a little bit of an impact on the law (chuckle) . . . we weren't from Montreal or Toronto . . ." Shymka Interview II, above note 5.
58 Shymka Interview I, above note 3.
59 Shymka Interview II, above note 5.
60 Shymka Interview I, above note 3.
61 Shymka Interview II, above note 5.
62 Shymka Interview I, above note 3.
63 Shymka Interview II Part II, above note 49.
64 Shymka Interview I, above note 3. An order for maintenance prior to judicial separation could be sought pursuant to the *Maintenance Order Act*, RSA 1955, c 188, while an order for maintenance after judicial separation, including a divorce, could be sought under the *Domestic Relations Act*, RSA 1955, c 89.
65 *Re Whiteley* (1974), 4 OR (2d) 393, 48 DLR (3d) 161 (CA). The beneficial interest is presumed to be proportionate to the financial contribution made to acquire the property. See, for example, Bruce Ziff et al. *A Property Law Reader: Cases, Questions, and Commentary*, 2nd ed. (Toronto: Thomson Carswell, 2008) at 446-47.
66 By contrast, where a husband has contributed financially to the property and registered title in the name of the wife, the court presumed that the husband intended to make a *gift* of the monies to the wife and did not intend to retain an interest in the property. This is referred to as a presumption of advancement. As with the presumption of resulting trust, it could be rebutted if it could be shown that the husband did not intend to make a gift, but rather intended to acquire an interest in the property for which the contribution was being made: *Pecore v Pecore*, [2007] 1 SCR 795 at paras 27-28; *Kerr v Baranow*, [2011] 1 SCR 269 at para 20. These rules have been altered in whole or in part in the coomon law jurisdictions in Canada: see Bruce Ziff, *Principles of Property Law*, 5th ed (Toronto: Thomson Carswell, 2010) at 230-32.

67 See further AH Oosterhoff et al, *Oosterhoff on Trusts: Texts, Commentary and Materials* (7th ed. 2009) at 642*ff*. Claims based on the "common intention" resulting trust continued to be advanced by unmarried couples in domestic property cases, but the Supreme Court of Canada has recently concluded that "there is no continuing role for the common intention resulting trust" in resolving property and financial disputes in domestic cases: *Kerr v Baranow*, above at para 15.

68 The wife worked in the fields, operated farm machinery and helped to build the house. She had also made a financial contribution to the fund realized from the sale of grain and livestock which was used to pay for the home at issue: *Murdoch* SCC, 434.

69 *Trial Transcript*, above note 5 at 103.

70 Shymka Interview I, above note 3.

71 Shymka Interview II, above note 5.

72 Louis Knafla and Robert Klumpenhouwer, *Lords and Ladies of the Western Bench: A Biographical History of the Supreme and District Courts of Alberta, 1876-1990* (Calgary: The Legal Archives Society of Alberta, 1997) at 90.

73 Shymka Interview I, above note 3.

74 Shymka Interview II Part I, above note 5.

75 *Trial Transcript*, above note 5 140-141.

76 *Murdoch v Murdoch*, above note 4 at para 6.

77 Shymka Interview I, above note 3.

78 Shymka Interview II, above note 5.

79 *Murdoch v Murdoch* (1971) 95 AR 119, 1971 CarswellAlta 142 (TD) at paras. 2-3, 12 (*Murdoch* ASC). With respect to whether Frederich suffered abuse, Irene testified at trial that although Alex did not physically abuse their son, he "speaks quite rough" to Frederich and agreed that he had an "explosive temper." *Trial Transcript*,153. As to the custody question, the trial judge concluded as follows: "I grant custody of the child to the defendant. I have discussed this matter of custody with the boy William. I questioned him and had him tell me a good deal about his school life and his daily life. I am satisfied that he is interested in the school where he is. This is where he has attended all his life, where he has his friends and his interests, other than for a short period of time, when he went to some other school. I think he went for a while in Edmonton, and I have had evidence given in this trial that he went in Nanton for a while. However, basically, the school he is attending is the school that he has attended. He is interested at the moment in pursuing his education, and also of, perhaps, seeking his occupation in the area of ranch and farm life. I did not question him in any way that I felt would embarrass him, or suggest the existence of any conflict, or misunderstanding between his father and mother, and he expressed no feeling in that respect to me. I will grant reasonable access to the plaintiff but, in light of the boy's age, I feel that this must be worked out between the plaintiff and the boy himself, in order that his normal responsibilities are not upset and that his own personal interests are given proper consideration."

80 *Ibid* at para 11.

81 Shymka Interview I, above note 3.

82 Shymka Interview II Part II, above note 49.

83 *Ibid.*

84 *Murdoch v. Murdoch* (1972) 95 AR 118, 1972 CarswellAlta 161 [(*Murdoch* ASCAD)], Clements JA concurred.

85 Shymka Interview I, above note 3.

86 *Murdoch* ASCAD, para. 8.

87 Shymka Interview II Part II, above note 49.

88 Shymka Interview II Part I, above note 5.

89 Shymka Interview I, above note 3.

90 *Murdoch* (ASC).

91 Shymka Interview II, parts I and II, above notes 5 and 49.

92 See Dennett, "Ranch Wife" above note 1 and Rockett, "Human Stories," above note 45. $200 in 1973 is equivalent to roughly $1,070 in 2012, $80 = $420, $60 = $320 and $2000 = $10,680.

93 Shymka Interview II, above note 5.

94 See RSC, 1970, c s-19 at s 36. See also James G. Snell and Frederick Vaughan, *The Supreme Court of Canada: History of the institution* (Toronto: University of Toronto Press, 1985), 238.

95 Lillian MacLennan, *The Do-Gooders: A History of the Calgary Local Council of Women, 1895-1975*, edited by Marjorie Barron Norris (Calgary: Detselig Enterprised Ltd., 2011), 117-18; 324-27. See also Carol Conway, "Calgary Council of Women. Test Case Helps Promote Cause," *Calgary Herald*, 30 April 1974, p. 6. See also the Calgary Local Council of Women fonds at the Glenbow Archives, Calgary, Series 7 (correspondence) M-5841-91 and Series 8 (financial records) M-5841-97.

96 See, for example, Geoffrey Cowper, "The Honourable Ronald Martland: reflections on a Canadian judicial conservative" (2000) 11 Sup Ct L Rev 547.

97 *Murdoch* SCC, 437. Peter Jacobson notes that it was open to the majority to find that the money was a payment which was intended to benefit both of spouses as Martland J had done in *Calder v Cleland* (1971) 16 DLR (3d) 369. Jacobson argues that this would have allowed the Court to more easily expand the resulting trust doctrine in favour of Mrs. Murdoch. See Peter M. Jacobson, "*Murdoch v. Murdoch*: Just about what the Ordinary Rancher's Wife Does," 20 *McGill Law Journal* (1974) 308 at 313.

98 [1971] AJ No 109 [*Trueman*]. In this case, the Court found that in addition to doing the usual work of a farm wife, Mrs. Trueman worked in the fields, operated farm machinery, and contributed to the fund which was used to pay for the property purchased under the husband's name. She also helped to build the farmhouse. Her work meant the couple had no need to hire outside help and, as her husband was frequently ill, Mrs. Trueman performed extra duties as required. The trial judge had held that Mrs. Trueman made "a very substantial contribution to the acquisition of this property." It was arguably determinative in that case that the husband expressed an intention to have the farm be a common venture with his wife.

99 *Murdoch* SCC, above note 4 at 436.

100 Quoted in Laskin's dissent, *ibid*, at 444.

101 Shymka Interview II, above note 5.

102 *Murdoch* SCC, above note 4 at 439.

103 *Ibid* at 454-55.

104 Laskin J cited *Garver v Garver* [(1959), 334 P 2d 408]; and *Engebretsen v Engebretsen* [(1942), 11 So. 2d 322 (Fla)] from the USA and *Pettitt v Pettitt* [[1970] AC 777]; *Gissing v Gissing* [[1971] AC 886]; and *Falconer v Falconer* [[1970] 3 All ER 449] from the UK.

105 Laskin J's dissent was welcomed because it rejected the proposition that non-domestic labour by a wife could not form the basis of a claim to property. Nevertheless, it is important to highlight that he clearly distinguished domestic labour performed by a wife, which would not be compensated. See Chambers, "Women's Labour," above note 9 at 83 and *Murdoch* SCC, above note 4 at 439.

106 Clapton, "*Murdoch v Murdoch*," above note 12 at 203.

107 Shymka Interview II, above note 5.

108 See, for example, Mrs. H. Humen, Letter to the Editor, *Toronto Star* (27 October 1973) B-3; Helen and Peter Coxe, Letter to the Editor, *Toronto Star* (27 October 1973) B-3; "The case of the rancher's wife," Editorial, *Toronto Star* (5 October 1973) B4; Anne W. Millyard, Letter to the Editor, *Toronto Star* (10 October 1973) B5; Alisa Schwartz, Letter to the Editor, *Toronto Star* (10 October 1973) B5; V.J. Gardiner, Letter to the Editor, *Toronto Star*, (15 October 1974) C5; "End sexual nepotism," Editorial, *The Globe and Mail*, (8 October 1973) 6; Robin Field, "A woman's work undone by court" *The Globe and Mail* (11 October 1973) W-1L; Mary Harris, Letter to the Editor, *The Globe and Mail*, (15 October 1973) 7; R. Sutherland, Letter to the Editor, *The Globe and Mail*, (19 October 1973) 6; Leslie Diane and Kaye Johnston, Letter to the Editor, *The Globe and Mail*, (24 October 1973) 7; Mrs. Jo Wilkins, Letter to the Editor, *The Globe and Mail*, (24 October 1973) 7; "Fund set up" *The Globe and Mail* (11 April 1974) 13 (Electronic: *Globe and Mail*); "Bales pledged bill to prevent a Murdoch case here, women say" *The Globe and Mail* (30 November 1973) 16 (Electronic: *The Globe and Mail*); Kathleen Rex, "Political clout beats placards, Mrs. Sabia tells women's group" *The Globe and Mail* (8 February 1974) 10 (Electronic: *The Globe and Mail*); and Rockett, "Human Stories," above note 45.

109 Robert Remington, "Revisiting the Court's Key Cases: *Murdoch* Decision" *National Post* (Calgary) 6 April 2000, B4 (Electronic: *Factiva*).

110 Dennett, "Ranch Wife," above note 1.

111 Mrs. Rathwell ultimately succeeded in her claim, arguably aided by the uproar following the *Murdoch* case. See above note 4.

112 Rockett, "Human Stories," above note 45; see also Dennett, "Ranch Wife," above note 1.

113 *Ibid.*

114 The move away from purely fault-based grounds for divorce was controversial, and the compromise whereby fault and no-fault grounds were combined was continued in the *Divorce Act*, 1985. See Kristen Douglas, "Divorce Law in Canada," (30 September 2008), online: Parliamentary Information and Research Service www2.parl.gc.ca/Content/LOP/ResearchPublications/963-e.htm.

115 *Murdoch v Murdoch* [1976] AJ No. 40, [1977] 1 WWR 16 at para. 18 (*Murdoch* II). Notably, this case proceeded with counsel Henry M. Beaumont, QC and not Ernest Shymka.

116 The decree nisi is the provisional decree granted by the court until satisfactory proof is given in support of the dissolution of the marriage.

117 *Murdoch* II, above note 5 at para 5.

118 Suzanne Zwarun, "Woman continues fight for share of ranch," *The Globe and Mail* 28 September 1976 (Electronic: *The Globe and Mail*) at 2.

119 *Murdoch* II, above note 115 at paras 14. Justice Bowen also commented that both parties were at fault in their unhappy marriage, stating "There is no doubt it was an unhappy marriage but the evidence adduced does not lead me to find fault on one party or the other. They were both at fault" (para 11).

120 Until 1970's *Feldman v Feldman* ((1970) 14 DLR (3d) 222) in 1970, only a handful of lump sum payments had been ordered across Canada. (See, for example, *Switzer v Switzer* (1969), 7 DLR (3d) 638, 70 WWR 161; *Kumpas v Kumpas* (1969), 71 WWR 317 [motion to quash granted [1970] SCR 438, 74 WWR 625]; *Straka v Straka*, [1970] AJ No. 145 (Alta SC) (a case on related issue where a lump sum had been ordered); *Jankov v Jankov*, [1970] NSJ No. 228 (NASC). Feldman resolved the legal controversy over the availability of lump sum payments. Various Courts had help that lump sum payments were not available; still others found that such payments were within their jurisdiction. The first Canadian lump sum payment was 1914's *Berlet v Berlet*, ((1914), 26 O.W.R. 817 (Ont SC). where the defendant husband's property was encumbered, and so a lump sum was granted in lieu of monthly maintenance. Other early cases such as *Cohen v Cohen*, ([1947] OJ No. 304 (Ont SC H Crt J). turned to British authorities (in particular *Mills v Mills* [1940] 2 All ER 254) for the holding that Courts had no jurisdiction to order a lump sum payment. As such, early lump sum awards were often awarded on consent. The earliest lump sum payment ordered on consent was *Maynard v Maynard*, [1949] OJ No. 499 (Ont CA); *Moshenko v Moshenko*, [1969] MJ No. 66 (Man QB); *Marsh v Marsh*, [1970] SJ No. 28 (Sask Crt QB). Lump sum payments became more common in the late 1960s, as the doctrine of lump sum payment availability was gradually widened. In *Kumpas v Kumpas*, ([1969] MJ No. 39 (Man CA), leave to appeal quashed because of delay [1970] SCR 438) the Court re-interpreted the *Divorce Act* and ordered a lump sum payment in addition to monthly maintenance. Such orders were traditionally prohibited, as Courts had held that periodic maintenance and lump sum payments were "either-or" propositions and they could not order both for the same plaintiff. After *Feldman* definitely declared the availability of lump sum payments, such payments increased in frequency. For instance in *Wener v Wener*, [1970] AJ No. 126 (Alta SC).

121 Mossman, *Families and the Law*, above note 14 at 372.

122 See, for example, Editorial, *Toronto Star* (29 December 1973), A15.

123 Clapton, "*Murdoch v Murdoch*," above note 12 at 201.

124 See, for example, Mossman, *Families and the Law*, above note 14 at 372; "Working paper says Murdoch case shows family law deficiencies" *The Globe and Mail* (27 May 1975) 13 (Electronic: *The Globe and Mail*); "Wives shortchanged by property law, federal report says" *The Globe and Mail* (18 March 1974) 1 (Electronic: *The Globe and Mail*); and "40-page report on women's rights tells what's been done, still to do." *The Globe and Mail*, (11 April 1974) 13.

125 Reg Vickers, "Seeking balance of sexes" *The Globe and Mail* (27 April 1974) 8 (Electronic: *The Globe and Mail*); see also Rex, "Political clout beats placards" and "Bales Pledged Bill."

126 [1978] 2 SCR 436, 1978 CarswellSask 36.

127 [1980] 2 SCR 834, 1980 CarswellOnt 299.

128 *Peter v Beblow*, [1993] 1 SCR 980, 1993 CarswellBC 44.

129 Mossman, *Families and the Law*, above note 14 at 372. For a full list of the reformed statutes by province see M. Elizabeth Atcheson et al, *Women and Legal Action: Precedents, Resources and Strategies for the Future* (Ottawa: Canadian Advisory Council on the Status of Women, 1984) at 28.

130 Laskin J's dissent, and its significance for the Court, for the former Chief Justice's career, and for family law reform generally, has been the subject of much academic commentary. See, for example, Philip Girard, *Bora Laskin: Bringing Law to Life* (Toronto: University of Toronto Press for the Osgoode Society for Canadian Legal History, 2005); John D. McCamus, "Chief Justice Dickson and the Law of Restitution" (1991) 20 Man LJ, 345; and Kent Roach & Robert Sharpe, *Brian Dickson: A Judge's Journey* (Toronto: University of Toronto Press for the Osgoode Society for Canadian Legal History, 2003).

131 See Robert Leckey, *Contextual Subjects: Family, State and Relational Theory* (Toronto: University of Toronto Press, 2008) at 70.

132 Peter Mosher, "Women given more rights but not a half share of house," *The Globe and Mail*, 13 May 1975, 17 (Electronic: *The Globe and Mail*).

133 Chambers, "Women's Labour," above note 9 at 75, 85.

134 For a more full description of the feminist, women's liberation and women's movements during this time see, for example, Judy Rebick, *Ten Thousand Roses: The making of a feminist revolution* (Toronto: Penguin Books, 2002); Marguertie Andersen, ed, *Feminist Journeys/Voices feminists* (Ottawa: Feminist History Society, 2010); and Clapton, "*Murdoch v Murdoch*," above note 12 at 204-08.

135 Clapton characterizes this as an "ideal narrative." See "*Murdoch v Murdoch*," above note 12 at 198.

136 See, for example, Sarah Evans, "The Women's Movement in the United States in the 1960s," in Constance Backhouse and David H. Flaherty, *Challenging Times: the Women's Movement in Canada and the United States* (Montreal: McGill Queen's University Press, 1992).

137 Backhouse, "Contemporary Women's Movement," above note 38 at 19.

138 *Ibid.*

139 Mary Jane Mossman, "Becoming Lawyers," above note 14 at 32.

140 Dennett, "Ranch Wife," above note 12.

141 See Doris Anderson, "Two court cases where women lost heavily," Editorial, *Chatelaine* (January 1974) 1; and Dennett, "Ranch Wife," above note 1.

142 See, for example, Rex, "Political clout beats placards," above note 108 and Mosher, above note 132.

143 Eleanor Wachtel, "The 10 Lousiest Legal Judgments of the Seventies" *Chatelaine*, March 1978 at 56.

144 See, for example, Rebick, *Ten Thousand Roses*, above note 134 at 25 and Clapton, "*Murdoch v Murdoch*," above note 12 at 218-19. More recently the Murdoch case has inspired a radio drama CKUA Radio Network and the Alberta Law Foundation, *Great Alberta Law Cases*, "The Sign: *Murdoch v Murdoch*" online: www.albertasource.ca/lawcases/civil/murdoch/murdoch_people_imurdoch.htm.

Morgan and Jacobson v Attorney General for Prince Edward Island

Margaret McCallum

In February 2010, a couple from Florida, Melvin and Sylvia Griffin, were ordered to pay fines of close to $40,000 for purchasing, through an intermediary, 188 acres (seventy-six hectares) of land on Prince Edward Island. As non-residents, the Griffins needed Cabinet approval to acquire more than five acres of land or more than 165 feet of shore frontage.[1] The *Lands Protection Act* (LPA), which the Griffins violated, had survived a Charter challenge in the Island courts in the 1980s.[2] In two earlier cases, almost a century apart, the Supreme Court of Canada had rejected landowners' challenges to Island legislation limiting the extent of individual land holdings. In the first of these, in 1877, the newly established Supreme Court upheld Island legislation compelling resident and non-resident owners of more than 500 acres to sell their estates to the government.[3]

In *Morgan and Jacobson v Attorney General for Prince Edward Island*, 1975, the Supreme Court again upheld the right of the provincial legislature to restrict the right of non-resident individuals to hold Island land.[4] This chapter tells the story of the *Morgan* case.

Historical Context

Absentee ownership was a major component of what nineteenth-century Islanders referred to as "the land question." After the Treaty of Paris (1763), when France transferred sovereignty over what became Prince Edward Island to Great Britain, the imperial government divided the Island into sixty-seven lots, or townships, of about 20,000 acres each, and allocated all but one of these in a single day to about 100 individuals. The grantees were required to assume the risks and benefits of populating their lots with immigrants, and many chose to rent lands to settlers, rather than granting freeholds. For the next century, Islanders tried various means to persuade proprietors to convert leasehold grants to freeholds. Restrictions on the rights of aliens to hold land were part of the received law in the British North American colonies, but these did not apply to proprietors who remained in the United Kingdom, as many did. In 1859, Prince Edward Island modified these restrictions, setting a 200-acre limit on alien land holdings. The campaign against the proprietorial system continued until 1875, when the Island, by then a Canadian province, enacted legislation to expropriate large private land holdings. Although by 1875 the proprietor with the largest holdings lived on the Island, those who opposed monopoly control of land often strengthened their arguments by invoking the image of absentee owners living off the labour of Islanders.[5]

That image continues to resonate with Islanders, and is invoked in contemporary policy debates over how Islanders should protect their land base. The Speech from the Throne at the opening of the Legislature in 1974, for example, referred to the "long, tempestuous and sometimes, passionate history connected with our land and our people's relationship to the land . . . the citizens of Prince Edward Island, individually and through their Government, are prepared to utilize the lessons of history and deal with the problems of land use and land ownership in a resolute and vigorous fashion."[6] For Island politicians, one lesson of this history was that voters, who would resist restrictions on what they considered to be their rights as landowners, would support different rules for non-residents. Richard Alan Morgan and Alan Max Jacobson, American citizens who lived in Rochester, New York, learned that lesson in 1972 when they attempted to purchase thirty-six acres (fourteen and a half hectares) of wooded land on an unpaved road in Prince County, about three miles from Cedar Dunes Provincial Park. Sol Mednick, the registered owner, had purchased the land the previous year from Eleanor MacWilliams.[7]

Non-Resident Land Ownership in the 1970s

Mednick and his partner, Marvin Taylor, owned Canadian Estate Land Corporation, which marketed vacant rural land in Canada as recreational lots.

Mednick and Taylor knew that the sale of thirty-six acres to Morgan and Jacobson violated the Island's restrictions on non-resident land ownership, enacted in 1972. Since 1939, the Island's *Real Property Act* had included the pre-Confederation limitation on alien land ownership, but with a proviso permitting aliens to apply to the Lieutenant-Governor in Council (Cabinet) for permission to acquire more than 200 acres. In 1964, that limit was reduced to ten acres of land and no more than five chains (330 feet) of shoreline, and in 1972, the restriction was amended so as to apply to non-residents of the Island, whether aliens or Canadian citizens.[8] Concerned that the Prince Edward Island approach would be adopted in other provinces, particularly in Nova Scotia, where Mednick and Taylor were working on a major recreational development, the partners brought a test case, using Morgan and Jacobson as the named plaintiffs, to challenge the province's constitutional power to restrict non-resident land ownership.[9]

The 1972 amendments were enacted by the Liberal government of Premier Alex B. Campbell, who had led the Liberal Party to victory in the Island election in 1966. Campbell focused on modernization and economic development, with funding and research assistance provided by the federal government under an agreement signed in 1969. During a federal presentation to the province on the Island's possibilities, Campbell was shocked and stunned by a map that showed considerable stretches of Island land, particularly along the shore, in the hands of non-residents. In response, he created a Special Committee of the Legislature to solicit public opinion.[10] The Committee Report recommended that the government regulate land acquisition and land use by foreign owners, to discourage speculation in land, and to ensure that "the use of agricultural land be left to bona fide resident farmers." The Committee noted with concern that if current trends continued unabated, the amount of Island land held by non-residents — 5 percent of all land and 10 percent of shoreline — would almost triple by the end of the century. Committee members, however, were unwilling to recommend restrictions on land ownership that would interfere with the right of private owners to sell to the highest bidder.[11] Campbell declared that his government supported rules to keep "the land resources of our province [from] once again falling into non-resident ownership and control," and described the amendments to the *Real Property Act* as a stopgap pending appointment of a Royal Commission to look at the issue more fully.[12] By year's end in 1972, Cabinet had rejected only thirty-eight of 213 applications for non-resident land purchases.[13]

In the early 1970s, Islanders were not the only Canadians concerned about foreign ownership of Canadian resources. Two books published in 1970, *Silent Surrender* and *Close the 49th Parallel Etc.*, warned Canadians that they were losing control of their land, resources, and economy.[14] In 1973, the federal government established the Foreign Investment Review Agency to prohibit takeovers of Canadian business enterprises by non-Canadians unless the takeover would significantly benefit Canada, and provincial governments considered various strategies to monitor and control non-resident land acquisition, particularly of recreational or agricultural land.[15] In 1969, Nova Scotia enacted legislation requiring non-resident land owners to report their land holdings to the government, and periodically thereafter considered whether to adopt more stringent measures. Late in 1972, the government of Gerald Regan considered, but did not enact, legislation to prohibit sales to non-residents unless the sale was approved by a land sales review board, with the province to have the right of first refusal on the sale of prime recreation land.[16] In 1971, Quebec Premier Robert Bourassa ordered an inquiry into foreign land acquisition after news broke that American investors were buying up large tracts of land in Abitibi, a region of lakes and rivers that was attractive to tourists.[17]

At the First Ministers' conference held in Halifax in August 1972, Campbell defended his government's restrictions on non-resident land ownership. Reminding his audience that the Island land base was less than 1.4 million acres, Campbell claimed that in the eighteen months prior to the new legislation, non-residents had been purchasing Island land at the rate of 700 acres per month. Saskatchewan Premier Allan Blakeney supported Prince Edward Island in insisting that provinces needed to control land purchases by non-residents if the purchases took land out of productive use.[18] The following year, the First Ministers' Conference created a Federal-Provincial Committee to consider the problem of alien and non-resident land ownership. The Committee Report, presented to the next First Ministers' Conference in August 1974, summarized the various approaches across the country, emphasizing that most provinces preferred to control land use and development, rather than regulate land ownership. Ontario, British Columbia, and the Northwest Territories and the Yukon, however, were reviewing policy options for limiting alien acquisition of recreational land, while Manitoba and Saskatchewan wanted to keep agricultural land in the hands of resident farmers. The Saskatchewan legislature had just rejected a proposal to prohibit the sale of agricultural land to non-residents, and instead enacted legislation setting land acquisition limits for non-agricultural corporations and non-residents that were much more generous than those in Prince Edward Island: non-residents could not hold property with an assessed value for municipal tax purposes of more than $15,000, excluding buildings, and corporations other than agricultural corporations required the permission of a newly established Saskatchewan Farm Ownership Board to hold more than 160 acres.[19]

The Royal Commission on Land Ownership and Land Use

The Royal Commission that Campbell had promised was appointed in August 1972 to consider the interest in non-Island markets in acquiring Island recreational properties, the effects of rising land prices on family farms, the preservation of prime coastal land for future public recreation, and the protection of the Island's environmental quality and heritage.[20] The government had declared that the Commissioners would be committed to preserving the Island way of life, but only two of the three commissioners were Islanders — James Wells, a retired businessman and lawyer, and Charles Jones, a farmer and then director of the PEI Federation of Agriculture. The dominant voice in the final report was that of the chair, Charles Raymond, a professional geographer with New Brunswick roots. As a federal civil servant in the late 1960s, Raymond had worked on plans for Prince Edward Island's economic development, and co-authored a federal report on the subject.[21] In a brief to the Commission, the Civil Liberties Association of Prince Edward Island supported government intervention to protect the environment from "unbridled selfishness," but only through controlling land use, not land ownership:

> The present practice with respect to restricting purchase by non-residents is discriminating, arbitrary and inefficient. It should be abolished at once . . . There is nothing to prevent the exercise of the control in an arbitrary manner. In addition, such a restriction is contrary to the very concept of Confederation, and inimical to the rights of landowners.[22]

The Law Society of Prince Edward Island was more circumspect in its brief, recognizing the need for regulation to ensure that farmers could lease agricultural land from owners who had taken it out of production, and supporting the limit of five chains on the amount of shore frontage that non-residents could purchase.[23]

The Commission Report, released in July 1973, predicted that, absent controls on land acquisition, half the Island would belong to non-residents

Map by Maritime Resource Management Service from the Report of the Royal Commission on Land Ownership and Land Use (Charlottetown, 1973), page 30. Black blocks are land held by non-residents.

by the year 2000; even with the existing restrictions, the figure would be one-quarter. A map included in the Commission Report showed pockets of non-resident ownership scattered across the Island. Responding to concerns of Island farmers about competing with well-capitalized agri-business, the Commission recommended that corporations and partnerships, whether foreign or domestic, be subject to the 200-acre limit that had applied to alien land holders from 1859 to 1964, with the right to apply to Cabinet for permission to exceed those limits. Otherwise, the Commission rejected restrictions on non-resident ownership generally, calling instead for regulation of land use, including minimum maintenance measures to compel owners to be good stewards of their land. A consultant's report for the Commission explaining this concept revealed the influence of Aldo Leopold.[24]

By the time the Commission reported, *Morgan* was working its way through the courts. Rather than implementing the Royal Commission's program to support and compel land stewardship, the Campbell government created a permanent Land Use Commission to advise Cabinet on land policies, which included a land identification system to restrict land to specific uses. The government also increased the restrictions on land acquisition, extending the 1972 limit of ten acres and five chains of shorefront to corporations. Further amendments in 1975 permitted land acquisition by non-residents through inheritance from spouses or parents resident on the Island.[25]

Morgan in the Island Supreme Court

IN DECEMBER 1972, Alan K. Scales, founder of the Charlottetown law firm of Scales, Macmillan, Ghiz, applied to the Island Supreme Court for a declaration that section 3 of the *Real Property Act* was *ultra vires* the province, and a writ of mandamus ordering Leo Blacquiere, the Registrar of Deeds for Prince County, to register the deed from Mednick to Morgan and Jacobson. Taylor and Mednick informed the Toronto media, and *The Globe and Mail* reported that real estate agents, "who have been enjoying booming business in recent years," approved of the "test case." The paper quoted Charlottetown realtor John Mackenzie who denounced government control of land sales as "dictatorial and a selling down the river of free enterprise."[26] The province was just beginning a year-long celebration of the centenary of Prince Edward Island's entry into Confederation, prompting some Islanders to reflect on whether the Island had benefitted from the relationship. An anti-celebration group called the Brothers and Sisters of Cornelius Howatt, named after one of the two members of the Island Assembly who had voted against Confederation in 1873, identified farm mechanization and consolidation, tourism, and sale of land to non-residents as serious threats to Island autonomy.[27]

In January 1973, Bell J granted a motion to reserve the Morgan and Jacobson application for consideration by the Supreme Court in Banco. Chief Justice Trainor and Bell J and Nicholson J heard the arguments in Charlottetown on 25 July 1973, interrupting the Court's customary "Long Vacation" in July and August.[28] Charles St. Clair Trainor, the chief justice since 1970, was born in Albany, Prince County, in 1901. A Liberal, he won a seat in the Legislative Assembly in 1935 but failed in his bid for re-election in 1939. Trainor then served as a Crown prosecutor until 1942, when he was appointed to the bench of the County Court. He was elevated to the Supreme Court in 1976. John Paton Nicholson, a Charlottetown practitioner, was appointed to the Supreme Court in 1970; like Trainor, he had been a Crown prosecutor. Richard Reginald Bell had been appointed to the Supreme Court in 1960, after serving as a Conservative MLA from 1947 to 1959. Bell described himself as a farmer; in the late 1940s he acquired Highland View Farms, where he raised Shorthorn cattle, Yorkshire hogs, and Cheviot sheep.[29]

Bernard Chernos, the 1957 gold medallist graduate from the University of Toronto Faculty of Law, represented the plaintiffs. An Ontario practitioner, and an unknown on the Island (a local paper identified him as Cernas), Chernos benefitted from recent regulatory changes to permit lawyers who were not members of the Law Society of Prince Edward Island to make occasional appearances in Island courts.[30] Both parties filed written arguments prior to the trial, but there was no agreed statement of fact beyond the pleadings, and neither party called witnesses. The written argument was thus the only evidentiary basis for the Court's ruling, and it contained no information about the extent of non-resident ownership of Island land.[31] Chernos began his oral argument by commenting that a few years earlier he had spent "a very pleasant month vacationing" with his family at Stanhope, which is on the edge of the sand dunes and beaches of the Prince Edward Island National Park. He may have regretted this attempt to establish a connection with the Island when he saw that Trainor CJ, in his reasons for the decision, linked the restrictions on non-resident land ownership to the creation of the national and provincial parks. Trainor CJ observed that the attention the parks brought to the Island's "beauty as a tourist resort" led to such an increase in non-resident landownership that Islanders became alarmed "as to the possibility of the Island once more falling under the control of absentee owners."[32]

The Statement of Fact and Law filed by Bertrand Plamondon, who represented the Attorney General, could have contributed to Chernos' perception that he was an outsider in an insular world. Plamondon asserted, without citing any authority, that "[T]he province is primarily an agricultural community and this community has an unchallenged right to impose restrictions on how the owner uses his property. Your Lordships are well aware of the amount of land owned by non-residents, which is not contributing to the economic development of the provincial community." Plamondon supported claims that the impugned legislation was concerned with the use of land by noting that the form for applying for permission to acquire land beyond the legislated limit "stresses the use that will be made of the lands." The legislature's intention could be inferred, too, "from what has been taking place in the province since the statute has been enacted," specifically, the Royal Commission on Land Ownership and Land Use, and a speech given by the Premier at the Federal-Provincial Conference of First Ministers held in May 1973. Neither reference was supported by quotations.[33]

Chernos' task might have been easier if his clients had been challenging the pre-1972 provisions which applied only to aliens. In his written and oral submission, he argued that the Island legislation was invalid because it infringed on the federal power over naturalization and aliens in section 91(25) of the *British North America Act*. Chernos also argued that the Island's restrictions on non-resident ownership conflicted with provisions of the *Can-*

adian Citizenship Act and of a treaty of 1899 granting aliens the same rights to acquire and hold land as enjoyed by Canadian citizens.[34] The Court asked: "Supposing [the legislation] had a preamble . . . which . . . stated a lot of the Island recreation land was being purchased by non-residents and allowed to fall into disuse and for that reason we are passing this law?" Chernos conceded that legislation providing that non-residents would lose their land if they did not keep it in good repair would be valid legislation, but he reiterated that the impugned legislation dealt with status, not land.[35]

The idea of the status of a citizen was central to Chernos' attempt to characterize the legislation as infringing on the federal legislative authority over citizenship. A province did not have the authority to legislate restrictions on the right to own land, Chernos argued, if the legislation created distinctions based on status, such as the distinction between slaves and free men or the distinction between those who were denied civil rights because of their religion and those who had the full rights of citizens. The Island legislation, Chernos asserted, dealt with "the status of Canadian citizens . . . you are making two classes of Canadian citizens with regard to the ownership of property . . . this sort of fundamental discrimination between Canadian citizens" violated "a basic trust of the federal system," and, so as a "basic national issue," came within the federal government's residual power to legislate with respect to "Peace, Order, and Good Government."[36]

The court responded by asking Chernos which level of government had the right to legislate with respect to "the status you are speaking of," but Chernos tried to avoid giving an answer. "You are putting the question to me the wrong way," he said.

The appropriate question, or at least the question that Chernos was willing to answer, was whether the province had the power to pass this legislation. To answer that question affirmatively, he said, the province would have to bring the legislation within a head of power enumerated in section 92 of the *British North America Act*. If the provisions dealt with property, they would be within section 92(13), Property and Civil Rights, but not if they dealt with status. Nor could the provisions be justified under the residual provincial power in section 92(16) — "Generally all Matters of a merely local or private Nature in the Province" — Chernos argued, as the legislation affected rights "throughout the Canadian community . . . [It affects] the status of Canadian residents outside the province and [their] status to own property within the province." Queried again as to what head of power gave the federal government the authority to legislate with respect to this status, so as to preclude the province from doing so, Chernos referred again to the residual power over "Peace, Order and Good Government" in the opening words of section 91.[37]

The Island Supreme Court released its decision upholding the legislation in November 1973. Chief Justice Trainor wrote for the Court. Although neither party to the action had presented evidence on the pattern of land holding in the Island, the judgment offered an accurate enough account of what the Chief Justice called "the Land Question," emphasizing the historical roots of Islander's antipathy to absentee owners. After reviewing the cases and legislation referred to by counsel, Trainor CJ observed that the plaintiffs had not found "any federal legislation attempting to determine what the rights of Canadian citizens are with respect to the holding of property. This is not surprising, because the power to determine what the rights of property are within a province has been assigned to the Provincial Legislature." Different provinces had different rules with respect to property rights, such as the age at which a person could make a valid will or enter into binding contracts with respect to land. The provisions of the federal *Citizenship Act* and the Treaty of 1899 could not be taken as doing more than conferring on aliens the right to be treated equally with Canadian citizens, that is, as having the rights with respect to property defined by provincial legislation. As federal legislation could not confer on aliens any greater rights than those enjoyed by Canadian citizens, including those who were not Island residents, the provincial legislation was validly enacted under the province's power to legislate with respect to property and civil rights.[38]

Appeal "To the Top"

Marvin Taylor was not surprised by the loss on the Island; Chernos had expected a "hometown decision" and had warned his clients that they would have to take their case "to the top."[39] The parcel of land at issue in *Morgan* was worth about $2,000, according to the plaintiffs, and as such was well below the $10,000 that would have given them an appeal to the Supreme Court as of right. The justices, perhaps welcoming the opportunity to rule on a question of considerable public interest, granted leave, and by April 1974, the Attorneys General of Canada and all of the provinces had been granted leave to intervene.[40] An editorial published by *The Globe and Mail* urged the intervenors to oppose Prince Edward Island's position "on behalf of Canada . . . Reasonable people would not deny that there is a need to start treating land as what it is — a limited resource which must be used for the benefit of all and not just for the pleasure or profit of a few . . . By trial and error we can find ways of handling the ownership of land so that it serves all of the people without causing undue injury to those who own it now . . . But whatever measures are adopted, they must be equal for all Canadians." Invoking the image of the many Canadians who left their home provinces to find work, the editorial asked: "Are they to be forbidden to keep a toehold in the particular piece of this country which most commands their hearts?"[41] Despite the editorial's exhortations to stand firm against the Balkanizing of the country, only Canada supported the position of the appellants in the *Morgan* appeal. Saskatchewan's new *Farm Ownership Act* would be vulnerable if the appeal succeeded, and none of the provinces wanted to cede any authority to the federal government.[42]

All nine judges of the Supreme Court sat on the appeal in *Morgan*, which occupied four days in February 1975.[43] Sharpe and Roach describe the Court in 1973 as an "aging and conservative institution . . . [that] embraced a follow-the-rules approach." Even with the appointments of Brian Dickson in March 1973 and of Louis-Philippe de Grandpré and Jean Beetz in January 1974, six of the justices had been born before World War I: three had been appointed in the late 1950s, and two in the 1960s. Bora Laskin's elevation to Chief Justice less than four years after his appointment had been widely criticized, and was a slight to Ronald Martland, the senior sitting judge. Both Martland and Roland Almon Ritchie — who had been appointed to the court a month after Martland — were regarded as "conservative black-letter" lawyers for whom "adherence to precedent was all important." Sharpe and Roach describe de Grandpré, too, as "very conservative . . . and frequently at odds with the more liberal and centralist views of Laskin." Sharpe and Roach say that he tended to favour provincial power. Louis-Philippe Pigeon, the third judge from Quebec, had been a legal advisor to Quebec Premier Jean Lesage. Wishart Flett Spence and Wilfred Judson, the two oldest justices, were both appointed to the Supreme Court after serving on Ontario's High Court of Justice.[44]

Argument in the Supreme Court

Bernard Chernos again represented the plaintiffs in the Supreme Court, assisted by Alan Scales and Richard N. Poole. Chernos, in his afternoon and morning at the podium, tried to convince the court that the principles of a federal union required that all of its citizens have the right to own land in any jurisdiction in the union. Chernos argued that legislation that discriminated against Canadians resident in other provinces "impair[ed] the nature of Canadian citizenship" and so was invalid legislation in relation to "the peace, order and good government of this federal union."[45] By emphasizing that the legislation discriminated on the basis of residence, Chernos was attempting to avoid the implications of several cases dealing with race-based restrictions on economic or political rights of naturalized or natural-born Canadians, relied on by the respondents and the provincial intervenors.[46]

In one of these cases from British Columbia, *Union Colliery v Bryden* (1899), the Privy Council struck down a provincial statute that prohibited the employment of boys under twelve, females, and "Chinamen" of any age in employment below ground in a coal mine. The Privy Council regarded the provisions respecting "Chinamen" as an invalid exercise of provincial legislative authority because, in their application to aliens or naturalized subjects, they trenched upon the exclusive authority of Parliament.[47] Yet in *Cunningham v Tomey Homma* (1903), the Privy Council upheld a British Columbia statute denying the vote to persons "of pure Indian blood," and to persons of the Chinese and Japanese races, regardless whether they were naturalized or natural-born British subjects.[48] In a subsequent decision, *R. v Quong Wing* (1914), the Supreme Court upheld a provincial statute, enacted in Saskatchewan in 1912, that prohibited the employment of white females in restaurants, laundries, or other businesses "owned, kept or managed by any Japanese, Chinaman or other Oriental person," declaring that the legislation was validly enacted under the provincial power over property and civil rights.[49] The apparent protection afforded to aliens and naturalized British subjects in *Union Colliery* was further constrained by the Privy Council decision in *Brooks-Bidlake* (1923), upholding a British Columbia statute providing that licences to cut timber on Crown land were subject to the condition that the licence holder not employ Chinese or Japanese labours.[50] It seemed, then, that the federal power over aliens and naturalized citizens could be invoked to enable employers in some resource sectors to hire the cheapest labour available, but not to ensure that racialized minorities could vote, obtain access to provincial Crown resources, or hire whom they chose.

What about restrictions on the right to own land? During the Second World War, Alberta enacted legislation that prohibited land transfers to "enemy aliens" or to Hutterites. As members of the Hutterian Brethren, a pacifist Christian community whose faith forbids individual ownership of property, Hutterites held their land communally. When the federal government disallowed the statute because of the reference to "enemy aliens," Alberta promptly enacted replacement legislation that applied only to Hutterites. [51] A new post-war statute, entitled the *Communal Property Act*, prohibited land transfers to "colonies," defined as including land held communally by Hutterites or Doukhobors.[52] In *Walter v the Attorney General of Alberta*, the Supreme Court upheld the legislation as a valid exercise of the provincial power to legislate with respect to property. Justice Martland, for the court, rejected the argument that the prohibition interfered with the Hutterites' religious freedom, on the ground that religion "must mean religion in the sense that it is generally understood in Canada." Thus, the court did not have to decide whether there was any conflict between the *Act* and a possible federal power at common law to protect fundamental liberties.[53] In the Island Supreme Court, Chernos had conceded that *Walter* was authority for the proposition that a province can enact valid legislation to control land ownership, but argued that provinces could do so only where there was no federal power to which the legislation related. Chief Justice Trainor, in rejecting that argument, relied in part on the decisions in *Tomey Homma* and *Quong Wing*.[54]

GW Ainslie, representing the Attorney General of Canada on the appeal to the Supreme Court, attempted to distinguish the restrictions on communal land ownership at issue in *Walter* from the impugned provisions of the *Real Property Act* on the basis that the former applied to all people who held land in Alberta, regardless of their residence. Like Chernos, Ainslie tried to characterize Prince Edward Island's restrictions on non-resident land ownership as limits on citizenship rights, not property rights. In his written submission, Ainslie asserted that an "essential attribute of citizenship is that all citizens of Canada residing without a province should have the same capacity as persons residing within a province without discrimination based solely and exclusively on the criteria that they are not resident within the province." Federally incorporated companies, Ainslie argued, were immune from provincial legislation restricting their capacity or status to hold or acquire land on the basis of their "federal domicile," and natural persons should not have lesser rights. Justice Martland, in draft reasons for decision, described Ainslie's argument as "probably [the] Appellants' strongest argument," even though, as Martland J had observed during the oral argument, Ainslie could not demonstrate that the right to hold land is an attribute of citizenship.[55]

The government of Prince Edward Island retained MH Fyfe, an Ottawa lawyer, to present the case for upholding the legislation. Among the provincial intervenors, Ontario and Saskatchewan filed the most comprehensive factums.[56] Ken Lysyk presented the argument for Saskatchewan. Lsysk had returned to Saskatchewan, his birth province, in 1972 as Deputy Attorney General after a dozen years as a law professor, first at the University of New Brunswick and then the University of Toronto. The year after *Morgan,* he became Dean of Law at the University of British Columbia, and in 1983, was appointed to the Supreme Court of British Columbia.[57] Ontario was represented by Morris Manning, a 1965 graduate of University of Toronto Faculty of Law who had been appointed as Ontario's Senior Crown Counsel, Civil Litigation and Constitutional Law, in 1973. Manning's subsequent career included being reprimanded by the Supreme Court of Canada for encouraging the jury to acquit Drs. Morgentaler, Scott, and Smoling of charges of conspiring to procure miscarriages, despite the law, and being found liable for defamation for his part in a press conference in which he announced that his client, the Church of Scientology, was bringing criminal contempt proceedings against a Crown Attorney.[58] Manning led in presenting the oral argument for the provincial intervenors, taking over two hours of court time. Lysyk took twenty-five minutes to present his argument, and the remaining provincial intervenors spoke about forty minutes in total.[59]

The *Walter* precedent was central to the argument of the respondents and the provincial intervenors, and they deployed it to limit the implications of Rand J's statement in *Winner v SMT (Eastern) Ltd.* (1951), relied on by Ainslie, that a province cannot prevent a person from entering it except temporarily because of some local situation such as a health risk.[60]As the provinces argued, one did not need the right to acquire land anywhere in Canada in order to move freely across provincial boundaries. In oral argument, according to the press reports, Manning went a step further, arguing that legislation stipulating that only Island residents could acquire more than ten acres of Island land was "in reality an invitation for other Canadians and aliens to take up residence in Prince Edward Island." Some in the courtroom laughed appreciatively when the Chief Justice said that he did not read the restrictions as a plan to develop the province.[61]

Manning in his factum argued that the rights of Canadian citizenship necessary to the effective working of democracy encompass freedom of speech, freedom to travel, freedom of religion, freedom of the press, and freedom to participate in the democratic process, but that the right to hold land is not an essential attribute of citizenship:

> The problem is to reconcile the federal power to legislate in relation to "Naturalization and Aliens" and in relation to "Peace, Order and Good Government" with preservation of the legitimate interests of the Provinces in the ordering of their domestic affairs. Each aspect of the matter is in its own way essential to the preservation of the federation. Since land ownership affects the everyday life of the majority of people obviously and directly, Provincial governments have a great political interest in being masters in their own house in this context.[62]

Victory for the Provinces

THE DECISION, RELEASED IN June 1975, upheld the Prince Edward Island legislation. Chief Justice Laskin, writing for the court, began with the points of agreement among the parties: provincial legislatures may regulate how land in the province may be held, and how it may be used, whether it is privately held or held by the Crown; the federal Parliament alone has the power to define citizenship and how it may be acquired and lost. These two principles, according to Laskin CJ, were not brought into conflict by the restriction on land acquisition in the *Real Property Act*, nor was it necessary to decide whether the right to acquire land anywhere in Canada was a right of citizenship, because the impugned provisions did not prevent anyone, citizen or alien, from acquiring land in Prince Edward Island, if they moved there. According to the Chief Justice: "Absentee ownership of land in a Province is a matter of legitimate provincial concern, and, in the case of Prince Edward Island, history adds force to this aspect of its authority over its territory." Referring to *Walter*, Laskin CJ noted that neither in that case nor in the one before him was the Court "concerned with the wisdom or utility of the provincial land policy but only with whether the Province has transgressed the limits of its legislative authority. I recognize, of course, that there may be cases where the line between wisdom and validity may be difficult to draw, but I find no such difficulty here."[63]

About one-third of the reasons for decision in *Morgan* dealt with the *Union Colliery* and *Tomey Homma* cases. During oral argument, Laskin CJ had observed that there was conflict between these cases,[64] and he reiterated that view in his decision. In *Tomey Homma*, the Privy Council had characterized the legislation at issue in *Union Colliery* as excluding Chinese from British Columbia by depriving them of the ability to earn a livelihood, and thus interfering with the federal power over aliens. Chief Justice Laskin commented caustically that "I would not myself have thought that the mere prohibition against employment of Chinese persons in underground mining could be taken to be a general prohibition against their earning a living in British Columbia and, however distasteful such legislation was, that it was beyond provincial competence." In any case, Prince Edward Island was not excluding aliens from acquiring residence in the Island or driving out those already there. If a province enacted regulatory legislation within its sphere of constitutional authority, the federal government could not, in the *Citizenship Act* or elsewhere, render aliens or citizens immune to that legislation "simply because it may affect one class more than another or may affect all of them alike by what may be thought to be undue stringency."[65]

Premier Alex Campbell, responding to the decision, emphasized that his government did not discourage outsiders from moving to the Island: "What we were, and are, concerned about is the rapidly developing problem of increasingly large acreages of farmland and Prince Edward Island prime shore frontage ending up in the hands of those people with little or no interest in the ongoing community life or economic future of this province." He thanked the other provinces for their support in the litigation, noting that the arguments presented by Ontario and British Columbia "were most helpful," and called for further discussions of the matter at a First Ministers' meeting.[66]

Taylor, who attended the Supreme Court hearing, was disappointed that Chernos had not persuaded even one justice to write a dissenting opinion, but relieved that the decision did not produce a flood of provincial legislation to keep out foreigners.[67] The report on foreign ownership of land presented to the First Ministers Conference in August 1974 had suggested, among other possibilities, some delegation of administrative authority from the federal government to the provinces to regulate the terms on which aliens could acquire land, provided the regulations did not discriminate between people resident in the province and those resident elsewhere in Canada. These recommendations were incorporated in the new *Citizenship Act*, passed in March 1976 but the Island did not change its legislation.[68] Mednick and Taylor divided the thirty-six acres they had been unable to transfer to Morgan and Jacobson into four separate parcels, each small enough that a non-resident could acquire them without permission. By 1981, all were sold, all to non-residents. The lots, still owned by non-residents, remained undeveloped thirty years later.[69]

Restricting Non-Resident Ownership in Prince Edward Island after *Morgan*

At the time of the *Morgan* decision, non-residents owned over 100,000 acres of land on Prince Edward Island, about 8 percent of the total Island land base.[70] After the Conservative election victory in 1979, the new government, led by Angus McLean and then James Lee, held extensive public consultations before enacting new restrictions on land acquisition in the *Lands Protection Act*. The new Act limited all individuals, resident or non-resident, to land holdings of 1,000 acres; corporations were limited to 3,000 acres. Non-residents and corporations in addition had to apply for permission to hold more than ten acres of land and five chains of shore frontage, unless they were farm corporations controlled by bona fide Island farmers.[71]

With adoption of the Canadian *Charter of Rights and Freedoms* in 1982, the legislation faced a constitutional challenge, prompted by Cavendish Farms' plans to expand its land holdings on Prince Edward Island. Cavendish Farms was part of the vertically integrated business empire founded by New Brunswick–born KC Irving. Between 1980 and 1984, it quadrupled the value of its exports of French fries, mostly to the USA, and quickly became a major employer and purchaser of farm products on the Island.[72] The government's public consultation leading to enactment of the LPA had been motivated in part by a Cavendish Farms decision to purchase additional land. Gordon Lank, chair of the Legislature's Standing Committee on Agriculture, tersely summarized the popular view as "Don't let Cavendish Farms do what they want to do," and Premier James Lee responded, "We won't let the Irvings or Cavendish Farms take control of our lands."[73] In 1984, when Cavendish Farms applied for permission to buy more land, Cabinet denied the application, and required the company to divest itself of 1,400 acres it held over the 3,000 acre limit. Instead, Cavendish Farms challenged the government's interpretation of the LPA, arguing that land that it leased to others should not be included in calculating its aggregate holders.[74]

The government asked the Island Supreme Court for a ruling. Justice McQuaid, writing for the court, noted that the LPA was intended to prevent the creation of land monopolies: "The memories of the troubles occasioned by the system of absentee landlords prevalent in pre-Confederation days dies hard." Despite this nod to the historical and cultural context of the legislation, McQuaid J upheld Cavendish Farms' interpretation of the Act.[75] The Court, however, rejected the argument that the Act violated section 7 of the

No! No! Don't Sell PEI

[Words by Reverend Andrew P. Macdonald; music from a Latin American protest song,"No Basta Rezar" (Praying is not Enough), transcribed from a compilation created by Marie Burge (2009) to celebrate the 50th anniversary of Father Andrew's ordination. Father Andrew is an Island-born social activist and a founder of the Cooper Institute, an education and community development centre named for radical nineteenth-century Island land reformer, William Cooper. The words and music, published in the 2nd issue of the *Cooper Review* (1987), were dedicated to the National Farmers Union "in their struggle against Vertical Integration."]

Chorus: No, no, don't sell PEI.
It's our homeland; it's our heritage and we want to make it free.
No, no, don't sell PEI!
It's a gift from the Almighty, made for sharing equally.

When the Micmacs walked our Island, back in those days of yore,
They loved and they respected every hill and field and shore.
They preserved it for this day of ours, for their children and for us;
The land was only to be used and handed on "in trust."

Chorus

When Acadians came and lived here, they tilled and cropped the soil.
It gave food and clothing, shelter, and rewarded all their toil.
But the British came and drove them out and sent them far away.
Ils sont exilés de l'Île Saint-Jean, bannis de ses foyers.

Chorus

When the British lotteried PEI to landlords far from here,
Tenant farmers raged against their plight for full one hundred years.
It was only a determined fight that got the Island back.
Shall we return to serfdom now or halt the invading pack?

Chorus

Just think! When the King of Glory comes on that dire and fateful day:
He'd be told the Island's Irving-owned — and if he wants it, he must pay!
But the earth would be so mined out that it's just a pile of sand,
And the Lord himself couldn't grow a thing if he *could* buy back the land!

Chorus

So, let the legislators make the laws to stop this present threat
Of corporate speculators, buying all the land they get.
Let the Premier and his Ministers not have to take the rap,
For allowing themselves to fall into a multinational trap!

Chorus

Charter of Rights and Freedoms, which protected the right to life, liberty, and security of the person. Justice Mitchell, writing on this issue only, considered that section 7 encompassed a limited right to acquire enough property to provide for basic needs of physical survival, such as food and shelter. The LPA restrictions did not infringe this right.[76]

The Supreme Court released its ruling on the *Reference* in July 1987. The new Liberal government led by Joe Ghiz — whose election victory the previous year had ended seven years of Conservative government — did not immediately introduce legislation to include land leased to others in calculating aggregate land holdings.[77] Instead, following the strategy employed successfully by Premier Campbell in 1972, the government appointed a Royal Commission on Land Ownership, Land Use, and the Landscape, and enacted legislation to halve the limits of ten acres and 330 feet of shore frontage for non-resident and non-farm corporate owners. After public hearings and research into land legislation in other jurisdictions, the Commission concluded that Cabinet rejected so few applications for permission to exceed the specified acquisition limits that the legislation was "a virtual open-door policy to non-resident land ownership."[78]

As in the early 1980s, concern about land ownership was a response to an Irving move to acquire more land. In April 1990, the public learned that Island resident Mary Jean Irving, granddaughter of KC Irving, and her husband, Stewart Dockendorff, owners of Indian River Farms, had recently spent $10 million to buy 4,000 acres of Island agricultural land. Farmers marched to Premier Joe Ghiz's office to protest. A marcher's sign summarized people's fears in three words: "Prince Irving Island." The government immediately enacted amendments to the LPA providing that farm corporations, like other corporations, would require the government's permission to acquire more than five acres or 165 feet of shore frontage. In his capacity as Minister of Justice, Ghiz demanded that Indian River Farms and its owners disclose their land holdings, and divest themselves of any excess holdings. Six months later, Mary Jean Irving acquiesced, complaining that any "legal proceedings against me would be used to explore other private aspects of the Irving family's business interests."[79]

Since 1992, applications under the LPA are reviewed by the Island Regulatory and Appeals Commission (IRAC), which forwards a recommendation to Cabinet.[80] From 2000 to 2009, IRAC handled an average of 110 applications per year for permission to exceed the statutory limits on non-resident land holdings, and recommended approval of most of these; on the few applications that IRAC denied, Cabinet often granted permission anyway. Permission, though, is generally subject to restrictions on subdividing or developing the land. As of 2010, IRAC had ordered fines for violation of the Act in only four cases. Two, in 2003 and 2008, involved Island residents, including a cluster of Irving companies, for failing to file the necessary land ownership disclosure statements and for holding more land than permitted under the Act.[81] The others were the Griffins and a would-be Islander from British Columbia, who, like the Griffins, acquired land without the permission of Cabinet by acting through an Island title-holder.[82]

In his argument in the Island Supreme Court defending restrictions on land ownership, Bertrand Plamondon suggested that the focus of the legislation was land use, not land ownership. However, in its 1990 Report, the Land Commission appointed by Premier Ghiz noted the lack of support for the 1973 Land Commission's call for land use regulations that would restrict owners' use rights. The later Commission did little better with its recommendations for measures to limit the proliferation of unplanned subdivisions and to promote agricultural practices that would curb soil degradation and erosion.[83] In 1995, during another round of debate on the LPA, an Island paper published an editorial cartoon portraying Alan Buchanan, the Cabinet minister responsible for the legislation, as focusing on the wrong threat. While he kept watch out the window, a villain labelled "soil erosion" was stealing the Island away. In December 2009, yet another government commission confirmed the public's continuing support for the LPA, and noted the failure of governments to adopt a comprehensive land use plan for the Island.[84]

The current provisions of the *LPA* were developed in response to recurring perceived threats to what politicians and their constituents describe as Island values or the Island way of life. The idea that Islanders had struggled to wrest control over their land from absentee landlords is central to popular constructions of Island history, and judges in the Island Supreme Court and the Supreme Court of Canada invoked this idea in upholding legislation that set limits on how much land people and corporations could hold. The idea appears, too, in a preamble added to the LPA identifying the "singular challenges with regard to property rights" facing the Island because of "historical difficulties with absentee land owners, and the consequent problems faced by the inhabitants of Prince Edward Island in governing their own affairs, both public and private," as well as the province's small size and high population density, and the fragility of its ecology, environment, and lands,

Provincial Affairs Minister Alan Buchanan introduces amendments to the *Prince Edward Island Lands Protection Act*. Charlottetown *Guardian*, 18 April 1995. Used with permission by Dean Johnstone.

which necessitated "the exercise of prudent, balanced and steadfast stewardship" to protect the Island's "ecology, environment, and lands."[85]

In Manitoba and Saskatchewan, legislation setting limits on agricultural land holdings is justified as necessary to ensure that resident agriculturalists have access to agricultural land.[86] The LPA is expected to achieve that goal, too, but, as a government official commented in 1987, "there has never been a consensus within our society on the purpose of the Act and how it should operate . . . The public interest that the Act is presumably designed to protect has never been adequately defined."[87] Nonetheless, the focus and justification of the Act reflect Islanders' perception of their history. That perception creates the possibility for government to enact what might be seen as extraordinary constraints on the rights of property owners, directed primarily at owners who can be characterized as "other" — non-residents or entities that want too much land, a limit that is currently defined as 1,000 acres for an individual and 3,000 acres for a corporation.[88]

Throughout the Island's history as a British colony and then as a Canadian province, some Islanders looked to government to ensure that land was broadly distributed among those who would use it to make a livelihood, while other Islanders expected government to protect the freedom of private property owners to amass large estates and do with them what they wanted.

For nineteenth-century proprietors, that included the right to hold land for speculative gains, or lease land rather than sell it; more recently, some Island landowners want the right to sell to the highest bidder, regardless whether that bidder is a corporation or an alien. Given Islanders' fears of foreign, corporate, or monopoly control of their limited land base, these disparate expectations are reconciled with rules that severely restrict land acquisition by non-residents and corporations, but allow ample exceptions.

Notes

1 Prince Edward Island, Island Regulatory and Appeals Commission, *In the Matter of alleged violations of the Prince Edward Island Lands Protection Act by Melvin C. Griffin and Sylvia J. Griffin*, Order TLF10-001, 18 Feb 2010; "American fined for buying P.E.I. land" *CBC News: Canada* (13 November 2009), online: CBC News www.cbc.ca/canada/prince-edward-island/story/2009/11/13/pei-american-land-fine-584.html; "Americans fined $37,800 over P.E.I. land buy" *CBC News: Canada* CBC (24 February 2010), online: CBC News www.cbc.ca/canada/prince-edward-island/story/2010/02/24/pei-americans-land-fine-584.html.

2 *Reference Re Lands Protection Act* (1987), 40 DLR (4th) 1, (PEI SC).

3 *Kelly v Sulivan* (1877), 1 SCR 3; Rusty Bittermann and Margaret McCallum, "Upholding the Land Legislation of a 'Communistic and Socialistic Assembly': The Benefits of Confederation for Prince Edward Island" (2006) 87(1) *Canadian Historical Review* 1; Rusty Bittermann, "Lady Landlords and the Final Defence of Landlordism on Prince Edward Island: The Case of Charlotte Sulivan" (2005) 38 *Histoire Sociale/Social History* 203.

4 *Morgan and Jacobson v Prince Edward Island (A.G.)*, [1976] 2 SCR 349 [*Morgan* (SCC)].

5 Ivan L Head, "The Stranger in Our Midst: A Sketch of the Legal Status of the Alien in Canada" (1964) 2 *Canadian Yearbook of International Law* 107 at 109-11; John Spencer, "The Alien Landowner in Canada" (1973) 51 *Canadian Bar Review* 389 at 391, 393; SPEI 1859 (22 Vict), c 4; Margaret McCallum, "The Sacred Rights of Property: Title, Entitlement and the Land Question in Nineteenth-Century Prince Edward Island" in J Phillips and B Baker, eds, *Essays in the History of Canadian Law: Vol. VIII — In Honour of R.C.B. Risk* (Toronto: University of Toronto Press for the Osgoode Society, 1999) 358.

6 Speech from the Throne, 5th Session of 52nd General Assembly, PEI, 7 March 1974.

7 Prince County Registry Records, Deed, Eleanor MacWilliams to Sol Mednick, 144/252, signed 6 May 1971, registered 28 June 1971.

8 Spencer, above note 5 at 395-96; *Real Property Act*, SPEI 1939, c 44; *Real Property Act*, SPEI 1964, c 27; *Real Property Act*, RSPEI 1951, c 138, s 3, as enacted by SPEI 1972, c 40, s 1. The text of s 3 read as follows:

> 3. (1) Persons who are not Canadian citizens may take, acquire, hold, convey, transmit, or otherwise dispose of, real property in the Province of Prince Edward Island subject to the provisions of sub-section two (2) here next following.
>
> (2) Unless he receives permission so to do from the Lieutenant-Governor-in-Council, no person who is not a resident of the Province of Prince Edward Island shall take, acquire, hold or in any other manner receive, either himself, or through a trustee, corporation, or any such the like, title to any real property in the Province of Prince Edward Island the aggregate total of which exceeds ten (10) acres, nor to any real property in the Province of Prince Edward Island the aggregate total of which has a shore frontage in excess of five (5) chains.

(3) The grant of any such permission shall be at the discretion of the Lieutenant-Governor-in-Council, who shall notify the applicant in writing by means of a certified copy of an Order-in-Council of his decision within a reasonable time.

(4) An application for any such permission shall be in the form prescribed, from time to time, by the Lieutenant-Governor-in-Council.

(5)(a) For the purposes of this section, "Canadian citizen" means persons defined as Canadian citizens by the Canadian Citizenship Act (R.S.C. 1970, Vol. 1, Cap. C-19).

(b) For the purposes of this section "resident of the Province of Prince Edward Island" means a bona fide resident, animus et factum of the Province of Prince Edward Island.

(c) For the purpose of this section "corporation" means any company, corporation or other body corporate and politic, and any association, syndicate or other body, and any such the like, and the heirs, executors, administrators and curators, or other legal representatives of such person, as such is defined and included by The Domiciled Companies Act (Laws of Prince Edward Island 1962).

9 *Statement of Claim*, Prince Edward Island, Prince Edward Island Public Archives and Records Office (Supreme Court Records, File A-12750); Jack McAndrew, "Attempts to curb land sales to outsiders face another hurdle," *The Globe and Mail* (16 December 1972) 8; personal communications with Sol Mednick and Marvin Taylor, Jan. and Feb. 2010.

10 Wayne MacKinnon, *Between Two Cultures: The Alex Campbell Years* (Stratford, PEI: Tea Hill Press, 2005) at 17, 97, 171-3; Edward MacDonald, *If You're Stronghearted: Prince Edward Island in the Twentieth Century* (Charlottetown: Prince Edward Island Museum and Heritage Foundation, 2000) at 297-99; the map was one of many prepared as part of the Canada Land Inventory, a project of the federal Department of Regional and Economic Expansion and Environment and subsequently Environment Canada, to assess and map land capabilities for agriculture, forestry, recreation, and wildlife. Much of the data is now available on the public internet site GeoGratis, online: http://geogratis.cgdi.gc.ca/CLI/index_agriculture.html.

11 Prince Edward Island, Legislative Assembly, "Report of the Committee on Land Acquisition and Land Transfer to Non-Resident Corporations and Private Individuals, March 1971" in *Journal of the Legislative Assembly of Prince Edward Island*, (1971) at Appendix F, 88-94.

12 "Prudent Land Use is Goal of Commission," *[Charlottetown] Guardian* (1 April 1972) 1.

13 MacDonald, above note 10 at 308.

14 Kari Levitt, *Silent Surrender: The Multinational Corporation in Canada* (Toronto: Macmillan, 1970); Ian Lumsden, ed, *Close the 49th Parallel Etc: The Americanization of Canada* (Toronto: University of Toronto Press, 1970).

15 Stuart McFayden, "The Control of Foreign Ownership of Canadian Real Estate" (1976) 11 Canadian Public Policy 65 at 69.

16 "N.S. to tax non-residents for land buys," *The Globe and Mail* (30 December 1972) 2; Nick Fillmore, "Conflict over control of land sale" *The Globe and Mail* (13 January 1973) 8.

17 Maurice Cutler, "Are we Alienating Too Much Recreational Land and Too Much of Our Best Agricultural Land?" (1975) 90 *Canadian Geographical Journal* 18 at 29.

18 Lyndon Watkins, "Provinces will not tolerate encroachment on their rights in urban affairs, Ottawa warned" *The Globe and Mail* (4 August 1972) 3.

19 Federal-Provincial Committee on Foreign Ownership of Land, *Report to the First Ministers* (Ottawa: Information Canada, 1975); *The Saskatchewan Farm Ownership Act*, SS 1974, c 98, ss 7 & 11; Douglas Brunton, "The Land of the Dispossessed" (1979) 23 Harrowsmith 24.

20 Prince Edward Island, Royal Commission on Land Ownership and Land Use, *Report of the Royal Commission on Land Ownership and Land Use*, (Charlottetown: Royal Commission on Land Ownership and Land Use, 1973) at 3.

21 "Prudent Land Use is Goal of Commission", *[Charlottetown] Guardian* (1 April 1972) 1; "Royal Commission Members Appointed", *[Charlottetown] Guardian* (15 August 1972) 3. See CW Raymond, JB McClellan, & JA Rayburn, *Memoir #9, Land Utilization in Prince Edward Island, Geographical Branch, Mines and Technical Surveys* (Ottawa: Queen's Printer, 1963).

22 Prince Edward Island Public Archives and Records Office, RG 24.3, Brief to the Royal Commission on Land Ownership and Land Use Presented by the Civil Liberties Association of PEI 11 December 1972.

23 *Brief of the Law Society of Prince Edward Island to the Royal Commission on Land Ownership and Land Use*, Prince Edward Island, Prince Edward Island Public Archives and Records Office, (RG 24.3).

24 *Report of the Royal Commission*, above note 20 at 5-6, 15, 31, 41-2, 67-70; Mary Rawson, "Minimum Maintenance: A Report for the Royal Commission on Land Ownership and Land Use, Prince Edward Island, April 1973" at 2.2-2.3, quoting from Aldo Leopold, *A Sand County Almanac* (New York: Oxford University Press, 1949).

25 *An Act to Establish the Land Use Commission*, SPEI 1974, c 22; *An Act to Amend the Real Property Act*, SPEI 1974, c 84; *An Act to Amend the Real Property Act*, SPEI 1975, c 80.

26 *Writ of Summons*, Prince Edward Island, Prince Edward Island Public Archives and Records Office (Supreme Court Records, File A-12750); Scales' firm is now part of the large Atlantic Canadian firm, Stewart, McKelvey; Jack McAndrew, "Attempts to curb land sales to outsiders face another hurdle," *The Globe and Mail* (16 Dec 1972) 8.

27 Lyndon Watkins, "How PEI became 'Ottawa's ward,'" *The Globe and Mail* (30 Dec 1972) 1; MacDonald, above note 10 at 318.

28 *Transcript*, Prince Edward Island, Prince Edward Island Public Archives and Records Office (Supreme Court Records, File A-12750); RA MacKimmie, *The MacKimmie Report* (Charlottetown: Queen's Printer, 1973) at 11-13.

29 Blair Weeks, *Minding the House: A Biographical Guide to PEI MLAs* (Charlottetown: Acorn Press, 2002) at 195-6, 11-12; "Judge C. St. Clair Trainor Named Chief Justice of Supreme Court" *[Charlottetown] Guardian* (11 July 1970) 1; "John Nicholson Named Supreme Court Judge" *[Charlottetown] Guardian* (11 Nov 1970) 1.

30 "Bernard Chernos Graduate Scholarship" *[University of Toronto] Nexus* (Spring 2002) online: www.law.utoronto.ca/visitors_content.asp?itemPath=5/7/3/1/0&contentId=1063; "Concerted Attack Brought Against Island's Real Property Act," *[Charlottetown] Guardian* (26 July 1973) 2.

31 *Transcript*, above note 28 at 1.

32 *Transcript*, above note 28 at 1, 2; *Morgan and Jacobson v Attorney General for Prince Edward Island* (1973), 5 Nfld & PEIR 129 at 134 (S.C.) [*Morgan* (PEI SC)]; on the development of the Park in the late 1930s, see Alan MacEachern, *Natural Selections: National Parks in Atlantic Canada, 1935-1970* (Montreal: McGill-Queen's University Press, 2001) at 73-97.

33 *Statement of Fact and Law Submitted on Behalf of the Defendants* (24 July 1973), Prince Edward Island, Prince Edward Island Public Archives and Records Office (Supreme Court Records, File A-12750).

34 Specifically, *The Canadian Citizenship Act*, RSC 1970, c 19, s 24 and Articles I and V of *The Real and Personal Property Convention 1899 between Her Majesty and the United States of America relative to the Disposal of Real and Personal Property*, United States and United Kingdom, 2 March 1899, (made applicable to Canada by Convention of 21st October, 1921).

35 *Transcript*, above note 28 at 3, 17, 25-26, and 30.

36 *Transcript*, above note 28 at 27-28 and 4.

37 *Transcript*, above note 28 at 28-29.

38 "Court Upholds Law on Land Ownership," *[Charlottetown] Guardian* (20 November 1973) 1; *Morgan*, above note 32 at 133-34, quotation at 140.

39 Conversation with Marvin Taylor, 7 February 2010.

40 *Notice of Appeal and Appeal Case*, Ottawa, Library and Archives Canada (RG 125, 1953, 13360-1); Robert J Sharpe and Kent Roach, *Brian Dickson: A Judge's Journey* (Toronto: University of Toronto Press for the Osgoode Society for Canadian Legal History, 2003) at 144-45.

41 "Is the land ours?," *The Globe and Mail* (15 Feb. 1974) 6.

42 *Farm Ownership Act*, SS 1973-74, c 98; "Provinces will not tolerate encroachment on their rights in urban affairs, Ottawa warned," *The Globe and Mail* (4 August 1972) 3.

43 *Notice*, above note 40.

44 *Brian Dickson*, above note 40 at 140-44; Supreme Court of Canada, "About the Court – Judges of the Court" online: www.scc-csc.gc.ca/court-cour/ju/index-eng.asp.

45 *Notice*, above note 40.

46 These cases have attracted considerable scholarly attention because of what they reveal about popular and judicial racial prejudice. See, for example, Patricia E Roy, *A White Man's Province* (Vancouver: University of British Columbia Press, 1989); Peter Ward, *White Canada Forever* (Montreal and Kingston: McGill-Queen's University Press, 1990), Alan Grove and Ross Lambertson, "Pawns of the Powerful: The Politics of Litigation in the *Union Colliery* Case" (1994) 103 *BC Studies* 3; James W St G Walker, *"Race," Rights and the Law in the Supreme Court of Canada* (Waterloo: Osgoode Society for Canadian Legal History and Wilfrid Laurier Press University Press, 1997) at 67-77.

47 *Union Colliery Company of British Columbia, Limited v Bryden*, [1899] HL 580.

48 *Cunningham and Attorney-General (British Columbia) v Tomey Homma and Attorney-General (Canada)*, [1903] AC 151 (PC).

49 *R v Quong Wing* (1914), 39 SCR 440; Quong Wing was denied leave to appeal to the Privy Council. See *"Race," Rights and the Law*, above note 46 at 51 and 90-106.

50 *Brooks-Bidlake and Whittall, Ltd v Attorney-General of British Columbia*, [1923] AC 450.

51 *The Land Sales Prohibition Act*, SA 1942, c 16; GV La Forest, *Disallowance and Reservation of Provincial Legislation* (Ottawa: Queen's Printer, 1955) at 82, 101. David Flint, *The Hutterites: A Study in Prejudice* (Toronto: Oxford University Press, 1975) at 65-66, 110-116; Simon M. Evans, "Spatial Bias in the Incidence of Nativism — Opposition to Hutterite Expansion in Alberta" (1974) 6 *Canadian Ethnic Studies* 1.

52 *The Communal Property Act of 1947*, SA 1947, c 16, specifically excluded land held by "any church or other religious organization or congregation" from the definition of land held by a colony. The restrictions were finally repealed in 1973. See John Hostetler, "The Communal Property Act of Alberta" (1961) 14 *University of Toronto Law Journal* 125; Douglas E. Sanders, "The Hutterites: A Case Study in Minority Rights" (1964) 42 *Canadian Bar Review* 225.

53 [1969] SCR 383.

54 Chernos did not note the federal government's disallowance of the earlier Alberta legislation. *Transcript*, above note 28 at 2; *Morgan*, above note 32 at 136-40.

55 *Notice*, above note 40, Factum of the Attorney-General of Canada paras 16, 18-20; Louis-Philippe Pigeon Fonds, *Morgan v PEI*, Ottawa, Library and Archives Canada (MG 31 E36,Vol. 19, File 40); Ronald Martland Fonds, *Morgan v PEI*, Ottawa, Library and Archives Canada (MG 31 E48, vol. 29, File 9).

56 *Notice*, above note 40; Nova Scotia, represented by JW Kavanaugh, adopted the Factum of the Respondent, and Manitoba, represented by Brian F Squair, adopted the Factum of the Attorney-General of Alberta, prepared by William Henkel. Ross Goodwin represented Quebec, DH Vickers represented British Columbia, WG Burke-Robertson represented Newfoundland (as it then was), and David M Norman represented New Brunswick.

57 Albert McClean, "Kenneth Martin Lysk," online: www.law.ubc.ca/news/2003/august/kenneth_lysyk.html.

58 "Morris Manning Lawyer Profile," online: www.martindale.com; *R v Morgentaler*, [1988] SCJ No. 1 at para 60-64; *Hill v Church of Scientology of Toronto*, [1995] SCJ No 64.

59 *Notice*, above note 40.

60 [1951] S.C.R. 887.

61 "Ontario Defends P.E.I. Land Ownership Laws," *[Charlottetown] Guardian* (13 Feb 1975) 1.

62 *Notice*, above note 40, Factum of the Intervenant, The Attorney General of Ontario, at paras 42-5, 62.

63 *Morgan* (SCC), above note 4 at 358; Philip Girard, *Bora Laskin: Bringing Law to Life* (Toronto: University of Toronto Press for the Osgoode Society for Canadian Legal History, 2005) at 468, observes that this is one of Laskin's few references to history in a constitutional case.

64 Louis-Philippe Pigeon Fonds, above note 55.

65 *Morgan* (SCC), above note 4 at 363-64.

66 "Premier Hails Court Ruling", *[Charlottetown] Guardian* (27 June 1975) 21.

67 Personal communications with Sol Mednick and Marvin Taylor, January and February 2010.

68 *Report to the First Ministers*, above note 19 at 35-6, 41-3. The *Citizenship Act* was proclaimed in force on 15 February 1977. So far, Alberta is only province to coordinate its land ownership restrictions with the federal legislation. See *Foreign Ownership of Land Regulations*, SOR/79-416, made pursuant to the *Citizenship Act*, RSC 1985, c C-29 and the *Agricultural and Recreational Land Ownership Act*, SA c A-9. This legislation is cited specifically in the North American Free Trade Agreement, Reservations for Existing Measures and Liberalization Commitments, Annex I, Schedule for Canada, which means that it cannot be challenged under the Article 1102 of the NAFTA, the National Treatment Article.

69 Prince County Registry Records, Deed, Mednick to Pickston, 210/83, signed 15 July 1977 and registered 29 September 1977; Deed, Mednick to Victor, 218/69, signed [ ] April 1978 and registered 1 May 1978; Deed, Mednick to Nesling, 235/33, signed 16 May 1979, registered 6 June 1979; Deed, Mednick to Davis & Davis, 268/58, signed [ ] March 1981 and registered 7 April 1981.

70 Royal Commission on the Land, *"Everything Before Us": Report of the Royal Commission on the Land*, vol 1 (Charlottetown, 1990) at 205.

71 *Lands Protection Act*, SPEI 1982, c 16; for a more detailed account, see Margaret McCallum, "The Prince Edward Island *Lands Protection Act*: The Art of the Possible" *University of New Brunswick Law Journal* 58 (2008), 148-66.

72 *Report of the Royal Commission on the Prince Edward Island Potato Industry* (Charlottetown: Queen's Printer, 1987) at 190-193 and 197.

73 Lank quotation from "3,000 Maximum Limit Urged on Ownership of PEI Land", *The Globe and Mail* (30 Jan. 1982) 14; Lee quotation from Douglas How & Ralph Costello, *K.C.: The Biography of K.C. Irving* (Toronto: Key Porter, 1993) at 363.

74 Special Legislative Committee on the Lands Protection Act, *Final Report* (March 1993) at 5-6.

75 *Reference*, above note 2 at 4, 8, and 11.

76 *Reference*, above note 2 at 16-17.

77 The effect of the Supreme Court ruling on the *Lands Protection Act* was reversed by SPEI 1995, c 22, s 1.

78 SPEI 1988, c 37; *Everything Before Us*, above note 70 at 33. The Commission was chaired by Douglas Boylan, former secretary to the provincial Cabinet, who represented Prince Edward Island on the Federal-Provincial Committee on Foreign Ownership of Lands of 1974. Other members were Gail Wellner, a Charlottetown business consultant; Elmer MacDonald, a farmer, businessman, and past president of the Prince Edward Island Potato Marketing Board; and Hugh Robbins, a retired engineering consultant living in Montague in Kings County.

79 John DeMont, *Citizens Irving* (Toronto: Doubleday, 1991) at 185-86; Harry Sawler, *Twenty-First Century Irvings* (Halifax: Nimbus, 2007) at 58-62; Prince Edward Island, Legislative Assembly, *Journal 1990*, 144, 162, 168, 169, and 173; Kevin Cox & Charles

Duerden, "K.C. Irving's Granddaughter Told to Reduce Land Holdings on PEI," *The Globe and Mail* (16 May 1990) A11; SPEI 1990, c 28.

80 SPEI 1992, c 38, s 3.

81 Prince Edward Island, Island Regulatory and Appeals Commission, *Annual Report 2008-2009* online: www.irac.pe.ca at 11; *In the Matter of Alleged Violations of the Prince Edward Island Lands Protection Act by Walter E. Wells*, Order TLF03-001, 4 April 2003; *In the Matter of Alleged Violations of the Prince Edward Island Lands Protection Act by Grand Forest Holdings Incorporated et al.*, Order TLFO8-001, 27 February 2008. The other companies were Island Holdings Ltd., Cavendish Agri-Services Limited, Simmac Packaging Ltd., JD Irving, Limited, and MF Schurman Company, Limited. Other landowners who failed to file their disclosure statements may have admitted the failure and paid a penalty without going through a formal hearing. See Island Regulatory and Appeals Commission, *Annual Report*, 2008-2009.

82 *Griffin*, above note 1; Prince Edward Island, Island Regulatory and Appeals Commission, *In the Matter of an investigation pursuant to Section 15 of the Prince Edward Island Lands Protection Act* (Frank G. Honisch), Order LF09-002, 5 February 2009.

83 *Everything Before Us*, above note 70 at 28-29, 72, 204-11, 223-29, 264, 476-77, 492-93, 584-86, 588-91, and 599-600.

84 *New Foundations: Report of the Commission on Land and Local Governance* (Charlottetown: Communications PEI, December 2009) online: www.gov.pe.ca/photos/original/ReportEng.pdf.

85 SPEI 1998, c 79, s 20.

86 Manitoba Dept. of Agriculture, Food, and Rural Initiatives, "Farm Lands Ownership Board" online: web2.gov.mb.ca/agriculture/programs/index.php?name=aaa23s03; Saskatchewan Ministry of Agriculture, Farm Land Security Board, "An Overview of The Farm Ownership Portion of T*he Saskatchewan Farm Security Act*" online: www.farmland.gov.sk.ca/ownership/overview.shtml.

87 John McClellan, "Land Ownership: Patterns and Problems" (1988) 3 *Cooper Review* 87 at 91.

88 Under s 17 of the *Lands Protection Act*, Cabinet can by regulation exempt specific land owners or specific kinds of land holdings from an individual's or a corporation's aggregate holdings. Since December 2009, "environmentally significant" land holdings may be exempt, including land taken out of agricultural production to minimize soil erosion, forested land, hedgerows, and wetlands. See *Prince Edward Island Lands Protection Act Exemption Regulations*, s 35, online: www.gov.pe.ca/law/regulations/pdf/L&05-1.pdf; Wayne Thibodeau, "Province Changing Lands Protections Act," *[Charlottetown] Guardian* (3 Dec. 2009) online: www.theguardian.pe.ca/Living/Environment/2009-12-03/article-1292647/Province-changing-Lands-Protection-Act/1; "An Important Victory for Land Stewardship" *[Charlottetown] Guardian* (14 Dec. 2009) online: www.theguardian.pe.ca/Opinion/Editorials/2009-12-14/article-1375423/An-important-victory-for-land-stewardship/1.

The Zoroastrian Temple in Toronto: A Case Study in Land Use Regulation, Canadian-Style

Eran Kaplinsky[*]

Introduction

ON A QUIET CUL-DE-SAC in Toronto at the southwest corner of Bayview Avenue and Steeles Avenue stands a stately two-storey residence overlooking the ravine that separates it from the busy intersection. The mansion stands out among the upscale suburban homes of the neighbourhood for its large size and 1920s Tudor Revival architecture. A gate and wrought iron fence guard the main entrance to the south. A well-worn paved road off Bayview Avenue leads to a second entrance. At various times the house was known as "Tudor Hill," "Windrush Hill," the "Rudd house," and the "Mazo de la Roche mansion" after the famous Canadian author who, as a small plaque notes, once lived there. The sign now reads simply, "Zoroastrian Temple: 3590 Bayview." The controversy that engulfed the house over thirty years ago, highlighted in *H.G. Winton Ltd. v North York*,[1] is the quintessential story of zoning regulation in Canada.

The Zoning Power

ZONING BYLAWS ARE THE best known and arguably the most important means of regulating the use of land in Canada. Municipal zoning powers are derived

* I would like to thank Brandon Mewhart and Tim Groves for their research assistance.

View of the Mazo de la Roche house from Creekside Road. (Photo: E.R.A. Architects.)

from enabling provincial legislation, and while the specific arrangements vary from jurisdiction to jurisdiction, zoning bylaws typically consist of a map dividing the municipal territory into districts or "zones," and a text document setting out for each district the uses that may be made of land and the development standards, such as height and bulk limitations, that apply to buildings. The effect of zoning is to establish or stabilize the predominant character of the various areas in the municipality, be it residential, commercial, or otherwise.

Zoning emerged in North America in the early decades of the 20th century. Local governments had previously exercised limited public control over the built environment through various health and building codes aimed chiefly at containing fire and contagion, but the patterns of land use within each community were determined largely by topography, the location of ports and railways, and common business sense, and were unregulated except by the common law of nuisance and the use of private restrictive covenants.[2] However, with rapid urbanization, industrialization, and increased immigration came a demand for new municipal powers over land use and development, which was met by the enactment of suitable enabling legislation by the various provinces. For example, in 1900, municipalities in British Columbia were permitted to define the streets or areas within which "laundries or wash-houses may be established, maintained or operated."[3] Similarly, Ontario municipalities were authorized in 1903 "to prevent, regulate and control the location, erection and use of buildings for laundries, butcher's shops, stores and manufactories."[4] In 1924, Kitchener, Ontario, became the first Canadian municipality to adopt a zoning bylaw that divided the whole municipal territory into use districts in accordance with a comprehensive town plan.[5] The practice of zoning spread across Canada soon after, and then in the United States once the constitutionality of zoning was settled by the US Supreme Court in 1926.[6]

Comprehensive zoning was championed by an emerging planning profession captivated by ideals such as the "City Beautiful," and later the "City Efficient." Zoning also appealed to professional surveyors, architects, and engineers, as well as reformers and housing advocates, who shared the planners' belief that it would promote orderly growth and a more salubrious urban environment. In the US, the federal administration actively encouraged the proliferation of zoning as a means to expanding home ownership.[7] Planning and zoning were consonant with the tenets of the Progressive Era in their promise to ameliorate society through scientific expertise and good governance, and were endorsed in Canada largely on similar premises.[8]

Despite its promise to promote the public good, however, zoning would not have gained popularity if it had not appealed to the private interest of homeowners and developers. New modes of transportation introduced in the early parts of the 20th century — first the electric streetcar and then the private automobile — created new opportunities for development and fundamentally altered land use patterns across North America. A "suburban century" began, as manufacturers no longer needed to build their factories next to ports or railways, and workers no longer needed to live near their place of employment. The suburbs beckoned to the middle class in particular, offering better neighbourhood amenities and a new social status. But the same ease of access that made exclusive residential enclaves so attractive also made them vulnerable to intrusion by uses and users deemed "undesirable," including multifamily housing.[9] Zoning was to the middle class a defender of their newly found suburban ideal. By entrusting zoning to locally elected councillors carefully attuned to their wishes, privileged homeowners could obtain the next best thing to a direct vote on who may be admitted to their neighbourhoods.[10] This de facto right to exclude was also a boon to real estate interests, because it protected land values and promoted investment in real property. It especially strengthened the position of large builders who became adept at manipulating municipal councils.[11]

Of course, zoning also had its share of opponents. Landowners who were adversely affected by zoning regulations were quick to challenge them in the courts — for why should a landowner's neighbours be entitled to the benefit of restrictions that go beyond the rules of common law nuisance and for which they did not covenant? Not surprisingly, it was the public interest arguments that ultimately won the day for zoning. The answer given by the United States Supreme Court in its landmark decision in *Village of Euclid v Ambler Realty Co.*,[12] was that zoning could be justified as a way to promote the health, safety, and general welfare of the community. *Euclid* concerned a landowner's challenge to the village's comprehensive zoning scheme, which segregated commercial, industrial, and residential uses and excluded apartment buildings from single-family neighbourhoods, on the ground that the ordinance amounted to a deprivation of the landowner's liberty and property without due process, in violation of the fourteenth amendment to the US constitution.

In dismissing the challenge, the Court relied on expert opinion that the segregation of uses would promote fire safety and prevent street accidents, decrease noise and conditions that produce nervous disorders, and even "increase the safety and security of home life" and "preserve a more favorable environment in which to rear children."[13] The same rhetoric was used by the Court to justify not only the spatial segregation of different uses, but also the exclusion of apartment buildings from single-family neighbourhoods. The court famously rationalized such use of zoning by drawing on the law of nuisance and pointing out the physical impact associated with high density development:

> Moreover, the coming of one apartment house is followed by others, interfering by their height and bulk with the free circulation of air and monopolizing the rays of the sun which otherwise would fall upon the smaller homes, and bringing, as their necessary accompaniments, the disturbing noises incident to increased traffic and business, and the occupation, by means of moving and parked automobiles, of larger portions of the streets, thus detracting from their safety and depriving children of the privilege of quiet and open spaces for play, enjoyed by those in more favored localities – until, finally, the residential character of the neighborhood and its desirability as a place of detached residences are utterly destroyed. Under these circumstances, apart-

> ment houses, which in a different environment would be not only entirely unobjectionable but highly desirable, come very near to being nuisances.[14]

The Court having accepted that zoning ostensibly deals with nuisance-like spillover effects was not prepared to hold that it bore no relationship to welfare objectives. Zoning thus fell squarely within the government's "police power" over private property. But the Court's emphasis of the supposed relationship between zoning and welfare objectives was not merely the means of persuading its audience of the mana of zoning: it was necessary (as proponents of zoning predicted!) to sustain the institution of zoning against a constitutional challenge.[15]

The Court's endorsement of the theory and principles of zoning shaped its legal structure and doctrine, and continues to influence the law today. Under "Euclidean" zoning (as it came to be known), whether a parcel of land could be put to a particular use would depend on whether that use fell within a predefined class of uses deemed appropriate in the district, regardless of that use's actual impact on nearby properties.[16] Ideally, uses would be grouped together and the municipality divided into fixed districts guiding all future development to its "proper" location with minimal administrative supervision. Euclidean zoning was expected to avert land use conflicts and produce healthy and prosperous communities. And to ensure that zoning is used only in the pursuit of these and other public ends, it would be wholly subordinate to expert city planning.[17]

In reality, the *practice* of zoning has been more strongly affected by social, political, and economic forces than by the ideals of planning, and despite the Court's assertions in *Euclid*, has rarely been as concerned with nervous disorders or the security of home life, as with the protection of private property values.[18] A year before *Euclid* was decided, the Committee on Community Planning of the American Institute of Architects observed that experience had shown zoning to be "concerned only feebly and incidentally with the community function the land will best serve; it focuses attention mainly upon the stabilizing of the existing uses and the values that are derived from them, whether these are to be the best advantage of the community or not."[19] The Canadian experience has been substantially similar. A study of early use of zoning in Toronto, for example, revealed that zoning restrictions were typically adopted by city councils on a case-by-case basis and in response to petitions from single-family homeowners to exclude apartment buildings and other so-called undesirable development.[20] In Vancouver, historian

John Weaver observed, "Businessmen have defined the instruments of land use control and directed their outcome."[21] Planning principles and the public interest have played only a minor role in the development of land-use regulations, as the administrative and political apparatus of zoning was captured by the private interests it was intended to regulate.[22]

Nevertheless the myth inculcated by the *Euclid* decision lingers in Canadian law. In the absence of constitutional protection for private property in Canada,[23] the validity of zoning bylaws never hinged on their actual or theoretical contribution to the welfare of the community (as it does in the US), but only on the scope of the enabling legislation. Yet the language of welfare found its way into provincial legislation that binds zoning to "the health, safety and general welfare of the inhabitants of the municipality,"[24] or requires that zoning "carry out the intent of a municipal planning strategy."[25] Such views also pervade judicial interpretation of zoning powers in other provinces. While judicial statements of the purpose of zoning are rare, in the words of one commentator, "the regulation of the physical impact of land uses continues to be the touchstone of a valid zoning regulation."[26]

Derived from this fiction is the rule developed by the courts that limits attempts by local councils to regulate not the *use* of land, but *who* may use it. Accordingly, a zoning bylaw that purported to prohibit in a particular residential zone the sharing of occupancy by persons unrelated by blood or marriage was struck by the Supreme Court as *ultra vires*.[27] However, municipal efforts to reserve certain neighbourhoods to single-family use can strain the distinction between *use* and *user*, as illustrated by the well-known duo cases of *R. v Brown Camps Ltd.*,[28] and *Barrie (City) v Brown Camps Residential & Day Schools*.[29] In both cases, the Ontario Court of Appeal was asked to decide whether the terms of the relevant zoning bylaw operated to exclude group homes in which children were placed under the supervision of professional staff. In the first case, the court held that the accommodation and care provided to the children by the operator had all the essentials of a "business." Further, the court refused to extend the definition of a "family" to paid staff and unrelated "inmates" placed in the group at the operator's discretion. The group home was therefore excluded from a district restricted to "single family residential" use. In the second case, *Barrie v Brown Camps*, the court reached the opposite result. The court concluded that the premises exhibited all the physical characteristics of a family home and were being used for the care and upbringing of the children "in the same manner as if they were being used by parents with special expertise."[30] The group home therefore fell squarely within the definition of the permitted use in the district. Commentators suggested that in both cases there was no planning justification to exclude a group home whose purpose was to rear children in essentially the same manner as a "conventional" family household, and that produced none of the physical impact (such as noise and traffic) associated with institutional and commercial uses that would make it inappropriate in a residential district.[31] This approach denies the full nature of neighbours' opposition to group homes.

Another noteworthy example of the courts' difficulties reconciling zoning theory and praxis can be seen in the judicial suspicion of municipal attempts at "spot zoning," i.e., the regulation of one or more selected parcels of land, as opposed to entire geographic districts.[32] Any expectations for rigid zoning supported by long-term comprehensive plans soon proved naïve, as the dynamics of real estate markets frequently rendered city plans obsolete or irrelevant, and pressures from private interests eroded the boundaries of designated land use districts and their homogeneity (as a look at the zoning map of any Canadian city will confirm).[33] As ad hoc zoning and rezoning became the norm, the courts searched for a way to distinguish between exercises of legislative authority in the public interest and instances of favouritism or maltreatment of specific owners. The leading authority for the proposition that spot zoning may be permitted if it can be supported by a public-interest justification remains *Scarborough (Township) v Bondi*.[34] There, the municipality passed a zoning amendment that was directed at one corner lot in a registered plan of subdivision and that had the effect of prohibiting the owner of that lot from developing more than one dwelling unit on the property. The owner in question applied to quash the amendment on the ground that it was discriminatory, enacted in bad faith, and *ultra vires*. In Canadian municipal law, the term "discrimination" does not necessarily imply prejudicial treatment of individuals based on certain characteristics, but refers to any regulatory distinction made by a municipality without statutory authority. As a rule of construction, "when the municipality is given the right to regulate . . . all it can do is to pass general regulations affecting all who come within the ambit of the municipal legislation. It cannot itself discriminate, and give permission to one and refuse it to another."[35] In the Ontario High Court, McRuer CJ expressed doubt whether that statement of the doctrine of discrimination is applicable to zoning:

> All restrictive by-laws in one sense are discriminatory. Owners of land who come within a restrictive by-law are prohibited from doing what owners who are without it may do with their land and it might well be that a municipality, acting in the public interest, might restrict a piece of property to certain uses while for good reasons other property in the neighbourhood might not be affected by the restriction. Likewise, and it frequently happens, a wider use of certain property is permitted than that allowed in the contiguous area. In a case of this kind I think the matter must be approached from the point of view of whether or not the municipal council in passing the by-law acted in good faith in the public interest or acted to promote some private interest.[36]

McRuer then reviewed the circumstances of the case. The bylaw that governed the area before the spot zoning allocated development rights based on street frontage and would have allowed the owner of the corner lot in question to take advantage of its peculiar features and build two houses, each having less than a quarter of the ground area typical to other houses in the neighbourhood. McRuer concluded that the amending bylaw was passed for no other reason than to maintain the general character of the district; Council therefore acted *intra vires*. The case reached the Supreme Court of Canada, where Judson J shared the reservations expressed by the Chief Justice of Ontario with respect to the applicability of the doctrine of discrimination.[37] But in any event, Judson J, too, held that the amendment was enacted in good faith and in the interest generally of the area, and was permissible inasmuch as it had the effect of compelling the owner to fall in with the local standards and preventing him from taking advantage of the neighbourhood amenities. In other words, spot zoning could be acceptable if it could be shown to promote some planning objective.

What such an objective might be may be gleaned from the following statement found in *Congrégation des témoins de Jéhovah de St-Jérôme-Lafontaine v Lafontaine (Village)*[38]: "The purpose of zoning bylaws is to organize a municipality's territory so as to protect citizens' interests and maintain order."[39] A remarkably frank view of zoning was expressed by Monnin CJ of the Manitoba Court of Appeal in *Alcoholism Foundation of Manitoba v Winnipeg (City)*.[40] The case dealt with restrictions on the location of group and rehabilitation homes. The court held that even if the city could legally exclude the institutional operation of group homes from residential districts, it could not define such homes by reference to the attributes of their occupants. But in one passage the Chief Justice reveals that the exclusionary force of zoning is decidedly *not* restricted to matters of physical impact or the public interest:

> Ratepayers building $150,000 or $200,000 single-family homes are entitled to expect that only similar homes will be built in their vicinity, and that the integrity of that particular zoned area of the community will not be interfered with or reduced by allowing homes having one-third the value to be built next to them or near them, or occupied by more than one family. That was and should still be an entirely legitimate concern of the City councillors.[41]

Why single-family homeowners should be entitled to the set the admission standard for their neighbourhood has never been explained satisfactorily by the courts.[42] Yet widespread socioeconomic segregation is carried out through minimum lot and house size and other regulations designed to reserve certain neighbourhoods to those with sufficient economic means. Moreover, it is standard practice in disputes over proposed development to cloak any objections to the prospective uses or users in "traffic," "parking," "environmental," or other concerns about supposed tangible impact.

The Rezoning of the Mazo de la Roche Mansion

The Mazo de la Roche Mansion

In 1976, the residence at 3590 Bayview Avenue formed part of an estate of nine acres in the Borough of North York. A year earlier, the property had been sold by its owner and occupant Dr. Rudd to JFM Developments Ltd., who planned to demolish the house and subdivide the land for single-family homes. In April 1976, the North York planning board endorsed the developer's plan of subdivision, dispensing in the process with petitions to preserve the house where the writer Mazo de la Roche — famous for her series of *Jalna* novels[43] — lived from 1939 to 1945. Among the most active and vociferous proponents of preservation was the thirty-year-old banker and Alderman, Michael Smith. He regarded the house as a tangible link to the borough's past even if the house itself was not of very great historical significance.[44]

On the basis of the planning board's recommendations, the developer's plan of subdivision was referred to the borough council for approval. After hearing representations, including an appeal to save the house by the Dean of English and Communications at Seneca College on behalf of concerned faculty, and after being entreated by Alderman Smith, council decided to defer its vote for several weeks in the hope that a buyer would be found for the house, so that the proposed subdivision could be developed around it.[45] Meanwhile, the wisdom of preserving the house was questioned by one of Mazo de la Roche's biographers, who pointed out that the author resided in not one, but several Toronto houses during her life, including five residences in which she wrote. In a letter to the editor he wrote: "Frankly, I would not bother with the Rudd house, for of the 33 full-length books she published, only three were written there, and it was the one place where she was plagued with ill-health and worry." The biographer cited two addresses in the neighbourhood of Forest Hill as more deserving locations for preservation, but argued that "to establish a shrine . . . for Mazo de la Roche, who set her face against canonization . . . is an elegant waste of time."[46]

But Smith's efforts succeeded and in May 1976, it was announced that local real estate developer Harry Winton (through his corporation, HG Winton Ltd.) had purchased the Mazo de la Roche residence. Under the terms of the deal, which were made public, Winton paid $250,000 for the house and an additional $70,000 for an adjoining lot. The borough sweetened the pot by conveying to Winton title to the ravine lands east of the house, on condition that they revert to the municipality should the house be demolished within twenty years. Although the deal was generally lauded by council, some members expressed concerns that the municipality was giving up useful public lands to preserve a house of dubious public significance. It was also hinted that JFM Developments was coerced into the deal, having been led to understand that its proposed plan of subdivision would face obstacles from council unless it agreed to sell the house.[47] On his part, Winton declared his intention to restore the mansion as a residential estate: "I just did it to satisfy the people, just to make the public happy."[48]

Winton did make several improvements to the property. He also closed off the private road leading to the house from Bayview Avenue and opened up a new entrance facing the cul-de-sac in the new subdivision in progress, giving the house a second address: 35 Creekside Road. But he never moved into the house and it stood empty.[49] He briefly entertained the idea of converting the mansion into a museum, but never obtained the requisite rezoning (it is unclear if he ever made the necessary application). By October 1977, Winton had become disillusioned with these plans and, after recovering from a medical operation and declaring his intentions to move to Florida, the mercurial developer applied to the borough for permission to demolish the Mazo de la Roche mansion. When it became clear that the municipality would not permit the house to be demolished, Winton decided to sell it.[50]

Enter the Zoroastrian Society of Ontario

Not long after Winton put the Mazo de la Roche mansion on the market, he was approached by the Zoroastrian Society of Ontario (ZSO) who expressed interest in purchasing it for use as a temple. Zoroastrianism is an ancient religion that originated in the Asian Steppes and is based on the teachings of the prophet Zoroaster. According to the leading authority, "Zoroastrianism is the oldest of the revealed credal religions, and it has probably had more influence on mankind, directly and indirectly, than any other single faith."[51] Zoroastrianism was the state religion of the Persian empires from the sixth century BCE until Muslim conquest in the seventh century CE, after which it was increasingly marginalized. In the tenth century, many Zoroastrians fled Iran to escape persecution, settling first in Gujarat, India, then migrating to Bombay in the seventeenth century, and from there, as merchants, around the world, where they became known as Parsis ("Persians"). A small Zoroastrian minority survived in Iran, and beginning in the 1970s, some of its members also immigrated to the Western world.[52] The first Zoroastrian whose presence in Canada was recorded was a gentleman prospecting for gold in British Columbia in the 1860s; Zoroastrians enrolled at the University of Toronto as early as 1922. But it was in the 1960s when a group of Zoroastrian students in Toronto succeeded in obtaining landed immigrant status, and it was they who in 1966 established a local Zoroastrian fraternity (informal associations were also established in Montreal and Vancouver around that time). It soon became easy for Zoroastrians to immigrate to Canada, as the Canadian authorities became convinced that they were people of high education and achievement.[53] In 1971, the Zoroastrian Society of Ontario (ZSO) was formally incorporated and set out as its immediate goals to obtain legal recognition of Zoroastrian marriage ceremonies and to educate its members in the traditions and religious practices of Zoroastrianism. By 1975, Toronto was home to about 250–300 Zoroastrian families, and the city's growing significance as a Zoroastrian centre was recognized by hosting the annual North American Zoroastrian conference. By the following year, the local community was seeking to establish a community and worship centre.[54]

In 1977, the Zoroastrian benefactor Rustom Guiv pledged $600,000 for this purpose (he also made donations for acquiring buildings in Vancouver,

New York, Chicago, and San Jose). He wished the building to be known as Darbe Mehr ("the door of love") and that it should be open to Zoroastrians and non-Zoroastrians alike.[55]

With the donation in place, a trustee on behalf of ZSO entered into an agreement to purchase the house from HG Winton Ltd. The purchase agreement, dated 16 February 1978 was conditional on the assurance that the property could be used lawfully as a temple. Several days earlier, Dr. Russi Balsara, a member of the Faculty of Dentistry at the University of Toronto and president of ZSO, had written to the borough building commissioner to seek written confirmation of the lawfulness of its intended uses of the property, which he described as, "(1) place of worship; (2) religious education at Sunday school; (3) practice of religious customs and traditions; (4) celebration of religious feasts on auspicious days; and (5) a source library for religious books and scriptures."[56]

It is important to put this description in context. The first practitioners of Zoroastrianism were nomadic and many of their rituals did not require a temple. In the temples of present day India and Iran, worship continues as personal acceptance of divine blessings in front of a sacred eternal fire. But in the diaspora, where Zoroastrians have made their homes wherever their career paths take them, congregational worship assumed a critical function of bringing the community together during religious festivals and other important occasions. To date, no Zoroastrian building in North America has been fully consecrated as a temple, but each functions as a focal point for the community and features a prayer room where members may congregate to attend ceremonies during which a temporary fire is lit.

Such were ZSO's plans for the Mazo de la Roche mansion. The Society emphasized in its letter to the North York building commissioner that regular religious services would not be held at the temple, but that its members would worship individually at various times in accordance with Zoroastrian practices. The Society undertook further that any alterations to the property would be carried out in conformity with the applicable building regulations. The building commissioner replied that the uses described in the letter came within the borough's zoning bylaw's definition of a "church," and would be, according to that bylaw, permitted as of right on the portion of the property zoned "R.3 residential."

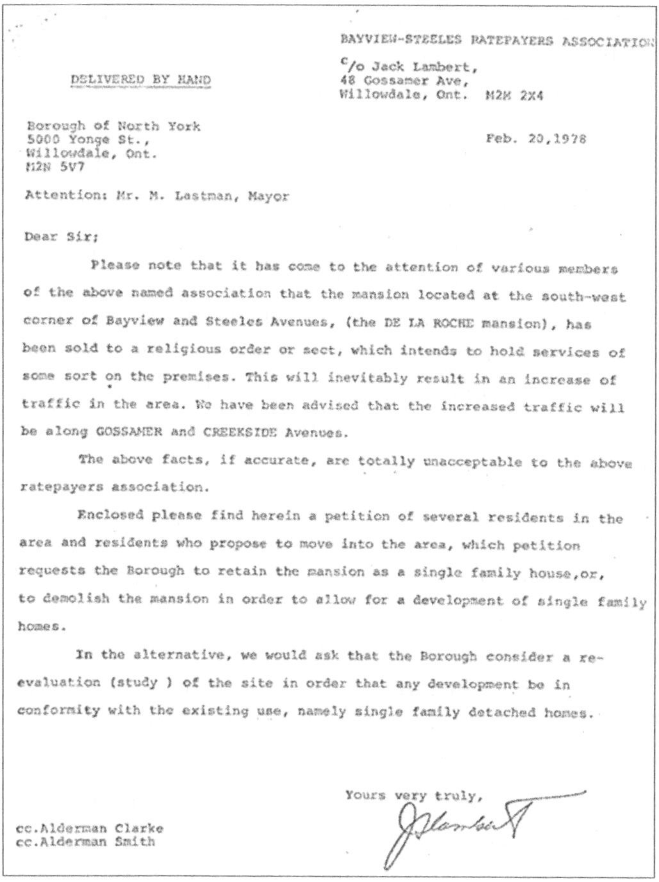

BAYVIEW-STEELES RATEPAYERS ASSOCIATION

DELIVERED BY HAND

c/o Jack Lambert,
48 Gossamer Ave,
Willowdale, Ont. M2M 2X4

Borough of North York
5000 Yonge St.,
Willowdale, Ont.
M2N 5V7

Feb. 20,1978

Attention: Mr. M. Lastman, Mayor

Dear Sir;

Please note that it has come to the attention of various members of the above named association that the mansion located at the south-west corner of Bayview and Steeles Avenues, (the DE LA ROCHE mansion), has been sold to a religious order or sect, which intends to hold services of some sort on the premises. This will inevitably result in an increase of traffic in the area. We have been advised that the increased traffic will be along GOSSAMER and CREEKSIDE Avenues.

The above facts, if accurate, are totally unacceptable to the above ratepayers association.

Enclosed please find herein a petition of several residents in the area and residents who propose to move into the area, which petition requests the Borough to retain the mansion as a single family house,or, to demolish the mansion in order to allow for a development of single family homes.

In the alternative, we would ask that the Borough consider a re-evaluation (study) of the site in order that any development be in conformity with the existing use, namely single family detached homes.

Yours very truly,

cc.Alderman Clarke
cc.Alderman Smith

Ratepayers' letter to the mayor of North York.

The Rezoning of Mazo de la Roche Mansion

As soon as the plans to convert the mansion into a Zoroastrian temple became known, local residents moved to defeat the deal. Within a week, the local ratepayers association delivered a letter to North York Mayor Mel Lastman together with a petition signed by 250 residents to retain the mansion as a private residence or to demolish it for single family detached homes. The letter cited the ratepayers' concerns about increased traffic on Gossamer Avenue and Creekside Road that bounded the mansion to the north and to the west, which would inevitably occur during services.

On 27 February 1978, borough council responded to the neighbours' petition by enacting a zoning amendment bylaw. Both the substance of the bylaw and the unusual circumstances of its adoption came under the scrutiny of the Ontario Divisional Court in *H.G. Winton Ltd. v North York (Borough)*,[57] and require some explication. The amendment restricted to single-family use all lands zoned "R.3 residential" within the area defined by the amendment — which comprised about four residential blocks, including Winton's property — and prohibited all other uses of such lands, including, importantly, churches and other institutional uses. The practical effect of the amendment was to render the proposed Zoroastrian temple unlawful and frustrate the sale of the Mazo de la Roche mansion. The amendment applied only to the lands identified in the bylaw and not to any similar lands elsewhere in the municipality, and was the first of its kind, as zoning had never been used before to exclude religious uses from residential districts in North York.

The bylaw was proposed as a new item on the agenda at a regularly scheduled council meeting and given three readings on the same day, after council agreed to Mayor Lastman's request to waive the usual two weeks' notice. A public hearing was not held, and neither Winton, nor the Zoroastrian Society, were invited to make submissions — in fact, they were not informed that a zoning amendment initiated by those opposing the temple was submitted to a vote of council. Furthermore, contrary to standard practice, the new zoning restrictions were not reviewed by the borough's planning board prior to the vote. No reports or studies supporting a change to the existing zoning were presented. Not even the correspondence between the Zoroastrian Society and the borough's building commissioner, which would have indicated the purchaser's good faith reliance on the municipality's assurances, was considered by council. The only material available to council when it voted to restrict the lands in question was the ratepayers' petition and accompanying letter.[58]

The exceptional bylaw amendment was made even more unusual by its recitals and council's resolution, which prefaced it. After council had dealt with several other matters on the agenda, the ratepayers' petition and letter were introduced together with a motion and the proposed bylaw amendment. Then, on a motion by Mayor Lastman, council resolved to request borough planning staff to prepare a general policy on religious uses in the municipality, as well as a report and specific recommendations with respect to the permitted uses of the lands to be affected by the amendment. After making this resolution, council enacted the bylaw amendment, indicating in the recitals to it that a review of the permitted uses was underway but not yet complete. It was never disputed, however, that prior to the meeting council had not manifested any intention to review the permitted uses in residential areas or its policies with respect to the location of religious institutions.[59]

The *Toronto Star* reported Council's decision, contrasting the neighbours' alleged concerns about increased traffic with the assurance given by the purchasers to the borough's building commissioner that weekly services would not be held on the property. Harry Winton was interviewed, and he pointed out that the Mazo de la Roche mansion was only accessible from Creekside Road, where only 13 of the 250 petitioners resided, and that the mansion would be totally isolated from the neighbourhood once he reopened the access road off Bayview Avenue. Finally, the borough solicitor was interviewed about council's decision to adopt the bylaw without holding a public hearing or obtaining planning staff's advice. "Well, they have done it," he said, and predicted that the courts will have to determine the validity of the amendment.[60]

While a legal challenge was imminent, the parties were also gearing up for an approval hearing at the provincially appointed Ontario Municipal Board (OMB) during which the merits of the bylaw would be discussed.[61] Council held a public meeting on 8 May (presumably to improve its position), and after hearing several submissions in support and in opposition to the bylaw affirmed it by a 10 to 5 vote. It was a victory for the ratepayers association. Their president insisted that the neighbours would welcome any single family who intended to make the mansion its home, but would oppose all institutional uses insofar as those generate traffic, endanger children, and threaten the residential character of the neighbourhood.[62] The Zoroastrian purchasers, however, felt that given their plans to sequester the temple from the neighbourhood, the neighbours' opposition could only be explained by prejudice. Their indignation was fuelled by the ratepayers' letter to the mayor, which described the Zoroastrians as "a religious order or sect, which intends to hold services of some sort on the premises." The newspaper picked up the sentiment by quoting the resident of 27 Creekside Road who spoke at the public hearing in support of the amendment. She described her encounter with several of the Zoroastrians who apparently visited the street to look at their future temple: "They would not even speak to me. They were speaking some language which I did not understand. I can't even pronounce the name."[63] These conflicting explanations of the opposition to the Zoroastrian temple were echoed by elected officials when the matter came before Metro Toronto council. North York Mayor Lastman insisted it was a local planning issue. Toronto Alderman John Sewell called it "straightforward bigotry."[64]

Because the Borough of North York formed part of the municipality of Metropolitan Toronto, the latter's support for the amendment at the scheduled OMB hearing was important. Metro council announced ultimately that it would formally oppose the borough's amendment.[65] By then, as anticipated, HG Winton Ltd. had applied to the Divisional Court to quash the amendment on the grounds that it was discriminatory and enacted in bad faith. An application for an early hearing was granted.

The Legal Proceedings and Decision in *HG Winton*

HG Winton Ltd.'s application for judicial review was referred to a panel of three judges, which included Robins J, Holland J, and Goodman J. Justice Sydney Robins, who delivered the opinion of the court, had been appointed to the Supreme Court in 1976. Prior to that he studied at the University of Toronto, Osgoode Hall Law School, and Harvard Law School, and had a distinguished career that included a Queen's Counsel appointment and office as Treasurer of the Law Society of Upper Canada. Three years after his decision in *H.G. Winton*, Robins was elevated to the Court of Appeal. There, he wrote a majority opinion in the important decision *Re Leonard Foundation Trust*,[66] in which it was held that a charitable trust written to exclude from its benefit "all who are not Christians of the White Race, and who are not of British Nationality or of British Parentage, and all who owe allegiance to any Foreign Government, Prince, Pope or Potentate, or who recognize any such authority" violated public policy.[67] Justice Robins also wrote the decision in one of the Eaton Centre trespass cases discussed elsewhere in this collection.[68] Both decisions hint at the judge's sensitivity to issues of privilege, power, and exclusion, which arise from private property.

The application was decided on the basis of the parties' affidavits, cross-examinations, and statements. Harry Winton and the president of ZSO gave evidence on behalf of the appellant, while North York offered the testimonies of the borough's deputy clerk and Alderman Smith. Smith described his previous experience dealing with proposals for institutional uses within established single-family neighbourhoods, which had led him to the conclusion that such residential areas were not adequately protected by the community's outdated land use policies and were becoming increasingly vulnerable to intrusions by nonresidential uses. He claimed a special familiarity with the site in dispute, even without the benefit of specific planning studies or reports, because he was the member of Council who previously "saved" the mansion.[69] According to Smith, he believed that the amendment was in the public interest and he regarded it necessary to give planning staff sufficient time to recommend a general policy with respect to institutional uses in residential neighbourhoods; he urged his fellow council members to adopt the amendment summarily in order to avert a *fait accompli*.[70]

During his cross examination, Alderman Smith reiterated that he was "influenced principally by the impact on the community of an institutional type use,"[71] but he was unable to adduce evidence of the harmful effects of the proposed temple from which he was trying to shield the surrounding homes. Moreover, his personal disdain for Harry Winton was obvious. At various points the Alderman referred to what he perceived as Winton's opportunistic character and unpredictable movements and to his attempts to "exploit" the situation to make a profit. In Smith's view, Winton was to blame for thrusting the Zoroastrians into unnecessary conflict with the ratepayers, because he broke his promise to the community to keep the mansion as a private residence. And while the problem of institutional uses was not specific to any one residential district in the borough, Smith admitted, other property owners who proposed to convert residential properties to institutional uses could be trusted — but not Winton, due to his acrimonious relationship with the municipality — to negotiate mutually acceptable terms upon which those uses could be accommodated. Accordingly, there was no reason, Smith submitted, for a sweeping exclusion of all institutional uses from every residential district in the borough, but only for an amendment directed at this limited area.

Smith's testimony proved critical to the case. Robins J found that it disclosed "the presence of factors neither relevant nor proper to the zoning process," and quoted several excerpts of Smith's cross-examination in support of this conclusion, including the following:

> . . . I have an intimate understanding and knowledge of that site, of the community that's around it and has been around it for some years, and the history and the unpredictable movements of its present owner, Mr. Winton. When I was made aware by the item being on the agenda that Mr. Winton was going off on another tangent to try and sell this property . . . I understand very well the course of action that was left open to Council, the fact that we had a very unpredictable owner and a person who I didn't feel we could rely on to act in good faith to protect the community's interests.

> . . . in this instance here, where you had a developer who is exploiting the situation, and that's my view of it, then it's incumbent upon a member of Council and, indeed, Council to take whatever steps necessary to protect the community . . .
>
> . . . The man is obviously motivated by profit. I think we have to recognize that and then we can simply address ourselves to the main issue. Then, who protects the community, who protects the interests of that community. I think it has to be North York Council.[72]

Justice Robins acknowledged the conceptual and practical difficulties in ascertaining legislative intent and that not all members of council necessarily shared Smith's views, but Smith's testimony was the Borough's own evidence, and the court gave it considerable weight. Given his finding of improper and irrelevant purposes, coupled with the unusual circumstances surrounding the amendment, Robins J held that the amendment could not be upheld on the basis of its ostensible terms. While Council purported to demarcate a new land use district in which all lands zoned "R. 3 residential" were reserved exclusively for single-family use, Robins J determined that the amendment's true purpose was to restrict the use of the Mazo de la Roche property alone. In his opinion, the scope of the bylaw was illusory, and the inclusion of other properties to the south and to the west was superfluous, if not a sham intended to disguise the amendment's true purpose, which was to block the imminent use of the Mazo de la Roche as a Zoroastrian temple.[73] Justice Robins reasoned further that if there had been concerns about possible intrusions of institutional uses into residential neighbourhoods, as council's resolution claimed, and danger of *fait accompli*, then those would apply to all similarly zoned lands in the municipality and not only the small area to which the bylaw applied.[74] There was nothing on record, however, to show that the lands contained in the new district differed from similar lands elsewhere in the municipality.

The new restrictions could be sustained therefore only if the amendment could be upheld as valid spot zoning. Justice Robins concluded, however, that the restrictions and the process by which they were adopted were tainted by bad faith. He explained the meaning of the doctrine in the context of municipal law:

> To say that council acted in what is characterized in law as "bad faith" is not to imply or suggest any wrongdoing or personal advantage on the part of any

> of its members. But it is to say, in the factual situation of this case, that council acted unreasonably and arbitrarily and without the degree of fairness, openness, and impartiality required of a municipal government.[75]

The court found abundant evidence of bad faith on the part of the municipality in its abuse of the zoning process — including the summary adoption of the bylaw, the abandonment of the borough's standard practices and procedures, the keeping of Winton and the Zoroastrian Society in the dark, and the attempt to cloak the spot zoning by creating a phantom zone. Bad faith was also indicated by the arbitrary and detrimental singling out of the Mazo de la Roche mansion, and the improper and irrelevant motives disclosed by Alderman Smith's testimony.[76]

According to the court, in addition to being tainted by bad faith, the spot zoning also constituted impermissible discrimination by the municipality. Justice Robins noted the special meaning of the doctrine of discrimination in municipal and planning law in Canada,[77] and contrasted the facts of the case with the spot zoning considered by the Supreme Court in *Bondi*.[78] That decision, too, involved a bylaw amendment enacted in response to a ratepayers' petition and directed at a single parcel, but in Robins J's opinion, the amendment under attack in *H.G. Winton* contrasted sharply with the spot zoning in the *Bondi* case:

> It is, of course, well recognized that every zoning by-law is discriminatory, in the sense that the municipality chooses the types of uses it will permit in certain or all parts of the land under its jurisdiction, and is not invalid on that account. But there must be proper planning grounds or standards to warrant discriminatory distinctions between property owners in the same position, classification or zoning category. Here, no planning purpose has been shown to explain, let alone justify, the selection of a single spot in the borough as the subject of this amendatory zoning by-law. There is no rhyme nor reason, in a planning sense, for it . . . The situation in this case is unlike that in cases such as *Bondi* . . . where the land use prohibitions . . . enacted were in the context of a planning policy or in furtherance of planning considerations.[79]

The court could find no credible planning rationale for the amendment. On the one hand, the bylaw could not be explained as a way to preserve the Mazo de la Roche mansion, not only because the bylaw's recitals and council's preceding resolution spoke to a different motive, but also because the Zoroastrian Society did not intend to demolish the house. On the other hand, given the purchasers' plans to close off the main entrance to the mansion, and in the absence of any traffic or parking studies to show any special problems associated with the temple (as opposed to all religious institutions in residential areas in North York[80]), the restrictions could not be said to be aimed at preventing inconvenience to the neighbours. This kind of spot zoning could not be tolerated, let alone intended by the legislature. That Robins J gave no credence to the neighbours' complaints is plain from his telling choice to quote from their letter only the first sentence ("a religious order or sect . . . intends to hold services of some sort on the premises"), but not the second ("This will inevitably result in an increase of traffic in the area"). In the judge's mind, the case was never about land use regulation, and that view is reflected in the decision.

Lessons for Zoning

H.G. Winton stands as a landmark decision in Canadian planning law. Robins J's statement of the doctrines of bad faith and discrimination remains influential.[81] The result of the case is perhaps less surprising, given council's egregious conduct, than North York's decision to defend its bylaw in court (perhaps it was easier for members of council to place the blame on the court, than to deny the petition and face the political wrath of their constituents — but that is speculation). When the Borough solicitor was interviewed after the decision was announced, he suggested that "if Council had followed the rules of the game, the bylaw would not have been declared discriminatory . . . [I]t was a mistake not to have notified the owner of the land, H.G. Winton Ltd., and the Zoroastrian Society that Council was considering the bylaw."[82] However, inasmuch as the finding of bad faith rested also on what the court held was an unreasonable and arbitrary singling out of the Mazo de la Roche property, it would appear that the bylaw would not have been saved even if the borough had adhered to the strictures of process, and even if Winton and the purchasers had been given an opportunity to make representations to council. The decision makes it clear that council was empowered to enact a general text amendment excluding religious institutions from *all* residential districts, but to restrict in this manner one property, or even one neighbourhood, without proper planning grounds would be discriminatory and indicative of bad faith.

That all forms of spot zoning are not illegal is also clear from the decision. For example, according to Robins J, spot zoning could be permitted in principle if enacted "in the context of a planning policy."[83] He did not cite, but may well have been referring to, the decision in *Re North York (Township)*.[84] The case may be regarded as an extension of the principles established in *Bondi*. There, the municipality proposed to rezone selected parcels along a major street. Parcels whose owners agreed to provide certain public amenities at no cost would be rezoned to allow development at a greater height and twice the number of dwelling units allowed as of right. The Ontario Municipal Board refused to approve the requisite zoning amendments on the grounds that only an "area" of land could be the subject of a zoning bylaw, and moreover, that the amendments constituted preferential spot zoning. Acting then as counsel for the appellant, Robins argued that the language of the *Planning Act* allowed the municipality to regulate an area of any size — even a single parcel. He argued further that the regulation was in the public interest even if it resulted in preferential treatment, inasmuch as a study commissioned by the municipality recommended spot zoning as a technique to break the monotony of the streetscape. The Court of Appeal concurred and remitted the bylaw for a new hearing.[85]

But even spot zoning ad hoc may be upheld, which is not made pursuant to some existing planning policy, and even if initiated by a local petition, as the decision in *Bondi*[86] demonstrates. Robins J's distinction of North York's illegal amendment from the spot zoning held to be permissible there is illuminating. In *Bondi*, the original zoning bylaw permitted the development of one dwelling unit per 100 feet of street frontage, which would have allowed the owner of the affected corner lot to take advantage of its frontage on two streets in order to build two houses much smaller than the ample neighbourhood standard. Judson J pointed to the homogeneity and reciprocity of advantage among all lands in the district as a legitimate planning purpose that justified the spot zoning. Under one reading of *Bondi*, although the amending bylaw (which permitted only one house to be constructed on the lot) did constitute spot zoning in the technical sense, it did not single out the affected property for any special treatment; rather, the purpose of the amendment was to impose substantive equality of treatment among all landowners. But couldn't the same be said of the amendment impugned in *H.G. Winton*? Was its purpose not also to create an exclusive single-family residential district within the municipal territory, much like the one enforced in *Bondi*? Robins J refused to recognize this use district because it was created for no other reason than the neighbours' opposition to the Zoroastrian temple.

Nor did the illegality of the *H.G. Winton* amendment lie with its interference with the buyers' expectation to use the land for a purpose that was expressly permitted by the regulations in force and confirmed by the borough's building commissioner (in contrast, the amendment in *Bondi* could have been said *not* to interfere with the landowner's expectations, as it merely gave effect to the clear purpose of the original restrictions). It is a longstanding principle of planning law, that the right of landowners to use and develop their land in accordance with the land use regulations in force may be negated by the adoption of subsequent regulations pursuant to the enabling legislation.[87]

What distinguished the *H.G. Winton* amendment, in the eyes of Robins J, from the *Bondi* case was that the exclusion of the Zoroastrian temple did not relate to a proper planning purpose. This prompts two questions: First, what might constitute proper planning grounds as a matter of law? And second, why (as *H.G. Winton* suggests) can't neighbours' opposition *per se* constitute sufficient planning grounds? The answers to both questions are found in the historical account of zoning and, specifically, the ascendancy of the public welfare, contrasted with the private interest view of zoning.[88] In light of this view of zoning, it is no surprise that the *H.G. Winton* court saw no planning reason for the exclusion of the Zoroastrian temple. The purchasers proposed no changes to the house itself, and planned to isolate it physically from the rest of the neighbourhoods. There was also no existing planning policy that the municipality could rely on to justify the exclusion, and failure to consult with planning staff proved fatal to the amendment.

This is not to say that courts have always insisted on planning evidence. For example, in *Toronto Roman Catholic Separate School Board,*[89] Duff J of the Supreme Court of Canada needed no evidence in order to characterize the impact of locating a separate school in the heart of a residential street as "very grave detriment and hardship" to the neighbours.[90] No planning evidence was adduced in the *Bondi* case either. While the result in *Bondi* is often explained by reference to the irregular shape of the lot in question, it is important to note that the neighbours' petition, cited by the lower court, complained that the backyards of the two houses proposed by the affected landowner would be plainly visible from the street.[91] It would be naïve, however, to think that the petitioning homeowners in *Bondi* were concerned with the visibility of backyards in their neighbourhoods. Their real complaint was also made explicit in their petition: that the existence of houses on 10,000 feet squared (roughly 930 metres squared) "is certain to detract from the neighbourhood and tend to reduce the value of surrounding properties."[92] This was well understood by council, and also by Judson J who wrote succinctly: "[t]he objection to the proposed buildings on comparatively small lots in a neighborhood such as this is apparent and needs no further comment."[93]

H.G. Winton demonstrates the continued adherence of Canadian courts to the notion that the purpose of zoning is to enhance welfare and promote the public interest embodied in the goals of planning — a myth inherited from the *Euclid* decision — and their reticence to discuss private interest and property values.[94] By the time the *H.G. Winton* decision was written, property law scholars had already begun to argue that it was unhelpful to analyze zoning by reference to its original, idealized welfare justifications. A better understanding of zoning could be obtained, they argued, by focusing on what zoning actually accomplishes.[95] Professor Dan Tarlock was one of the first to recognize that the zoning of existing neighbourhoods might be explained — and perhaps justified — as a simulation of a market in which potentially affected landowners could enter into a scheme of enforceable restrictive covenants to exclude undesirable uses:

> This is, in effect, applying a doctrine of prior appropriation to zoning. The first users appropriate the amenity level, and subsequent users must buy their way in. This is consistent with the principle that economic efficiency will be furthered if property rights are assigned so that the transaction costs associated with the initiation of negotiations will be minimized. Assigning property rights to existing users rather to those who wish to initiate a new use will minimize the costs of forming a coalition.[96]

Certainly, neighbours of the Mazo de la Roche mansion felt they were entitled to the status quo. A letter to the editor, published in the *Toronto Star*, criticizing the court's decision in *H.G. Winton* contended:

> The "bad faith" described in the decision lies elsewhere. Here is an institution that was being allowed to move onto a quiet residential street without any regard for the residents. The residents were there first, and these residents chose this type of street for its private nature.[97]

The writer was mistaken: the neighbours were not there first. They had bought homes in a subdivision that was created around the mansion with the knowledge that it was not restricted. It was only when the neighbours perceived an imminent threat to their suburban environment that they lobbied their council to use its power in order to impose essentially a restrictive covenant that the builder failed to exact from the original owner.

If property owners held a collective property right to the neighbourhood environment, they could vote on what uses (but not which users[98]) to admit to the neighbourhood. They could elect to admit some religious uses, but not others, as another letter to the editor, this time published in *The Globe and Mail*, reveals:

> [I]t should be remembered that the basis for this bylaw exemption for churches and schools was based on the old concept that such churches would be servicing the immediate community and responding to local demand. The bylaw probably did not envisage exemption in residential areas for churches or temples whose membership is small and drawn not from the immediately surrounding area but from a large region. While ratepayers may have the deepest respect for Zoroastrians, they can hardly be expected to be overjoyed by the establishment of institutions, religious or otherwise, which do not serve a number of residents in the surrounding area. Such, I submit, was not the original intention of the North York zoning bylaw.[99]

If the neighbours could not as a matter of law choose which religious institutions to admit, then perhaps they would have preferred to admit none than to admit all of them. The decision in *H.G. Winton* denies even this second-best choice.

Aftermath and Conclusions

In the aftermath of the Court's decision to quash the bylaw, North York council voted not to pursue an appeal.[100] The Zoroastrian Society took possession of the house, and in 1980 inaugurated it as their temple. The Society's newsletter reported a speech by Mayor Lastman, who at first supported the neighbours' fight to stop the temple, but now admitted that their fears were unnecessary.[101]

In 1985, plans by the Zoroastrian community to construct a centre in West Vancouver were met by strong opposition from the neighbours.[102] A ratepayers' petition to the West Vancouver community council cited traffic concerns, but *The Vancouver Sun* quoted one of the residents as stating: "To be really honest with you, [the neighbours] didn't want an Iranian church in the neighbourhood. It's a high-class neighbourhood. Put yourself in the same position. You've got a $250,000 house and they put an East Indian church in there and the value of your house is going to drop by half."[103] In the face of these objections, the plans were withdrawn and in their stead, a vacant church property in Burnaby was purchased and converted for use as a Zoroastrian centre with a donation from the same benefactor of the Zoroastrian temple in Toronto. The episode was described by Rastin Mehri as part of his portrayal of the Zoroastrian community in British Columbia. Mehri quotes a trustee for the centre, who explained the community's decision to back down from a struggle over the original site: "Our religion is based on peace and harmony, so when we saw it was creating problems we felt it would be best to withdraw and look for a neighbourhood where we would be accepted."[104] In light of this statement, how can the decision of the Toronto Zoroastrians to challenge North York's zoning amendment be explained? Perhaps they were worried about losing the funds pledged by their benefactor to a Zoroastrian centre elsewhere in North America.[105] But another reason may be that Winton had regarded the letter from the borough's building commissioner, assuring ZSO of the conformity of the propose use with the borough's zoning bylaw, as sufficient to remove the vendor's conditions, and that the purchasers were now bound to close the deal. It is possible (and indeed alluded to in Winton's cross-examination) that he threatened ZSO with legal action, forcing them to join the application for judicial review.[106]

In 2006, the house at 3590 Bayview Avenue was listed on the inventory of Toronto's heritage properties as the "Mazo de la Roche House" — the only Toronto house among the many that the author occupied during her life, that is officially associated with her name.[107] (Benares Historic House in Mississauga, considered the inspiration for the *Jalna* series of novels that earned Mazo de la Roche her reputation, is nationally recognized by the Historic Sites and Monuments Board of Canada.) In 2008, the public was invited to tour the temple and view the prayer room as part of the City of Toronto's Doors Open program. Several months earlier, the Zoroastrian Society filed plans with the city of Toronto to demolish the house and construct a modern temple more suitable to the current needs of the community, which is now the largest in North America. The application is still under review.

H.G. Winton exemplifies the presumption that the exclusionary power of zoning, and spot zoning in particular, is exercisable only for the purposes of promoting some formally recognized planning policy or preventing some undesirable physical impact. It also demonstrates the tendency of the courts to view spot zoning with greater suspicion than land use regulations that apply to all lands in the municipality. On a more general level, *H.G. Winton* reveals the legal assumptions underlying the exclusionary power of zoning, as well as the sensitivities of the realities of zoning practice and the difficulty of the courts in confronting the dominant function of land use regulations as a municipal service to existing homeowners. It provides a useful example of the protection from prejudice afforded to minority religious uses even prior to the *Charter*. Other uses are not immune from exclusion. While residents may not harness the coercive power of zoning to against religious minorities,[108] they still have a *de facto* right to exclude affordable housing, for example — so long as they can couch their motives in terms of planning and the public interest.

Notes

1 [1978] 20 OR (2d) 737, 88 DLR (3d) 733, 6 MPLR 1 (Div Ct) [*H.G. Winton*, cited to MPLR].

2 See Raphaël Fischler, "Development Controls in Toronto in the Nineteenth Century" (2007) 36:1 *Urban History Review* 16 (arguing that early bylaws contained the rudimentary elements of modern zoning). For discussion of covenants, see Philip Girard's essay, in this collection.

3 RSBC 1897, c 144, s 50(91), am. SBC 1900, c 23, s 4.

4 *Consolidated Municipal Act*, SO 1903, c 19, as amended by SO 1904, c 22, s 19. The section was amended subsequently several times to include (or more precisely, to *ex*clude) such uses as horse stables, dog kennels, blacksmiths, pits and quarries, manure pits, theatres, plumber shops, and apartment or tenement houses. See JB Milner, *Community Planning: a Casebook on Law and Administration* (Toronto: University of Toronto Press, 1963) at 605–07.

5 The plan was drawn by Thomas Adams and Horace Seymour, two pioneers of planning in Canada. See Elizabeth Bloomfield, "Reshaping the Urban Landscape: Town Planning Effects in Kitchener/Waterloo, 1912–1926" in Gilbert A. Stelter & Alan FJ Artibise, eds, *Shaping the Urban Landscape: Aspects of the Canadian City-Building Process* (Ottawa: Carleton University Press, 1982) 256.

6 American cities had experimented with land use controls since the turn of the century, and while New York City's 1916 zoning ordinance is hailed as the first comprehensive zoning scheme implemented in the US, the legality of zoning was not settled until the ruling in *Village of Euclid v Ambler Realty Co.* (1926) 272 US 365 [*Euclid*].

7 The context in which land use planning and regulation evolved in Canada, as well as its intellectual sources and early objectives are described in Gerald Hodge & David LA Gordon, *Planning Canadian Communities: an Introduction to the Principles, Practice and Participants*, 5th ed (Toronto: Nelson Thomson, 2008) at 50–108. See also Michael Allan Wolf, *The Zoning of America: Euclid v. Ambler* (Lawrence, Kan.: University Press of Kansas, 2008), Chapter 3.

8 See Robert H. Nelson, "Zoning Myth and Practice: From Euclid into the Future" in Charles M. Haar, ed, *Zoning and the American Dream: Promises Still to Keep* (Chicago: Planners Press, 1989) 299; Walter van Nus, "Towards the City Efficient: The Theory and Practice of Zoning, 1919–1939" in Alan FJ Artibise & Gilbert A. Stelter, eds, *The Usable Urban Past: Planning and Politics in the Modern Canadian City* (Toronto: Macmillan, 1979) 226.

9 In Ontario, for example, municipalities with a population of 100,000 or higher were given the power to exclude building containing three or more suites in 1912: see *Consolidated Municipal Act*, SO 1903, c 19, as am. by SO 1912, c 40, s 10.

10 See Nelson, above note 8.

11 See, for example, John C. Weaver, "The Property Industry and Land Use Controls: The Vancouver Experience, 1910–1945" (1979) 19:3 Plan Canada 211.

12 Above note 6.

13 *Ibid* at 397.

14 *Ibid* (per Sutherland J).

15 Alfred Bettman, the Cincinnati lawyer credited with winning over the US Supreme Court in *Euclid* by submitting an amicus brief in support of zoning correctly predicted in 1917: "A comprehensive city plan, based on a thorough, expert study and upon the promotion of the health, safety and comfort of the whole community, will surely sooner or later — and probably sooner — be upheld by the supreme court of the United States as a modern form of the regulation of the use of private property for the promotion of general public safety and comfort and welfare": see Alfred Bettman, "City planning progress" (1917) 6:3 *National Municipal Review* 351 at 351–52. Indeed, two years after *Euclid*, the Court struck down a zoning ordinance which placed some of the appellant's industrial lands in a residential district, having concluded on the facts that the ordinance bore no rational relationship to the health, safety, convenience, or general welfare of the community: See *Nectow v City of Cambridge*, 277 US 183 (1928).

16 It's been suggested that "performance zoning," that is, the regulation of the location of uses on the basis of their measured impact (e.g., noise, traffic volume) would produce a more desirable mixture of uses: see, for example, Luther L McDougal, III, "Performance Standards: A Viable Alternative to Euclidean Zoning" (1972-1973) 47 *Tulane Law Review* 255. Such proposals have not been adopted widely.

17 See Charles M. Haar, "In Accordance with a Comprehensive Plan" (1955) 68 Harv L Rev 1154.

18 For the classic authority providing empirical evidence see Richard F. Babcock, *The Zoning Game: Municipal Practices and Policies* (Madison: University of Wisconsin Press, 1966).

19 American Institute of Architects, *Report of the Committee on Community Planning (to the Fifty-Eighth Annual Convention, 1925)*, reprinted in Roy Lubove, ed, *The Urban Community: Housing and Planning in the Progressive Era* (Englewood Cliffs, NJ,: Prentice-Hall, 1967) [Lubove, *The Urban Community*] 116 at 127–28. A study of the famous 1916 zoning ordinance of New York confirmed systematic efforts under the guise of promoting the general welfare of the city's residents (by regulating such matters as the height and bulk of skyscrapers) to segregate the city's residents into different districts according to their socioeconomic status: see Raphael Fischler, "Health, Safety, and the General Welfare: Markets, Politics and Social Science in Early Land-Use Regulation and Community Design" (1998) 24:6 Journal of Urban History 675. The City justified the regulations as welfare enhancing measures: "There is an intimate and necessary relation between conservation of property values as here proposed and the conservation of public health, safety, and general welfare. Throughout a city the areas in which values have been depressed by the invasion of inappropriate uses or lack of building control as to height, courts, and open spaces, are the areas in which the worst conditions as to sanitation and safety prevail": see City of New York, Board of Estimate and Apportionment, *Final Report of the Commis-*

sion on Building Districts and Restrictions (1916) reprinted in Lubove, *The Urban Community* at 97.

20 See Peter W. Moore, "Zoning and Planning: The Toronto Experience, 1904-1970" in Alan FJ Artibise & Gilbert A. Stelter, eds, *The Usable Urban Past: Planning and Politics in the Modern Canadian City* (Toronto: Macmillan, 1979) 316. See also Richard Harris, *Creeping Conformity: How Canada Became Suburban, 1900–1960* (Toronto, ON: University of Toronto Press, 2004) at 124.

21 Weaver, above note 11 at 221.

22 See further Michael C. Poulton, "Externalities, Transaction Costs, Public Choice and the Appeal of Zoning: A Response to Lai Wai Chung and Sorensen" (1997) 68:1 The Town Planning Review 81.

23 See, for example, Doug Harris's essay in this collection.

24 *The Planning and Development Act*, SS 2007, c P-13.2, s 45.

25 *Municipal Government Act*, SNS 1998, c 18, s 219.

26 See Stanley M. Makuch, Neil Craik & Signe B. Leisk, *Canadian Municipal and Planning Law*, 2nd ed (Toronto: Thomson Carswell, 2004) at 197 and 199.

27 *R. v Bell* [1979] 2 SCR 212, (1979), 9 MPLR 103, 98 DLR (3d) 255. For analysis of this decision see Felix Hoehn, *Municipalities and Canadian Law: Defining the Authority of Local Governments* (Saskatoon: Purich Pub., 1996) at 175–77; Makuch, Craik & Leisk, above note 26 at 198–99.

28 [1969] 2 OR 461 (CA).

29 *Barrie (City) v Brown Camps Residential & Day Schools*, (1973), 2 OR (2d) 337, 42 DLR (3d) 681, (CA) (leave to appeal refused (1974), 2 OR (2d) 337n, 42 DLR (3d) 681n (SCC)) [*Barrie v Brown Camps*].

30 (1973), 2 OR (2d) 337 at 443–44. An approach focusing on the actual attributes of the use instead of the zoning bylaw's taxonomy was also favoured in *Aurora (Town) v Anglican Houses* (1990), 50 MPLR 62, 72 OR (2d) 732 (HC).

31 Hoehn, above note 27 at 178–79, 182; Makuch, Craik & Leisk, above note 26 at 197–98. Makuch points out that this was the reasoning of the trial judge in the second *Brown Camps* case.

32 Spot zoning may be more broadly defined as the designation of a small (often a single) parcel of land for a use category inconsistent with that of similar lands in the surrounding area. This may be done for the benefit of the owner of such lands and at the expense of others (such as when one parcel in a single-family district is zoned for multifamily housing), or to the detriment of the owner and for the benefit of owners of surrounding lands.

33 See van Nus, above note 8. No different is the American experience: see, for example, Robert C. Ellickson & Vicki L. Been, *Land Use Controls: Cases and Materials*, 3rd ed (New York, NY: Aspen Publishers, Inc., 2005).

34 [1959] SCR 444, 18 DLR (2d) 161, affirming on other grounds 11 DLR (2d) 358, [1957] OR 643, 1957 (CA), reversing [1957] OJ 699, 7 DLR (2d) 733, [1957] OWN 257 (HC) [*Bondi*].

35 *Forst v Toronto (City)*, [1923] OJ No. 42, 54 OLR 256 (CA), at 278–79 (Middleton J). See further Stanley M. Makuch, "Discrimination and Municipal By-Laws" (Paper

presented to the Canadian Institute for the Administration of Justice Conference, Kananaskis, Alta., Oct. 11–14, 1989) in Walter Surma Tarnopolsky et al, eds, *Discrimination in the Law and the Administration of Justice* (Montréal: Éditions Thémis, 1989) 98; Hoehn, above note 27 at 37–40, 173–75.

36 7 DLR (2d) 733 at para. 16.

37 [1959] SCR 444 at 451: "The mere delimitation of the boundaries of the area affected by such a by-law involves an element of discrimination. On one side of an arbitrary line an owner may be prevented from doing something with his property which another owner, on the other side of the line, with a property which corresponds in all respects except location, is free to do." Compare Judson J's statement with the recent judgment of McLachlin CJ, for the majority of the Supreme Court in *Sacré-Coeur (Municipality) v Lacombe*, (2010), 75 MPLR (4th) 1, 324 DLR (4th) 625, [2010] 2 SCR 453. The case dealt with a zoning bylaw that permitted aerodromes in one part of the municipality, but banned them in an adjacent zone that was otherwise identical. The Chief Justice held that the bylaw "purports to regulate the location of aerodromes without reference to the underlying land use regime. It does not function as zoning legislation, but rather, is a stand-alone prohibition. It treats similar parcels differently, and different parcels the same, *belying the first principle of zoning legislation*" (*ibid*, at para. 56, emphasis added).

38 [2004] 2 SCR 650, 49 MPLR (3d) 157, 2004 SCC 48, 241 DLR (4th) 83 (LeBel J, dissenting).

39 *Ibid* at para. 81 (LeBel J).

40 [1990] 6 WWR 232, 69 DLR (4th) 697, 65 Man R (2d) 81, 49 MPLR 1 (C.A.) [*Alcoholism Foundation of Manitoba*] (provisions in the city's zoning bylaw, which referred to disabled and substance-dependent individuals stuck down for being in violation of the *Charter*).

41 *Ibid* at para. 45.

42 Meanwhile, several scholars have offered an economic justification for exclusion under certain conditions: see, for example, Bruce W. Hamilton, "Zoning and Property Taxation in a System of Local Governments" (1975) 12:2 *Urban Studies* 205; Robert C. Ellickson, "Suburban Growth Controls: An Economic and Legal Analysis" (1977) 86 *Yale Law Journal* 385; Robert H. Nelson, *Zoning and Property Rights: an Analysis of the American System of Land-use Regulation* (Cambridge, Mass.: MIT Press, 1977); William A. Fischel, *The Economics of Zoning Laws : A Property Rights Approach to American Land Use Controls* (Baltimore: John Hopkins University Press, 1985).

43 Mazo de la Roche published her first work in 1902, but became an internationally famous, best-selling author after her novel *Jalna* won the *Atlantic Monthly* book award in 1927. She went on to publish numerous other works, including fifteen more *Jalna* books. The curious reader may refer to one of her published biographies, including: Ronald Hambleton, *Mazo de la Roche of Jalna* (New York,: Hawthorn Books, 1966); Joan Givner, *Mazo de la Roche: the Hidden Life* (Toronto: Oxford University Press, 1989); and Daniel L. Bratton, *Thirty-two Short Views of Mazo de la Roche* (Toronto: ECW Press, 1996).

44 "North York plans to flatten Mazo de la Roche's house" *The Toronto Star* (8 April 1976), B01; Michael Keating "Jalna author's home may be doomed" *The Globe and Mail* (8 April 1976), 51. The developer reportedly paid $1.6 million for the property. As a curious side note, the vendor of the property, Dr. Rudd, who bought the estate in 1954, claimed that he defeated a previous attempt in the 1960s by Metro Toronto to expropriate the land and demolish the house for the purpose of improving Bayview Avenue, by invoking "a century-old law that said the municipality could not deprive him of the enjoyment of the tributary of the Don River running along an area which would have been paved"; *ibid.* The precise nature of these riparian rights is unclear. Only a few days after the borough's planning board recommended the developer's plans, but before council could vote on the application, fire officials were called in to stop a fire in the house, which was started by Dr. Rudd when he was burning papers in one of the mansion's fireplaces: "De la Roche home saved from wreckers and fire" *The Toronto Star* (13 April 1976), B1.

45 Borough of North York, *Council Minutes* (20 April 1976) at 20.

46 Ronald Hambleton "Mazo's homes" *Globe and Mail* (23 April 1976), 7.

47 "Buyer saves author's home from wreckers" *The Toronto Star* (26 May 1976), B2.

48 "Developer buys home of Mazo de la Roche" *The Globe and Mail* (26 May 1976), 4.

49 In fact, the court records show that at the time, HG Winton Ltd.'s rights in the property were held under his agreement to purchase the land from JFM Development Ltd, and although a deposit was paid for the property, the company did not yet complete the transaction and take title. See Applicant's Statement, No. R.E. 8150/78; and Cross Examination of Harry Winton (both on file with the author).

50 A sense of Winton's mercurial movements can be obtained from reading some of the new reports: see Warren Potter "Home to be a museum" *The Toronto Star* (4 June 1976), B2; "'Whispering pines' got chop, owner says" *The Toronto Star* (17 May 1977), B2; Warren Potter "Owner can't raze writer's home" *The Toronto Star* (7 October 1977), C2.

51 Mary Boyce, *Zoroastrians: their Religious Beliefs and Practices* (London: Routledge, 2001) at 1.

52 John R. Hinnells, "The Zoroastrian Diaspora in Britain, Canada, and the United States" in Harold G. Coward, John R. Hinnells & Raymond Brady Williams, eds, *The South Asian Religious Diaspora in Britain, Canada, and the United States* (Albany, NY: State University of New York, 2000) 35 at 36–37. For a comprehensive account of the Zoroastrian diaspora in Canada see John R. Hinnells, *The Zoroastrian Diaspora: Religion and Migration* (New York: Oxford University Press, 2005); for additional information on Iranian Zoroastrians see Richard Foltz, "Iranian Zoroastrians in Canada: Balancing Religious and Cultural Identities" (2009) 42:4 *Iranian Studies* 561.

53 The *Toronto Star,* while reporting in 1976 on the local Zoroastrian community's building drive, noted the Zoroastrian "passion for education" reflected in the high percentage (more than half) of local Parsis employed as teachers, accountants, engineers, and so forth. "One is a deputy minister in the Ontario government; another is chairman of a department in a leading medical school." The reporter noted also that Parsis "resemble very fair-skinned Indians" and that they have a reputation for

honesty, charity, and being liberal-minded: see Tom Harpur "Toronto Zoroastrians strive to keep their identity" *The Toronto Star* (17 July 1976), A17.

54 *Ibid.*

55 In India, non-Zoroastrians are prohibited from entering fully-consecrated temples. But in the diaspora, where inter-faith marriage are common, the admission of non-Zoroastrians is a live issue. See further Hinnells, above note 52 at 462–65.

56 *HG Winton*, above note 1 at 4.

57 Above note 1.

58 *HG Winton*, above note 1 at paras 7–8.

59 Borough of North York, *Council Minutes* (27 February 1978). See also *HG Winton*, above note 1 at 8–9.

60 Warren Potter "Group's opposition blocks purchase of author's home" *The Toronto Star* (21 March 1978), A4.

61 At the relevant time, all zoning bylaws adopted by municipalities in Ontario required OMB approval. Following legislative reforms introduced in 1983 by Ontario's new *Planning Act*, zoning bylaws took immediate effect unless appealed to the OMB.

62 James Jefferson "Zoroastrians to challenge North York law" *The Globe and Mail* (10 May 1978), 5.

63 *Ibid.* The language spoken by many Parsi Zoroastrians in addition to English is Gujarati.

64 "Metro opposes North York law that prohibits religious temple" *The Globe and Mail* (31 May 1978), 4. The following month, Mr. Sewell entered the Toronto mayoral race, which he won in December of the same year. Mr. Lastman continued to serve as Mayor of North York until January 1998, when he himself became Mayor of Toronto.

65 See Municipality of Metropolitan Toronto, *Minutes of Metropolitan Council* (30 May 1978) at 185, 192; "Planners oppose law barring Zoroastrians" *The Globe and Mail* (18 May 1978), T6.

66 *Canada Trust Co. v Ontario Human Rights Commission*, (1990), 69 DLR (4th), 321, 74 OR (2d) 481.

67 See further, Bruce H. Ziff, *Unforeseen Legacies: Reuben Wells Leonard and the Leonard Foundation Trust* (Toronto: University of Toronto Press, 2000).

68 See *Cadillac Fairview Corp. v R.W.D.S.U.* [1989] OJ No. 2291, 64 DLR (4th) 267, 71 OR (2d) 206 (CA), discussed in Eric Tucker's essay in this collection.

69 See cross-examination of Michael Paul Smith (on file with the author) at 12.

70 As a general rule, zoning changes do not affect existing (legally protected non-conforming) uses and building: see e.g., *Saint-Romuald (Ville) v Olivier*, 204 DLR (4th) 284, [2001] 2 SCR 898, 22 MPLR (3d) 1. The classic authority (which bears some similarity to the facts in *H.G. Winton*) is *Toronto (City) v Central Jewish Institute*, [1948] 2 DLR 1, [1948] SCR 101. In that case, the appellant purchased property in a residential neighbourhood for the purpose of operating on the premises a school, which was a permitted use under the zoning in force. When the appellant got wind of the City's plan (in response to the neighbours' agitation) to rezone the land so as to prohibit the proposed use, it was able to take early possession of the building and make limited use of it as a school before the municipality completed the rezoning process.

The Supreme Court found that the appellant established a legal non-conforming use of the building and was not bound by the new restrictions.

71 Above note 69 at 33.

72 *H.G. Winton*, above note 1 at 10.

73 *Ibid*, at 8.

74 *Ibid*, at 9.

75 *Ibid*, at 11 (citations omitted).

76 *Ibid*, at 8–11.

77 See above notes 32–36 and accompanying text.

78 Above note 34.

79 *H.G. Winton*, above note 1 at 12 [citations omitted].

80 *The Globe and Mail* comment pointed out that within a few blocks from the Zoroastrian temple were several religious institutions, including two churches, a synagogue, a bible college, and a seminary: see Dick Beddoes "Paving path to a temple" *The Globe and Mail* (5 July 1978), 8.

81 For a sample of decisions adopting Robins J's formulations see *Grosvenor v East Luther Grand Valley (Township)* (2006), 53 RPR (4th) 176, 32 MPLR (4th) 20 (Ont Div Ct.); *Brantford (City) v Konakov*, (2004), 181 OAC 187, 69 OR (3d) 97, 45 MPLR (3d) 1 (CA); *Sivulliik Development Corp. v Iqaluit (Town)* (1998), [1998] NWTJ No. 116, 47 MPLR (2d) 323 (CA); *Canada Mortgage & Housing Corp. v North Vancouver (District)* (1998), 51 BCLR (3d) 351, 45 MPLR (2d) 214, 70 LCR 161 (BC SC); *Equity Waste Management of Canada Corp. v Halton Hills (Town)* (1997), 35 OR (3d) 321, 103 OAC 324, 40 MPLR (2d) 107 (CA) [*Equity Waste*]. For other analysis of HG Winton, see Hoehn, above note 27 at 173–74, 184; Makuch, Craik & Leisk, above note 26 at 101, 203, 206.

82 "North York to accept Zoroastrian ruling" *The Globe and Mail* (14 July 1978), P5.

83 See text accompanying note 79, above.

84 [1960] OR 374, 24 DLR (2d) 12 (CA) [*Re North York*].

85 *Ibid*. One might question what planning purpose is served by artificial height and density restrictions, which a municipality imposes, but is willing to waive for a price.

86 Above note 34.

87 *Toronto (City) v Trustees of the Toronto Roman Catholic Separate School Board*, [1926] AC 81, [1925] 3 DLR 880 (PC), reversing [1924] SCJ No. 17; [1924] SCR 368; [1924] 3 DLR 113 [*Toronto Roman Catholic Separate School Board*]. In that case, the separate school board acquired residential properties in order to convert them to a school building, which was a lawful use. Upon learning of this plan, neighbours' petitioned council to pass a zoning bylaw prohibiting all uses except residential on their street block. The school board then made an application for a building permit which the city refused. The school board then sought a writ of mandamus, but by the time the matter came before the courts, the city had completed the rezoning process. On appeal from the Supreme Court of Canada, the Judicial Committee of the Privy Council held that the although the school board had a *prima facie* right to a building permit, that right was defeated by the passing of the bylaw.

88 See "The Zoning Power" above.

89 Above note 87.
90 [1924] 3 DLR 113 at 118.
91 7 DLR (2d) 733 at para 9.
92 *Ibid.*
93 *Bondi*, above note 34 at 450.
94 But see Monnin's unabashed acknowledgment in *Alcoholism Foundation of Manitoba*, above note 40.
95 This line of argument is strongly inspired by Nelson, above note 8.
96 A. Dan Tarlock, "Toward a Revised Theory of Zoning" (1972) Land Use Controls Annual 141, reprinted in Randall W. Scott, David J. Brower & Dallas D. Miner, eds, *Management & Control of Growth: Issues, Techniques, Problems, Trends*, vol. i (Washington, D.C.: Urban Land Institute, 1975) 228 at 232 (footnotes omitted). Professor Tarlock's argument was influenced, of course, by Ronald Coase's 1960 seminal article, "The Problem of Social Cost" (RH Coase, "The Problem of Social Cost" (1960) 3 Journal of Law and Economics 1). If the original understanding of land use regulation was based in externalities, Tarlock explained, the case for regulation must be evaluated in light of Coase's work, which showed convincingly that in many cases, social costs can be internalized by private negotiations if property rights are clearly defined. For an assessment of the advantages of zoning over restrictive covenants, see Herbert Hovenkamp, "Bargaining in Coasian Markets: Servitudes and Alternative Land Use Controls" (2002) 27 J Corp L 519.

This was not merely theory. For example, the City of Toronto's 1927 zoning bylaw was enacted at the request of the residents of the prestigious Lawrence Park neighbourhood and imposed the same restrictions contained in a scheme of covenants that attached to the area and that was set to expire: see Moore, above note 20 at 322–23.
97 T. Saltzman "Letter to the editor" *The Toronto Star* (17 July 1978), A9.
98 Zoning follows the law of restrictive covenants in refusing to uphold such restrictions: see Bruce Ziff, *Principles of Property Law*, 5th ed (Toronto: Carswell, 2010) at 402–404; compare notes 27–32, above and accompanying text.
99 Henry J. D. Turman "Zoroastrians" *The Globe and Mail* (12 July 1978), P7.
100 "North York to accept Zoroastrian ruling," above note 82.
101 See Hinnells, above note 52 at 501 (citing a ZSO Newsletter dated 1 November 1980).
102 The episode is documented in Rastin Mehri, "Zoroastrians in British Columbia" in Don Baker, Daniel L. Overmyer & Larry DeVries, eds, *Asian Religions in British Columbia* (Vancouver: University of British Columbia Press, 2010) 85 at 94–96.
103 N. Knickerbocker "Racism Charges Levelled as Group Drops Church Bid" *Vancouver Sun* (26 July 1985), A14 (Cited by Mehri, above note 102 at 94.)
104 See Mehri, above note 102 at 95.
105 Harry Winton's affidavit states that Winton was informed about ZSO's concern by Mr. Shroff: see Winton's affidavit, 1 May 1978 at ¶4.
106 See cross examination of Harry Winton, pages 23–24.

107 A search of Toronto's inventory of heritage properties indicates that of the four other houses in Toronto where Mazo de la Roche wrote, only 3 Ava Crescent is listed as a heritage property, but not for its connection with the author.

108 Now see *Lafontaine,* above note 39.

Manitoba Fisheries v The Queen: The Origins of Canada's De Facto Expropriation Doctrine

Jim Phillips and Jeremy Martin[1]

Introduction

In October 1978 the Supreme Court of Canada decided *Manitoba Fisheries v The Queen*,[2] the first case in which the court held that a statute — the federal *Freshwater Fish Marketing Act*[3] (FFMA) — that did not expropriate title to property nonetheless had the effect of taking away, and giving to the government, a citizen's property. *Manitoba Fisheries* established in Canadian law a doctrine that in US law has been around since the early twentieth century and is known as "regulatory takings"; in Canada it is known by either that term or, more commonly, as "*de facto* expropriation." A *de facto* expropriation occurs when the state does not take title to property, but regulates in such a way and to such an extent that it is considered to have effectively taken it. Most claims for *de facto* expropriation, in the US and in Canada, concern regulation of land use, but they are not limited to that. *Manitoba Fisheries* came out of broader economic regulation, which had an incidental effect on property other than land. Indeed it is fair to say that clever lawyering turned an issue of economic regulation into a property case, and thus enabled one set of economic actors to receive compensation that is not otherwise given for losses occasioned by changes to a regulatory framework.

In the second part we will first briefly describe the case. The third part deals with the pre-litigation background, looking at the state of Canada's freshwater lake fishery before a new regulatory regime was brought in, analyzing the various federal and provincial enactments that made up that regime, and examining the demands for compensation by some Manitoba corporations as they were played out in the politics of the province in the early 1970s. To this point the story is largely an economic and political one. Part four deals with the litigation, beginning in 1974 when a young and rather inexperienced sole practitioner found a way to make the matter a legal case. From then on the story becomes a legal one. We conclude with a brief account of the effects of the Supreme Court judgment.

The *Manitoba Fisheries* story contains a number of interrelated themes. In part it is a very Canadian story, one about a willingness to employ government intervention in the economy to remedy socioeconomic ills caused by the operation of the free market. In part, like so many other Canadian legal stories, it is about federalism. As an exercise in legal archeology, however, it is ultimately a tale of lawyers and judges. The principal player is Ken Arenson, a young sole practitioner who through an inventive argument was able to turn what everybody, including four federal court judges, thought was a hopeless case into a winner. Equally important in the end were the men who decided the case at the Supreme Court of Canada, who arguably allowed their broadly small-p political views to influence their judgment.

A Brief Account of *Manitoba Fisheries v The Queen*

In 1969, pursuant to an agreement among the federal government, the provinces of Alberta, Manitoba, Ontario, and Saskatchewan, and the Northwest Territories, the federal parliament passed the FFMA. Its principal provisions were the establishment of a federal crown corporation, the Freshwater Fish Marketing Corporation (FFMC), and the granting to that corporation of a monopoly of international and inter-provincial trade in freshwater fish caught in the provinces noted. The Act went into force in those provinces only when each made an agreement with the federal government, and in each province parallel provincial legislation was to be passed giving the FFMC an internal monopoly in the buying and selling of freshwater fish. Such are the needs of federalism; the federal government can only legislate with regards to international and inter-provincial trade, not intra-provincial trade.

The effect of the Act and the operations of the FFMC was to put out of business all the private companies that had operated as middlemen — dealers, processors and exporters — taking the fish from the primary producer and getting it to market. The federal-provincial legislative scheme included provision for some compensation for these companies, but it was considered inadequate by those who had operated in Manitoba. When neither the provincial nor the federal government would yield to demands for higher compensation, eight Manitoba companies sued the federal government in federal court, with *Manitoba Fisheries* becoming the test case for the group. The company argued that the effect of the federal statute had been to take away their goodwill and to give it to the FFMC, an agent of the crown. Since goodwill is a recognized species of property, the crown had in effect taken property.

The claim failed at the trial level and on appeal, but was accepted by a unanimous Supreme Court of Canada. The Court accepted that there were many customers of Manitoba Fisheries who could no longer do business with the company after 1969, but were "compelled to do business only with the Corporation." That process represented a transfer of property from the company to the Crown, for goodwill "although intangible in character" was "a part of the property of a business just as much as the premises, machinery and equipment employed in the production of the product whose quality engenders that goodwill." Since goodwill was property, and since that goodwill necessarily flowed to the corporation, "the appellant was deprived of property which was acquired by the Crown." For this Manitoba Fisheries should be compensated. Although there was and is no constitutional protection for property in Canada, the common law's respect for private property gives rise to a presumption of statutory interpretation, which provides that while in a system of parliamentary supremacy, Parliament has the power to take property, if it wishes to do so without paying compensation it must say so "clearly."[4] Since the FFMA did not do so, compensation was payable.

Background to the Litigation

Canada's Freshwater Fishery and Government Intervention

Commercial fishing in the Prairie provinces had begun in the late-nineteenth century, and it expanded rapidly by century's end, as a ready market was found in the US. Aboriginal and Euro-Canadian fishers contributed to the catch.[5] The American demand was fuelled largely by the substantial Jewish communities of the North East and Midwest, who used various species of lake fish to make gefilte fish. The industry enjoyed its most successful years up to 1930, after which it suffered a series of crises, including over fishing, an American import ban, and parasitic infestation. Particularly affected were the large southern lakes, so that by the second half of the century the northern lakes became increasingly important, with the consequence that the primary producers were increasingly aboriginal in all the provinces.

By the 1950s and 1960s, Canada's freshwater fishery had recovered somewhat and was a significant player in provincial economies.[6] Among the provinces/territories that came under the federal-provincial scheme, Manitoba had by far the largest share; over half of the roughly 6,000 fishermen involved in the industry were in Manitoba, as were two-thirds (198 of 285) of the dealers. Manitoba exported more fish than the other two Prairie provinces combined, and more than Ontario, if the Great Lakes fisheries, which were much larger and more prosperous, are excluded. Fish came from very large lakes (Lake Manitoba, Lake Winnipeg, Lake Winnipegosis, Reindeer Lake, and Great Slave Lake) and from hundreds of small ones.

The patterns of marketing varied from place to place. For "whole," or unprocessed, which means not filletted, some fishermen in Manitoba and elsewhere sold directly to American importers. This was very much the exception, however, being only possible when distances to markets were small. A more common method often employed when distances were moderate was for a group of fishermen to sell to dealer/exporters, who then sold the catch on to the US. Most fishermen, however, sold to dealers who in turn consolidated their purchases and sold the collective catch on to exporters; this was how almost all "whole" fish from the Prairie provinces' lakes reached market. Exports of filleted fish were the purview solely of exporters who necessarily also had processing plants. There were thirty-two licensed exporters in the Prairie provinces, of which twenty were substantial operations, and of those twenty, thirteen were in Manitoba, mostly in Winnipeg. The result was that almost all fish exported from Manitoba moved through various stages before reaching the retail market.

By the 1950s the freshwater fishing industry outside the Great Lakes was in a sorry state, and had been in that condition for some time. The primary producers eked out a subsistence income only, and the socioeconomic problem was exacerbated by the substantial representation in the industry in the prairies of Aboriginal — Indian and Métis — fishermen. Prices were chronically low. A very small number of American importers in Chicago, Detroit, and New York controlled the wholesale market, and within Canada the industry had too many small players and too much competition. In Manitoba there was one dealer for every seventeen fishermen, and most processing plants were small and inefficient. Canadian exporters, in the absence of rationalization or co-operative marketing, had very little room to negotiate the best price for their produce. The result was a highly impoverished sector marked by what a 1965 federal commission of inquiry under former Wheat Board chair George McIvor called an "atmosphere of pessimism and doom." McIvor also asserted that he was "not aware of a worse pocket of poverty in Canada than the northern segments of the inland fishery." Noting that many of the fishermen did not own their own boats or equipment, and borrowed money for them from dealers and exporters, money that they could not repay at the end of the season, he went so far as to draw comparisons with indentured servitude.[7]

Governments were aware of these problems at least as early as the 1930s.[8] But our story begins a little later, in 1953, when a confidential report to the federal Commercial Fishing Commission drew attention to the inefficiencies of the Prairie fisheries compared to those of the Great Lakes, and the bare subsistence income of most fishermen.[9] A 1956 report to the federal government, part of the Royal Commission on Canada's Economic Prospects chaired by Walter Gordon, identified hyper-competition in fish exporting in general and the comparative under-production in the Prairie lakes in particular.[10] In addition, in 1963 Manitoba premier Duff Roblin's conservative government's Committee on Manitoba's Economic Future (COMEF) found that 90 percent of primary producers made only a supplementary income from fishing, that most of the fishermen were Métis or Aboriginal, and concluded that "fishermen in general have incomes and standards of living among the lowest of any industry group in Manitoba." It called for "extraordinary measures necessitating the closest co-operation between all interests concerned," including coordinated marketing of the inter-provincial and international trade in fish.[11] The faith in government intervention by Manitoba conservatives should not surprise us. In the prairies marketing boards were and are prevalent in rural industries, and at this time were generally strongly supported by farmers.[12] Indeed small-time dealers in the fishery had attempted to form their own co-operative in the 1920s to combat the power of the import firms, but the attempt came to nothing.

These recommendations produced some activity.[13] Sterling Lyon, then Manitoba's Minister of Mines and Natural Resources, approached the January 1964 Federal-Provincial Conference on Fisheries in Ottawa, the result of Lester Pearson's promise of a national fisheries policy, with a plan to implement the COMEF report's marketing and other suggestions. He aggressively promoted the idea of federal-provincial co-operation, and persuaded federal ministers and the premiers of Alberta, Saskatchewan, Manitoba, and Ontario to undertake a study of the usefulness of a marketing board. At the conclusion of the conference, Hédard Robichaud, federal Minister of Fisheries, announced a national fisheries development program. The future of the freshwater fisheries would be bright, he said, if a "progressive program of education, modernization and economic encouragement [were to be] adopted." The creation of a marketing board was to be the first step. In October 1964 a committee of deputy ministers recommended that an export monopoly be given to some body established by federal legislation, that that body "purchase . . . such products offered to it under contract by licensed dealers," and that provincial governments "provide for the appropriate re-organization of the primary and secondary fishing industries in their jurisdiction."[14] It is thus quite clear that at this time a marketing board would have little or no involvement in production and processing; private operators would continue to be involved, with the only change being that they would sell all their produce to the board directly rather than to US buyers. The new agency would operate very similarly to that most Canadian of institutions, the Wheat Board.

Nonetheless, some concerns were expressed about this by processors and exporters. As *The Winnipeg Tribune* put it, they felt that "the wedge would be set for driving fish companies out of business." These concerns do not appear to have derailed official plans, however, and by the end of November 1964, Alberta, Saskatchewan, Manitoba, Ontario, and the Northwest Territories had all accepted the idea and the federal government began drafting legislation for a new marketing board to be established sometime in 1965. The drafting came to naught in 1965 when Prime Minister Pearson established a Commission of Inquiry into Freshwater Fish Marketing.[15] It was to be chaired by McIvor, and its mandate was to report on "the nature of the factors which give rise to the weakness of prices for freshwater fish, particularly in the export market," and "the possibility and desirability of establishing an export monopoly to achieve more efficient marketing and thus provide better returns to primary producers." It is not clear why the government waited until six months after a broad consensus on the need for intervention had been reached to set up the inquiry. But it is reasonable to suggest that some differences of opinion had emerged during the drafting process. It may be — and we have only the circumstantial evidence of later developments to support this assertion — that the differences were principally over whether the board should function simply as a marketing board or whether it should take over other aspects of the chain of supply.

The McIvor Commission worked quickly, producing a report in a little over a year.[16] McIvor held public hearings in thirteen places, received a substantial number of written submissions, and visited wholesalers and Department of Trade and Commerce officials in the United States. The commission did not only look into the export trade, but also at the domestic "handling and processing" of fish, because to McIvor marketing involved the entire process "of moving freshwater fish from the primary producer to the consumer." Most of the major export/processing firms gave evidence in some form and, not surprisingly, in McIvor's words, were "opposed to an export monopoly." The *McIvor Report* produced a highly critical picture of the industry. Among its seven principal findings were that prices were weak because there were "too many exporters to counter the control exercised by a few importers." This was in part the cause of returns to fishermen being "unduly small" and "far too low." But an additional problem was that the domestic handling and processing of the fish was "inefficient and costly," leading to a lack of "effective quality control and of product standardization." None of this was particularly new, but the seventh listed finding was. McIvor stated his general agreement with the existing proposals for an export monopoly, but went on to "disagree strongly" with the idea that fish "be bought from licensed fish dealers and not directly from fishermen."

McIvor's attitude to both the fishermen and the other players in the industry was succinctly summarized in the body of the report: "The fisherman is the first and essential participant in marketing Canadian freshwater fish. This obvious fact appears to be often forgotten by the other participants in their relationships with the fishermen."

The Commission's substantive recommendations — seventeen in total — stressed the need to improve the lot of the freshwater fisherman by establishing a national marketing board for freshwater fish which would be responsible for improving prices and returning more profit to the primary producers. McIvor recommended that a marketing board for freshwater fish deal directly with primary producers, bypassing extant processing and export firms.

The Freshwater Fish Marketing Act

THE *McIvor Report* WAS tabled in Parliament on 18 October 1966, and discussion of its recommendations with the provinces began immediately. Yet it would be almost three years before federal legislation passed. In November 1967 the federal government stated that it disagreed in principle with some of the recommendations of the *McIvor Report*.[17] Given that compensation payments by the provinces were written into the final deal, it is likely that the need, politically if not legally, to provide compensation, was at least part of the problem. More generally, Ottawa did not want to act alone. The provinces took the federal government's objection seriously, with the result that in February 1968 they agreed that a freshwater fish marketing corporation be established as a joint venture, something that would require both federal and provincial legislation in order to give the corporation powers to operate with respect to both extra-provincial trade and intra-provincial production. Ottawa was now prepared to move, although nothing happened in the early months of 1968 because the governing Liberals were engaged in the leadership race that resulted in Pierre Trudeau's election as leader. His elevation was followed, on 25 June, by a federal election that saw the liberals win a majority government. Among the items in Trudeau's first throne speech, on 12 October, was a marketing board for freshwater fish.[18] A bill to that effect was introduced in late October, and it quickly passed, receiving royal assent on 27 February 1969. The Act was to come into force on proclamation, which turned out to be 1 May.

As the Bill went through Parliament, there were meetings between officials from the federal Ministry of Fisheries, their counterparts from the Manitoba government, and the representatives of Manitoba companies involved in the trade.[19] According to Manitoba Fisheries' later court filings, but denied by the federal government, the companies were told that either their businesses would be purchased or that full compensation for losses would be paid. The government's version was different: "there were indications given that compensation in some form would be taken into consideration."

The FFMA had two principal purposes. One was to establish the FFMC. Testament to the prominence of Manitoba in the freshwater fishing industry, the head office of the Corporation was to be in Winnipeg. The second main purpose of the Act was to give the FFMC a monopoly of the international and interprovincial trade in freshwater fish. This was achieved in the "participating provinces" by sections 21 and 23, which read:[20]

> 21 (1) Except in accordance with the terms and conditions set out in any licence that may be issued by the Corporation in that behalf, no person, other than the Corporation or an agent of the Corporation, shall
>
> (a) export fish from Canada;
>
> (b) send, convey or carry fish from a participating province to another participating province or to any other province;
>
> (c) in a participating province, receive fish for conveyance or carriage to a destination outside the province; or
>
> (d) sell or buy, or agree to sell or buy, fish situated in a participating province for delivery in another participating province or any other province, or outside Canada.
>
> 23 (1) . . . [T]he Corporation has the exclusive right to trade in and to market fish in interprovincial and export trade and shall exercise that right, either by itself or by its agents, with the object of
>
> (a) marketing fish in an orderly manner;
>
> (b) increasing returns to fishermen; and
>
> (c) promoting international markets for, and increasing interprovincial and export trade in, fish.

The only exception to the monopoly to be given to the FFMC was section 21 (2), which allowed it to issue licences to others.

There were other provisions of the Act that empowered, and in some cases required, the corporation to take a much larger role than that of mere marketing board. Section 7 stated that the FFMC was "established for the purpose of marketing and trading in fish, fish products and fish by-products in and outside Canada," and gave it powers "for that purpose" to "buy fish and dress, fillet, freeze, package or otherwise prepare fish for market" and to "buy, manufacture or produce fish products and fish by-products and package or otherwise prepare fish products and fish by-products for market." In other words, although the Act did not in terms give the FFMC a monopoly over the purchasing and processing of fish, as it did over their export, it did permit the corporation to not only buy fish but also to process it. Although the power to buy "fish" meant fish in whatever stage of production, and thus included fish bought from dealers and processors, section 23 (2) required the corporation to purchase fish directly from fishermen if the latter offered them. In short, the corporation had full power not only to act as a marketing board in dealing with out of province buyers, it could play, and was to some extent required to play, the role of intermediary between primary producers and ultimate buyers. It could also deal directly with the primary producers, to "make loans of working capital on a seasonal basis to persons engaged in fishing for commercial purposes in a participating province."

The federal-provincial nature of the undertaking was expressed in section 25, which dealt, *inter alia*, with compensation. The section provided that the federal Minister could make an agreement with any province for a variety of purposes. The two most important of these agreements were, first, an agreement to allow "the performance by the Corporation, on behalf of the province, of functions relating to intraprovincial trade in fish," and, second, a compensation agreement covering "the undertaking by the province of arrangements for the payment, to the owner of any plant or equipment used in storing, processing or otherwise preparing fish for market, of compensation for any such plant or equipment that will or may be rendered redundant by reason of any operations authorized to be carried out by the Corporation." Section 25 provided in effect a condition precedent for the FFMA's going into force in a province. The export monopoly set up under section 21 applied only to "participating provinces," and "participating province" was defined as a province or territory that had signed a section 25 agreement.

As noted above, the bill received an easy passage in parliament, although a few MPs noted that some businesses would go under as a result, and expressed concerns about compensation.[21] Otto Lang, Minister without Portfolio and the minister responsible for the bill in the Commons, was reassuring: "the provinces have accepted the responsibility for compensation for redundancy resulting from the operations of the corporation." More generally, he countered the few oppositions concerns by noting that the provinces had been "consulted all the way along" and "[t]here is complete agreement among the provinces and with the Federal Government about the content of the bill."

Provincial Legislation and Federal Provincial Agreements

Ontario, Alberta, Saskatchewan, and the Northwest Territories passed legislation to confer on the FFMC the powers to operate a monopoly within the provinces.[22] Pursuant to section 25 of the FFMA, the same provinces and territories also made agreements with the federal government about responsibility for compensation. Manitoba's turned out to be one of its last acts of the conservative administration before it was defeated in an election. Signed on 4 June 1969, the Canada-Manitoba agreement read: "The Province undertakes to make any arrangements necessary with the owner of any plant or equipment in . . . Manitoba used in storing, processing or otherwise preparing fish for market, for compensation for any such plant or equipment that will or may be rendered redundant by reason of any operations authorized to be carried out by the Corporation under the Act."

The agreement also committed to giving the FFMC "authority . . . to exercise powers of regulation in relation to the marketing of freshwater fish locally within the Province."[23] But uniquely among the provinces that passed similar enabling legislation, the Manitoba *Fisheries Act* of 1969 engendered heated debate and only just passed.[24] Such controversy is surprising, because the Conservatives had taken part in the federal-provincial negotiations, signed the agreement with Ottawa, and had actually drafted the legislation. Before it could be introduced in the legislature, premier Walter Weir resigned, calling an election for 25 June 1969.[25] Only weeks before the election, the New Democratic Party was embroiled in a leadership contest between MLA Sidney Green, a labour lawyer, and Edward Schreyer, then federal MP for Selkirk. Schreyer won easily — 506 votes to 177 — and carried the momentum of publicity into the election, which he also won. The NDP was the largest single party, with 28 seats, one fewer than all other MLAs combined.[26] Its minority in the Assembly was overcome when Liberal Laurent Desjardins chose to sit as a "Liberal Democrat," supporting the NDP despite his dislike of their economic policies in order to pursue his agenda of better minority language rights.

Although it was their own legislation, the Conservative opposition raised a number of objections to it, principally over the compensation provisions. They claimed that the FFMC had begun operations and that their effect was that existing companies were being substantially displaced. This was correct: the FFMC quickly took over all aspects of the industry in Manitoba and elsewhere, including processing, and continues to do so to this day.[27] As a result, the new NDP government had a lot more trouble than it expected. Nearly every major fish company submitted briefs to the Law Amendments Committee (LAC),[28] and they were able to persuade a number of opposition members that the FFMC was appropriating, rather than incorporating, their businesses. When the bill came out of the LAC and was debated in the house, for example, Warner Herbert Jorgenson, Conservative MLA for Morris, stated that the processors had "pretty well convinced [the LAC] that there were some difficulties being experienced," specifically that "the restructuring of the industry" was going to result in "putting them out of business." He claimed that this outcome was "[not] contemplated when the bill was first drafted."[29]

It is strange that the Conservatives believed that private operators would be integrated into the FFMC's overall control of marketing, because the legislation they drafted established a regime in which any participation by those companies would be at the sufferance of the FFMC. Section 3 of the Manitoba *Fisheries Act* gave the FFMC "in respect of the marketing of fish locally within the province . . . all the powers and rights that it has" under the FFMA in regard to the export trade. Section 9 prohibited anybody from selling fish "within the province" to "any person other than the corporation or an agent of the corporation," and similarly prohibited anybody from buying fish other than from the FFMC or one of its agents. The Conservatives presumably believed that existing operators would be the "agents" referred to in the legislation, but nothing in the legislation said so, and it was surely not difficult to imagine that the FFMC would rather work through its own employees than maintain a network of small firms that would eat up part of the profit derived from fish sales and thus limit its ability to fulfill one of its key mandates — increasing the incomes of primary producers.

The conservatives fought over a variety of issues, principally the bill's compensation clause, which read:

> Where, in the opinion of the minister, any real or personal property that, before the coming into force of this Act, was used by the owner thereof in, or in connection with, his business as a fisherman, fish dealer or fish processor, as an earning asset in that business, can no longer be used by the owner because of the operations of the corporation, the minister may, at any time, not later than the first day of May, 1971, for and on behalf of the government, purchase the property. [30]

The provincial legislation was slightly differently worded from the federal act and the Canada-Manitoba agreement. They talked of "plant or equipment . . . rendered redundant," the provincial bill of "any real or personal property that . . . can no longer be used." But the Manitoba bill clearly did not envisage compensation for loss of business, and this drew the ire of many opposition members. They argued that because they had believed prior to May 1969 that the fish processors and dealers would be largely integrated into the FFMC, they had drafted the legislation to include only compensation for redundant equipment. They did not conceive that there would be any loss of business for the dealers, merely that they would be restricted to selling to a single buyer. Conservative MLA Sidney Spivak of River Heights proposed an amendment to expand the scope of compensation to include loss of business.[31] The government prevailed in a close vote, 23–21.

The NDP administration took the view that compensation was not a right, but an unusual and generous gesture. There was no right to compensation for those who lost out when the economy was regulated. Leonard Evans, Minister of Mines and Natural Resources, put it this way: "It must be clearly understood by the industry that the compensation for redundancy is only being considered by the government because of the very special problems of the industry." Evans also pointed out what he saw as the hypocrisy in the opposition position, insisting that it was only the rate of redundancy, not the fact of it, that had not been foreseen by the former administration. The conservatives "knew darned well that there was going to be some redundancy and they had to decide on how they were going to handle the redundancy, whether it's one company or a hundred companies. So don't tell us that we're all of a sudden being big monsters about this and unfair and so on."[32]

Although the government received some unflattering press,[33] it is not surprising that it was unwilling to bend, and took the view that the opposition was just playing politics. Schreyer himself was very much committed to fisheries reform, an issue that the federal and provincial governments had spent many years negotiating. There would have been pressure to fall into line with the other provinces and get that reform properly off the ground.[34] The government presumably also did not see the companies as deserving of much consideration, not only legally but morally. They were perceived as responsible for the social malaise among the northern fishing communities, and as having done well out of the system for years. Manitoba was home to a disproportionately large number of fish dealerships affected by the FFMC, and compensating so many and to such a large extent as would be required to make up for "loss of business" would have been a heavy financial burden. Finally, the government's position was no doubt influenced by the fact that one of the principal planks in their election platform had been public auto insurance, and they wanted no part of conceding a right to compensation from economic regulation.

The Fishery Companies and Compensation, 1970–1974

THE EIGHT PRINCIPAL FISHERY companies spent the best part of the next four years trying to get the compensation for loss of business they thought they deserved. The largest was Northland Fisheries, a family business owned by one Peter Lazarenko, who was the best-known figure in the industry.[35] It operated in northeastern Manitoba and northwestern Ontario, owned processing plants in the north and in Winnipeg, and from the early 1950s used aircraft — in 1960 it had eight — to bring in supplies to camps and to transport fish to the south. It went into receivership in the early 1970s, but remained as a formal corporate entity able to pursue litigation.[36] The company that became the test litigant in the Supreme Court of Canada was Manitoba Fisheries (MF), a much smaller player.[37] It had begun operations in 1920 at Oak Point, Manitoba, as Lake Manitoba Fisheries. Its owner, Isaac Bercovitch, moved its headquarters to Winnipeg in 1928. When he died in 1948, the business passed to his widow, Sophia. An employee, Harry Gordon Marder, married Sophia Bercovitch in 1951, and became one of the two principal shareholders (with Sophia Marder) and president. Marder was not popular in the business. He was considered rude and a tough businessman, a *parvenu* who had married into the business and made no effort to be likeable.

Like the other exporting companies, MF bought fish in Manitoba, and to a small extent from other provinces, from dealers and fishermen; the latter were frequently financed by MF. MF then prepared and processed the fish in the province, and sold the product in the US (85–90 percent of sales) or elsewhere in Canada. In the peak season, MF employed between 200 and 250 people. In the mid-1960s it owned five fishing stations, with equipment and docks, and eight boats of varying sizes. From 1965 to 1969 the company's annual operating profit averaged just under $45,000. In court Marder claimed that the value of its assets, tangible and intangible, was some $450,000, rather more than the $118,000 they were valued at in April 1964 when Marder signed an option with Arni Swanson, a Winnipeg investment dealer, for Swanson to buy the company.

The government set up a "Committee for the Acquisition of Assets of Freshwater Fish Producers,"[38] but the amounts it offered did not satisfy the companies. MF was offered $1,500 in 1971 for what was termed a "disposal allowance," a sum of money to be used in helping the company sell its equipment, and $4,104 in 1972 under the same rubric. Both offers were refused because the Corporation's monopoly meant there could be no buyers. Northland did rather better, in March 1970 receiving $150,000 for its equipment; Lazarenko later claimed that a short time earlier he had received a verbal offer from Manitoba to purchase the same assets for $350,000, but that offer was withdrawn before he could accept. He later testified that "he had no alternative" but to execute the agreement, even though the goods were worth much more. All the companies wanted more, and wanted the value of their businesses as on-going concerns. This, the province would not countenance. We have no direct evidence why not. The government was not simply unable to pay — the first Schreyer administration of 1969–1973 returned balanced budgets every year, and the issue was one of principle, not pecuniary shortfall. As noted above, a government with an ambitious program of reform did not wish to set a precedent by compensating those affected by reforms,[39] nor, perhaps more importantly, did the government see any justice in the companies' demands. They had done well for decades and were responsible at least in part for maintaining northern residents, many of them aboriginal, in abject poverty. In the government's view, they were being treated generously in getting any compensation at all. To this general explanation we need to add a more individual factor, the personality and attitudes of the man responsible for compensation — Minister of Mines and Natural Resources Sidney Green. A brilliant debater, highly intelligent, a labour lawyer, he was generally considered the leader of the "hard liners" in the Schreyer government.[40] Although Green took a moderate position on at least some issues, including that of labour picketing rights on private property,[41] and while he did not believe in uncompensated expropriation, his sympathies were wholly with the primary producers. Green likely carried the ball alone on the compensation question, which was probably never debated in cabinet.[42] Even if it had been, presumably Green's voice on a relatively minor issue directly within his area of responsibility would have prevailed, even if he had not been a dominating figure in cabinet discussions. And he was not a compromiser: he "was a man who believed that everything had to be thought out and fought out." His combative personality, which one friend described as his "Achilles heel," made him "abrasive, abusive, argumentative, combative . . . impulsive, intense, pugnacious."[43] His principles about this issue and his personality both came through very clearly in one back room off-the-record meeting recalled by MF's lawyer Arenson: "I'm going to fuck [the companies]," he said. They had "fucked the Indians for fifty years," and now they were getting theirs.[44]

After some years spent trying to negotiate better terms with government, in 1973 the eight principal Manitoba companies combined to hire Aikins Macaulay, the leading Winnipeg law firm, to represent them.[45] But the Aikins lawyers could not come up with any basis on which to sue. Senior litigator and leading liberal John Lamont took the lead, and he concluded that the fact that the companies had been taken out of business through government regulation was legally irrelevant. Governments legislate in a variety of ways in many areas of the economy, and such economic regulation almost always produces some winners and some losers. The losers must seek change in the ballot box or by influencing sitting governments, not in the courts. The companies received the same kind of answer from another Winnipeg law firm, Thompson Dorfman, which would not take the case.[46] Joe O'Sullivan, one of the city's top litigators, a man with an encyclopedic knowledge of the law, and later a judge of the Court of Appeal, also shared this view when MF's lawyer Ken Arenson (see below), went to speak with him about it.

Consistent with their view of the law, Lamont and John Macaulay, the dominant partner in the firm and a major force within both the provincial and federal liberal parties, offered a political rather than a legal solution. Macaulay counted some liberal cabinet members as personal friends, and lobbied the federal government to either pay more compensation or to put pressure on Manitoba to do so. He flew back and forth to Ottawa on a number of occasions, but ultimately all he was able to wring from his Ottawa friends was a statement by federal Fisheries Minister Jack Davis.[47] Davis noted that at the time the federal-provincial deal had been made in the 1960s "it was generally agreed compensation was with respect to assets" — that is, not with respect to on-going business values. Nonetheless the federal government was "now prepared to accept for purposes of compensation, that the assets could be valued on the basis of ongoing business."

So far so good — the policy of higher compensation was approved by the federal government. Even better, Davis went on to indicate that the federal government would pay 50 percent of any compensation. But, and this was a big but, Davis also insisted that responsibility for negotiating the amounts and for paying half the cost "rests with the provinces." The federal government would not compensate unilaterally. Davis was adamant on the point despite at the same time expressing disappointment at Manitoba's policy and indicating that he had written "to the minister responsible in Manitoba" [Green] requesting a review of the level of compensation, only to be refused.[48]

Manitoba Fisheries and the Courts

Going to Court

Aikins Macaulay did what they could, but achieved only the moral victory of the Davis letter. A card game now changed everything. Harry Marder regularly played pinochle with one Sam Arenson, and one night, as he sounded off about how he was getting nowhere with Aikins Macaulay, Arenson told him to "go see my young nephew" who was a "smart boy, just starting out." So Marder went to see Ken Arenson in the fall of 1974. Arenson had been called to the Manitoba bar only four years previously, in 1970.[49] A Winnipegger, and one of six brothers, three of whom became lawyers, Arenson attended what was then the Manitoba Law School, which was run by the profession and held classes at the law courts. He was in the last class to graduate from that school, for in 1970 it became the Faculty of Law at the University of Manitoba. He spent his first three years after his call to the bar working as the director of the Agassiz Centre for Water Studies, at the law school. He resigned to run for the Liberal party in the 1973 provincial election, recruited by new Liberal leader Izzy Asper, but came third in Winnipeg Centre. After the election Arenson set up his own general practice at 695 Wolseley Avenue in a then down-at-heel area of Winnipeg, doing what sole practitioners usually do — everything. Working out of what he described as "a very small office, 100 square feet on two floors, with murals painted on the walls," he bailed people out of jail, helped buy and sell houses, took on small claims, defended drug possession cases, etc.[50] He was briefly in partnership with Morris Kaufman, now a judge of the Manitoba Court of Queen's Bench, but otherwise worked on his own, employing two or three articling students and/or young lawyers, including at different times his younger brothers Murray and Alexander, and Larry Allen, scion of the family that owned Keystone Fisheries.[51] Arenson stayed with the *Manitoba Fisheries* case until its triumphant (for him) end. He still practices, but in Toronto, having moved there in 1982 and, after eighteen months working for well-known civil litigator Marty Teplitsky, he went out on his own. He is a self-confessed "lone wolf," and his Toronto practice has been exclusively in personal injury. He is now best-known for his work on cases arising from the tainted blood scandal, including one that went to the Supreme Court of Canada.[52] But despite these later and more high-profile successes, *Manitoba Fisheries* remains his "all-time favourite case," according to his no longer live website.

It was Arenson who came up with the ultimately successful strategy of litigating on the basis that the FFMC had taken the goodwill of MF. Goodwill, variously defined as reputation, customer lists, trade advantage, etc., and measured as the amount a business will sell for above and beyond its other tangible and intangible assets, has been recognized as property at common law in a variety of contexts. The argument Arenson came up with was that in taking over the export trade, the FFMC had effectively acquired the goodwill that the companies had built up over the years. As he put it, it was late at night, and he was poring over the MF file, "when it occurred to me that goodwill had been acquired." It was "an odd and ecstatic moment."[53] A theory was one thing, a case to support it was another, and Arenson dispatched his articling student David Miles to the library to find one. Miles spent eight hours a day for a week or so looking at anything and everything in the library, and came up with just one[54] — the Northern Ireland Court of Appeal case of *Ulster Transport Authority v James Brown and Sons Ltd*,[55] decided in the 1950s and that seemed highly apposite.

In 1935 the Government of Northern Ireland legislated to give a government board a monopoly over freight and passenger road transport. At the same time it provided for the compulsory acquisition of all affected motor transport undertakings, with compensation paid to the owners of the businesses. The 1935 Act exempted a number of areas of the road transport business, including furniture movers. In 1948 the scheme was altered so as to no longer exempt most furniture movers. The change in the scheme was not accompanied by compulsory acquisition and compensation provisions. James Brown challenged the constitutionality of the 1948 legislation when prosecuted for carrying furniture, on the basis that it violated the constitution of Northern Ireland, the *Government of Ireland Act* (1920), which prohibited legislation that "either directly or indirectly . . . take[s] any property without compensation."

Lord McDermott CJ, author of the court's principal judgment, held that the company had lost goodwill, and that goodwill was property. He also concluded that "the natural consequence of the . . . prohibition would be to divert to the [Authority] . . . the business, or at least the substantial part of the business, which their erstwhile competitors were no longer allowed to transact." His judgment did not simply rest, however, on an analysis of the effect of the legislation. He also found that it was the intention of the legislature to effect this taking. He reasoned that given that the Authority's predecessor had competed with the exempted private firms since 1935, and given that the Authority wished to acquire a monopoly, and given that the consequences of changing the scheme by removing the exemption were known to the legislature, "the intention was to enable the [Authority] … to capture the prohibited business." It was, he said, a "colourable device" to avoid paying compensation. That is, compensation had been paid in 1935 to those not exempted, and the more recent legislation had removed the exemption without providing compensation. This conclusion that the legislation was "designed . . . to achieve acquisition" was returned to on a number of occasions: "Parliament must be presumed to intend the necessary effect of its enactments," he stated a little later, and he also noted that "I can find no other intention which offers a more likely explanation of the provisions." *Ulster Transport Authority* certainly seemed to be a case on point. But it was ambiguous in one critical respect — it was not clear whether it was sufficient to find that the effect of the legislation was to move property from one person to the crown, or whether one also had to find that that was the intent of the legislation. This would become an important question in the litigation.

Coming up with a viable legal strategy changed much. Once Marder had boasted to his colleagues about what his smart young lawyer had found, three of the others also left Aikins and went to high profile trial lawyer D'Arcy McCaffrey instead. McCaffrey was very well known, principally at that time through his work as counsel to Manitoba's Royal Commission on Forest Products. Seven other companies filed suits, using Arenson's goodwill theory, and McCaffrey for three of them and Lamont for four were content to let Arenson take MF's case forward as the "test case." McCaffrey and Arenson made it what Arenson calls "a joint venture," with both working on the case, while Lamont was happy to "coattail" (his words, according to Arenson) on them.[56]

McCaffrey, a "big gun" and a "legendary Winnipeg lawyer," was a leading litigator, then with his firm McCaffrey, Akman, Carr, and Starr, which is now Taylor McCaffrey LLP. [57] He was also a liberal party politician, and briefly interim leader of the Manitoba party. McCaffrey was a very flamboyant character, known for his wild drinking parties and bar fights. Arenson remembers him as captivating, larger than life, and "an almost hypnotic character." Perhaps not surprisingly given his lifestyle, he died of a stroke at the relatively young age of sixty-one, in 1998. The case obviously meant a lot to him as well as to Arenson; he kept the exhibits after the Supreme Court had handed down its decision, and they were on display at his funeral, a remarkable event in itself, held in an amphitheatre with some 2,000 people in attendance.

Arenson and McCaffrey took the cases on a contingency basis — 25 percent of any settlement. They consulted regularly throughout the proceedings as they stretched over the next few years. But despite McCaffrey's public profile, and despite Lamont's position with the major law firm, it was Arenson and his juniors who did the work on the file.[58] McCaffrey, says Arenson, was "fun to bounce ideas off, but he was not always very good on the law."[59]

A few months after getting Marder as a client Arenson filed a statement of claim.[60] The venue for the litigation was the still young Federal Court of Canada, created in 1971, one of the Trudeau-era reforms to legal doctrines and institutions.[61] The Federal Court was to some extent a successor to the Exchequer Court, founded in 1875 along with the Supreme Court of Canada. Like the Exchequer Court, the Federal Court had jurisdiction, concurrent with provincial superior courts, in actions against the crown and in cases of exclusive federal jurisdiction, such as admiralty and intellectual property and tax law. MF's statement of claim briefly described the facts, and then asserted that because Canada had failed to exempt MF from the FFMA, and because the Corporation had not granted it a licence, it could no longer do business. Since the FFMC had a monopoly, the result was that "property of the plaintiff, namely its goodwill, has been taken from it and vested in the Corporation."[62]

The crown lawyer on the file was Sherwin Lyman, a Winnipegger based in the Department of Justice office in Winnipeg.[63] His route to law school and law practice was an unusual one. Brought up by a single mother after his parents divorced in 1945, he did not finish high school, leaving during his senior year to support the family. He finished high school at night, went to United College (then a college of the University of Manitoba but now the University of Winnipeg), and after two years was admitted to the same law program as Ken Arenson — indeed Arenson and he were "friendly classmates" at law school, something that their involvement on opposite sides of the MF case over many years did not change. Lyman had stints with Canadian Pacific and with the Combines Investigation Branch, based in Ottawa. In 1974 he joined the Department of Justice and moved to its Winnipeg office. His new job involved having the FFMC as a client. He had no knowledge, however, of any of the events described here before he was assigned to respond to MF's statement of claim.

Lyman's immediate reaction was that MF had no case, an opinion shared by Doug Rutherford, then Regional Counsel in the Winnipeg Office of the Department of Justice, and who subsequently became Associate Deputy Minister of Justice and an Ontario Superior Court judge. Hence they decided to take the first shot in the court battle and go for summary judgment. In retrospect, while Lyman thinks this was a good decision, he believes the crown should also have added Manitoba as a defendant. This was not suggested at any time, largely because nobody on the government side thought MF could win. Lyman was sympathetic to the position the companies found themselves in, but blamed it on Manitoba, which he thought had offered paltry compensation.

The crown's motion to strike the statement of claim as disclosing no cause of action was filed on 11 March 1975, and heard in Winnipeg on 24 March, before C. Rhodes Smith DJ, a former Chief Justice of Manitoba (1967–1971).[64] On the motion, Arenson appeared on his own because McCaffrey had business elsewhere, and Lyman also appeared without assistance. The crown made four arguments.[65] First, that MF was suing the wrong party — Manitoba should have been the defendant, not Canada. Smith DJ succinctly dismissed this; it was a statute of Canada that had prevented MF from operating, and if anybody was legally responsible for the consequences it had to be Canada. Second, the crown argued that no property had been taken because goodwill was not a form of property. Deputy Judge Smith also dealt expeditiously with this argument, citing a House of Lords case that defined goodwill as a form of property and stating that it was "the very sap and life of the business, without which the business would yield little or no fruit. It is the whole advantage . . . of the reputation and connection of the firm."[66]

The crown's third and fourth arguments were related, and for ease of understanding we will present them in the opposite order to which they appear in the case report. The fourth was that no compensation was payable for taking property unless that compensation was specifically authorized by statute. The crown cited a handful of cases for this proposition, all of which contained short statements, which, if taken out of context, supported it.[67] But there was a competing line of cases, of which *Attorney-General v De Keyser's Hotel*,[68] is usually seen as emblematic. These stand for the proposition that while in a system of parliamentary supremacy with no constitutional right to property the state can take away property from a citizen, and can choose to do so without compensation, "[t]he recognized rule for the construction of statutes is that, unless the words of the statute clearly so demand, a statute is not to be construed so as to take away the property of a subject without compensation." The compensation rule is the most important of a number of "presumptions of intent" that the legislature does not intend to take away common law "rights," presumptions collectively dubbed the "Common Law Bill of Rights" by John Willis.[69] Deputy Judge Smith did not decide whether this line of cases or the crown's cases were correct; he only had to find that the point was arguable. As he could not rule on "uncertain points of law," the crown's application was denied.

Finally, we return to the third argument, which we think was the strongest. Accepting the presumption of compensation, the crown contended that the mention of compensation in section 25 of the FFMA disposed of the issue. By the *expressio unius est excliusio alterius* doctrine, if the statute said compensation for "plant and equipment" rendered redundant, it meant only that and precluded compensation for an intangible like goodwill. Deputy Judge Smith's response was a strange one. He noted that section 29 of the Manitoba *Fisheries Act* did not preclude compensation for goodwill because it referred to any "real or personal property" and thus was not limited to tangible property. This was true, but, as he himself had earlier stated, the relevant statute was the FFMA. It was surely inconsistent to assert that MF was right to sue the federal crown because a federal statute was involved, and to then use the provincial statute to decide that "property" could include goodwill. In suggesting that the *expressio unis* argument was a good one, we do not think that it was sure to win. Had it been seriously considered at any level of the litigation — and it was not — the courts would have had to decide what the words "clearly so demand" meant in the *De Keyser's* test. Must the words be express or will necessary implication suffice? The cases are unclear on this and thus it was not, and is not, obvious that the FFMA exempted compensation for goodwill.[70] But it is a sufficiently important point that it is surprising that the issue was not given a full airing at any stage.

The Federal Court: Trial and Appeal

Deputy Judge Smith's decision was given on 25 April 1975,[71] but it was another year and a half before the case was tried, in November 1976. The principal cause of the delay was a set of ultimately fruitless negotiations to agree on certain facts and on the formulation of questions for the trial judge arising out of them.[72] By September 1975, Arenson and Lyman had agreed on a final draft, but that draft was never formalized because Saul Froomkin, the lawyer in the Ottawa office overseeing the file, decided that Lyman was conceding too much. Lyman acknowledges that Froomkin was probably right, that he had more experience and thus a better understanding of trial tactics.[73] The major point of contention was what was said to the companies when they met with fisheries officials in early 1969. MF claimed it and others had been told that either compensation would be paid or its business would be purchased; the crown insisted that no such undertakings had been given.[74]

For the trial Ottawa decided it wanted a more experienced lawyer, and assigned the case to Luther P. Chambers, of the Department of Justice's civil litigation section. Chambers had been called to the Bar in 1965 in Ontario, and was a government lawyer for his entire career, specializing in tax cases.[75] Lyman and Chambers disagreed over the best argument to make, discussed below. The trial occupied three days in Winnipeg in November 1976, with the judgment being released just before Christmas.[76] The trial judge was Frank Collier, a British Columbian lawyer appointed to the court in September 1971 at the age of forty-nine. He was one of three appointments made in 1971 to bring the trial division of the court to its full complement of eight; the other five were holdovers from the old Exchequer Court.[77] The crucial factual question was whether MF had had goodwill. Chambers decided that his best argument was to try to show that there was none,[78] but this proved to be a mistake. The crown's accountant witness testified that goodwill was ignored by accountants in valuing a business except when the business is purchased and one can determine the difference between the sale price and the value of the physical assets. But that was the loophole Arenson needed, and on cross-examination the accountant admitted that "a practical businessman, with market experience, might well have concluded that there was . . . goodwill in a business sense and pay for it." This testimony was bolstered by Arenson's own witness Walter Dubowec, and by the fact that Arenson was able to present an option agreement Marder had signed in 1964 with Ari Swanson, an investment dealer, to buy the company; the accompanying list of assets included as part of the sale price "Goodwill including the right to use the name Manitoba Fisheries Limited," valued at $9,500.[79] Arenson was also able to show, through documents and *viva voce* testimony, that the FFMC had put MF out of business.

The evidence satisfied Collier J that MF and other companies had "over the years, built up individual clienteles . . . [The] company enjoyed a good reputation . . . it retained a competitive position and individual custom of its own." Thus there had been goodwill, even if its value was small.[80] Trying to prove that MF had no goodwill was obviously a mistake on Chambers' part, but of greater significance, we think, was that he ignored Lyman's suggestion that they go with an alternative argument, that the goodwill had not been transferred to the FFMC. A company could have goodwill only against a competitor, not in the abstract, and thus as there was a monopoly given to the FFMC, it neither had nor needed goodwill.[81] Since the FFMC had no competitors in selling Manitoba fish, it simply could have no goodwill in that market. This argument is quite a good one, although it is susceptible to the rejoinder that MF and the other companies had built up goodwill in the product — Manitoba fish — and without their efforts the FFMC would have had a smaller overall market. This is correct, but it remains the case that the suit was about MF's goodwill in particular, not the industry's as a whole.

Despite his factual finding on goodwill, Collier J decided the case in favour of the crown. MF's written arguments relied heavily on the *Ulster Transport Authority* case, but Collier J read it as requiring that the legislature intend to take property. After quoting at considerable length from that case, he concluded that the case before him "is distinguishable" because it lacked the "colourability" element: "the clear purpose" of the Northern Irish legislation was "to take over the furniture moving business." Conversely, the FFMA did not represent "any attempt . . . to capture or take the existing property" of MF. Rather, "the intent or purpose" was "to set up a corporation for the purpose of marketing or trading in fish." This, "an exclusive marketing" power, was "subject to a licensing system," but "the Corporation has, in its wisdom, decided not to issue any licences."

While that did have the "practical effect" of putting MF out of business, there was "no intention to take or confiscate . . . any property" expressed in the FFMA itself. Justice Collier expressed sympathy with the fact that, as he saw it, MF and other companies had been "unfairly treated" by Manitoba, had become "entrapped in policy differences between two levels of government" and as a result had been "economically erased." They "ought to receive better treatment" from both governments. "The law . . . compels rejection of the plaintiff's claim," he said at the end, but "[i]t does not follow that justice, in the true sense, has been done."[82]

A few minor issues were also dealt with in the judgment, but the need to find an intention to take was the crucial one. The distinction drawn by Collier J seems highly formalistic, perhaps even unrealistic. The FFMA, which not only set up the export monopoly, but also gave the FFMC such broad powers to operate in other areas of the industry, could certainly have been interpreted as indicating that Parliament's intention was to take the businesses of the private operators. At the same time it must be acknowledged that the case on intention is less strong than it was in *Ulster Transport Authority*. There was no history of legislative intervention in the industry against which to compare the FFMA, and the federal statute was only permissive, not mandatory. Arenson now concedes that *Ulster Transport Authority* can be read as requiring an intention, but remains perplexed that Collier J chose to do so.[83]

MF appealed, the argument taking place on 28 and 29 June 1977, again in Winnipeg, with the judgment being released a month later, on 25 July 1977.[84] The lawyers on the appeal were the same men who had appeared at trial. The three-judge panel comprised Darrel Heald JA, presiding, John Urie JA, and Mackay DJ. Heald was from small-town Saskatchewan, son of the owner of a general store who liked to fish in Last Mountain Lake, part of the Saskatchewan freshwater fishery.[85] A graduate of the University of Saskatchewan law school, he had a general practice in Regina before being elected a liberal MLA and serving as Attorney General of Saskatchewan from 1964 until appointment to the federal court trial division in 1971. He was elevated to the Court of Appeal in December 1975. John Urie, born in Guelph, Ontario, graduated from Osgoode Hall and then over twenty-five years built himself a litigation practice in Ottawa which included a number of appearances in the Supreme Court of Canada.[86] A self-described "good liberal," his political connections helped him get an appointment directly to the Federal Court of Appeal at the age of fifty-three in April 1973. The appointment surprised him, for he thought himself a "practical lawyer" and not of a particularly academic turn of mind. There was one very unusual aspect of the proceedings. The day after oral argument concluded, on 30 June 1977, Luther Chambers wrote to the court that he had that day discovered a very recent judgment of the Privy Council, *Government of Malaysia v Selangor Pilot Association*[87] (discussed below) that was directly relevant to the appeal. The court ordered the parties to provide written submissions on the case.[88]

The crown won again, in a Court of Appeal judgment penned by Urie JA that is not a model of judgment writing. Justice Urie accepted, although one can read between the lines some unhappiness with it, the factual conclusion reached by Collier J that MF had goodwill in its business when the FFMA was passed. But on the question of whether that goodwill had been taken by the crown, he seemed to agree with Collier J that such was not the intent of the FFMA. The legislation was concerned with the "orderly marketing of fish," and did not evince "a clear intention to take the goodwill of [MF]," either "expressly or impliedly."[89] While this language of intention seems to evoke Lord MacDermott in *Ulster Transport Authority*, Urie JA did not cite the case at all, despite Collier J's reliance on it, and despite the fact that MF's lawyers relied on it and invited the court to hold that effect, not intention, was what should matter.[90] Justice Urie probably did not feel that he needed to stress lack of intention because he also went on to hold that there had been no acquisition, intentional or otherwise. A compensable taking, he insisted, "must be one which involves the actual, physical assumption of possession or use of property by the crown." A "mere negative prohibition" is not a taking. Justice Urie thus concluded that only if the FFMC had used MF's property, which in the case of goodwill probably required it to have operated as Manitoba Fisheries, could they be said to have "taken" or "acquired" anything.[91] He reiterated this point, along with his finding of no intention, in his conclusion:

> it is clear from the stated objects and purposes of the . . . Act, from the whole scheme of the Act and from a plain reading of the statute as a whole that it neither directly nor indirectly discloses an intention to take from anyone any kind of property . . . . The Corporation did not purchase, confiscate or in any other way acquire possession, in fact or in law, of any of the physical or intangible assets belonging to the appellant. There was no "taking," "taking away," or "taking over" of any such assets in any realistic interpretation of those words.

The finding that there had been no acquisition was, as we shall see, later ridiculed by the Supreme Court of Canada. Given his conclusions on taking and intention, Urie JA did not have to consider whether the FFMA provided that no compensation would be paid, a point the crown had argued in its factum.

Selangor Pilots, the case discovered after the oral arguments, was very similar to the MF case. A group of harbour pilots argued that they had been deprived of property (goodwill) when a Port Authority legislated that only persons employed by it could provide pilotage services. Previously such services were provided by a pilots' association or by other pilots employed by the association. The association sued for loss of goodwill, even though it had been compensated for loss of use of physical assets, which were bought by the Port Authority. A majority of the Privy Council found against the pilots, 4–1. Viscount Dilhorne, for that majority, held that the pilots had lost only the right to act as pilots unless employed by the public authority, and the right to employ others as pilots — and neither of these "rights" was property. An analogy was drawn to driving licences — Parliament could alter licence conditions and qualifications whenever it wanted without depriving a holder of property. Viscount Dilhorne rejected the goodwill argument, holding that any goodwill lost was not acquired by the Port Authority. He did not explain why the goodwill was not acquired, but he did distinguish the *Ulster Transport Authority* case on the colourability question: that was a case in which "the statutory prohibition was a colourable device to secure property without compensation."[92]

The crown insisted that *Selangor Pilots* helped it, that the facts of the case were "in all their essential elements" the same.[93] In both cases "all the legislation . . . did was to prohibit the operators in an industry from carrying on their activities, unless they were employed or licensed by the statutory body," and in both cases "that body had the exclusive right to carry on, and it did carry on these activities." Arenson had the trickier case to make, because there were very substantial similarities between his claim and the facts in *Selangor Pilots*. Nonetheless, he insisted on one particular distinction. The Privy Council had said that if the pilots' association had had goodwill, it was not acquired by government. Arenson argued that MF's deprivation of property had been accompanied by an acquisition. As he put it with a flourish, the goodwill "was not lost or destroyed," but rather it was "transferred, obtained, taken, diverted, acquired — the verb does not matter" by the FFMC. He went on to provide a much better reasoned answer for why the pilots should have lost than the Privy Council had done. He contrasted the factual circumstances to show that the pilots, unlike MF, had not created any goodwill. Pilots do not produce shipping, no matter how good a service they provide: "The shipping industry used the port because there were goods to be conveyed to and from Malaysia. The custom of the port had given rise to the need for pilots." That was why, even if the pilot association had lost goodwill, the Port Authority had not acquired it: "because the custom of the Port was not created by the pilots . . . nothing was acquired which had first been created by the expense and effort of the . . . Association."

It is impossible to know how influential *Selangor Pilots* proved to be. In asserting that MF had not been deprived of property, Urie JA adverted to *Selangor Pilots*, saying that he found "considerable support" for this part of his reasons in that case and quoting extensively from it. He then shortly stated his conclusion that there had been no deprivation of property: "What the appellant lost was not property but was its right to carry on the business in which it had been engaged, without a licence. If that loss included whatever goodwill the appellant had, it was not taken by the Corporation." In short, he saw it as another case where nothing had been taken, although he did not make it at all clear why it supported his conclusion. Like Collier J, Urie JA took pains to criticize the result he believed he was compelled to reach; it was "harsh."[94]

The Supreme Court of Canada

The fishery companies were intent on taking the case to the Supreme Court. But before they did, some hope for a settlement appeared. In October 1977 the NDP lost the Manitoba general election, with the Conservatives under new leader Sterling Lyon taking thirty-three seats to Schreyer's NDP twenty-three. The premier was now the man who, as Manitoba's Minister of Mines and Natural Resources, had been so instrumental in bringing about a federal-provincial agreement that lead to the FFMA, and the party in power was the same one which had so vociferously demanded better compensation for fishery companies in 1969. In November, Arenson asked the Supreme Court for more time to submit his application for leave to appeal, on the ground, *inter alia*, that Manitoba now had a government "with whom it was thought that a negotiated settlement of the Plaintiff's claim was possible."[95] Arenson got his delay, but it produced no result. The negotiations, if any took place, must have been perfunctory, for Sherwin Lyman cannot recall anything about them, and just two weeks after his request for a delay Arenson submitted materials for the leave application. It seems reasonable to think that the companies, whose resort to law to this point had been unavailing, would have been willing to compromise, and in turn this suggests that it was Manitoba that was not interested in a settlement. It perhaps seems strange given the party's position in 1969 that the Lyon Conservatives would have so quickly dismissed the possibility of a settlement, and we can only speculate about why. Lyon might have taken the view that the FFMC was responsible for the mess because it had not worked with the existing companies. Less creditably, Lyon may have agreed with compensation for ongoing businesses in principle, but have been reluctant to provide the kind of money required; even if the case went in favour of the companies in the SCC it was the federal government which would have to pay.

The oral hearing of the leave to appeal application took place before the three Quebec judges, Pigeon, Beetz, and Pratte JJ, and they granted leave on 17 December 1977.[96] The written materials and the facts of the case clearly touched a nerve for the judges. Arenson knew he was going to win not only leave but also, he says, the case itself, within minutes of the hearing starting. As he got up to make his pitch, Pigeon J, who was presiding, said that the panel did not need to hear from him, a sure sign that the court had decided in his favour. And when Chambers stood up, Pigeon said: "if a private citizen had done this, we would have called it theft." The panel grilled Chambers for what must have been an uncomfortable thirty minutes. There really was no response to Pigeon's question, other than to make the obvious point that a private person had not been responsible, that it was government, and government does things all the time, including, of course, taxation, that has the effect of "taking" property from some for public purposes. For Pigeon to have asked his question meant that he had a lot of difficulty seeing that point.

The appeal was heard six months later, on 22 June 1978. Seven of the nine judges sat on the panel, including Brian Dickson, whose career included eighteen years as a corporate lawyer with Aikins Macaulay in Winnipeg.[97] Arenson, McCaffrey, and Lamont represented MF, but Sherwin Lyman was joined by George W. Ainslie, QC, who replaced Chambers. Ainslie was the head of civil litigation at the Department of Justice; he was also dying of cancer at the time.[98] Argument took all day, with an hour and a half for lunch. McCaffrey led off for MF, and was up for fifty minutes. Arenson followed, for fifty-two minutes separated by a brief break, and Lamont completed the appellant's case in the morning with a half-hour argument. Lamont spoke again for seven minutes in the afternoon, and then the court heard Ainslie for just over an hour. McCaffrey put in a thirty-nine-minute reply at the end.[99] Judging from the written materials, the arguments were the same as before. Arenson concentrated on the fact that goodwill had moved from MF to the crown, and denied the significance of lack of intention.[100] He found a colourful way of talking about how goodwill is acquired: "The Appellant can claim no credit for hunger pangs felt by U.S. customers, not for the existence of fish in Canadian lakes. But appetite is different than hunger, and appetite for Manitoba fish, rather than beef or fowl or salt water fish . . . was the unique creation of the Appellant and other firms in the industry."

The crown's arguments were largely familiar also.[101] It rested its case on taking on the lack of intention. It conceded that the FFMA had "materially affected the Appellant's business," but insisted that "there is nothing to disclose that it was the intention . . . to take or acquire any portion of the Appellant's goodwill." Rather, "the true purpose and intent of the legislation" was to market freshwater fish better. The crown did add one new argument: Sherwin Lyman's idea that goodwill could not "exist independently of a business." Hence "[i]f a business has not been acquired, then the goodwill could not have been acquired." This was quite a good argument, and it is unfortunate that it emerged only in the Supreme Court and was not subjected to analysis by the lower courts. Lyman was able to persuade Ainslie that it had merit, but it would perhaps have been better had Chambers listened to it earlier. The contrast between the way the crown handled the case — bringing in senior men and changing counsel twice — and the fact that the young and inexperienced Arenson controlled the case on the other side is stark.

The Supreme Court issued its judgment fairly quickly, on 3 October 1978, a little over three months after the hearing, reversing the lower courts. It accepted that goodwill was property and could be treated separately from other forms of property. Justice Ritchie then dealt with Urie JA's conclusion that while the FFMA had put MF out of business, there had not been an acquisition of property. He had "great difficulty in following this reasoning" because the factual record clearly indicated that there were many customers of MF who after 1969 were "compelled to do business only with the Corporation."[102] Since goodwill was a species of property, and since that goodwill necessarily flowed to the corporation, "it seems to me to follow that the appellant was deprived of property which was acquired by the Crown." Ritchie J's dismissive attitude to the courts below was perhaps unfair. Both Collier J and Urie JA had found that whether or not MF had a case depended on whether the statute intended that result. We must assume that Ritchie J saw no distinction based on the intent of the statute, that if it had the effect of moving goodwill from one party to the other that was enough. But he did not say so explicitly; rather he cited long passages from *Ulster Transport Authority* and then tersely remarked that it "strongly supports the appellant's contention in the present case."

Once the court had concluded that property had been in effect transferred, there was no issue about compensation, given the *De Keyser*'s rule. The court nonetheless dealt with a few other issues. Having recounted the facts of *Selangor Pilots* Ritchie J baldly asserted that "the factual differences existing between the Malaysian case and the present one are so fundamental as to make the opinion of the Privy Council inapplicable to the present circumstances." One expects a judge who relies on factual differences between cases to say how the cases are so factually different, and it ought to be an easy task when such differences are "fundamental." That Ritchie J did not do so suggests that the differences were not so easy to explain. *Ulster Transport Authority, Manitoba Fisheries,* and *Selangor Pilots* are not very different. If the pilots' association had goodwill then exactly the same thing had happened to it as happened to MF. If, conversely, *Selangor Pilots* really is just a licensing case, so too, arguably, was *Manitoba Fisheries;* one could have said that all directors and employees of MF had simply lost the privilege of engaging in whatever trade they wished, but they could always go to work for the FFMC.[103] The conservative Ritchie J was, we would speculate, averse to saying that the Privy Council had simply got it wrong.

In addition to his jurisprudential conservatism, Ritchie J also seems to have been willing to allow his feeling, shared with Collier J and Urie JA, about unfairness to shape his decision. He cited both those judges' comments, as well as Jack Davis' letter that agreed that compensation should be paid for lost business and expressed disappointment that Manitoba refused to do so. He suggested that the Davis letter was "very close to an acknowledgment of the propriety of awarding compensation for the loss of goodwill." That may be correct, but propriety was irrelevant to the legal issues. Arenson thinks the letter was very important. It convinced the court that whatever the FFMA said, the original deal was that companies would be compensated for business losses, not just plant and equipment. Lyman does not concede this point, but agrees on the importance of that letter — it turned out to be a tactical mistake, giving ammunition to those who thought the events unfair to the companies.[104]

MF was awarded "compensation in an amount equal to the fair market value of its business as a going concern as at May 1, 1969, minus the residual value of its remaining assets as of that date." Justice Ritchie's judgment also gave MF 5 percent a year in interest on the fair market value from 1 May 1969. The interest ruling turned out to be a very important one for the companies, because with almost ten years between May 1969 and the Supreme Court judgment, and a few more years before matters were all settled, the final settlements were more than half as much again as the 1969 values.

Manitoba Fisheries attracted relatively little comment at the time. One author thought it was an "obviously just result" but also pointed out that the case espoused no workable theory of *de facto* expropriation.[105] Since there is "no general legal principle which requires Parliament or a Legislature to provide for fair compensation to everyone who is harmed by new legislation," it behooved the court to consider a variety of questions — "what sorts of harm or loss will the courts say entitle a person to compensation . . . will the line be drawn at the taking of property . . . what exactly is property and when is it taken?" In the absence of such guidelines, Jones concluded, "one is left wondering precisely what legal basis the Supreme Court of Canada used to uphold the appellant's claim."

Postscript and Conclusion

Following the Supreme Court judgment, the other seven Manitoba companies involved in the litigation received summary judgment against the crown, and all the litigants were reasonably handsomely compensated although it took further litigation in a number of cases. We do not know exactly what MF received, but it was in the $300,000–$400,000 range.[106] Bodners settled for $442,500 plus interest, and Canadian Fish Producers also settled. Main Fisheries got only $66,161 plus interest. The largest company Northland ended up with $747,241 plus interest for almost fifteen years ($564,422) for a total award of $1,311,633.[107]

If we move beyond the individual companies to broader consequences it would appear that *Manitoba Fisheries* has had very little effect on Canadian law, at least in the courts. There have only been two other successful regulatory takings claims, both involving regulations curtailing mining in British Columbia provincial parks.[108] All other litigated claims have failed. Some cases have involved land use regulation — Nova Scotia's *Beaches Act*,[109] Winnipeg's historical building designation[110] — while others have involved different kinds of regulations affecting property — examples include rent controls and changes to a milk-marketing scheme.[111] Perhaps ironically, claims have failed on the two main grounds of the test established in *Manitoba Fisheries*. First, the need to find a separate and identifiable interest in property that has been taken, met in *Manitoba Fisheries* by goodwill, has proved a difficult requirement to satisfy. The right to use property in a particular way is not property itself and thus does not meet the test, nor is a diminution in value considered a loss of property. These principles have recently been reaffirmed by the Supreme Court of Canada in *Canadian Pacific Railway Co v Vancouver*,[112] discussed elsewhere in this volume. Second, the need for the state to acquire what has been taken away, another key aspect of *Manitoba Fisheries* that makes Canadian regulatory takings law distinct from American, has been a very difficult hurdle to overcome. In *Mariner Real Estate*, for example,

Cromwell JA found that even if it could be argued that extremely onerous regulation of land use could be said to amount to destroying the fee simple, the regulations did not transfer any interest to the crown. In *La Ferme Filibier Ltee v The Queen*[113] the regulation under attack had prohibited fish farming in the area, and thus nothing had been acquired. Justice Marceau's comment in that case that if every regulation was treated as an expropriation "with respect to anyone whose commercial activities were interfered with" then a "proliferation of claims" would follow, is correct, and suggests why courts have been reluctant to extend *Manitoba Fisheries*.

Thus, since 1978 the courts have essentially confined *Manitoba Fisheries* to its rather unique facts. It is, in the words of one commentator, "one of the most liberal applications" of the *De Keyser's* compensation doctrine, and concerns that dire consequences for the ability of government to regulate were it to be expanded have not been borne out.[114] Thus perhaps the best way to understand the case is to see it as a "palm tree justice" decision, a ruling in favour of a particular plaintiff for whom a group of Supreme Court judges had sympathy. It was a sympathy perhaps born of their small-c conservative politics, but one that has had to be restrained thereafter for fear of the consequences.[115] Even if this is true, sympathy alone cannot win cases, and the real hero of the case was the person who found a legal way for the court to express that sympathy — Ken Arenson. The goodwill argument was crucial in that it provided a legal theory that could be married to the judges' "common sense" understandings of right and wrong, it turned an economic regulation case into one about property.

But if we move beyond decided cases and speculate, it is possible that *Manitoba Fisheries* has been more significant, in two ways. First, it is possible that the decision has had the effect of making governments apprehensive about regulating areas of the economy when that regulation might produce similar litigation. We have no evidence for this, and indeed it would be difficult to find such negative evidence. But people always act "in the shadow of the law," and the shadow cast by *Manitoba Fisheries* could be a long one indeed.

Second, *Manitoba Fisheries* may have been influential in the early 1980s when the details of Canada's new *Charter of Rights* were being fleshed out.[116] The *Charter* does not contain a guarantee of property rights, unlike the American *Bill of Rights* or the Diefenbaker *Bill of Rights* of 1960. Right-wing politicians and pressure groups continue to press for its inclusion — in 1988 the House of Commons voted for it, albeit with only 124 members present.[117] The issue is usually cast in simple left-right terms. But the fact is that in the early

1980s property rights were not a contentious issue in the negotiations, and not an issue that saw a split between liberal/NDP provincial governments and conservative ones. While the federal government supported a right to property, all provincial governments, of whatever stripe, were opposed. In part they were concerned that such a right would trench on provincial power, "property and civil rights" being a very important aspect of provincial jurisdiction. But they also feared that the inclusion of a right to property would threaten a variety of regulatory schemes, from provincial crown corporations to Prince Edward Island's limitation of non-resident ownership of land. The fear was that a constitutionally entrenched right to property would introduce into Canada a version of American regulatory takings doctrine, which is much broader; rather than require the government to have acquired the property taken, it asks only if the owner has been denied "economically viable" uses.[118] The decision in *Manitoba Fisheries* showed a willingness in the Supreme Court to adopt an expansive approach to "takings," and could only have reinforced these concerns. In these two senses, *Manitoba Fisheries* may indeed have been a much more influential case than it would seem merely by looking at later judicial decisions.

Notes

1 We thank Ken Arenson, Philip Girard, Norm Larsen, Thomas Lederer J, Brian Mayes, David Percy, Lisa Piper, and David Schneiderman for comments on earlier versions of this chapter. We also benefitted substantially from the discussions held at the symposium on this volume at the University of Alberta, Faculty of Law in June 2010. We also thank the participants at various presentations of this work at: the Toronto Legal History Group, the Faculties of Law at Dalhousie University, the University of Windsor, Macquarie University, and the Australian National University. We also thank members for comments received at a joint meeting of the Francis Forbes Society and the New South Wales Bar Association, especially the chair of that meeting, the Honourable Brian Preston, Chief Judge of the New South Wales Land and Environment Court. This paper has benefitted greatly from the oral recollections of participants. Ken Arenson, lawyer for Manitoba Fisheries, was very helpful to us and generous with his time, as was Sherwin Lyman, one of the counsel for the crown throughout the proceedings. Others who shared their recollections with us were Robert Carr, David Miles, and Howard Pawley. Financial assistance was provided by the Osgoode Society for Canadian Legal History.

2 [1979] 1 SCR 101

3 SC 1968-69, c 21, now RSC 1985, c F-13, as am.

4 The principle is usually referred to *Attorney-General v De Keyser's Hotel*, [1920] AC 508 (HL).

5 For the history of the fishery before c 1950 see an excellent article by Lisa Piper, "Parasites from 'Alien Shores': The Decline of Canada's Freshwater Fishing Industry," (2010) 91 *Canadian Historical Review* 87, and Thomas A. Judson, "The Freshwater Commercial Fishery of Western Canada," Ph.D. thesis, University of Toronto, 1961. See also, *inter alia*, F. Tough, "The Establishment of a Commercial Fishing Industry and the Demise of Native Fisheries in Northern Manitoba," (1984) 4 *Canadian Journal of Native Studies* 303, and Anne Bryden, "Dreams and Claims: Icelandic-Aboriginal Interactions in the Manitoba Interlake," (2001) 36 *Journal of Canadian Studies* 164. The broader background is treated in a recent excellent environmental history, Liza Piper, *The Industrial Transformation of Sub-Arctic Canada* (Vancouver: University of British Columbia Press, 2009).

6 This section on the fishery in the 1950s and 1960s is drawn principally from *Report of the Commission of Inquiry into Freshwater Fish Marketing*, Commissioner: George H. McIvor (Ottawa, 1965), p. 19 [hereafter *McIvor Report*]. See also *Winnipeg Tribune*, 22 April 1964, p. 1. There is also much useful background information in some of the cases produced by disputes over the level of compensation that should be awarded following the Supreme Court of Canada judgment: see especially *Main Fisheries Ltd. et al v The Queen*, [1982] FCJ No. 214 (TD) and *Northland Fisheries Ltd. et al v The Queen*, [1983] FCJ No. 221 (TD).

7 Quotation at *McIvor Report*, p. 10. This "indentured servitude" was a long-established practice in the industry: see Piper, "Decline of Canada's Freshwater Fishing Industry" at 103.

8 See Piper, above note 5 "Decline of Canada's Freshwater Fishing Industry," pp. 101 et seq.

9 Canada, Commercial Fishing Commission, *Confidential Resumé of the Verbal Report of W.A. Kennedy*, Director, Central Fisheries Research Station, 10 November 1953.

10 Department of Fisheries of Canada and the Fisheries Research Board, *The Commercial Fisheries of Canada: Report to the Royal Commission on Canada's Economic Prospects*, September 1956.

11 *Report of the Committee on Manitoba's Economic Future* (COMEF) (Winnipeg: Government of Manitoba, 1963) at V-4-1.

12 See on this point Royden Loewen, *Diaspora in the Countryside: Two Mennonite Communities and Mid Twentieth-Century Rural Disjuncture* (Toronto: University of Toronto Press, 2006).

13 For this paragraph see "Lyon Wants National Policy on Fisheries," *Winnipeg Free Press*, 22 January 1964, p. 33; "Fishermen to Get Same Federal Aid as Farmers," *Winnipeg Tribune*, 25 January 1964, p. 12; "Fisheries Plan," *Winnipeg Tribune*, 24 January 1964, p. 2; "Fishing Monopoly," *Winnipeg Tribune*, 1 February 1964, p. 9; Ben Ward, "Agency May Handle All Fish Exports," *Winnipeg Free Press*, 30 November 1964, p. 11.

14 *McIvor Report*, pp. vii-viii. For this see also "Price-Fixing for Prairie Fish Backed by Provinces," *Winnipeg Tribune*, 14 October 1964, p. 3; "Fishing Industry Problems," *Winnipeg Tribune*, 16 October 1964, p. 21; Ben Ward, "Agency May Handle All Fish Exports," *Winnipeg Free Press*, 30 November 1964, p. 11.

15 See *McIvor Report*, p. iii for what follows in this paragraph.

16 For the commission's operations see Piper, "Decline of Canada's Freshwater Fishing Industry," pp. 105-6. See also Victor Mackie, "Probe Finds Fish Prices are Weak," *Winnipeg Free Press*, 18 October 1966, p. 1. For the rest of this paragraph and the next see *McIvor Report*, *passim*, and especially pp. vi-viii, 1-2, 11, 63, and 80.

17 "Fish Marketing Board Scuttled," *Selkirk Enterprise*, 29 November 1967, p. 2, and Victor Mackie, "Fish Board 'Torpedoing' is Denied," *Winnipeg Free Press*, 30 November 1967, pp. 1 and 4. See also these sources for the rest of this paragraph, and "Fish Marketing Now Near," *Selkirk Enterprise*, 21 February 1968, p. 1.

18 *Commons Debates*, 12 October 1968, p. 8.

19 Information given in this paragraph is from Statement of Claim, 7 February 1975, paras 3-5, and Notice to Admit Facts, 10 October 1975, both in Federal Court Trial Division File, Case T-358-75 [hereafter FCTD File], and Statement of Defence, 6 May 1975, in FCTD File. See also the case report of the motion to strike the statement of claim, [1976] 1 FC 8, para 3, and Interview with Ken Arenson [hereafter Arenson Interview.]

20 SC 1968-69, c 21. These sections are numbered differently in the current Act.

21 See the statements by Lloyd Crouse, Nova Scotia PC, Arnold Peters, Ontario NDP, William Gordon Ritchie, Manitoba PC, and Ralph Harding, British Columbia NDP, in *Commons Debates*, 16 January 1969, p. 4373, 4378, and 4382. Lang's reassurance is at House of Commons, Standing Committee on Fisheries and Forestry, Freshwater Fish Marketing Act, in *Minutes of Standing Committee on Fisheries and Forestry*, 28 January 1969, at 175.

22 *Fish Marketing Act*, SA 1969, c 36; *Freshwater Fish Marketing Act*, SO 1969, c 40; *Freshwater Fish Marketing Ordinance*, ONWT 1969, c 6, now *Freshwater Fish Marketing Act*, RSNWT 1988, c F-11, as am. Saskatchewan did not pass legislation, but it gave the FFMC a monopoly within the province by a regulation made under its *Fisheries Act*: see *Saskatchewan Regulations*, 1969, p. 264. The Ontario legislation pertained only to parts of northern Ontario, once the Minister had made regulations to define the area. The designated area was west of Longitude 86 degrees and encompassed the districts of Cochrane, Rainy River, and Kenora: Ontario Regulation 302/69, 24 July 1969; Ontario Order in Council 2932/69, in Manitoba Fisheries Case File, Library and Archives Canada, RG 125, Vol 2826, File 14925 [hereafter LAC — MF].

23 The full text of the short agreement is in FCTD File.

24 *Fisheries Act*, SM 1969, c 9.

25 This paragraph on Manitoba politics in 1969 is from JA McAllister, *The Government of Edward Schreyer: Democratic Socialism in Manitoba* (Kingston and Montreal: McGill Queens University Press, 1984), ch 2, and Sidney Green, *Rise and Fall of a Political Animal: A Memoir* (Winnipeg: Great Plains, 2003).

26 The Conservatives won 22 seats, the Liberals 5, Social Credit 1, and Gordon Beard won Churchill as an Independent.

27 For details see the FFMC's website, online: www.freshwaterfish.com.

28 For the briefs submitted by the companies see *Main Fisheries v R.*, [1980] 1 FC 104; *Northland Fisheries Ltd. v Canada* (1984), 56 NR 333 (FC-TD); Arenson Interview. No records of the LAC's deliberations are available prior to the early 1970s, but it is reasonable to assume that the issues that dominated discussion there were the same ones debated in Committee of the Whole in early October, from which our evidence is taken.

29 Manitoba, Legislative Assembly, *Official Report of Debates (Hansard)*, [hereafter *Manitoba Debates*], 6 October 1969, p. 1324. See to similar effect the comments of Conservative MLA from Fort Garry, Robert Louis "Bud" Sherman, who asserted that "we heard testimony over and over again in Law Amendments Committee, [that] the legislation as originally conceived and drafted has not worked out the way it was intended to. It's turned out to be extremely arduous and onerous and discriminatory and oppressive for the representatives of a particular industry in this province, . . . despite the good intentions of the previous administration": *Manitoba Debates*, 6 October 1969, pp. 1326-27.

30 Above note 24.

31 For the proposed amendment see *Manitoba Debates*, 2 October 1969, pp. 1246-47. The opposition also wanted to replace the section on purchase with broader wording requiring the Minister to buy redundant property, and to extend the time for doing so by two years. They also wanted recourse to the courts, both to get a declaration of redundancy if the government did not find one, and to appeal the Minister's determination of the level of compensation. See *Manitoba Debates*, 6 October 1969, pp. 1325–1326.

32 *Manitoba Debates*, 25 August 1969, pp. 137-38, and 2 October 1969, pp. 1254-1255.

33 The *Winnipeg Tribune*, 7 October 1969, p. 6, ran an editorial calling for fair compensation for the firms' loss of business.

34 As Schreyer said in the legislature, the bill was identical to that being passed "by the sister provinces of Saskatchewan and Alberta, in order to accommodate the Federal Marketing Board's operations": *Manitoba Debates*, 6 October 1969, p. 1338.

35 Much information on Northland is in *Main Fisheries Ltd. et al v The Queen*, [1983] FCJ No. 221, and *Northland Fisheries Limited v The Queen*, (1984), 56 NR 333 (Fed CA).

36 See *Sasnella Contractors Ltd v Lazarenko and Northland Fisheries Ltd*, [1976] MJ No. 231

37 Information given in this paragraph and the next on the history of the company is from [1976] 1 FC 8; [1977] 2 FC 457; Arenson Interview; *Winnipeg Free Press*, 4 October 1978, p. 4; and FCTD File.

38 For the little that we know of the negotiations between government and the companies see Elswood F. Bole to Harry Marder, 8 September 1972, and Statement of Claim, 7 February 1975, paras 12-13, both in FCTD File; [1976] 1 FC 8, para 3, and [1977] 2 FC 457, para 41; *Main Fisheries Ltd. et al v The Queen*, [1982] FCJ No. 214 (TD) and *Main Fisheries Ltd. et al v The Queen*, [1983] FCJ No. 221. The 1972 offer to MF stemmed from the committee valuing its equipment at $16,416, and the "disposal allowance" was for 25 percent of this.

39 As noted above, the government's major first term initiative was public auto insurance, an especially contentious issue with the man responsible for it, Municipal Affairs, Housing and Government Services Minister and future premier Howard Pawley, needing police protection because of threats on his life: see Interview with Howard Pawley [hereafter Pawley Interview.] Manitoba did in fact compensate insurance agents in some small degree for loss of business, although not the insurance companies.

40 Information and quotations in this paragraph are from Green, *Memoir*, pp. 62-63, unless otherwise referenced

41 See the discussion of his role in another famous Supreme Court case from Manitoba, P. Girard and J. Phillips, "A Certain Mallaise: *Harrison v Carswell*, Shopping Centre Picketing, and the Limits of the Postwar Settlement," in J. Fudge and E. Tucker, eds, *Work on Trial: Canadian Labour Law Struggles* (Toronto: Irwin Law and Osgoode Society for Canadian Legal History, 2010).

42 Howard Pawley cannot remember a cabinet discussion on this issue: see Pawley Interview. None of the memoirs of members of the Schreyer administration mention it: see McAllister, *The Government of Edward Schreyer*; Green, *Memoir*; H. Schulz, *A View from the Ledge: An Insider's Look at the Schreyer Years* (Winnipeg: Heartland Associates, 2005); Russell Doern, *Wednesdays Are Cabinet Days: A Personal Account of the Schreyer Administration* (Winnipeg: Queenston House, 1981); Lloyd Stinson, *Political Warriors: Recollections of a Social Democrat* (Winnipeg: Queenston House, 1975).

43 Doern, *Wednesdays Are Cabinet Days*, pp. 38, 131, and 134

44 Arenson Interview. Perhaps ironically Green, who was identified as a leftist for much of his career, left the NDP in 1979 in what was really a defection to the right. He became disillusioned with labour, opposing anti-scab legislation and generally unhappy with the rise of feminism and a human rights agenda in the labour move-

ment. He also opposed the equal division of marital property legislation of 1977, and the government's French language legislation: see Pawley Interview.

45 Arenson to Registrar of the Federal Court, 20 October 1975, FCTD File. Unless otherwise referenced, the rest of this paragraph is from Arenson Interview.

46 Information from email from Robert Carr to Jim Phillips, 17 January 2010, on file. Thompson Dorfman is the current name of the firm.

47 Federal Fisheries Minister Davis to the Northern Lakes Fisheries Company, 24 January 1974, reproduced at [1977] 2 FC 457. Para 42.

48 The experience of the Manitoba companies is in stark contrast with those from Alberta, which were rather well compensated, at least judging from the experience of Quality Fish Producers Ltd: see *Quality Fish Producers Ltd et al v Minister of Lands and Forests for Alberta*, [1973] 4 WWR 720 (Alta CA). The Alberta legislation allowed for an appeal to the courts, and Quality Fish received $52,000 for a company that had made $7,650 a year.

49 Our information on Arenson is principally derived from Arenson Interview and Interview with Sherwin Lyman, November 2009. See also the various court files and judgments in the *Manitoba Fisheries* case.

50 Email from Norm Larsen to Jim Phillips, 11 July 2010, on file.

51 For the lawyers and students who worked with him see Arenson Interview and various items of correspondence with their names on the letterhead: Arenson to Federal Court, 20 October 1975 and 15 September 1976, FCTD File; Arenson to Registrar of Supreme Court of Canada, 5 April 1978, LAC — MF, RG 125, Vol 2826, File 14925.

52 See *Walker Estate v York Finch General Hospital* [2001] 1 SCR 647.

53 Arenson Interview.

54 Phone Interview with David Miles, 16 August 2010. Miles is now a Winnipeg lawyer and Chair of the Manitoba Horse Racing Commission.

55 [1953] NILR 79 (QB) and 101 (CA); quotations at 109-110 and 112-113.

56 For all this see Arenson Interview. McCaffrey represented Bodner Fish, Canadian Fish Producers, and Keystone Fisheries. The companies still represented by Lamont were Main Fisheries Ltd., Northern Lakes Fisheries Company Ltd., Northland Fisheries Ltd., and Mid-Central Fish Company: see Arenson to Registrar of the Federal Court, 20 October 1975, FCTD File.

57 The information given here on McCaffrey is from: University of Manitoba Law School website; Law Society of Manitoba *Communique*, February 2009; Taylor McCaffrey LLP website; Arenson Interview; and Roland Penner and Norm Larsen, *Tales from the Underworld and Other Stories* (Heartland: Winnipeg, 2009), *passim*.

58 This is how Arenson remembers the case, and his memory is borne out by language in later decisions about costs: See Decision of Smith DJ on Costs, 2 June 1979, in FCA File.

59 Arenson Interview.

60 Statement of Claim, 7 February 1975, in FCTD File.

61 For the history of the court see I. Bushnell, *The Federal Court of Canada: A History, 1875-1992* (Osgoode Society for Canadian Legal History and University of Toronto

Press, 1997), esp ch. 14. See also R. Pound, *Chief Justice W.R. Jackett: By the Law of the Land* (Osgoode Society for Canadian Legal History and McGill-Queens University Press, 1999).

62 Statement of Claim, 7 February 1975, para 15, in FCTD File.

63 The information provided in this paragraph and the next is from Lyman Interview.

64 [1976] 1 FC 8; FCTD File; Appeal Book, p. 7, in Supreme Court of Canada, Manitoba Fisheries, Court File 14925 [hereafter SCC File]. Like its predecessor the Exchequer Court, the new federal court used deputy judges where necessary. They were invariably supernumerary or retired judges from provincial superior courts, and in the 1970s were often used on appeal panels because of the need for three judges at a time when the court had no more than three or four members of the appeal division: Bushnell, *The Federal Court*, pp. 193-194. At least one member of the Federal Court did not like this practice, thinking it "totally inappropriate" to use people who were in some cases "too old to sit as regular judges" and who had had little or no experience with the Federal Court's jurisdiction: Osgoode Society for Canadian legal History, Oral History Collection, John Urie [hereafter Urie Interview — Osgoode Society].

65 We have not been able to locate any documents from the summary judgment process other than the judgment, and so must deduce the crown's arguments from that, with assistance from the Sherwin Lyman Interview.

66 *Trego v Hunt*, [1896] AC 7 at 24.

67 The major case cited was the decision of the Judicial Committee of the Privy Council in *Sisters of Charity of Rockingham v The King*, [1922] AC 315, para 3, to the effect that "[c]ompensation claims are statutory and depend on statutory provisions. No owner [of expropriated property] . . . is entitled to compensation . . . unless he can establish a statutory right." This sounds like strong support for the argument, taken in isolation, but the *Sisters of Charity* case involved the question of whether a landowner who had had lands expropriated was entitled not just to compensation for the expropriation but also to compensation for "injurious affection" of lands not expropriated by work done on the expropriated land. The case turned on the meaning of the term "injurious affection" in the Dominion *Expropriation Act*. In context the passage quoted was not only irrelevant to the decision, it was a "throw away" statement.

68 [1920] AC 508 (HL); quotation below at 542.

69 J. Willis, "Statute Interpretation in a Nutshell" (1938) 16 *Canadian Bar Review* 1 at 17.

70 In *London and North Western Railway Co v Evans* [1893] 1 Ch 16 at 28 the test is stated as "clear words shewing . . . intention" not to compensate, and "plain expressions of such a purpose." In *Central Control Board (Liquor Traffic) v Cannon Brewery Company Limited* [1919] AC 744 (HL) it is stated as "intention . . . expressed in unequivocal terms," and in *Belfast Corporation v O.D. Cars* [1960] AC 490 at 523 Lord Radcliffe held that the courts must find "the presence of the most explicit words before an acquisition could be held to be sanctioned by an Act of Parliament without full compensation being provided." More recently the British Columbia Court of Appeal has seemingly reversed the onus on intention, arguing that if the legislation is silent

there is no obligation to pay compensation: *Cream Silver Mines Limited v British Columbia* (1993), 99 DLR 199, p. 208.

71 Appeal Book, p. 9, SCC File; FCTD File.

72 Much of this is described in Arenson to Registrar of the Federal Court, 20 October 1975, FCTD File.

73 Lyman Interview.

74 Statement of Defence, 6 May 1975, para 6, in FCTD File.

75 He still practices in the Tax law section of the federal government. Mr. Chambers did not answer requests for an interview.

76 [1977] 2 FC 457 (TD).

77 For Collier see Bushnell, *The Federal Court*, pp. 188 and 349, and Osgoode Society for Canadian Legal History, Oral History Collection, Darrell Heald [hereafter Heald Interview — Osgoode Society].

78 Lyman Interview. The rest of this paragraph, unless otherwise referenced, is from the Arenson and Lyman Interviews, and the trial judgment, [1977] 2 FC 457 (TD).

79 Memorandum of Agreement, 6 April 1964, in FCTD File.

80 [1977] 2 FC 457, paras 4 and 7.

81 Lyman Interview

82 [1977] 2 FC 457, paras 24, 25, 32, 33, 43, and 45.

83 Arenson Interview.

84 List of Documents, in FCA File.

85 For Heald see Heald Interview — Osgoode Society, and Bushnell, *The Federal Court*, pp. 188, 192, and 349. Last Mountain Lake is some 80 miles long and 2-3 miles wide.

86 For Urie see Urie Interview — Osgoode Society, and Bushnell, *The Federal Court*, pp. 189 and 349.

87 [1977] 2 WLR 901 (PC).

88 Luther Chambers to Federal Court, 30 June 1977, in FCA File; Appellant's and Respondent's Submissions on *Selangor Pilots* case, in FCA File.

89 [1978] 1 FC 485 (CA); quotations below from paras 3, 17, 18, 19, and 22.

90 See Appellant's factum, FCA File.

91 For the conclusion that there had been no taking he evoked *France Fenwick and Co. Ltd v The King*, [1927] KB 458, an English case involving the detention of a coal carrying ship for twenty-one days under emergency powers legislation. The crown did not use or sell the coal; they merely prevented its owners from getting it to market for a period of time.

92 *Selangor Pilots*, pp. 907-908 and 909.

93 For this paragraph see Chambers to Federal Court, 8 July 1977, Respondent's Submission Regarding . . . *Selangor Pilots Association*, and Appellant's Brief on ... *Selangor Pilots Association*, 7 July 1977, all in FCA File.

94 [1978] 1 FC 485, paras 33 and 36.

95 For this paragraph see Application to extend the time to seek leave to appeal, 23 November 1977; Affidavit of Ken Arenson, 7 November 1977; SCC Order, 30 November 1977 (Ritchie J); Arenson to SCC Registrar, 7 December 1977, in LAC- MF, RG 125, Vol 2826, File 14925; and Lyman Interview.

96 For this paragraph see Order Granting Leave, 17 December 1977, Appeal Book, p. 26, SCC File; Clerk's Note, 19 December 1977, in LAC — MF, RG 125, Vol 2826, File 14925; Arenson Interview.

97 See Robert Sharpe and Kent Roach, *Brian Dickson: A Judge's Journey* (Toronto: Osgoode Society for Canadian Legal History and University of Toronto Press, 2003), ch. 4. In addition to Dickson the panel comprised Beetz, Estey, Pigeon, Pratte, Ritchie (who wrote the judgment) and Spence JJ.

98 See also email communication from Sherwin Lyman, 28 September 2009, on file, also noting that Ainslie was the most senior litigator in the Department of Justice.

99 See Clerk's Note, in LAC — MF, RG 125, Vol 2826, File 14925

100 For what follows see Factum of Appellant, SCC File.

101 For what follows see Factum of Respondent, SCC File

102 [1979] 1 SCR 101; quotations here and below at pp. 106, 110, 111, 115, 116, and 118.

103 The similarity is noted in economic terms in Jack L. Knetsch, *Property Rights and Compensation: Compulsory Acquisition and Other Losses* (Toronto: Butterworths, 1983), pp. 84-89.

104 Arenson and Lyman Interviews.

105 We have found only one contemporary comment: David Jones, "No Expropriation Without Compensation: A Comment on *Manitoba Fisheries Limited v The Queen*," (1978) 24 *McGill Law Journal* 627. It has been discussed in later articles: see Richard Bauman, "Exotic Appropriations: Government Action and Compensation," (1994) 52 *The Advocate* 561, and Barry Barton, "Case Comment on *British Columbia v Tener*," (1987) 66 *Canadian Bar Review* 145. The quotations below in this paragraph are from the Jones comment at 627, 633, and 634.

106 Arenson Interview.

107 For all this see *Bodner Fish Producers Ltd. v The Queen; Canadian Fish Producers Ltd. v The Queen* (1980), 113 DLR (3d) 644 (FCTD); *Main Fisheries Ltd. et al v The Queen*, [1983] FCJ No. 221; *Northland Fisheries Limited v The Queen*, (1984), 56 NR 333 (Fed CA)

108 See *Tener v Attorney-General of British Columbia*, [1985] 1 SCR 533; *Casamiro Resource Corporation v British Columbia*, (1991), 80 DLR (4th) 1 (BCCA)

109 *Attorney General of Nova Scotia v Mariner Real Estate Limited et al*, (1999), 177 DLR (4th) 696 (NSCA).

110 *Harvard Investments Ltd. v Winnipeg* (1994), 54 LCR 163 (Man QB); 56 LCR 241 (CA).

111 *A and L Investments Ltd et al v Ontario* (1993), 32 RPR (2d) 1 (Ont GD); (1997), 152 DLR (4th) 692 (Ont CA) *Sanders v British Columbia (Milk Board)* (1991), 77 DLR (4th) 603 (BCCA).

112 (2006) SCJ No 5.

113 [1980] FC 120; quotation below at 128.

114 Bauman, "Exotic Appropriations," p. 562

115 More than one person has suggested to us that more than "small c" politics might have been involved, given that the NDP was the party in power in Manitoba. We would disagree, for two reasons. First, the NDP was not in power when the SCC judgment was given. Second, Manitoba was not being sued, the federal government was the defendant.

116 For what follows see A. Alvaro, "Why Property Rights were Excluded from the Canadian Charter of Rights and Freedoms," (1991) 24 *Canadian Journal of Political Science* 309; Sujit Choudhry, "The Lochner Era and Comparative Constitutionalism," (2004) 2 *International Journal of Constitutional Law*, esp pp. 15 et seq; Richard Bauman, "Property Rights in the Canadian Constitutional Context," (1992) *8 South African Journal on Human Rights* 344; Jean McBean, "The Implications of Entrenching Property Rights in Section 7 of the Charter of Rights," (1988) 26 *Alberta Law Review* 548. For the attitudes of federal and provincial governments see also constitutional advisor Barry Strayer's memoir of the Charter negotiations, on file with the author. We say that *Manitoba Fisheries* may have contributed to this concern, but should note that none of the authors cited here refer specifically to the case, despite it being decided just four years before the Charter's terms were finalised.

117 See, *inter alia*, Editorial, *National Post*, 8 February 1999; L. Gunter, "Property Rights in Jeopardy in Canada," *The Windsor Star*, 23 October 2003, comparing Canada unfavourably with China.

118 See, *inter alia*, *Keystone Bituminous Coal Association et al v Nicholas Debenedictis, Secretary, Pennsylvania Department of Environmental Resources et al*, 107 S. Ct. 1232 (1987).

The Malling of Property Law?: The Toronto Eaton Centre Cases, 1984–1987, and the Right to Exclude[1]

Eric Tucker

Introduction

The Toronto Eaton Centre (TEC) opened its doors on 10 February 1977 and instantly become one of Toronto's top attractions, drawing in millions of tourists, shoppers, and people who just wanted to hang out.

But it also soon became the site of contests over the ancient action of trespass. Cadillac Fairview , TEC's principal owner,[2] asserted it enjoyed an absolute right to exclude people from its private property, while members of the public, trade unionists, and political activists claimed that common areas of the mall were like city streets. These conflicting claims were transformed into legal disputes in three cases. The first arose out of a union organizing drive by the Retail, Wholesale and Department Store Union (RWDSU). RWDSU had organized retail workers at six Eaton's department stores in southern Ontario and was attempting to organize workers at Eaton's flagship store in the TEC. Both Eaton's and Cadillac Fairview invoked their property rights to exclude union organizers from their premises. The union filed an unfair labour practices (ULP) complaint with the Ontario Labour Relations Board (OLRB) claiming that the exclusion of organizers from the common areas of the mall interfered with their statutory right to organize under the *Labour Relations Act* (LRA). The OLRB agreed with the RWDSU and its decision was subsequently upheld by the Ontario Court of Appeal.[3] In the second case, then city councillor Jack Layton was assisting RWDSU by handing out

Figure 1. Aerial Photograph of the Toronto Eaton Centre, October 1976. Toronto, Archives of Ontario, T. Eaton Co. Fonds, F229-308-0-450. Used with the permission of Sears Canada Inc.

leaflets to Eaton's employees arriving for work while standing on TEC property. A Cadillac Fairview manager directed Layton to leave and when he refused to do so, police were called and he was charged under the *Trespass to Property Act* (TPA). Layton was convicted at trial but successfully appealed based on a claim that the *Charter of Rights and Freedoms* guarantee of freedom of expression trumped the absolute right of property owners to exclude under the TPA.[4] The third case also involved a charge under the TPA, but the defendant was Keith Medcalf, a volunteer in Layton's office. Medcalf's case was unrelated to the organizing drive; rather his case arose out of Cadillac Fairview's policy of excluding persons that it found undesirable. Medcalf defended himself on the ground that Cadillac Fairview had entered into a public access agreement with the City of Toronto to secure planning approvals and had no right to exclude.[5] Subsequent litigation between Medcalf and Cadillac Fairview was eventually settled without concessions by either party.

These three cases are not leading cases in any conventional sense of the term, but they are important. First, they provide a glimpse of property law on the ground, so to speak, where it arguably matters most, but is not often seen by law students whose training is centred on appeal court judgments. Second, these case histories illuminate the processes and contingencies that produce or don't produce leading cases. Finally, these cases reveal a tension within property law between two models of ownership: an absolutist one and a socially contextualized one. According to the absolutist model, owners should enjoy complete discretion to decide how property is used and who is permitted to enter, based entirely on self-interest. Opposed to that view is the socially contextualized model, which requires owners to take into account the interests of non-owners when making decisions about the use of and access to property.[6] There is no easy reconciliation of these competing views within a liberal rights framework and the stakes of the debate are often high, engaging deep concerns over human freedom and autonomy. For non-owners, limits on where they can be may entail a significant restriction on their freedom if the effect of those limits is to exclude them from locations that are important or meaningful to their ability to realize their goals. As Jeremy Waldron made clear in the context of the homeless, "No one is free to perform an action unless there is somewhere he is free to perform it."[7] Yet a limit on property owners' right to exclude necessarily restricts owners' freedom and autonomy to use their property to realize their goals. After all, John Locke told us the state was called into existence to protect the rights of property owners.[8] The resolution of these cases, and their legal aftermath, provide us with a rich empirical case study of the way this recurring tension was resolved in a liberal property regime at a particular time and place and in a particular context.

In order to set the stage for this case study, the chapter begins with a brief history of the right to exclude and its application to a new property form, the shopping mall. It then proceeds to the three cases, each beginning with the legal and factual background, followed by the actual case and its aftermath. The final section examines the legal aftermath of the cases and provides a brief summation.

The Right to Exclude and the Rise of the Mall

Blackstone famously characterized the right of property as "that sole and despotic dominion which one man claims and exercises over the external things of the world, in total exclusion of the right of any other individual in the universe,"[9] and one of the ways in which private property owners exercise that sole and despotic dominion is by an unfettered right to determine who is allowed to enter onto their property. Of course, even in Blackstone's time, the institution of private property did not accord owners an absolute right to exclude. But following parliamentary enclosures in the eighteenth century, which strengthened exclusive private property, common law and customary limits on the right to exclude became truly exceptional and steadily diminished thereafter.[10] Indeed, whether one agrees with the argument of Thomas Merrill that the right to exclude is now the *sine qua non* of ownership, takes the view that it is one of a bundle of rights that must be present for property to exist, or that it is simply one of the ways in which owners set the agenda for how an object will be used, there is comparatively little disagreement over the strength of private property owners' legal right to exclude.[11]

Not much has been written about the history of the law of trespass in Canada. For example, RCB Risk's study of property law from 1841–1867 mentions trespass in passing and affirms that the right of an owner to exclude was not the subject of dispute.[12] The first incarnation of the TPA in Ontario was enacted in 1834. The statute provided for a summary power to prosecute minor offences, including common assaults and petty trespasses to real and personal property, before a justice of the peace. The offence of petty trespass was defined as willfully or maliciously committing any damage, injury, or spoil to real or personal property, either of a public or private nature, provided that the offending behaviour had not already been made a felony by law. It also provided that a trespasser could be apprehended without a warrant by a police officer or by the owner or the owner's agent. Persons convicted of trespass could be fined up to five pounds, and in cases of private property, the fine was payable to the owner. It was a defence to a charge of trespass to show that the accused "acted upon a fair and reasonable supposition that he had a right to do the Act complained of."[13]

In subsequent legislation, trespass began to be separated out from other criminal offences[14] and in 1858 a petty trespass act for Upper Canada was enacted that defined petty trespass as any unlawful entry upon wholly enclosed land, whether or not damage was caused.[15] In post-Confederation Canada, the constitutional division of powers conferred upon the federal government exclusive power to enact criminal law and upon the provinces exclusive power to regulate property and civil rights. This arrangement required that a sharp distinction be drawn between the two. Apparently without debate, pre-Confederation petty trespass acts were treated as laws within provincial jurisdiction, not criminal law, as evidenced by the inclusion of the 1858 statute in the first Ontario statute consolidation in 1887.[16] Further amendments followed, so that by the 1970s the Act prohibited unlawful entry onto enclosed land, gardens or lawns, and posted lands.[17] But as well, some forms of trespass were covered by the criminal law.[18]

It is fair to say that from the beginning, the Canadian state strongly protected the right to exclude. Not only did property owners enjoy common law rights, enforceable by damage actions and injunctions, but also criminal and regulatory legislation provided property owners with quasi-police powers to protect their property against intruders. Clearly, protecting the right of private property owners to exclude was an important public policy that was never seriously contested — that is until the advent of the shopping plaza and mall.

The mall was the brainchild of Victor Gruen, a Jewish socialist who fled from Austria to the United States in 1938, after the Nazi *anschluss.* Already a successful, innovative store designer, Gruen first proposed the idea for large regional shopping centres in a 1943 article. He envisaged numerous shops enclosed in a single building, surrounded by a landscaped area and parking lots. In addition to retail spaces, these developments would contain public facilities, including a post office and library, and meeting rooms and auditoriums for community activities.[19] Beginning with Northland, a regional shopping centre built outside of Detroit in the 1950s, the popularity of the suburban mall soared, often accelerating the hollowing out of downtown retail areas. In turn, municipalities promoted the construction of malls in city centres as a way of attracting shoppers back downtown by providing "sanctuaries of civility in an otherwise uncivil society."[20] But as the mall grew more popular, the public dimension of Gruen's vision increasingly fell by the wayside. As Gruen himself bemoaned in a 1978 article, "The environmental and humane ideas underlying, though not perfectly expressed, in the original centres were not only not improved upon – they were completely forgotten. Only those features which had proved profitable were copied."[21]

Gruen's disillusionment may be a bit disingenuous,[22] for at the heart of the mall concept was an unresolved tension between its public and private dimensions. Gruen never discussed property rights, but he understood that the mall was to be constructed by private developers on privately owned land, and that its primary appeal to investors was that it would generate greater revenues than more traditional shopping formats.[23] It was not surprising, then, that in the event of a conflict between public uses and private profits, mall owners would give priority to the latter, and assert their legal right to do so on the theory that members of the public were simply licensees whose permission to be on the premises could be revoked by the owner at any time and for any reason.[24] As one journalist characterized the situation, "shopping malls are only private buildings masquerading as public property."[25] Any change in their owners' legal position and actions would have to be externally imposed.

Interest in making mall owners behave otherwise grew with the malls' success. In suburban areas, malls provided civic spaces that were largely missing in the new suburban landscape, while the colonization of downtowns by malls[26] not only drew people off the streets into privatized spaces, but often literally entailed the privatization of public spaces, including the closing off of public streets and the sale of public lands to developers.

The push to make mall owners behave otherwise came from several sources. Some urban politicians and planners were concerned that malls would replace the town centre and that public life would suffer if mall owners were allowed to exclude those who engaged in activity that detracted from the shopping environment the owners wished to promote.[27] For example, Stephen McLaughlin, the Toronto Planning Commissioner in the mid-1980s, expressed the view that, "In Toronto, we have to be wary of giving up the public realm to the private sector."[28] These concerns were well grounded. Mall managers frequently developed "public filtering"[29] techniques to exclude people who did not look as if they were participating in the shopping process. Youth, who were drawn to the malls as much for socializing as for shopping, were often given shorter rein than adults.[30] Indeed, their presence was often viewed as a threat to the mall's operation.[31] Minority youth felt they were victims of discrimination, and were frequently targeted by mall security. Planners urged more public control to counter this trend,[32] and, as we shall see, others turned to the law to challenge their exclusion.

For political activists, malls could be attractive sites for expressive activities because of the large number of people who gathered there and, sometimes, because it contained a business they wanted to target. For union organizers, access to mall property was sometimes seen as necessary. They could not go into the stores to organize and it was difficult to distinguish store employees from the crowds of people entering and exiting the mall from public property. As well, if the unionized employees of a mall tenant struck, the ideal place to picket would be at the entrance to the store, which was on mall property. But mall owners would not willingly permit picketing on their property.

Let's Go to the Mall: The Eaton Centre Cases

THE TEC CASES PROVIDE an excellent opportunity to observe how the tensions in Gruen's concept and the emerging social conflict over the mall owner's right to exclude played out in the heart of Toronto in the mid-1980s. From a legal point of view, these challenges were based on three sources: public access laws and agreements, statutory labour rights, and the *Charter*. Each of the three cases tracks one of these grounds.

Public Access Laws and Agreements

THE ISSUE OF ACCESS to private property that was normally open to the public did not first arise in the context of the mall. For example, prior to World War II a number of cases were brought to challenge racial segregation. The courts took the view that, apart from the ancient duty of an innkeeper to serve all members of the travelling public, merchants were free to refuse to sell a ticket or to provide service to a prospective patron.[33] The absolutist position was infamously embraced by the Supreme Court of Canada (SCC) in *Christie v York Corporation* (1940), upholding the right of a tavern owner to refuse to serve a black man.[34]

Since the courts would not limit the owner's right to exclude to accommodate the human rights of non-owners, activists turned to the legislature, where organized campaigns met with much greater success.[35] In 1947, Saskatchewan became the first province to prohibit discrimination in the provision of services in public places, such as hotels and restaurants, on the grounds of race and religion.[36] It took several more years before other provinces followed Saskatchewan's lead, but by the mid-1960s, businesses in Canada providing services to the public were barred from refusing to permit entry onto their premises on prohibited grounds.[37]

Modern anti-discrimination law was the first significant and successful challenge to the absolutist right to exclude, but its impact was limited: it only applied to property owners who normally provided service to members of the public and it still left those owners free to exclude on non-prohibited grounds. For example, store owners could exclude people arbitrarily or because they were engaging in unapproved expressive activities. While the former power made it difficult for persons alleging discrimination to prove that their rights had been violated (they might have been arbitrarily excluded), the latter limitation only became significant when appropriate public spaces for expressive activities were unavailable. This was not typically a problem in urban areas, where stores fronted on public streets and there were public spaces suitable for demonstrations and protests.[38] The rise of the shopping mall in the 1960s, however, changed the physical landscape and resulted in a second round of efforts to expand public access laws.

The issue came to the fore during the lengthy planning process for the TEC. The first attempt by Eaton's to construct a mall on its downtown Toronto site failed in the 1960s because the plan called for the demolition of a heritage building, Old City Hall (Figure 2). It is fitting that this plan was prepared by none other than Victor Gruen and an associate, James A. Murray. An examination of the proposal reveals it did not include much in the way of public facilities. Rather, the site was to be dominated by the Eaton department store, retail space, office towers, and an 800 room hotel. Out of over 10 million square feet of development, only 263 thousand was designated as publicly used space (e.g., a galleria).[39]

Figure 2. Panoramic view from the south of the Gruen-Murray Model for their Toronto Eaton Centre Proposal. Toronto, Archives of Ontario, T. Eaton Co. Fonds, F229-308-0-423 (Photo of Model by Ezra Stoller). Used with the permission of Sears Canada Inc.

Subsequent proposals left Old City Hall intact, but other concerns emerged. Part of the problem was that city planners initially embraced Gruen's original vision and wanted a centre that would contain a public library, learning facilities, and galleries. These features did not emerge in later designs.[40] But the issue of public access remained and concerned municipal politicians had a good opportunity to press their demands, because Cadillac Fairview needed the city to agree to close public streets and convey the underlying land for it to assemble a large enough block of land in a prime downtown commercial area (Figure 3).

As well, Cadillac Fairview needed to negotiate an agreement with its neighbour, the Holy Trinity Church, which owned some of the land Cadillac Fairview required for the development, and Cadillac Fairview wanted subway entrances within the mall, which required public access. As part of the protracted negotiations, Cadillac Fairview granted a number of pedestrian rights of way, including one through the enclosed mall to provide access to the church from Yonge Street, and ones to provide access to the Toronto Transit Commission (TTC) subway stations, which had entrances into the mall property (Figure 4).[41] Cadillac Fairview also agreed to provide 40,000 square feet of "private open space accessible to the public."[42]

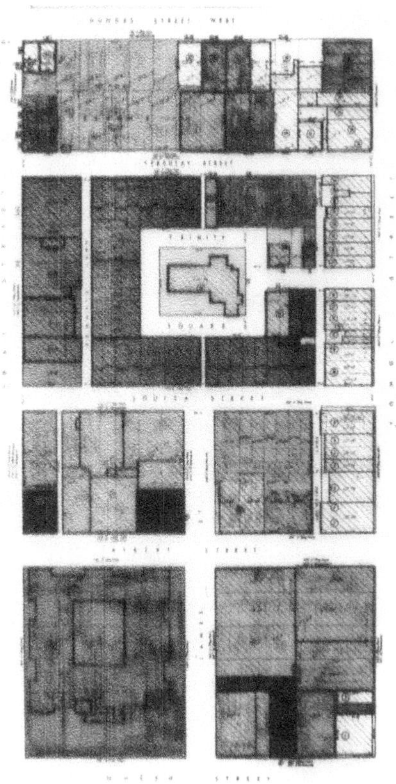

Figure 3. Map of area between Dundas and Queen Streets and Bay and Yonge Streets, 1964. Toronto, Archive of Ontario, T. Eaton Co. Fonds, F229-301-0-63. Used with the permission of Sears Canada Inc.

The principal concerns of the politicians were the impact of the development on the surrounding streets, and the ability of members of the public to cross through the mall. The right of members of the public to engage in expressive activities while on mall property was not specifically raised.[43]

While the legal nature of a right of way is reasonably clear, its implications in the context of a mall were not, and neither was the effect of the public access commitment. Clarification was first sought in the context of the drive to organize Eaton's employees at the TEC store. Union organizers went onto TEC property in order to make contact with employees as they entered the store before it opened to the public, but Cadillac Fairview management had

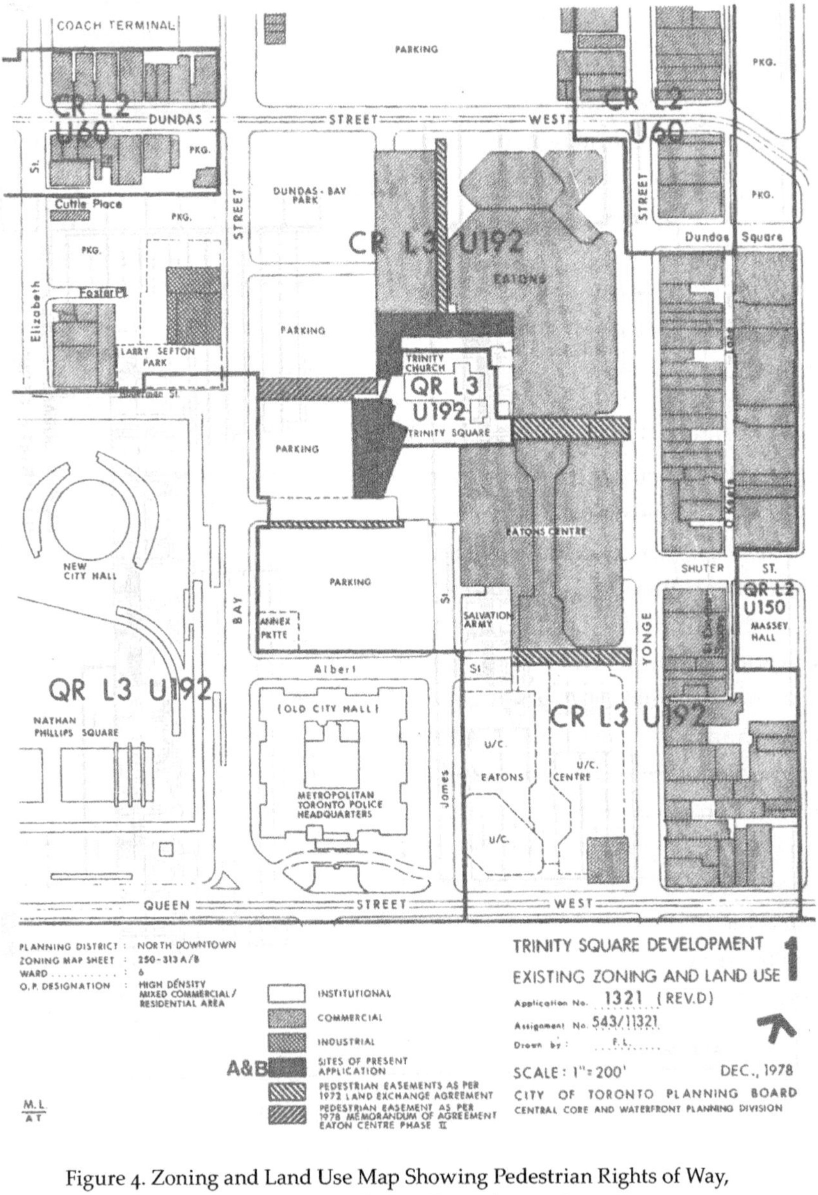

Figure 4. Zoning and Land Use Map Showing Pedestrian Rights of Way, Toronto Eaton Centre, December 1978.

them evicted. We will come back to the legal challenges that arose out of this confrontation, but efforts were also made to use the public access agreement as leverage with Cadillac Fairview. Submissions were made to the Neighbourhoods Committee of City Council by Carole Currie, a key RWDSU organizer; Jack Layton and Dale Martin, city councillors representing downtown wards (that included the TEC) who were union supporters; and Alan Borovoy and Erika Abner, on behalf of the Canadian Civil Liberties Association. Borovoy and Abner's submission was the most detailed. They reviewed a number of planning documents related to the TEC development approval and argued that the underlying concept was that "the areas in question were designed to serve a number of public functions, not simply the commercial or property interests of the owners . . . . Indeed, a reading of the planning reports conveys the impression that the idea was to render the mall areas, as far as possible, an indoor counterpart of streets and parks."[44] On the basis of these submissions, the Neighbourhoods Committee called for a meeting between then mayor Art Eggleton and Cadillac Fairview management, and requested a report from the city solicitor on whether Cadillac Fairview's expulsion of labour organizers constituted a breach of its agreement with the city.[45] The solicitor's report reviewed the building scheme agreement and concluded that the "two-below area," where the organizing activity was being conducted, was not included in the required open space area, so that Cadillac Fairview's actions did not violate the agreement.[46] Cadillac Fairview also refused to meet with the mayor on the ground that there were legal proceedings pending with the union.[47] This put an end to the political route for seeking to limit the exclusion of union organizers, but not to the question of the legal implications of the public access agreement and rights of way for Cadillac Fairview's right to exclude.

Keith Medcalf was nineteen years old and had just graduated from high school when he moved to Toronto from Cambridge, Ontario. He quickly burned through the savings he had accumulated in high school by working on computers for a local manufacturer. He soon found himself living on the street and in trouble with the law. By 1984 he had started to turn his life around, working temporary jobs and volunteering at the Union of Injured Workers and then in Layton's office. His anti-authoritarian streak and feistiness, however, were still strong. On the afternoon of 5 November 1984, Medcalf was on his way to work at Layton's office when he stopped at Simpson's, a department store across the street from the TEC, to buy cigarettes. There he ran into a friend. The two crossed Queen Street and entered the

TEC. They walked in a northerly direction and stopped to talk and smoke. A few minutes later, a private security guard, employed by Intercon Security, the company then under contract with Cadillac Fairview to patrol the TEC, came over. He recognized Medcalf's friend as someone who had previously been banned from the mall. The security guard instructed Medcalf's friend to leave and when Medcalf intervened he was also ordered to leave. Medcalf insisted that he had a right to be in the TEC and additional security guards were called. They attempted to detain Medcalf and his friend. A scuffle ensued. Medcalf and his friend were forcibly taken to the security office and police were called. The officer who arrived on the scene issued a ticket to Medcalf's friend but refused to issue one to Medcalf, advising Intercon guards that they should issue an exclusion notice, which they did. Medcalf was angered and upset by what he viewed as the exercise of arbitrary power over what he considered a public space.[48]

The exclusion of Medcalf and his friend was not an isolated incident. It was reported that in 1984 more than 32,000 people were removed from the TEC and that hundreds of tickets were being issued each month by the police for trespassing.[49] If the sworn testimony of John Dennis, the TEC manager, is any indication, mall management felt besieged.[50]

> We have a lot of problems with just general youth hanging out in the centre with nothing better to do than to spend six, eight, ten hours a day hanging out. We have problems with drunks and derelicts who try to use the centre as a place of residence. We have problems with runaways who use the centre because of its prominence – they know that if they come to that centre that if they want to make a connection with the lower element or the unlawful element, they can usually make a connection there. We have problems with people trying to deal drugs from time to time and we have problems with different groups who espouse a particular philosophy or a particular political point who would try to use the centre as their forum from time to time, and we constantly have to remove these people and keep them removed.

Medcalf told Layton what had happened. Layton was already quite familiar with the issue. In addition to having been involved in the city hearings looking into the public access agreements, Layton had been recently charged with trespassing while handing out leaflets for RWDSU's union organizing campaign (see below). Layton informed Medcalf about the public access agreements between the city, the TTC, and the TEC. Medcalf was convinced he had a legal right to go through the TEC and decided to defy the ban.

On the evening of 11 January 1985, Medcalf left Layton's office for home. He entered the TEC on his way to the subway and was recognized by a security guard who attempted to arrest him. Medcalf informed the guard that he was on a TTC easement and continued walking. The guard pursued and forcibly detained him. A police officer was called and a trespass charge was laid.

The case was heard in May in provincial court, criminal division, by Justice J Belobradic. Mr. Rutter, who was not a lawyer, appeared for the crown and Medcalf defended himself. Medcalf came prepared with a copy of the agreement between the TTC and Cadillac Fairview, as well as with a copy of *Harrison v Carswell*, a Supreme Court of Canada judgment, which he thought supported his case.[51] The crown was unprepared to deal with Mecalf's legal arguments and an adjournment was granted. The trial resumed on 22 May. Medcalf was beginning to feel comfortable and confident in the courtroom. Rutter introduced a copy of the minutes of the City of Council executive committee at which the city solicitor had reported on the public access agreement, and argued that it superceded the TTC right of way. As Belobradic J questioned Rutter about his submissions, Medcalf intervened. "My friend the Crown is trying to say that my argument regarding the City guaranteeing me access is that the Eaton's Centre [sic] doesn't apply. Is that correct?" His Honour responded: "That is all right, Mr. Medcalf. You can assume that I get the purport of what he is saying." A few questions later, Medcalf intervened again and Belobradic J cut him off: "Let Mr. Rutter tell me what he has to say then you can correct anything he says in your submissions. If we do not do it this way I will not know where I am going." In the end, Belobradic J was dismissive of Rutter's legal submission, questioning at one point Rutter's qualification to make a legal argument given that he was not a lawyer. Justice Belobradic acquitted Medcalf on the basis that the right of way agreement deprived Cadillac Fairview of a right to exclude people who were accessing the subway. The crown did not appeal.[52]

TEC management reacted dismissively to the acquittal and asserted that it would continue to issue tickets,[53] a statement it made good on. Not only did the exclusions and the ticketing keep up, but also, on 19 February 1986 there was another confrontation between Medcalf and Intercon. The guard issued Medcalf a written warning and escorted him off the premises.

One week later, Medcalf commenced a lawsuit against Cadillac Fairview in which he claimed $10 million in general damages as well as punitive and exemplary damages. A fair bit of legal wrangling ensued. Cadillac Fairview was represented by the large Toronto law firm, Weir, Foulds (WF). On

24 March WF unsuccessfully moved to have Medcalf's amended statement of claim struck. Subsequently, Medcalf obtained an order noting Cadillac Fairview in default for failing to deliver a statement of defence. WF had the order set aside and delivered a statement of defence on 14 April, which set out Cadillac Fairview's version of the facts and its legal arguments. Medcalf served his reply on 16 April, providing more factual details about his run-ins with Intercon. WF unsuccessfully sought to strike out Medcalf's reply and appealed the Master's decision.

While the appeal was pending, Medcalf had two more confrontations with Intercon. On 12 May, an Intercon guard ordered Medcalf to stop as he was entering the TEC with his German shepherd at the Trinity right of way. Medcalf ignored the guard and continued walking. Cadillac Fairview alleged Medcalf unleashed his dog, ran through the TEC, out the other side of the Trinity right of way, and back in through the Albert right of way, where he again unleashed his dog and yelled abusive language. Cadillac Fairview also claimed that he later phoned their lead lawyer on the case, WAD Millar, and threatened to have his dog attack any security guard who tried to stop him entering the TEC. A more serious incident occurred on 26 May when an Intercon guard again stopped Medcalf as he entered the TEC with his dog and advised him that no dogs were allowed. Medcalf defied the guard's order to leave and a confrontation followed as the guard attempted to arrest Medcalf for trespassing. By this time a crowd had gathered. Medcalf and the security guard scuffled and other guards came to restrain Medcalf and his dog. He was forcibly taken to the security office and a police officer was called who charged Medcalf with trespass.

After the last May incident, Medcalf made a motion for an interlocutory injunction restraining Cadillac Fairview from interfering with his and the public's use of the right of way. The motion was denied by Gray J. According to Medcalf, it was sometime after this that he had a discussion with Cadillac Fairview's lawyers and they agreed that he would drop the case and they would not seek costs. Cadillac Fairview made no concession about its right to exclude but they agreed to permit Medcalf on TEC property, unless there were grounds to exclude him. A consent order ending the action was issued on 18 July. The agreement was honoured and Medcalf experienced no further difficulties entering the TEC.

Just as Medcalf was winding up his conflict with TEC in the spring of 1986, he began having problems at the nearby College Park mall when he was stopped by an Intercon Security guard while walking with his dog through the mall on his way to the subway. A series of confrontations led to Medcalf being banned and then a charge of trespass followed. This time around, Medcalf appeared before provincial court judge Robert Dnieper, noted for his "sometimes harsh and always unconventional sense of justice."[54] He was convicted on 19 November 1986. Medcalf launched an appeal but confusion over which court had jurisdiction eventually left the matter in limbo. As a result of further confrontations between Medcalf and College Park security, Medcalf launched a lawsuit on 19 January 1987, in which he sought various declarations as well as general damages of $1 million and punitive damages of $10 million. In his statement of claim, Medcalf reviewed the confrontations and disputed the right of the mall owner to exclude based on various legal arguments, including that a right of way had been granted to provide access to the TTC entrances within the mall. For reasons that Medcalf does not recall, he let the matter drop in September 1987 and did not appear on his own motion for judgment.[55] However, he also remembers that Intercon guards at College Park also stopped trying to prevent him from entering.

Property Rights and Statutory Labour Rights Meet at the Eaton Centre

Property rights and labour rights did not first meet at the mall. Rather, labour law grew up in the shadow of property law and always confronted its restrictions on where and in what manner workers could engage in organizing activity and picketing. Prior to modern statutory collective bargaining schemes, it was clear that employers could exclude union organizers from their premises. Of course, employees had an implied right to come on to the employer's premises for the purpose of performing their work, but nothing more. So when workers occupied factories on a few occasions in the 1930s, these were clearly acts of trespass and were treated as such by all levels of government, notwithstanding the claim made by progressives that under modern industrial conditions the "plant and its machines are by morals and equity as much the property of the men that work them as the men who draw dividends."[56] The law regulating picketing was far more complicated. Although it was clear that picketers could not enter onto the private property of the targeted firm, the question of picketing on public property adjacent to its entrances was more vexed, although clearly mass picketing that blocked access to private property was a legal nuisance, which would be enjoined at the behest of the employer.[57]

During and in the aftermath of World War II, statutory collective bargaining schemes were enacted in Canada that required employers to bargain with unions that obtained majority support from a unit of employees. These statutes also protected the freedom of employees to join unions and engage in their lawful activities, and gave workers the right to be free from employer interference in organizing activity.[58] Property rights were not explicitly addressed initially, but the right of the employer to exclude organizers from its premises was never seriously questioned.[59] One small exception to the absolutist position empowered the labour board to order employers in remote locations to permit organizers onto their premises.[60] A second was that the labour board had the power to order the employer to provide the union access to its property after it had been found guilty of committing unfair labour practices during a union organizing drive.[61]

The first cases to consider labour rights on mall property arose in British Columbia as a result of picketing on the common areas of the Dell Shopping Centre by striking workers employed at Zellers. The results were mixed. In the first case, Zellers, the mall tenant, sought an injunction on the basis that the picketing constituted unlawful interference with the easement it enjoyed over the mall's common areas. An interim injunction was granted and affirmed on appeal. Writing for the majority, Tysoe JA held that the union's picketing would almost certainly constitute a substantial interruption of the employer's enjoyment of the right of way and thus would be unlawful.[62] The court, however, left open a small possibility that picketing on the common areas might not always unlawfully interfere with the enjoyment of the right of way, giving the union another chance to test the legal waters by continuing to picket peacefully. Zellers brought an application for contempt and the picketers were convicted, but on appeal a differently constituted panel of the Court of Appeal held that the picketing was lawful. "No significant distinction can be drawn in this case between picketing on a public sidewalk and on the privately owned right of way."[63] However, the judgment raised the possibility that the landlord could have obtained an injunction based on trespass.[64]

This set the path for future litigation: from now on, mall owners, not tenants, appeared as the plaintiffs. So in 1964, when striking employees of Loblaws picketed on the premises of the Grosvenor Park Shopping Centre in Saskatchewan, the mall owners obtained an injunction based on trespass. A unanimous Court of Appeal lifted the injunction on the ground that the owners were not in actual possession because of the multiple easements granted to tenants and the practice of opening the mall to the public.[65] Some appeal court judges were taking into account the mall context and qualifying the absolutist position.

This openness soon began to close. In 1969 James Peters, president of the Brampton Labour Council and of United Auto Workers, Local 1285, was charged under the *Petty Trespass Act* for picketing the Safeway supermarket in the Shoppers' World shopping centre in support of a boycott of California grapes called by the United Farm Workers.[66] At trial, Provincial Court Judge Ord acquitted Peters on the basis of the *Grosvenor Park* case. "I don't see how [picketing] becomes unlawful when it is done on property over which the owner has control but not exclusive possession."[67] The crown successfully appealed and Peters was fined $10 by County Court Judge Grant. On further appeal, Gale CJ, writing for a unanimous court of appeal, rejected the *Grosvenor Park* reasoning: "[I]t is our opinion that an owner who has granted a right of entry to a particular class of the public has not thereby relinquished his or its right to withdraw its invitation to the general public or any particular member thereof, and that if a member of the public whose invitation to enter has been withdrawn refuses to leave, he thereby becomes a trespasser."[68] The court also rejected an argument that the *Petty Trespass Act* was beyond the power of the province to enact, because it fell within criminal law, a matter of federal jurisdiction. The SCC unanimously disposed of the appeal with a brief affirmation of the Ontario Court of Appeal's judgment.[69]

The high noon confrontation between the absolutist and the socially contextualized positions occurred in the now famous majority and dissenting opinions of Dickson J and Laskin CJ, respectively, in *Harrison v Carswell*, a case involving picketing on a Cadillac Fairview shopping centre in Winnipeg.[70] The case's history has already been well told by Philip Girard and Jim Phillips,[71] so we can turn directly to the judgments. For Dickson and the majority of the Court, the issue was resolved by the recent precedent of *Peters*. However, Dickson did not stop there and went on to reject the argument that the Court should balance the rights of property owners and the rights of picketers. He defended the Court's refusal to do so on two arguably inconsistent grounds. The first was that such balancing entailed consideration of "important and difficult political and socio-economic issues, the resolution of which must, by their very nature, be arbitrary and embody personal economic and social beliefs."[72] This was a legislative, not judicial, function.

The second ground was that: "Anglo-Canadian jurisprudence has traditionally recognized, as a fundamental freedom, the right of the individual to the enjoyment of property and the right not to be deprived thereof, or any interest therein, save by due process of law."[73] In other words, the common law balance was already struck in favour of property rights over labour rights and for that reason the legislature would have to intervene if it wished to rebalance those rights.[74]

Laskin CJ, a former labour lawyer and academic who had been harshly critical of the courts' picketing decisions in the 1930s, was, as his biographer Philip Girard put it, a legal modernist[75] who believed deeply that it was the role of the court to "search for an appropriate legal framework for new social facts."[76] For Laskin, the application of the absolutist view of the right to exclude to the context of the mall, which was opened to the public, "does not make sense"[77] and the court was perfectly justified in rebalancing the interests of the owner with competing interests of non-owning members of the public in the public areas of the mall. Laskin's proposed solution was to limit the mall owner's right to exclude by giving members of the public a qualified right to remain as long as their activities did not interfere with the owner's legitimate interests.

The triumph of the absolutist position in *Harrison*, however, did not establish a uniform position across the country and in some provinces the right of mall owners to exclude on a non-discriminatory basis was limited. Courts in Saskatchewan continued to apply *Grosvenor Park* on the ground that the province did not have legislation equivalent to the *Petty Trespass Act*.[78] Legislative measures also added to the legal mosaic. The first New Democratic Party (NDP) government in British Columbia's history passed labour legislation in 1973 that did not allow trespass actions with respect to picketing on property to which members of the public normally had access.[79] And in Manitoba the legislature effectively overruled *Harrison* by amending its petty trespass and the Queen's Bench acts to permit communicative activities on outdoor areas attached to businesses to which the public is normally admitted.[80] Nevertheless, the absolutist position remained in force in Ontario when the drive to organize Eaton's workers at the TEC began in 1984.[81]

Organized labour and Eaton's also did not meet for the first time in 1984, but all previous efforts to organize employees at Eaton's had gone badly. In 1912 the Toronto branch of the International Ladies Garment Workers Union struck Eaton's garment production facilities. Despite substantial support from the local labour movement and suffragists, the strike was lost.[82] The next attempt to organize Eaton's workers started in 1947, when the fledging RWDSU began seeking support among the more than 10,000 Eaton's employees at its extensive Toronto facilities, which included several stores, a factory, a warehouse, mail order offices, delivery-dispatch depots and administrative offices. Four years later, the campaign was abandoned and the department store sector in Ontario remained mostly union-free for the next thirty years.[83]

The 1984 organizing drive at Eaton's stores in southern Ontario began serendipitously when Mike Danyluk, a RWDSU business agent, was shopping in late December 1983 at the Eaton's store in Brampton, Ontario, for a video cassette recorder. An off-hand comment made by commission salesperson Paul Wannamaker about the low rate Eaton's paid set in motion a lightening-quick organizing drive. The first meeting of employees at that store was held on 2 February 1984 and eight days later the union filed for certification, which it was granted on 28 March.[84] Five more Eaton's stores in southern Ontario were quickly organized, and shortly thereafter so were six Simpson's stores.[85] Clearly, more than serendipity was at work; union organizers were tapping into a deep well of dissatisfaction among department store workers.[86]

Yet despite these successes, the union still faced the challenge of organizing Eaton's flagship store in the TEC. The store was crucial to the union's success because without it the union's bargaining power for the other Eaton's stores would be diminished. Both Eaton's and the union understood its significance and the store soon became a battleground. The organizing challenge was formidable. The store employed 3,000 workers, nearly half working part time. Moreover, because of the store's location within the TEC, union organizer access to the employees from public property was difficult. This led the union to push the boundaries of property law.

The campaign began on 8 March when organizers went through the store, handing out informational material and business cards to Eaton's employees. This action itself was of dubious legality, since labour legislation did not permit organizing during working hours, even by in-house organizers, let alone outside organizers. In-house organizers were recruited and meetings were planned. The first confrontation between outside organizers and Cadillac Fairview security occurred on 11 April when organizers attempted to distribute notice of a meeting on mall property, near the link to the Dundas TTC subway station, which was used by large numbers of Eaton's employees coming to work. A Cadillac Fairview employee advised them that they were not permitted to distribute leaflets and so the organizers moved to the adjacent TTC property and continued their activity. Inspectors from the

TTC, however, told them they were not permitted to solicit on TTC property. In short, there was no place where the organizers were permitted to be at this crucial site for contacting Eaton's employees.[87]

Outside organizers responded with guerilla tactics. Drops of literature inside the store continued but were met by a letter from Eaton's declaring that further such entries would be regarded as a violation of the TPA.[88] At some point during these events, union organizers reportedly encountered Frederik Stefan Eaton, president of Eaton's, who told the organizers to leave, stating, "This is my store."[89] On 27 June, the RWDSU filed an ULP complaint alleging that Eaton's and Cadillac Fairview, acting on behalf of Eaton's, had violated the workers' statutory right to organize without employer interference.[90]

Following the complaint, the union ceased making floor drops, but continued distributing leaflets early in the morning outside the Eaton's store on TEC property near the TTC Dundas subway link. James Hayes, the union's lawyer, recommended this time and location for two strategic reasons: first, most of the pedestrian traffic at this time consisted of Eaton's employees and, second, Hayes wanted to "create the facts" that would be most favourable for the ongoing ULP complaint if Cadillac Fairview interfered.[91] Cadillac Fairview did not initially object, but toward the end of September Cadillac Fairview changed its mind and informed the union it would no longer allow leafleting.[92] In response, employee organizers began distributing literature in restaurants used by Eaton's employees that were located inside the Eaton's store. As well, outside organizers occasionally distributed leaflets near the Dundas subway link. On 11 October, Cadillac Fairview security ejected outside organizers, as well as a reporter who was watching nearby.[93] The following week, outside organizers appeared again, this time accompanied by Toronto alderman Layton. Cadillac Fairview security conversed with Layton but took no action. On 15 November, Cadillac Fairview security called police when Layton and other union organizers refused to leave the area. Two police officers attended but no one was arrested or charged with trespass.

In the following weeks a *modus vivendi* seemed to have been established; union organizers greeted incoming employees but did not hand out literature or impede traffic. However, after a brief time, literature distributions resumed. By this time, the union's priorities and resources began to shift toward negotiating a first agreement for the Eaton's and Simpson's stores it had already organized. On 30 November, employees at the unionized Eaton's stores went on strike and set up picket lines on sidewalks outside the malls where the stores were located. Apparently, the union did not wish to open another front on the property rights battle, focusing instead on a consumer boycott.[94]

It was in this context that Layton, accompanied by his children, then ages nine and six, and two union supporters, entered the TEC on Saturday morning, 1 December, to hand out leaflets to employees coming through the Dundas subway link. John Dennis, the TEC manager, was called to the scene and ordered Layton and the others to leave the premises. Layton refused, the police were called, and they issued him a ticket (tickets were not issued to his children or the two other organizers) when he continued his refusal. Layton and the others finally left when police warned that they would be arrested if they remained.[95] In a statement to the press, Layton expressed his view of the law: "But just because they've been fortunate enough to have delivery of customers right to their property — built at public expense I might add — doesn't mean they have the same exclusive rights as the average property owner."[96] We will come back in the next section to Layton's case. For now we will focus on the ULP complaint.

Hearings in the case commenced on 13 August 1984 before a tripartite panel composed of Mort Mitchnick, a former management labour lawyer who had been appointed vice chair of the OLRB in 1979,[97] and A. Grant and LC Collins, the labour and employer sides respectively. RWDSU was represented by James Hayes, a labour lawyer with Cavalluzzo's;[98] Eaton's was represented by Harvey Beresford, QC, a partner in Hicks, Morley;[99] and Cadillac Fairview was represented by WJ McNaughton from Weir, Foulds. The hearings dragged on for twenty-one days over eight months, ending in April 1985. The length was partly a function of the mass of evidence, but was also due to the parties' own actions. Journalist David Olive described the cross-examination of Carole Currie, one of the key organizers, by Beresford.

> By accident or design, great chunks of time pass between the posing of his every question. And Currie, wary of traps that may be concealed in the most innocuous query, hesitates sometimes half a minute before issuing usually a monosyllabic answer. Even after these, though, there is much scribbling by the dozen or so lawyers and their assistants — some of them using three pens, no less, each a different color — after every answer . . . Currie is unyielding and Beresford is abrasive . . . . Throughout she is locked into an expression of defiance and fear, like the patient who is preparing to object as her dentist decides which drill to use next. As for Beresford, in his courtroom

> manner one detects the charismatic impulses of someone who might have trained guard dogs.[100]

The union's complaint covered Eaton's practices of limiting literature distributions and discussions by employees on its premises, but our focus is on Cadillac Fairview's exclusion of union organizers from the mall. In the written complaint and in argument before the Board, Hayes submitted that any act of the employer or its agent (in this case Cadillac Fairview) that unnecessarily limits union organizers' access to employees violated the LRA. He emphasized the public character of the mall and the importance to the organizing campaign of being able to make contact in this space. With respect to the TPA, Hayes argued that the LRA gives "a right or authority conferred by law" to conduct organizing activity on mall property so that organizers were not trespassing. Finally, the union raised the *Charter*, claiming that to the extent the TPA limits freedom of expression and association, it was unconstitutional and that, at the very least, the interpretation of the LRA ought to be informed by these *Charter* rights.[101]

For its part, Cadillac Fairview denied it was acting on behalf of Eaton's. Rather, Cadillac Fairview claimed it was protecting its own commercial interests, which required it to maintain tight control over the mall because of its great popularity. Outside groups were permitted to use the mall "solely on the basis of what Cadillac Fairview feels enhances the commercial purpose of the Mall, or enhances Cadillac Fairview's image in the City as a 'good corporate citizen.'"[102] McNaughton argued that Cadillac Fairview was legally entitled to take this position because previous decisions of the SCC recognized a mall owner's right to exclude "as it feels its interests dictate."[103] With respect to the *Charter*, Cadillac Fairview argued there was no authority for holding that section 2 freedoms overrode the TPA, and that in any event the source of their property rights was not the TPA but the common law, so the *Charter* did not apply.[104]

In a unanimous decision, the Board sidestepped the *Charter* argument, preferring instead to balance the interests of property owners and labour organizers within the confines of the LRA.[105] The Board extensively reviewed American and Canadian case law, ultimately embracing the general principle, articulated in a US Supreme Court decision, *Babcock & Wilcox*, that it should strive to achieve a balance between organizing and property rights "with as little destruction of one as is consistent with the maintenance of the other."[106]

The big legal hurdle for the union and the Board was the SCC's holding in *Harrison,* which Eaton's and Cadillac Fairview argued embraced legal absolutism. The Board distinguished *Harrison* on the basis that unlike picketing, organizing was protected by a statute that could be interpreted to limit property rights. In the mall context, the balance between the statutory right to organize and the common law right to exclude depended on whether the mall owner was protecting its own legitimate commercial interests. In this case, because of the facts Hayes' legal advice helped produce, Cadillac Fairview could not demonstrate an independent interest in stopping the leafleting. Therefore, the board concluded that Cadillac Fairview was not acting on its own behalf but rather was excluding organizers as an agent of Eaton's and unlawfully interfering with the right to organize. The Board ordered Cadillac Fairview to permit union organizers access to mall property at times and places when contact with customers would be minimal.[107]

The decision had no impact on the organization drive because, by the time it was issued, the organizing drive had been abandoned while RWDSU focused on the strike and its aftermath.[108] The OLRB's decision, however, created a potentially valuable precedent for future organizing drives of retail stores operating in malls.[109] For this reason, it caused Eaton's some concern, particularly in regard to the parts of the board's decision that required Eaton's to allow limited literature distributions on its premises by employee organizers. The Board's decision was a more significant blow to Cadillac Fairview and its legal position that it had an unfettered right to exclude, a position that the Board had described as "extreme." In an interview shortly before the Board's decision was issued, Cadillac Fairview's lawyer WJ McNaughton had told the press, "You want people there to shop. You don't want your people distracted by public rallies or such." Moreover, apart from union organizers, mall owners were increasingly concerned about the presence of young people and others who were perceived to be disturbing the malls' commercial purposes, and had stepped up their enforcement of the TPA.[110] These concerns prompted both Eaton's and Cadillac Fairview to request the OLRB to reconsider its decision.

Eaton's argument for reconsideration focused on management rights, not property rights. Cadillac Fairview, however, was most interested in defending its right to exclude, and its submission argued that the Board's decision was inconsistent with the TPA, that it condoned the creation of a nuisance, and that it had unreasonably put a third party non-employer in a worse position than an employer by requiring the third party, but not the employer, to allow union organizers onto its premises.[111] The Board rejected Cadillac Fairview's request on the ground that it did not introduce new evidence or arguments, although it did address some of Eaton's concerns.[112]

Cadillac Fairview had more at stake than Eaton's, so it alone applied for judicial review of the Board's decision. The factum was prepared by McNaughton and J. Gregory Richards, and filed on 21 August 1986, more than nine months after the Board's reconsideration decision. With respect to the property rights issue, Cadillac Fairview's lawyers essentially refined the claims they had made earlier: the Board's interpretation of the LRA abrogated Cadillac Fairview's rights under the TPA; courts had consistently held that legislation should not be interpreted in a manner that derogated from existing property rights; and the LRA expressly allowed non-employee organizers to enter an employer's property under limited circumstances, but made no provision to allow organizers onto third-party property. Each of these alleged errors took the Board beyond its statutory jurisdiction and justified striking down its decision in a judicial review application.[113]

Oddly, the OLRB's brief defended its restriction on Cadillac Fairview's right to exclude as an aspect of its broad remedial authority. Indeed, the Board denied that its decision was based on an interpretation of the LRA that made the exclusion itself the ULP.[114] But this was inconsistent with a plain reading of the decision. After all, the ULP was the unjustified exclusion of union organizers, so the power of the board to limit the right to exclude did not derive from its remedial authority but from the statutory right of employees to organize without interference by employers or parties acting on behalf of employers. The OLRB seemed to be minimizing the implications of its own decision.

The union, represented by Paul Cavalluzzo, endorsed the OLRB claim regarding its remedial authority, but also defended the more significant point that the right to exclude could be limited by the right to organize under the LRA. To hold otherwise, the union argued, would allow mall owners' property rights to put them beyond the reach of the act.[115]

The case was argued before a panel of the Divisional Court, comprised of Van Camp, Gray, and Bowlby JJ on 15 April 1987. The court unanimously upheld the Board's decision. The court's reasoning, however, was not strong: it held that the right to exclude under the TPA was not absolute but qualified, insofar as a person who made entry pursuant to "a right or authority conferred by law" did not commit the statutory offence of trespassing. It then distinguished *Harrison* on the basis that the picketing employees in that case had no prior sanction to be on mall property. This case, according to the court, was different, because the entry was made "as the result of an otherwise valid order issued by the Labour Relations Board."[116] But that was wrong: the entry had taken place before the LRB had issued an order. The real question was whether the statutory right to organize provided legal authority to enter onto private property in the circumstances of this case. The court did, however, accept the union's argument that *Harrison* should not be read to immunize a mall owner from the reach of decisions and orders issued pursuant to the LRA.[117]

Given what was at stake for Cadillac Fairview and a relatively weak Divisional Court decision, Cadillac Fairview sought and obtained leave to appeal to the Ontario Court of Appeal. This turned out to be a mistake. Cadillac Fairview's factum, again prepared by McNaughton and Richards, shifted its focus from the board's finding that Cadillac Fairview was acting on behalf of Eaton's to the property rights issue. It canvassed a line of cases, starting in 1765,[118] that emphasized the absolute right of property owners to exclude and submitted that the Divisional Court had erred in holding that the LRA limited this right by implication. Indeed, it insisted that any derogation of the right to exclude required express legislative action. The factum also pointed out the flaw in the Divisional Court's reasoning with regard to its assertion that there was prior OLRB authorization for the entry onto mall property by union organizers.[119]

Stephen Goudge's brief for the OLRB and Cavalluzzo's for the union emphasized that the board correctly held that the LRA's protection of the right to organize could limit the right to exclude under the common law and the TPA. The union's brief also invoked the *Charter*, submitting that the LRA should be interpreted in the manner that best protects the fundamental freedoms of expression and association. It noted that *Peters* and *Harrison* were pre-*Charter* decisions, implying that they might be decided differently in a post-*Charter* world.[120]

The case was argued before Sydney Lewis Robins, Walter Tarnapolsky, and John Hartey Osler JJ. Prior to his appointment in 1983, Tarnapolsky had taught at several Canadian law schools and had been dean at Windsor. More importantly, he had been a human rights activist who had published widely in the area.[121] Robins had spent many years in private practice before his appointment to the bench in 1976 and had practiced labour law, representing unions in a number of cases. He also served as treasurer of the Law Society of Upper Canada from 1971 to 1974.[122]

The court issued a unanimous judgment, written by Robins JA, on 20 December 1989, five years after the events that gave rise to the case.[123] The court emphasized that the LRA protected the freedom to organize and noted that for this freedom to be meaningful, employees must have access to union communications and opportunities for organizational activity. In the context of the TEC, all the employee entrances to the Eaton's store were within the mall and under the control of Cadillac Fairview, making organizing on public streets impracticable. It followed that, "If private property rights are indeed absolute, the result is that . . . the shopping centre itself creates a buffer of private property between employees and the union which precludes the exercise of s. 3 organizational rights at the entrance to the workplace where the activity can most effectively be conducted."[124]

There was a clear conflict between property rights and organizing rights and the board was not obliged as a matter of law to treatCadillac Fairview's property rights as absolute: "In my opinion, notions of absolutism have no place in the determination of issues arising under a statute designed to further harmonious labour relations and to foster the freedom of employees to join a trade union of their choice."[125] *Peters* and *Harrison* could be distinguished because statutory rights were not being asserted in those cases. The outcome was a clear defeat for Cadillac Fairview's absolutist property rights position.

Constitutional Rights to Freedom Expression

Although Cavalluzzo raised the *Charter* in the context of the ULP complaint, the OLRB and the courts preferred to deal with the matter wholly within the principles of the LRA. The defence of Jack Layton against trespass charges, however, provided another opportunity to raise those arguments.

Layton's trial in provincial offences court began on 26 June 1985. Two weeks earlier the OLRB had issued its decision that the exclusion of labour organizers from the mall property was a ULP. This opened up an obvious line of defence to the trespass charge — that Layton had "a right or authority, conferred by law" to be on Cadillac Fairview's private property.[126] Layton's lawyer was Susan Ballantyne, a former union organizer who had been called to the bar in 1984, and was with the firm of Cavalluzzo and Hayes.[127] She served notice that she intended to raise the OLRB decision and to make constitutional arguments regarding freedom of speech and association. The prosecutor was Stan Berger, who had been a crown since being called to the bar in 1981.[128] The judge was Garry Hunter, a former crown prosecutor.

From early in the trial Hunter took a very narrow view of the case. For example, when the OLRB decision was first raised, Hunter intervened, "I have difficulty in understanding what relevance that has to this charge. I mean I don't doubt they have certain rights, but I understand that we are talking about private property and the right of the managers or management of that property to determine what can go on on that property."[129] Later on, in response to Ballantyne's objections to Berger's questioning of a police officer, Hunter expressed the view that "The facts are straightforward. It's a simple trespass case."[130]

Berger's principal witness was Cadillac Fairview's property manager, John Dennis. The facts were not in dispute and so much of the questioning was designed to lay a foundation to counter potential legal defenses. Ballantyne's chief witness was Layton, and most of his evidence addressed his understandings of the law and his motivations for being at the TEC. Layton testified he was passing out leaflets in that area because he was convinced it was the only effective way to communicate with the workers and that he had been allowed to do so in the past. He also stated his belief that important issues of freedom of expression and association were at stake and that he saw this as something of a test case. Finally, he asserted that city council, in approving the TEC, understood that the mall would provide a pedestrian environment similar to a public street.

Berger's cross-examination went on for some time. In Berger's view, Layton appeared self-righteous and went on too long, and in so doing alienated the judge.[131] Perhaps this is true, but the only importance of the case to Layton was its potential to change the law. The transcript does not record the legal arguments made by counsel at the end of the trial, but it does record Hunter's brief judgment, which rejected Layton's claim that he had a legal right to be on TEC property. "I find as a fact that the decision of the Labour Relations Board is not binding on this court, and I do not accept that the accused in fact had a right to be there, in law."[132] Hunter also dismissed the *Charter* argument. "I am of the opinion that those rights do not exist to the detriment of somebody else's rights. In other words they are limited, given the circumstances." He did not elaborate further, except to say that Layton was obliged to leave the mall property when requested to do so by management. Hunter acknowledged that union organizers faced obstacles contacting Eaton's employees but was skeptical that no other means were available. He fined Layton $53, the amount set on the ticket.[133]

Cavalluzzo took over the appeal to the Ontario Provincial Court (Criminal Division), where he raised two arguments: first, that the LRA conferred on union organizers a right to be on mall property, and second, that Layton's actions were protected by the *Charter*. Both of these claims were vigorously opposed by Stan Berger, who argued the case for the crown. The case was heard by David Scott J, the brother of Ian Scott, then Ontario's Attorney General. He issued his judgment on 26 May 1986, one month before his brother appointed a task force to inquire into trespass on mall property (see below).

The first issue raised an interesting administrative law point; was a decision of an administrative tribunal interpreting its own statute binding on a court? Interestingly, the crown attorney chose to attack the merits of the OLRB decision, in addition to denying that it was binding.[134] Justice Scott agreed that the Board's decision was not binding, but saw it as persuasive and concurred with the Board's conclusion that the LRA created an exception to the TPA in appropriate circumstances. That said, he then excluded Layton from the class of persons protected by the LRA (union organizers and union representatives) on the basis that Layton's "main interest in the matter was to establish that these common areas in the TEC were public space to be used by any member of the public for peaceful purposes."[135] In short, he saw this as a test case and intended to treat it as such.

The case was argued and decided before the SCC's judgment in *Retail, Wholesale and Department Store Workers' Union, Local 580 v Dolphin Delivery*,[136] which held that the *Charter* does not apply to private litigation relying on the common law. Moreover, given the lack of clarity about the state action requirement, no court had considered whether the *Charter* applied to the TPA. Justice Scott simply assumed that it did and turned directly to the issues of whether Layton was engaged in expressive activity covered by the *Charter* at the time of his arrest, whether the application of the TPA violated his freedom of expression, and whether the violation was justified under section 1.

The first issue was the easiest. The peaceful distribution of literature was clearly expressive activity. But crown counsel argued that the definition of freedom of expression was internally limited and did not extend to expression on private and public property, a position that crown attorneys pursued in subsequent cases.[137] Justice Scott rejected that view because it was founded on the erroneous "contention that the *Charter* does not diminish or modify any common law rights concerning the enjoyment of property." He noted that while some sections of the *Charter* reflect concern for the protection of property, property itself was not protected. Therefore, the door was open "to a new assessment of statutes such as the *Trespass to Property Act*, and indeed of property rights at common law, as regards the extent to which they may be affected by the *Charter*."[138]

Justice Scott did not address the common law rights of property owners further, but focused on whether the TPA infringed Layton's freedom of expression. In his view, this was a simple matter once the idea of an internal limit on location was rejected. Layton's freedom of expression "was clearly infringed. Indeed, it was denied."[139] The question then was whether the infringement could be demonstrably justified under the *Oakes* test, issued earlier that year.[140] The purposes of the TPA — to protect property from unjustified invasions — were clearly of sufficient importance to get by the first branch of the test. More problematic was the question of whether the means chosen were demonstrably justified. Scott's phrasing of the question suggested his answer. "Why is it reasonable that the occupier of the mall be empowered by the *Trespass to Property Act* to deny a member of the community, acting peacefully on mall property, his freedom of expression?"[141] Crown counsel could not provide Scott J with a satisfactory answer. He rejected the argument based on the additional expenses that might flow from being required to tolerate expressive activities, especially in the mall context, where property is generally open to the public. It was no longer acceptable to argue that mall owners could be driven solely by commercial considerations. "In my view, the occupier cannot set a condition on its invitation whereby the invitees enter the mall with money in hand but must leave their *Charter* rights and freedoms outside the mall property."[142] Finally, Scott J also rejected the argument that the balancing of competing rights is best left to the legislature, and quoted Laskin's dissent in *Harrison* justifying judicial action to revise the legal framework in response to new social facts.[143]

In the result, Scott J dismissed the charge against Layton. James Hayes, one of Layton's lawyers, told the press that the decision would provide legal guidelines for balancing between private property interests and other social values.[144] But the crown was not satisfied and successfully sought leave to appeal to the Ontario Court of Appeal. Dana Venner took over the case for the Crown and prepared the factum, which was submitted prior to the SCC judgment in *Dolphin Delivery*. Venner first argued that the *Charter* did not apply in this situation because it was not intended to "create additional new rights to use someone else's property for the purpose of such expression."[145]

Alternatively, if the *Charter* did apply, Venner argued that the provisions of the TPA were a reasonable limitation under section 1.

Cavalluzzo's factum challenged the argument that the *Charter* is "merely declaratory of existing rights."[146] He emphasized the primacy of freedom of expression and the need to give it an expansive interpretation, including one that limited absolute property rights. It followed that the TPA infringed Layton's freedom of expression and was unconstitutional unless saved by section 1. Cavalluzzo then went through the *Oakes* test, and argued that the government failed to show that owners of publicly used private property were entitled to the same level of protection as owners of privately used property. He also argued that the TPA did not impair as little as possible freedom of expression to achieve its purpose and that there was no proportionality between its effects and its objective.

The case was argued on 11 February 1987, before a panel consisting of Associate Chief Justice MacKinnon and Martin and Blair JJ. Justice MacKinnon began working on a judgment immediately and a draft was prepared.[147] Unfortunately, MacKinnon ACJ died suddenly of a heart attack on 19 June at the age of sixty-six, before a judgment had been issued.[148] A copy of the draft judgment has not been located and MacKinnon's law clerk at the time, who worked on the draft, does not recall its contents.[149] What we do know from an annotation on the back of the appeal book by Howland CJ is that the surviving two justices, Martin and Blair, were divided. As a result, Howland scheduled a rehearing before a panel of five judges to be held on 19 October. That hearing never took place. On 8 October 1987, Dubin JA granted a request by the crown to delay the appeal because the government was planning to amend the TPA, making the appeal moot. On 17 June, ten days after Ian Scott introduced amendments to the TPA into the legislative assembly, the crown abandoned the appeal.[150]

Winning the Battles but Losing the War: The Triumph of Near Absolutism

If we stopped our stories here, the result might be interpreted as evidence of the legal triumph of a socially contextualized property regime over an absolutist one. After all, in each of our three cases, the alleged trespassers were at least partially victorious: Medcalf was acquitted of one trespass charge because the court found that a public access agreement limited the mall owner's right to exclude; RWDSU was successful in gaining a limited right to conduct organizing activities on common areas of the mall based on statutory labour rights; and Layton was acquitted because his constitutional right to freedom of expression trumped the right to exclude. Yet at the time of writing most lawyers and lay people would find the suggestion that mall owners do not enjoy a broad right to exclude surprising — and with good reason. The common law has not changed; property owners, including owners of property normally open to the public, enjoy a near absolute right to exclude,[151] and, as we shall see, neither statutes nor the *Charter* have significantly limited that right.

Public Access Laws

With the exception of Manitoba, provincial governments have shown little enthusiasm for limiting mall owners' right to exclude. Manitoba amended its *Petty Trespass Act* in the aftermath of *Harrison* to allow communication of true statements on areas of property to which the public is normally admitted. It also amended its *Court of Queen's Bench Act* to prevent injunctions from being granted in this circumstance. One might think that on their face these provisions substantially limit the mall owner's right to exclude, but that is not the case. In *Gameday Publication(s) Ltd. v Keystone Agricultural and Recreational Centre Inc.*, a unanimous Manitoba Court of Appeal held that the common law right to exclude remains unaffected by these laws, so that even if the mall owner cannot get an injunction to prevent or end a trespass, or prosecute trespassers under the trespass statute, a "property owner is not restrained . . . from exercising his common law right to evict trespassers from his property, as long as the force used is reasonable for that purpose."[152] Moreover, the court held that the legislation "had no impact upon a landowner's other remedies against a trespasser . . . "[153] which would include an action for damages.

The more significant story, however, is that no other province has enacted any public access law limiting the right of mall owners to exclude. The fate of such an initiative in Ontario is both instructive and directly related to our narrative, since the TEC was in the eye of the storm. As noted earlier, the TEC had adopted strict policies to limit the presence of individuals who were simply hanging out in the mall. Youth and minorities were particularly affected. In 1986, Ron Stubbert, program manager for Mercury Youth Services, which operated in the area, estimated that at least 90 percent of the thousand teenagers it served every year had been charged with trespassing either in the TEC or nearby College Park.[154] Complaints about this pattern of conduct were made to Ian Scott, then the province's Attorney General and a former labour-side lawyer, and on 23 June 1986, he appointed the Task Force on the Law Concerning Trespass to Publicly-Used Property as it Affects Youth and Minorities. Raj Anand, who had articled with Scott's firm, was its chair.

The task force held hearings in which a number of our protagonists participated. Layton lost no time in writing to Scott to let him know of his case and of the confusion about the applicability of the TPA to "quasi-public places such as the Eaton's Centre."[155] Later that summer Layton and fellow councillor and partner, Olivia Chow, were banned from the TEC for a year after they intervened with security guards who had told some minority youth to leave. Layton told the task force that since that time he had been stopped by Cadillac Fairview security guards on several occasions while exiting or entering the subway through the mall. The Task Force's sought an explanation from McNaughton, Cadillac Fairview's lawyer, who confirmed that Layton was banned, but provided a very different account of the events that caused it, suggesting that the incident was manufactured.[156] In his communications with the Task Force, Layton also cited Medcalf's research and experiences.

McNaughton's lengthy brief emphasized the important role of the TPA as a tool for malls to maintain order and denied that mall management discriminated against youth and minorities. The TEC was presented as a special case because it had become a regional attraction and McNaughton provided figures to demonstrate that the press had overstated the extent of it use of bans and arrests under the TPA.[157] No one mentioned the recent organizing drive, the labour rights issue, or, for that matter, the potential impact of the *Charter* on the right to exclude.

Anand's task force reported in March 1987. He completely rejected the absolutist property rights position advanced by owners, developers, and managers of publicly used property. Not only did he find convincing the evidence of user groups that the mall owners' absolute discretion to exclude under current law was being exercised discriminatorily, but he also adopted the view that because mall owners "have been given (or have created) a virtual monopoly . . . over prime settings for community life – in short the privatization of the town square" they must assume a corresponding obligation to permit activities like hanging out that did not contribute to the profitability of the mall.[158] He proposed two alternatives reforms: amend the TPA to require just cause to evict from publicly used property, or subject publicly used property to the same legal regime that governs the public square.[159]

On 7 June 1988, Scott introduced Bill 149, the *Trespass to Property Amendment Act*, in response to Anand's report. The bill limited the right of owners of publicly used property to exclude to situations where an individual's behaviour was not compatible with public use or contravened posted rules. It also allowed a person charged with trespassing to challenge the reasonableness of the posted rules or the owner's action. Bans were limited to thirty days.[160] The bill was debated at second reading on 14 February 1989. Positions were predictable. The NDP members were critical, claiming that it did not go far enough to protect labour and political rights on mall property, while the Progressive Conservative members viewed the bill as one that unduly restricted the rights of property owners.[161]

Outside of the legislative assembly, property owners mounted a major campaign to stop the bill. The spectre of youth gangs was raised by the Retail Council of Canada as well as by Rick Grange, then executive vice-president of Intercon Security, the company providing security at the TEC. Other groups representing mall owners and senior citizens added their voices to the opposition and *The Globe and Mail* supported them, claiming that the "vitality of Canadian shopping malls rests on an atmosphere of civility and public security" that presumably would be weakened if the law passed.[162] The labour movement was ambivalent about the legislation since it did not directly address the legality of organizing and picketing on mall property, and so it did not mount a lobby to support it. That work largely fell to Anand, who had since been appointed head of the Ontario Human Rights Commission. He argued that the criminal law was the appropriate tool for dealing with youth gangs, not property regulations. The bill also got editorial support from the *Toronto Star*, which argued that malls should be treated as public places and that the new law would not prevent police or private security guards from dealing with swarming or other illegal activities.[163] However, this support was not enough and the Liberal government let the bill die.

And so the law stands now where it stood when Medcalf challenged the TEC, Cadillac Fairview, and Intercon Security. Mall owners cannot discriminate on prohibited grounds and they must respect rights of way that were granted during the development approval process. However, the notion that common areas of the mall are quasi-public and should be treated as such by the laws of trespass has gained no legal traction and a public access requirement is not normally imposed on mall developers by the City of Toronto.[164]

It is also noteworthy that Saskatchewan, the one province in Canada that did not have trespass to property legislation and whose courts permitted picketing on mall property, passed a trespass statute in 2009. During the debates, the opposition NDP specifically objected to the impact this would have on access to mall property, but its efforts to amend the law to exclude peaceful assembly and expression on privately owned, publicly used property failed.[165] So if there is a trend in Canada, it is toward the restriction, not the expansion, of public access.

Statutory Labour Rights

THIS IS THE AREA where the gains made in the TEC cases have fared best, although the picture is still mixed. The case limits the right of mall owners to exclude labour organizers in the absence of an independent, legitimate business justification. Organizing activity that interferes with mall activity, therefore, could be banned by mall owners on the basis they are protecting a legitimate business interest and not acting on behalf of a tenant-employer. As well, the decision does not affect mall owners' right to prohibit picketing on mall property, since there is no statutory right to picket in most of Canada. *Harrison* continues to govern.[166]

Little has changed legislatively or otherwise since the judgment. Outside of remote worksite provisions, few labour relations statutes provide union representatives access to employer property, including property that is normally open to the public. In Ontario, legislation providing a limited right to organize and picket on privately owned, publicly used property was enacted by the NDP government in 1993, but the provision was repealed in 1995 by the newly elected Conservative government.[167] Presumably this leaves the *Cadillac Fairview* precedent in place, although there have been no subsequent Labour Board cases applying it. In non-labour cases, the Ontario Court of Appeal has relied on its decision in *Cadillac Fairview* to find that legislation may by implication limit private property rights.[168]

In British Columbia the judiciary has narrowly interpreted the *Labour Code* restriction on the right of private owners of publicly used land to bring actions for trespass against union organizers and picketers. In a case that involved picketing on a parking lot leased by the employer for the exclusive use of its employees, Hood J required that all statutory restrictions on private property rights be explicit.[169] In a subsequent case, again involving a parking area, the court of appeal interpreted a 1975 amendment to the

Labour Code, which substituted "petty trespass" for "trespass." The court determined that, notwithstanding any evidence that the distinction between the two terms has ever been ascribed legal meaning, the change must reflect a legislative intent to preserve the right of property owners to bring actions for acts of trespass that are not petty.[170]

Overall, it would be fair to conclude that the inroads made by labour law on the right to exclude have been minimal. Except in very unusual circumstances employers remain free to exclude non-employee union organizers and mall owners are only required to permit union organizing (or picketing in British Columbia) to the extent that the activity does not impair business operations. This approach throws serious doubt on the claim that the law fairly balances workers' statutory organizing rights and property and managerial rights.[171]

The Charter and the Right to Exclude

BECAUSE OF THE UNUSUAL circumstances of MacKinnon J's death and the decision of the crown to withdraw its appeal, the Ontario Court of Appeal did not pronounce on the constitutional validity of the TPA. Moreover, Scott J's judgment has had no legal traction. Indeed, it has never been cited by another court and the weight of other judgments is clearly against the view that the *Charter* limits the right to exclude, whether at common law or under trespass statutes. An earlier judgment of the Federal Court of Appeal set the tone for the dominant view: "The freedom guaranteed by the *Charter* is a freedom to express and communicate ideas without restraint . . . . It is not a freedom to use someone else's land or platform to make a speech, or someone else's printing press to publish his ideas."[172] The SCC's judgment in *Dolphin Delivery*, holding that the *Charter* does not apply to private litigation between private parties relying on the common law, provided a firmer jurisprudential basis for this view, and was given more traction by McLachlin J in *Committee for the Commonwealth of Canada*.

> Freedom of expression does not, historically, imply freedom to express oneself wherever one pleases . . . . For example, it has not historically conferred a right to use another's private property as a forum for expression. A proprietor has had the right to determine who uses his or her property and for what purpose. Moreover, the *Charter* does not extend to private actions. It is

> therefore clear that s. 2(b) confers no right to use private property as a forum for expression.[173]

This view does not rule out a *Charter* challenge to the TPA, but courts have questioned whether a TPA prosecution meets the state action requirement. For example, in *Russo v Ontario Jockey Club*, Boland J upheld the absolute right of the racetrack owner to decide who may enter or remain on the premises. She rejected the *Charter* argument made by the bettor on the ground that the *Charter* did not apply to the private actions of the racetrack owner relying on its common law rights. Yet the owner had not relied exclusively on its common law rights; the plaintiff in the case had been served a notice of exclusion under the TPA. Justice Boland never addressed this point, perhaps because of her view, expressed earlier in the judgment, that the TPA merely enforces common law rights.[174] As such, it might not have occurred to her, or the lawyers appearing before her, that reliance by a private party on the TPA arguably meets the state action requirement.[175] The submission that the *Charter* applies to TPA prosecutions was successfully made in a subsequent case, but that holding was dismissed out of hand on appeal.[176]

Of course, the absence of state action does not preclude the *Charter* having an influence on the common law. As *Dolphin Delivery* recognized, the common law should develop in a manner that is consistent with *Charter* values.[177] In the *Pepsi* case, the SCC abolished the tort of secondary picketing precisely on this basis.[178] At least one SCC judge opened the door to a reconsideration of *Harrison*, but to date nothing has come of this[179] and it seems unlikely that the *Charter* will be used successfully in the near future to make private mall owners behave otherwise.[180]

In sum, for a moment in time it looked as if a near perfect storm would overwhelm the near absolutism that has characterized the right of mall owners to exclude. However, for both contingent and conjunctural reasons the storm passed, leaving behind only minor changes and near absolutism remains the norm.[181] There are many who decry this situation,[182] but there is little reason to believe that in the near future private owners of publicly used space will be required to behave otherwise.

Notes

1 Research funding for this project was provided by the Social Science and Humanities Research Council. Tim Groves provided outstanding research assistance. I also benefited from comments by David Hayman and other participants in the June 2010 Law Stories workshop in Edmonton.

2 The TEC was owned by T.E.C. Leasehold Limited, which in turn was owned by Cadillac Fairview (60%), the Toronto-Dominion Bank (20%), and Eaton's (20%).

3 *R.W.D.S.U. v T. Eaton Company Limited,* [1985] OLRB Rep. June 941 [OLRB Decision]; upheld at (1988), 62 OR (2d) 337 (HCJ, Div. Ct.) [Divisional Court Decision]; affirmed (1990), 71 OR (2d) 206 (CA)[CA Decision].

4 *R. v Layton* (1986), 38 CCC (3d) 550 (ON Prov. Ct, Crim. Div.)

5 Beverly Bowen, "Judge's Ruling Opens Eaton Centre Door" *The Globe and Mail* (23 May 1985) M1.

6 For a helpful discussion of this tension, see Joseph William Singer, *Entitlement: The Paradoxes of Property* (New Haven: Yale University Press, 2000) at 1-55.

7 Jeremy Waldron,"Homelessness and the Issue of Freedom" (1991) 39 UCLA L Rev 295 at 296.

8 John Locke, *Two Treatises of Government* (1689), c 9 at para 124.

9 William Blackstone, *Commentaries on the Laws of England: A Facsimile of the First Edition of 1765-1769,* Stanley N. Katz, ed, 4 vols (Chicago: University of Chicago Press, 1979) vol 2 at 2.

10 A variety of legal historians claim there was a substantial gap between the image of absolute private property and legal reality. However, they are unable to identify significant limitations on the right to exclude. For example, see Robert W Gordon, "Paradoxical Property" in John Brewer & Susan Staves, eds., *Early Modern Conceptions of Property* (London: Routledge, 1996) at 95-110. His most significant counter-example to absolute property is the right to public grazing in the United States. However, a more recent study demonstrates that rights to roam had largely disappeared by the twentieth century. See Eric Freyfogle, *On Private Property: Finding Common Ground on the Ownership of Land* (Boston: Beacon Press, 2006) at 29-60. The gap is also emphasized by David Sugarman & GR Rubin, "Towards a New History of Law and Material Society in England, 1750-1914" in David Sugarrman & GR Rubin, eds., *Law, Economy and Society, 1750-1914: Essays in the History of English Law* (Abington, Oxon: Professional Books, 1984) at 23-36, but none of the examples they cite relate to limits on the right to exclude.

11 Thomas W Merrill, "Property and the Right to Exclude" (1998) 77 Neb L Rev 730; Larissa Katz, "Exclusion and Exclusivity in Property Law" (2008) 58 UTLJ 275. There is a growing literature opposing the primacy of the right to exclude, which advocates for greater recognition of rights of entry onto private property that serves a public function. For example, see Kevin Gray and Susan Francis Gray, "Civil Rights, Civil Wrongs and Quasi-Public Spaces" (1999) 4 Eu Hum Rights L Rev 46; Hanoch Dagan, *Property: Values and Institutions* (New York: Oxford University Press, 2011), 37-55. These authors emphasize the breaches in the wall around private property, but their

normative arguments are more compelling than their positive claim that the right of private owners to exclude has already been eroded.

12 RCB Risk, "The Last Golden Age: Property and the Allocation of Losses in Ontario in the Nineteenth Century" (1977) 27 UTLJ 199 at 204.

13 *An Act to provide for the Summary Punishment of Petty Trespasses and other offences*, SUC 1834, 4 Wm 4, c. 4, s.3. According to one brief account, the legislation was motivated by a sense that civil lawsuits were too cumbersome a method for enforcing the right to exclude trespassers, however no source is given. See Ontario, Ministry of the Attorney General, *Discussion Paper on Occupiers' Liability and Trespass to Property* (Toronto: Ministry of the Attorney General, 1979) at 13.

14 For example, see An Act for consolidating and amending the Laws in this Province relative to Malicious Injuries to Property 4&5 Vic c 26 (1841).

15 *An Act respecting Petty Trespasses in Upper Canada*, 22 Vic c 98 (1858). The act also applied to persons who let their horses, cattle, sheep or swine to go onto another's land. This part of the offence was repealed in 1862 by 25 Vic c 22.

16 An Act respecting Petty Trespasses, RSO 1887, c 101.

17 *The Petty Trespass Act*, RSO 1970, c 347.

18 For current criminal law protections, see *Criminal Code of Canada*, RSC 1985, c C-46, ss 40-43. Willful damage to property is now covered by the offence of mischief, s 430.

19 M Jeffrey Hardwick, *Mall Maker: Victor Gruen, Architect of an American Dream* (Philadelphia: University of Pennsylvania Press, 2004); Malcolm Gladwell, "The Terrazo Jungle" *The New Yorker* 80:4 (15 March 2004) 120; Lizabeth Cohen, *A Consumers' Republic: The Politics of Mass Consumption in Postwar America* (New York: Alfred A Knopf, 2003) c. 6; William Severini Kowinski, *The Malling of America* (New York: William Morrow, 1985) c. 12.

20 Jon Pahl, *Shopping Malls and Other Sacred Places* (Grand Rapids, MI: Brazos Press, 2003) at 74. On the challenge of shopping malls to existing town centres, see George Baird & Barry Simpson, "Main Street: Can it Survive the Shopping Centre" in James Lorimer & Carolyn MacGregor, eds., *After the Developers* (Toronto: Lorimer, 1981) at 32-45. Also, see Michael C Ircha, "Regulating Shopping Centres: Canadian and International Experience," in Lorimer & MacGregor at 68-76.

21 Victor Gruen, "The Sad Story of Shopping Centres" (1978) 46:7-8 *Town and Country Planning* 350 at 351.

22 Hardwick, above note 19 at 216-18. Also, see text accompanying footnote 39.

23 John A Dawson & J Dennis Lord, "Introduction" in *Shopping Centre Development: Policies and Prospects*, John A Dawson & J Dennis Lord, eds, (London: Croon Helm, 1985) 1. They observe that "the essence of the shopping centre lies in the concept of a managed and controlled retail environment…The purpose of this management and administration generally is the maximization of the retail power of the centre as a whole."

24 For example, see Joel E. Pink, *Loitering, Disturbances and Shoplifting: Landlords' and Tenants' Rights Versus Shoppers' Rights* (Halifax: Continuing Legal Education Society of Nova Scotia, 1980).

25 Susan Delacourt, "Task Force to Study Use of Trespass Law in Shopping Malls" *The Globe and Mail* (16 July 1986) A12.

26 See Frederic Jameson, "Future City" (May-June 2003), 21 *New Left Review* 65 at 70. He observes that: "The older city centre – blighted by suburbs and the new supermarkets, and then the malls themselves – now, with postmodernity and gentrification, catches up: not only by housing new malls within itself, but by becoming a virtual mall in its own right." This image does not quite fit downtown Toronto which has retained significant unplanned commercial areas characterized by small stores and boutique operations. See Jim Simmons, "Commercial Structure and Change in Toronto" (Centre for Urban and Community Studies, University of Toronto, Research Paper 182, September 1991).

27 Dawson and Lord, above note 23 at 1. They observe that:

> Increasingly, because this retail power is now considerable within urban areas, the agencies responsible for overall urban management are themselves looking for ways to control, maybe limit, but certainly direct this power, such that social costs do not result from the potential abuse of economic power.

See also Bruce Krushelnicki, "Shopping Centres: Public Agora or Privileged Place" *City Magazine* 7:4 (Fall 1985) 22; David Brown, Pieter Sijpkes & Michael MacLean, "The Community Role of Public Indoor Space (1986) 3 *Journal of Architectural and Planning Research* 161 at 172. They observe: "These projects must also be expected to contribute to the variety of experiences available both with respect to built form and social opportunity."

28 Marina Strauss, "Property Rights of Malls Contested" *The Globe and Mail* (10 June 1985) M1.

29 Suzanne Stephens, "At the Core of the Apple" (1978) 8 *Progressive Architecture* 72.

30 David Brown, Michael MacLean & Pieter Sijpkes, "The Indoor City – Can it Be Successfully Integrated into the Urban Fabric?" *City Magazine* 7:4 (Fall 1985) 16.

31 The fear of delinquent youth was visceral. For example, prominent Halifax lawyer Joel Pink, above note 24, spoke of shopping centres attracting "dope users and pushers." Also, see the comments of Haines J in *R. v Page* [1964] OJ No 383, an early case upholding the right of shopping plaza owners' right to exclude.

32 For example, see Brown, MacLean & Sipkes, above note 30 at 21; where they observe that "the fundamental importance of public places suggests that local government should assume primary responsibility for the design and management of both outdoor and indoor environments." See also Robert W. Collier, *Contemporary Cathedrals: Large-Scale Developments in Canadian Cities* (Montreal: Harvest House, 1975) at 133, where he observes: "When a private owner takes over block after block – who in fact becomes the civic authority and who exercises the power and control over the new town?"

33 The earliest cases succeeded on the basis that the exclusion took place after an entrance ticket had been sold, making the removal a breach of contract. *Johnson v Sparrow* (1899) 8 Que QB 379 aff'd at (1899), 15 Que SC 115; *Barnswell v National Amusement Company, Limited* (1914), 21 BCR 435. See Constance Backhouse, *Colour-Coded: A Legal*

History of Racism in Canada, 1900-1950 (Toronto: Osgoode Society and University of Toronto Press, 1999) at 250-60; James W. St. G. Walker, *"Race," Rights and the Law in the Supreme Court of Canada* (Waterloo, ON: Osgoode Society and Wilfred Laurier University Press, 1997) at 144-51.

34 *Christie v York Corporation* [1940] SCR 139 at para 6. For an extended discussion, see Walker, *ibid* at c. 3.

35 Carmela Patrias, "Socialists, Jews, and the 1947 Saskatchewan Bill of Rights" (2006) 87 *Canadian Historical Review* 265; Carmela Patrias & Ruth A. Frager, "'This Is Our Country, These Are Our Rights': Minorities and the Origins of Ontario's Human Rights Campaigns" (2001) 81 *Canadian Historical Review* 1; Walker, above note 33 at 172ff ; and Arnold Bruner, "The Genesis of Ontario's Human Rights Legislation: A Study in Law Reform" (1979) 37 UT Fac L Rev 236.

36 *Saskatchewan Bill of Right Act*, SS 1947, c. 35. On earlier efforts to fight discrimination at the municipal level, see Ross Lambertson, *Repression and Resistance: Canadian Human Rights Activists, 1930-1960* (Toronto: University of Toronto Press, 2005) at 237-38.

37 Ontario was the first province to enact a fair accommodation practices act that applied to "the accommodation, services or facilities available in any place to which the public is customarily admitted." *Fair Accommodation Practices Act*, SO 1954, c 28, s. 2. For a catalogue of similar legislation enacted by other provinces, see Walter Tarnapolsky, *Discrimination and the Law* (Don Mills, ON: Richard De Boo, 1982) at 28-29.

38 It would be a mistake to assume that public spaces were freely available for expressive activities. As Blomley's chapter (this volume) demonstrates, public authorities commonly impose restrictions on the use of public streets. There is a burgeoning literature on the subject. For example, see Charles Tilly, *Contentious Performances* (New York: Cambridge University Press, 2008) at 71-78 on the development of freedom of assembly. For a sample of the Canadian literature, see Peter Goheen, "Negotiating Access to Public Space in Mid-Nineteenth Century Toronto" (1994) 20:4 *Journal of Historical Geography* 430; Kathleen Lord, "Permeable Boundaries: Negotiation, Resistance, and Transgression of Street Space in Saint-Henri, Quebec, 1875-1905" (2005) 33:2 *Urban History Review* 17; Michael Barnholden, *Reading the Riot Act: A Brief History of Riots in Vancouver* (Vancouver: Anvil Press, 2005); Richard Moon, *The Constitutional Protection of Freedom of Expression* (Toronto: University of Toronto Press, 2000) at 148-181; and W. Wesley Pue, "Trespass and Expressive Rights" (Paper prepared for the Ipperwash Inquiry, 2005).

39 *James A Murray-Victor Gruen Associates, Supplemental Report*, (25 September 1964), Toronto, Archives of Ontario, T. Eaton Co. Fonds, F229-501-135. Gruen's proposal was severely criticized by Associate Professor James Acland of the University of Toronto as an example of "unbridled competitive development," which reduces public spaces and amenities to a minimum. He contrasted this approach with the older European tradition of blending private enterprise and superb civic space. James Acland, "A new challenge from the old City Hall," *The Globe and Mail* (29 January 1966), A9.

40 Adele Freedman, "By Design: Is It 'Our Centre' or Just a Place to Go and Shop?" *The Globe and Mail* (13 April 1985) E13; Rod McQueen, *The Eatons: The Rise and Fall of Canada's Royal Family*, rev ed (Toronto: Stoddart, 1999) at 163-64, 193-96.

41 A copy of the agreement, dated 1 May 1973, can be found in Ontario Superior Court, Civil Division. See *Keith Medcalf v The Cadillac Fairview Corporation Limited*, File No. 9724/86 [*Medcalf v Cadillac Fairview*].

42 *Agreement between Church of the Holy Trinity, Fairveiw Corporation and Eaton's* (14 November 1972) Toronto, Archives of Ontario (*T. Eaton Co.* Fonds, F299-501-135) [*T.Eaton Co.*]; *Building Scheme Agreement* (14 November 1972), referred to in Toronto, Council of the Corporation of the City of Toronto, *Minutes of proceedings for the year 1985*, Appendix A, 143 [*Minutes*].

43 For example, see John Sewell, "Eaton Centre Agreement Called Too Lax" *The Globe and Mail*, (23 November 1972) A7. A public right of way was also included in the development agreement for Rideau Center in Ottawa, which also involved Cadillac Fairview and Eaton's. See "Eaton Pickets Get Access to Mall" *The Globe and Mail* (18 April 1985) M7. On the politics of the Rideau development, see Caroline Andrew, "Ottawa: Progressives in Power" in Lorimer & McGregor, above note 20 at 96-108.

44 *Minutes*, above note 42 at 140.

45 "City Investigates Eviction of Union" *The Globe and Mail* (16 November 1984) M3.

46 *Minutes*, above note 42 at 143-44. In fact, the city subsequently took the position that Cadillac Fairview's public space obligation was satisfied by park space outside the mall at the corners of Bay & Dundas and Dundas & Yonge. See the written notes of Raj Anand from the oral submissions of John Phillips and Allen Appleby, City of Toronto, Planning and Development Department, *Task Force on the Law Concerning Trespass to Publicly-Used Property as it Affects Youth and Minorities* (6 December 1986), Toronto, Archives of Ontario (RG 18-543).

47 Lorne Slotnick & Stephen Brunt, "Eaton's Stores Face Boycott Called by CLC" *The Globe and Mail* (5 December 1984) M1.

48 The account of events is derived from statements of claim, defence, and reply in *Medcalf v Cadillac Fairview* and from author interviews with Keith Medcalf, 6 Feb. 2010; 13 March 2010. Efforts to interview the lawyers at Weir, Foulds who acted for Cadillac Fairview in this matter were unsuccessful.

49 "Eaton Pickets Get Access to Mall" *The Globe and Mail* (18 April 1985), M7.

50 Ontario Court of Appeal, File 843/86, Transcript, *R. v Layton* at 24.

51 *Harrison v Carswell*, [1976] 2 SCR 200 [*Harrison*], discussed below.

52 A transcript of the hearing on 22 May 1985 is contained in *Medcalf v Cadillac Fairview*, above note 41. Also see Bowen, above note 5. A month earlier two union activists, Geoff Bickerton and Michael Hurley, were charged with trespassing when they refused to stop handing out leaflets in front of the Eaton's store in the Rideau Mall. The prosecutors withdrew the charge when they concluded that the Bickerton and Hurley were on the public right of way contained in the development agreement between the city and the Rideau Centre. See "Public City, Public Centre" *Our Times* (June 1985) 8 and email from Geoff Bickerton to the author, 22 February 2010.

53 Bowen, above note 5.

54 Donn Downey, "Judge provided oasis in judicial wasteland" *The Globe and Mail* (27 March 1993) A8.

55 *Keith Medcalf v Toronto College Street Centre Limited et al*, Toronto 143/87 and 17592/87 (Sup. Ct. (Civ. Div.)). Interview with Keith Medcalf, above note 48.

56 "Is the Sit Down Strike a Crime?" *Canadian Forum* (April 1937) 7. More generally, see Judy Fudge & Eric Tucker, *Labour Before the Law* (Oxford: Oxford University Press, 2001) at 206-08.

57 For a good overview, see AWR Carrothers, *Collective Bargaining Law in Canada* (Toronto: Butterworths, 1965) at 415-88.

58 For example, see *Labour Relations Act*, SO 1950, c.34, s. 3, 45, 47 & 48.

59 *Adams Mine, Cliffs of Canada Ltd.* [1982] OLRB Rep. 1767. For an insightful and critical discussion, see Patrick Macklem, "Property, Status, and Workplace Organizing" (1990), 40 UTLJ 74. For a critical discussion of American labour law on this issue, see Cynthia Estlund, "Labor, Property, and Sovereignty after *Lechmere*" (1994), 46 Stan L Rev 305.

60 *Labour Relations Amendment Act, 1970 (No. 2)*, SO 1970, c. 85, s. 7. The law was passed in the aftermath of the decision of the Ontario Court of Appeal upholding the trespass conviction of a union organizer for entering onto a private logging road without the permission of the owner, the Chapleau Lumber Company. Chief Justice Porter held: "Nothing . . . in . . . the Labour Relations Act . . . gives the right to any organizer or other person to go upon lands against the wish of the owner" (*R. v Labelle* (1964), [1965] 1 OR 321 (OCA) at 326). Many other jurisdictions have analogous provisions. For a general discussion of the law, see George W. Adams, *Canadian Labour Law*, looseleaf (Aurora: ON: Canada Law Book, 1993) at para 10.570 *ff*.

61 Adams, *ibid* at para 10.2080; *K-Mart Canada*, [1981] OLRB Rep. 60.

62 *Zeller's (Western) Ltd. v Retail Food and Drugs Clerks Union, Local 1518* (1962), 36 DLR (2d) 581 at 584, Wilson JA dissenting. Tysoe wrote, in part, "The appellant has no more right to enter upon the lands over which the respondent has easement rights and to so interfere with those rights as to injure the respondent than it has to enter upon lands without the consent of the owner of those lands."

63 *Zeller's (Western) Ltd. v Retail Food and Drugs Clerks Union, Local 1518* (1963), 42 DLR (2d) 582 at 586.

64 *Ibid* at 586-87. For a discussion of the Zellers cases, see HW Arthurs, "Labour Law: Picketing on Shopping Centres" (1965) 43 Can Bar Rev 357. Also, see Judy Fudge & Eric Tucker, "'Everybody Knows What a Picket Line Means': Picketing Before the British Columbia Court of Appeal" (Summer 2009) 162 *BC Studies* 53 at 66-67.

65 *Grosvenor Shopping Centre Ltd. v Waloshin* (1964), 46 DLR (2d) 750.

66 "Grape boycott causes arrest of union chief" *Toronto Daily Star (Peel/Hamilton)* (11 September 1969) 41.

67 "It's not a crime to picket plaza judge decides" *Toronto Daily Star* (1 October 1969) 63.

68 *R. v Peters* (1970), 16 DLR (3d) 143 (OCA).

69 *R. v Peters* (1971), 17 DLR (3d) 128 (SCC).

70 [1976] 2 SCR 200.

71 Philip Girard & Jim Phillips, "A Certain Mallaise: *Harrison v Carswell*, Shopping Centre Picketing, and the Limits of the Postwar Settlement" in Judy Fudge & Eric Tucker, eds, *Work on Trial: Canadian Labour Law Struggles* (Toronto: Irwin and the Osgoode Society for Legal History, 2010), 249.

72 *Harrison*, above note 51 at 218.

73 *Ibid* at 219.

74 It should be noted, however, that Dickson's judgment was not entirely rooted in the common law. This was, after all, a case of a prosecution under Manitoba's *Petty Trespass Act* and Dickson went on to argue that the policy to protect property owners' absolute right to exclude was a legislative one. While accepting that society had recognized that the public interest was served by permitting picketing, Dickson did not consider that Manitoba's labour statute implicitly limited the rights of private property owners to exclude. Rather, the change would have to be explicit, as was the case in British Columbia. For a further discussion of Dickson's judgment, see Robert J. Sharpe and Kent Roach, *Brian Dickson: A Judge's Journey* (Toronto: Osgoode Society, 2003) at 148-52.

75 Philip Girard, *Bora Laskin: Bringing Law to Life* (Toronto: Osgoode Society, 2005).

76 *Harrison*, above note 51 at 209.

77 *Ibid* at 207.

78 *Broadway Park Shopping Plaza Ltd. v Lakin* [1975] SJ No 354 (QB); *Wildwood Mall Ltd. v Stevens* [1980] 2 WWR 638 (QB).

79 *Labour Code of British Columbia Act*, SBC 1973 (2nd Sess.), c 122, s 87. In 1975 the legislation was amended to bar actions or proceedings for "petty trespass." See SBC 1975, c 33, s 21. This change had unanticipated implications. See accompanying note 170.

80 An Act to Amend the Queen's Bench Act and the Petty Trespass Act, SM 1976, c. 71.

81 In Ontario, the government issued a discussion paper on occupiers' liability and trespass to property in 1979, motivated largely to provide more protection for rural landowners. *Harrison* was not mentioned in the report. See Ontario, Ministry of the Attorney General, *Discussion Paper on Occupiers' Liability and Trespass to Property* (Toronto: Ministry of the Attorney General, 1979). The government followed up by introducing Bill 203 to implement the paper's recommendations. NDP members objected that the bill would prevent picketing on malls, seemingly quite unaware that the law already did so.

82 Mercedes Steedman, *Angels of the Workplace* (Toronto: Oxford University Press, 1997) at 78-84; Ruth Frager, *Sweatshop Strike* (Toronto: University of Toronto Press, 1992) at 127-30.

83 Eileen Tallman Surfin, *The Eaton Drive* (Don Mills, ON: Fitzhenry & Whiteside, 1983). Also see Bradley J. Pragnell, *Organizing Department Store Workers: The Case of the RWDSU at Eaton's, 1983-1987* (Kingston, ON: Industrial Relations Centre, Queen's University, 1989) at 34-42 and Donica Belisle, "Exploring Postwar Consumption: The Campaign to Unionize Eaton's in Toronto, 1948-1952" (2005) 86 *Canadian Historical Review* 641. In 1980, about 4 percent of retail workers, including the highly organized supermarkets, were union members. See Wilfred List, "Union Campaign

Organizers See Potential in Certification at Eaton's Store" *The Globe and Mail* (27 February 1984) P4.

84 "First Union Certified at Brampton Store of Eaton's Chain" *The Globe and Mail* (29 March 1984) M1; Ann Finlayson, "Shopping for Unionists at Eaton's" *Maclean's* (12 March 1984) 65; and Paul McGrath, "Timothy Would Be Shocked" *Canadian Business* (August 1984) 58-60.

85 Lorne Slotnick, "Retail Workers' Union Nets First Sears" *The Globe and Mail* (21 August 1984) M4; Yves Lavigne, "Simpsons Takes Stock" *The Globe and Mail* (6 October 1984) L5.

86 Pragnell, above note 83 at 42-46; Carol Currie & Geri Sheedy, "Organizing Eaton's" in Robert Argue, Charlene Gannagé & DW Livingstone, eds, *Working People and Hard Times* (Toronto: Garamond, 1987) 247 at 247-54; Nik Habermel, "Organizing in Eight Days" *Our Times* (April 1984) 27; Donna Johansen, "Getting Organized" *Our Times* (June 1984) 30; Lorne Slotnick, "Union Drive Ignites Firebrands at Eaton's" *The Globe and Mail* (7 May 1984) P1; Maya Gallus, "Rousing the Rabble" *The Globe and Mail* (2 June 1984) L5; and Duncan McMonagle & Ann Silversides, "Layoffs Add to Troubles of Ailing Retail Industry" *The Globe and Mail* (12 July 1984) M3.

87 OLRB Decision, above note 3 at paras 2-6.

88 Letter from Ronald Hubert, Company Employee Relations Manager to Mr. A Scott, Director, Department Store Organizing Committee, RWDSU, 18 May 1984, cited in *T. Eaton Co., ibid* at para 8.

89 David Olive, "Trouble at Canada's General Store" *Toronto Life* (March 1985) 33.

90 OLRB File 0861-84-U.

91 Author Interview with James Hayes, 10 September 2010.

92 OLRB Decision, above note 3 at paras 9-13.

93 Lorne Slotnick, "Management at Eaton Centre Ejects Workers, Union Organizers" *The Globe and Mail* (12 October 1984) M4.

94 Transcript of *R. v Layton*, a copy of which is located in Ontario Court of Appeal, File 843/86. Lorne Slotnick & Robert MacLeod, "Strikers Start Picketing Outside 6 Eaton's Stores" *The Globe and Mail* (30 November 1984) P1; Lorne Slotnick, "Eaton's Boycott Gathering Steam After Slow Start" *The Globe and Mail* (13 February 1985) M1. He observes:

> The labor council's strike support committee has already discussed tactics such as sit-downs at Eaton's stores, but there is some division on the issue. The retail, wholesale union appears reluctant to have the strikers engage in unconventional actions.

95 Transcript, *R. v Layton, ibid.*

96 Bill Schiller, "Labor Congress to Call for Boycott of Eaton's Stores" *The Globe and Mail* (4 December 1984) A6.

97 For biographical information, see online: www.blgcanada.com/en/home/our-professionals/Pages/Mitchnick-Morton-OTT.aspx.

98 Hayes was assisted by Patrick Macklem, then an articling student, now a professor of law at the University of Toronto, and author of a critical article of the subordination of labour rights to property rights. See above note 59.

99 He was accompanied by Nancy Ebert, then an articling student and later a government lawyer, and RA Hubert, Eaton's employee relations manager at the time.

100 Olive, above note 89 at 51.

101 Complaint of RWDSU, in OLRB Decision, above note 3 at paras 20-28.

102 OLRB Decision, *ibid* at para 309.

103 *Ibid* at para 41.

104 The case was argued and decided before this view was adopted by the SCC in *RWDSU v Dolphin Delivery Ltd.* [1986] 2 SCR 573 [*Dolphin Delivery*].

105 OLRB Decision, above note 3 at para 48.

106 *NLRB v Babcock & Wilcox*, 351 US 105 (1956), quoted in OLRB Decision, *ibid* at para 65.

107 OLRB Decision, *ibid* at paras 62-74, 83-84.

108 To end the lengthy strike the union signed a weak agreement over the heads of its members and was facing the threat of decertification. Pragnell, above note 83 at 50-57.

109 Marina Strauss, "Union Given Recruiting Rights on Eaton Centre's Property" *The Globe and Mail* (14 June 1985) P1.

110 Marina Strauss, "Property Rights of Mall Contested" *The Globe and Mail* (10 June 1985) M1.

111 *RWSU v T. Eaton Co. et al.* [1985] OLRB Rep. 1683, para 2 (Reconsideration Decision).

112 *Ibid* at paras. 4-14.

113 *Re Cadillac Fairview Corporation Limited and RWDSU*, Supreme Court of Ontario, Divisional Court (Factum of the Appellant).

114 *Ibid.*, OLRB Factum (17 March 1987) at para 14. The OLRB was represented by Stephen T. Goudge and Ross Wells, of Gowling & Henderson.

115 *Ibid*, RWDSU Factum (10 April 1987) at para 30.

116 Divisional Court Decision, above note 3 at 350.

117 *Ibid* at 350.

118 *Entick v Carrington* (1765), 19 How St Tr 1029. The case held that "every invasion of private property, be it ever so minute, is a trespass. No man can set his foot on my ground without any license, but he is liable to an action, though the damage be nothing . . . ."

119 *Cadillac Fairview Corp. Ltd. v R.W.D.S.U.*, Supreme Court of Ontario, Court of Appeal, Factum of the Appellant, at paras 28-42.

120 *Ibid*, OLRB Factum, at paras 6-14; RWDSU Factum, at paras 32-37.

121 Tarnapolsky, above note 37.

122 Goodman's LLP, "Sydney Robins biography" online: Goodman's LLP Directory www.goodmans.ca/index.cfm?ce=details&cm=employee&primaryKey=137; Law Society of Upper Canada, *Sydney Robins* fonds, online: Law Society of Upper Canada Archives http://rc.lsuc.on.ca/library/FindingAids/PF188.pdf. Osler was a high court judge sitting as an appellate judge on an ad hoc basis.

123 CA Decision, above note 3 at para 25.

124 *Ibid* at para.29.

125 *Ibid* at para.31.

126 TPA, s. 2(1).

127 Raven, Cameron, Ballantyne & Yazbeck LLP/s.r.l., "Susan Ballantyne" *Lawyers Directory*, online: Ravenlaw www.ravenlaw.com/Susan-Ballantyne.html.

128 Interview by author with Stanley Berger, 2 February 2010.

129 Ontario Court of Appeal, File # 843/86, Transcript of Hearing at 28.

130 *Ibid* at 44.

131 Beger Interview and email to author, 9 September 2010; Alden Baker, "Centre Space Like Street, Court Told" *The Globe and Mail* (27 June 1985) M6.

132 Transcript, above note 129 at 135.

133 *Ibid* at 136-37.

134 Crown position is stated in *R. v Layton*, above note 4 at para 16. According to Stan Berger, Crown Counsel was under no obligation to accept a tribunal decision which conflicted with his own principled view of the facts and law, and were free to argue the facts and the law as they saw fit. They guarded their independence jealously. Email communication with author, 3 February 2010.

135 *Ibid* at para 23.

136 [1986] 2 SCR 573.

137 See, for example, *Committee for the Commonwealth of Canada v Canada* [1991] 1 SCR 139 [Committee for the Commonwealth of Canada].

138 *R. v Layton*, above note 4 at para 27.

139 *Ibid* at para 30.

140 *R. v Oakes* [1986] 1 SCR 103 (decided 28 February 1986). The test has two components: first the Crown must show that the restriction on the *Charter* right has a "pressing and substantial objective," and second that the restriction is rationally connected to the objective and proportional to the objective with a minimal infringement on rights.

141 *R. v Layton*, above note 4 at para 45.

142 *Ibid* at para 48.

143 *Ibid* at paras. 52-56. Judge Scott also briefly considered and accepted the argument that the TPA violated freedom of association. See para 64.

144 "Alderman Acquitted in Eaton Trespassing" *The Globe and Mail* (27 May 1986) A15.

145 Ontario Court of Appeal, File 843/86, Factum of the Appellant at para 22.

146 Factum of the Respondent, *Ibid* at para 25.

147 Memorandum from James Morton to MacKinnon J, 23 February 1987, in which Morton notes that he has attached an edited copy of the draft judgment in *Layton*, *Ibid*. Also see a memo from James Morton to Justice MacKinnon, dated 17 April 1987, in which he refers to some cases that he thought might be helpful in the *Layton* case, *Ibid*.

148 "Bert James MacKinnon, Judge sought to curb drinking and driving" *The Globe and Mail* (20 June 1987) A13.

149 Interview with James Morton, 5 April 2010. On a little note in the file Justice MacKinnon wrote out a quote from Abraham Lincoln. "Property is the fruit of Labour; property is desirable; it is a positive good in the world."

150 Letter from Dana L. Venner, Crown Counsel, to William Shaughnessy, Registrar, Ontario Court of Appeal, 17 June 1988, in Ontario Court of Appeal, *R. v Layton*, File 843/86.

151 For example, see *Ontario Harness Horse Association v Ontario Racing Commission* (2002), 62 OR (3d) 44 (ONCA) at para 32.

152 *Gameday Publication(s) Ltd. v Keystone Agricultural and Recreational Centre Inc.* (1999) 170 DLR (4th) 617 at 621.

153 *Ibid.* at 622.

154 Susan Delacourt, "Task Force to Study Use of Trespass Law in Shopping Malls" *The Globe and Mail* (16 July 1986) A12.

155 Jack Layton to Ian Scott (27 June 1986) in materials of the Task Force on the Law Concerning Trespass to Publicly-Used Property as it Affects Youth and Minorities, Toronto, Archives of Ontario, RG 18-543.

156 Handwritten notes from 22 August and 4 November 1986, *ibid*; Letter from WJ McNaughten to Raj Anand, 27 January 1987, *ibid.*

157 *Ibid*, Submission on Behalf of Cadillac Fairview Shopping Centres, 15 September 1986.

158 Task Force on the Law Concerning Trespass to Publicly-Used Property as it Affects Youth and Minorities, *Report* (Toronto: Ontario Ministry of the Attorney General, 1987) at 61.

159 Anand also called for greater public controls over the design features of malls. *Ibid* at 112-32.

160 Bill 149, *An Act to amend the Trespass to Property Act*, 1st Sess., 34th Leg., Ontario, 1988, s. 2.

161 Ontario, Legislative Assembly, *Official Report of Debates* (*Hansard*) (7 June 1988, 14 February 1989).

162 Peter Moon, "Mall owners fear new law will be 'devastating'" *The Globe and Mail* (30 May 1989) A14; Kim Honey & Nomi Morris, "Trespass changes stir alarm" *Toronto Star* (13 June 1989) W1; Anne-Marie Waters, "Abuse of shoppers could get worse, mall owners warn" *Toronto Star* (20 June 1989) E1; Royson James, "Seniors fear youths in malls, Givens says" *Toronto Star* (9 August 1989) ME2; Editorial, "Security in the mall" *The Globe and Mail* (31 May 1989) A6.

163 Nomi Morris, "Rights chief defends trespass bill" *Toronto Star* (28 April 1989) A5; Editorial, "Sensible trespass bill" *Toronto Star* (14 June 1989) A24. It is no small irony that Anand later became a partner in Weir, Foulds, the firm that defended Cadillac Fairview's absolute right to exclude before his taskforce.

164 Author interview with Michael Swan, Planning Department, City of Toronto, 20 September 2010.

165 Trespass to Property Act, SS 2009, c T-20.2; Saskatchewan, Legislative Assembly, *Debates and Proceedings (Hansard)*, 26st Leg, 2nd Sess, No 18A (25 November 2008) at 1845-47 (Sandra Morin); Saskatchewan, Legislative Assembly, Standing Committee on Intergovernmental Affairs and Justice, in *Hansard Verbatim Report*, No. 17 (20 April 2009) at 340-41 (Frank Quennell).

166 For example, on 3 June 1985, nine days before the OLRB ruling, two trade unionists in St. Catharines, Ontario, were convicted of trespassing and fined $200 each for picketing on shopping plaza property in support of striking Eaton's workers. See "Two Fined $200 Over Protest" *The Globe and Mail* (4 June 1985) M4. Similarly, in 1990 striking hairdressers at two salons located in Simpsons stores lost a bid for a court order permitting them to picket in the Simpsons store itself. See Thomas Claridge, "Can't picket in Simpsons, judge rules" *The Globe and Mail* (21 December 1990) A10.

167 The right was limited to organize or picket at or near the entrance to the targeted employers' premises and the board was authorized to restrict organizing or picketing activity to avoid undue disruption to the mall. See SO 1992, c 21, s 11.1. For the repeal, see *Labour Relations Act*, RSO 1995, c 1, Sch A.

168 Ontario Harness Horse Association v Ontario Racing Commission (2002), 62 OR (3d) 44 (CA).

169 *RMH Teleservices International Inc. v British Columbia Government and Service Employees' Union* (2003), 223 DLR (3d) 750 (BCSC).

170 *Gateway Casinos LP v British Columbia Government and Service Employees' Union* (2007), 67 BCLR (4th) 225 (CA).

171 For example, see Adams, above note 60 at para 10.570 and Macklem, above note 59.

172 Re New Brunswick Broadcasting Co. Ltd. and Canadian Radio-Television & Telecommunications Commission (1985), 13 D.L.R. (4th) 77 at 89.

173 Committee for the Commonwealth of Canada, above note 137 at 228.

174 *Russo v Ontario Jockey Club* (1987), 62 OR (2d) 731 (HCJ) at 733. "There is a general principle in common law, which is enforced by the *Trespass to Property Act*, that a landowner has the exclusive right to decide who is allowed to remain on his or her land."

175 Also, see *R. v Weitz* [1991] OJ No. 2827 (holding that the Charter does not apply when the Clarke Institute of Psychiatry invoked the TPA to exclude demonstrators because the Clarke Institute is not a government actor). In *R. v Buhay*, [2003] 1 SCR 631, the SCC held that private security guards were not government actors subject to the *Charter*. It does not appear the argument was made that they became state actors when exercising powers conferred by the TPA.

176 See *R. v N.S.* [2004] OJ No. 290 overruling [2002] OJ No. 3028. The Ontario Court of Appeal's short judgment relied entirely on the SCC's judgment in *R. v Buhay*, *ibid*.

177 *Dolphin Delivery*, above note 104 at 603.

178 *R.W.D.S.U., Local 558 v Pepsi-Cola Canada Beverages (West) Ltd.*, [2002] 1 SCR 156.

179 For example, in *Committee for the Commonwealth of Canada* at 197, Justice L'Heureux-Dubé left it open for another day to consider the impact of the *Charter* on expressive activities on private property. See above note 136.

180 For a similar view, see Moon, above note 38 at 171-75.

181 For a similar view, see Linda McKay-Panos and Brian Seaman, "Do You Have a Right to be at the Mall?" online: (July-August 2007) 31:6 *Law Now* www.lawnow.org.

182 In addition to the authors cited in above in note 11, see Jennifer Niles Coffin, "The United Mall of America: Free Speech, State Constitutions, and the Growing Fortress of Private Property" (2000) 33 U Mich JL Reform 615; Note, "The Impermeable Life:

Unsolicited Communications in the Marketplace of Ideas" (2005) 118 Harv L Rev 1314; Anne Bottomley, "A Trip to the Mall: Revisiting the Public/Private Divide" in Hilary Lim and Anne Bottomley, eds, *Feminist Perspectives on Land Law* (New York: Routledge – Cavendish, 2007), 65; Lisa M. Austin, "Person, Place, or Thing? Property and the Structuring of Social Relations" (2010), 60 UTLJ 445.

Regina v Stewart: Is Information Property?

C. Ian Kyer[1]

Regina v Stewart,[2] a 1988 decision of the Supreme Court of Canada, has been said to "represent a milestone in Canada's march into the Information Age."[3] Cited in many common law texts in Canada and elsewhere as standing for the proposition that confidential information is not property and cannot be stolen,[4] it was one of a series of cases in the 1980s that heralded the dawn of Information Technology ("IT") law in Canada.[5]

The case both reflected and stimulated a lively debate in the 1980s about the nature of property and whether confidential information should be treated as such. Could a business be said to own its confidential information? If someone gained unauthorized access to that information could that person be said to have stolen property of the business and be prosecuted for theft? If so, what effect might the threat of such a criminal prosecution have on the free flow of information and knowledge? These were the questions that were asked in and about the *Stewart* case as it made its seven year journey through the Canadian legal system from the laying of charges to the trial to the Ontario Court of Appeal and ultimately to the Supreme Court of Canada.

One would expect that such a frequently cited and much debated case would be well understood, but there are many aspects of this case that have remained unknown or not fully appreciated. My intention is to look beyond the proposition for which *Regina v Stewart* is said to stand and the debate it engendered to explain how it arose, why it became a test case, what the Ontario Attorney General's office was seeking to achieve in prosecuting the case and why they never attained that goal. In the process, there are several lessons in law reform to be learned.

Regina v Stewart is a case replete with irony. It arose out of an attempt by a trade union to obtain the names and addresses of waiters and waitresses at an airport strip hotel in an effort to unionize the employees and yet it was in no way treated as a labour law case. It was a harbinger of the Information Age and computerization, but it was as "low tech" as could be. No computers were involved — just computer printouts stored in a file cabinet. It was a case about the stealing of information but it did not involve the taking of anything. No information was copied or even accessed. In a case that would make its way to the Supreme Court of Canada no one lost anything and, as we shall see, no one's liberty was at risk. Furthermore, this case about confidential information did not involve any valuable confidential business information. There was no carefully guarded business formula stolen through industrial espionage, just the names and addresses of restaurant wait staff.

How is it that what was at first blush a simple, relatively insignificant act — the unsuccessful counselling of the copying of some seemingly innocuous employee information — was prosecuted at all and that when it was it became a leading case? Interestingly, it was its very simplicity (and the fact that the defendant had a young counsel barely out of law school) that led the Ontario Attorney General's office to select the Stewart prosecution as a test case on several important legal issues with broad social and business implications.

Judges, lawyers, academics, and government representatives all were active participants in a debate about whether confidential information should be treated as property. It was a question that concerned and troubled many at the dawn of the Information Age. But as we shall see there was another aspect of this case that was undisclosed and of practical importance to the Ontario Attorney General's office and to a series of other cases before the courts.

The immediate context of the case, a long standing and very bitter labour dispute, would play no part whatsoever in the judicial analysis and treatment of the case or in the debate that it stimulated. *Regina v Stewart* arose out of the strenuous efforts of the owner and operator of the Constellation Hotel to resist unionization of his waiters, waitresses, and kitchen staff. Once selected as a test case, however, the labour issues were intentionally suppressed. In different circumstances one could imagine a very different approach to this case. It might have served as a companion case to *Harrison v*

Carswell.[6] In each instance the rights of unionized labour to conduct union business came into conflict with the property rights of others. In *Harrison v Carswell,* judges were asked to balance the labour rights of picketers and the property rights of a mall owner.[7] Six judges of the Supreme Court of Canada held that a mall owner could eject any person he or she wanted to, for any or no reason, while three dissenting judges favoured the rights of picketers over these property rights. The *Stewart* case might have been seen as requiring the balancing of the rights of a union to obtain certain basic information needed to facilitate a union certification vote against the right of employers to treat that information as confidential proprietary information. There was, however, no balancing of labour rights and property rights in *Regina v Stewart*. There was no discussion of labour law at all. Nevertheless, the facts can only really be understood if we look at the labour's unsuccessful efforts to unionize the hotel.

The Constellation, a large hotel near what was then known as the Toronto International Airport, employed approximately 600 full- and part-time staff. Throughout the summer and fall of 1981, the Hotel, Restaurant & Cafeteria Employees Union, Local 75 had been trying to unionize its waiters. A prior unsuccessful attempt had been made in the 1970s. In 1974 the union had obtained an order of the Ontario Labour Relations Board for a certification vote.[8] The employees had rejected the union, but the union had asked for a new vote based on the Board's "no propaganda rule." On 19 November 1974 the Board had directed the taking of a second pre-hearing vote[9] but as in the first vote the union did not receive support sufficient for certification.

The union, although twice defeated in a certification vote, had not given up. On a number of occasions union organizers were told to stay off the hotel property but it was an employee termination that brought the matter again before the Board. Tom Grougiannis, a waiter in the Burgundy Room, had recruited six others for the union. In late July he was called to a meeting with the hotel's general manager and his supervisor, and was warned about harassing and molesting employees. About a month later Grougiannis was involved in another exchange with management. He had been working in the kitchen when his supervisor came in and said that he was to be sent home for talking to certain women about the union. Finally, in September, after a female personal assistant alleged that he had sexually harassed her, Grougiannis was asked to put his explanation in writing. When he failed to produce the written explanation for which he had been asked, a termination letter was prepared and he was let go.

The union filed a complaint under the Labour Relations Act alleging that the dismissal from employment constituted a violation of the Act. The Labour board stated that it was "clear on the evidence that Mr. Kalmar, the president and owner of the hotel, would prefer to operate without a trade union . . . . However, the preference of an employer to operate union free does not in itself support a finding that the employer is prepared to or has unlawfully threatened those who actively pursue the right to unionize." The complaint was dismissed.

By the fall of 1981, the union was growing desperate. As a result of complaints by some employees and a subsequent management decision, the hotel's Chief of Security had delivered a letter to advise the union that its agents and representatives were to be barred from the hotel. In order to solicit members, the union had to find other means to contact the employees. It needed the names, telephone numbers, and addresses of the hotel's employees. The union organizers knew from past experience that it would be useless to make a written request of the hotel management for such a list. The union began to consider alternative methods of obtaining the employee information that it needed.

The union approached Wayne John Stewart, a self-employed, experienced thirty-two-year-old private investigator.[10] He was asked to obtain the employee information needed by the union in soliciting employees. Through inquiries, Stewart soon learned that this information was to be found in personnel files as well as on a computer printout entitled "Payroll." The information for computer processing was sent weekly by special courier to the Bank of Nova Scotia Computer Centre and the resultant computer printout was returned to the hotel by special courier. The computer printout and the individual personnel files were kept in locked filing cabinets under the control of a payroll supervisor. The filing cabinets were kept in the payroll office adjacent to the executive offices. This office was secured by a locked door from 5:00 p.m. each day to 9:00 a.m. the following day. The payroll supervisor had the only key to the filing cabinets and she and her two assistants possessed the only keys to the payroll office. These people worked from 9:00 a.m. to 5:00 p.m. each day.

In the course of his inquiries, Stewart also learned that he had previously worked with one of the hotel's security guards, Jan William Hart. On 29 September, he contacted Hart and asked if he would help him procure the required information. During this and several subsequent conversations, Stewart suggested methods by which Hart could collect the information.

Stewart had determined that to access and record the information for the employees would require someone to work for about an hour for every thirty names. He offered to pay Hart $2 per name. What Stewart did not know is that on being first contacted, Hart had gone to his employer to reveal what was being tried. Armed with Hart's statement, the hotel went to the police who then arranged for Hart to record his telephone conversations with Stewart.[11]

Collecting this evidence was the easy part. The question was whether Stewart had committed any crime. Certainly counselling someone to commit theft was itself a crime even if the theft was not committed.[12]

So the crucial question was whether it would have been an offence under the *Criminal Code* for the security guard to have copied the employee information. The law on the theft of information was unclear. As one commentator would later say, "The cases are far from consistent, reasons are seldom articulated, and there is much conceptual confusion."[13] Another commentator agreed, saying "The cases do not yield any insights of real significance for policy-makers or theorists, but solve particular disputes in relatively crude terms."[14] The police and the Crown had to be creative in determining what charges they could bring. They were where English prosecutors had been in 1878 when a disgruntled government clerk had made a copy of a secret treaty and sold it to a newspaper. In that circumstance, because it was thought to be impossible to steal the information itself, the clerk had been charged with stealing the paper upon which the treaty had been copied.[15] This and other cases like it had led the British Government to pass an *Official Secrets Act* which made it an offence to communicate government information to a foreign power or to obtain or retain any such information for such purpose or to induce or incite another to do so. The Canadian government had quickly followed suit. But, of course, the information here was not government information and Stewart was no spy seeking to pass the information to a foreign power. The *Criminal Code* of Canada had no equivalent of the *Official Secrets Act* for non-governmental information. Nevertheless, they charged Stewart with three offences under the *Criminal Code* — counselling Hart to commit fraud,[16] counselling him to commit theft,[17] namely: to steal information that was the property of the Constellation Hotel and its employees, of a value exceeding $200; and counselling him to commit mischief to the private property of the Constellation Hotel and its employees.[18] None of these charges were well founded in the law as it then existed. They were, as people say, "a stretch" but of course that was the idea. This was a conscious attempt to establish a new offence of wrongful taking of confidential information. The precise foundation for such an offence in the Criminal Code had not yet been established. Each of these three charges was arguable, they thought. One, they hoped, would provide the basis for the offence they sought to create. So from the beginning the *Stewart* case was meant to test the extent to which the courts would recognize such an offence.

In determining why these charges were brought against Stewart and why the Crown sought to establish an offence of wrongful taking of confidential information, it is important to look at the broader social context — what was happening in Canada in the early 1980s. Without a doubt, that context was important in making *Regina v Stewart* the leading case that it would become. There are three trends that need to be examined — computerization and the development of information technology, increasing concerns about how best to deal with improper collection and misuse of information, and the debate over fundamental rights.

The early 1980s were a time when computers were being widely used in business for the first time. Programs were being written to permit computers to store and manipulate large volumes of data. People had begun to create computer databases and software to manage them. For the first time, the task of collecting, storing, indexing, comparing, and accessing very large volumes of information became widespread and commercially feasible. Banks, insurance companies, and many other businesses that needed to collect and manipulate large volumes of information, or data as it had come to be called, were either acquiring their own mainframe or mini computers or were sharing the use of computers through third-party computer centres operating as service bureaus. In 1984, I wrote:

> It is becoming popular to talk of our times as a post-industrial age, the age of the information revolution or as the computer age. Whether or not one uses such terms, there can be no doubt that more and more corporations and individuals are purchasing computers and storing information in them . . . At the same time there has been heightened concern over incidents of computer theft, *i.e.*, the taking or copying of information stored on computers.[19]

Dan Brooks, a leading American computer law expert, recalls this time and the burgeoning interest in how the law ought to deal with computerization:

> . . . the microcomputer was emerging from the garages and basements of early adopters into the limelight of what have become known as the personal computer industry, Silicon Valley and the overall technology boom.

> In March, 1980, Paul Bent, General Counsel of Century Financial Services, organized a very successful program in San Francisco entitled "Computer Law: Developing, Marketing, and Acquiring Software." . . . In October, 1981, Mike Keplinger, of the Copyright Office, organized a wildly successful program in Washington, DC entitled "Computer Software Protection: A Pragmatic Approach." High powered speakers from government, industry and private practice such as Jon Baumgarten, Mort Goldberg, Roger Milgrim, George Bosworth, and Tom Lynch played to packed houses filled with eager practitioners. In uncertain times of an evolving technology sector, they produced unusually valuable materials for the growing number of practitioners encountering their first technology enterprises and transactions. What had been a modest Association with a few hundred members, only a handful from foreign countries, suddenly doubled in size and reach.[20]

The growth of the Computer Law Association (CLA) to which Brooks was referring is instructive. It had begun in 1971 with only seven members. A fall meeting that first year had attracted thirty-eight attendees. By 1981 there were 516 members listed in the CLA Directory, but supplements were published in September 1982 and in March 1983 adding 152 and 231 respectively, a number of them Canadians. Clearly lawyers on both sides of the border were seeking to better understand the interplay between law and computerization.

The rise of the business of collecting and selling access to information led lawyers to ask some fundamental questions. How could this information, often collected, organized, and analyzed at great effort and expense, be protected from competitors? Copyright was slowly coming to be used to protect computer software. Would it also prove capable of protecting databases generally? What of individual pieces of data? What of the information itself? If copyright could not be stretched sufficiently to protect information *per se*, what of the law of trade secrets? The tort of breach of confidence existed but was seen by many as inadequate. What of the criminal law? Could one charge an industrial spy with theft? As noted there had been cases dating back over 100 years where people taking pieces of paper containing information had been successfully charged with theft of the paper, but in the Information Age could one sustain a charge of theft of nothing but the bare information? If nothing physical was taken, could someone be guilty of theft? Many pointed out that surely it was ludicrous to prevent people from stealing paper when it was the information recorded on the paper that gave it real value. Could that not be protected? These and other like questions were on the minds of many at the beginning of the 1980s.

A decision of the Supreme Court of Canada in 1980 seemed to invigorate this debate. A student who, without authorization, had obtained information from a University of Alberta computer had been charged with the improper obtaining of a telecommunications service under the *Criminal Code*.[21] The Supreme Court had ruled that a computer did not qualify as a telecommunication service and had acquitted the student.[22] In reaction, the Canadian Bar Association, the Canadian Data Processing Association, and the Canadian Law Information Council had petitioned the federal government to take action to remedy the perceived flaw in the *Criminal Code*. A private member's bill was even introduced into Parliament to create new computer crimes.[23] Rather than supporting the opposition member's bill, the federal Department of Justice initiated a study as part of its omnibus review of Criminal Law.

It was also a time when much thought was being given to the use and misuse of information both in the public and the private sector. In Ontario, following a 1977 revelation that health records were being improperly accessed and used by insurers, Horace Krever J had been appointed to conduct a Royal Commission on the confidentiality of such records. It had come to light that certain private investigators were obtaining health records on behalf of insurance companies seeking to defend health-related insurance claims. Justice Krever studied the matter for three years before reporting in September 1980, one year before Stewart's attempt to gain access to the hotel records. He found widespread, regular abuse of the confidentiality of health information. Justice Krever made a number of recommendations, both practical and legal, to try to curb the abuses. But it would be wrong to think that he sought to lock such information away to preserve its confidentiality and patient privacy. Early in his report he quoted Dean Jack R. London of the Faculty of Law at the University of Manitoba as standing for the proposition that "in the absence of competing interests in the disclosure of information, free and unqualified disclosure ought to be the rule." Justice Krever saw such competing interests with health records, namely, society's desire for the privacy of such records. But even as he made this case for the confidentiality of health records, it was clear that he saw value in free and uninhibited disclosure of information generally.[24]

Federally another royal commission was looking into misuse of information — in this case by the RCMP. The McDonald Commission on RCMP

Law Society of Upper Canada Archives, Paul Lawrence fonds, "Photograph of Justice Horace Krever," 2001088-102.

activities reported in 1981 after several years of study. Their analysis, which would lead to the creation of the Canadian Information Security Service, included an extensive consideration of the legal aspects of National Security and specifically of the *Official Secrets Act* that had been adopted almost a century before to deal with the wrongful taking of government information. A separate study on the legal dimensions of National Security prepared for the Commission by Martin L. Friedland was published in 1979.[25] But unlike the Crown in the *Stewart* case, which was seeking to broaden the law of the wrongful taking of information, the Macdonald Commission, adopting the recommendations of Friedland, had encouraged a narrowing of the offences created under the *Official Secrets Act* and the creation of a freedom of information act.[26]

The debate was lively between those who sought to protect confidential information by legal means and those who advocated free flow of information. For everyone who suggested that the criminal law should protect information, there were many who feared the consequences of such an extension. If people could own information, what would happen to the freedom of the press, freedom of expression, and scientific inquiry? Many were advocating freedom of information for government and saw the free flow of information as crucial to fundamental rights.

These individual rights and freedoms were also much on people's minds in the early 1980s. In February 1980, after the parliamentary defeat of the short-lived Joe Clark minority Conservative government in December 1979, Pierre Elliott Trudeau had returned to power federally with a majority. After the 20 May 1980 Quebec referendum was held with 59.56 percent voting against separation, Trudeau introduced a *Charter of Rights and Freedoms*.[27] The joint address of the Commons and Senate seeking the British amendment to the *British North America Act* was passed the very month that the *Stewart* case was heard.

At almost the same time as the union was considering how to wrest the desired information from the unwilling hotel management, a New Zealand scholar transplanted to Dalhousie Law School was writing an article that put the issues to be raised in *Stewart* into their legal, social, and economic context. R. Grant Hammond would prove to be a crucial player, perhaps the most crucial player in the debate about information and property. In an article that foreshadowed the *Stewart* case, Hammond issued several warnings.[28] First, he noted that the "article [was] set against the construct of an information-based economy, which is a particular abstraction. Modern societies are too complex to be viewed through any single construct or prism." He went on to say that "although this article [was] concerned in a broad way with the ascription of property rights to information, it [did] not purport to offer any answers to narrowly defined issues. Its primary purpose [was] to disrupt unquestioning faith in the appropriateness of conventional proprietary notions in the formal ordering of information." Prophetically he stated that "North American lawyers [were] about to experience different kinds of problems than they [had] heretofore had to deal with." He cautioned that "[t]hose problems [would] require different ways of thinking." He noted that

> the history of legal responses to new information and knowledge suggest[ed] two critical challenges. The first relate[d] to the ability of the profession and the commercial community to devise new social arrangements that [would] ensure both the creation and the effective and profitable utilisation of new information and technology. The second challenge[d] a liberal society to protect its basic political and human values from unwise applications or withdrawals of that new knowledge. The real question [was] whether the institution of "property" [was] an appropriate vehicle for addressing those challenges.

Hammond's conclusion made it clear that he did not favour the broad application of property rights to information. He warned that:

> The employment of proprietary theory with respect to information could have adverse consequences for society. For example: (a) It may result in a "locking up" of information for private advantage. Even in pure economic terms this must be counterproductive since information begets information. (b) A less than appropriate concern for the moral dimensions of the law may be engendered. Ideas are the common heritage of mankind. Reliance on the market, which necessarily posits the existence of exclusionary rights to information, to produce adequate social accommodations to new knowledge is terribly hazardous when so many of the proposed uses of such knowledge may destroy basic human values, i.e., privacy, human dignity and the physical quality of human life as affected by the new genetics, and, democratic values as they are subverted by an increasingly technocratic bureaucracy.[29]

It was against this backdrop, that the charges were brought against Stewart. Clearly the Ontario Attorney General would have known of the Federal Parliamentary study that was underway but they were unwilling to await its outcome. They were eager to engage in some old fashioned judicial lawmaking notwithstanding Hammond's warnings.

Stewart was represented by Robert A. McNeely, then an eager young lawyer. McNeely, who had articled with the noted criminal firm of Cooper & Sandler, had been called to the bar in 1979 and was practising with a partner in Mississauga as McNeely Crouch. What he lacked in experience he more than made up for in determination, energy, and enthusiasm. He poured himself into what he recognized could be the most important case of his career.[30]

At Stewart's first appearance the senior Crown attorney assigned to the case, Lloyd Budzinsky, took McNeely aside and explained that the Crown was not looking to punish Stewart.[31] Their goal was to clarify the law on the wrongful taking of confidential information at the dawn of the Information Age. Budzinsky explained that if the taking of confidential information constituted fraud, theft, or mischief, they were confident that based on the evidence they could convict Stewart for counselling such offences. What they wanted from McNeely and his client, Stewart, was their agreement to a statement of facts that would isolate the information counselled to be taken from any physical object so that they could clearly establish a precedent that the taking of confidential information *per se* supported one or more of the charged offences. By the time that the trial came in April 1982, the Crown had agreed that if Stewart was found guilty, it would not oppose an absolute discharge.

Young McNeely became an eager participant in the seemingly academic exercise that the Crown was proposing. With no fear for his client's freedom, he saw himself as engaged in a highly important philosophical debate. What was the nature of information generally and confidential information specifically? He gave Stewart's defence all of his attention. He carefully studied the words of the *Criminal Code*. The fraud charge required that the Crown prove that Stewart had dishonestly deprived the hotel of property, money, or valuable security.[32] Could it be said that the copying of employee names had deprived the hotel of anything? Surely not. McNeely was even less concerned about mischief since it required the Crown to prove that Stewart in counselling the copying of the employee names had counseled an act that would obstruct, interrupt or interfere with the lawful use, enjoyment or operation of property. It was the Crown's position that the property obstructed was the physical premises of the hotel. How would the copying of employee names interfere with these premises? McNeely, however, had more concerns about the theft charge. He saw that as the most challenging for his client. On first read, the theft section seemed very broad. The words "anything whether animate or inanimate" seemed to catch confidential information and if the information was revealed to others the owners could be said to have been deprived of its confidentiality. He read every Canadian, British, and American case he could find on the taking of information, going so far as to look at the Roman Law and the origins of our concept of property. In seeking to answer the question of whether the mere copying of that information without more constituted theft, he fastened upon a quote from a respected County Court Judge, Stephen Borins. A few years before Borins had held that a physician's prescription, being a written communication, was not "property" for the purposes of a charge of fraud within the meaning of the *Criminal Code*.[33] Borins had said

> I have no doubt that a person can claim a property interest in his or her words, for example, to enforce a right of intellectual property such as copyright. However, we are here concerned not with copyright law but with criminal law where the words of the Criminal Code must be strictly defined and construed in favour of the accused person.

McNeely would stress the fact that a criminal law provision ought to be narrowly construed in favour of the accused. Based on the English and Canadian case law to date, he would argue that for confidential information to be anything within the meaning of the theft section it had to be property.

The quality of McNeely's "highly important philosophical debate" was improved immensely by the fact that it was Horace Krever J who came to serve as the trial judge. As we have seen, Krever J was no stranger to the legal treatment of confidential information. In September 1980 as Commissioner in a Royal Commission he had written a three volume report for the Ontario Commission of Inquiry into the Confidentiality of Health Information.[34] From 1977 to 1980 he had heard from 500 witnesses and had collected evidence on the techniques used by lawyers and private investigators hired by insurance companies and others to gather confidential health information about people under investigation or involved in litigation. His study demonstrated not only the care with which he worked but also his intellect and the depth of his analysis of the nature and appropriate legal protection for confidential information. He had even come to the attention of the US Congress. In 1979 he had testified in Washington, DC, before the House Subcommittee on Government Information and Individual Rights.[35] It is hard to imagine anyone being better prepared and more appropriate to join this philosophical debate.

When first presented with the charges against Stewart, Krever J wondered if he would get the chance to sit in judgment.[36] He had dealt with Stewart before. In fact it was likely that Stewart was then working as an independent investigator because of Krever J. Stewart had previously been a field investigator employed by Centurion Investigation Ltd. For fifty-five months he had inappropriately gathered confidential health information for Centurion. Justice Krever in his report had been quite critical of the acts of Centurion Investigation and its principals. His report had specifically mentioned Stewart and had discussed some of his actions such as the making of calls to hospitals under false pretences.[37] Although Krever J had recommended against criminal charges being brought against anyone as a result of his report,[38] he expected to be asked to recuse himself on the basis of a pre-existing prejudice against Stewart. McNeely, however, was delighted when he saw that Krever J would be seized of the case. He was aware that Krever J had been the Commissioner for the confidentiality of health records but he also had enormous respect for him. He knew that Krever J was a former professor of law and medicine and former chair of the medical legal society that made rulings on ethical issues. He was confident that Krever J could excise any feelings about his client from his mind and moreover he was exactly the sort of thoughtful, academic judge that he so wanted for his client's case. As it happened, Krever J proved to be an active participant in McNeely's debate, asking a number of probing questions of the parties.[39]

Influenced no doubt by McNeely's complete confidence in Krever and supported by the Crown, Stewart elected to be tried by a judge without a jury. The trial proceeded in April 1982 upon the agreed statement of facts. This was supplemented by the *viva voce* evidence of the investigating police officer, the written statement of Jan William Hart, the security guard, the tape recording of the intercepted telephone conversation between Stewart and Hart and a transcript of that recording. The statement, recording, and transcript were entered into evidence with McNeely's consent.[40]

The case was presented in such a way as to ensure that the real issues in the case were legal and not factual in nature. Nothing at all was made of the labour context or the nature of the information being sought by the union.[41] Nor was there any question that Stewart had counselled Hart to copy the information. The question before the court was whether what Hart had been asked to do amounted to fraud, theft, or mischief.

The Crown's desire to have a clear foundation for its proposed offence of wrongful taking of confidential information was brought out clearly in its submissions to Krever J. They asked that if Krever J found that the facts supported a conviction on more than one of the charged offences, Stewart ought to be convicted of only one. Moreover, if counselling theft was one of the proven charges, he should be convicted only of that offence.[42]

The Crown argued most strenuously for theft. The agreed statement of facts made it clear that the act that Stewart asked Hart to carry out did not involve the taking or converting of any physical object or anything corporeal. The Crown referred to it as the "cloning of information."[43] The Crown lawyers acknowledged openly that they were seeking to broaden the current law by asking Krever J to find that confidential business information *per se* could be the subject of theft. W. Nesmith, the junior Crown prosecutor, conceded that if one took a traditional approach, it could not be said that information was property and thus the subject of theft. But the Crown submitted that the law ought to be permitted to evolve or grow with the times and with the new technology. Besides, they noted, a careful analysis of the theft section of the *Code* disclosed that property was not a requisite of the definition of theft. Paragraphs (a) and (d) of that section did not speak of property. The word used was "anything." They argued that everyone, who fraudulently and without colour of right takes or converts to his own use or to the use of another person, anything, whether property or not, provided the requisite intent was present, commits theft. Anything, they submitted, should, in this modern age, include information. In support of this argument, they referred Krever J to the language of the extortion section of the *Code*, which makes it an offence to use various means, with intent to gain anything, to induce another to do anything or cause anything to be done. The Court of Appeal of British Columbia had held that the word "anything" in the phrase "with intent to gain anything" should be construed widely enough to include sexual intercourse and was not to be restricted to some tangible or material thing.[44] That same court had also decided that credit in a bank account was "anything" capable of being stolen, stating that the word should be construed in its widest sense.[45] They also referred Krever J to a number of US cases that dealt with the prohibition against the interstate transport of any goods, wares, merchandise, securities, or money of the value of $5,000 or more knowing the same to have been stolen, converted, or taken by fraud.[46] Another series of US cases cited by the Crown[47] concerned the theft or conversion of "any record, voucher, money, or thing of value of the United States."[48] These cases had held that information about the identity of potential informants and the status of various drug traffic investigations taken from a government drug enforcement administration computer, on the one hand, and about aircraft flight times, on the other, fell within the prohibition of the statute.

McNeely argued that "anything" in this context meant anything capable of being property. He observed that the theft section was found in Part VII of the *Code* entitled "Offences Against Rights of Property" and that the second count of the indictment itself alleged that Stewart had counselled Hart "to steal information, the property of the Constellation Hotel." He noted that such was in keeping with Canadian and English case law which required that "anything" must partake of the nature of property. He had been unable to find any Canadian authority supporting the view that confidential information was property.

Krever J rendered his judgment on 25 June 1982. Dealing with the charge of counselling mischief, he noted that the Crown had argued that the taking of the information would result in the loss of its confidentiality and interfere with the operation of the hotel by jeopardizing the contract between the hotel and its employees. The hotel, they had pointed out, had undertaken to maintain this information in confidence. Krever found it difficult to understand how the hotel could be said to be in breach of its contract if the loss of confidentiality occurred by reason of the unauthorized and surreptitious conduct of an employee acting in breach of trust. Neither did he accept that, in the light of the hotel's opposition to the union, the disclosure of the information would interfere with the "overall operation" of the hotel.

He dealt more fully with the more difficult question of whether the conduct could amount to counselling theft of the information. After a review of relevant Canadian, US, and British cases, he concluded that to be "anything whether tangible or intangible," must be capable of being property and that confidential information was not property for the purpose of the law of theft in Canada. Being concerned that he might have stated the proposition too widely, he added that he was confident that it was correct to say that a person who takes or converts confidential information alone does not take or convert "anything" as that word is contemplated by the theft section.

In answer to the Crown's request to broaden the law he added:

> If this interpretation should be thought to be inadequate to meet the needs of modern Canadian society, particularly because of its implication for the Computer Age remedy must be a change in the law by Parliament. It is not for a court to stretch the language used in a statute dealing with the criminal law, to solve problems outside the contemplation of the statute. If an accused person's conduct does not fall within the language used by Parliament, then, no matter how reprehensible it may be, it ought not to be characterized as criminal. In this connection see the language of Chief Justice Laskin and Estey J. in Regina *v* McLaughlin (1980), 53 C.C.C. (2d) 417 at pp. 420-421 and 425 respectively.

He also dismissed the charge of counselling fraud, even though the Crown had clearly established the element of dishonesty. The difficulty, he noted, was whether deprivation was involved. He pointed out that the fraud section of the *Code* required that there be deprivation of "any property, money or valuable security." Certainly no valuable security was involved in the confidential information at issue nor was there any property. What was left was money. He had no difficulty in attributing a notional value to the confidential information but there still had to be deprivation. In response to the Crown's suggestion that the hotel was denied the sale value of the information he noted that there was no suggestion in the facts that the hotel would ever sell the information. Indeed, the undertaking by the hotel, as employer, to maintain the confidentiality of the employees' information entirely negated the suggestion. In short, the element of deprivation had not been shown and in the absence of the element, there was no fraud.

The Toronto newspapers gave Krever J's decision little notice. *The Globe and Mail* ran a few lines on page 4 in their Saturday 26 June issue in the "In Brief" section under the heading "Private Information Cannot be Stolen." The same day the *Toronto Star* ran a brief piece on page A8 under the heading "Secret Data Cannot be Stolen Top Court Rules." The *Star* emphasized that this was one of the first cases of its kind. They quoted Crown prosecutor Lloyd Budzinsky as saying that Krever J had been asked "to resolve a novel issue."

While McNeely and his client were thrilled with the result, they were not surprised when the crown appealed.[49] The Attorney General of Ontario chose to appeal Stewart's acquittal on the charges of counselling fraud and theft of information. Even though he was being paid only a modest fee, young McNeely eagerly agreed to take the appeal. JF Casey appeared for the Crown, the appellant. The appeal was heard by three senior judges, Lloyd Houlden, Peter Cory, and Maurice Lacourciére.

One day almost exactly one year after Krever J's trial judgment, Lloyd Houlden J, whose office in Osgoode Hall was beside Krever J's, dropped in to tell him that the appeal panel was split but it seemed that the majority was against him. Krever J had the impression that Houlden J had sided with him but he had not.[50] Justice Houlden wrote the majority judgment overturning the trial decision. He agreed with the interpretation given to the word "anything" in *R v Scallen*.[51] Being a word in everyday use, it had a broad general meaning wider in scope than the words "anything capable of being stolen" used in the *Criminal Code* prior to the 1953–54 amendments. He stated that while clearly not all information was property, he saw no reason why confidential information that had been gathered through the expenditure of time, effort, and money by a commercial enterprise for the purposes of its business should not be regarded as property and hence entitled to the protection of the criminal law. He, however, made nothing of the fact that the information in question in the *Stewart* case did not meet the criteria that he himself had set out. Could it be said that the employee names and addresses had been gathered through the expenditure of time, effort, and money by a commercial enterprise for the purposes of its business? How much time and effort had it taken the hotel management to take down the names and addresses of its employees? Justice Houlden was clearly dealing with this issue in the abstract rather than within the confines of the *Stewart* case itself. In justifying his interpretation Houlden J stated that the "last half of the twentieth century has seen an exponential growth in the development and improvement of methods of storing and distributing information. I believe that section 283(1) of the Code is wide enough to protect the interests of those who compile and store such information and to restrain the activities of those who wrongfully seek to misappropriate it."

In finding that Stewart had the requisite intent he noted that if Hart had taken the information as requested by Stewart, the hotel would not have been deprived of possession of the information; but the character of confidentiality would have been gone. In his opinion, Stewart had intended to deal with the information in such a manner that it would not be returned in the condition it was in at the time it was taken or converted.

Justice Peter Cory wrote a concurring judgment. He too noted that the word "anything" was very wide in its scope and he too justified taking a broad interpretation based on changes in society. He noted that "[f]or many businessmen their confidential lists may well be the most valuable asset of their company. Their security will be of utmost importance to the firm." He added:

> Information and its collection, collation and interpretation are vital to most modern commercial enterprises. Compilations of information are often of such importance to the business community that they are securely kept to ensure their confidentiality. The collated, confidential information may be found in many forms covering a wide variety of topics. It may include painstakingly prepared computer programmes pertaining to all aspects of the firm's business; meticulously indexed lists of suppliers with comments as to their efficiency, reliability and time required for delivery; laboriously compiled lists of customers and their needs; instructions as to manufacturing processes learned from months of experimentation and trial . . .

Unlike Houlden J, Cory J then addressed the type of information involved in the case before him by adding to his litany "lists of employees, including reference to their physical well-being and disciplinary history that may be required to be kept confidential in compliance with the terms of a collective bargaining agreement."

He also noted that copyright was a significant property right of substantial importance to modern commercial enterprises and that copyright constituted property of a nature that falls within the scope of the widely encompassing phrase "anything whether animate or inanimate" in section 283(1).

Justice Maurice Lacourciére dissented. Impressed with Krever J's analysis, he wrote of "the learned judge's careful reasons delivered after reserving judgment"[52] and of his "scholarly analysis of a number of Canadian, American and English cases."[53] He stated that:

> In any event, Canadian courts have grafted a property concept on the definition of the words "anything whether animate or inanimate", and thus confidential information per se is not protected under the Criminal Code. I agree with Krever J.'s conclusion that it is for Parliament to broaden the criminal definition of the property concept if the needs of modern Canadian society require it.

Turning to the fraud charge, he stated:

> Although the respondent would have received some money for the information I find it difficult to see how the hotel suffered the requisite deprivation or detriment within the meaning of R. v. Olan, supra. The deprivation would be clear if the confidential information had been in the nature of a trade secret or copyrighted material having a commercial value intended to be exploited by the victim: see judgment of this court, R. v. Kirkwood, released June 27, 1983, unreported [since reported 42 OR (2d) 65].

The next day *The Globe and Mail* reported the ruling on page 5 under the heading "Called Valuable Asset: Firm's secret data ruled 'property.'" They stated:

> The value of confidential business information has received a boost from an Ontario Court of Appeal ruling that a man who paid a hotel employee for a computerized employee list is guilty of counselling theft of property.[54]

The case was referred back to Krever J for the sentencing. NcNeely and the Crown had earlier agreed that an absolute discharge would be sought. Justice Krever was inclined to agree. There was, however, a problem. As one reads Krever J's comments on the problem, one cannot help but smile at the lesson in logic and criminal procedure that Krever J proceeded to teach to the appellate court that had overruled him. He pointed out that the Act said that a discharge could be imposed, "instead of convicting the accused" but the Court of Appeal had imposed a conviction. He was, nevertheless, able to "interpret the order of the Court of Appeal, as reflected in the reasons for judgment of Mr. Justice Houlden, with whom Mr. Justice Cory concurred, as intending to exercise the powers conferred by section 613(4) (b) to substitute a verdict of guilty rather than a verdict of conviction, notwithstanding the language which the court chose to use."[55]

The decision of the Court of Appeal spurred much academic comment.[56] Christopher Millard, recently returned to his native England after graduating from the University of Toronto LL.M. program, saw it as an indication "that Canadian judges [would] eschew the reticence of their English counterparts and instead treat information per se as property that can be stolen . . . the majority departed radically from traditional Anglo-Canadian jurisprudence and may have greatly expanded the scope of the theft offence in Canada."[57]

Not all commentators regarded this radical departure as a good thing. The most notable critic was R. Grant Hammond, who, as we have seen, both anticipated and supported the reasoning used in the original trial judgement. This New Zealander by birth who had received a Master of Laws from Illinois had become the Director of the Institute of Law Research and Reform in Edmonton and a member of the Federal Provincial Working Party on Trade Secrets.[58] In 1992 he would be appointed to the High Court of New Zealand. He wrote a case comment in the *Law Quarterly Review*.[59] He was critical of the majority holding. Hammond noted that the majority finding that information was property for criminal law purposes was "an example of unwarranted judicial activism which [was] at odds with certain law reform and parliamentary initiatives in Canada."[60] He added that the technical handling of the authorities was suspect. Finally, and most tellingly, he commented that the practical consequences of the decision were far reaching and had not been adequately addressed by the court.

He noted that the issue before the Court of Appeal in *Stewart* had been the subject of much study and considered analysis and that the majority decision was out of step.[61] He reminded his readers that the matter had been referred to a subcommittee of the Commons Standing Committee on Justice and Legal Affairs. The consultative process on this issue had been underway at exactly the time that the Court of Appeal had been hearing the appeal. He pointed out that some data industry members had pushed for the creation of a broad theft of information offence as was done by the Ontario Crown in *Stewart* but this had been resisted by the Department of Justice and its advisers. The consensus had been that an offence of the theft of information was "altogether too broad."[62] It was thought that other means of social control were available, namely civil actions for misappropriation of information. Just a few days after the Court of Appeal issued its ruling, much narrower, more focused reform had been proposed in a government information paper. In this context, how, he asked, could the majority have knowingly stretched the existing law to create an offence of theft of information?

After pointing out several technical flaws in the legal analysis of the earlier authorities, Hammond turned to "the consequences of the decision." He began by pointing out that the only qualifier on this broad offence of theft of information was that the information should be confidential. This was even further than some US states had gone in making it a crime to steal trade secrets. He feared that given the facts in Stewart there would be little room for strict construction in the interpretation of the offence. As we have seen, the information that was to be copied in Stewart was not commercially valuable or sensitive trade secrets. It was a list of employee names and addresses.

One significant problem that the majority decision would create was for employee mobility. How was the court to deal with the case of an employee who, in contravention of an employee covenant, took "confidential information" with him when he left the employ of his employer? He noted that courts had long struggled with the need to protect businesses while at the same time permitting employees to take their knowledge and skills to another employer. Judges had had trouble drawing this line. How was an employee to know what he could take without committing a crime?[63]

Hammond acknowledged that questions of the entitlement to information would surface more frequently given the changes in the economy. But he stressed that:

> The need to maintain the free and open transmission of ideas and information is the cornerstone of the western liberal tradition and should be viewed as the overriding norm. Departures, or suggested departures, from this norm should be rigorously scrutinised and granted only in compelling cases and then only in sufficient, but no more than sufficient terms.[64]

Hammond's criticism undoubtedly helped shape the Trade Secrets report of the Institute of Law Research and Reform in Edmonton and a Federal Provincial Working Party in July 1986. That report stated

> The proposition that information – even confidential information – is or should be "property" for legal purposes seems to us to involve difficulties at both a technical level, and in the effects which such a proposition would . . . give rise to.[65]

It is interesting to note that Crown prosecutor Lloyd Budzinsky, who had handled the *Stewart* case at trial, was the Ontario representative on the Task Force. There can be little doubt that he and Hammond debated the need for the crime of the theft of confidential information. In the final analysis the Report recommended the use of criminal law to protect trade secrets, but to meet Hammond's concerns it stated:

> The countervailing societal interests in freedom of information and mobility of labour suggest that any criminal offence should be "customized": to respond precisely to the conditions that warrant the use of the Criminal Law.

In contrast to the majority in the *Stewart* case, the Report set out in detail its recommendations as to the "particularly reprehensible conduct" that the criminal law ought to be reserved for. It stressed that what was being sought was an offence "directed at wrongful interference with the economic advantage derived from knowledge of a trade secret."[66] In looking at the nature of the information to be protected, the Task Force concluded that the information should be the same as was protected by the civil law. They stressed not the nature of the information but the reprehensible conduct involved in the taking. The offence ought to require the fraudulent acquisition, disclosure, or use of the information without colour of right with the intent to interfere with the economic advantage to be derived from the trade secret or the intent to deprive a person of the control of the trade secret. They further recommended a separate offence of fraudulently inducing the consent of the trade secret holder to the acquisition, disclosure, or use of the information. The Task Force then dealt at some length with included offences and with defences. They distinguished their proposed offences from reverse engineering or independent development of the trade secret. Those should remain valid exercises, they noted, provided that nothing was improperly taken to facilitate them. They also advocated a public interest defence in situations where the public interest in access to the information clearly outweighed the need to condemn such conduct.

The decision of the Court of Appeal had been a terrible disappointment to McNeely. He took some solace in the fact that Lacourciére J had dissented but he could not accept that the majority had rejected his arguments. Stewart, his client, was not as concerned. Based on the Crown's recommendation and his own sense of justice, Krever J had given him an absolute discharge. Nevertheless, NcNeely met with his client after the Court of Appeal to try to convince him to appeal. He noted that Stewart had the right to appeal to the Supreme Court of Canada on the basis of the Lacourciére J dissent. He agreed to take the case pro bono and did all of the initial work to perfect the appeal at his own expense. He began to realize, however, just how expensive this was going to be. The printing cost for the record and the appeal books alone came to between seven and nine thousand dollars.[67]

Then McNeely received a call from a much more experienced and very able criminal lawyer. Clayton Ruby explained that he had a strong interest in the appeal and in clarifying the law because he had another client facing similar charges. Ruby, a partner with the law firm of Ruby & Edwards in Toronto, was a rising star and would become, if he was not then already, one of Canada's leading defence lawyers. He was also an outspoken proponent of personal freedoms and an ardent supporter of the new *Charter of Rights and Freedoms*. He had received his LL.B. from the University of Toronto and his LL.M. from the University of California, Berkeley. Ruby prided himself on devoting his professional career to ensuring that those who were underprivileged and those who faced discrimination were given equal access to the legal system. One of those that Ruby saw as persecuted on religious grounds was the Church of Scientology — the client that faced similar charges. McNeely encouraged Stewart to call Ruby but did not participate any further in the preparations for the appeal, which Ruby assumed with Stewart's consent.

Ruby's appearance on the scene after the Court of Appeal ruling revealed that there was more to *Regina v Stewart* than the test case that the Crown had first discussed with McNeely. *Stewart* was an attempt by the Crown to clarify the law in support of their ongoing prosecution of the Church of Scientology without having to face Ruby and the other lawyers for the Church. The Crown was engaged in a battle by proxy.

In order to better understand the Crown's strategy, we need to look at the lengthy struggle by the Crown in Ontario to prosecute the Toronto branch of the Church for certain alleged criminal activities. The Church had been founded in the mid 1950s by L. Ron Hubbard, a former science fiction writer, who claimed his methods could cure or prevent many diseases, increase IQs, and produce superior beings with power of mind over matter. The Church vigorously defended its reputation and its interests. It sued the Hamilton and Etobicoke libraries for defamation when they added anti-Scientology books to their collections.[68] When former members spoke out against the Church, they too were sued for defamation.[69] In defending itself it sought out every avenue to obtain information on its perceived enemies. At public hearings into the RCMP, for example, the Church sought access to the RCMP files.[70] But the methods that it used were not always lawful. In 1975 two members of the Church pleaded guilty to possessing lock-picking tools after they were found trying to enter the offices of Weir & Foulds, a law firm defending former members of the Church who were being sued. In August 1976 John Marshall of *The Globe and Mail* alleged that the Church had even organized an anti-cult crusade as a front to uncover the names of their "enemies."[71]

The Ontario Attorney General's office would be involved in years of litigation against the Church as a result of certain events in the late 1970s. In May 1976, *The Globe and Mail* had reported that the Ontario Medical Association was asking the College of Physicians and Surgeons of Ontario to conduct an investigation of Scientology on the grounds that its members had been practising medicine without a licence.[72] The Church promptly launched an action against the newspaper for libel. The action could not have come as much of a shock since, as we have seen, the Church had earlier sued many others for libel. One group that had attracted such action were the three members of the Committee on the Healing Arts for their 1970 report that had the reviewed the Church's alleged unlicensed medical practice. Coincidentally, Horace Krever J had been one of commissioners. The action against the commissioners would ultimately be abandoned and the one against the newspaper lost.[73] More important for our purposes, in 1976 the Church of Scientology of Toronto, faced with a need to understand the government's intentions, had resorted to a technique similar to the one later used unsuccessfully by Stewart. They had infiltrated the offices of the Ontario Medical Association to obtain information about the intended investigation. A scientology member, Nanna Anderson, had been instructed to take documents and give them to another scientology member to be copied and to then return them to the files.[74] Nothing but the information was taken. But this seems to have been only one instance of what was a much more widespread technique that the Church used against those that it perceived as enemies. The fuller extent of the practice came out when thousands of documents were seized by the FBI in a massive 1977 raid of US Scientology offices in Los Angeles and Washington DC.[75] About 33,000 of the seized documents were submitted as evidence by federal attorneys in the Washington prosecution of US leaders of the Church on charges of conspiring to steal government documents and obstructing justice by coverups and by kidnapping an informant.[76] In 1978, before the full impact of US seizures was realized in Ontario, the Church sued five ministers of the Ontario government — Roy McMurtry, Larry Grossman, Thomas

Wells, Dennis Timbrell, and George Kerr — alleging that they were conspiring to bring about the demise of the Church.[77] It was only in 1980 when *The Globe and Mail* ran a series of articles by John Marshall known as "The Scientology Papers"[78] that the public learned that confidential documents from various Ontario Government offices including a communication from the Attorney General about police intelligence operations had been found in the Scientology files seized in the US. The Canadian material seized in the US also included private documents from non-governmental agencies like the Ontario Medical Association and private papers of the Committee on the Healing Arts including the 274-page pre-publication draft of the committee's report on sectarian healing and hypnotherapy, which had been written by Professor John A. Lee and published in 1970. Among the seized documents were reports from and about Church members who worked in government and non-government offices where they could gather information to help the Church defend itself from those who sought to take action against it. Hubbard's followers in the United States and Canada claimed that there had been thirty years of civil rights violations against them by the US Government. It was these violations that had led them to use Church members to gain access to information in various government files.

The Ontario prosecution of the Church would continue for a decade. In early March 1983, between the *Stewart* trial and the initial appeal, more than one hundred Ontario Provincial Police raided the premises of the Church on Yonge Street in Toronto. Some 39,000 files and books totalling about 2,000,000 pages as well as tapes were removed in a massive two-day search.[79] The warrant was issued on the basis of an information approximately 1,000 pages in length. In addition to counts of possible tax fraud and other fraud was the following:

> And further that L. Ron HUBBARD, Mary Sue HUBBARD, CHURCH OF SCIENTOLOGY OF TORONTO . . . and others unlawfully did between January 1, 1972, and February 15, 1983 at Toronto, in the Judicial District of York, and elsewhere in Canada, commit an indictable offence, to wit: did conspire together and with other persons to effect a lawful purpose, the operation of Scientology-owned and controlled companies and organizations, by unlawful means, to wit: the use of the GUARDIAN OFFICE OF SCIENTOLOGY to commit indictable offences, including theft and break, enter and theft, when perceived necessary by the said persons to protect the interests of Scientology contrary to Section 423(2)(b) of the Criminal Code of Canada. (Offence #3).

The theft that was alleged would seem to have been the theft of information from government and non-governmental files. In 1984 after the Crown had successfully appealed *Stewart* and had established the crime of theft of information, charges were brought against the Church of Scientology and eleven individuals, as well as numerous unindicted co-conspirators, for theft of information from numerous organizations including Canadian and Ontario medical and mental health organizations, the Ontario and Toronto Police, the Attorney General of Ontario, and the Royal Canadian Mounted Police.[80] In 1985, Nanna Anderson, the scientologist who had been charged in the indictment with stealing documents from the Ontario Medical Association at the request of church officials, pleaded guilty. The judge discharged her because she had "suffered enough." Other guilty pleas by individuals followed. The Church itself, however, continued to fight.

During and after the *Stewart* case, over a period of many years, the Ontario Crown and the Church of Scientology engaged in a complex mass of litigation. The Church challenged every aspect of the Government's actions including the validity of the search warrants, the charges, and the value of the stolen documents, and claimed priest/penitent privilege of confidentiality for much of the seized documentation. The Church's largely unsuccessful attempt to quash the search warrants, for example, continued over fours years and led to a large number of motions, many hearings and a 1987 ruling of the Ontario Court of Appeal.[81]

The two combatants fought at every step. Each side accused the other of misinforming and misleading the public.[82] Morris Manning, one of the lawyers for the Church of Scientology, even attacked the reputation of Casey Hill, the Crown Attorney who was preparing the case for the prosecution. In September 1984, Manning appeared in his barrister's robes at a press conference on the steps of Osgoode Hall in Toronto and alleged that Casey Hill had misled a Supreme Court judge and had breached the court order sealing certain of the seized documents. The order in question had been made on 11 July 1984, by Osler J who had ruled that solicitor-and-client privilege applied to 232 of the seized documents he had reviewed and ordered that they remain sealed pending further order of the court. Manning alleged that Casey Hill had allowed government officials in the Ministry of Consumer and Commercial Relations to access these sealed documents in connection with the processing of an application by the Church to have its president, Earl Smith, authorized to solemnize marriages pursuant to section 20(2) of the *Marriage Act*[83] and subsequently with the defence of the Church's application for judicial review of the Ministry's failure to approve that application. A motion for contempt based on these allegations was filed with the court. Within days, however, the Church of Scientology learned that at least some of the allegations were untrue but it continued to press them. The contempt trial was heard by Cromarty J for eleven days beginning 5 November 1984. After the Church had put in its case, Cromarty J dismissed the application on a motion for non-suit.[84] He found that there was no evidence that Hill participated in any stage of the application made by the Church. Casey Hill then successfully sued Manning and the Church for libel and slander. The Church, of course, appealed. For seven years that case would make its way through appeals to the Supreme Court of Canada where the verdict for Hill would ultimately be upheld.[85]

The *Stewart* case was motivated in large part by the desire of the Crown to clarify the law to assist them in the prosecution of the Church and its members and to do so without the many challenges, motions, and hearings that plagued them in the actions against the Church itself. Clayton Ruby certainly thought so and thought that the best way to defend the Church was to assume Stewart's appeal to the Supreme Court of Canada. That appeal effectively became one more skirmish in the very lengthy battle between Ontario and the Church.

As Ruby prepared his Supreme Court appeal, the Alberta courts were wrestling with the same legal issues. In *Regina v Offley* the accused was a former RCMP sergeant who operated a security firm that did background checks on job applicants. It was alleged that after Offley was told that only police agencies could access the Canadian Police Information Centre (CPIC), a database of pooled police information, he befriended an Edmonton police constable and offered him money to run security checks for him through the CPIC. The Police constable reported the offer to his superiors and was told to play along. Doing so, he received two lists from Offley and ran the requested security checks through the CPIC. On delivering the information to Offley, the constable received $65,000. Offley was then charged with counselling theft of information. The trial judge, following the Ontario Court of Appeal decision, found Offley guilty. On appeal, however, the Alberta Court of Appeal declined to follow their Ontario brethren. They were of the view that Krever J had been correct and that information, even when qualified as confidential, was not "anything" within the meaning of the *Criminal Code*, because it was intrinsically incapable of being an inanimate thing.[86] In so finding they relied upon Glanville Williams' text on Criminal Law[87] and the

1978 English case of *Oxford v Moss*.[88] Echoing but not citing Hammond and the Alberta led Task Force, Belzil JA writing for the unanimous court, said

> the definition of theft does not well fit the cases of industrial espionage. There is a strong case for extending the criminal law to the protection of trade secrets and other valuable confidential information (such as the scenario of a play) deliberately obtained by industrial espionage or knowingly in breach of confidence, but the way to achieve this is somehow to goad Parliament into action on the subject.

While *Regina v Offley* provided unexpected support for Ruby's appeal, it also spurred Arnold Weinrib, a professor of property law at the University of Toronto, to write in support of the majority view in the Ontario Court of Appeal. Professor Weinrib was noted for beginning his first year property classes with the famous US Supreme Court case of *International News Service v The Associated Press*. This was a case in which the Court granted an injunction against the unauthorized copying of news stories and their transmission to members of news service for a fee on the basis that news "must be regarded as quasi property."[89] On the eve of the Supreme Court hearing of the *Stewart* appeal, Weinrib's as yet unpublished article was delivered in typescript to the court by the Office of the Attorney General of Ontario.[90] After some deliberation the court decided to accept the soon to be published article for consideration.

Weinrib began with the telling comment that people were then living in an age when information had assumed unprecedented importance in the operation of commercial enterprises. He pointed out that a great deal of time and money could be spent in gathering that information and that methods needed to be created to protect it from misappropriation. After alluding to the split between the Courts of Appeal in Ontario and Alberta and the resultant uncertainty in the law, he acknowledged the novelty of the *Stewart* decision and stated that his thesis was that *Stewart* was a natural and appropriate application of the law of property.[91] He went on to point out that property had become "de-physicalized." It ought to be seen not as a thing but as a bundle of divisible rights in or to things. Property was a conclusory term that did not define in what circumstances rights should be awarded.

Weinrib's careful analysis of the American, Canadian, and English treatment of property and of confidential information was much more thorough and less easy to criticize than the majority judgments from the Ontario Court of Appeal. How, he asked, can it be a theft to take the paper upon which the information is written but not the information itself? The paper only draws its value from the information.[92] He then turned to Hammond's dire warnings about the consequences of *Stewart*. He pointed out that the Ontario Court of Appeal had not intended to create the broad theft of information offence that people feared. He noted the qualifying remarks from both Houlden and Cory JJ. Clearly the Court had only intended that confidential information that had been gathered through the expenditure of time, effort, and money would be capable of being stolen. He had earlier noted that the information in *Stewart* itself was not commercially valuable confidential information but he did not ask whether that information satisfied this criteria, being but employee names and addresses. Turning to the issue of the alleged stretching of the words of the *Criminal Code*, he pointed out that the plain meaning of the word anything needed no stretching to capture intangibles like information. He dismissed those who argued that this ruling challenged the freedom of information by noting that those that misappropriated confidential business information were not aiming for broad public dissemination. They wanted the information for their own private gain. Finally, he challenged those who saw the Ontario Court of Appeal's decision as unjustified legal activism.

> . . . the essence of the argument must be that, because no Canadian court had previously ruled that confidential information could be the subject of theft, it was up to Parliament to change 'the law'. This reasoning reflects a curious view of the legal process . . . . The common-law is judge-made; it has evolved through the ability of judges to adapt the law to meet changing circumstances . . .
>
> A legislative solution to a problem of this type may in fact be preferable, but in the absence of any action by the legislators it is not helpful to anyone for the court to defer the solution to them.

On 1 December 1987, the *Stewart* appeal was heard by Dickson CJ and by Beetz, Estey, McIntyre, Lamer, Wilson, and Le Dain JJ. Clayton Ruby and Mary Bartley argued for the appellant. Jeff Casey appeared for the Crown. Jeff Casey adopted the majority's reasoning in the Ontario Court of Appeal as buttressed by Weinrib's article. Clayton Ruby looked to the Alberta Court of Appeal and Hammond's work. Each argued public policy. Casey noted the need to adapt the law to the Computer Age. Ruby pointed out the many practical problems that a holding for the Crown would create. He tried to convince the court that the offence of theft contemplated only physical objects and that whether information might be property in certain limited, non-criminal cases was irrelevant.

The decision of the court came down on 26 May 1988. Willard Z. Estey J had retired from the Court a month earlier on 22 April and took no part in the judgment which was delivered by Lamer J, the acknowledged criminal law specialist on the Court. In his view, the wording of the *Criminal Code* limited the meaning of "anything" in two ways. "First, whether tangible or intangible, 'anything' must be of a nature such that it can be the subject of a proprietary right. Second, the property must be capable of being taken or converted in a manner that results in the deprivation of the victim." He did not, however, close the door entirely on future developments in the treatment of confidential business information.

> It is possible that, with time, confidential information will come to be considered as property in the civil law or even be granted special legal protection by statutory enactment. Even if confidential information were to be considered as property under civil law, it does not however automatically follow that it qualifies as property for the purposes of criminal law. Conversely, the fact that something is not property under civil law is likewise not conclusive for the purpose of criminal law. Whether or not confidential information is property under the Criminal Code should be decided in the perspective of the criminal law.

He stressed that in criminal law consideration had to be given to more than just the interests of the parties. Society had other interests.

He noted that conservatism in the interpretation of criminal law was appropriate. "If the unauthorized appropriation of confidential information becomes a criminal offence, there would be far reaching consequences that the courts are not in a position to contemplate."

He accepted the argument that many practical problems could arise from a finding that information was property. He acknowledged that "given recent technological developments, confidential information, and in some instances, information of a commercial value, is in need of some protection through our criminal law." But the extent and the manner of such protection was "best left to be determined by Parliament rather than by the courts."

Turning to the issue of fraud, he said that "one cannot be deprived of confidentiality, because one cannot own confidentiality. One enjoys it. Therefore, appellant should not have been convicted on the sole basis that he might have had the intent set out in section 283(1)(d) since the commission of the actus reus was not and could not be established."

What of the argument that the information was protected by the provisions of the *Copyright Act*? He stated that a "mere copier of documents, be they confidential or not, does not acquire the copyright nor deprive its owner of any part thereof. No matter how many copies are made of a work, the copyright owner still possesses the sole right to reproduce or authorize the reproduction of his work. Such copying constitutes an infringement of the copyright under section 17 of the Act, but it cannot in any way be theft under the criminal law."

He then provided a useful summary.

> in a schematic way: "anything" is not restricted to tangibles, but includes intangibles. To be the subject of theft it must, however: 1. be property of some sort; 2. be property capable of being (a) taken — therefore intangibles are excluded; or (b) converted — and may be an intangible; (c) taken or converted in a way that deprives the owner of his proprietary interest in some way.

Finally after almost six years of legal battles, Ruby and the Church of Scientology had won on at least this one front. Hammond's arguments had bested Weinrib's. The taking of confidential information was not a crime in Canada. *The Globe and Mail* ran a front-page story of the ruling under the heading "Secrets can't be stolen, Supreme Court decides." Clayton Ruby, in a quote intended to catch the attention of the press, is reported as saying,

> If you could steal information, any reporter who had a tip on what the Government is doing, would be in possession of stolen goods. Why criminalize a reporter's tip?

Not all were pleased. In an interesting turn of phrase, Richard Potter, a thoughtful practitioner in the new field of computer law, stated that it reflected the "radically conservative side of the Supreme Court."[93] He noted the difficulty of implementing the sort of legislative reform that the court called for. It was fine to talk of amending the *Criminal Code* but integrating this with the provincial laws relating to trade secrets required "complete cooperation between the Parliament to amend the Criminal code and ten provincial legislatures each to enact an Act protecting trade secrets." This was not likely to be achieved.

Certainly those in the Ontario Attorney General's office who had seen *Stewart* as a way to shape the law to deal with the Church of Scientology were not pleased. Although the Crown could no longer support a charge of theft of confidential information, the war between the Church and the Provincial Crown in Ontario was not yet over. In September 1990 certain Scientologists and the Church of Scientology of Toronto were charged with theft and/or possession of stolen documents and with breach of trust by a public officer (disclosing to unauthorized persons information coming to his or her knowledge or possession by reason of his or her office). Then in February 1991, the Ontario Attorney General, Howard Hampton, filed an additional preferred indictment against the Church and ten of its members. The indictment charged the defendants with infiltrating, stealing documents, or breach of trust at a number of law firms and organizations between April 1975 and January 1978.[94] The indictment originally included twelve counts, consisting of seven counts of theft and five counts of breach of trust. The theft counts related to theft of documents from government agencies and other organizations. They were eventually severed from the indictment, and acquittals were entered on the theft charges.

The Church argued that it was not legally responsible for the actions of its "renegade members" in the Guardian's Office who had failed to follow Church doctrine. They also contended that the information-gathering functions carried out by the Guardian's Office in Toronto were assigned to it by the Church of Scientology of California (UK) (Guardian Office World Wide), not by the Church of Scientology of Toronto. They further submitted that the doctrine of corporate criminal liability did not apply to non-profit religious corporations. The theory of defence put forward on behalf of Jacqueline Matz was based on gaps in the Crown's case with respect to each of the counts. In relation to the charge involving the OPP, she argued that there was no breach of trust since the information obtained by the agent was unimportant. With respect to the count involving the Ministry of the Attorney General, she argued that the Crown's evidence was unreliable and that, in one of the incidents relied on by the Crown, no confidential information seems to have been obtained.

On 25 June 1992, the Church of Scientology of Toronto and Jacqueline Matz were each convicted of two counts of breach of trust contrary to the *Criminal Code*,[95] following a trial before Southey J and a jury. It was a long and complex trial in which virtually everything was in issue. The jury convicted on breach of trust in relation to the Ontario Provincial Police and the Ministry of the Attorney General of Ontario but acquitted on a second count involving the Ontario Provincial Police and on charges relating to the Metropolitan Toronto Police, and the Royal Canadian Mounted Police. The Church was fined $250,000 and Jacqueline Matz was fined $5,000.

The Church of Scientology of Toronto appealed both the convictions and the sentence. Jacqueline Matz appealed the conviction only. In September 1996 the Ontario Court of Appeal heard arguments for seven days.[96] Counsel for the Church put forward numerous grounds of appeal, some of which were abandoned at the hearing. The principal remaining issues in the appeal were whether the jury was properly constituted having regard to the exclusion of certain persons, such as non-citizens, from the array; whether the identification doctrine of corporate liability applied to a non-profit corporation without share capital established for religious purposes; and whether there was sufficient evidence to meet the test for corporate criminal liability, and, alternatively, whether the jury was adequately directed with respect to corporate criminal liability.

After a lengthy review of the various bases for the appeal, the Court of Appeal rejected all of the appeals and upheld both the convictions and the sentences given.

The *Stewart* case is instructive in several ways. In one sense it is the classic test case. The Crown wanted to determine the limits of the law as it related to a new perceived threat, in this case the theft of confidential information. The crown sought out a suitable case. As part of a deal with the accused, the facts were shaped in an agreed upon statement of facts. The case was then argued by the Crown on the basis of the legal issues they wished resolved rather than strictly on the merits of the particular matter before the court. Generally the academic community and the courts played their assigned roles, considering the legal issues generically rather than in the narrow context of the labour dispute that was really the heart of the matter in *Stewart*. Looked at in this way, it is an interesting chapter in the history of criminal law reform. Those who favour the flexibility of the common law approach looked with some satisfaction on the decision of the Ontario Court of Appeal which was able to interpret the law to create the new offence sought by the Crown. Those who favour the shaping of the law by Parliament after careful study by law reform commissions, criticised the lack of precision in the Court of Appeal's judgment and were encouraged when the Supreme Court left the law largely unchanged and referred the matter to Parliament.

But as we have seen much more was going on behind the scenes. The *Stewart* case was chosen because it raised the same issues as did a number of incidents of unauthorized access to and copying of information by members of the Church of Scientology. Not only did the case offer suitably malleable facts but it offered the prospect of arguing the case against a young and inexperienced, if eager, counsel in a small office rather than against the very capable, aggressive, and thorough Clayton Ruby and his office.

Looked at as an attempt to develop the law to assist in the prosecution of the Church of Scientology of Toronto, *Stewart* was a failure. The Crown's end run around the defences offered by Ruby and his team ran into its first hurdle in the person of Horace Krever J, an able, well-informed judge who knew this area of the law better than anyone and who favoured a different approach to the criminalization of information theft. The second hurdle was the respect that Maurice Lacourciére J had for Krever J's trial judgment. The dissenting voice at the Ontario Court of Appeal gave the opportunity for the intervention of Clayton Ruby in the appeal to the Supreme Court of Canada. But even more important in the ultimate decision was the work of the Federal Provincial Task Force on Trade Secrets that both reflected and was shaped by the persuasive arguments of R. Grant Hammond.

In a case full of ironies, perhaps the ultimate irony was the fact that Hammond's carefully thought out and thorough analysis of how the law ought to be shaped to deal with the wrongful taking of trade secrets was never implemented. The referral of the issue of law reform to Parliament first mentioned by Krever J in his trial judgment and later endorsed by both Lacourciére J at the Ontario Court of Appeal and by the unanimous Supreme Court fell on deaf ears. The recommendations of the Federal Provincial Task Force on Trade Secrets were never implemented.[97] The law as determined by the Supreme Court of Canada in *Regina v Stewart* remains the law in Canada. Those like Weinrib and Potter who said that judge-made law, although imperfect, would at least result in reform were proved correct.

In the end, the value of *Regina v Stewart* came from the debate it engendered. It provided an opportunity and a forum for a thorough analysis of a newly developed social and business concern. Although the law did not change, Canadian society was better informed of the issues and their consequences. That is the legacy of *Stewart*.

Notes

1 I should point out that I have several personal connections to the subject. I was one of the participants in the debate on the case in the 1980s. In 1984 I wrote an annotation for the Business Law Reports on the Court of Appeal decision and I assisted my mentor, Dick Potter, in an op-ed piece for *The Globe and Mail* on the Supreme Court of Canada judgment in 1988. I count as friends both the trial judge Horace Krever and one of the Court of Appeal judges that ruled on the case, Peter Cory. I also consider Roy McMurtry, the Ontario Attorney General who led the prosecution of the Church of Scientology and the founder of the Osgoode Society, a friend. Finally, my law firm, Fasken & Calvin, as it was known before 1988, was one of the victims of the theft of information by the Church of Scientology. Notwithstanding all of the foregoing, I have approached this subject as I would any historical project with what I trust is a non-partisan, objective perspective.

2 *R v Stewart*, [1988] 1 SCR 963 an appeal from a judgment of the Ontario Court of Appeal (1983), 42 OR (2d) 225, 149 DLR (3d) 583, 5 CCC (3d) 481, 74 CPR (2d) 1, 35 CR (3d) 105, allowing the Crown's appeal from a judgment of the Ontario High Court of Justice (1982), 38 OR (2d) 84, 138 DLR (3d) 73, 68 CCC (2d) 305, 74 CPR (2d) 4, acquitting the accused on charges of counselling to commit the offence of theft and fraud. Appeal allowed.

3 Richard B Potter, "If someone steals a secret has theft been committed?," *The Globe and Mail* (22 September 1988) A7.

4 See for example, Robert WK Davis and Scott C Hutchison, *Computer Crime in Canada* (Toronto 1997) at 144 and John Hull, *Commercial Secrecy: Law and Practice* (London 1998) at para 2.38.

5 *La Societe d'informatique RDG Inc v Dynobec et autres* [1984] CS 1189; *IBM Corp v Ordinateurs Spirales Inc* (1985), 27 Business Law Reports 191; *Apple Computer Inc v Mackintosh Computers Ltd et al* (1985), 3 Canadian Patent Cases (3d) 34; and *Apple Computer Inc v Mackintosh Computers Ltd et al* (1986), 10 CPR (3d) 1.

6 [1976] 2 SCR 200.

7 See P Girard and J Phillips, "A Certain Malaise: *Harrison v Carswell*, Shopping Centre Picketing and the Limits of the Post-War Settlement" in J Fudge and E Tucker, eds, *Work on Trial: Canadian Labour Law Struggles* (Toronto: Osgoode Society for Canadian Legal History and Irwin Law, 2010) 241.

8 Dated 10 July 1974

9 Cited in [1981] OLRB Rep. December 1763

10 *The Globe and Mail* (26 June 1982) 4. Confirmed in an interview with Stewart's counsel, Robert A McNeely, conducted by telephone in October 2009.

11 *Toronto Star* (26 June 1982) A8.

12 Now s 464 of the Criminal Code.

13 Arnold Weinrib, "Information and Property" (1988) 38 UTLJ 117 at 128.

14 R. Grant Hammond, "Quantum Physics, Econometric Models and Property Rights to Information," (1981) 27 McGill L J 47 at 68.

15 See Macdonald Commission, National Security: the Legal Dimensions by ML Friedland, (June 1979) at 31-32.

16 Now s 380.

17 Now s 224.

18 Now s 430.

19 Annotation, *R v Stewart*, (1984) 24 BLR 53 at 55.

20 Personal email to the author in connection with the writing of the history of the Computer Law Association on its 35th anniversary.

21 Now s 326.

22 *R v McLaughlin* (1980), 53 CCC (2d) 417; (1980) 18 CR (3d) 339 (SCC).

23 See the discussion in R Grant Hammond, "Theft of Information" (1984) 100 LQR 252 at 253.

24 See his discussion in *Report of the Commission of Inquiry into the Confidentiality of Health Information*, Vol 1 (Toronto: Queen's Printer, 30 September 1980) (The Hon. Mr. Justice Horace Krever) at c 1.

25 I was a research assistant on this project. See Martin L. Friedland, *My Life in Crime and Other Academic Adventures* (Toronto: University of Toronto Press, 2007) at 234-253.

26 The cases brought against Peter Treu in 1978 and against *The Toronto Sun* in 1979 had been much criticized.

27 For a discussion of this political context see John English, "Pierre Elliott Trudeau" in *Canada's Prime Ministers Macdonald to Trudeau* (2007) 441. There is a fuller discussion in John English, *Just Watch Me: The Life of Pierre Elliott Trudeau 1968-2000* (2009), cc. 14 & 15.

28 At pp 51-52.

29 At page 69.

30 Personal interview of McNeely (October 2009).

31 Budzinski, a graduate of New College at the University of Toronto, would later be appointed to the Ontario bench and become a judge noted for his interest in dealing with defendants with special needs and in encouraging programs to allow young people to better understand the judicial process. See, for example, *Ontario Justice Education Network Update* (Fall 2004) 8.

32 Justice Dickson's reasons for judgment in *Regina v Olan, Hudson and Hartnett* (1978), 41 CCC (2d) 145 at 150.

33 *Regina v Falconi* (1976), 31 CCC (2d) 144 at 148.

34 *Report of the Commission of Inquiry into the Confidentiality of Health Information*, (Toronto: Queen's Printer, 30 September 1980) (The Hon. Mr. Justice Horace Krever).

35 See Robert Gellman, "Trafficking in Health Information: A Widespread Problem" online: http://bobgellman.com/rg-docs/rg-health-traffic.pdf at 3-5.

36 Based on interview of Horace Krever (30 September 2009)

37 *Report of the Royal Commission*, vol 1 at 274-77.

38 *Report of the Royal Commission*, vol 1 at 3.

39 Based on interview of McNeely (October 2009).

40 *R v Stewart* [1982] OJ No. 635, Ontario Supreme Court - High Court of Justice, Krever J. Heard: 5 and 30 April 1982, Judgment: 25 June 1982. (24 pp) at pp 1-2.

41 From personal interview of Horace Krever (September 2009).
42 *R v Stewart* [1982] OJ No. 635 at para 4 page 5.
43 At para 10, page 10.
44 In *Regina v Bird*, [1970] 3 CCC 340, 9 CRNS 1
45 In *Regina v Scallen* (1974), 15 CCC (2d) 441
46 These cases included *United States v Seagraves*, 265 F 2d 876 (3rd Circ. 1959), *United States v Lester*, 282 F 2d 750 (3rd Circ. 1960) and *United States v Bottone* 365 F 2d 389 (2nd Circ. 1966)
47 *United States v Lambert*, 446 F Supp. 890 (D. Conn. 1978), aff'd *sub nom United States v Girard*, 601 F 2d 69 (2 Circ. 1979), cert. denied 444 US 871, 100 S. Ct. 148, (1979) and *United States v May*, 625 F 2d 186 (9th Circ. 1980)
48 18 USCA 564 (1970)
49 From interview of McNeely (October 2009).
50 From interview of Krever (September, 2009).
51 (1974), 15 CCC (2d) 441 at p. 473, [1974] 4 WWR 345.
52 Para 2 page 2.
53 Para 6 page 3.
54 *The Globe and Mail* (15 July 1983) 5.
55 *Ibid* at paras. 7-18.
56 See, for example, Amos, Note (1984) 1 *Intellectual Property Journal* 77; Hayhurst, Note (1983) 12 *European Intellectual Property Review* 261; Hitchcock, "Intellectual Property Infringement as Criminal Fraud" (1984) 1 *Canadian Intellectual Property Review* 182; and CI Kyer, Annotation to *R v Stewart* (1984) 24 Business Law reports 55.
57 Christopher Millard, *Legal Protection of Computer Programs and Data* (London: 1985) at 158-161.
58 See Alberta, Institute of Law Research and Reform and a Federal Provincial Working Party, *Report 46: Trade* Secrets (Edmonton: Institute of Law Research and Reform, July 1986) at 2-3.
59 R Grant Hammond, "Theft of Information" (1984) 100 LQR 252.
60 *Ibid* at 253.
61 *Ibid* at 253.
62 *Ibid* at 255.
63 *Ibid* at 259.
64 *Ibid* at 263.
65 Above note 58 at 138.
66 At page 221.
67 From personal interview of McNeely (October 2009).
68 *The Globe and Mail* (10 December 1974) 5.
69 *The Globe and Mail* (22 July 1974) 1-2; *The Globe and Mail* (26 July 1974) 5; *The Globe and Mail* (27 December 1975) 5.
70 *The Globe and Mail* (19 December 1974) 5.
71 *The Globe and Mail* (17 August 1974) 5.
72 *The Globe and Mail* (18 May 1976) 2.
73 The decision is reported at 19 Ontario Reports 62.

74 In December 1985 Nanna Anderson pleaded guilty to stealing documents from the Ontario Medical Association, at the behest of the Church of Scientology, between November 1976 and March 1983.

75 *The Globe and Mail* (9 July 1977) 5.

76 *The Globe and Mail* (8 August 1978) 5 and *The Globe and Mail* (7 December 1979) 20. Of twelve indicted, nine were convicted and sentenced by a US District Court in Washington. The highest-ranking of the nine was Mary Sue Hubbard, who received the maximum sentence of a $10,000 fine and five years in prison. Her husband, Scientology founder L. Ron Hubbard, was one of twenty-three people named as unindicted co-conspirators.

77 *The Globe and Mail* (9 June 1980) 5.

78 The articles in the series were entitled "Hubbard Still gave orders, records show" *The Globe and Mail* (14 January 1980) 11; "Secret Ontario documents found in US cult's files" *The Globe and Mail* (22 January 1980) 1-2; "Cult harassment, spying in Canada documented" *The Globe and Mail* (23 January 1980); "Files show spy reported woman's intimate words" *The Globe and Mail* (24 January 1980) 10; "The Hidden Hubbard" *The Globe and Mail* (25 January 1980) 4.

79 "100 Officers Raid Scientology Centre" *The Globe and Mail* (4 March 1983) 1-2

80 The subsequent 1991 indictment on these charges forms the case in chief, i.e., *The Queen v Church of Scientology of Toronto, et. al.*

81 *Re Church of Scientology and The Queen (No. 1)* (1984), 13 CCC (3d) 93, 9 DLR (4th) 721, 46 OR (2d) 449; *Re Church of Scientology and The Queen (No. 2)* (1984), 13 CCC (3d) 97, 10 DLR (4th) 312, 47 OR (2d) 86; *Re Church of Scientology and The Queen (No. 2)* (1984), 15 CCC (3d) 190n, 13 DLR (4th) 639n, 47 OR (2d) 765n (Addendum); *Re Church of Scientology and The Queen (No. 3)* (1984), 13 CCC (3d) 353, 10 DLR (4th) 711, 47 OR (2d) 90; *Re Church of Scientology and The Queen (No. 3)*, above; *Re Church of Scientology and The Queen (No. 4)* (1985), 17 CCC (3d) 499; *R. v Church of Scientology (No. 5)* (1985), 18 CCC (3d) 244; *Re Church of Scientology et al. and The Queen (No. 6)*; *Re Walsh et al. and The Queen* (1985), 21 CCC (3d) 147, 15 CRR 23. *R v Zaharia and Church of Scientology of Toronto* (1985), 21 CCC (3d) 118 & 23 CCC (3d) 192, 5 CPC (2d) 92). Also see Court of Appeal 1987 CanLII 122 (ON CA).

82 See, for example, *The Globe and Mail* (11 March 1983) 5.

83 RSO 1980, c 256.

84 On 7 December 1984. See 13 WCB 231.

85 For a detailed review of the facts see *Hill v Church of Scientology of Toronto*, [1995] 2 SCR 1130.

86 In *R v Offley* (1986), 28 CCC (3d) 1

87 2nd edition at p. 717.

88 *Oxford v Moss*, (1978) Cr. App. R 183.

89 See his discussion of the case in Arnold S Weinrib, "Information and Property" (1988) 38 UTLJ 117 at 123.

90 *Ibid*. It was ready for publication but not yet published in the *University of Toronto Law Journal*. In an interview Weinrib admitted that he provided his soon to be pub-

lished article to Jeff Casey of the Ontario AG's office and also provided advice on how to counter certain arguments made by Hammond.

91 At pages 117-18.

92 At page 140.

93 Richard B Potter, "If someone steals a secret has theft been committed?" *The Globe and Mail* (22 September 1988) A7.

94 The firms and organizations were Fasken & Calvin, a law firm of which I would become a partner in 1988; Goodman & Goodman; the College of Physicians and Surgeons of Ontario; the Ontario Medical Association; the Canadian Mental Health Association; the Ontario Provincial Police; the Metropolitan Toronto Police; the Attorney General of Ontario; Royal Canadian Mounted Police.

95 Then s. 111 of RSC 1970, c. C-34 (now RSC 1985, c C-46, s 122)

96 *R v Church of Scientology of Toronto*, (1996) 33 OR (3d) 65, 116 CCC (3d) 1 CanLII 1650 (ON CA).

97 Changes were made to create certain computer related crimes. See Robert WK Davis and Scott C Hutchison, *Computer Crime in Canada* (Toronto: Carswell, 1997).

Begging to Differ: Panhandling, Public Space, and Municipal Property[1]

Nicholas Blomley

Introduction

THE *FEDERATED ANTI-POVERTY GROUPS of B.C. v Vancouver* case,[2] concerning the constitutionality of a City of Vancouver bylaw regulating panhandling, marks the first and (to my knowledge) only time that the recent wave of Canadian municipal panhandling regulation has received constitutional scrutiny. It has been overshadowed somewhat by *Banks*,[3] which upheld provincial law regulating panhandling and squeegeeing in Ontario and the 2008 *Adams*[4] case, involving the constitutionality of the City of Victoria's bylaw regulating camping in public property.

Yet it is worth exploring. What is the significance of the case to a discussion of property in Canadian law? At its core is a conflict over the nature and function of public property.[5] While several chapters in this collection track the state's relationship to private ordering (Phillips and Martin, Harris, Kaplinsky), the dominant focus tends to be private property itself. However, public property is far from a residual concern, but deserving of attention in its own right. Indeed, *Federated* echoes themes evident in many of the other cases reviewed in this book, including the vexed and important question of the relation between property and social power, or the contested nature of the public interest.

More immediately, I want to argue that *Federated* reveals an important and often overlooked tension concerning the uses to which public property is to be put. For opponents and proponents of the bylaw beyond the state, the sidewalk is the material manifestation of the public sphere, a site for democratic dialogue, the production of citizenship, and the exercise of rights. The sidewalk, therefore, is to be understood as public space. Conversely, for the City (and, ultimately, the court), the sidewalk is municipal space, to be governed according to a narrowly defined public interest, that being understood as circulation.

I begin by providing a brief overview of the regulation of panhandling in Canada, and then note its more recent controversial history in Vancouver, including the decision to launch a *Charter* challenge. I note the manner in which both sides engaged in the public controversy around panhandling regulation, deployed a common understanding of public property as serving important political ends. Rights, whether those of the panhandler to express herself, or the pedestrian to freely circulate, are appropriately exercised in such publicly owned spaces. In the third section of the paper, which reviews the legal arguments made in the case, and the ultimate judgment, I contrast this view with a very different rendering of the sidewalks of Vancouver. Viewed as municipal property, the City successfully argued for a view of its sidewalks as serving functional, apolitical ends, notably the facilitation of circulation, and the prevention of obstruction. The panhandler, consequently, was re-imagined as neither a rights-bearer nor a threat to rights, but simply as a potential obstacle. I conclude with some reflections on the prevalence of this latter view, and its broader implications.

In keeping with the theme of this collection, I thus consider the case by telling some of its stories, of which there are several. Those who lobbied the City for panhandling regulation, for example, projected stories of the city's uncertain trajectory in the face of mass public homelessness. Protagonists in the judicial dispute also deployed conflicting stories of public property. But given that histories are necessarily tied up with the spaces and places of social and legal life,[6] I also point to the important spatial dimensions at issue in these various narratives. The conjunction of circumstances that gave rise to the regulation, at issue in *Federated*, can be understood with reference to the particularities of Canadian downtowns as platforms of consumption and investment in an era characterized by the increasing mobility of capital. Moreover, the decision itself turns, in one sense, on competing representations of the spaces of public property. Is a sidewalk an agora, or a conduit of circulation?

Vagrancy Law and the City

THE REGULATION OF VAGRANCY has been a long-standing concern within Canada, even prior to Confederation.[7] In 1869 the Canadian Parliament passed a vagrancy act substantially similar to the *English Vagrancy Act* (1824) entitled *An Act Respecting Vagrants*[8] by which those "persons who . . . wander about and beg . . . shall be deemed vagrants, loose, idle or disorderly persons." Offenders were subject to up to two months incarceration and a fine not exceeding $50. By 1874, the period of incarceration was increased to six months.

Provisions dealing with begging and vagrancy were included in the *Canadian Criminal Code* upon its introduction in 1892, making it an offence to beg "from door to door in a public place" and to not have any apparent means of support when found "wandering abroad and trespassing." In 1972, these sections were repealed.[9] The underlying rationale for these reforms " . . . was the overwhelming belief that vagrancy – and in particular, begging and wandering in public without apparent means of support – was not a crime, that vagrants were not criminals, and this problem posed little harm to society, if any. If however, these matters needed to be addressed legislatively, the criminal law was seen as the inappropriate tool."[10] Liberal-minded reformers also characterized the vagrancy offence as a violation of equality rights. As the Minister of Justice, Otto Lang, argued in Parliament:

> The offence of vagrancy has been applied in many different ways in the legal system . . . . Here we have an offence which has been applied differently to the rich and to the poor in our society and we propose to move against this difference in application . . . . [T]he changes are necessary in order to try in some way to attain greater fairness in our law as applied to the privileged and to those who are less privileged, to the rich and to the poor.[11]

The Parliamentary debates also reveal the licence granted to local governments to deal with vagrancy. Vagrancy, it was asserted, was not a matter of criminal law.[12] As such, municipalities and provinces were said to be better suited to dealing with the local vagaries of the issue. For the Minister of Justice:

> the sections dealing with vagrancy here are being repealed as really being too vague for the purposes of the criminal law. With respect to the vagrancy offence of begging, it is not considered that this is a proper matter to continue

> as part of the criminal law. *We believe that if legislation is needed in this regard, it would be best to have it by way of municipal bylaw or provincial legislation.*[13]

Thus it was that, two years later, on 22 January 1974, Vancouver enacted section 70A of the *Streets and Traffic Bylaw,* which amounted to an absolute ban on panhandling ("Other than the holder of a licence to solicit for charity no person shall use any street or any part thereof for the purpose of begging or seeking or receiving alms for himself or herself or on behalf of any other person"). Judging by local media coverage, this was not deemed a significant event, *The Vancouver Sun* devoting only a few paragraphs to it.[14] However, just a few months later, Sedgwick J overturned the bylaw in the British Columbia Provincial Court, ruling that the Vancouver Charter did not provide the requisite authority for a regulation that made no reference to pedestrians, traffic, or the control of those who impede traffic, leaving the City without direct regulation of panhandling.[15]

This lacuna does not seem to have been a pressing concern, at least initially. However, subsequent decades saw important shifts in the landscape of Canadian cities such as Vancouver.[16] Cities in general, and downtowns in particular, became increasingly socially polarized. On the one hand, downtown Vancouver became home to a growing middle class population. While in the early 1970s, workers in advanced services were underrepresented in the Canadian central city, by the 1990s "one [was] more likely to meet a senior white collar white worker on an inner-city street than in a suburban mall."[17] By 1996 the decline in relative inner city income had been halted for several metropolitan areas, including Vancouver.[18] Yet downtowns also saw a growing population of low-income people. Scholars have documented a growing economic gap in the Vancouver CMA between 1990 and 1995,[19] such that the "glittering new inner-city landscapes and the increasingly marginalized communities of the Downtown Eastside and other sites of deprivation present a far more polarized profile of urban form and social conditions . . . ."[20] Although exact numbers are hard to come by, Canadian downtowns also saw a burgeoning population of homeless people.

With this general increase in street homelessness, the 1990s saw a growing number of panhandlers on city streets, prompting debate and disagreement concerning the appropriate response to visible public poverty. While some Vancouverites grappled with the moral challenges that panhandling presented,[21] or sought to come to an understanding of the panhandler him or herself, noting that "panhandlers have become so prevalent they have become part of the city's fabric,"[22] others lamented the decline in the Canadian city occasioned by the "swelling number of aggressive indigents,"[23] complaining that on downtown streets, "hundreds of vagrants can be found in strategic locations with palms extended or caps set before them . . . . Panhandlers block pedestrian passage and aggressively plant themselves in front of bank entrances and bus stops."[24] Merchants characterized panhandlers as "hunters," as a "disgust [sic] and embarrassment,"[25] and as "professional street extortionists."[26] "On every street corner," warned a restaurant owner, "lurks a panhandler, ready to prey on whomever they judge to be their next likely benefactor."[27]

A number of working groups and task forces were formed during the 1990s to develop and implement panhandling strategies, including public education and outreach programs. Various city Business Improvement Associations funded outreach and "redirected giving" programs, or hired security officers to encourage panhandlers to relocate. Downtown merchants and other businesses placed increasing pressure on the City to regulate panhandling. The Downtown Vancouver Business Improvement Association and Tourism Vancouver hosted a visit by "broken-windows" advocate George Kelling on 6 March 1997 where he presumably advocated for a crackdown on panhandling, echoing his influential argument that to tolerate such forms of "disorder" was to invite more serious crime.[28] As part of its deposition in *Federated*, the City submitted a sample of correspondence it had received from 1992–1999 on panhandling , the vast majority of which favoured either regulation or an outright ban on panhandling, urging the City to "get these people off of the streets," as one correspondent put it. The authors include individual citizens, condo strata councils, and aggrieved tourists, as well as powerful players such as Eaton's Department Store, Heritage Canada, the Robson Street BIA, the Vancouver Hotel Association, and Tourism Vancouver.

These business anxieties concerning panhandling were fully predictable, reflecting the political economy of downtown investment (although one must note, in passing, the interesting irony whereby small monetary transactions are deemed problematic in a locale predicated on the transfer of money). Canadian downtowns have long consumed a high proportion of investment in the built environment, historically commanding higher land prices. Downtown cores in cities such as Vancouver have seen significant investments in office development, as well as waterfront redevelopment, sports complexes, and residential construction.[29] The development of the Concord Pacific property in downtown Vancouver is a striking example, still unfolding. When completed, it is estimated that it will house 15,000 people, at a total cost of C$3 billion.[30] Downtowns also retained a significant proportion of retail investment.

Yet the 1990s also saw growing anxiety about the stability of these investments, particularly given a heightened sense of both the benefits as well as the potential costs of liquid capitalism. A *National Post* article in 2000 argued that "you have to keep investing in downtowns, they are very fragile."[31] Even Vancouver's relative success in sustaining a strong downtown provided no guarantee of future success. The "beggar my neighbour" character of contemporary urban competition fostered a highly uncertain environment. While much less intense than the "voices of decline" observable in US cities,[32] a growing number of pundits and observers began expressing concern at the stability of the Canadian downtown, with some worrying at the possibility of US styled "doughnut cities."[33] This was understandably more intense in economically challenged inner cities such as that of Winnipeg, yet even shiny Vancouver was far from immune.

The stability of the downtown retail sector was a particularly pressing concern. Canadian commerce became increasingly suburbanized, with large format retail and "power centres" developing to serve a growing suburban population. The 1990s saw significant declines in the level of downtown retail sales (down 15.7 percent between 1990 and 1998). Vancouver did not fare so poorly, yet it did experience a 2.5 percent drop (although downtown sales did see a modest increase between 1999 and 2001). In 1989, about twelve cents of every retail dollar in the Vancouver metropolitan area was spent downtown. By 1998, this had declined to just under 10 cents.[34]

While the causes of these shifts in market share are undoubtedly complex, the growing number of the public poor in general, and the panhandler in particular, provided an easy and obvious target. Advocates of panhandling bylaws across Canada argued that the activities of beggars had to be proscribed in order to preserve the economic vitality of downtown areas, and in particular the viability of retailing.[35] It was suggested by both city governments and merchants' associations that downtown retailers lost significant custom as a result of the presence of panhandlers, who deterred shoppers from particular stores by standing near their doors, and perhaps from visiting the downtown core altogether. Although such claims are seldom verified, anti-poverty groups worried at their effects upon municipal public policy in Canada.[36]

Similarly, the panhandler became an obvious target of urban-economic anxieties in Vancouver. One concerted campaign of public pressure came from the Gastown Business Improvement Association, a tourist district within the low-income Downtown Eastside. Members were encouraged by the BIA to submit letters, to be forwarded to City Hall, explaining how aggressive panhandling affected their business. These letters warned, repeatedly, of the negative image that panhandling portrays. For example, the manufacturer of Gastown's landmark steam clock sent a stern letter with photos of a recumbent street person lying in front of the clock, wondering "What is the image about the community of Gastown that visitors will take home with them?"[37] For another, "[e]ach time one person has a bad experience in the Gastown area they tend to tell their friends, and down the line it goes, resulting in Gastown having a poor public image."[38] The City was accused of abandoning Gastown: "One thing has now become abundantly clear to those of us who love this area enough to try to sustain the businesses that will keep it vibrant – and that is not to hold your breath thinking that the City will help, as it is obviously both powerless and rudderless . . . . "[39] Another drew on biological metaphors, noting that "in nature, the parasite generally doesn't kill the host as it is not in its best interest. What we are seeing now is that . . . the host is dying."[40]

Faced with such pressures, City politicians began exploring regulatory options. In 1997, Inspector Dave Jones of the Vancouver Police Department filed an information report on panhandling for City Council.[41] Jones could not resist editorializing, offering some striking characterizations of the various categories of panhandler, such as the "street kid wannabees . . . engaged in a minor rebellion against what they might view as constrained lives"[42]; offered exposes of frauds, such as the "blind" panhandler who, without benefit of divine intervention, reacquired their sight and ability to walk without a crutch once they passed from sight into a lane; and warned that, in the case of the addicted beggar, the giver "defeats their own social system, enabling the panner to continue their life of substance abuse and rejection of personal responsibility."[43]

Jones considered a variety of options for regulation, highlighting problems with attempts at a blanket ban on panhandling (as reportedly proposed by the Board of Trade, which also proposed restraining the act of giving to panhandlers). It was also suggested that such blanket bans may "run the risk of triggering a local social conscience."[44] A bylaw in Winnipeg was noted as a useful template, in combination with a consistent program of police enforcement of "no let up and no different message,"[45] with the added suggestion that a nighttime ban be imposed.

Jones' report appears to have been influential. A City Report in April 1998 noted that:

> while enforcement is apparently an attractive option, it is difficult to achieve. A previous City by-law to prohibit begging was struck down. By-laws to regulate panhandling have been passed in both Winnipeg and New Westminster, although the Winnipeg by-law is currently being challenged. The New Westminster by-law is relatively new, and to date, has not been challenged in court. When considering the introduction of a by-law, it is important to note that the broader the by-law, (and hence the more effective), the more likely it will be successfully challenged. In view of the fact that the city's earlier attempt to create an absolute prohibition of begging on all city streets without a licence was not successful, should Council choose to enact a by-law regulating panhandling, it should apply only to areas and in circumstances identified as those where panhandling has created the greatest problems.[46]

Accordingly, the Director of Legal Services proposed a bylaw based on the Winnipeg and New Westminster templates.[47] On 30 April 1998, the City passed bylaw number 7885. This forbade panhandling within ten metres of the entrance to a bank or liquor store, ATM, bus stop or shelter, or from the occupant of a motor vehicle. It also disallowed panhandling from sunset to sunrise; sitting or lying on a street while panhandling; and panhandling from a person after a refusal, with fines ranging up to $2,000.[48] Speakers from Tourism Vancouver and several BIAs and Merchant Organizations spoke in support at Council, expressing concern at the increasing numbers of aggressive and persistent panhandlers, which was said to constrain tourism and threaten the City's reputation as a safe, clean, and enjoyable city.[49] One observer celebrated the fact that, finally, "bums and beggars will not rule the streets."[50]

At Council, anti-poverty organizers and civil libertarians countered with claims that the bylaw penalized the poor, was intolerant, and violated expressive rights. An activist complained that "[i]t's horrible to divide the sidewalk between the rich and poor. What they've done here is put up a fence so people can ignore panhandlers, because the whole idea makes them feel uncomfortable."[51] But criticism came from more established interests. Unexpectedly, the editorial board of *The Vancouver Sun* called for the bylaw to be "run out of town" as "an assault on civil liberties." A city's sidewalks, it noted, are "public property that belong to everyone." Council was attempting to make "non-crimes in public places illegal" and as such, the bylaw deserved to be overturned by the courts.[52] John Dixon of the BC Civil Liberties Association concurred, claiming that "[m]y Labrador retriever could get a successful judicial review of this bylaw . . . ."[53] Anti-poverty activists stormed City Council in June in protest at the bylaw, leading to several arrests. A subsequent meeting between Council and protestors saw the latter raising issues of the rights of people to use public spaces, and the argument that the bylaw "just sends a strong message to poor people that they're pieces of crap."[54] Activists went so far as to openly challenge the bylaw by staging a "Pan-in," alleging that police and private security were using the bylaw to abuse their authority.[55] Nevertheless, many other Canadian cities, including Saskatoon, Calgary, and Burnaby began considering similar bylaws, modelled on the Vancouver regulations.

In May 1999, the BC Public Interest Advocacy Centre (BCPIAC), acting on behalf of three anti-poverty organizations — National Anti-Poverty Organization (NAPO), federated anti-poverty groups of bc (fapg), and End Legislated Poverty (ELP) — petitioned the British Columbia Supreme Court to declare the bylaw unconstitutional, arguing that the bylaw was *ultra vires* the *Vancouver Charter*, and a violation of sections 2, 7, and 15 of the *Charter*. In its newsletter, BCPIAC characterized the bylaw as an attack on the poor, and a capitulation to the wishes of businesses.[56] *The Vancouver Sun* again editorialized that it was time to rescind a bylaw deemed ineffective, and now entangled in costly litigation.[57]

BCPIAC is a non-profit formed in 1981, with the mission of advancing the interests and rights of under-represented groups and interests through litigation. Patricia McDonald, counsel for BCPIAC, noted that ELP, a Vancouver organization, was the catalyst for the challenge, organizing a series of community meetings, and subsequently approaching BCPIAC to query the legality of the bylaw. NAPO was simultaneously involved in a challenge to Winnipeg's bylaw. The involvement of ELP and fapg gave BCPIAC an association with national, provincial, and municipal anti-poverty organizations. Attempts were made to have individuals charged under the bylaw so as to trigger a test case, but this proved difficult, with suggestions that the authorities were reluctant to ticket in order to avoid triggering a constitutional challenge.[58] As a result, the anti-poverty organizations acted on behalf of panhandlers.

Matters became complicated, however, when the City of Winnipeg repealed its panhandling bylaw in 2000 in the face of a similar *Charter* challenge, initiated by NAPO, after a judge questioned its constitutional validity during pre-trial hearings. NAPO reached an out of court settlement with the City, agreeing to discontinue a legal challenge to the bylaw.[59] In return, the City repealed its panhandling bylaw and replaced it with a bylaw "to control obstructive solicitation for donations" that simply made it an offence to solicit in a manner that causes an obstruction (that is, to obstruct or impede, to continue to solicit after a negative response, to verbally threaten to insult a pedestrian, or to solicit in a group of three or more).[60]

This was widely characterized in the media as a victory for NAPO, which called on other cities to "sit up and pay attention."[61] Indeed, they seem to have done so. In September 2000, Victoria considered abandoning its panhandling bylaw, with the mayor noting that he "was not interested in wasting money or time in court if we don't have to."[62]

In March 2001, just two weeks before the challenge was to be heard in court, Vancouver also elected to repeal its bylaw, to be replaced with slightly less sweeping regulations, formalized as amendments to the Streets and Traffic Bylaw. As one commentator noted, "[d]espite its concerns about vagrancy, city council is learning that even bums and beggars have rights under the Canadian Charter of Rights and Freedoms."[63]

As an aside, some suggested that maps (Figure 1), prepared for BCPIAC by a graduate student, Lorraine Chisholm, in the Department of Geography at Simon Fraser University, played a role in the City's decision to revise the original bylaw. These simply mapped out areas in which panhandling was forbidden along Granville Street, a major city thoroughfare. The effect, as was later noted in *Federated*, was "draconian."[64]

Despite the City's move, BCPIAC did not abandon its challenge, worrying that if the revised bylaw were allowed to stand, more punitive US style restrictions would be forthcoming (this during a period of provincial welfare cutbacks, and also at a time when Ontario was embroiled with protests over the proposed *Safe Streets Act*, itself facing judicial scrutiny). Sympathetic observers also concluded that the revised regulations still entailed a powerful form of depersonalization, being "part of a powerful, if subterranean, collective wish to erase the spectacle of people asking for money altogether" that ignored the fact that "panhandlers are people too."[65]

The revised bylaw was different in at least two senses. First, it was somewhat less wide ranging, both in time and in space. The ban on any night-

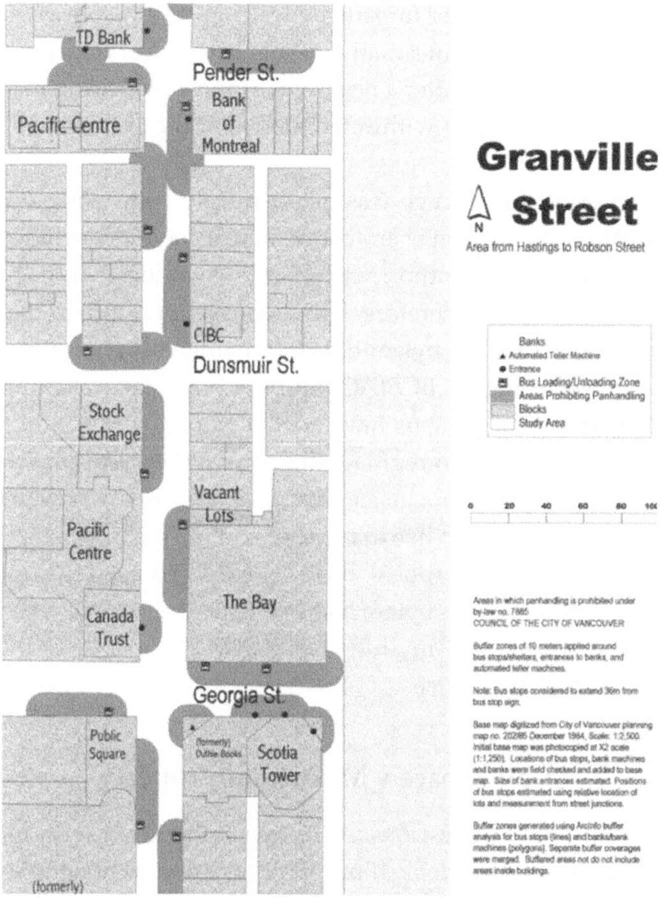

Figure 1. Areas in which panhandling is prohibited under bylaw number 7885: Granville Street, Vancouver.

time panhandling was dropped, as were prohibitions on panhandling at bus stops, bus shelters, or the entrance to liquor stores. Secondly, and, as we shall see, more importantly, unlike its predecessor, it used a language of obstruction and circulation, with no express reference to panhandling. As the City Manager noted in his report: "The proposed amendments consist of provisions which regulate the solicitation for donations carried out in a manner which obstructs free movement on streets and sidewalks and obstruction in the form of "persistent" panhandling. Their objective is to regulate the use of city streets in a manner that acknowledges the varied interests of all people who use the streets."[66] The bylaw forbade "solicitation" in a manner that "causes an obstruction." An obstruction was defined as sitting or lying in a street so as to obstruct or impede pedestrian traffic, soliciting from the occupant of a motor vehicle in a manner that obstructs or impedes vehicular traffic, continuing to solicit after a negative response, soliciting in a group of three or more, and soliciting within ten metres of the entrance of a bank or an ATM.

The constitutional challenge was heard in July 2001, with judgment in March 2002. The City won on every count. Justice Taylor concluded that the City of Vancouver had the authority to enact bylaw 8309; that the bylaw was not a criminal matter and, therefore, fell under section 92(16) of the *Constitution Act* (1867); and that the bylaw did not infringe sections 2(b), 7, and 15 of the *Charter*. Nevertheless, BCPIAC put on a brave face, arguing that the decision confirmed that persons have a right to panhandle, and that it set limits on the City's ability to regulate the panhandler. The case, moreover, "provided an opportunity to educate the public, the media and government about the rights of those who live in poverty and the discrimination they are subject to."[67] Electing not to appeal, BCPIAC consoled itself by arguing that the challenge to the original bylaw had been successful. Yet, that said, it is hard to conclude that it was anything but a clear affirmation of the validity of the City's regulatory scheme.

Public Space v Municipal Property

Federated entails many questions. At its heart, though, I wish to argue, is an important and often overlooked property question. While the streets and sidewalks of Vancouver are a form of public property, are they held by the people as a collective, to be used for civic means? Or are they municipal property, held by the City of Vancouver, to serve an administratively defined "public interest"?

The former view, interestingly, seems shared by proponents and opponents of public space regulations such as Vancouver's bylaw. Despite their differences, both rely upon characterization of the sidewalk as "political" (although, of course, with somewhat different readings of politics). In an influential call for the regulation of street disorder in the US, Ellickson characterizes "open-access public spaces," like the street, as "precious,"[68] in part because of their democratic potential, allowing for political "gatherings and mixings."[69] A diverse society, he argues, "requires venues where people of all back- grounds can rub elbows."[70] Similarly, leftists such as Don Mitchell see public space as a crucial site for civic engagement, encounters with difference, and the emergence of alternative claims to political standing.[71]

While both those who opposed the Vancouver bylaw, and those who advocated for it, would presumably recognize the sidewalk as public property, this frequently took on a particular meaning. While the state may be called upon to regulate (or desist from doing so), "public" ownership does not seem to be coterminous with state ownership. Rather, the public was characterized as necessarily and appropriately distinct from the state.[72] One variant of this, echoed in much of the public space literature, saw the sidewalk as the material manifestation of a Habermasian public sphere, set apart from both state and private actors. The sidewalk, in this sense, was "the people's property."[73] Others saw the sidewalk as a reflection of an ordered community of strangers, ideally predicated on respect and civility. For one editorialist,[74] given that public spaces are spaces we share with strangers, "we must be spared the things we absolutely would not have there . . . . If you want beggars in your living room, go right ahead. But public spaces shouldn't contain things that offend a significant number of people, and beggars do. It's time the cops moved them along." For opponents of the bylaw, the publicness of the sidewalk was compromised to the extent that panhandlers were constrained or excluded. Others insisted that the panhandler threatened the very publicness of the sidewalk, as their mere presence threatened norms of order and appropriate behaviour. Yet, in both cases, a coherent, organic public was invoked.

Obviously, proponents and opponents of regulation differ in how they view the place of law in the governance of public space. For Ellickson, law is a precondition for shared use; for Mitchell, it is potentially its undoing. But in both cases, rights play a crucial role. For Ellickson, rules of street behaviour must not be seen as a violation of freedom, but as a foundation of it. Like Roberts' Rules of Order, he argues, they serve as a precondition for the flow of speech and the publicness of space. Street law, he insists, must not only respect the rights of the homeless, but also that of other street users.[75] Opponents, conversely, tend to focus on the rights of the poor. Waldron, for example, argues from negative liberty, noting that regulation governing behaviour in public (such as laws forbidding sleeping in parks) act with particular force upon the homeless. Such law, he argues, constitutes "one of the most callous and tyrannical exercises of power in human times."[76]

Outside the courtroom, opponents and proponents of Vancouver's bylaw alike characterized public space in general, and the begging encounter in particular, as a political site. Rights claims — to circulation, freedom, and autonomy — were frequently deployed. The letters of Gastown BIA members, noted above, were redolent with rights, often rolled into a concern at the bottom line. Thus, a cabaret owner worried about allowing "panhandlers to infringe upon the freedoms and rights of the individuals that visit or work in the Gastown area, thus having a detrimental effect on the businesses and economy of Gastown itself."[77] "Our objective is to attract the local and tourist industry to come to Vancouver and Gastown," noted another, "not to scare them away, as we too have rights, which sometimes are forgotten."[78]

Others worried that the *Charter* challenge to the City's bylaw redistributed rights to the advantage of the panhandler: " . . . it seems the local 'problem people' enjoy special privelidges [sic] not extended to normal law abiding citizens."[79] A furniture storeowner argued: "I have the right to live and work in an area free of intimidation and abuse. My business has the right to succeed from my hard work and personal investment. My livelihood is being effected [sic], please communicate my rights and disgust to the public interest groups attempting to strike down any bylaw giving the above mentioned individuals the power and freedom that they have stolen from me and many others."[80] Implied here is a view of a public sphere, and a public space, that was out of kilter, as a fragile collective ecology of rights and responsibilities was distorted by a few. The bylaw, in reining in these distortions, would reconstitute a civil public. A pub owner similarly lamented " . . . any attempts to strike down a bylaw that grants rights and freedoms to individuals who in turn thrive on stealing rights and freedoms from others."[81] "I do not believe we have ever agreed to abandon our basic right to an orderly and law abiding community" worried a property owner: "Any overturning of the existing minimal laws we have to protect us against these 'predators' will send the worst signal that, as a society, we have given up on the protection of the most basic rights of civil and law abiding citizens,"[82] such as the right to " . . . walk our streets free of harassment and intimidation by panhandlers."[83]

What then of the legal arguments of the City and BCPIAC? In conversation, Patricia McDonald, who represented the anti-poverty groups, noted that they had contemplated staying with a jurisdictional argument, but elected to also include a *Charter* challenge given BCPIAC's goal of advancing an anti-poverty agenda, arguing that "we're trying to change society with the kind of arguments that we make. We're trying to change policy and law . . . . We're really trying to push the envelope." ELP also pushed for a *Charter* challenge, there being a sense that a jurisdictional victory would be essentially a "technical" win. A *Charter* argument also allowed BCPIAC, as McDonald put it, to "educate" the court: "there are so many stereotypes about people who panhandle, as you very well know, and judges are part of society who have those stereotypes. And so they don't know what the reality is, or they forget the reality. And so then you want to remind them. This is who people are that panhandle, and this is why it's really important that they have rights."[84]

While BCPIAC obviously deployed different arguments than the aggrieved merchants, they too treated the streets of the CCity as a political space, charged with rights significance and "publicness."[85] They characterized the purpose of the bylaw as exclusionary and biased, motivated by a desire "to restrict and prohibit the speech and conduct of a class of persons — those who panhandle — to achieve the overall effect of restricting and prohibiting the intimidating and unsightly people who panhandle."[86] The restrictions placed upon panhandlers, they argued, negated the publicness of the sidewalk, a space of and for the people in the broadest sense. In so doing, not only were the rights of panhandlers compromised, but also their standing as citizens of the polity. The bylaw denied panhandlers "recognition as citizens of Vancouver, equally deserving of respect and dignity."[87] The effect was to deny their " . . . right to the use and enjoyment of public places in the City of Vancouver and . . . distance these people from the rest of the population."[88] The City "ha[d] not regulated *how* people can use our sidewalks and streets but *who* can use our sidewalks and streets."[89]

This was evident in their treatment of the right to expression. BCPIAC argued for the significance of expression as something available to all Canadians, regardless of who they were and what they said. Panhandling was characterized as a form of expression that embodied valued principles of participation, human flourishing, self-fulfillment, and the pursuit of truth. BCPIAC noted the value of the interaction associated with panhandling on self-realization and enlightenment, it being argued that this entailed valued engagement with others. Such speech did not occur in a vacuum, moreover, but was predicated on the engagements with others that can only occur in a fully public place. This echoes the comments of public space advocates, such as Marshall Berman: "the glory of modern public space is that it can pull together all the different sorts of people who are there. It can compel and empower all these people to see each other, not through a glass darkly, but face to face."[90] Put this way, public space not only provided a site where the public sphere can be found. It was itself the site where the potential of the public sphere was realized. For political theorist Iris Marion Young:

> Politics, the critical activity of raising issues and deciding how institutional and social relations should be organized, crucially depends on the existence of space and forums to which everyone has access. In such public spaces people encounter other people, meanings, expressions, issues, which they may not understand or with which they do not identify.[91]

BCPIAC drew from the argument of l'Heureux Dubé J in *Commonwealth*,[92] in which the publicness of a place was defined as a function of multiple factors, including the symbolic significance of the property for the message being communicated, and the impact of the availability of such property for expressive activity on the achievement of section 2(b)'s purposes. BCPIAC argued that streets have traditionally been venues for free expression and, citing *Hague v CIO*, that streets were property held in trust for the public, as a forum for "purposes of assembly, communicating thoughts between citizens, and discussing public questions."[93]

The City's argument, however, was strikingly different. The streets and sidewalks belonged to the City. This is not to say, however, that the sidewalk is a form of private property. Rather, the City administered its property so as to advance the "public interest." Rarely defined, this did not entail the facilitation of politics and the production of the public sphere, but the more technical goal of the advancement of circulation and the prevention of obstruction. The panhandler was characterized not as a rights-bearing citizen, or as an objectionable affront to the "public," but as a potential obstacle, akin to other people or objects.

The difference between these two visions became strikingly evident in an interview I conducted with a City representative, in which I sought to explore the rights dimension to the case. He quickly resisted this line of enquiry, pointing out to me that as far as the City was concerned, the case was not about "civil rights," but rather about "civil engineering." Such a view was most clearly articulated by the affidavit of Rowan Birch, a Streets Administration Engineer with the City of Vancouver, which was quoted in the judgment. In it, he abstained from comments on poverty and rights, and simply described his work and its logic, which was governed, he deposed, by a quite particular mandate: "When carrying out my responsibilities, the most common and principal concern is the maintenance of a safe passage and a smooth and unobstructed pedestrian traffic flow on the City's sidewalks."[94] But "smooth" flow, he cautioned, is never guaranteed: "Streets and sidewalks constitute a finite public resource that is shared by a number of competing interests."[95] Strikingly, he categorized these interests according to their relative mobility (labelling them "moving and static elements.")[96] He then provided an extensive list of these elements based on his own observations, in which he moved seamlessly from people to things:

a) Pedestrians going from point A to point B, including pedestrians with visual or ambulatory disabilities;
b) Panhandlers;
c) Street vendors;
d) Street entertainers;
e) Pedestrians waiting for public transit;
f) Pedestrians waiting in line at an ATM;
g) Sundry workers needing sidewalk space to perform their duties (i.e. washing building windows, repairing underground utilities, etc.);
h) Sidewalk cafes;
i) Newspaper boxes;
j) Bus stops and bus shelters;
k) Street furniture;
l) Utility poles;
m) Parking meters;
n) Canada Post delivery boxes;
o) Trees;
p) Garbage bins;
q) Water fountains;
r) Fire hydrants;
s) Phone booths, etc. [97]

Pedestrians (going from point A to point B), it would seem, must navigate an exhaustively listed array of "static elements" that include people as well as inert things. The successful sidewalk, for Birch, is one in which the competition between the static and the moving resolved itself in favour of flow. Static objects are to be "positioned away from the flow of pedestrian traffic."[98] Unlike BCPIAC, Birch seemed uninterested in the inner life of the sidewalk user, or the effects of interactions between people. Moreover, circulation itself required no further justification, but appeared simply to be an uncontested and obvious end of civic regulation. Note also his characterization of the sidewalk as a "finite public resource" threatened by "competing interests," requiring state intervention. He attached numerous exhibits to his affidavit demonstrating Vancouver City Council's widespread concern "with the proper administration of the city's sidewalks"[99] and its "desire to facilitate pedestrian flow on its sidewalks,"[100] including memos, information packages, policy reports, and bylaws concerning street vending, produce and flower displays, sandwich board signs, sidewalk cafes, street entertainment programs, and newspaper boxes.

Such a view is remarkably widespread, although rarely analyzed. Elsewhere, I characterize this administrative logic as "pedestrianism," a view that understands the sidewalk as a finite public resource that is always threatened by multiple competing interests and uses.[101] The role of the authorities is to use law so as to arrange these bodies and objects in order to ensure that the primary function of the sidewalk is sustained: that being the orderly movement of pedestrians from point A to point B. Obstacles that impede flow are inherently suspect, according to this logic, and are to be limited or placed carefully so as to minimize blockage. The motivation or inner life of the pedestrian is not an issue, for pedestrianism, nor is their social standing. Beggars, protestors, commuters at a bus stop, or patrons at a sidewalk café are all potential obstructions. Some of those obstructions are manifested as things, such as fire hydrants or utility poles, and some as bodies, such as people waiting at a bus stop. The bus stop and the waiting transit user are in this sense comparable. Pedestrianism values public space not in terms of its aesthetic merits, or its success in promoting public citizenship and democracy. Rather, the successful sidewalk is one that facilitates pedestrian flow and circulation. Rather than seeking to promote and enhance a Habermasian public sphere that is distinct from the state, pedestrianism views the sidewalk as a form of unitary municipal property, held in trust for an abstract public. The municipality has a formal duty to regulate the sidewalk in the name of the public good. Other sidewalk users — such as the beggar, or the abutting merchant or homeowner — are not thought of as members of alternative publics, so much as they are deemed trespassers, impinging and encroaching upon municipal space.

Francois LeTourneux, Counsel for the City, drew heavily from such a characterization of the sidewalk, opening his written argument by drawing from Birch's affidavit, arguing that the amended bylaw must be characterized as a form of regulation that governs the "the solicitation for donations in a manner which obstructs free movement on streets and sidewalks and obstruction in the form of 'persistent' panhandling. Their objective is to regulate the use of city streets in a manner that acknowledges the varied interests of all people who use the streets . . . "[102] While rights arguments are necessarily considered, the City was at pains to characterize panhandling regulation as essentially apolitical, motivated by a desire to minimize obstruction and facilitate circulation. The sidewalk is not an agora, in other words, but a parcel of municipal property, to be governed according to administrative ends (the "proper administration of . . . sidewalks.")[103] The bylaw, the City insists, was not discriminatory, but was part of "a general regime which applies equally to all users of the City's streets and sidewalks."[104] The bylaw was not *ultra vires* the City, given that its main thrust is the regulation of obstruction, not the suppression of social difference. As such, the bylaw "does not deal with the morality of panhandling"[105]:

> It is submitted that the pith and substance of the Bylaw provisions is effective administration of traffic on the City's streets and sidewalks. An inherent feature of panhandling is its street activity component (such as street vending or busking). The Bylaw provisions simply ensure that the activity is carried out in a manner that does not impede pedestrian and vehicular traffic, in much the same way the City regulates other street activities such as street vending and busking, and in much the same way the City supervises the placement of static objects on its sidewalks, such as newspaper boxes, street furniture, utility poles, trees, phone booths, etc . . . . "[106]

The City conceded that panhandling was a form of expression. However "this expression is conveyed on the City's streets and sidewalks which, while owned by the City, consist of public property shared by a number of competing interests."[107] Lamer's conclusion in *Commonwealth* that picketing a highway is not compatible with the "principal function of the place, which is to provide for the smooth flow of pedestrian traffic"[108] was cited as applying "squarely to the case at bar." As a public forum, the City acknowledged that sidewalks are "places of social interaction." However, this was quickly minimized, it being noted that "another important function of streets and sidewalks is to ensure smooth pedestrian and vehicular traffic from point A to point B. To that extent, it is submitted that panhandling carried out in a manner that obstructs pedestrian traffic is incompatible with the function of the City's sidewalks and streets."[109] The bylaw did not prohibit expression to the extent that it did not prohibit panhandling, except in narrowly defined zones. Even if expression was overly curtailed, the bylaw was said to pass a section 1 test, it being argued that the "proper administration of the City's streets and sidewalks for the benefit of all competing interests utilizing this public resource is a pressing and substantial concern."[110]

The section 7 argument of the City also relied upon a "pedestrianist" logic concerning the uses of public space. The bylaw, it was argued, did not deny panhandlers the use and enjoyment of public places or distanced them from other citizens, but only placed reasonable restrictions, akin to that prohibiting street vending so as to obstruct traffic. The bylaw did not, therefore, draw an invidious distinction between panhandlers and all other people, given that all other legitimate street activities that carry a transactional component with the public were also regulated. Such discriminations, as applied to panhandlers, were said not to be a violation of the purpose of section 15, which was to prevent the violation of essential human dignity. Indeed, by regulating the panhandler, she was affirmed as a legitimate street user. To not regulate the panhandler, by extension, was to deny him full citizenship.

That the court agreed with the City's characterization was soon clear from the judgment. In his analysis of the jurisdictional question, Taylor J, began by accepting the City's characterization of the begging regulations as a matter of traffic regulation, and thus within the authority of the City. The purpose of the bylaw was not to prohibit panhandling, but rather to regulate the sidewalk so as to minimize the potential for obstruction. Indeed, he commended the City for not caving in to narrow-minded parochial interests who would politicize the sidewalk. Rather, the bylaw embodied a higher-minded balancing of competing interests in pursuit of technical ends:

> notwithstanding the considerable public debate in which the [Downtown Vancouver Business Improvement] Association played a loud and public role in decrying the conduct of panhandlers and would have preferred the outright banning of such activity, the respondent has enacted Bylaw 8309 in a manner that recognizes both the paramount duty to provide for the safe and efficient movement of pedestrians, and the need for other forms of activity to be conducted on its streets.[111]

Evident here also was the acceptance of the view that the "paramount" purpose of the sidewalk was circulation. This is evident in the court's evaluation of expressive rights as they related to panhandling. Panhandling was quickly acknowledged as "a tool used by those in poverty to engage in dialogue with the rest of society about their plight. As such, it is a form of expression."[112] The crucial question then, following *Ramsden*,[113] becomes whether the expression on public property was protected by section 2 (b).

Here, Taylor followed the reasoning of Lamer CJ in *Commonwealth* who argued that: " . . . it must be understood since the government administers its properties for the benefit of citizens as a whole, that it is the citizens who have an interest in seeing that the properties are administered and operated in a manner consistent with their intended purpose."[114]

As owner, the state "is accordingly responsible for ensuring that such places serve the specific purposes and function for which they were intended."[115] The interests of the person wishing to access a public space in order to engage in expression must therefore be balanced by the state's obligation to sustain such functions: " . . . the individual will only be free to communicate in a place owned by the state if the form of expression he uses is compatible with the principal function or intended purpose of that place."[116]

As has been noted, there are problems with such a characterization.[117] We might worry, for example, at the view that a public place has one "purpose" (interestingly, Lamer slid from a plural to singular reading of such a purpose). Even so, others might argue that the "principal function" of a public place is political — the exercise of rights and citizenship. This relies, in turn, on a view of the sidewalk as fully "public" property. However, Taylor simply characterized the sidewalk as municipal property, to be governed according to administrative criteria, the acme of which was the prevention of obstruction in the service of circulation:

> the dominant purpose of Bylaw 8309 is the safe and efficient movement of pedestrians. All other activities, whether active such as permitted conduct, or passive such as the setting of stationary objects, are governed by this predominant function. Activities, whether or not they engage forms of expression, are subordinate to the purpose of safe and efficient movement of pedestrians.[118]

This was echoed in his section 15 analysis, in which Taylor rejects the petitioner's argument that the bylaw drew a distinction between those who panhandle and those who did not, thus discriminating on the basis of poverty. A better comparator group, Taylor suggested, given that the bylaw is "merely an extension of the general regime of governing conduct on the streets as it relates to the movement of pedestrians,"[119] is those who use the streets for activities that may have the effect of impeding circulation. As such, the bylaw could not be said to be discriminatory, "given that all [street users] are proscribed from being obstructive."[120] The bylaw thus did not deny the human dignity of the panhandler, but affirmed it. Taylor approvingly adopts the City's argument that:

> Far from constituting a violation of human dignity . . . the Bylaw provisions confirm the status of [non-obstructive] panhandling as a legitimate street activity, subject to regulations, in the same way other legitimate street activities are subject to regulations, and foster[s] a climate of mutual respect on the [Respondent's] streets and sidewalks.[121]

Conclusion

It is interesting to reflect on why the City's view of public property was so persuasive to the court.[122] I think there may be two factors at work here. The first is the fact that Taylor's characterization not only echoes a bureaucratic mindset, but also conforms to common law understandings of the sidewalk as a particular parcel of state owned property. The sidewalk is understood as a "highway," that being "a way over which there exists a public right of passage, that is to say a right for all Her Majesty's subjects at all seasons of the year freely and at their will to pass and repass without let and hindrance."[123] Historically, the land over which highways ran remained privately held, with the public only acquiring an easement in the road, this being the right of passage over it. Any interference with the soil, other than that necessary to the full enjoyment of this right, was regarded as an interference with the rights of the owner. The use of streets and highways was thus seen as conditional upon adherence to the function of passing and repassing. Thus, "[t]he primary and overruling object for which the streets exist is passage. The streets are public, but they are public for passage."[124] This has been a long-standing judicial preoccupation. For example, in a Vancouver decision, Rinfret J noted that municipalities are owners of the street but only insofar as they are trustees for the public: "The streets remain subject to the right of the public to 'pass and repass' and that character, of course, is the very essence of the street."[125] As such, it surely becomes easier to characterize Vancouver's sidewalks as sites of circulation, rather than loci of politics.

The logic of obstruction, so central to Rowan Birch's account of "static objects" is also echoed by common law treatments of public nuisance, defined by Blackstone as "an offence against the public order and oeconomical regimen of the state; being either the doing of a thing to the annoyance of all the king's subjects, or the neglecting to do a thing which the common good requires."[126] First on his list of offences against the public are: . . . annoyances in highways, bridges and public rivers, by rendering the same inconvenient or dangerous to pass: either positively, by actual obstructions, or negatively, by want of reparations."[127] Highway obstruction is thus construed as an unwarranted private encroachment upon the rights of the Crown (and thus the public). Fulminating against a stagecoach owner who used the public highway near Charing Cross to take on passengers to the obstruction of the public, for example, Ellinborough CJ insisted that no private actor may make a "stableyard of the King's highway."[128]

The convergence between an administrative and judicial view of the sidewalk is a powerful one. The effect, frequently, is to deactivate urban rights claims, transmuting normative claims premised on personhood and human dignity into the logic of circulation, flow, placement, and blockage. In this sense, *Federated* and related decisions are not to be understood as battles between competing rights discourses, but rather as collisions entailing incommensurable logics — between civil rights and civil engineering, in other words. Valverde[129] makes a related argument in her discussion of the ways in which municipal law tends not to govern through persons, but focuses on things, activity, and space. Contemporary municipal law, she notes, tends to regulate through categories such as use, and is neutral with respect to persons. This is important, she argues, given that governing urban problems through "uses" is different from governing through the person. While the regulation of things and space entails the regulation of people, it rests upon a different protocol. Liberal rights rest upon claims of personhood. Thus, people have rights: uses, things, and space do not. This makes the translation of rights arguments into the terrain of municipal regulation much harder to make. Either rights based arguments are simply deflected by municipal logics (panhandling law is said to be not regulatory of persons, just of actions in particular spaces), or rights arguments are refracted into arguments around uses, things, and spaces. As she argues, arguments around urban homelessness often turn into arguments around urban uses: the discourse is not about the rights of the poor to shelter, but about the location of homeless shelters (and thus about density, setbacks, and parking spaces).

Those interested in making such rights-based claims need, therefore, to take these municipal logics, such as pedestrianism, seriously, on their own terms. In so doing, however, it may be tempting to characterize these logics as obvious manifestations of the privatization of public space, much discussed in the literature. However, we should be cautious of such a reductive reading.

While there is little doubt that City politicians were swayed by the interests of merchants, it is also very clear that pedestrianism cannot be reduced to such concerns. It may serve inequality, in other words, without manifesting it.[130] Further, once treated on its own terms, it becomes clear that it has its own egalitarian logic. This can be seen by the particular ways in which it, in fact, may rely upon claims to equality whereby all sidewalk users, whether beggars or bus stops, commuters and indigents, are treated as equally subject to, and protected by, the law. It can also be seen, more immediately, in the ways in which it is also put to work to police established, commercial users of sidewalks, such as news media companies, that wish to place boxes selling newspapers on city streets. To the courts, as the engineers, such uses may be treated as obstructions, nuisances or even trespasses, in much the same way that the obstructions of the panhandler were regarded.

And, finally, what of the panhandlers themselves? Their voices are absent from the judicial record, being represented by well-meaning advocates and lawyers. How do they envisage the sidewalk: as a space of rights, or of circulation? On the former, the evidence is mixed. Rights are clearly important to a sample of Vancouver panhandlers, including rights to expression. However, these rights do not appear as actionable. Indeed, given a general feeling that law does not work for them, but rather applies against them, several indicated that to assert their rights was to risk an aggressive response from the authorities.[131] Evident here, and in several interviews I conducted with panhandlers (with Mario Berti's assistance) is a clear sense of marginalization and dehumanization, of being ignored, insulted, and brutalized (one described having cockroaches dropped on his head, for example). The sidewalk may be a public space, in other words, but it is not one that is fully open to all. Rights are experienced either as an absence, or as a dangerous card to play.

For the panhandlers, however, the sidewalk is not simply a space for rights, or their negation. Echoing administrative logics, it is also seen as a site of circulation. Panhandlers constantly described how they situated themselves (or were moved on by private security and police) so as not to impede circulation, whether in relation to the entrances of private stores, or upon the public thoroughfare. So, for example, a panhandler in Vancouver's West End poignantly described how he governed his behaviour according to pedestrianist logic. When compelled to sleep on the sidewalk, he sought to make himself non-obstructive:

> I usually put myself in a position where I'm using up as much space as a mailbox or something like that. And I sleep close to something that people walk around anyways . . . . So that way I'm not getting in anybody's way . . . . So I feel like having somebody sleep, like, right up against the wall and stuff like that, it's not getting in anybody's personal space or anything like that. Because when I sit up, I take up more room than I do when I lie down.[132]

Yet he still characterized the sidewalk as public property: "the streets . . . and the public space belongs to everybody . . . . [I]t belongs to everybody who walks on it and everybody who pays taxes . . . . [I]t doesn't matter if you're homeless or not." But, as *Federated* reveals, "public" property, such as Vancouver's sidewalks, does not "belong to everybody," but is owned and regulated by the state, acting on behalf of the public. Consequently, the manner in which the "public interest" is defined in relation to such property becomes a crucial matter.

Notes

1 Many thanks to the discussants at the "Property Stories" workshop, Steve Penney and Erin Black, for their comments, as well as those of the editors, other participants in the workshop, and reviewers of this chapter. This project was supported by funding from the Social Science and Humanities Research Council. This chapter also draws on an earlier chapter prepared for the Law Commission of Canada written with Damian Collins (Damian Collins & Nicholas Blomley "Private needs and public space: politics, poverty and anti-panhandling bylaws in Canadian cities" In Law Commission of Canada, eds, *New Perspectives on the Public-Private Divide* (Vancouver: University of British Columbia Press, 2003) 40-67. I should note that I was asked to provide a submission concerning panhandling and expression on behalf of the petitioner in this case.

2 *Federated Anti-Poverty Groups of B.C. v Vancouver (City)* 2002 BCSC 105.

3 *R v Banks* (2001), 45 CR (5th) 23; (2005) 248 DLR (4th) 118; 84 OR (3d) 1; (2007) 84 OR (3d) 1.

4 *Victoria (City) v Adams* (2008) BCSC 1363; (2009) BCCA 563.

5 This is not to say, however, that private property is irrelevant to the situation at the centre of the case given that it concerns a population that is largely, although not exclusively, defined by their negative relation to property (Nicholas Blomley, "Homelessness, rights, and the delusions of property" 30 *Urban Geography* 6 (2009) 577-590). Interestingly, private property does not figure in the pleadings: while the petitioner did make the argument that poverty should be recognized, by analogy, as one of the enumerated grounds upon which a section 7 argument for equality can be made, they did not question the hierarchies of power enshrined in the built landscape by the prevailing regime of private property. The case also does not explicitly concern the "privatization" of public space, where a public asset is increasingly governed by private interests, either directly, through the actual transfer of public property to private actors, or through attempts by private interests to enlist the power of the state to regulate public space in the interests of profit maximization. Such omissions are worth reflecting upon.

6 Nicholas K Blomley, David Delaney & Richard Ford (eds) *The Legal Geographies Reader: Law, power, and space* (Oxford, Blackwell, 2001).

7 Jim Phillips, "Poverty, Unemployment and the Criminal Law: The Administration of the Vagrancy Laws in Halifax, 1864-1890," in Philip Girard and Jim Phillips, eds, *Essays in the History of Canadian Law: Volume Three - Nova Scotia* (Toronto: University of Toronto Press and Osgoode Society for Canadian Legal History 1990), 128-162.

8 32 & 33 Vict., c 28.

9 Similarly, this era saw many public order regulations in the US struck down, notably *Papachristou v City of Jacksonville* (405 US 156, 1972), in which the US Supreme Court overturned a Jacksonville, Florida, vagrancy ordinance as overly vague and granting excess discretionary powers to police.

10 Prashan Ranasinghe, "*The refashioning of vagrancy and the (re)ordering of public space* (University of Toronto, PhD dissertation, 2009) 97.

11 Dominion of Canada, House of Commons Debates: 27 April 1972: 1703.

12 Ranasinghe, above note 10.

13 *Dominion of Canada, House of Commons Debates, Minutes of the Proceedings and Evidence on Justice and Legal Affairs*, 9 May 1972: 5:35; emphasis added, quoted in Ranasinghe, above note 10.

14 "Alderman OK anti-begging bylaw", *The Vancouver Sun*, 23 January 1974, B2. Echoing later typologies, elected officials identified four types of panhandler: "the lone panhandler; musicians who accept offerings; religious groups who solicit money; and organized groups of toughs who intimidate and obstruct people." Three left-of-centre aldermen opposed it: Harcourt, Marzari, and Rankin, who likened it to "using a 14-pound sledge hammer to smash a gnat." On the unintended consequences of constitutional oversight of public order law, see Katherine Beckett & Steve Herbert "Dealing with disorder: social control in the post-industrial city" (2008) 12 *Theoretical Criminology*, 5-30. Historically, Vancouver had a Vagrancy Bylaw (No 135, 1892), section 4 of which noted that "all vagrants and mendicants without any visible means of support . . . shall be subject to the penalties of this Bylaw."

15 *R v Snobollen* (27 November 1974) Vancouver Registry (BC Prov Ct),

16 Collins And Blomley, above at 1.

17 David Ley, *The new middle class and the remaking of the central city*. (Oxford: Oxford University, 1996) 84.

18 Robert Murdie & Carlos Texeira "The city as social space." In Trudi Bunting and Pierre Filion, eds, *Canadian Cities in Transition*. (Oxford, Oxford University Press, 2000) 198-223.

19 Ley, above at 17.

20 Thomas Hutton, (2004) "Post-industrialism, post-modernism and the reproduction of Vancouver's central area: re-theorizing the twenty first century city" 41 *Urban Studies*, (2008) 10, 1953-82 at 1967.

21 Murray Mcmillan, "What's the sense in handing out money when it just perpetuates misery? Murray McMillan discusses the ethics of the endless cadge" (1993) *The Vancouver Sun* 10 April C10.

22 Andrew Robulack, "It's not easy when you're down and nearly out" (1993) *The Vancouver Sun*, 10 April C10.

23 Parker Shafer, "Don't feed the bears: protected by the courts, beggars forage for cash and threaten to despoil Vancouver" (1998) 9 *British Columbia Report* 28, 16 March 21-22.

24 Parker Shafer, "Bums and beggars will be busted: Vancouver and New Westminster pass anti-panhandling bylaws" (1998) 9 *British Columbia Report*, 39, 25 May, p 28. Shafer laments the City's regulatory gap, the subtitle of his article being: "protected by the courts, beggars forage for cash and threaten to despoil Vancouver."

25 Letter El Sol Imports to Leanore Sali, Gastown BIA, 25 October 2000. Copy with author.

26 Email, Reliance Holdings, to Leanore Sali, Gastown BIA, 26 October 2000. Copy with author.

27 Letter, The Irish Heather, Letter, to Leanore Sali, Gastown BIA, 25 October 2000. Copy with author.

28 James Q Wilson & George Kelling "Broken windows" (1982) *Atlantic* March, 29-37.

29 Larry Bourne & Antony E Olvet "New urban and regional geographies in Canada: 1986-91 and beyond" (1995) *Major Report 33* (Toronto, Centre for Urban and Community Studies, University of Toronto).

30 Trevor Barnes & Thomas Hutton "Situating the new economy: contingencies of regeneration and dislocation in Vancouver's inner city" (2009) 46 *Urban Studies* 5&6 1247-1269.

31 Brent Paul "Big box stores thump retailers downtown: flight to suburbs as sector becomes Americanized" (2000) *Financial Post.* 7 July, D3.

32 Robert A Beauregard, *Voices of decline: the postwar fate of U.S. cities* (New York, Routledge, 2000).

33 Anon. "The doughnut city: downtown has died in many US cities. Canada's urban politicians hope to avoid the same fate" (1996) 61 *Canada and the World Backgrounder* 5 March, 13-15.

34 Tony Hernandez & Ken Jones "Downtowns in transition: emerging Business Improvement Area strategies" (2005) 33 *International Journal of Retail and Distribution Management* 11, 789-805.

35 G Lepage "The underlying problem with panhandlers" (1999) *Ottawa Citizen* (Letter), 27 June: A17; Lindsay D "Easy pickings for transients in Kelowna: young drifters and job-seekers take advantage of the Okanagan city's charity" (1997) 8 *British Columbia Report* 49, 15; Wicksen R "Panhandling Bylaw Must Change" (2000) *Business Examiner,* October 2.

36 NAPO (National Anti-Poverty Organization), 1999: *Short-Changed on Human Rights: A NAPO Position Paper on Anti-panhandling By-laws.* (Ottawa, NAPO).

37 Letter, Landmark Clocks International to Leanore Sali, Gastown BIA, 22 October 2000. Copy with author.

38 Letter, the McLean Group to Leanore Sali, Gastown BIA, 25 October 2000. Copy with author.

39 Letter, Spirit Wrestler Gallery to Leanore Sali, Gastown BIA, 23 October 2000. Copy with author.

40 Letter, Spirit Wrestler Gallery to Leanore Sali, Gastown BIA, 23 October 2000. Copy with author.

41 Memo: Vancouver Police Department, Patrol Division, 28 October 1997, To Deputy Chief Constable T Blythe, From Inspector D Jones. Copy with author. As an aside, the report noted that from a police perspective, panhandling had actually decreased in the city centre. Jones subsequently left the VPD to work for the Downtown Vancouver Business Improvement Association, where he played a leading role in successfully lobbying for provincial regulation of panhandling (the *Safe Streets Act*).

42 *Ibid*, 1.

43 *Ibid*, 3-4.

44 *Ibid*, 6.

45 *Ibid*, 6.

46 Vancouver, City (1998) *Administrative Report* April 21: To Standing Committee on Planning and Environment. From: City Manager. Subject: Panhandling copy with author, 6.

47 City staffers noted that downtown businesses had raised the concern that the New Westminster bylaw would lead to an influx of panhandlers into Vancouver unless similar regulation was enacted (Vancouver, City, above at 46).

48 There is evidence that the police were informally regulating panhandlers according to some of these criteria before the creation of the bylaw. A Vancouver Police Department letter of 29 August 1997 described an attempt to crack down on "aggressive panhandlers" on Granville St, noting that offenders had been informed "of our 'in-house' rules regarding distances from bank machines and bus shelters" (copy with author).

49 Vancouver, City "Report to Council, Standing Committee of Council on Planning and Environment" (1998) 30 April 4-5. Copy with author.

50 Shafer, above at 24.

51 Doug Ward & Petti Fong "Panhandling bylaw passed, lawsuits likely" *The Vancouver Sun* (1998) 1 May, A1.

52 Vancouver Sun, The "Panhandling bylaw best run out of town" (1998) *The Vancouver Sun* (Editorial) 4 May, A1.

53 Ward And Fong, above at 51.

54 Catherine Porter "Begging bylaw critics meet council" (1998) *The Vancouver Sun*, 19 June, B1.

55 Jack Keating "Panhandlers rally against city bylaw" (2000) *The Province*. 18 May, A29

56 Vancouver's Anti-Panhandling bylaw" *In the Public Interest*, 1999 3:2, p 1, online: http://bcpiac.com/wp-content/uploads/2007/08/newsletter1999june.pdf.

57 "It's time to rescind the city's panhandling bylaw" (2000) *The Vancouver Sun* (Editorial) 25 May A12.

58 Bob Sarti, "Courting disaster, and getting nowhere" (2000) *The Vancouver Sun*, 13 May H5.

59 Minutes of Settlement, National Anti-Poverty Organization and the City of Winnipeg. 2000. Copy with author.

60 The Obstructive Solicitation Bylaw, No 7700/2200. This was later amended to include a prohibition on soliciting from a "captive audience," such as pedestrians waiting at a bus stop, and any pedestrian using the city's extensive Indoor Walkway network.

61 Anon. "Winnipeg dumps panhandling bylaw" (2000) *Kamloops Daily News*, 21 Sept, C7.

62 *Ibid*, 57. Following debate, Victoria decided to await the outcome of the Vancouver Charter challenge.

63 Yvonne Zacharias, "Vancouver may scrap panhandling bylaw" (2001) *The Vancouver Sun*. 5 Mar B1.

64 *Federated*, above at 2, para 37.

65 Carellin Brooks, "Oh, those bothersome beggars" (2001) *The Vancouver Sun*. 19 Mar, A10.

66 Vancouver, City Of *Administrative Report* (2001) 22 February. To Vancouver City Council. From City Manager. Subject: Panhandling Bylaw. Copy with author, no page.

67 BCPIAC (2001) "Panhandling update." *In the Public Interest,* February, online: http://bcpiac.com/wp-content/uploads/2007/08/newsletter2001feb.pdf.

68 Robert C Ellickson, "Controlling chronic misconduct in city spaces: of panhandlers, skid rows and public-space zoning" (1996) Yale LJ, 105 1165–1248, 1168.

69 *Ibid,* 1173.

70 *Ibid,* 1173.

71 Mitchell, Don *The Right to the City: Social Justice and the Fight for Public Space.* (New York: The Guilford Press, 2003).

72 This is echoed in some legal scholarship. For example, Joseph Sax has pointed to the enduring significance and value of the public trust doctrine to Anglo-American property law, which vests ownership in the public, not the state (JL Sax "The public trust doctrine in natural resource law: effective judicial intervention" Mich LR (1970) 68, 471-566). While the state may act as trustee, there is still a recognition of "the public at large, which despite its unorganized state seems to have some property-like rights in the land held in trust for it – rights that may be asserted against the state's own representatives" (Carol Rose *Property and persuasion: Essays on the history, theory and rhetoric of ownership* (Boulder, Westview Press, 1994) 121-122; compare Carol Rose "Romans, roads and romantic creators: traditions of public property in the information ago" Research Paper No. 10 (Yale Law School: Public Law and Legal Theory, 2002).

73 Don Mitchell & Lynn Staeheli *The people's property: power, politics and the public* (New York: Routledge, 2009).

74 John Robson, "Should begging be legal? No: we need protection from harassment in public spaces" (1999) *The Ottawa Citizen,* 24 June D5.

75 Ellickson, above at 68.

76 Jeremy Waldron, "Homelessness and the issue of freedom" (1991) UCLA L Rev 39 295–324.

77 Letter, General Manager of The Purple Onion Cabaret to Leanore Sali, Gastown BIA, 24 October 2000. Copy with author.

78 Letter, Rossinis, to Leanore Sali, Gastown BIA, 27 October 2000. Copy with author.

79 Letter, OK Boot Corral, Email, to Leanore Sali, Gastown BIA, 24 October 2000. Copy with author.

80 Letter, Inform Interiors to Leanore Sali, Gastown BIA, 20 October 2000. Copy with author.

81 Letter, Steamworks Brewing Company to Leanore Sali, Gastown BIA, 24 October 2000. Copy with author.

82 Email, Reliance Holdings, to Leanore Sali, Gastown BIA, 26 October 2000. Copy with author.

83 Letter, Water Street Café, to Leanore Sali, Gastown BIA, 27 October 2000. Copy with author.

84 Interview with author, BCPIAC, 2 August 2006.

85 Petitioner's arguments, 2001. Copy with author.

86 *Ibid*, para 51.

87 *Ibid*, para 85.

88 *Ibid*.

89 *Ibid*, para 100, original emphasis.

90 M Berman, "Take it to the streets: Conflict and community in public spaces" (1986) 33 *Dissent* 4, 470–494 at 482.

91 Iris Marion Young, *Justice and the politics of difference* (Princeton NJ: Princeton University Press, 1990) 240, my emphasis.

92 *Committee for the Commonwealth of Canada v Canada* (1991) 77 DLR (4th) 385 (SCC).

93 *Petitioner's arguments*, 2001. Copy with author, para 240.

94 Rowan Birch, *Affidavit* (2001) Copy with author, p 2.

95 *Ibid*, 2.

96 *Ibid*, 2.

97 *Ibid*, 2-3.

98 *Ibid*, 2.

99 *Ibid*, 3.

100 *Ibid*, 4.

101 Nicholas Blomley, *Rights of passage: sidewalks and the regulation of public flow* (New York: Routledge, 2011).

102 City of Vancouver *Written argument of the Respondent City of Vancouver* (2001) para 3. Copy with author.

103 *Ibid*, para 4.

104 *Ibid*, para 33.

105 *Ibid*, para 73.

106 *Ibid*, para 58.

107 *Ibid*, para 77.

108 *Ibid*, para 79 (p 396 in Commonwealth).

109 *Ibid*, para 81.

110 *Ibid*, para 100.

111 *Federated*, above at 2, para 141.

112 *Ibid*, para 151.

113 *Ramsden v Peterborough* (City) 2 SCR 1084, 106 DLR (4th) 233.

114 *Commonwealth*, above at 88, p 394.

115 *Ibid*, p 394.

116 *Ibid*, p 394.

117 R Moon "Out of place: comment on *Committee for the Commonwealth of Canada v Canada*" (1993) McGill LJ, 38, 204–232.

118 *Federated*, above at 2, para 157-8. Although he does note, although almost as an afterthought, that " . . . it must not be forgotten that the street plays an important role in providing a public forum for the expression of ideas and thoughts" (para 158).

119 *Ibid*, para 262.

120 *Ibid*, para 264.

121 *Ibid*, para 189. Taylor J went on to invert the petitioner's use of Anatole France's famous ironic pronouncement, intended to point to the cruel inequalities of laws that conform to the narrow constraints of formal equality ("The majestic equality of the law forbids the rich as well the poor to sleep under bridges, to beg in the streets and steal bread"). For Taylor "What underlies this statement is the caveat that if the rich and the poor do so sleep together under a bridge, they must do so respectful of one another.... The Bylaw does no more than to enunciate that caveat" (para. 303). For a critique of the social "flattening" that seems at work here, see Nicholas Blomley, "How to turn a beggar into a bus stop: law, traffic and the "function of the place" (2007) 44 *Urban Studies* 9 1697-1712.

122 The judgment in *Banks* is broadly comparable (see Blomley, above at 121). More generally, common law courts have tended to characterize sidewalks through a broadly similar lens (see Blomley, above at 101).

123 *Ex parte Lewis* (1888) 21 Qbd 191 at 197.

124 *Metra v Magistrates of Edinburgh*, 1913, SC 1059 at 1073.

125 *Vancouver v Burchill* (1932) SCR 620 at 625, 1932 4 DLR 200.

126 W Blackstone, *Commentaries on the Laws of England: Volume 4: Of public wrongs.* (Chicago: The University of Chicago Press, 1979/1769) 167.

127 *Ibid.*

128 *R v Cross* [1803-1813] All ER Rep 296.

129 Mariana Valverde, "Taking 'land use' seriously: toward an ontology of municipal law" (2005) *Law Text Culture*, 9, 34–59.

130 Skeptics may characterize pedestrianism as simply a convenient smokescreen, behind which lurk more sinister "hidden" motives. While there is no doubt that it made the bylaw bulletproof, I think this underestimates its "commonsensical" nature as a form of urban legal knowledge. For the many street engineers I have spoken to in Vancouver and elsewhere, it is simply the way things are done. A city representative in Vancouver also resisted seeing the insertion of the panhandling regulations in the Streets and Traffic Bylaw as anything other than an appropriate decision (it was "a logical place to put it"), given that panhandling was obviously a matter of street use, circulation and potential obstruction (Interview with author, 19 October 2006: Representative of City of Vancouver).

131 Mario Berti, *The way of rights and the right of way: panhandling and rights in public space* (2009) MA Thesis; Department of Geography, Simon Fraser University.

132 Interview with Research Assistant, 12 July 2006.

Pirate or Prophet?
Monsanto Canada Inc. v Schmeiser

Patricia L. Farnese[1]

Introduction

THE SUPREME COURT OF Canada's (SCC) decision in *Monsanto Canada Inc. v Schmeiser* is likely most remembered for what it did not decide.[2] By beginning the majority's decision with an outline of what the court would not address, McLachlin CJ and Fish J, clearly understood that much of the public's interest in this case concerned a number of broader issues. Specifically, the court stated:[3]

> we emphasize from the outset that we are not concerned here with the innocent discovery by farmers of "blow-by" patented plants on their land or in their cultivated fields. Nor are we concerned with the scope of the respondents' patent or the wisdom and social utility of the genetic modification of genes and cells – a practice authorized by Parliament under the *Patent Act* and its regulations.

Nonetheless, the story of *Monsanto v Schmeiser* is as much the story of how this case drew global attention to these broader issues as it is about the narrow issue of patent infringement. This story is also about two fascinating protagonists, Monsanto and Percy Schmeiser, in what has often been described as a modern battle between David and Goliath.[4] For many, Schmeiser, like David, remains a folk hero whose ongoing public life continues to draw attention to this case.

Monsanto

Monsanto is the leading agricultural biotechnology company. Its 2009 net sales from its seeds and genomics and agricultural productivity divisions were close to $12 billion USD.[5] The seeds and genomics division sells products with biotechnology traits while the agricultural productivity division mainly refers to the company's agricultural chemical business.[6] The company's sale of glyphosate, branded as Roundup, constitutes the majority of its chemical business.[7] Monsanto's commodity crop seeds — such as canola, cotton, soybeans, and corn — are globally available.[8] Monsanto's global reach comes through both the direct marketing of its own branded seeds and chemicals, and through the licensing of its patented technology and genetic material to other companies.[9]

Monsanto, however, did not begin as an agriculture company and for many, what Monsanto was cannot be separated from what Monsanto has become. In 1901, John F. Queeny formed a company and purchased the materials and technology to produce saccharine. Queeny chose to use his wife Olga's maiden name, Monsanto, as his new company's name. Derived from benzoic sulfimide and significantly sweeter than sucrose, Queeny hoped to provide a local source of saccharine in the US. His investment was rewarded when The Coca Cola Co. purchased all of the saccharine Monsanto produced in 1903 and 1905. By 1905, Monsanto had developed other chemical additives for use in food products including vanillin[10] and caffeine.[11]

Fueled by its success in the food additive business, Monsanto continued to expand and diversify its chemical business. Monsanto began to manufacture styrene and polystyrene plastics, which, by the 1940s, were the central focus of its business. In 1947, Monsanto had the misfortune of becoming involved in what has been described as the "most devastating industrial accident in US history."[12] A French freighter, the S.S. *Grandcamp*, was unloading ammonium nitrate fertilizer[13] when it caught fire in the Texas City harbour. Monsanto was located dockside. Thus, when the S.S. *Grandcamp* exploded, it triggered fires at the Monsanto facility resulting in hundreds of deaths and thousands of injuries.[14] In addition to the loss of many of its employees, Monsanto's polystyrene facility suffered considerable damage and released fuel oil, benzene, and styrene into the environment.[15] The Texas City disaster introduced most of the public to Monsanto.

Monsanto's involvement with polychlorinated biphenyls (PCBs) during the 1960s and 1970s likely underlies some of the public distrust of Monsanto that surrounded *Monsanto v Schmeiser.* In 1935, Monsanto purchased the Swann Chemical Company, located South of St. Louis, Missouri, in the community of Carondelet.[16] The importance of this acquisition to Monsanto is perhaps reflected in the fact that St. Louis is now home to Monsanto's corporate headquarters. Through Swann, Monsanto began selling PCBs. Although the sale of PCBs is now banned, the issue of when Monsanto knew or should have known about the adverse health effects of PCBs is featured prominently in many indictments of Monsanto's corporate practices.[17]

Edgar M. Queeny took over the company in 1928 when his father was diagnosed with incurable cancer. Edgar Queeny was somewhat of a renaissance man. He also farmed near St. Louis and was an innovative documentary filmmaker. He frequently made films about wildlife and the natural environment. In fact, Edgar Queeny made several films on waterfowl whose proceeds were donated to Ducks Unlimited, where he served as National Trustee.[18]

Edgar Queeny also took the company in new directions; Monsanto's interest in agriculture is attributed to him. He charged Monsanto's research department to develop agricultural applications for their chemical products. Thus, when the US government was looking for a defoliant to remove the advantage the jungle provided to North Vietnamese soldiers during the Vietnam War, Monsanto and other American chemical manufacturers were asked to produce a product that became known as Agent Orange. One of the active ingredients in Agent Orange was dioxin. Dioxin is now understood to have significant adverse health effects.[19] Like PCBs, when Monsanto knew or should have known about the lasting consequences of dioxin exposure is the subject of much speculation and criticism.[20]

The development and production of Agent Orange was not the first time Monsanto was called upon by the US government to collaborate in a military project. Under the leadership of Dr. Charles Allan Thomas, Monsanto scientists collaborated on the Manhattan Project. Monsanto's research team developed the polonium triggers used in the atomic bombs dropped on Hiroshima and Nagasaki. Monsanto, therefore, contributed a key technical component to the development of atomic weapons.[21] For his efforts, Dr. Thomas was named Monsanto's president in 1951.[22]

Glyphosate

For many the story of *Monsanto v Schmeiser* begins with saccharine and continues with PCBs, Agent Orange, the Manhattan Project, and finally, agricultural biotechnology. For Monsanto, however, the story begins with the 1970 discovery of the herbicidal properties of N-phosphonomethyl glycine, also known as glyphosate, by its scientist, Dr. John E. Franz. One reason why the story begins with glyphosate's discovery is that the Monsanto Corporation has been broken apart in recent years into separate entities. Today's Monsanto is solely focused on agricultural products.[23] The non-agriculture, chemical products business is now Solutia Inc.[24]

In 1952, Monsanto began routinely testing all chemical compounds it developed for herbicidal activity.[25] The compound that would be synthesized into glyphosate was one of two compounds sent to Franz for herbicidal testing after they were deemed unsuitable for use as water softeners. Although the compounds were deemed not to be active enough to act as a commercial herbicide, Monsanto's herbicide screening manager, Dr. Philip Hamm, felt further exploration was justified as they demonstrated some properties that inhibited plant growth.[26] According to Franz, glyphosate was the third compound he synthesized from the original two compounds he was sent.

Franz's initial laboratory tests indicated that glyphosate was a potent, broad-spectrum herbicide that killed both the foliage and rootstocks of plants.[27] Because the whole plant was killed, glyphosate had the potential to combat both annual and perennial weeds. Glyphosate also seemed effective on all plant species that could be a one-size-fits-all herbicide, thereby eliminating the use of multiple herbicides. Moreover, glyphosate worked by inhibiting the functioning of EPSP synthase, an enzyme essential to photosynthesis, but not present in animals or humans. Consequently, glyphosate was thought to pose little adverse health risk.[28] In addition, glyphosate was water-soluble and readily broke down into carbon dioxide, phosphoric acid, and ammonia. As all of these compounds occur naturally in the environment, glyphosate was also thought to have minimal adverse environmental impacts. Likewise, glyphosate was not volatile and thus posed little risk of becoming airborne after being applied to fields.[29] From Franz's laboratory, glyphosate appeared as an effective, safe, environmentally friendly herbicide with significant market potential.

Because the initial laboratory tests of glyphosate were so promising, the product was rushed to field trials.[30] The report to Monsanto's management with the results of the initial field trials from Dr. Douglas Baird, the plant physiologist tasked with evaluating the field trials, was titled "EUREKA," reflecting perhaps both the herbicidal and market potential of glyphosate.[31] This optimism reflected the understanding that weeds pose significant economic, health, and environmental costs. In Saskatchewan alone, the annual cost to control weeds is estimated to be $1.36 billion. This amount does not include the reduction to crop yields despite control efforts.[32] Further, there are economic costs associated with the infrastructure damage and control costs on non-agriculture land such as on road allowances and in urban areas. Likewise, pollens from weeds are the most significant cause of seasonal allergies in North America.[33] There are also additional health costs associated with the use of chemicals to control weeds. Last, many weeds are invasive, meaning they are aggressive and out-compete native species thereby imposing ecological costs. It is estimated that the ecological costs of invasive species in the US, in the form of habitat destruction and species disruption, is approximately $120 billion per year.[34]

Once the glyphosate field trials were complete, Monsanto focused on preparing the product for market. After Monsanto received US Patent No. 3985773 on 12 October 1976, glyphosate became commercially available. Consistent with the cowboy theme Monsanto had developed to brand all its agricultural chemicals, Roundup was named by Monsanto secretary Dottie Mills. Mills received $50 for her suggestion.[35]

Since its introduction, glyphosate has become the most used pesticide in the United States.[36] Interestingly, hindsight has revealed how fortunate Monsanto is that no one beat it to this discovery. Although initially thought to be an entirely novel compound, a thorough review of the literature, likely while preparing a patent application, revealed that the compound had been patented by the Stauffer Chemical Company in 1964 for use in the preparation of phosphonic acids.[37] Likewise, one of Monsanto's competitors, Ciba-Geigy, had access to glyphosate as early as 1958, but never tested its herbicidal properties.[38]

The significance of glyphosate's discovery is likely foremost evident by its acceptance and use by farmers and other land managers around the world. From a scientific perspective, glyphosate's founder Franz has been granted numerous awards attesting to the impact of his invention. In 1987, he received the National Medal of Technology and Innovation from US President Ronald Reagan.[39] He was also inducted into the National Inventors Hall of Fame in the US in 2007.[40]

Roundup Ready Canola

Perhaps the most important reason why, for Monsanto, the story of *Monsanto v Schmeiser* begins with glyphosate's discovery, is because glyphosate became the central focus of Monsanto's agriculture business. According to Monsanto's executive vice-president and chief technology officer, Dr. Robert Fraley, the potential market for glyphosate resistant plants was recognized immediately.[41] Monsanto's global dominance in agricultural biotechnology is the result of a deliberate strategy of investment.

Glyphosate is an effective, broad-spectrum herbicide. While this can be a desirable trait for a herbicide in certain circumstances, glyphosate's indiscriminate effect limits its application in agriculture. Roundup cannot be used on conventional agricultural crops after the crop has emerged from the soil without damaging the crop. Thus, conventional farmers would likely still need to apply another herbicide to deal with weeds that compete with crops as they mature in the field. Moreover, the exceptionally lucrative patent on glyphosate would one day expire. If Monsanto's research department could develop Roundup resistant seed varieties, the natural limit on the timing of glyphosate's use would be removed. In addition, the market for Roundup could continue past the end of its patent. Competition from manufacturers of generic brands of glyphosate could be mitigated by tying access to glyphosate-resistant seed to use of Monsanto's Roundup.

Therefore, Monsanto scientists were tasked with developing seeds that were resistant to Roundup. The emerging field of agricultural biotechnology held promise that such a goal could be achieved although the science was mainly theoretical at that time. Nonetheless, a team of molecular biologists developed techniques to move biological traits into plants, located a Roundup resistant gene that could be moved into a plant cell, and ultimately genetically engineered a seed to become Roundup resistant. Given the state of the science at the time, Monsanto's investment in the molecular biology team was risky.[42]

In 1983, Monsanto scientists became the first to modify a plant cell using biotechnology and to grow a plant from a genetically modified seed — a petunia.[43] It had been modified with a gene that allowed a plant to grow in the presence of plant inhibitor. The discovery of a glyphosate-resistant gene was still a few years off. Ultimately, the trait was found in a bacterium in an effluent treatment pond at one of Monsanto's glyphosate manufacturing facilities in Luling, Louisiana.

By 1996, Roundup Ready (RR) seeds were made available for sale.[44] RR canola was one of the first genetically engineered seeds available to farmers. Canola is also the only RR seed variety introduced into Canada before becoming available in the US. Canadian farmers had commercial access to

RR canola in 1996, three years before it was available to US growers.[45] In that first year, approximately 600 farmers planted RR canola on 50,000 acres. In 2010, Canadian farmers planted almost seventeen million acres of canola;[46] approximately 80 percent of it was genetically modified.[47]

Initially, Monsanto licensed its patented Roundup resistant genes to seed companies to sell to farmers. Monsanto, however, soon began an aggressive strategy of acquiring prominent seed companies in order to direct their business towards the marketing of Roundup resistant seeds themselves. Today, Monsanto is the world's largest seed company.[48] Monsanto's dominance in the global seed market has attracted criticism. When *Monsanto v Schmeiser* was before the courts, Schmeiser's supporters regularly questioned the appropriateness of patenting seeds because of the ability of a patent-holder to restrict access to its invention. That question, however, is an example of one of the broader questions not before the court in *Monsanto v Schmeiser.*

Percy Schmeiser

Monsanto's relationship with Schmeiser began when Monsanto received an anonymous phone call to a tip line that it had established to report unlicensed sales and plantings of its RR seeds.[49] Not surprisingly, the tipster, David Leuschen, was someone from Schmeiser's community, as it is unlikely that anyone else would have occasion to discover the canola. What reason would someone have to report Schmeiser? The answer may simply be that the caller felt it was unfair that Schmeiser had access to the RR seed without paying the $15 per acre licensing fee. In the alternative, the call may have been the result of existing animosity between the caller and Schmeiser. An examination of Schmeiser's public and community life makes the latter reason a possibility although Schmeiser has stated that he did not know Leuschen before the lawsuit.

Schmeiser was born 5 January 1931, the middle child of Charles and Elsie Schmeiser. Schmeiser has an older brother and sister and two younger brothers. One of his brothers, Douglas, is the former Dean of the College of Law at the University of Saskatchewan. Although Douglas played no formal role in Schmeiser's defence, he recommended the law firm that ultimately would take the case. Schmeiser also often turned to Douglas for advice. Schmeiser's confidence was undoubtedly bolstered by the knowledge that his brother recognized the viability of his defence. Douglas did not publicly support his brother, but in Douglas' recent novel, *A Settling of Accounts*, Monsanto is portrayed critically.[50]

In addition to a potential professional interest in the legal questions raised in this case, Douglas had a more personal reason to be interested in how the court defined the scope of Monsanto's patent rights. One of the fields where RR canola was found was land Schmeiser rented from Douglas. If Monsanto's patent rights were broadly defined, as a landowner with unlicensed RR canola on his property, Douglas may also have faced liability. The issue of land owned versus rented by Schmeiser was not discussed at trial, thus the liability of a landowner who is found to have unlicensed patented crops on his land remains uncertain.

Schmeiser grew up, and continues to reside in, Bruno, Saskatchewan. Bruno is a small rural community of approximately 500 people that is located ninety kilometres east of Saskatoon. For many years, Bruno was home to an Ursuline convent and Catholic boarding school for girls.[51] Like most people in Bruno, Schmeiser was raised Roman Catholic. In fact, Catholicism was responsible for the Schmeiser family coming to Canada and settling in the Bruno area. Schmeiser's grandfather, Karl Schmeiser, emigrated to Collegeville, Minnesota, from Austria in 1892 to work at St. John's Abbey, a Benedictine Monastery. In 1904, Karl moved to Canada because of the offer of free land to those who would settle and begin farming. Karl chose to settle in the Bruno area because one of the priests from St. John's Abbey, with whom Karl had a close relationship, joined a mission in Bruno. Schmeiser's grandmother and father followed a year later.

Perhaps the influence of Catholicism in the Schmeiser family life is best demonstrated by the fact that Schmeiser's youngest brother, James, became a Professor of Philosophy and Religious Studies at King's University College, a Catholic college affiliated with the University of Western Ontario. Similar to his brother, it is likely that Catholicism left its mark on Schmeiser. In fact, Schmeiser's opposition to the patenting of seeds may be rooted in his strong Catholic upbringing. Many Catholics view the patenting of seeds as violating the Catechism of the Catholic Church.[52] When asked, however, Schmeiser stated that his initial objection to patenting seeds was the associated prohibition on seed saving.[53]

The Schmeisers may have shared a Catholic upbringing with their neighbours, but in other ways, they were not the typical rural Saskatchewan family. First, farming was just one of Charles' business ventures. Prior to starting to farm, Charles was co-owner of a hotel in Davidson, Saskatchewan. He then returned to the Bruno area to farm and opened a service station. He also received a contract to sell and repair JI Case farm equipment, a business Schmeiser would later take over. Charles' experience in business likely contributed to his assumption of leadership roles in the community. For example, Charles served as the first president of the Bruno Savings and Credit Union.

In addition, Charles and Elsie placed a high value on formal education. Charles himself was well read and literate during a time when many of his peers would not have been. As mentioned, two of Schmeiser's brothers became professors and his sister, Doreen, became a teacher. Schmeiser went to Toronto and attended the Radio College of Canada, where he specialized in RADAR and received a diploma in communication technology. He became an associate officer in the North American Air Defence and returned home to Saskatchewan.[54] Schmeiser would later take over the family businesses when his younger brother James decided not to return home to farm.[55]

Many members of the Schmeiser family also took the opportunity to travel, not only outside of Saskatchewan, but outside of Canada as well. All of the siblings, save Kenneth, would leave home for post-secondary education. James studied in Ottawa and Germany and Douglas obtained his post-graduate degrees in the United States.[56] Doreen, with her teaching training, became a missionary in Papua, New Guinea. While teaching abroad, Doreen met and married an Australian and settled in Australia. Charles and Elsie were not left behind. In 1950, they travelled throughout Europe on a six-week tour and religious pilgrimage — an exceptional voyage for a couple from the prairies during that time.

In 1952, Schmeiser married his classmate, Louise Weyland. Louise joined Schmeiser on the family farm. Schmeiser took over the farm from his father in 1947.[57] Like his parents, Schmeiser has five children. At trial, MacKay J described Schmeiser as having "an extensive history in municipal and provincial politics, and as a businessman and an adventurer,"[58] a description that also could have applied to his father.

From reading the family history prepared by Schmeiser's father for *Up to Now*, a local history project prepared by the Bruno History Book Committee in 1984, one gets the sense that Schmeiser, in the eyes of his father, fulfilled the role of the underachiever in his family. If the amount of space devoted in the family history to Douglas, Doreen, and James' achievements are any indication, staying home and taking over the family businesses was somehow less impressive than his siblings' accomplishments. Over time, however, Schmeiser's notoriety likely outshines the rest.

Like his father, Schmeiser was involved in many business ventures, including the garage he took over from his father. When his lawsuit was initiated, Schmeiser farmed approximately 1,400 acres, the majority of which was seeded to canola. In 1996, when RR canola first appeared on Schmeiser's farm, the average farm size in Saskatchewan was 1,152 acres.[59] While Schmeiser farmed more than the average amount of acres, his operation would generally be considered a medium-sized farm based on his annual farm receipts of $142,625 from the sale of the 1998 canola crop.[60] Like many family farm operations in Canada, the farm was organized as a corporation. The control of the farm operation was transferred to Schmeiser Enterprises Ltd. in 1996.[61] Interestingly, the timing of this transfer does not appear to have become an issue at trial. That this attempt to limit the Schmeisers' personal liability occurred at the same time as Schmeiser was gathering RR canola seed without a licence could be viewed as suspicious. During that time, however, many family farms restructured to corporations.[62]

Schmeiser also operated a seed breeding business in conjunction with the farm operation. In a counterclaim that was delayed until the conclusion of Schmeiser's infringement case and then later abandoned, Schmeiser would allege that this seed breeding business was ruined after his seed stock was contaminated with RR canola. Although Schmeiser would later state that he regrets initiating the counterclaim because it gave the appearance that his actions were motivated by money, the loss of his seed stock was a significant personal blow.[63] At trial, Schmeiser broke down during his testimony when recalling the decision to destroy his seed stock.[64]

Following his father's example, Schmeiser assumed leadership roles in his community. Schmeiser was Bruno's mayor from 1966 to 1983. He was also elected to the provincial legislature and served as the Liberal member for the Watrous riding from 1967 to 1971. As a member of the Saskatchewan Liberal Party, the timing of Schmeiser's entrance into provincial politics was unfortunate. After many years in government, the Liberal Party was defeated in the next election.[65] In 2003, Schmeiser was elected as town councillor in Bruno.

Despite farming, operating the garage, and being active in local politics, the Schmeisers spent many winters travelling. They have travelled to Africa, Central America, and Asia, foregoing the tourist sites for more adventurous travel. On one trip, they spent two months camping across the Sahara Desert. Schmeiser also climbed Mount Kilimanjaro.[66] When asked during the trial why he had not yet visited Antarctica, Schmeiser replied, "Because I have a lawsuit with Monsanto."[67] Schmeiser attributes some of his motivation for choosing to defend his patent infringement claim to his experiences travelling in other countries where poverty and lack of access to the courts prevent others from defending their rights.[68]

Even though Schmeiser's long-term involvement in municipal politics demonstrates that he has many supporters in his community, it would be difficult for anyone to have this long of a career in local politics and not alienate some people. Some of that acrimony surfaced in 1994. Two town employees complained that Schmeiser's interactions with them were abusive. One had an emotional breakdown that led to a leave of absence. In 1996, a second employee complained to the Department of Labour, who conducted an investigation and subsequently issued a Notice of Contravention that directed the town to pass a resolution barring Schmeiser from physically attending at the town office.[69] Council for the town passed a motion requiring Schmeiser to communicate with the town solely in writing and the matter settled down.

In the spring of 2003, the Schmeisers' water line froze and consequently broke. Schmeiser began, once again, to visit the Town Office, and the Town Clerk alleged Schmeiser was making excessive demands of her. In the fall of 2003, however, he was elected by acclamation to Town Council. One of the last actions of the previous Council was to pass a motion barring Schmeiser from physically attending Town Council meetings as they were held at the Town Office. Upon his arrival at what was to be the first meeting of the new council, Schmeiser was informed that there was a court order barring him from being at the Town Council. In fact, no such order existed. Schmeiser was informed that he could attend meetings by conference call. He refused and meetings were held without him. After Schmeiser had missed a number of meetings, the Council tried to have him removed from office for non-attendance pursuant to the *Urban Municipality Act* (1984).

Schmeiser took the matter to court. Schmeiser asked the court to declare that the Council's actions were a violation of the *Urban Municipality Act* and that any business conducted at the meetings in his absence was null and void. The court ultimately found in Schmeiser's favour with respect to the first issue, but not the second. The court felt Schmeiser could have attended the meetings by conference call while he awaited the outcome of his court application.[70]

His dispute with the Town of Bruno was not the first time Schmeiser looked to the courts to resolve a dispute with local government. In 1978, after years of complaining, Schmeiser initiated a legal action to recover damages for crop loss associated with flooding from the Rural Municipality of Bayne.[71] Schmeiser alleged that a municipal road built adjacent to his property between 1959 and 1961 prevented the natural flow of water from leaving his farmland. In 1990 the matter was resolved in Schmeiser's favour at the Court of Appeal.[72]

In choosing Schmeiser to test the scope of its patent, Monsanto chose someone willing to fight. If Monsanto was looking for a test case, Schmeiser was the ideal defendant; he was neither likely to back down nor to resolve the matter quietly. Two other high profile litigants in disputes with Monsanto at the same time as Schmeiser, the Nelson Brothers of North Dakota and Troy Roush of Indiana, ultimately settled lawsuits alleging each had grown RR soybeans without a licence.[73] According to Schmeiser, the stress of the litigation became too much for the other litigants. At a meeting between the Nelson, Roush, and Schmeiser families, however, the other families offered to support Schmeiser if he would continue the fight against Monsanto.[74]

Getting to Court

The Lawyers

Initially, Schmeiser went to his local lawyer who soon realized that patent law was well beyond his expertise and suggested that Schmeiser look to a specialized intellectual property firm. Terry Zakreski became Schmeiser's lawyer after a referral by Schmeiser's brother. Zakreski was encouraged by members of his firm to take the lead on this file as he had litigated trademark disputes and was interested in intellectual property law.[75] When Schmeiser first approached Zakreski's firm, Monsanto was accusing Schmeiser of knowingly purchasing seed from an unlicensed seller to avoid paying Monsanto the associated licensing fee. Zakreski states that in addition to the interesting legal issue this case presented, the case was appealing because Schmeiser was so adamant about his innocence. It is not difficult to see how having a tenacious client like Schmeiser would be attractive to a litigator.

Zakreski was born and raised in Saskatoon and attended law school at the University of Saskatchewan. He had been practicing law for about ten years when this case began. Although not a new lawyer by any means, this case presented many firsts for Zakreski. It was his first patent litigation, his first case to reach the SCC, and his first case to attract international media attention. This final first would have been true for almost any lawyer in Saskatoon, thus Zakreski had few mentors in the Saskatoon legal community that could help him prepare for the media frenzy surrounding this case.

From the beginning, concerns were raised about whether Schmeiser would be "out gunned" by the legal team Monsanto would mount for this case. Schmeiser, however, states that Zakreski's competency was never an issue. The only concern Schmeiser had about Zakreski was the lasting health impact this case may have had. Zakreski suffers from multiple sclerosis and the physical demands of litigating can be significant. When asked, Schmeiser was exceptionally complimentary about the quality of Zakreski's representation and his dedication to the case.

Zakreski continues to practice law in Saskatchewan. A subsequent, high-profile case, *Hoffman v Monsanto*, demonstrates his ongoing commitment to representing farmers.[76] In that case, organic farmers unsuccessfully attempted to certify a class action lawsuit to recover losses they alleged to have suffered as a result of the introduction of genetically modified seed into Saskatchewan. The farmers assert that because organic crops cannot be meaningfully segregated from genetically modified crops, like RR varieties, they can no longer market certain crops as organic.

Monsanto's legal team was based in Toronto and led by Roger T. Hughes, now a judge of the Federal Court. Hughes was an accomplished patent lawyer who had worked for Monsanto on their intellectual property law issues since the 1970s. [77] He was particularly suited for the technical nature of intellectual property law, as he had earlier achieved his professional engineer designation.[78] This training was no doubt put to use building the scientific evidence needed to challenge Schmeiser's version of how RR canola found its way onto his fields. This background and his significant experience in the Federal Court practice made him an obvious choice for appointment to the Federal Court in 2005.[79]

Hughes was assisted by associates in his firm, Arthur B. Renaud and LE Trent Horne. Both Renaud and Horne believe this case will likely be their most remembered. The interest in the case during the pre-trial process, the packed courtroom at trial, and the ongoing interest in this case only served to reinforce this belief. Renaud and Horne describe a memorable night, in 2005, when they attended a performance of the play *Seeds – Monsanto v Schmeiser* by Annabel Soutar. Despite, as Renaud describes it, "sticking out like a sore thumb," they were invited backstage after the performance to meet the cast. Although Hughes, Renaud, and Horne no longer litigate alongside one another, the three continue to collaborate. In 2008, the second edition of their publication *Federal Courts of Canada Service* was released.[80]

The Investigation

Science played a leading role at trial in establishing that Schmeiser knowingly planted RR Canola. Although not ultimately persuasive, Zakreski identified how elements of Monsanto's investigation of Schmeiser could be perceived as problematic. Because the origin of Schmeiser's RR seed was never determined, many of Schmeiser's supporters, and Schmeiser himself, continue to question the legitimacy of the scientific arguments presented by Monsanto. Some of the questions Schmeiser's defence raised about Monsanto's scientific evidence helps to explain why Schmeiser remains a credible advocate for the rights of farmers despite being found to have knowingly planted RR canola without a license.

First, questions were raised about the integrity of the samples of Schmeiser's canola. As mentioned, Schmeiser was reported by a neighbour who called one of the toll-free phone numbers Monsanto advertised for reporting unlicensed use of RR seeds throughout North America. To investigate these reports, to conduct audits of licensed growers in Saskatchewan, and to randomly test land-growing canola for RR varieties, Monsanto hired Robinson Investigations Ltd. Investigators also collected samples of plant material, including seeds and leaves, for further testing by Monsanto. Robinson Investigations Ltd., comprised mainly of former police officers, began conducting spray tests for Monsanto in the summer of 1997.[81] In a spray test, canola plants are sprayed with Roundup and left for ten to fourteen days to see if they survive the spray.[82] Plants that do not die are suspected to be grown from RR seed.

Monsanto's investigators could only use canola seed sprayed with Roundup in the ditches and public road allowances adjacent to canola crops without the landowner's permission, or risk trespassing on private land. Monsanto has repeatedly been accused of trespassing to obtain their samples throughout North America.[83] Schmeiser also accused Monsanto of trespassing to obtain canola samples from his land. As proof of the trespass, Schmeiser produced a battered pen embossed with Monsanto's name, which he stated he found in the centre of his field. The trial judge, however, did not find the pen persuasive proof of trespass and accepted all of Monsanto's field samples into evidence.

Permission to use granted by etcgroup.org.

Likewise, a persistent rumour exists that Monsanto has employed helicopters or planes to swoop down and aerially spray Roundup on farmer's fields.[84] Despite being unfounded, this rumour conjures up images of the secretive and illegal actions of oppressive police states and effectively casts Monsanto on the opposite side of democratic values and freedom. This image was further fueled by the use of former police officers and an admission by the owner of Robinson Investigations Ltd., Michael Robinson, that he "turned up the heat" on three farmers suspected of selling unlicensed seed to Schmeiser. At trial, Robinson admitted to lying about the existence of evidence that confirmed Schmeiser obtained unlicensed seed in an attempt to gain a confession from these farmers.

Although trespassing was the only unlawful action Monsanto employees were explicitly accused at trial of engaging in, the lawfulness of Monsanto's tactics continued to be raised by Schmeiser. For instance, he drew this author's attention to the fact that Robinson pled guilty in Saskatchewan Provincial Court and agreed to pay a $20,000 fine for unlawfully accessing an RCMP computer database to obtain information about individuals his private investigations firm was hired to investigate.[85] If Robinson was willing to engage in unlawful behaviour in other cases, what would prevent him from doing so in Schmeiser's case?

In August 1997, Wayne Derbyshire, a Robinson Investigations Ltd. employee from Regina was sent to collect canola samples from the fields of three farmers in the area around Bruno, Saskatchewan. Interestingly, samples from one of the other farmers sampled that day tested positive for the presence of RR canola.[86] No information exists, however, as to what consequences flowed from that discovery. Normally, an investigator from Saskatoon would have been sent to Bruno, but Derbyshire was sent to cover for someone on summer holidays. As such, Derbyshire was out of his usual territory. Unable to locate Schmeiser, Derbyshire purchased a map from the Rural Municipality Office and sampled two of Schmeiser's fields. He gathered pods of canola seeds from three locations on the edges of the two fields. These samples were sent to Monsanto employee Aaron Mitchell in Saskatoon.

Derbyshire's samples were one of three sets of samples Monsanto relied upon to prove the presence of RR canola in Schmeiser's fields during the 1997 and 1998 growing seasons. In August 1998, Monsanto obtained a court order to sample all of Schmeiser's fields including those he rented. Don Todd, of Robinson Investigations Ltd. and Jim Vancha from Monsanto, gathered six samples from each of Schmeiser's nine fields seeded with canola in 1998. Three samples from each field were left with Schmeiser, and the remaining samples were sent to Mitchell at Monsanto.

The final set of samples came from Humboldt Flour Mills (HFM), a seed cleaning and treatment plant in Bruno where Schmeiser treated his seed with a fungicide before planting in 1998. Unbeknownst to Schmeiser, HFM collected samples of their clients' seeds before and after treatment for quality control purposes.[87] Monsanto representative Rob Chomyn obtained the HFM samples and also delivered them to Mitchell.[88] Thus, all of Monsanto's samples were in Mitchell's sole custody at one time. Although there is no evidence that Mitchell tampered with the samples, he had the opportunity to do so. In fact, despite not providing any specific evidence of tampering by Mitchell, Zakreski's questions on cross-examination raised enough suspicion that Hughes felt the need to explicitly ask Mitchell if he tampered with the samples in redirect.[89] Mitchell categorically denied any interference with the evidence.

One of the ways Zakreski proposed the seeds could have been tampered with was by using a "quick test" that detects the presence of the RR gene within minutes. The quick test could have allowed Monsanto's investigators to select only RR plants to sample, thereby misrepresenting the amount of the RR canola in Schmeiser's fields. Although Monsanto regularly used the quick test method to test for the RR gene, no evidence was presented to support the assertion that samples from Schmeiser's fields were selected after being identified as RR by the quick test. Moreover, when asked, Todd and Vancha explicitly stated that they did not have quick testers with them when they gathered samples from Schmeiser's fields.[90] Likewise, Mitchell testified that he did not use the quick test to prescreen Schmeiser's samples.[91]

Nonetheless, the integrity of Monsanto's samples remains under suspicion particularly as the only set of samples that did not pass through Mitchell on the way to testing had a lower concentration of RR canola. Schmeiser sent half of the court ordered samples he received from Todd and Vancha to Monsanto and the other half to its own expert to test for the presence of the RR gene. While the majority of samples revealed virtually the same concentrations of RR seed as Monsanto samples, there was one discrepancy. Samples from one field tested by Friesen indicated a 68 percent concentration rather than a concentration in the 90-percent range as reported by Monsanto.[92]

Another, perhaps less sinister, challenge to the integrity of Monsanto's samples arises from how the seeds were collected by Monsanto. At trial, investigators from Robinsons Investigations Ltd. described a process of sampling each field by collecting plant material from multiple plants from at least three locations in each field.[93] If, however, the investigators did not diligently follow this sampling protocol, as suggested by Zakreski, and collected plant material from one plant or from one area of the field, the amount of RR canola in Schmeiser's fields may have been misrepresented.

Finally, the legal land description was mislabelled on every sample taken from Schmeiser's land by Todd and Vancha. The samples were labelled as being taken from land west of the third rather than second meridian. Given that the distance between meridians is hundreds of kilometres, the court accepted Todd's explanation that he mistakenly wrote the third meridian as he had just been working in that area.[94] For those looking for malice, that Monsanto built a case against Schmeiser using samples obtain from the wrong fields is not beyond reason.

In addition, Zakreski raised questions about the independence of the testing Monsanto relied upon to establish the presence of RR canola in Schmeiser's canola. Monsanto's in-house laboratory facilities at St. Louis conducted the majority of the scientific tests that verified the presence of the RR gene in Schmeiser's canola. Mitchell also contracted researchers at the University of Saskatchewan and Prairie Plant Systems to conduct grow-out tests whereby seeds are planted and grown until they have a few leaves and can be sprayed with Roundup.[95] Mitchell, however, designed the testing protocol, provided the seeds, and applied Roundup to the plants.[96] Thus, Monsanto was actively engaged in all of the testing at these independent facilities.

When asked why independent testing was not undertaken, Monsanto's counsel indicated that in-house testing kept costs down. In-house testing was also not seen as an unusual practice in patent litigation, as often few people beyond the patent holder have the necessary skills to conduct the testing. Moreover, where there is competence, it is often housed in the laboratories of the patent holder's competitors.[97] At trial, Monsanto demonstrated that its scientists at its St. Louis head office followed meticulous protocols for documenting their research methods and findings. For example, the chain of custody was recorded whenever the samples moved through the laboratory.[98] The content of each page of a scientist's laboratory book was acknowledged and also signed by another scientist within a week of the first scientist recording her notes. The integrity of their research findings is, therefore, difficult to call into question without alleging that multiple Monsanto employees were involved in a conspiracy to frame Schmeiser. No evidence of such a conspiracy emerged from the trial.

In Court

The Experts

At trial, Monsanto relied on testimony from in-house experts to establish that its patented RR gene was found on Schmeiser's field and that it had not licensed its use to Schmeiser. Beyond questioning the integrity of the science as previously described, the defence did not present any evidence to dispute these findings. Therefore, Schmeiser had the burden of showing that although RR seed was found in his fields, he did not knowingly infringe the patent. As a result, much of the trial was spent testing the veracity of Schmeiser's account of how RR canola had ended up in his fields. If Monsanto had found any evidence of how Schmeiser obtained brown-bagged RR canola seed as it alleged, expert evidence challenging Schmeiser's account would have been unnecessary.

According to Schmeiser, in 2006 he discovered canola plants around power poles adjacent to his field that did not die when sprayed with Roundup.[99] Having heard about the growing problem of pesticide resistance associated with overuse of pesticides, Schmeiser thought he may have the same problem. He investigated this further by spraying an area in his field adjacent to those power poles. Most of those canola plants also did not die. When it was time to harvest, Schmeiser, who was laid up recovering from a farming accident, directed his hired man, Carlyle Moritz, to first combine the area he had sprayed. Moritz unloaded the first collection of canola seed from the combine into the back of an old truck. The truck was later placed in a garage, where the seed sat, under a tarp, until the next spring. This seed was used to plant his fields in the spring of 2007. When it became clear that his plants were resistant to glysophate because they contained RR gene, Schmeiser speculated that the seed blew into his field from trucks moving harvested canola to the elevator. Without a specific known incident of when RR canola blew onto his fields, Schmeiser's defence aimed to establish the reasonableness of such an assertion.

In anticipation of Schmeiser's defence, Monsanto called two experts from academia to challenge Schmeiser's account of how RR canola entered his fields. The first was Dr. Philip Barry Hertz, a mechanical engineer from the University of Saskatchewan. His research focused on the dispersal of particles through the air. He provided his expert opinion that given the height of the trucks carrying the canola seed and the prevailing wind speed, canola seed blown from trucks was not the source of the RR canola seed in Schmeiser's fields.[100]

Schmeiser's defence attempted to counter the opinion offered by Hertz by questioning the assumptions Hertz made about prevailing wind speeds.[101] In addition, Hertz's analysis did not consider the possibility that seed dropped on frozen ground or into run-off waters may continue to travel after it originally was blown out of a truck.[102] Schmeiser also provided photographs of trucks with mature canola plants caught in their undercarriage and a number of truck drivers admitted that trucks are not always covered when canola is being hauled.[103] Two farmers who had problems with volunteer RR canola and had Monsanto representatives come to their land and remove the volunteer plants also provided evidence about their experience with the uncontrolled spread of RR canola.[104]

In the event that the court accepted Schmeiser's assertion that the potential existed for seed to have blown onto his field, Monsanto called Dr. R. Keith Downey to provide his expert opinion. Downey is often referred to as the Father of Canola, due to his pivotal role in breeding rapeseed into the viable agricultural commodity renamed canola. Although not an employee, Downey had received research support from Monsanto in the past. His objectivity, therefore, was questioned by the defence.[105] Although no evidence was presented to suggest that Downey's analysis was not conducted at arm's-length from Monsanto, one incident at trial did suggest that he did not view the case objectively. Downey, for no apparent reason other than to raise questions about Schmeiser's character, chose to inform the court, while under cross-examination, that the old farm truck was unlicensed when Schmeiser said it was used to transport the combined RR seed. In Downey's opinion, Schmeiser's account could not explain the amount and concentration of RR canola in Schmeiser's fields.[106] Downey's conclusions would ultimately prove insurmountable.

Findings

When this case went to trial, the legality of a patent on life, including seeds, was uncertain. The Federal Court of Appeal had yet to release its decision in *Harvard Mouse,* although at trial, a mammal was held to be unpatentable.[107] Thus, Schmeiser challenged the validity of Monsanto's patent on the ground that it claimed unpatentable subject matter. In support of this assertion, Schmeiser pointed to the *Plant Breeder's Rights Act*[108] as evidence of Parliament's intention to exclude plants from the *Patent Act*.[109] Justice MacKay rejected Schmeiser's claim that *Harvard Mouse* was a relevant authority as *Harvard Mouse* dealt with claims on an entire mammal, not its components.

Likewise, the court rejected Schmeiser's argument that Monsanto's uncontrolled release of the RR Canola and its subsequent inability to control its spread, waived its patent right to exclusive possession. Instead, Monsanto's use of Technology Use Agreements (TUAs) to control access to the seed, subsequent enforcement of these agreements and removal of unwanted plants were found to be sufficient efforts to control the patented seed. Finally, MacKay J held that Schmeiser infringed Monsanto's patent when he planted RR canola. Planting, whether intentional or not, was an unlicensed use of Monsanto's patented invention.

Monsanto was granted an injunction restraining Schmeiser from any continued infringement of Monsanto's patent. Schmeiser was also ordered to deliver all plants and seeds from his 1997 and 1998 crops to Monsanto. Monsanto also received an order for profits of $19,832.[110] Monsanto did not succeed in persuading the court that Schmeiser's actions warranted exemplary damages.

By the time the appeal was argued before Sharlow JA, the Federal Court of Appeal had reversed the trial judge's decision in *Harvard Mouse*; the genetically engineered mouse could be patented.[111] Consequently, it is not surprising that MacKay J's decision was affirmed. One distinction worth noting is that Sharlow JA was not prepared to dismiss the relevance of intention to the question of infringement as had been done by MacKay J. The appeal decision appears to lay the foundation for the "innocent" farmer exception to patent infringement articulated in the SCC's decision.

A detailed analysis of the legal significance of the SCC's decision in *Monsanto v Schmeiser* can readily be found in one of the many articles written about this case.[112] From the perspective of Monsanto's lawyers, this case filled a hole left by the SCC in the *Harvard Mouse* case.[113] In *Harvard Mouse*, the SCC overturned the Federal Court of Appeal, and reaffirmed the longstanding prohibition of patenting higher life forms in Canadian patent law.[114] What remained unclear, however, was where the line should be drawn between lower and higher life forms. In addition, it was not known whether the patenting of genes and cells of a higher life form was also precluded by the prohibition.

Monsanto v Schmeiser did not definitively answer the first question. Cells and genes of plants, however, can be patented even if the effect of granting the patent allows for restrictions on the use of plants that contain the patented material. The effect of the patent is not limited to the patented material isolated in a laboratory as suggested by the dissent.

From Schmeiser's perspective, the SCC's decision was certainly a disappointment. Briefly, by gathering and replanting canola that contained what Schmeiser should have known was the RR gene, Schmeiser used Monsanto's patent even though he derived no benefit from the RR characteristic. A majority of the SCC did not accept Schmeiser's argument that following *Harvard Mouse*, patenting a seed violated the prohibition on the patenting of higher life forms. The court also rejected his alternative argument that the Plant Breeder's Rights regime precluded seeds from becoming patented. Schmeiser had infringed Monsanto's patent.

The SCC held, however, that because Monsanto had sought the remedy of an accounting of profit rather than damages, it was not entitled to the profits awarded in the lower courts, as Schmeiser derived no profit from Monsanto's property. Had Schmeiser sold his seed at a higher price because it was RR, or used Roundup while growing the crop, the Court likely would have awarded a remedy. In addition, as there was a split result, there was no order as to costs. For Schmeiser, the SCC provided him with the best loss possible given that both the trial and appeal courts awarded damages for infringement and costs to Monsanto.

Despite an ultimate finding of infringement, another win for Schmeiser was that Monsanto did not prove its allegation that he deliberately acquired the RR seed through an unlicensed purchase. After Monsanto failed to produce any evidence to support this allegation at trial, Zakreski made an application for summary judgment and Monsanto was forced to abandon this claim. It is interesting to speculate whether Monsanto was disappointed that it could not pursue the piracy claim. Monsanto likely realized, whether successful or not, the issue risked raising other concerns about agricultural biotechnology among the general public.

First, Monsanto only made RR canola available to growers through licensed seed dealers grown by licensed seed stock producers. Anyone who purchased the seed had to sign a TUA which prohibited the sale of RR canola for seed. Thus, if Schmeiser was able to acquire brown-bagged seed, the source would have been a Monsanto licensee. A breakdown in Monsanto's control of its patented seed would likely attract criticism from those who express concern about the ability to control this technology.

No doubt Monsanto was aware of the 2000 Starlink recall in the United States.[115] Corn that had been genetically engineered and marketed under the name Starlink had received approval for introduction in the animal feed market only. Starlink was not approved for human consumption. Nonetheless, tests revealed that Starlink corn was present in a number of processed foods. A large recall of corn products contaminated with Starlink was subsequently initiated. Moreover, many people called for a ban of agricultural biotechnology or, at a minimum, stricter regulation. If Monsanto pursued the source of the RR canola in Schmeiser's fields, it risked providing evidence to support the argument that agricultural biotechnology potentially poses a health and safety risk because it is difficult to control once introduced into the market.

Furthermore, if unsuccessful in its attempt to prove that Schmeiser was a seed pirate and the court accepted Schmeiser's description of how he acquired the seed, the degree to which bioengineered seed varieties can spread would come under scrutiny. To this day, Schmeiser maintains that RR canola blew onto his field after the first harvest of RR canola in Canada.

While the SCC did not find that Schmeiser had purchased unlicensed seed, they did accept the trial judge's conclusion that Schmeiser's story did not adequately explain the degree of concentration of RR canola in his field. This result is not surprising as the trial judge was asked to weigh the scientific explanations regarding the spread and concentration of RR canola in Schmeiser's fields by Monsanto's experts with the somewhat anecdotal evidence presented by the defence. Ultimately, a majority of the court held that by harvesting and replanting seed, Schmeiser ought to have known that it contained Monsanto's patented RR gene; Schmeiser was not an innocent bystander. The court distinguished Schmeiser from those who just happen upon unexpected RR canola plants in their fields. In that circumstance, if the landowner did not use the seed in any way, Monsanto's patent would not be infringed. Thus, the often spoken fear that a finding of infringement in this case would result in liability for farmers who had no control over RR seeds blowing into their fields was unfounded.

Even though Monsanto abandoned the piracy claim, maligning Schmeiser's character appeared to be deliberate strategy to counter the bad publicity it was receiving. One attempt to portray Schmeiser as dishonest during trial was not successful. Instead, it revealed the limits of the research Monsanto's Toronto-based lawyers had undertaken to become familiar with the underlying context of the case. While questioning Schmeiser on the stand, Hughes tried to demonstrate Schmeiser's dishonesty by comparing a receipt for the purchase of seed with Schmeiser's records.[116] One recorded the purchase as wheat, the other grain. When asked to explain the discrepancy, Schmeiser did not know how to respond. Wheat, of course, is a grain.

Conclusion

Monsanto v Schmeiser is certainly a case that will continue to be studied by property law and patent infringement scholars and litigators. The SCC's decision provides an instructive outline for how patents can be infringed by unauthorized use. Likewise, the adoption of a comparable approach to determine that an award of profits was not warranted has been identified as novel.[117] Nonetheless, the case will primarily be remembered for its vocal and unyielding defendant, Percy Schmeiser, and the number of broader issues this case has been used to draw attention to.

Although conclusive proof of this assertion is likely not possible, it is not unreasonable to suggest that much of the interest in this case was a result of its timing. In particular, global use of the Internet was reaching a tipping point. Civil society began to feel they had the means to connect and mobilize in a way that could challenge the perceived unrestrained, self-interested power exercised by transnational corporations. Schmeiser emerged as a champion of civil society because his fight with Monsanto provided a proxy for this struggle between civil society and transnational corporations.

It is, therefore, not surprising that the finding of infringement did little to deter the Schmeisers' supporters. Together they have won numerous awards and accolades including the Right Livelihood Award, often referred to as the alternative Nobel Prize. The Right Livelihood Award is given to honour and support those "offering practical and exemplary answers to the most urgent challenges facing us today."[118] In addition, Schmeiser is regularly invited to speak at conferences, workshops, and other public events. One memorable invitation came from the Prince of Wales. Schmeiser had the opportunity to meet the Prince in Turin, Italy, after a meeting between the two was deemed inappropriate due to the ongoing legal dispute when the Prince visited Saskatchewan in 2001.[119]

While Schmeiser lost at the SCC, these awards recognize his success in drawing attention to some of the concerns associated with agricultural biotechnology. Principal among these concerns is the question of whether Monsanto is liable for any harm that results from the use of the patent seed. In 2005, Louise Schmeiser asked the court to address the issue in an application in Small Claims Court. Louise sued Monsanto to recover the costs associated with removing unwanted RR canola that had blown into her garden. The matter was settled out of court with Monsanto agreeing to reimburse Louise for these costs.[120] The question of whether Monsanto is liable for any harm that results from the use of its patented seed is an important question now that there is evidence of Roundup resistance in weed species.[121]

Postscript

Monsanto's patent for the variety of RR canola found in Schmeiser's fields expired in February 2010. Monsanto, however, remains able to benefit from its discovery of the herbicidal properties of glyphosate. Monsanto is marketing many new, patented varieties of RR canola and other seed crops. Monsanto's successful transformation from a chemical company to a seed company, however, continues to attract criticism. Legal action is ongoing to prevent the introduction of RR seed varieties into markets that currently do not have RR varieties.[122]

As for the Schmeisers, they are no longer actively farming. During the 2010 growing season, their remaining farmland was rented out. Nonetheless, the Schmeisers have not retired. Interest in the case does not seem to be waning. They continue to be widely sought after speakers and consultants on the regulation of biotechnology in agriculture. Schmeiser and Zakreski also recently met with the producers of an upcoming feature film about the case. While a farmer's right to save seed remains a central concern of the Schmeisers, possible health and environmental effects of agricultural biotechnology increasingly underlie their ongoing hostility to the continued introduction of these crops. This shift is perhaps fitting given that for much of the public, especially the non-farm public, these issues, not property rights, motivated their interest in this case.

Notes

1 Assistant Professor, College of Law, University of Saskatchewan. I wish to acknowledge Jared Craig, Zeke Zimonick, and Deirdre Bryant who provided excellent research assistance as I prepared this piece.

2 *Monsanto Canada Inc. v Schmeiser* [2004] 1 SCR 902 [*Monsanto v Schmeiser*].

3 *Ibid* at para 2.

4 *Percy Schmeiser: David versus Monsanto*, (DENKmal-Film 2009).

5 Monsanto, *Growing Together: 2009 Annual Report* (2009), at ii.

6 *Ibid* at 4.

7 Above note 5 at 4.

8 Above note 5 at 5.

9 Above note 5 at 5.

10 "Monsanto sells vanillin business" *The Day* (12 October 1986), online: Google News http://news.google.com/newspapers?nid=1915&dat=19861012&id=cywrAAAAIBAJ&sjid=HnIFAAAAIBAJ&pg=6081,2885176.

11 "Monsanto Company" online: Reference for Business, www.referenceforbusiness.com/history2/92/Monsanto-Company.html.

12 "April 16, 1947: Texas City explodes" online: A&E Television Networks www.history.com/this-day-in-history/texas-city-explodes.

13 Ammonium nitrate is extremely explosive. Its use in improvised explosive devices has recently resulted in more stringent monitoring of its movement and sale (See *Restricted Components Regulations*, SOR/2008-47 of the *Explosives Act*, RS, 1985, c E-17).

14 Fire Prevention and Engineering Bureau of Texas and the National Board of Fire Underwriters, "Texas City, Texas, Disaster Report" at 8, online: www.local1259iaff.org/report.htm.

15 *Ibid* at 9.

16 "History" online: ICWUC/UFCW Local 81C www.local81c.com/history.html.

17 See, for example, Michael Grunwald, "Monsanto Hid Decades of Pollution" *The Washington Post* (1 January 2002), online: www.washingtonpost.com/ac2/wp-dyn?pagename=article&contentId=A46648-2001Dec31; Eric Coppolino, "Pandora's Poison" 7-8 *Synthesis/Regeneration* (Summer 1995), online: www.greens.org/s-r/078/07-50.html.

18 "Walk in the Fields of Our Fertile History" online: Monsanto Company www.monsanto.com/whoweare/Pages/monsanto-history.aspx.

19 Health Canada, "It's Your Health: Dioxins and Furans" (Ottawa: Health Canada, 2005) online: www.hc-sc.gc.ca/hl-vs/alt_formats/pacrb-dgapcr/pdf/iyh-vsv/environ/dioxin-eng.pdf.

20 See, for example, "Monsanto Wins Dioxin Lawsuit Filed by Seven" *The New York Times* (1 May 1985) online: www.nytimes.com/1985/05/01/us/monsanto-wins-dioxin-lawsuit-filed-by-seven.html; Cate Jenkins, "Monsanto Corporation Criminal Investigation Cover-up of Dioxin Contamination in Products Falsification of Dioxin Health Studies," Report to John West, Special Agent in Charge Office of Criminal Investigations

Center US Environmental Protection Agency (15 November 1990) online: www.mindfully.org/Pesticide/Monsanto-Coverup-Dioxin-USEPA15nov90.htm.

21 Jim DeBrosse, "Dayton shunned, stunned by exclusion from bomb history: Area faces hard fight to win place in nation's park system linked to Manhattan Project" *Dayton Daily News* (8 December 2004) online: www.atomicheritage.org/index.php?id=83&option=com_content&task=view.

22 Ralph Landau, "Charles Allen Thomas," in National Academy of Engineers, *Memorial Tributes: National Academy of Engineering, Volume 2* (Washington, DC: National Academy Press, 1984) at 281.

23 On 9 February 2000, Monsanto was incorporated as a subsidiary of Pharmacia Corporation. Pharmacia, itself, is a subsidiary of Pfizer Inc. Today, no control relationship exists between Monsanto, Pharmacia, or Solution. The three companies, however, remain linked through indemnification, service and supply agreements.

24 "Company History" online: Monsanto Company www.monsanto.com/who_we_are/monsanto_relationships.asp.

25 John E. Franz, Michael K. Mao, James A. Sikorski, *Glyphosate: a Unique Global Herbicide* (Washington, DC: American Chemical Society, 1997) at 6.

26 John E. Franz, "Discovery, development, and chemistry of glyphosate" in E. Grossbard, D. Atkinson, eds, *The Herbicide Glyphosate*, (London: Butterworths, 1985) at 4.

27 *Ibid* at 3.

28 Above note 25 at 8.

29 Above note 26 at 3.

30 Above note 25 at 7.

31 Above note 25 at 7.

32 Saskatchewan, Standing Committee on the Economy, *Hansard Verbatim Report*, 26th Leg. 1st sess., No. 26 (27 April 2010) online: www.legassembly.sk.ca/committees/Economy/Verbatim/100427Economy.pdf.

33 Bobbie Hasselbring, "Weed Pollen," online: Discovery Health http://health.discovery.com/centers/articles/articles.html?chrome=c16&article=LC_13&center=p01.

34 Pimentel, D., Zuniga, R., and D. Morrison. 2005. "Update on the Environmental and Economic Costs Associated with Alien-Invasive Species in the United States." 52 *Ecological Economics* 273-288.

35 Above note 18.

36 US Environmental Protection Agency, "2000-2001 Pesticide Market Estimates: Usage" online: www.epa.gov/oppbead1/pestsales/01pestsales/usage2001_2.htm#3_6. In 2001, one year after Monsanto's patent on glyphosate expired, glyphosate overtook atrazine for the top selling pesticide

37 Above note 2525 at 21. Phosophonic acids are commonly used as chelating agents that are used to bind metal ions for a variety of industrial applications.

38 Above note 25 at 22.

39 "Recipient List of National Medal of Technology and Innovation" online: US Patent and Trademark Office www.uspto.gov/about/nmti/recipients/1987.jsp (note his name is listed incorrectly as John F. Franz).

40 "Profile for John E. Franz" online: National Inventor Hall of Fame www.invent.org/hall_of_fame/333.html.

41 Above note 18.

42 Above note 18.

43 *Monsanto v Schmeiser* (5 June 2000), Saskatoon T-1593-98 (F.C.T.D.) (Opening Remarks, plaintiff).

44 Above note 18.

45 "Evaluation Canola" online: Monsanto Company www.biotechknowledge.com/biotech/bbasics.nsf/biotech01_canola.html.

46 Rod Nickel, "UPDATE 3-Canada farmers to plant record canola area" (26 April, 2010) online: Reuters www.reuters.com/article/idUSN2121826720100426.

47 "Canola Quick Facts" online: Canola Council www.canolacouncil.org/facts_gmo.aspx.

48 Jack Kaskey, "Monsanto to Charge as Much as 42% More for New Seeds (Update3)" (13 August 2009) Online: Bloomberg.com www.bloomberg.com/apps/news?pid=20601103&sid=aLW8VZBkP3PA.

49 *Monsanto Canada Inc. v Schmeiser* 12 CPR (4th) 204 at para 37.

50 Douglas A. Schmeiser, *A Settling of Accounts* (Ottawa: Borealis Press, 2009) at 52.

51 David McLennan, "Bruno," *The Encyclopedia of Saskatchewan* (Regina, SK: Canadian Plains Research Center, 2005) at 133.

52 See, for example, The National Catholic Rural Life Conference, *Agricultural Biotechnology: A Catholic Rural Life Perspective* (June 2002) online: www.ncrlc.com/NCRLC_GE_webstatement.html.

53 Interview of Percy Schmeiser by Patricia L. Farnese (24 June 2010), Bruno, SK.

54 Above note 43 (Examination-in-chief, P. Schmeiser).

55 Above note 53.

56 *Ibid.*

57 Interview of Percy Schmeiser, online: TUC radio http://emma2.radio4all.net/pub/files/tuc@tucradio.org/0107schmeiser.mp3.

58 Above note 49 at para 7.

59 Statistics Canada, *Census of Agriculture, Saskatchewan Highlights* online: www.statcan.gc.ca/ca-ra/saskatchewan-eng.pdf.

60 Statistics Canada classifies farms as small, medium, large, and very large based on annual revenues. Medium farms have annual revenue of $100,000 to $249,999. Given that a large majority of the Schmeisers' 1998 crop was planted to canola, it is unlikely that sales of their remaining crop would exceed $250,000.

61 Above note 49 at para 6.

62 Between 1981 and 2001, the number of family farm corporations in Canada quadrupled (AAFC, *Next Generation of Agriculture and Agri-Food Policy. Economic Backgrounder: Changing structure of primary agriculture* at 6).

63 Above note 53.

64 Above note 54.

65 "Historical Provincial Vote Summaries, online: Elections Saskatchewan www.elections.sk.ca/historicalgeneralelectionsarchive.php.

66 Interview of Percy Schmeiser by Paul Goettlich (27 May 2004) online: www.mindfully.org/GE/2004/Percy-Schmeiser-Persistent27may04.htm.

67 Above note 54.

68 *Ibid.*

69 *Bruno (Town) v Schmeiser* (2008) Sask R 207 at para 6.

70 *Ibid* at paras 25 and 41.

71 *Bayne No. 371 (Rural Municipality) v Saskatchewan Water Corp.* [1990] SJ No 265.

72 *Ibid.*

73 Above note 53.

74 *Ibid.*

75 Email from Terry Zakreski to Patricia L. Farnese (15 September 2010).

76 220 DLR (4th) 542; 227 Sask R 63.

77 Telephone Interview of Arthur B. Renaud and LE Trent Horne by Patricia L. Farnese (9 July 2010).

78 "The Honourable Roger T. Hughes" online: Federal Court of Canada http://cas-ncr-nter03.cas-satj.gc.ca/portal/page/portal/fc_cf_en/Hughes.

79 "Judicial Appointments 2005" online: Department of Justice www.justice.gc.ca/eng/news-nouv/index.asp?action=tdetail&tid=4&year=2005&ssum=1.

80 Roger T. Hughes, Arthur B. Renaud & LE Trent Horne, *Federal Courts of Canada Service, 2nd Edition* (Toronto, LexisNexis Canada, 2008).

81 Above note 43 (Examination-in-chief, Michael F. Robinson).

82 Above note 43 (Examination-in-chief, Wayne Derbyshire).

83 See, for example, Robert Schubert, "Monsanto goes after Indiana farm family," *CropChoice News* (25 September 2001) online: www.cropchoice.com/leadstry4901.html?recid=470.

84 See, for example, Linn Cohen-Cole, "Genetically Modified Seeds: Monsanto is Putting Normal Seeds out of Reach" (14 Feb 2009) online: Global Research www.globalresearch.ca/index.php?context=va&aid=12309.

85 "Private eye fined for accessing police computer system" (15 December 2006) online: CBC Radio-Canada www.cbc.ca/canada/saskatchewan/story/2006/12/15/robinson.html.

86 Telephone Interview of Wayne Derbyshire by Patricia L. Farnese (23 June 2010).

87 Above note 43 (Examination-in-chief, G. Pappenfoot).

88 Above note 43 (Examination-in-chief, R. Chomyn).

89 Above note 43 (Reexamination, Aaron Mitchell).

90 Above note 43 (Cross-examination, D. Todd) and (Cross-examination, J. Vancha).

91 Above note 43 (Cross-examination, A. Mitchell).

92 Above note 43 (Examination-in-chief, L. Friesen).

93 See, for example, above note 43 (Examination-in-chief, Wayne Derbyshire).

94 Above note 43 (Examination-in-chief, D. Todd).

95 Above note 43 (Examination-in-chief, Aaron Mitchell).

96 *Ibid.*

97 Above note 77.

98 Above note 43 (Examination-in-chief, Doris Dixon).

99 Above note 53.
100 Above note 43 (Examination-in-chief, PB Hertz).
101 Above note 43 (Cross-examination, PB Hertz).
102 *Ibid.*
103 Above note 43 (Examination-in-chief, P. Schmeiser) and (Examination-in-chief. E. Borstmayer).
104 Above note 43 (Examination-in-chief, L. Gerwing) and (Examination-in-chief, C. Boser).
105 Above note 43 (Cross-examination, RK Downey).
106 Above note 43 (Examination-in-chief, RK Downey).
107 *Harvard College v Canada* (Commissioner of Patents), 146 FTR 279.
108 SC 1990. C 20.
109 RSC, 1985, c P-6.
110 *Monsanto Canada Inc. v Schmeiser* (2002), 19 CPR (4th) 524, 2002 FCT 439.
111 President and Fellows of Harvard College *v* Canada (Commissioner of Patents), [2000] 223 F.T.R. 320.
112 See, for example, Philippe Cullet, "A Landmark Decision concerning Farmer Liability and Transgenic Contamination: *Monsanto Canada Inc. v Schmeiser*," (2005) J Env L 17:83-108; Robert Burrell, Stephen Hubicki, "Patent Liability and Genetic Drift," (2005) 7 Envtl L Rev 278; Bruce Ziff, "Travels with My Plant: *Monsanto v Schmeiser* Revisted," (2005) 2 U Ottawa L & Tech J 493; Robert Stack, "How Do I Use This Thing? What's It Good for Anyway? A Study of the Meaning of Use and the Test for Patent Infringement in the *Monsanto Canada Inc. v Schmeiser* Decisions," (2005) 18 IPJ 277; Sean Robertson, "Re-Imagining Economic Alterity: A Feminist Critique of the Juridicial Expansion of Bioproperty in the Monsanto Decision at the Supreme Court of Canada," (2005) 2 U Ottawa L & Tech J 277; Siddharth Khanijou, "Patent Inequity: Rethinking the Application of Strict Liability to Patent Law in the Nanotechnology Era," (2007) 12 J Tech L 179.
113 *Harvard College v Canada (Commissioner of Patents),* [2002] 4 SCR 45.
114 *Ibid.*
115 *Re Starlink Corn Prods. Liability Litigation,* 212 F. Supp. 2d 828 (ND Ill. 2002).
116 Above note 43 (Cross-examination, P. Schmeiser).
117 Kurtis Andrews and Jeremy De Beer, "Accounting of Profits to Remedy Biotechnology Patent Infringement," (2010) 47 Osgoode Hall LJ 619.
118 "About the Right Livelihood Award" Online: www.rightlivelihood.org/award.html?&no_cache=1.
119 Above note 53.
120 Monsanto, Media Release, "Percy Schmeiser Settles Small Claims Issue with Monsanto Canada" (19 March 2008), online: www.monsanto.ca/about/news/2008/03_19_08.asp.
121 University of Guelph, News Release, "U of G Researchers Find Suspected Glyphosate-Resistant Weed" (7 May 2009), online:www.uoguelph.ca/news/2009/05/u_of_g_research_19.html.
122 See, for example, *Monsanto Company, et al. v Geertson Seed Farms,* 130 S. Ct. 2743; *Center for Food Safety v Thomas* J *Vilsack* 2010 US Dist LEXIS 92369.

A Railway, a City, and the Public Regulation of Private Property: *CPR v City of Vancouver*

Douglas C. Harris[1]

The Arbutus Corridor winds ten kilometres north-south through the west side of the City of Vancouver. Owned in fee simple by the Canadian Pacific Railway (CPR), this fifty- to sixty-six foot-wide strip of land is, depending on one's perspective, forty-five acres of enormously valuable real estate, or a precious ribbon of automobile-free urban land (Figure 1). The CPR carved most of the corridor out of the provincial land grant that induced the company to move the terminus of its transcontinental railway from a planned location at the eastern end of Burrard Inlet to the western end — to what would become Vancouver. Built in 1902 to carry freight and passengers from the commercial centre of Vancouver to the northern arm of the Fraser River and beyond to the fish canning town of Steveston, the Arbutus Corridor line ceased passenger service in 1954, but continued to move freight until 2001. One year before the last train rolled along the line, and as the CPR explored development options, the City passed the Arbutus Corridor Official Development Plan (Appendix A). Intended to preserve the linear strip from development, the plan limited use of the corridor to a "public thoroughfare" for rail, transit, or cycling, or to some mix of park and paths that the City labelled a "greenway." Automobiles were expressly excluded and other development would not be considered. The company turned to the courts, arguing that the City had taken its property for which compensation was due, and *CPR v City of Vancouver* was born.[2]

This chapter considers the intertwined histories of a railway company and a city that gave rise to *CPR v City of Vancouver*. It begins with the land grants that gave the CPR such a strong corporate presence in Vancouver. The company was one of the city's principal employers and by far its largest landholder, and it used its position to establish basic patterns of urban land use; industrial, commercial, and residential districts all followed the CPR's lead. As the city grew and the CPR sold its land, the company's influence waned, but it retained the capacity to shape the urban form when, in the early 1960s, the CPR turned, through its subsidiary, Marathon Realty, to real estate development. This chapter describes these initiatives, particularly those involving rail lands that were to be converted to other, usually residential, uses. It then turns to the Arbutus Corridor, to the CPR's development planning, and to the city's official development plan.

The final two sections of this chapter analyse the progression of *CPR v City of Vancouver* to the Supreme Court of Canada (SCC), and then reflect on what the decision means for the city and what it reveals about the role of the courts in Canada as arbiters of the boundary between public regulation and private property. In its first engagement in nearly twenty years with the doctrine known in the United States as regulatory taking and in Canada, variously, as *de facto* expropriation, constructive taking, or *de facto* taking, the SCC, in a brief twelve paragraphs, ruled public regulation of private property would amount to a taking of that property that warranted compensation only if the state effectively acquired the interest *and* prevented all reasonable uses of that interest by its owner.[3] The Arbutus Corridor Official Development Plan did not meet either criteria and therefore the city need not choose between compensating the company for its loss of a property interest or rescinding the development plan. As a result, the plan and the railway remain in place; the property remains unused and undeveloped by its owner. Beyond this particular outcome, *CPR v City of Vancouver* appears to confirm the reluctance of Canadian courts to patrol the regulation of private property. Indeed, the courts in Canada have seldom intervened to require public compensation for regulations that limit the uses of private property,[4] and this chapter concludes by locating this judicial reticence within a legal framework that does not include constitutional guarantees of rights to private property.

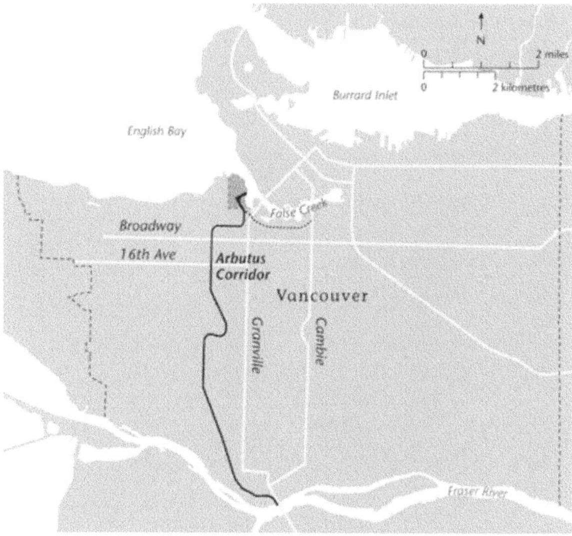

Figure 1. Arbutus Corridor.

CPR and the Making of Vancouver

Once upon a time, a city gave itself away in order that a great railway might be induced to establish its terminus there.[5]

THE CITY OF VANCOUVER arrived with the Canadian Pacific Railway, but might well have been otherwise.[6] The town site of Port Moody at the eastern end of Burrard Inlet on the Pacific Ocean was to have been the transcontinental line's western terminus. The Federal government had announced as much in 1881 when it passed the *CPR Act* and identified Port Moody as the end of the line.[7] In anticipation of the railway's completion and the economic activity that a terminus would bring, investors and speculators acquired land in and around the town site, bidding up its value, even shutting out the railway builder itself. As a result, the CPR looked elsewhere for a location where it might benefit, as a landholder, from the economic activity that the railway would generate. Another small settlement which had emerged around the Hastings lumber mill and the adjacent Granville town site lay nearly twenty kilometres west on Burrard Inlet. With a population of approximately 400 people in the early 1880s, Granville sat just east of a 480-acre provincial government reserve (District Lot 541). Most of the surrounding land was subject to timber leases, but not otherwise alienated, and in 1885 the CPR received the government reserve and a larger parcel (District Lot 526) in exchange

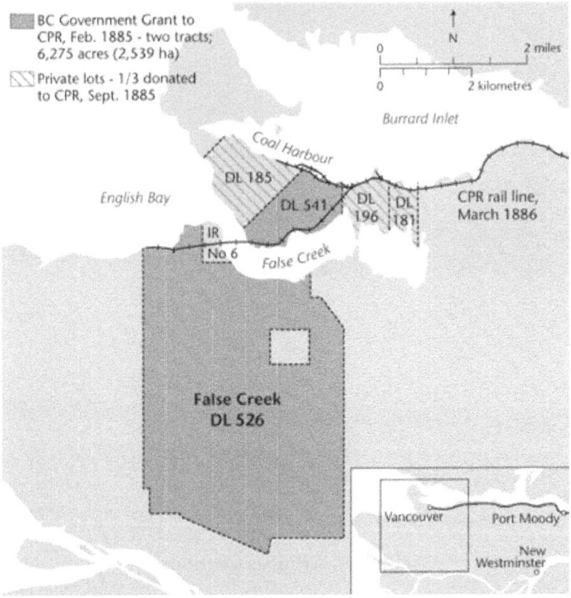

Figure 2. CPR Land Grant, 1885. (Source: Based on a map in Frank Leonard, "'So Much Bumph': CPR Terminus Travails at Vancouver, 1884–89" (2010) 166 BC Studies 7–38 at 13.)

for extending the rail line to Granville. The two parcels, together 6,458 acres, would comprise the largest land grant to the railway company within any Canadian city.[8]

The CPR set about maximizing the value of its land and building the City of Vancouver in the process. The city was not so much given away, as the epigram at the beginning of this section suggests, as it was created by the land grant to the railway, a sentiment captured and extolled as part of a reified colonial narrative of progress in the following inscription on a plaque in downtown Vancouver:

Here stood
HAMILTON
First Land Commissioner
Canadian Pacific Railway
1885
In the silent solitude
Of the primeval forest
He drove a wooden stake
In the earth and commenced

To measure an empty land
Into the streets of
VANCOUVER[9]

The provincial land grant established the CPR as the central force in Vancouver's early development. On the basis of this landed position, and wielding threats to move the terminus elsewhere, the CPR induced the existing land owners in lots 185, 196, and 181 on either side of its 480-acre parcel on the peninsula to give the company one-third of their holdings (Figure 2). The CPR then set about moving the locus of economic activity from the Hastings mill and the old Granville town site to its land — lot 541.[10] The intent and effect was to increase the value of the CPR land grant, but the reorientation of the commercial centre also symbolized a shift in the economic base. Lumbering (the early industry around the inlet) remained important, and an industrial salmon fishery expanded rapidly at the mouth of the Fraser River, but work associated with the railway and with the sale and development of land quickly dominated the urban economy. "Railroad and real estate interests," suggests historian Robert McDonald, "rather than wholesale merchants, lumbermen or salmon canners were Vancouver's initial city-builders."[11] In these early years, real estate development and a range of supporting commercial activities underwrote Vancouver's economy, not the resource-rich hinterland. By 1891, after six years of rapid growth, the industrial camp of 400 had grown to a town of nearly 14,000.

As Vancouver grew, its relationship with the CPR changed. The city's early supplication and deference was replaced, by the early 1890s, with "a more matter-of-fact, businesslike tone."[12] The relationship became strained when, in 1892, Vancouver funded a competitor railway to build a link with the Northern Pacific Railway in Washington State. The link was not built, but the fact that Vancouver would encourage it revealed a different city from the one that just a few years earlier had so assiduously courted the CPR. Indeed, through much of the 1890s, the city would battle the railway company to the Supreme Court of Canada over a right of public access across CPR land to the waterfront.[13] The City eventually lost this dispute — the SCC denied it the right to extend Gore Avenue across company land — but access to the waterfront, much of it CPR controlled, remained disputed.

Following its early efforts in the commercial core, the CPR turned to subdividing and selling the large tract of land south of False Creek — lot 526. It marked out a grid, establishing a pattern of numbered east-west avenues and named north-south streets. Ontario Street, the eastern boundary of the CPR land grant, marked the dividing line between a working class east and more affluent west.[14] An increasingly dense network of electric street-rail lines, known as the inter-urban railway, served, and in some cases preceded, residential development. Replicating the federal and provincial governments' strategies of land for railways, the CPR gave lots to the Vancouver Electric Railway & Light Company in exchange for building and operating streetcar lines.[15] In 1902, the CPR built its own rail line from False Creek to Steveston, the centre of the salmon-canning industry on the Fraser River. Operated by a subsidiary, the Vancouver & Lulu Island Railway, it began as a steam-hauled passenger and freight service, but was converted to an electric inter-urban line when the British Columbia Electric Railway Company took over its operation in 1905. Passenger service continued until 1954 and freight service until 2001. This was the line, the Vancouver portion of which is shown in Figure 1, that became known as the Arbutus Corridor.

CPR and the Re-Making of Vancouver

Statistically speaking, Vancouver is Canada's third largest urban area. In fact, Vancouver is nothing but an overblown company town. The company, of course, is the CPR. Vancouver was a creation of the CPR and its fate has always been intimately tied to the railway company.[16]

The decision of the CPR to build its rail yards on the north shore of False Creek established the inlet and the land around it as the industrial workshop of Vancouver. By 1891, six of the eight sawmills in the city clustered around False Creek. They were followed by bricks, cement, lime, sand, and gravel works, and by manufacturers of furniture, doors, and windows, many of them serving the local market as the city grew rapidly around the inlet. In the early twentieth century, various metal works and machine shops located on False Creek, and then, with the outbreak of World War I, several shipbuilding yards.[17] The large shipbuilding yards closed shortly after the war, and by the late 1920s, parcels of vacant and under-utilized land marked an industrial region in decline. The depression of the 1930s hastened False Creek's demise as the city's industrial workshop, and squatting communities settled portions of shoreline between the factories and mills.[18] World War II reversed the decline only temporarily. Part of the problem was access. Shipping raw materials to the inlet and finished products out had become increasingly difficult as the city grew around False Creek. Local residents were also increasingly vocal about the problematic by-products of industry, particularly air and water pollution.

The City's initial response was to retain and revitalize the industrial character of the area. The influential Bartholomew Report, prepared for Vancouver's Town Planning Commission in 1928, recommended as much: "it [False Creek] should be encouraged as an industrial entity of extreme usefulness to Vancouver."[19] And as late as 1967, Vancouver city council passed a bylaw declaring "the land abutting False Creek be retained as an industrial area."[20] This bylaw was city council's response to a motion from Vancouver's elected parks board to establish a 1,000-foot-wide strip of parkland around the inlet, part of an effort to create a natural amenity that would attract residents to high-density, inner-city living.[21] The parks board was not alone in beginning to re-think the uses of False Creek, and city council, not six months later, re-examined its recently stated intent to maintain False Creek's industrial character.[22] Then in 1968, the City became one of the principal landowners around the inlet when it acquired most of the south shore of False Creek in a land swap with the provincial government. This led, beginning in 1974, to the City's redevelopment of the south shore and to what geographer David Ley describes as "a picturesque, medium-density, human-scale landscape, with mixed residential, commercial and leisure uses."[23] The federal government contributed as well, remaking its industrial land on Granville Island as public market.[24]

The CPR was also beginning to rethink its large rail yard on the north shore of False Creek. In the early 1960s, as part of a significant corporate reorganization, the CPR created subsidiary companies to operate its component businesses. One was Marathon Realty, established to manage and develop land that the parent company did not require for its railway operations. In Vancouver, this included the remnants of the original land grant (several golf courses and a large 250-acre parcel in the middle of the original grant) and the expendable parts of its rail operations. Marathon Realty began with the non-railway lands, but then turned to its rail yards on False Creek.[25] In December 1968, several months after the City reversed its industry-first policy for False Creek, Marathon Realty announced plans for a massive housing complex to occupy much of its rail yards.[26] False Creek, one of the early iterations of the proposal began, "is an unplanned conglomeration of logbooms, railyards, dilapidated buildings and congested waterways. It is the home of warehouses and industry dependent on rail and water transportation to service a complex urban structure, Vancouver. While the city grew around it with alarming speed, False Creek deteriorated."[27] The concept drawings and scale model proposed a modernist marvel of urban redevelopment, including twenty high-rise towers (averaging thirty-five stories) intermixed with terraced housing and parks, and served by an expressway: "In essence," said the designers, without any apparent irony, "a suburb of 20,000 people" in the heart of the city.[28]

Marathon refined the proposal over the next few years, reducing the proposed residential development to 14,000 people and changing the mix of residential and commercial uses, but it was not until June 1974, that the City rezoned the Marathon lands from "industrial" to "comprehensive development" so as to allow a development of this nature to proceed.[29] This rezoning, which massively increased the value of the land, provoked criticism that the company was the undeserving recipient of windfall profits, and the conclusion, expressed above, that Vancouver, Canada's third-largest city, remained a company town.[30] But Marathon Realty did not develop these lands. The City thought the proposed density too high and insisted on more non-market housing than Marathon was prepared to build.[31] While the land lay in limbo, its remaining industry on short-term leases, the parcel came to the notice of the provincial government. In 1980, it acquired the large parcel on False Creek from Marathon Realty as the future site for the world exposition to be held in Vancouver in 1986. When Expo '86 ended, the province, in a controversial single transaction, sold the land to one of Hong Kong's most prominent and successful developers, Li Ka-shing. He would develop the property under the auspices of Concord Pacific.[32] Marathon Realty turned its attention to the redevelopment of its land on the other side of the downtown peninsula at Coal Harbour.[33]

Among its land holdings around False Creek, the CPR retained a rail line that extended parallel to the south shore of the inlet and behind the city-owned land at the waterfront (Figure 3). Known as the False Creek Right-of-Way, the spur, which connected to the Arbutus Corridor, had served the industries on the south shore of False Creek. The CPR decommissioned the line in 1989 and entered negotiations for its sale to the City, which imagined this fifty-foot-wide strip as part of an electric streetcar network. Negotiations broke off in 1993, and in 1995 the CPR turned to the City to request that the right-of-way be re-zoned to permit multi-family housing. However, several parcels at the western end of the right-of-way were already zoned for commercial use and, early in 1995, the CPR sold a single lot to a private developer who built a coffee shop and leased it to Starbucks, effectively severing the right-of-way from the Arbutus Corridor (Figure 3).[34] Responding to criticism that the City had not acted early or quickly enough to forestall the sale and preserve the right-of-way, the City's director of land use and development argued that "a municipality cannot use its zoning powers to limit use of privately owned lands so as to preserve an historic corridor for future transportation purposes. The land on which the new Starbucks is being constructed could not be 'sterilized' as Ward [the critic] would seem to prefer."[35] The City would do just that several years later with the Arbutus Corridor. In the meantime, fearing loss of more of the False Creek right-of-way, the City acquired a portion of the remainder, approximately 1.5 kilometres, from the CPR for $8.95 million.

One other parcel of CPR land needs mention before turning to the Arbutus Corridor. In 1886, to bring its line across False Creek to English Bay, the CPR acquired a strip of land through Squamish Indian Reserve No. 6, False Creek.[36] The reserve, allotted in the 1860s and expanded by the federal-provincial Joint Indian Reserve Commission in 1876, sat at the entrance to False Creek and, after 1886, was surrounded by the CPR land grant (Figure 2).[37] Instead of crossing the inlet to adjoin its land on the south shore of False Creek, something it could easily have done given that it owned most of the land around the inlet, the CPR used 3.5 acres of Indian reserve. It reduced the reserve by another seven acres in 1901 to connect the Vancouver and Lulu Island Railway line (later the Arbutus Corridor) to the trestle bridge across False Creek. In 1913, the City and Province induced the Squamish residents to leave the reserve. After this, the reserve was further reduced for other purposes until, in 1947, it was formally surrendered.[38] That surrender and the circumstances leading to it precipitated a specific claim and legal action that, in 1999, produced a $92.5 million settlement to compensate the Squamish Indian Band for the entire False Creek reserve, except the portion acquired by the CPR.[39] When the federal government learned that the CPR had listed for sale the former Indian reserve, it turned to the courts to recover the land on the grounds that the land reverted to Canada when the CPR ceased to use it for railway purposes. The Squamish, Musqueam, and Burrard Indian Bands claimed that if the land reverted to Canada, it did so as Indian reserve held in trust for the bands. In 2002, the British Columbia Court of Appeal ruled that the ten acres of land reverted to the Squamish as Indian reserve.[40] This decision excised the first few hundred metres of the Arbutus Corridor from the city's jurisdiction (Figure 3).

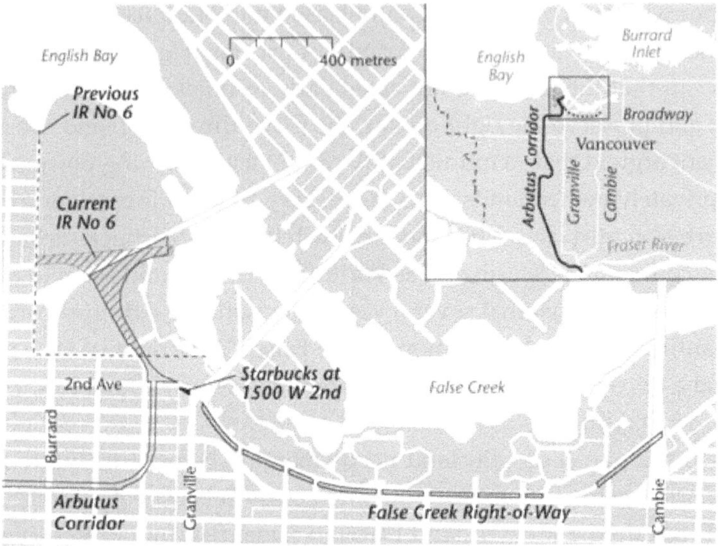

Figure 3. False Creek Right-of-Way. (In 1996, the City acquired the False Creek Right-of-Way between the Arbutus Corridor and Cambie Street from the CPR after the company sold a small segment to a developer who built a coffee shop and leased it to Starbucks, severing the right-of-way from the Arbutus Corridor. In 2002, the British Columbia Court of Appeal ruled that ten acres of CPR land, which had been Indian Reserve, should be reserve again. This decision removed the northern-most portion of the Arbutus Corridor — the crescent-shaped portion that was part of the Indian reserve — from the city's jurisdiction.)

Such was the urban, corporate, and political context from which the dispute over the Arbutus Corridor emerged. By the end of the 1970s it was clear that False Creek's industrial era was ending. The federal government and the City had re-made Granville Island as a public market and much of the inlet's south shore as a moderate-density residential neighbourhood with a mix of parks, townhouses, and apartments. The province had acquired most of the CPR's railway lands on the north shore for a world exposition, then for massive residential development. The transformation of False Creek from an industrial zone to a dense, residential neighbourhood has been hailed as a model of inner-city redevelopment,[41] but it also sealed the fate of the Arbutus Corridor as a viable freight line. Without industrial customers, the CPR began looking at other uses for its forty-five acre corridor. Under the auspices of Marathon Realty, the CPR had become a land developer. Although its False Creek lands were developed by another firm, the company was working on other large development projects and the Arbutus Corridor presented such an opportunity.[42] Finally, it was clear that the City was actively seeking to preserve the remaining rail corridors in the city. It had purchased the False Creek Right-of-Way from the CPR, but that was a relatively small parcel compared to the ten kilometre, forty-five acre Arbutus Corridor, which, in 2000, the City regulated to preserve as a transportation corridor for trains, public transit, or human-powered locomotion.

The Arbutus Corridor Official Development Plan

WITH THE DEMISE OF an industrial False Creek, the CPR concluded that the Arbutus Corridor was no longer economically viable for hauling freight. Recognizing this, and the possibility that the unique strip of land might again transport people by rail, city council passed a resolution in 1986 declaring that "the Arbutus rail corridor (V and LI Line) be preserved as a potential rapid transit corridor between downtown Vancouver and Richmond."[43] The council passed a similar resolution in 1992 "reiterat[ing] its desire to maintain the Arbutus right-of-way as a transportation corridor."[44] Over the next few years, a series of plans and policy statements — the Vancouver Greenways Plan (1995), the Vancouver Transportation Plan (1997), and the Vancouver Regional Context Statement Development Plan (1999) — announced a similar intention to preserve several rail corridors, including the Arbutus Corridor, for rail or transit, or as greenways.[45] The Regional Context Statement of 1999, Vancouver's component of the greater metropolitan area's strategic plan, provided that "the existing rail corridors along the Arbutus corridor and Grandview Cut are considered for a combination of rail, transit and Greenways uses."[46] In September 1999, the City adopted this document as an Official Development Plan.[47]

The 1999 Regional Context Statement situated Vancouver's planning within the four broad goals of the region-wide strategic plan: 1) protect the green zone; 2) build complete communities; 3) achieve a compact metropolitan region; and 4) increase transportation choice.[48] The provision for the Arbutus Corridor was included within the first goal — to protect the green zone — and was an apparent restatement of existing policy. However, the choice of language — "considered for" rather than a stronger "designated for" — suggested that this was still a subject for discussion. Nonetheless, under the *Vancouver Charter* (the provincial statute conferring Vancouver's municipal powers), the effect of adopting an official development plan (ODP) is to make it "unlawful for any person to commence or undertake any development contrary to or at variance with the official development plan" and to prohibit city council from authorizing any development that is contrary to the plan.[49]

Within this statutory framework, even the language of "considered for" concerned the CPR. Earlier in 1999, the company had informed the City that the Arbutus Corridor was no longer "economically viable for rail use" and that it was planning to discontinue rail service. In doing so, the company suggested that it was "open to working with the city to develop a vision for future uses of the Arbutus Corridor lands" and that it "would like to explore options that might exist to achieve our respective objectives. One possible opportunity," the company continued, "is for the re-introduction of the Arbutus Corridor into the adjacent neighbourhood in a way that achieves public objectives at no additional expense to taxpayers while achieving a fair return to CPR."[50] Given this redevelopment plan, an ODP that appeared to limit the corridor to transportation was problematic. In October 1999, the CPR filed a petition in the British Columbia Supreme Court to set aside the bylaw adopting the Regional Context Statement as an official development plan.[51] The company maintained that the ODP presented a "fundamental change" in city policy and an unacceptable limit on its use and development of the corridor.[52] Among various grounds, the CPR claimed that the bylaw "designates private lands for public use" and that it "constitutes a taking."[53]

At a meeting with city officials in March 1999, before the City had made the Regional Context Statement an official development plan, the CPR presented a "draft option for enhanced use of the Arbutus Corridor" and a plan for community consultation. The community consultation was part of a required process that the CPR hoped would lead the City to rezone the land to accommodate the proposed development. The draft included photographs of the corridor as it existed, accompanied by a landscape architect's sketches of segments of the corridor with various combinations of residential and commercial space, green-way and bike-way routes, parks, and community gardens.[54]

In 2000, with its legal action over the Regional Context Statement on hold pending discussions with the City on the future of the Arbutus Corridor, the CPR forged ahead with a round of community consultation about the corridor and its proposed redevelopment. In June, the company informed the City that approximately 80 percent of those who participated in the consultation felt that the lands should be purchased by a public body for public use.[55] The public uses included greenways, but possibly also the route for the proposed Vancouver-Richmond transit line. The building of this line depended on significant provincial and federal support, and on the Vancouver 2010 Olympic bid, none of which had yet been secured, but the regional transit authority had also identified the Arbutus corridor as a viable route and sought to preserve it as an option.[56]

It had become increasingly clear to the City that the CPR was preparing to sell or develop the Arbutus Corridor. The mooted price was $100 million, a figure that the CPR never confirmed, but then the City did not seem inclined to negotiate for the corridor.[57] However, the City was concerned about the future of the corridor and that the possibility of a continuous transit line or greenway might be lost. The lots in the corridor north of 16th Avenue were already zoned for mixed residential, industrial, and commercial uses so once the CPR decommissioned the line, it could apply for and would be entitled to receive development permits for projects that fit within the zoned uses. Remembering the Starbucks development on the False Creek Right-of-Way, which the City had been obliged to permit because it fit existing zoning, and fearing the same might happen on parts of the Arbutus Corridor, city council adopted an Arbutus Corridor Development Plan in June 2000, limiting the uses of the corridor to a public thoroughfare.[58] It also set in motion a process for public meetings so that the development plan might become a legally binding official development plan. In the meantime, council included a provision, permitted under the *Vancouver Charter*, which enabled the City to withhold requests for development permits pending the consideration of an official development plan.

Public hearings about the Arbutus Corridor ODP proceeded in July, as one scheduled evening for comment became four to accommodate all the speakers.[59] They included the CPR, which spoke out strongly against what it viewed as the sterilization of its property interests, but also many local residents who were concerned about the prospect of public transit, particularly elevated public transit, in their neighbourhood. Following these hearings, on 25 July 2000, council adopted the earlier development plan (approved in June) as the Arbutus Corridor Official Development Plan ("Arbutus Corridor ODP") (Appendix A).[60] The plan reserved the Arbutus Corridor as a greenway or for transportation, including rail, transit, or cycling, but not for motor vehicles or for elevated transit such as the SkyTrain system. This last provision had been added after the public hearings, confirming for some that the City treated its more affluent west side differently from its east side, through which the SkyTrain already ran.[61] At the public hearings a representative for the recently formed Arbutus Corridor Residents' Association, organized to lobby against public transit on the Arbutus Corridor, suggested that the west side had been and should continue to be treated differently: "We are the people that live in your neighbourhood. We are dentists, doctors, lawyers, professionals, CEOs of companies. We are the creme de la creme in Vancouver. We live in a very expensive neighbourhood and we're well educated and well informed. And that's what we intend to be."[62] By weight of numbers, influence, or both, SkyTrain would not run through the city's west side.

The Regional Context Statement ODP may have been of uncertain effect on the CPR's rail line, but there was no doubt that the Arbutus Corridor ODP dramatically curtailed the company's development options in the forty-five acre parcel. In a letter sent to the City between the passing of Arbutus Corridor Development Plan in June and the ODP in July, the company's vice-president of real estate demanded the production of numerous documents and more time before the public hearing. He added, "[t]he taking of such sudden and drastic action breeds cynicism with our governmental institutions, and simply serves to discourage parties from acting in the cooperative and open fashion that the CPR has." He continued that rail use in the corridor "can no longer be economically viable" and, therefore, "the bylaws amount to a downsizing to a public thoroughfare consisting of public uses and non-viable uses, all in the context of preserving the Corridor for future public use."[63] In August the CPR revived its court proceedings against the City, filing a new petition to quash the Arbutus Corridor ODP on the grounds that it was an unjustified and uncompensated taking of the CPR's private property for a public purpose.

CPR v City of Vancouver

THE CPR CLAIMED THE process that produced the Arbutus Corridor ODP had been unfair, that the City had no jurisdiction to pass such a bylaw, and that the bylaw amounted to a taking of its property for which it should be compensated. At trial, heard over nine days in June 2002, Brown J conflated the issues into a single question: Was the bylaw within the powers granted to the City under the *Vancouver Charter*?[64] She concluded that it was not. "The *Vancouver Charter* does not give the Cty the power to use the vehicle of an official development plan to denude a private property of all use, except as a public thoroughfare, without acquiring title to the property, or reaching some agreement with the land owner."[65] The City argued that, even if a taking had occurred, which it did not admit, then the *Vancouver Charter* excused the City from the need to compensate: under section 569(1), a zoning bylaw "shall be deemed as against the city not to have been taken or injuriously affected by reason of the exercise of any such powers or by reason of such zoning," and further, that "no compensation shall be payable by the city." However, Brown J concluded that this provision was insufficiently specific and that the legislature would need "much clearer language" to enable the City to designate private land as public thoroughfare without compensating the private owner. In doing so, she presented the following scenario:

> The City's interpretation leads to this result: a person may acquire a bare lot in the City of Vancouver which is zoned for residential development and is in every respect appropriate for residential development. Before that development occurs, the City may pass an official development plan which designates that particular lot as a public park, even though it remains zoned for residential development. Thereafter, the owner of that property may not develop the property in any way other than as a public park. The City need not acquire that property and may never acquire the property because the City is not compelled to undertake any of the developments shown on the plan. The individual has been deprived of all of the benefits of ownership of that land and has only the burden of paying taxes and, presumably, maintaining the property. Should the individual fail to keep the grass cut, the City would be able to cut the grass and charge the individual with the expense of doing so.[66]

This scenario blanched the corporate personality of the CPR or the uniqueness of the Arbutus Corridor from the case before the court, but it revealed for Brown J "an absurd result." "Legislation," she concluded, "should not be interpreted to produce an absurd result."[67] However, rather than declare, as the CPR had requested, that the Arbutus Corridor ODP constituted a taking for which compensation was due, she ruled that the bylaw creating the ODP was invalid and set it aside.

The CPR felt vindicated, and representatives of the business community and development industry expressed their strong support for the decision.[68] However, the City appealed, and the British Columbia Court of Appeal (BCCA) granted the appeal. Justice Esson, joined by Donald J and with whom Southin J (in separate reasons) concurred, found that the City had ample authority under the *Vancouver Charter* to pass the Arbutus Corridor bylaw.[69] Moreover, he held that the bylaw, while perhaps "unfair" from the CPR's perspective, was an entirely appropriate response given the public interest in preserving the corridor, the uncertainty of eventual uses and of funding for them, and the CPR's move to redevelop the land.[70] Having established the validity of the bylaw, Esson J, in a few short paragraphs and without citing case law, concluded that the Arbutus Corridor ODP did not amount to expropriation or to a taking of private property that entitled the CPR to compensation.[71] He then considered and dismissed the CPR's procedural arguments: that the City had failed to disclose pertinent documents, that the City had provided inadequate notice of the public hearings, and that the City had improperly changed the wording of the bylaw after the public hearings. Justice Esson also dismissed the argument that the City had improperly attempted to depress the value of the land in order to acquire it more cheaply.

Justice Southin concurred, but clearly thought the City should move to acquire the land. By the time the BCCA issued its decision in April 2004, the Olympics had been awarded to Vancouver and Cambie Street had been announced as the route for the Vancouver-Richmond transit line. The Arbutus Corridor would not be needed as the main north-south public transit thoroughfare. Given this development, Southin J, in her acerbic fashion, wrote "the bylaw in issue now can have no purpose but to enable the inhabitants to use the corridor for walking and cycling, which some do (trespassers all), without paying for that use. The shareholders of the CPR,"[72] she continued, "ought not to be expected to make a charitable gift to the inhabitants," and the City should move to acquire the land or the province should intervene to impose a settlement.[73] Although not agreeing with Brown J at trial that the bylaw produced an absurd result, she did think "[t]he present impasse is an absurdity unworthy of this Province which, on its way to the 2010 Olympic Games, is asserting to all and sundry that it is a marvellous place."[74]

Between trial and appeal, the CPR had applied to the City for permits to build twenty-four residences on parcels at the north end of the corridor. It was, claimed the CPR, a signal to the City that the company intended to sell the land, either to the City or, were it not prepared to pay market value, to another purchaser. The City refused the applications, announcing that it would not process them, unless forced by a court order, while the Arbutus Corridor ODP bylaw remained before the courts.[75] However, it was also clear that relations between the CPR and the City were strained beyond what one would expect from litigation. Justice Esson noted that "this proceeding has been litigated with an intensity which seems somewhat inconsistent" with a dispute over the interpretation of a municipal charter.[76] Construed as an exercise in statutory interpretation, the intensity may well have been surprising, but is less so if one understands the case, which the parties did, as a dispute over the rights of a holder of private property and the capacity of a public body to exercise its authority over those rights. Moreover, the dispute over the Arbutus Corridor had not arisen in isolation. The City was understandably vigilant, perhaps even distrustful of the CPR after the company "Starbucked" the False Creek Right-of-Way in clear contravention of the City's desire to keep that corridor intact. For its part, the CPR perceived that the City had not engaged in what the company thought were good-faith attempts to find a compromise that respected its property interests in the Arbutus Corridor while achieving the City's goals to enhance public amenities.

Opposition to the Court of Appeal's decision was as quick as its sources were predictable. The CPR announced immediately that it would appeal to the Supreme Court of Canada (SCC);[77] the Business Council of British Columbia suggested that the decision would "have a chilling effect on investors" and that it continued "a slow erosion of property rights in BC";[78] the Chamber of Commerce wondered "whose rights might other BC municipalities trample tomorrow";[79] and a former director of the Urban Development Institute, the association of real estate developers, concluded that the municipal legislation, as interpreted by the courts, "denies property rights to owners of land, regardless if the landowner is the CPR or an ordinary Vancouver homeowner."[80]

The litigation would continue with the CPR seeking and receiving leave to appeal to the SCC. Once there, McLachlin CJ, writing for the court, framed the appeal around three questions, the second of which brought the issue of private property and public authority to the fore:

1. Was the ODP Bylaw beyond the statutory powers of the City?
2. If not, must the City compensate CPR for the land?
3. Should the bylaw be set aside for procedural irregularities?[81]

On the first and third questions, the SCC agreed with the BCCA: the *Vancouver Charter* provided the City with ample authority to pass the bylaw[82] and there were no procedural irregularities that required setting it aside.[83] On the question of compensation, which had been argued before but never squarely engaged by the lower courts, the SCC took the opportunity to make its first statement on the law of *de facto* expropriation or regulatory taking — the SCC used the hybrid "*de facto* taking" — since its 1985 decision in *British Columbia v Tener*.[84]

In an efficient twelve paragraphs, the SCC set out the test for *de facto* taking and concluded that it had not been met. The Court drew, briefly, on a trio of cases, including its decisions in *Manitoba Fisheries Ltd. v The Queen*[85] and *Tener*, and the Nova Scotia Court of Appeal in *Mariner Real Estate Ltd. v Nova Scotia*,[86] to hold that a *de facto* taking required: "(1) an acquisition of a beneficial interest in the property or flowing from it, and (2) removal of all reasonable uses of the property."[87] Of the first requirement, the SCC held that "[t]he City has gained nothing more than some assurance that the land will be used or developed in accordance with its vision, without even precluding the historical or current use of the land;" it had not acquired a beneficial interest.[88] Of the second requirement, which it drew from *Mariner*, the SCC held that the bylaw did not prevent the CPR from using the land as it had done since 1902 — as a railway — and therefore that not all reasonable uses had been removed. Moreover, the SCC went on to say that even if the CPR could make out a claim for *de facto* taking at common law, the provisions in the *Vancouver Charter* immunized the City from such a claim.[89] Although evincing sympathy for the CPR's position at the beginning and end of her judgment, McLachlin CJ held that the bylaw was valid and that the City was not required to compensate the company for the restrictions on its use of the land.

City councillors were understandably pleased that the City's zoning power had been upheld. Business and developer organizations, on the other hand, called for legislative change to reduce municipal power because of the threat it posed to private property.[90] The CPR, which had initiated another visioning process for the Arbutus Corridor before the SCC released its judgment, felt it was back where it had been in 1999 when it told the City of its intent to sell the land.[91] In some ways it was, although, as an editorial in *The Vancouver Sun* suggested, the decision relieved the City of any pressure to negotiate: the land would remain zoned as a public thoroughfare, but the CPR had no intention of reviving passenger or freight rail service, and the City was not ready to purchase the land for what the CPR believed it was worth, so nothing would happen.[92] Indeed, nothing has happened.

"Trespassers All": Reflections on an Urban Landscape and a Constitution without Property

In May 2001, the last train rolled along the Arbutus Corridor. Vancouverites who use the corridor — "trespassers all," according to Southin J — do so with impunity. However, it is not obvious that one is a trespasser when walking, running, or biking along the Arbutus Corridor, as many do. The tracks are still in place, increasingly rusty from lack of use and overgrown in places with blackberry brambles, but the "Private Property No Trespassing" signs that once announced its perimeter have largely disappeared. There are no fences (Figure 4). Even if one knows that the CPR holds title to the land, the trespasser label hardly seems to apply. Garden plots occupy stretches of the municipal boulevards that border the corridor, their edges marking a boundary between public and private land that is otherwise indistinct. Generally the gardens occupy city land, but, in a few places, gardeners have used the rails themselves as one side of a raised bed.[93]

Discussions between the City and the CPR over the corridor have occurred sporadically since the SCC decision, but without any sense of urgency, at least not from the City.[94] The last visioning process, commissioned by the CPR but conducted independently by an eminent panel of academics, planners, and others, recommended in 2007 that the corridor and adjacent city streets should be used "to accommodate a continuous greenway and possible future transportation route with carefully considered opportunities for development in select locations."[95] The panel imagined that residential and commercial development along portions of the corridor would generate the funds for the City to acquire the land and build the recommended public infrastructure. Moreover, this development could fit with the city's "EcoDensity Initiative" to add affordable housing in ways that reduced the ecological footprint of the city's residents.[96] The panel also suggested that the development could be a showcase for sustainable urban infill development when attention turned to Vancouver for the 2010 Winter Olympics. However, perhaps because of that event and the City's preoccupation with its development of an athlete's village

Figure 4.The Arbutus Corridor, looking north towards 16th Ave., shortly after the SCC decision in February 2006. Photograph Glen Baglo, *The Vancouver Sun*.

on False Creek, the Arbutus Corridor received relatively little of the City's attention. The SCC's decision in *CPR v City of Vancouver* did not require it.

If little has happened to the much-debated urban land since the SCC decision, what is the effect of *CPR v City of Vancouver* on the law of constructive taking? Perhaps most importantly, the fact that the SCC declined to construct a taking for which the City would have to compensate the owner confirms that the courts will continue to play a relatively small role in balancing the interests of private property owners and public authorities, much smaller than they do in the United States. In the United States, the doctrine has developed under the constitutional protection for property — "nor shall private property be taken for public use, without just compensation"[97] — and the US Supreme Court's 1922 decision in *Pennsylvania Coal v Mahon* "that while property may be regulated to a certain extent, if regulation goes too far it will be recognized as a taking" requiring compensation.[98] Since that decision, and many others which have followed it, the spectre of regulatory taking and the possibility that a court will order compensation has loomed over municipal zoning and a great many other actions by public authorities in the United States that have the capacity to limit the rights of private property.

"At some point," writes Bruce Ziff in a rephrasing of *Penn Coal*, "admittedly hard to locate, excessive regulation must be seen as equivalent to confiscation,"[99] and in a small handful of cases Canadian courts have ordered compensation for a constructive taking. [100] But unlike the United States, where judicial review of the actions of public authorities has played an important role in determining that location, in Canada it hardly has. Canadian courts, while consistently expressing sympathy for property owners, seem reluctant to intervene. Gregory Alexander, in using Canada as an example of a liberal constitutional democracy without constitutional protection for private property, notes "surprisingly little case law" on how much state interference with the traditional incidents of ownership is too much.[101] However, the lack of judicial involvement is not surprising if understood in the very legal and political context that Alexander describes: that of a liberal constitutional democracy without constitutional protection for private property.

In her comparative analysis of constructive takings law in the United States, Australia, and Canada, Donna Christie suggests that "the constitutionalization of property enshrines the courts, rather than legislative bodies, as the primary arbiters of the private property/public interest conflict."[102] This has certainly been the result with the rights that did end up in the *Charter of Rights and Freedoms*; the courts have become much more active than they were pre-*Charter* in patrolling the lines that mark the boundaries between individual rights and state authority.[103] "Canada's decision," she continues, "*not* to constitutionalize property manifested the nation's intention that both the public and private aspects of property should continue to be fully realized through federal and provincial legislative action" rather than the courts.[104] How accurately the absence of a right to private property among enumerated constitutional rights reflects or manifests a national intention is debateable, and there have been various attempts since the *Charter* was adopted in 1982 without protection for private property to insert that protection,[105] but the non-constitutional nature of property rights in Canada has situated the balancing of public regulation and private property in legislatures and the democratic process, and not in the courts.

From various perspectives, some argue that this is as it should be. To constitutionalize property rights, suggests Jennifer Nedelsky, is to reinforce the idea of property rights as prior to the state, to place inappropriately the burden of justifying any interference in those rights for public purpose on government, and to establish an irresolvable conflict between private and public interests.[106] Others suggest that property owners are not a minority that need constitutional protection from systematic majoritarian bias against their interests.[107] In fact, property owners enjoy substantial statutory, if not constitutional, protection of their property rights in the expropriation acts that compel compensation, usually at market value, when the state takes private property. The acts are generally silent on the question of constructive taking: the provision in the *Vancouver Charter*, which expressly precludes a finding of a taking when the City regulates property, is rare.[108] Courts will still intervene when the regulation amounts to a complete or virtually complete confiscation of property rights; *CPR v City of Vancouver* affirms this, although it also confirms that the standard for establishing constructive taking will be difficult to meet.

Russell Brown has argued that courts need to become more involved in light of what he perceives to be "the unavoidable and likely imminent influence of NAFTA" in the realm of takings.[109] As one of the many foreign investment protection agreements that Canada has signed, the North American Free Trade Agreement (NAFTA) provides that expropriation of a property interest or "measures tantamount to expropriation" will give rise to a right to compensation for foreign investors.[110] Some have suggested that this provision imports the US law of regulatory taking into Canada, at least for foreign investors.[111] Ziff recommends vigilance, but offers a more ambiguous reading of the emerging body of NAFTA tribunal decisions, suggesting that it is not clear that the protections for foreign investors will diverge sharply from those for their domestic counterparts.[112] In either event, Brown castigates the SCC for its failure in *CPR v City of Vancouver* to construct a more robust doctrine of constructive taking.[113] The SCC's analysis of *de facto* taking in *CPR v City of Vancouver*, while more expansive than that offered in the lower courts, is certainly truncated. Partly, this may reflect a court that is led by a consensus-building chief justice with a penchant for crisp judgments. However, it is the absence of property rights in the constitution that has prevented the courts from becoming the principal arbiters in the balancing of property rights and public regulation. It may be the insertion of these rights in quasi-constitutional documents, such as NAFTA, that eventually compels greater domestic judicial attention.

Whether courts become more involved or not, it will remain difficult to establish a precise rule of general application for how much regulation is too much so as to amount to a taking of property. Whether regulation amounts to a taking should depend not only on the provisions that restrict use, but also on the nature of the property interest in question, the history of its use and past regulation, and perhaps even on the relationship between owner and regulating authority. When one considers whether the restricting of the Arbutus Corridor to a public thoroughfare amounts to a taking, it matters that the land in question is a long-standing rail corridor owned by an entity with extensive history of property sale and development in the city, and not simply the "bare lot" acquired by an individual who wishes to build a residence but is prevented from doing so when the lot is designated a public park, as in Brown J's imagined scenario in her trial court decision.

Because the SCC declined to find a taking in *CPR v City of Vancouver*, what occurs on the Arbutus Corridor, and how, is a major decision that lies primarily with the city. For such an important and unique parcel of land that was for most of a century a significant part of the city's transportation infrastructure, this is how it should be. However, the Arbutus Corridor remains a private rail corridor, although one that is not likely to be used again for this purpose as the city has changed around it. Public transit once seemed a possible use, but the choice of a different location for the main north-south line means that the Arbutus Corridor would be no more than a secondary transit route, if so used at all.[114]

When the CPR and the City will return to negotiations over the parcel remains an open question, as do the results of those negotiations. Will the

City acquire the land and direct its redevelopment as it did in the 1970s with the False Creek South neighbourhood? Will it acquire the land and then offer parcels on long-term leases to developers as it did with the Olympic village site in the 2000s? Will the CPR or another owner work with the City to develop a mix of privately held buildings and public amenities, as occurred on the former Expo lands on the north shore of False Creek? In a rapidly developing city with the highest residential land prices in Canada, it seems unlikely that the Arbutus Corridor will remain in its present state indefinitely, but redevelopment of the land will depend on basic agreement between the CPR and the City over the appropriate realms of the public and the private. This was the issue in *CPR v City of Vancouver*; it is this boundary that the doctrine of constructive taking attempts to define and which the CPR and the city continue to dispute. How this question is resolved over this ten kilometre, forty-five-acre strip of land will have a significant impact on the urban landscape that surrounds it.

Appendix A

Arbutus Corridor Official Development Plan[115]

Section 1: Background

1.1 Application

This plan applies to those lands in the City of Vancouver described as the Arbutus Corridor within the boundaries shown on Maps 1 to 25 attached to this plan.

1.2 Intent

The intent of this plan is to provide a context for the future of the Arbutus Corridor.

The Arbutus Corridor has been used for many years for a rail line and this plan accommodates this use, but also provides for a variety of other uses.

This plan is derived from broad public processes associated with the following existing City plans:

(a) CityPlan,
(b) Vancouver Transportation Plan, and
(c) Vancouver Greenways Plan,

which plans determined the importance of providing corridors for improved rapid transit and opportunities for increased walking and biking as part of the City's transportation network.

Section 2: Designations

2.1 Designations for the Arbutus Corridor

This plan designates all of the land in the Arbutus Corridor for use only as a public thoroughfare for the purpose only of:

(a) transportation, including without limitations:
    i) rail;
    ii) transit; and
    iii) cyclist paths

but excluding:

  - (iv) motor vehicles except on City streets crossing the Arbutus Corridor; and
  - (v) any grade-separated rapid transit system elevated, in whole or in part, above the surface of the ground, of which one type is the rapid transit system know as "SkyTrain" currently in use in the Lower Mainland;

- (b) greenways, including without limitation:
  - (i) pedestrian paths, including without limitation urban walks, environmental demonstration trails, heritage walks and nature trails; and
  - (ii) cyclist paths.

Notes

1 I thank Shea Coulson and David Volk for their research assistance, George Macintosh, QC, for providing access to the appeal books in *CPR v Vancouver*, and Michael Begg, Davin Gard, Cole Harris, Felix Hoehn, and the editors of this volume for their comments on earlier drafts. The research was supported with funds from Canada's Social Science & Humanities Research Council (SSHRC).

2 *CPR v Vancouver (City of)*, [2006] 1 SCR 227, 2006 SCC 5 [*CPR* SCC].

3 *Ibid* at para 30.

4 The two most notable exceptions are *Manitoba Fisheries Ltd. v The Queen*, [1979] 1 SCR 101, [1978] 6 WWR 496 [*Manitoba Fisheries*] (see the chapter by Phillips & Martin in this volume) and *The Queen in Right of British Columbia v Tener*, [1985] 1 SCR 533, 17 DLR (4th) 1 [*Tener*].

5 W. Playfair, "Vancouver and the Railways," (June 1911) *British Columbia Magazine* at 498, quoted in JMS Careless, "Aspects of Urban Life in the West, 1870-1914" in Gilbert A. Stalter & Alan FJ Artibise, eds, *The Canadian City: Essays in Urban History* (Toronto: McClelland and Stewart, 1977) at 131.

6 This discussion of Vancouver's early history is drawn primarily from Norbert MacDonald, "The Canadian Pacific Railway and Vancouver's Development to 1900" (1977) 35 *BC Studies* 3 [MacDonald, "CPR and Vancouver"]; Robert AJ McDonald, "City Building in the Canadian West: A Case Study of Economic Growth in Early Vancouver, 1886-1893" (1979) 43 *BC Studies* 3 [McDonald, "City Building"]; Frank Leonard, "'Diplomatic Forces of the new railroad': Transcontinental Terminus Entry at Vancouver and Seattle" (2007) 28 *Journal of Transport History* 21. See also Patricia E. Roy, *Railways, Politicians and the Development of the City of Vancouver as a Metropolitan Centre, 1886-1929* (MA Thesis, University of Toronto, 1963) [unpublished].

7 *An Act Respecting the Canadian Pacific Railway*, Canada Statutes, 1881, c 1, Sch, s 1.

8 For a detailed study of the CPR land grant see Frank Leonard, "'So Much Bumph': CPR Terminus Travails at Vancouver, 1884-89" (2010) 166 *BC Studies* 7-38 [Leonard, "CPR Terminus"].

9 Plaque reproduced in Donald Gutstein, *Vancouver Ltd.* (Toronto: Lorimer, 1975) at 13 [Gutstein, *Vancouver Ltd.*]. See also RE Watters, ed, *British Columbia: A Centennial Anthology* (Vancouver: Evergreen Press, 1958) at 69.

10 See Angus Everett Robertson, *The Pursuit of Power, Profit and Privacy: A Study of Vancouver's West End Elite, 1886-1914* (MA Thesis, University of British Columbia, 1977).

11 McDonald, "City Building," above note 6 at 28.

12 MacDonald, "CPR and Vancouver," above note 6 at 24, 25.

13 *City of Vancouver v Canadian Pacific Railway Co.* (1894), 23 SCR 1.

14 See the series of maps, by decade, revealing the expanding city in Bruce Macdonald, *Vancouver: A Visual History* (Vancouver: Talon Books, 1992).

15 Norbert MacDonald, "A Critical Growth Cycle for Vancouver, 1900-1914" (1973) 17 *BC Studies* 26.

16 Gutstein, *Vancouver Ltd.*, above note 9 at 11.

17 Robert K. Burkinshaw, *False Creek: History, Images, and Research Sources* (Vancouver: City of Vancouver Archives, 1984) at 28, 31 [Burkinshaw, *False Creek*].

18 See Jill Wade, "Home or Homelessness? Marginal Housing in Vancouver, 1886-1950" (1977) 25 *Urban History Review* 19.

19 Harland Bartholomew & Assoc., *A Plan for the City of Vancouver, British Columbia, Including a General Plan of the Region, 1928* (Vancouver: Town Planning Commission, 1928), 147. See also Burkinshaw, *False Creek*, above note 17 at 41-42.

20 City of Vancouver Archives, City Council Minutes, 24 October 1967, vol 97, at 140.

21 Burkinshaw, *False Creek*, above note 17 at 54.

22 *Ibid.*

23 David Ley, "Styles of the Times: Liberal and Neo-conservative Landscapes in Inner Vancouver, 1968-1986" (1987) 13 *Journal of Historical Geography* 40 at 42. Ley goes on to remark that the City's development was the "product of the ideology of liberal reform, emerging from the social innovation of the 1960s and reacting against the rationalism of an earlier general of municipal politicians, planners and designers."

24 See the discussion of the development of False Creek South in John Punter, *The Vancouver Achievement: Urban Planning and Design* (Vancouver: University of British Columbia Press, 2003) at 34-47 [Punter, *Vancouver Achievement*].

25 Gutstein, *Vancouver Ltd.*, above note 9 at 15-18, 84-89.

26 The plans were reported in *The Province*, 7 and 8 December 1968.

27 *Proposal for the North Shore of False Creek, Vancouver, BC* (circa 1970 at 2), City of Vancouver Archives, Marathon Realty (Location # 925-F-6 file 1).

28 *Ibid* at 18.

29 See the discussion in Frederick Joseph Elligott, *The Planning Decision-Making Process of Vancouver's False Creek: A Case Study 1968-1974* (MA Thesis, University of British Columbia, 1977) at 44-143. For a brief account from someone who was involved as an academic and city councillor, see Walter G. Hardwick, *Vancouver* (Don Mills, ON: Collier-Macmillan Canada, 1974) at 94-97.

30 Gutstein, *Vancouver Ltd.*, above note 9 at 11. See also Robert Chodos, *The CPR: A Century of Corporate Welfare* (Toronto: Lorimer, 1973).

31 Punter, *Vancouver Achievement*, above note 24 at 187.

32 For a summary of the land transactions and the subsequent development of the neighbourhood known as False Creek North, see *Ibid* at 186-214. For an analysis of Li Ka-shing's acquisition and its subsequent effects on Vancouver, see Kris Olds, *Globalization and Urban Change: Capital, Culture, and Pacific Rim Mega-Projects* (Oxford: Oxford University Press, 2001) at 57-140.

33 For an overview of the massive development project, see Punter, *Ibid* at 214-24.

34 *CPR* SCC above note 2 (Affidavit, David Rudberg, General Manager of Engineering Services and City Engineer, Vancouver, 20 October 2000, Appellant's Appeal Book, pp 1902-14, at 1903-05). See also John Mackie, "New coffee shop site steams streetcar fans, who fear end to plan," *The Vancouver Sun* (19 July 1995) A3.

35 Rick Scobie, "Land-law issues can be trickier than Robin Ward seems to realize," *The Vancouver Sun* (6 January 1996) D7, responding to Robin Ward, Architecture Column, *The Vancouver Sun* (9 December 1995) D3.

36 For details of the expropriation see Leonard, "CPR Terminus," above note 8.

37 On the construction of an Indian reserve geography in British Columbia, see Cole Harris, *Making Native Space: Colonialism, Resistance, and Reserves in British Columbia* (Vancouver: University of British Columbia Press, 2002).

38 See Jordan Stanger-Ross, "Municipal Colonialism in Vancouver: City Planning and the Conflict over Indian Reserves, 1928-1950s" (2008) 89 *Canadian Historical Review* 541.

39 The court cases included an action brought by the Squamish against Canada, begun in 1981, and then actions by the Musqueam and Burrard against Canada and the Squamish. The actions were combined in a single case, and then the Squamish claim against Canada settled after trial but before the Federal Court issued its decision. See *Squamish Indian Band v Canada* (2000), 207 FTR 1 (TD).

40 *Squamish Indian Band v Canadian Pacific Ltd.* 2002 BCCA 478, 217 DLR (4th) 83.

41 Punter, *Vancouver Achievement*, above note 24.

42 In 1996, CP Ltd., the holding company for Marathon Realty and CPR, sold the real estate development and management company as part of its effort to focus on what it understood to be its core businesses.

43 City of Vancouver Archives, City Council Minutes, 21 October 1986, at 7. "V and LI" refers to the Vancouver and Lulu Island Railway Company, a subsidiary of the CPR, that, in 1902, built the line that would become known as the Arbutus Corridor.

44 *Ibid* 16 June 1992, pp 4035, 4040.

45 *CPR* SCC above note 2 (Appellant's Appeal Book, pp. 1338-53, Affidavit, Ann McAfee, Director of City Plans and Co-Director of Planning, City of Vancouver, 18 September 2000, at 1340-47).

46 Vancouver City Council Minutes, 26 January 1999, adopting the Regional Context Statement Development Plan, online: http://vancouver.ca/ctyclerk/cclerk/990126/minutes.htm.

47 City of Vancouver, bylaw No 8060, *Official Development Plan - Regional Context Statement* (14 September 1999), online: http://vancouver.ca/ctyclerk/cclerk/990914/regmin.htm.

48 Greater Vancouver Regional District, *Livable Region Strategic Plan* (26 January 1996) at 9, online: www.metrovancouver.org/about/publications/Publications/LRSP.pdf.

49 *Vancouver Charter*, SBC 1953, c 55, s 563.

50 *CPR* SCC above note 2 (Appellant's Appeal Book p 130, Supplementary Affidavit, Andrew Massil, Exhibit A, letter from Massil, CPR Regional Manager, Real Estate Group, to Judy Rogers, City Manager, 17 February 1999) [Massil, Supplemental. Affidavit].

51 *Ibid*, (Appellant's Appeal Book, pp 1637-67, Petition to the Supreme Court of British Columbia, 14 October 1999) [CPR Petition, 1999].

52 *Ibid*, (Appellant's Appeal Book, pp 1-28, Affidavit, Andrew Massil, 14 October 1999, at 22-23).

53 CPR Petition above note 51, at 1643.

54 Massil, Supplemental Affidavit above note 50, Exhibit B, at 131-42.

55 *CPR* SCC above note 2 (Appellant's Appeal Book, pp 544-46, letter from JR Walsh, Vice President Real Estate, CPR, to Judy Rogers, City Manager, City of Vancouver, 7 June 2000).

56 *Ibid*, (Appellant's Appeal Book, pp 502-04, memo from Ken Dobell, TransLink CEO, to TransLink Board of Directors 11 February 2000).

57 Jason Proctor, "CPR plan off track," *The Province* (9 December 1999) A19; Karenn Krangle, "CPR's plans for arbutus corridor 'out of order,'" *The Vancouver Sun* (8 January 2000) B3.

58 Vancouver City Council Minutes, 13 June 2000, online: http://vancouver.ca/ctyclerk/cclerk/000613/regmin.htm. The approved Arbutus Corridor Official Development Plan, online: http://vancouver.ca/ctyclerk/cclerk/000613/p4.htm.

59 Vancouver, Special Council Meeting Minutes, 10, 12, 17 & 18 July 2000, online: http://vancouver.ca/ctyclerk/cclerk/000710/phmin.htm.

60 City of Vancouver, bylaw No 8249, *Arbutus Corridor Official Development Plan* (25 July 2000) [*Arbutus Corridor ODP*].

61 Michelle Cook, "Council rules out SkyTrain along Arbutus: The line will be preserved as a transportation corridor despite objections by CP Rail," *The Vancouver Sun* (26 July 2000) A1.

62 Pete McMartin, "Crème erred in failing to let money talk: A woman in Kerrisdale comments on the Arbutus Corridor and breaks the code of the rich," *The Vancouver Sun* (13 July 2000) A3.

63 Massil, Supplementary Affidavit above note 50, Exhibit 348, pp 583-89, JR Walsh, CPR VP Real Estate, to Judy Rogers, City Manager, 21 June 2002, at 584.

64 *CPR v Vancouver (City of)* (2002), 47 Admin LR (3d) 56, 2002 BCSC 1507 at para 55.

65 *Ibid* at para 76.

66 *Ibid* at para 78.

67 *Ibid* at para 79.

68 Neal Hall, "Court thwarts city plans for public use of Arbutus strip," *The Vancouver Sun* (31 October 2002) B1; Wyng Chow, "Chamber of Commerce applauds Arbutus decision," *The Vancouver Sun* (1 November 2002) C4; Maureen Enser, Urban Development Institute, "CPR's win on Arbutus a good sign for all land owners," *The Vancouver Sun* (7 November 2002) A23.

69 *CPR v City of Vancouver* 2004 BCCA 192 at para 28 [*CPR* (BCCA)]. See Ryan Goldvine, "In Good Faith to Whom?: An Analysis of Judicial Deference to Municipal Authority and the Dispute Over the Arbutus Corridor" (2006) 11 Appeal 39 for an analysis of the case following the BCCA decision.

70 *CPR* (BCCA), *Ibid* at para 41.

71 *Ibid* at paras 68-70.

72 *Ibid* at para 117.

73 *Ibid* at paras 118-19.

74 *Ibid* at para 120.

75 See Frances Bula, "West-side rail line eyed for housing," *The Vancouver Sun* (5 September 2003) B1; and "Vancouver won't process CP applications for development along Arbutus corridor," *The Vancouver Sun* (11 September 2003) B3.

76 *CPR* (BCCA) above note 69 at para 86.
77 Maurice Bridge, "CPR vows to appeal Arbutus ruling," *The Vancouver Sun* (8 April 2004) B.1.
78 Jerry Lampert, "Who's being railroaded? Business council fears investors will be scared off without guaranteed property rights," *The Vancouver Sun* (17 April 2004) C9.
79 John Winter, "This may be the thin edge of the wedge," *The Vancouver Sun* (27 April 2004) A18.
80 Bob Ransford, "CPR ruling isn't good for property owners," *The Vancouver Sun* (1 May 2004) I14.
81 *CPR* SCC, above note 2 at para 10.
82 *Ibid* at paras 11-26.
83 *Ibid* at paras 38-62.
84 *Tener*, above note 4.
85 *Manitoba Fisheries*, above note 4. See the chapter by Phillips & Martin in this volume.
86 *Mariner Real Estate Ltd. v Nova Scotia (AG)* (1999), 177 DLR (4th) 696 (NSCA).
87 *CPR* SCC, above note 2 at para 30.
88 *Ibid* at para 33.
89 *Vancouver Charter*, above note 49, s 569 (1): Where a zoning bylaw is or has been passed, amended, or repealed under this Part, or where Council or any inspector or official of the city or any board constituted under this Act exercises any of the powers contained in this Part, any property thereby affected shall be deemed as against the city not to have been taken or injuriously affected by reason of the exercise of any such powers or by reason of such zoning and no compensation shall be payable by the city or any inspector or official thereof.
90 Jerry Lampert, "Concept of private land must have meaning," *The Vancouver Sun* (20 March 2006) A9.
91 Mark Hume, "Vancouver wins right to decide fate of line," *The Globe and Mail* (24 February 2006) S1.
92 *The Vancouver Sun* (25 February, 2006) C6.
93 On the capacity of gardening in public spaces to establish a sense of ownership see Nicholas Blomley, "Un-real Estate: Proprietary Space and Public Gardening" (2004) 36 Antipode 614-41. On Vancouver's community gardens, see Ashleigh Keall, "Conceptions of Property in Community Gardens" (2007) [unpublished term paper, copy with the author].
94 Naoibh O'Connor, "Arbutus Corridor's fate in limbo," *Vancouver Courier* (16 May 2008) 18; "One track minds," *Vancouver Courier* (14 May 2010) 1.
95 Arbutus Lands Advisory Panel, "Arbutus Lands Visioning Process Final Report" (16 April 2007) at 28. The advisory panel included Dr. Nola-Kate Seymour, Dr. Patrick Condon, Dr. John Robinson, Dr. Warren Gill, Dr. Tsur Somerville, Ken Cameron, Jim Fulton, Heather Redfern, Jim O'Dea, Marta Farevaag, and the Honourable Mike Harcourt. Thanks to James Hoggan & Associates, one of the project team members, for supplying a copy of the report. See also the work of the Society for Promoting

Environmental Conservation, "All Aboard the Arbutus Corridor" design contest in 2004, online: www.spec.bc.ca/ArbutusCorridor/index.html.

96 Vancouver City Council Minutes, 18 July 2006, online: http://vancouver.ca/ctyclerk/cclerk/20060718/documents/regularminutes.pdf adopting the principles to guide the development of an "Eco-density charter," and 10 June 2008, online: http://vancouver.ca/ctyclerk/cclerk/20080610/documents/regmins.pdf adopting the EcoDensity Charter.

97 US Const amend V, § 1.

98 *Pennsylvania Coal Co. v Mahon*, 260 US 393 (1922) at 415. See the discussion in Stuart Banner, *American Property: A History of How, Why and What We Own* (Boston: Harvard University Press, 2011), pp. 59-69, 267-71.

99 Bruce Ziff, "'Taking' Liberties: Protections for Private Property in Canada" in Elizabeth Cooke, ed, *Modern Studies in Property Law*, vol 3 (Oxford: Hart, 2005) at 347 [Ziff, "'Taking' Liberties"].

100 *Manitoba Fisheries*, above note 4; *Tener*, above note 4; *Casamiro Resources Corp. v British Columbia (AG)* (1991), 80 DLR (4th) 1, 55 BCLR (2d) 346 (CA); *Rock Resources Inc. v British Columbia* (2008), 229 DLR (4th) 115, [2008] 8 WWR 680, 2003 BCCA 324, leave to appeal to SCC refused, [2003] SCCA No 375. See Raymond E. Young, "Canadian Law of Constructive Expropriation" (2005) 68 Sask L Rev 345.

101 Gregory S. Alexander, *The Global Debate over Constitutional Property* (Chicago: University of Chicago Press, 2006) 43.

102 Donna R. Christie, "A Tale of Three Takings: Taking Analysis in the Land Use Regulation of the United States, Australia, and Canada" (2007) 32 Brook J Int'l L 343 at 373 [Christie, "Three Takings"]. See also Rachelle Alterman, ed, *Takings International: A Comparative Perspective on Land Use Regulations and Compensation Rights* (Chicago: American Bar Association, 2010).

103 Although see the more nuanced view of the changing role of the court from the former SCC Chief Justice who led the court through the transition: Brian Dickson, The *Canadian Charter of Rights and Freedoms*: Dawn of a New Era? (1994) 2 Rev Constit Studies 1.

104 Christie "Three Takings," above note 102, 375-76 (emphasis in original).

105 See Alexander Alvaro, "Why Property Rights Were Excluded from the Canadian Charter of Rights and Freedoms" (1991) 24 *Canadian Journal of Political Science* 309; Jean McBean, "The Implications of Entrenching Property Rights in Section 7 of the Charter of Rights" (1988) 26 Alta L Rev 548.

106 Jennifer Nedelsky, "Should Property Be Constitutionalized? A Relational and Comparative Approach" in GE van Maanene & AJ van der Walt, eds, *Property Law on the Threshold of the 21st Century* (Apeldoorn, Netherlands: Maklu, 1996) 417 at 422. See also Joel Bakan, "Against Constitutional Property Rights," in Duncan Cameron & Miriam Smith, *Constitutional Politics* (Toronto: James Lorimer, 1992) at 117. Richard W. Bauman, "Property Rights in the Canadian Constitutional Context" (1992) 8 S Afr J on Hum Rts 344 offers a somewhat more equivocal view.

107 See Dan Cole, "Political Institutions, Judicial Review, and Private Property: A Comparative Institutional Analysis" (2007) 15 Sup Ct Econ Rev 141.

108 *Vancouver Charter,* above note 89.

109 Russell Brown, "The Constructive Taking at the Supreme Court of Canada: Once More, Without Feeling" (2007) 40 UBC L Rev 315 at 342 [Brown, "Constructive Taking"].

110 *NAFTA Between the Government of Canada, the Government of Mexico and the Government of the United States* (17 December 1992) Can TS 1994 No 2, 32 ILM 289, art 1110(2).

111 David Schneiderman, "NAFTA's Takings Rule: American Constitutionalism Comes to Canada" (1996) 46 UTLJ 499; Vicki Been & Joel C. Beauvais, "The Global Fifth Amendment? NAFTA's Investment Protections and the Misguided Quest for an International 'Regulatory Takings' Doctrine" (2003) 78 NYUL Rev 30.

112 Ziff, "'Taking' Liberties," above note 99 at 358.

113 Brown, "Constructive Taking," above note 109 at 335.

114 The 2007 Arbutus Lands Report, above note 95, considered and rejected a light rail option.

115 *Arbutus Corridor ODP,* above note 60.

Private Property and the Public Interest: (Re)Telling the Stories of Principles, Places, and Parties

Mary Jane Mossman

> What are the stories told to us of . . . conflicts and disputes that go to law, and become the stuff of which the law is made? Do these stories represent what was told, or have they been transformed by lawyers, judges and others, by law's procedures and practices? And what of the stories untold in law because the silent cannot speak or lawyers cannot hear?[1]

As these questions reveal, legal disputes and reported cases also tell "stories." However, as Katherine O'Donovan suggests, stories that are told by ordinary people may be transformed by law. Indeed, lawyers and judges assume that stories "in law" have a clearly defined purpose: "Storytelling in law is narrative within a culture of argument."[2] Thus, the goal of law's storytelling is to persuade the court that "one's story is true, to win the case . . . ."[3] Yet, as Carol Rose demonstrated in relation to ideas about the principle of possession, stories are also told within a community, one that includes the legal community but which may also resonate beyond it. That is, while stories have storytellers, they must also have an audience that can "hear" the story being told: the interpretive community. In the context of the nineteenth-century case of *Pierson v Post*,[4] for example, Rose argued that "the definition of first possession depended on a particular audience and its chosen symbolic context,"[5] that is, a legal rule that embodied effective communication of claims to the world, its audience. Thus, it seems that law always shapes the stories that are told in its special context.[6]

In addition, some legal scholars have claimed that storytelling, or narrative, has distinctive powers in law for "oppositionists" or outsider groups (including racial and other minorities, and women), whose claims have often been "silenced" by law:

> Telling stories (rather than simply making arguments) . . . has a distinctive power to challenge and unsettle the legal status quo, because stories give uniquely vivid representation to particular voices, perspectives, and experiences of victimization traditionally left out of legal scholarship and ignored when shaping legal rules.[7]

Thus, a number of scholars in the law and literature movement have employed narrative to provide more texture and detail about the law's impact on "outsiders."[8] Yet, even among these scholars, some have urged caution, arguing that the (neutral) methodology of storytelling provides no guarantee of their provenance: "Stories break stereotypes, but stereotypes are also stories, and stories can be full of them. . . Disembodied and decontextualized stories are also stories."[9] In the legal context particularly, Martha Minow expressed concerns about the limits of stories:

> Stories alone do not articulate principles likely to provide consistency in generalizations to guide future action; stories do not generate guides for what to heed or what additional stories to elicit. Stories on their own offer little guidance for evaluating competing stories.[10]

In spite of these debates within the law and literature movement about the role of stories in relation to law, histories of legal cases continue to attract our interest: sometimes because they reveal the back story of a legal conflict that was not reflected fully in the facts that were proved in the case, sometimes because they show that serendipity explains how a client's story was reframed to attract legal principles, and sometimes because stories about legal cases allow us to glimpse values or aspirations that fuelled human action in particular circumstances or unfamiliar contexts. In this way, telling and retelling stories about legal cases in the courts, about the politics of intervention by legislatures, and about the people involved in these disputes may provide different historical perspectives about the legal process: arguments that were employed or discarded, strategies that succeeded or failed, the impact of external social or political pressures or of missing voices, and a deeper understanding of the emergence of common law legal precedents out of individual disputes between parties. As the editors of *Property Stor-*

ies in the United States concluded, stories are important because "it is out of these conflicts involving real human emotions and desires that our regime of property law emerges and evolves."[11]

Like its American counterpart, this collection of property stories reflects a variety of perspectives and purposes, and they will enrich discussion about property law in many classrooms in Canadian law schools. As these essays reveal, stories may tell us more about legal cases in a variety of ways: stories about the evolution of principles, stories about how law defines "propertied" places, or stories about determined legal actors, including pugnacious parties as well as creative lawyers and judges — and sometimes stories that combine all these features. In addition, however, because many of the stories in this collection concern modern property cases of the twentieth and twenty-first centuries, they generally reflect how such claims renegotiate fundamental but ever-shifting boundaries between private property and the public interest,[12] a context in which property law must engage with social, economic, and political interests and must continue to evolve, sometimes in the unexpected ways demonstrated by the essays in this volume.

In providing this brief commentary about the essays in this collection, I focus on the ways in which ideas about relationships between private property and the public interest were reflected in the evolution of legal principles, in the redefining of propertied places, and in the legal aspirations of particular parties — and how some of these features overlapped in interesting ways. In concluding, I will comment briefly on how these stories sometimes seem to reflect the critiques of outsiders, but may also serve to reinforce the status quo.

The Evolution of Property Principles: Courts and Legislatures

Four essays in this collection focus on the evolution of common law principles in the courts and legislatures. Two essays focus on late nineteenth-century cases about principles of possession and nuisance, while a third case reveals how legislative intervention in the mid-twentieth century augmented common law nuisance principles and initiated standards for environmental regulation. The final case demonstrates similar tensions between protection for unfettered property rights in common law courts and legislative action to foster emerging principles of anti-discrimination in Canadian society in the second half of the twentieth century.

The earliest case concerned the principle of possession in property law, Bruce Ziff's essay about *Clift v Kane*,[13] which reveals how contextual nuances shaped the application of the principle in the context of the seal hunt off the coast of Newfoundland in 1869–70. His essay also examines the larger social and economic context to reveal how judges attempted to shape an outcome that achieved both individual justice and the overall economy of the seal hunt (arguably, a balancing of private property rights and the public interest). Although few archival records exist, Ziff tracked precedents about the seal hunt from 1858, showing how the generic rule of capture (killing an animal renders title absolute, and loss of possession does not constitute abandonment) seemed to have been augmented by a principle of "deemed abandonment." In these cases, evidence that a ship would not likely be able to recover seals piled on ice floes for later recovery (particularly because of poor weather) would result in cessation of the ship owner's property interest. Ziff's careful analysis of the trial and Full Court decisions reveals how different judges sought to uphold precedent in the context of the seal hunt in Newfoundland in the nineteenth century. In examining possession in these sealing cases, Ziff argued that a *sui generis* sealing custom emerged in this particular time and place, and suggested that radical changes in the mode of seal hunting (and particularly the adoption of steamships to replace schooners), along with the depletion of seal stocks, may provide a socio-economic explanation for the emergence of rules appropriate to a changing commercial environment. Ziff's essay represents a significant contribution to Canadian stories of the law of possession, and a fine effort to reveal the nuances of both sealing customs and the reasoning of nineteenth century Newfoundland courts about them.

The principle of nuisance in property law was explored in two essays in this collection. Eric Reiter's essay examines *Drysdale v Dugas*,[14] the first pronouncement on the law of nuisance by the Supreme Court of Canada in 1896. *Drysdale* was a dispute between a residential home owner in Montreal and the owner of a stable nearby, and Reiter's essay is important for its analysis of the intersection of property law and liability for nuisance, particularly because the reasoning also straddles principles within civil law and common law. In addition, the essay shows how legal principles intersected with a story of changing urban landscapes (the significance of place), and how the parties' interests and strategies reflected their differences of class and language within communities of nineteenth-century Montreal. Reiter's description of the parties clearly identified the plaintiff home owner as not only a member of the legal community, but also a judge of Montreal's lower criminal court, a fact that was never reported in the litigation. By contrast, Drysdale was a Scottish immigrant to Montreal who worked as a coachman and groom before opening his stable on St. Denis Street. However, Drysdale was also well connected to the Montreal Hunt Club with responsibility for its stables, and a number of prominent English Club members gave evidence on Drysdale's behalf in the trial. As Reiter also noted, the streetscape on St. Denis (the place) was also in a process of transition in the 1890s, a context that created space for social contestation and litigation, particularly because Montreal was relatively slow to initiate municipal regulation of stables. In addition to his description of the parties and place, Reiter provided a detailed exposition of the absolute nature of civil law (allodial) property ownership, and the contested principle of *voisinage* (use of property without injury to neighbours): a strict liability approach under the property-based approach, but a more general civil liability based on fault under article 1053 of the *Code Civil*. Reiter's examination of the interplay between these concepts, and their use in judicial reasoning in *Drysdale v Dugas* reveals the malleability of concepts of ownership, fault, injury, and abuse of rights. In the end, however, the Supreme Court of Canada failed to remove ambiguity about the role of fault in liability relating to the use of property, Drysdale closed his stable, Dugas relocated his home to another residential area, and the city of Montreal enacted a new building bylaw five years later, subjecting stables to strict limits: "The effect was to begin to replace the subjective appreciation of nuisance that drove private litigation with objective regulatory criteria like fire risk and hygiene, as interpreted and applied by public inspectors." Thus, the outcome of the case reveals the beginning of a transition to public regulation, augmenting common law nuisance principles, in disputes between owners of private property.

Half a century later, principles of nuisance also seemed to be at issue in the context of claims about industrial pollution of the Spanish River in Ontario by the Kalamazoo Vegetable and Parchment Company (*KVP v McKie*[15]). In James Benidickson's essay about this litigation and the riparian owners who launched it, he explained the broader context of such challenges posed by post–World War II industrialization in Canada and elsewhere, and early efforts to regulate the pollution it created. In the KVP trial before McRuer J in 1948, the rights of riparian owners were vindicated when McRuer J issued an injunction against KVP. Interestingly, the judge commented that the case was not about nuisance but about the quality of water for riparian owners, and that the economic significance of KVP's mill to the community was not a relevant matter for the court's legal analysis. Although the trial decision was upheld in the Ontario Court of Appeal and in the Supreme Court of Canada (and the Privy Council declined a further appeal), Benidickson described how KVP changed its strategy, engaging in media efforts about the impact of the injunction, and threatening to close the mill. In this highly charged political context, the Ontario legislature became involved in the controversy, with Premier Leslie Frost pledging to balance the rights of riparian owners to clean water with the need to ensure manufacturing productivity and industrial employment in Ontario, a balance perhaps more achievable in political rhetoric than industrial reality. After seeking advice from the Ontario Research Council, the government introduced the *KVP Company Limited Act*, dissolving the injunction and entrenching a research program concerning measures to limit the impact of industrial pollution. When further public action became necessary, the government created the Pollution Control Board of Ontario in 1952; after courts once again upheld claims by riparian owners who claimed damages for pollution resulting from outdated municipal sewage operations, the legislature intervened again by establishing the Ontario Water Resources Commission in 1957. In this property story, Benidickson focused on the shifting boundaries between private property and the public interest, as well as the seesaw roles of courts and legislatures, a story less concerned with individual parties than the larger story about the politics of pollution control in mid-twentieth-century Ontario.

Similarly, the essay by Frank Luce and Karen Schucher tells the story of *Bell v Ontario (Human Rights Commission)*,[16] a case that demonstrates the evolution of legal principles of anti-discrimination in the decades after World War II, and particularly how judicial concern to protect private property and legal processes tended to undermine protection for these human rights goals and the specialized administrative processes designed to promote them. The essay provides a detailed history of many of those involved in the broad social movement in Ontario, which campaigned against discriminatory practices, particularly in relation to employment, the provision of goods and services, and housing. It also reveals how the emergence of specialized tribunals in Ontario, particularly in relation to labour relations, created new issues about their roles for administrative law. When the Ontario legislature created the Human Rights Commission in 1962, its director, Dr Dan Hill, was among the strong proponents of its specialized procedure of complaint investigation, conciliation, a tribunal (Board of Inquiry) process, and a Minister's order for enforcement. However, *The Globe and Mail* lamented the assignment of these decisions to a tribunal rather than a court, and continued to advocate the need for judicial principles to protect the legal rights of employers and owners of businesses and rental housing. In this context, *Bell* became a test case. The case arose when a black man, Carl McKay, answered an advertisement for a flat, the upper level of a home owned by Kenneth Bell and his wife. Bell told McKay that the flat was taken, but when McKay requested a subsequent test of the flat's availability by a white woman (a typical practice in the anti-discrimination movement), Bell indicated to her that the flat was still available. On this basis, McKay filed a complaint with the OHRC, which appointed an investigator, who met with McKay and Bell, and then reported to Bell in writing that there was "sufficient evidence supporting Mr. McKay's allegations of discrimination to warrant further involvement of the Commission." These words were seized upon by Bell's lawyers to argue that the process had denied Bell natural justice or "legal rights," and they also challenged a jurisdictional fact about whether the flat was "self contained" within the meaning of the human rights statute.

The hearing before a Board of Inquiry was adjourned when Bell's lawyers sought prohibition, and the subsequent arguments before the High Court resulted in the court firmly upholding Bell's right to determine who could rent a flat in his home. Concern in the Ontario legislature that the court's decision had attacked the legislative purpose of the *Human Rights Code* may have encouraged the Attorney General to appeal the decision. In the Ontario Court of Appeal, the trial judgment was overturned, with Laskin J clearly acknowledging how the statute had changed the common law position of owners of housing accommodation, that is, recognizing that common law property rights had been altered by legislative action. In the subsequent appeal to the Supreme Court of Canada, however, the Court interpreted the flat as not self-contained and upheld the trial judge's decision on the prohibition issue. All the same, the legislature had the final word, enacting an amendment to enlarge the definition to encompass "any place of dwelling." In addition, however, the legislature eventually implemented procedural recommendations of the McRuer Report in the *Civil Rights Law Amendment Act* of 1971. In the end, although a number of significant changes have taken place in the structure and processes of the Ontario Human Rights Commission, the authors concluded that these developments have tended to place "social rights . . . in a much more competitive position vis a vis [sic] property rights than they were at the time of the *Bell* case." Thus, as with *KVP*, the *Bell* case reveals the ways in which courts and legislatures engaged in a rebalancing of the rights of owners of private property with the greater public interest in the second half of the twentieth century.

The Legal Politics of Property in Places

Contested relationships between private property and the public interest were also at issue in six essays that focused in different ways on the significance of propertied places. Moreover, all of these essays revealed, in rather different ways, tensions between the owners of private property and public planning processes. Two essays reveal these tensions in new kinds of property contexts in the second half of the twentieth century: in arrangements for shopping malls and in the regulation of sidewalks, both significant places for those who are poor or homeless.

Similarly, two essays examine the role of municipal planning and zoning bylaws in enhancing or diminishing private property interests, particularly when they threaten the homogeneity of urban communities or relationships between the interests of governments and private enterprise.

And two essays explore the significance of place and the evolution of legal principles in the context of recreational property, including a province's effort to preserve its limited recreational property for its own residents and the efforts of a group of like-minded university graduates to create an exclusive cottage community. In all of these contexts, there is a special emphasis on the idea of place in the application of property principles.

In Eric Tucker's essay about three Toronto Eaton Centre cases from 1984 to 1987,[17] the focus was the shopping mall and the limits (if any) on the rights of its corporate owners to exclude unwanted persons, based on an owner's private property rights. As Tucker noted, these cases reveal "a glimpse of property law on the ground" and the exigencies that sometimes transform ordinary persons into plaintiffs, and ordinary activities into legal cases. He also suggested that these mall cases provide good examples of the tension in property law between the absolute model of property ownership (claimed by the mall owner) and one that is socially contextualized (the mall as a new marketplace for civic activity), providing a case study of how such tensions in property law are resolved (or not). Tucker's essay offers a history of the emergence of the suburban mall in post–World War II America, developed by private enterprise but increasingly envisioned by citizens as providing necessary civic space: a new kind of "marketplace," strongly supported in the dissent of Laskin CJ in *Harrison v Carswell* (discussed in the essay).

Tucker's essay reviewed how the early negotiations for the Eaton Centre seemed to create rights of access, at least to some extent; and then how the mall engaged in energetic efforts to control access quite stringently pursuant to common law trespass principles. In addition to a detailed legal analysis, Tucker's essay told the story of Keith Medcalf, an ordinary young man who wanted to gain access to the Eaton Centre on a number of occasions, and how he ended up engaged in ongoing scuffles with security guards, court appearances, suits for damages against the Eaton Centre, and other arguments over several years — without ever really resolving the legal issue of trespass in relation to mall property. As well, Tucker analyzed two reported cases concerning labour organizing on mall property, both of which were ultimately successful for the union and for its supporter, Jack Layton. Yet, even though these labour cases appeared to negate the mall's absolutist property rights position, suggesting acceptance of the mall as a socially contextualized propertied place (a concept supported by legislative bills, a public inquiry, and the Supreme Court's decision upholding freedom of expression rights on government property), Tucker regretfully suggested that trespass law remains essentially unchanged: with respect to shopping malls and the private property rights of their owners, "near absolutism remains the norm."

In an analysis that is similar to Tucker's focus on shopping malls, Nicholas Blomley's assessment of private property in relation to public sidewalks in *Federated Anti-Poverty Groups of BC v Vancouver*[18] concluded that municipalities may use the public interest to regulate, even when the consequence is to exclude the poor from public property. Blomley's essay highlights how the absence of property negates a person's entitlement to inhabit any place, private or public. In particular, for homeless persons, there is no entitlement to place, a result that fails to respond to increasing inequality among Canadians or to confront how publicly owned property is often regulated in the interests of profit maximization for private enterprise — or privatized completely. After explaining the history of vagrancy law in Canada, Blomley described the phenomenon of increasing homelessness in Canadian cities in the latter part of the twentieth century, and rising concerns about its negative impact on commercial activity and tourism. In this context, Blomley analyzed the constitutional challenge launched by the BC Public Interest Advocacy Centre (on behalf of three anti-poverty organizations) against efforts by the City of Vancouver to enact bylaws regulating panhandling.

As Blomley's essay explains, the City eventually succeeded in enacting a valid bylaw by focusing it on the need to prevent obstruction and to promote circulation on city sidewalks. As he noted, the plaintiffs argued that this approach negated "the publicness of the sidewalk, a space of and for the people in the broadest sense," a place for "purposes of assembly, communicating thoughts between citizens, and discussing public questions." By contrast, it is significant that the City's bylaw characterized its streets and sidewalks as intended to promote the public interest in a different way: the facilitation of circulation and the prevention of obstruction. Although the City's definition may appear to promote equality for all persons to pass along sidewalks, with application to both pedestrian and commercial interests, the goals of circulation and prevention of obstruction may also tend to reinforce the status quo with respect to the use of sidewalks. Moreover, in spite of the City's stated goal of promoting equality, the voices of dispossessed panhandlers were not heard at all. Thus, while the sidewalk is public property and the City's bylaw is directed to the "public interest," Blomley concluded that regulatory municipal action has reinforced the exclusion of panhandlers: "The sidewalk may be a public space . . . but it is not one that is fully open to all."

Eran Kaplinsky's essay about *HG Winton v North York*,[19] also focuses on the municipal planning process, in the context of "spot zoning" to prevent the establishment of a Zoroastrian temple in North York. Kaplinsky described the emergence of municipal zoning in the twentieth century as a means of promoting health, safety, and welfare in cities, although in practice, of course, zoning also tends to preserve property values. In this context, Kaplinsky explained how principles had evolved to generally discourage spot zoning, that is, exercises of legislative authority that represented "instances of favouritism or maltreatment" of individual property owners, rather than the public interest. As Kaplinsky's essay reveals, a dispute resulted after HG Winton agreed to sell an unoccupied two-storey mansion (often known as the Mazo de la Roche mansion because the writer had lived there briefly) to the Zoroastrian community in Toronto, a highly educated immigrant community, with an interest in establishing a temple for use by the community. Although the Zoroastrians had obtained confirmation from the building commissioner that use of the property for the specified purpose was permitted, neighbouring home owners delivered a letter and petition opposing the sale to North York's Mayor Mel Lastman just a few days after Winton made his agreement with the Zoroastrian community. About a week later, the borough council enacted a zoning amendment bylaw prohibiting use of four blocks of residential lands (including the mansion) from use as churches and other institutional uses.

Kaplinsky provides a detailed analysis of "the substance of the bylaw and the unusual circumstances of its adoption," both of which were scrutinized by the court. For example, the bylaw proposal appeared suddenly as a new item on a regular council agenda, where it was given three readings on the same day, and a required two-week notice was waived. In addition, there was no public hearing, and neither Winton nor the Zoroastrians made submissions, mainly because they had not been informed of the proceeding. There were also none of the usual planning reports. Indeed, Kaplinsky notes that the only material provided to council was "the ratepayers' petition and accompanying letter." In the end, the court held that the borough's bylaw was based on bad faith and discrimination: as Kaplinsky concluded, "the case was never about land use regulation." In this way, the *Winton* case reveals how discrimination in property law may occur against "others" even when they are educated and economically successful, if they are religious minorities. Indeed, echoing Blomley's conclusion in relation to the homeless, Kaplinsky warns that outsiders may still be excluded according to planning law principles, so long as owners of private property can justify such exclusion "in the public interest."

Similarly, Douglas Harris' essay about *CPR v City of Vancouver*[20] focuses on a contest about a large tract of green space: the Arbutus Corridor that runs through the west side of Vancouver. The essay provides an analysis of a constructive takings of this Corridor after the CPR ceased its use for railway purposes, and it also reveals how a municipality may enact a bylaw about the use of private property that effectively stifles the owner's options "in the public interest." Harris situated the dispute within the historic development of Vancouver as a CPR town, based on significant land grants in return for railway development in the nineteenth century, and how the CPR's interests thereafter greatly influenced industrial, commercial, and residential development in the twentieth century. Tracing some of the changes in the urban landscape and studies by city planners, Harris noted especially the 1995 sale by CPR of a single lot to a developer, which resulted not only in the establishment of a Starbucks coffee shop on the parcel, but also the severance of a significant right of way related to the Arbutus Corridor. Because the Starbucks parcel had already been zoned for commercial use, however, the City was unable to intervene. Following this development, both the City and the CPR took steps to plan for the Corridor: the City developed several planning reports in the 1990s, while the CPR conducted a series of public meetings and later informed the City that about 80 percent of those who participated wanted the Corridor to be purchased by a public body for public use (the mooted sale price was $100 million).

In this context, and to prevent a reoccurrence of the Starbucks dilemma, City Council adopted the Arbutus Corridor Development Plan in June 2000. The plan was adopted as an Official Development Plan the following month, reserving the corridor as a greenway or for transportation, but (as a result of pressure from a wealthy homeowners' lobby group on the west side) not to include elevated transit such as the SkyTrain. In the face of the ODP, the CPR launched its petition to quash it as an "unjustified and uncompensated taking of the CPR's private property for a public purpose." At trial, the CPR succeeded, with the court concluding that the City did not have the power to denude private property of all use except as a public thoroughfare, and declared the bylaw invalid. However, the British Columbia Court of Appeal granted the appeal, holding that the City had authority to enact the bylaw, and that the bylaw was an appropriate response in the context of public support for preserving the corridor (with only Southin J concluding that some compensation might be needed). On a further appeal to the Supreme Court of Canada, however, the court very briefly reviewed the test for *de facto* taking, citing the few reported decisions on this issue, and concluded that it had not been met: the City had not acquired a beneficial interest, the CPR was not precluded from using the corridor as a railway (its traditional usage), and compensation was precluded under the terms of the City's Charter. In the end, Harris noted that the corridor is now used for walking, running, or biking, and gardens have been planted by "trespassers all," a result that Harris suggests confirms the small role for principles of *de facto* taking in balancing the rights of private property owners with the public interest in Canada — unlike the situation in the United States with its constitutional provisions for compensation in such cases. As he concluded, "the appropriate realms of the public and the private require continuing and repeated negotiation."

The politics relating to the public interest and the sense of place, and relationships between concepts of ownership and use, were also examined in Margaret McCallum's essay about Prince Edward Island's legislated restrictions on land acquisition by non-residents, focusing particularly on *Morgan and Jacobson v Prince Edward Island (AG).*[21] In this case, two American citizens who were resident in Rochester, New York, attempted to purchase thirty-six acres of wooded land in Prince Edward Island, contrary to the Island's statutory restrictions on the size of holdings for non-residents. As McCallum explained, Islanders' concerns about non-resident ownership of land had both a long history and a significant political resonance. Although the case was launched at the same time that the provincial government was appointing a Royal Commission on Land Ownership and Land Use, and arguments were heard by the Prince Edward Island Supreme Court just as the Commission released its report (recommending the regulation of land use rather than land ownership), the government did not implement the Commission's recommendations and they appear to have had no influence in the legal proceedings.

Augmented by archival documents and interviews with some of the protagonists, McCallum provided a detailed description of the parties, their lawyers and the judges, and a clear explanation of the plaintiffs' argument that these restrictions on non-resident land ownership in the *Real Property Act* infringed federal jurisdiction over citizenship; and that the province did not have jurisdiction to enact legislation that created distinctions based on status, i.e., distinctions between citizens who were, and who were not, resident in Prince Edward Island. When the court held that the provincial legislation was *intra vires* the province, the plaintiffs appealed to the Supreme Court of Canada, which also upheld the legislation as within provincial constitutional jurisdiction. McCallum's discussion of the legal arguments and judicial reasons, including the Court's assessment of earlier precedents concerning provincial legislation defining status (based on race), demonstrates how the court's reasoning distinguished issues of status from those of land regulation. McCallum's essay also details a number of later developments in Prince Edward Island, including the unsuccessful *Charter* challenge launched by Cavendish Farms in relation to restrictions on corporate land holdings in the 1980s, as well as similar efforts to protect land use and land ownership in other Canadian provinces. Although she cites a provincial official who suggested that "The public interest that the Act is presumably designed to protect has never been adequately defined," and suggests that non-residents became the "other" in this case, it seems clear that an important factor in this case was the strong sense of place in the traditions of Prince Edward Island and among its residents.

The same sensitivity to place was evident in Philip Girard's essay about a recreational community established in the late nineteenth century near Go Home Bay on Georgian Bay, and how the issue of enforcing its restrictive covenants eventually resulted in litigation in the Supreme Court of Canada in *Galbraith v Madawaska Club*.[22] In this case, covenants in the documents establishing the recreational community — a form of "private" planning designed to create a summer cottage community of scientists, scholars, and engineers associated with the University of Toronto — limited assignment of these cottage properties only to persons with connections to the university, and the letters patent conveying these lands from the Ontario government to the Club adopted these restrictions. About a decade later, the Club also acquired a collection of nearby islands owned by the federal government, and the Club then required the owners of these properties to insert in subsequent deeds of transfer a requirement that the grantee would convey only to Club members with the university connection. As Girard noted, such arrangements were relatively common in the early twentieth century and were intended by the governments to prevent speculation in recreational land. In addition, the covenants fostered a sense of purposefulness on the part of its members who engaged in a good deal of research with a sense of "sacred" stewardship in relation to these lands.[23]

The controversy that resulted in litigation related to the son of a founding Club member, John Galbraith, whose father (also John Galbraith) had been one of the original Club members. Some tensions between the Club and the younger Galbraith were created at his father's death in 1914, since his mother did not have the requisite University of Toronto qualifications to remain there. Although this situation was eventually resolved, Galbraith's dislike for the Club's rules increased when he decided to purchase an island property from Mrs. Firth, and the transfer deed to him in 1947 included the required covenants. In a challenge to their enforceability, Galbraith reconveyed the island property to himself and his wife (who was not a University of Toronto graduate) as joint tenants, and omitted the required covenants. For Galbraith (and probably for others), the Club's rules forbidding ownership of cottage properties by descendants without the requisite connections to the university created a sense of discrimination.

Indeed, as Girard suggested, Galbraith believed that denying the right of ownership because a person was not a Club member was a form of communism, a view that may have resonated strongly in the Cold War of the 1950s and 1960s. In his subsequent action to declare all the covenants invalid, his counsel relied on the distinction between the use of land and the identity of its owners to support Galbraith's claim. Galbraith partially succeeded at trial, but his claim was rejected in the Court of Appeal because the court concluded that the cottagers' interests were not fee-simple estates but only licences to which restrictions and conditions could be freely attached. In the face of this significant legal problem, Galbraith appealed to the Supreme Court of Canada, which concluded that the cottagers did have fee simple estates. In addition, the Court concluded that the restrictions were invalid for three reasons: they did not touch and concern the land, the Club had not retained land capable of being benefited, and the benefit had not been expressly annexed to the lands. However, since this result concerned only the island property purchased from Mrs. Firth, the invidious distinction between owners on the islands and on the mainland, all Club members, had to be resolved, eventually by the enactment of a private members' bill in the Ontario legislature in 1989. And, as Girard carefully explained, the *Galbraith* decision set a major precedent in Canada, one that was somewhat distinct from English legal principles about covenants, but consistent with different arrangements for the registration of title there. And, since the requirement to retain land makes such covenants more difficult to enforce, the *Galbraith* precedent may privilege development over stewardship, an ironic result for the "sacred" stewards of the Madawaska Club.

The Impact of Parties and Creative Lawyers

Four essays in this collection suggest how the persistence of parties or the creativity of their lawyers — and sometimes both — may be crucial elements in property law cases. Significantly, all these cases also reveal elements of test cases in relation to legal principles emerging in the context of new political, technological, scientific, and social developments. Two essays focus attention on the role of creative lawyers, both of whom were relatively young and inexperienced, but who demonstrated persistence and resourcefulness in defining the property issues at stake in cases that reached the Supreme Court of Canada. In the other two cases, it was the litigants themselves whose dogged belief in the justice of their causes resulted in decisions in the Supreme Court of Canada. While only one of them succeeded initially, the dissenting judgment in the other case eventually created a new jurisprudence about property for separating spouses. As all of these cases reveal, property law sometimes needs creative lawyers and intrepid litigants to evolve to meet the challenges of societal change.

In the essay concerning *Manitoba Fisheries v The Queen*,[24] Jim Phillips and Jeremy Martin traced the complex story of the creation of the Freshwater Fish Marketing Corporation, a federal-provincial initiative in the 1960s and 70s that was designed to reorganize the marketing of freshwater fish in Ontario and the three Prairie provinces. In doing so, the legislative initiative granted a monopoly to the Corporation and thereby closed down the businesses of privately owned fish marketing companies. As the authors note, the case is probably the "high water mark in Canadian takings law," since the result of litigation was an award of compensation for the loss of the companies' "goodwill," recognized by the Supreme Court of Canada as an intangible form of property. In explaining the larger context of the freshwater fish industry and its problems, as well as ongoing governmental studies (including the influential McIvor Report) in the efforts to solve them, the essay also provides an engaging history of the complicated federal-provincial negotiations that were required to establish the Corporation. Eventually, federal legislation establishing the Corporation was enacted in 1969, and complementary legislation was then enacted in the provinces (Manitoba's legislation passed with a very close vote). Unfortunately, the arrangements for compensating the fish marketing companies for their loss of business was both uncertain in the federal-provincial agreement, and politically contentious. A number of fish companies were unsatisfied with the compensation offered, especially in Manitoba where Premier Schreyer's social democratic government's commitment to "giving priority to public rather than private interests" resulted in intransigence on this issue. There is also some evidence that one member of Cabinet, Sidney Green, was particularly sympathetic to the plight of the primary producers (northern fishers, many of whom were Aboriginals) who lived in abject poverty and who had probably been treated poorly by the companies. Yet, the key player in the *Manitoba Fisheries* litigation was a young lawyer named Ken Arenson, who became involved in the compensation claim as a result of a chance encounter between his uncle and one of the business claimants. It was Arenson who created the strategy of claiming compensation on the basis that the government's Corporation had taken the goodwill of Manitoba Fisheries, and he then located a precedent from Northern Ireland to support his argument that goodwill constituted property. Although the argument was rejected at trial and in the Manitoba Court of Appeal, it succeeded in achieving unanimous support in the Supreme Court of Canada. As the authors conclude, the decision may have been based, at least to some extent, on sympathy for the plaintiffs, and if so, the "hero of the case was the person who found a legal way to express that sympathy — Ken Arenson." In terms of precedent, Phillips and Martin argue that it is possible that the case has had some impact by necessitating greater care with respect to governmental intervention in the regulation of the economy, even though a successful claim of *de facto* expropriation requires acquisition of an identifiable interest in property, a test that is not met when only usage is affected, as in *CPR v Vancouver.*

In addition, however, the authors suggest that *Manitoba Fisheries* may have bolstered support for those who opposed including protection for private property in the *Canadian Charter of Rights and Freedoms*, particularly because of its potential to derail provincial regulatory schemes such as Prince Edward Island's restrictions on land ownership by non-residents. In addition, while *Manitoba Fisheries* clearly reveals the importance of persistent parties and creative lawyering, it is also interesting to contrast the sympathy for Aboriginal fishers in the Manitoba Cabinet with the quite different focus of the judges' sympathy for business owners in the Supreme Court of Canada. In the result, the balancing of private property and the public interest may once again have contributed to voiceless outsiders.

Ian Kyer's essay about *R v Stewart*[25] similarly focused on the definition of property in a new context: specifically, whether confidential information (in relation to computer technology) constituted property for purposes of offences under the *Criminal Code*. In addition, however, this case also reveals the significance of "determination, energy and enthusiasm" on the part of another young lawyer, Robert McNeely. As Kyer explained, the criminal charges of counselling fraud, theft, and mischief against Stewart arose out of a highly contested union organizing effort at an airport strip hotel in Toronto. Stewart was charged after he requested the assistance of a security guard at the hotel to copy the names of hotel employees from a confidential computer print out, part of a strategy to contact employees to promote the union's organizing efforts that was foiled when the security guard notified police. Significantly, Stewart's unsuccessful effort to gain access to confidential information in this way did not, in itself, constitute a major legal issue. But, as Kyer pointed out, this case occurred in the context of three emerging trends in Canada: computerization and the development of information technology, increasing concerns about improper collection and misuse of information, and the debate over fundamental rights. In this context, the question of whether law should recognize information as property loomed large, and both academic views and the few decided cases varied in their approaches and outcomes.

At the instigation of the Crown to pursue the matter as a test case, McNeely agreed to a statement of facts, on the understanding that if Stewart were found guilty at law, the Crown would not oppose an absolute discharge. Thus, the case was argued on the basis of legal principles alone. Kyer provided a detailed description of the arguments presented by McNeely and the Crown before Krever J, who held that to be "anything whether tangible or intangible" pursuant to the theft provisions of the *Criminal Code*, the confidential information had to be property. Stewart was accordingly acquitted on all three charges. On appeal, however, the trial decision was overturned, with the majority of Houlden JA and Cory JA fashioning a conviction out of existing provisions of the *Code*, and a dissenting opinion from Lacourcière JA. This division of opinion was also reflected in academic critique, so that although Stewart had benefited from the promised absolute discharge, McNeely advised him to pursue his appeal as of right to the Supreme Court of Canada, and with Stewart's consent, McNeely filed the requisite documents to initiate the appeal. However, just as McNeely was becoming overwhelmed by the rising expenses of the appeal, he received an offer of assistance from Clayton Ruby, whose client, the Church of Scientology, was facing similar charges. As Kyer concluded, Ruby's intervention confirmed that the Crown had selected the *Stewart* case "as an attempt . . . to clarify the law in support of their ongoing prosecution of the Church of Scientology without having to face Ruby [and others]," a strategy that was undermined when Stewart agreed to be represented by Ruby in the Supreme Court of Canada. The Crown was assisted, however, when Professor Arnold Weinrib authored an article which supported the arguments of the majority of the Ontario Court of Appeal, and the Supreme Court accepted it (in typescript) for consideration. As Kyer noted, the Supreme Court's decision took into account the new technological context, but concluded that taking confidential information was not theft of property, an outcome that clearly served to create ongoing challenges for the Crown in its case against the Church of Scientology. It also consigned to Parliament the task of redefining theft in a computer age, a task largely ignored. Yet, in spite of its significance in engendering debate about this new technological challenge, the story of *R v Stewart* may also be important because it highlighted the contribution of another creative lawyer in defending an accused charged with an offence in this new context — a contribution that substantially succeeded, as in *Manitoba Fisheries*.

By contrast with these two cases involving creative young lawyers, Patricia Farnese's essay about *Monsanto Canada Inc v Schmeiser*[26] reveals how cases sometimes require a persistent, even pugnacious, defendant, such as Percy Schmeiser, as well as a committed lawyer — Terry Zakresky. Farnese's essay tells the story of a claim of patent infringement launched by the leading agricultural biotechnology company in the world, Monsanto, against Schmeiser, a Saskatchewan farmer. As Farnese explained, Monsanto's history in the twentieth century was closely connected to a number of scientific developments that have had serious health and other impacts, including PCBs, Agent Orange, and atomic weapons. In the 1970s, Monsanto researchers discovered glyphosate, a herbicide that was apparently effective, safe, and environmentally friendly, and with significant market potential to eradicate weeds. Indeed, Farnese reported that it has been accepted and used by farmers and land managers around the world. To ensure their market, Monsanto also engaged in research to develop genetically modified seed (resistant to the herbicide), and introduced Roundup Ready canola seeds in Canada in 1996.

The impact of this development is evident in the statistics: by 2010, there were seventeen million acres of canola in Canada, with about 80 percent of them genetically modified, and Monsanto has become the world's largest seed company. Farnese then explained how Schmeiser, from a prominent family in a small rural community in Saskatchewan, had both the personal qualities and the financial resources to defend against Monsanto's claim of patent infringement all the way to the Supreme Court of Canada. In a careful assessment of the scientific evidence of test results and the inconclusive testimony of some witnesses, as well as the legal arguments before the courts in Saskatchewan and at the Supreme Court, Farnese showed how Schmeiser's tenacity was ultimately rewarded when the Court held that there was a patent infringement, but refused to order an accounting for profits since he had not profited from the infringement; the Court also chose not to award costs in the case. In addition, Monsanto failed to prove its allegation that Schmeiser had deliberately obtained the patented seed, a victory for Schmeiser and his lawyer. As Farnese's essay reveals, however, it is possible that only a defendant with Schmeiser's willingness to go to court, evidenced by a number of earlier but unrelated litigation matters and his financial status as a successful farmer and businessman, would have accepted the challenge to defend against Monsanto's claim. Certainly, others had yielded to out of court settlements to avoid such a contest, characterized in the press as "a modern battle between David and Goliath." Indeed, in the view of many with concerns about the health and environmental effects of agricultural biotechnology (both farmers and the public), these issues remain ongoing matters of public interest. Thus, just as in the *Stewart* case, further developments in scientific technology will continue to require negotiation between the public interest and private property.

The final case about the impact of parties focuses on the role of Irene Murdoch, who claimed a share of ranch lands owned by her husband in her divorce action after twenty-five years of marriage in a case that was also appealed to the Supreme Court of Canada, *Murdoch v Murdoch*.[27] Irene Murdoch's situation was quite typical of farm wives in the 1960s and 1970s, when hierarchical farming and ownership structures frequently resulted in the invisibility of women's work and contributions to farm families. As Vanessa Gruben, Angela Cameron, and Angela Chaisson's essay about the *Murdoch* case explains, the rejection of Irene Murdoch's claims occurred after the enactment of the first federal divorce legislation in 1968 and prior to the introduction of property sharing statutes for spouses at divorce and separation. Although Irene Murdoch had laboured alongside her husband, and on her own when he was away for months at a time, and even though her work contributed to their acquisition of a number of ranch properties, her husband assaulted her physically (breaking her jaw in three places) when she refused to release her dower claim to enable him to sell their ranch and home.

In the trial court, Irene Murdoch's claims for judicial separation and support of $200 monthly succeeded, but the court awarded custody of her thirteen-year-old son to her husband, and denied her claim for exclusive possession of the matrimonial home. In addition, the trial court denied her claim to share the property by way of resulting trust or partnership, concluding that there was no intention of co-ownership. The Court of Appeal rejected her appeal on the basis that her monthly support award precluded any property interest. Although Irene Murdoch had few financial resources, and even though she had little desire for publicity, she pursued her claim with the assistance (on a contingency basis) of her lawyer Ernest Shymka to the Supreme Court of Canada. For Shymka, it seemed quite unfair for her husband to end up with all the assets after Irene Murdoch's major contributions over twenty-five years. Yet, pursuing the claim was difficult. As the authors suggested, Irene Murdoch was severely disabled by her husband's assault (she could not eat solid food for a few years and she was unable to speak easily at the trial in 1971), and she was emotionally and financially bereft. Unfortunately, after an extensive review of resulting trust principles, a majority of the Supreme Court rejected Irene Murdoch's claim on the basis that her efforts were simply the "work done by any ranch wife," a claim that seems to have been based on her husband's evidence at trial. By contrast, the dissenting judgment of Laskin J used the concept of constructive trust to conclude that her husband held a beneficial interest in his land for Irene Murdoch, based on her extensive contributions. While the significance of the dissenting judgment in terms of the legal principles concerning constructive trusts became much more significant in later years, the majority judgment seemed to provide an immediate catalyst or "lightning rod" for women and others demanding reforms to matrimonial property law in the 1970s, a campaign that eventually resulted in the enactment of statutory property sharing regimes by all the common law provinces by 1980. Moreover, when her husband finally petitioned for divorce, the court awarded Irene Murdoch lump sum support of $65,000, secured against one of the properties, an amount representing about half the value of the property. Beyond the parties themselves, moreover, Irene Murdoch's case probably contributed to more egalitarian views of marriage and marital property in Canadian society, and in courts and legislatures. As the authors concluded, "Irene's personal circumstances [and her perseverance] gave the feminist movement a public face for matrimonial property reform to which many 'average' Canadians of both genders could relate."

(Re)Telling Stories and Storytelling in Property Cases

As THE ESSAYS IN this collection demonstrate, there are many different property stories and many different perspectives on how stories are told in the legal context. Moreover, the essays also reveal some of the links among parties and their lawyers, sensitivity to the idea of place, and the evolution of legal principles within broader societal contexts in ways that are often full of serendipity as well as purposefulness. Sometimes the characters in the stories are as important as their location in time and space, and both of these elements may result in new ways of seeing traditional legal principles and processes.

As a number of these stories also reveal, however, the parties in legal cases (even the ones that take on the role of David against Goliath) are more often the sealing ship owners (not the crew members), or the plaintiffs with connections and resources (businesses and governments, as well as businessmen, middle-class home or cottage owners, or unions), and much less frequently an individual who may benefit, or not, as a result of a test case (such as the accused Stewart, the "real" claimants in the *Federated Anti-Poverty* case, or Irene Murdoch). Moreover, some property stories may silence outsiders, such as Medcalf in his unresolved shopping mall litigation, the northern Aboriginal fishers who remained invisible in *Manitoba Fisheries*, and other potential litigants' choices to settle when they were sued by Monsanto. These may be the litigants silenced by law whom CB Macpherson had in mind when he proposed to redefine property as "the right not to be excluded."[28]

Thus, in reflecting on these property law stories about principles, places, and parties, it remains necessary for teachers and students to attend carefully to those who are outsiders in these stories and to reassess the intersection of the public interest and private property in judicial analyses in the courts and in proposals for legislative intervention. In doing so, we need to practise Carol Rose's proposal for "a new way of seeing," an imaginative revisioning of current ideas about property and law:

> *[W]hat you see* in property is what you and others have talked yourselves into about . . . "things"; and given some imagination, you may always talk yourselves into seeing something else — with all the effects on understanding and action that a new "envisioning" may bring.[29]

Notes

1 Katherine O'Donovan, *Family Law Matters* (London: Pluto Press, 1993) at 106.

2 Paul Gewirtz, "Narrative and Rhetoric in the Law" in Peter Brooks and Paul Gewirtz, eds, *Law's Stories: Narrative and Rhetoric in the Law* (New Haven and London: Yale University Press, 1996) 2 at 5.

3 Ibid.

4 3 Cai R 175 (NY. Sup. Ct. 1805).

5 Carol Rose, "Possession as the Origin of Property" in Carol Rose, *Property and Persuasion* (Boulder, San Francisco, Oxford: Westview Press, 1994) 11 at 18.

6 For an argument that "narrative" in fiction should be completely separated from "facts" in law, see Alan M Dershowitz, "Life is Not a Dramatic Narrative" in Brooks and Gewirtz, eds, note 2 at 99. Particularly in the context of criminal trials, Dershowitz argued (at 105) that "human experience cannot be cabined into the structure of narrative," so that "law needs to develop its own rules of evidence, relevance, and prejudice" rather than relying on stories in literature: "life is not a Chekhovian narrative."

7 Gewirtz, note 2 at 5.

8 Some examples include Mari Matsuda, "When the First Quail Calls: Multiple Consciousness as Jurisprudential Method" (1989) 11 *Women's Rights Law Reporter* 7; Sharon McIvor, "Aboriginal Women: Working in Coalition to Advance Sex Equality" in Elizabeth Sheehy and Sheila McIntyre, eds, *Calling for Change: Women, Law and the Legal Profession* (Ottawa: University of Ottawa Press, 2006) 253; and Derrick Bell, *Faces at the Bottom of the Well: The Permanence of Racism* (New York: Basic Books, 1992).

9 Catharine A MacKinnon, "Law's Stories as Reality and Politics" in Brooks and Gewirtz, note 2, 232 at 235

10 Martha Minow, "Stories in Law" in Brooks and Gewirtz, note 2, 24 at 35.

11 Gerald Korngold and Andrew P Morriss, "Introduction: The Story of *Property Stories*" in Korngold and Morriss, eds, *Property Stories* (New York: Foundation Press, 2004) 1 at 2.

12 For example, see John Cribbet, "Concepts in Transition: The Search for a New Definition of Property" (1986) *University of Illinois Law Review* 1. In this article, Cribbet argued that older justifications for private property have become less useful than a theory of social utility.

13 (1870), 5 Nfld LR 327 (SC).

14 (1896), 26 SCR 20.

15 [1949] 1 DLR 38.

16 [1971] SCR 756.

17 *RWDSU v T Eaton Company Limited* [1985] OLRB Rep June 941; upheld (1988), 62 OR (2d) 337; affirmed (1990), 71 OR (2d) 206 (ONCA); and *R v Layton* (1986), 38 CCC (3d) 550. The third case was unreported and settled out of court.

18 [2002] BCSC 105. As Blomley notes, this case is also related to *R v Banks* in Ontario (2001), 45 CR (5th) 23; and to *Victoria (City) v Adams* 2008 BCSC 1363. *Banks* upheld provincial law regulating panhandling and squeegeeing; while *Adams* challenged

the constitutionality of Victoria's bylaw regulating camping in public property such as parks.

19 [1978] 20 OR (2d) 737 (Div Ct).

20 [2006] 1 SCR 227.

21 [1976] 2 SCR 349.

22 (1960) 23 DLR (2d) 6 (Ont CA); [1961] SCR 639.

23 As Girard noted, the Club published a retrospective every 25 years, detailing ecological changes, shifting social mores, and the literary and scientific output of Club members. See Girard's chapter at note 18 and accompanying text.

24 [1979] 1 SCR 101.

25 [1988] 1 SCR 963.

26 [2004] 1 SCR 902.

27 [1975] 1 SCR 423.

28 CB Macpherson, "Liberal Democracy and Property" in CB Macpherson, *Property: Mainstream and Critical Positions* (Toronto: University of Toronto Press, 1978) 199 at 201.

29 Rose, "Seeing Property" in Rose, note 5, 267 at 297 (emphasis in original).

Select Bibliography: Canadian Property Law Histories

Case Studies

Eric Adams, "Errors of Fact and Law: Race, Space, and Hockey in *Christie v York*" forthcoming (2012) 62 UTLJ

Constance Backhouse, "'Bitterly Disappointed' at the Spread of 'Colour-Bar Tactics': Viola Desmond's Challenge to Racial Discrimination, Nova Scotia, 1946" in *Colour-Coded: A Legal History of Racism in Canada, 1900-1950* (Toronto: Osgoode Society & University of Toronto Press, 1999) 226

Brian Bucknall, "*Pajelle Investmentss Ltd. v Herbold*: On the Importance of Having a Convenient Enemy" (1997) 35 OHLJ 685

Mysty S. Clapton, "*Murdoch v Murdoch*: The Organizing Narrative of Matrimonial Property Law Reform" (2008) 20 C JWL 197

Richard Daly, *Our Box was Full: An Ethnography for the Delgamuukw Plaintiffs* (Vancouver: University of British Columbia Press, 2005)

Hamar Foster, Heather Raven & Jeremy Webber, eds, *Let Right be Done: Aboriginal Title, the Calder Case, and the Future of Indigenous Rights* (Vancouver: University of British Columbia Press, 2007)

Philip Girard & Jim Phillips, "A Certain Mallaise: *Harrison v Carswell*, Shopping Centre Picketing, and the Limits of the Postwar Settlement" in Judy Fudge & Eric Tucker, eds, *Work on Trial: Cases in Context* (Toronto: Osgoode Society & Irwin Law, 2010) 249

Douglas C. Harris, "The Boldt Decision in Canada: Aboriginal Treaty Rights to Fish on the Pacific" in Alexandra Harmon, ed, *The Power of Promises: Rethinking Indian Treaties in the Pacific Northwest* (Seattle: University of Washington Press, 2008) 128

Virginie Marier & Tina Piper, "Early Twentieth-Century Canadian Medical Patent Law in Practice: James Bertram Collip and the Discovery of Emmenin" (2010) 60 UTLJ 855

Antonio Mills, *Hang on to These Words: Johnny David's Delgamuukw Testimony* (Toronto: University of Toronto Press, 2005)

Mark M. Orkin, *The Great Stork Derby* (Don Mills: General Pub. Co., 1981)

Mariana Valverde, "Families, Private Property, and the State: The Dionnes and the Toronto Stork Derby" (1994-95) 29 J of Can Stud 15

James W. St. Walker, "*Christie v York Corporation*" in *'Race', Rights and the Law in the Supreme Court of Canada: Historical Case Studies* (Waterloo, ON: Osgoode Society & Wilfrid Laurier University Press, 1997) 122

______________, "*Noble & Wolf v Alley*" in *"Race," Rights and the Law in the Supreme Court of Canada: Historical Case Studies* (Waterloo, ON: Osgoode Society & Wilfrid Laurier University Press, 1997) 182

Bruce Ziff, *Unforeseen Legacies: Reuben Wells Leonard and the Leonard Foundation Trust* (Toronto: Osgoode Society & University of Toronto Press, 2000)

Other Works

Christopher Alcantara, "Individual Property Rights on Canadian Indian Reserves: The Historical Emergence and Jurisprudence of Certificates of Possession" (2003) 23 Canadian J of Native Stud 391

S. Allen, "One Hundred Years of Solicitude – Judicial Resistance to Reform of Married Women's Property Law in the West" (1995) 4 Dal J Leg Stud 175

Harvey Amani Whitfield & Barry Cahill, "Slave Life and Slave Law in Colonial Prince Edward Island, 1769-1825," (2009) 38 Acadiensis 29

Constance Backhouse, "Married Women's Property Law in Nineteenth-Century Canada," 6 Law & Hist Rev 211 (1988)

Peter A. Baskerville, *A Silent Revolution?: Gender and Wealth in English Canada, 1860-1930* (Montreal: McGill-Queen's University Press, 2008).

______________, "Chattel Mortgages and Community in Perth County, Ontario" (2006) 87 Can Hist Rev 583

Jamie Benidickson, "Private Rights and Public Purposes in the Lakes, Rivers, and Streams of Ontario, 1870-1930" in David H. Flaherty, ed, *Essays in the History of Canadian Law* (Toronto: Osgoode Society & University of Toronto Press, 1983) 365

Rusty Bittermann, *Rural Protest on Prince Edward Island: From British Colonization to the Escheat Movement* (Toronto: University of Toronto Press, 2006)

Rusty Bittermann & Margaret McCallum, *Lady Landlords of Prince Edward Island: Imperial Dreams and the Defence of Property* (Montreal & Kingston: McGill-Queen's University Press, 2008)

______________, "Upholding the Land Legislation of a 'Communistic and Socialist Assembly': The Benefits of Confederation for Prince Edward Island." (2006) 87 Can Hist Rev 1

Peggy J. Blair, *Lament for a First Nation: The Williams Treaties in Southern Ontario* (Vancouver: University of British Columbia Press, 2008)

Bettina Bradbury, *Wife to Widow: Lives, Laws, and Politics in Nineteenth-Century Montreal* (Vancouver: University of British Columbia Press, 2011)

Bettina Bradbury, Peter Gossage, Evelyn Kolish & Alan Stewart, "Property and Marriage" (1993) 26 Histoire Sociale: Social History 9

JM Bumsted, "The Land Question on Prince Edward Island and the Quitrent Controversy of 1802-1806" (2000) 29 Acadiensis 3

Barry Cahill, "Slavery and the Judges of Loyalist Nova Scotia" (1994) 43 UNBLJ 73

Brian Calliou, "The Supreme Court of Alberta and First Nations Hunting Rights: Federalism and Respect for 'the Queen's Promises'" in Jonathan Swainger, ed, *The Alberta Supreme Court at 100* (Edmonton: Osgoode Society & University of Alberta Press, 2007) 133

Catherine Cavanaugh, "The Limitations of the Pioneering Partnership: The Alberta Campaign for Homestead Dower, 1909-1925" (1993) 74 Can Hist Rev 198

Lori Chambers, "Women's Labour, Relationship Breakdown and Ownership of the Family Farm" (2010) 25 CJL & S 75

______________, *Married Women and Property Law in Victorian Ontario* (Osgoode Society & University of Toronto Press, 1997)

Christopher A. Clarkson, "Property Law and Family Regulation in Pacific British North America, 1862- 1873," (1997) 30 Histoire Sociale: Social History 386

Douglas Cole, *An Iron Hand upon the People: The Law Against the Potlatch on the Northwest Coast* (Vancouver: Douglas & McIntyre, 1990)

Alvin J. Esau, *The Courts and the Colonies: The Litigation of Hutterite Church Disputes* (Vancouver: University of British Columbia Press, 2004)

Hamar Foster, "A Romance of the Lost: The Role of Tom MacInnes in the History of the British Columbia Indian Land Question" in G. Blaine Baker & Jim Phillips, eds, *Essays in Canadian Legal History, In Honour of R.C.B. Risk, Vol. VIII* (Toronto: Osgoode Society & University of Toronto Press, 1999) 171

Hamar Foster & Benjamin L. Berger, "From Humble Prayers to Legal Demands: The Cowichan Petition of 1909 and the British Columbia Indian Land Question" in Hamar Foster, Benjamin L. Berger & AR Buck, eds, *The Grand Experiment: Law & Legal Culture in British Settler Societies* (Vancouver: Osgoode Society & University of British Columbia Press, 2008) 240

Lillian F. Gates, "The Heir and Devisee Commission of Upper Canada, 1797-1805" (1957) 38 Canadian Historical Review 21

Philip Girard, "Married Women's Property Law, Chancery Abolition, and Insolvency Law: Law Reform in Nova Scotia, 1820-1867" in Philip Girard & Jim Phillips, eds, *Essays in the History of Canadian Law, Vol. III, Nova Scotia* (Toronto: Osgoode Society & University of Toronto Press, 1990) 80

Philip Girard & Rebecca Veinott, "Married Women's Property in Nova Scotia, 1850-1910," in Janet Guildford and Suzanne Morton, eds, *Separate Spheres: Woman's Worlds in the 19th Century Maritimes* (Fredericton: Acadiensis Press, 1994)

Douglas C. Harris, *Landing Native fisheries: Indian Reserves and Fishing Rights in British Columbia, 1849-1923* (Vancouver: University of British Columbia Press, 2008)

______________, *Fish, Law, and Colonialism: The Legal Capture of Salmon in British Columbia* (Toronto: University of Toronto Press, 2001)

______________, "The Nlha7kapmx Meeting at Lytton, 1879, and the Rule of Law" (1995) 108 BC Studies 5

R. Cole Harris, *Making Native Space: Colonialism, Resistance, and Reserves in British Columbia* (Vancouver: University of British Columbia Press, 2002)

R.E. Hawkins, "Dower Abolition in Western Canada: How Law Reform Failed" (1997) 24 Man L J 635

Trudi Johnson, "Defining Property for Inheritance: The Chattels Real Act of 1834" in Christopher English, ed, *Essays in the History of Canadian Law: Two Islands, Newfoundland and Prince Edward Island* (Toronto: Osgoode Society & University of Toronto Press, 2005) 192

__________, "Women and Inheritance in Nineteenth-Century Newfoundland," (2002) 13 J of Can Hist Assoc 1

Bruce Kercher & Jodie Young, "Formal and Informal Law in Two New Lands: Land Law in Newfoundland and New South Wales" in Christopher English, ed, *Essays in the History of Canadian Law: Two Islands, Newfoundland and Prince Edward Island* (Toronto: Osgoode Society & University of Toronto Press, 2005) 147

Arlene Kwasniak, "The Supreme Court of Alberta and Water Law" in Jonathan Swainger, ed, *The Alberta Supreme Court at 100* (Edmonton: Osgoode Society & University of Alberta Press, 2007) 193

Margaret McCallum, "The Sacred Rights of Property: Title, Entitlement, and the Land Question in Nineteenth-Century Prince Edward Island" in G. Blaine Baker & Jim Phillips, eds, *Essays in Canadian Legal History, In Honour of R.C.B. Risk, Vol. VIII* (Toronto: Osgoode Society & UTP, 1999) 358

__________, "Prairie Women and the Struggle for a Dower Law, 1905-1920" (1993) 18 Prairie Forum 19

__________, "Mechanics' Liens in the Mowat Era," (1986) 19 Histoire Sociale: Social History 387

John McLaren, AR Buck & Nancy E Wright, eds, *Despotic Dominion: Property Rights in British Settler Societies* (Vancouver: University of British Columbia Press, 2005)

John McLaren, "The Canadian Doukhobors and the Land Question: Religious Communalists in a Fee Simple World" in AR Buck, John McLaren & Nancy Wright, eds, *Land and Freedom: Law, Property Rights and the British Diaspora* (Aldershot: Ashgate Pr., 2001) 135

Kent McNeil, "Social Darwinism and Judicial Conceptions of Indian Title in Canada in the 1880s" (1999) 38 J of the West 68

Meera Nair, "The Copyright Act of 1889: A Canadian Declaration of Independence," (2009) 90 Canadian Historical Review 1

Jennifer Nedelsky, "From Private Property to Public Resource: The emergence of Administrative Control of Water in Nova Scotia" in Philip Girard & Jim Phillips, eds, *Essays in the History of Canadian Law, Vol. III, Nova Scotia* (Toronto: Osgoode Society & University of Toronto Press, 1990) 326

Bill Parenteau, "A 'VERY DETERMINED Opposition To The Law': Conservation, Angling Leases, and Social Conflict in the Canadian Atlantic Salmon Fishery, 1867–1914," (2004) 9 Env'l Hist. 436

David R. Percy, "Water Law of the Canadian West: Influences from the Western States" in John McLaren, Hamar Foster & Chet Orloff, eds, *Law for the Elephant Law for the Beaver* (Regina: Canadian Plains Research Centre, 1992) 274

Sean Purdy, "By the people, for the people: Tenant organizing in Toronto's Regent Park housing project in the 1960s and 1970s" (2004) 30 J of Urban Hist 519

William R. Riddell, "The Slave in Canada" (1920) 5 J. Negro History 261

Michele Stairs, "'The Duty of Every Man': Intestacy Law and Family-Inheritance Practice in Prince Edward Island" in Christopher English, ed, *Essays in the History of Canadian Law: Two Islands, Newfoundland and Prince Edward Island* (Toronto: Osgoode Society & University of Toronto Press, 2005) 217

Jordan Stanger-Ross, "Municipal Colonialism in Vancouver: City Planning and the Conflict over Indian Reserves, 1928–1950s" (2008) 89 Can Hist Rev 541

Greg Taylor, *The Law of the Land: The Advent of the Torrens System in Canada* (Toronto: Osgoode Society & University of Toronto Press, 2008)

John C. Weaver, *The Great Land Rush and the Making of the Modern World, 1650-1900* (Montreal: McGill-Queen's, 2003)

______________, "While Equity Slumbered: Creditor Advantage, A Capitalist Land Market, and Upper Canada's Missing Court" (1990) 28 OHLJ 871

Bruce Ziff & Sean Ward, "Squatters' Rights and the Origins of Edmonton Settlement" in Jim Phillips, R. Roy McMurtry & JT Saywell, eds, *Essays in the History of Canadian Law, Vol. X: A Tribute to Peter N. Oliver* (Toronto: Osgoode Society & University of Toronto Press, 2008) 446

Contributors

Jamie Benidickson of the Faculty of Law, University of Ottawa, has written elsewhere on the history of regulation and administrative decision-making in Canada. He is the author of *The Culture of Flushing: A Social and Legal History of Sewage* (University of British Columbia Press, 2007) and *Environmental Law* 3rd ed. (Irwin Law, 2008).

Nicholas Blomley is Professor of Geography at Simon Fraser University. He has a long standing interest in property, both public and communal, and private. He is the author of *Unsettling the City: Urban Land and the Politics of Property* (Routledge, 2004) and *Rights of Passage: Sidewalks and the Regulation of Public Flow* (Routledge, 2011).

Angela Cameron received her LLB from Dalhousie University in 1998, and was admitted to the Nova Scotia Bar in 1999. She received her LLM from the University of British Columbia in 2003 and her Doctorate from the University of Victoria in 2012. She was an SSHRC Doctoral Fellow, and a President's Research Scholar at the University of Victoria. Professor Cameron's research is generally in the area of social justice, with a particular focus on the equality interests of women. Professor Cameron's research areas include criminal law, restorative justice, property law, reproductive technologies law, family law, legal theory, sociological approaches to law, and human rights law. She is the administrator of Bloggingforequality.ca.

Angela Chaisson is a graduate of the University of Ottawa's faculty of law, where she focused on social justice and equality issues. She is a feminist lawyer practicing criminal, constitutional, and administrative law in Toronto.

Patricia Farnese, BA (Guelph), LLB (Saskatchewan), LLM (Arkansas), is an Assistant Professor of Law at the University of Saskatchewan where she teaches Property, Agriculture, and Wildlife Law. She also teaches courses related to resource management in the Indigenous Peoples Resource Management Program of the College of Agriculture and Bioresources. Professor Farnese clerked with the Saskatchewan Court of Appeal and is a member of the Saskatchewan bar. Currently, she serves as the vice-Chair of the Practitioner's Staff Appeals Tribunal for Saskatchewan.

Philip Girard is University Research Professor and Professor of Law, History and Canadian Studies at Dalhousie University, where he is based at the Schulich School of Law. He has published widely on Canadian and comparative legal history. His biography *Bora Laskin: Bringing Law to Life* (Osgoode Society, 2005) received the Chalmers Award for the best book published in Ontario history in that year, while his *Lawyers and Legal Culture in British North America: Beamish Murdoch of Halifax* (Osgoode Society, 2011) received the Clio Atlantic award from the Canadian Historical Association in 2012. He is the associate editor of the Osgoode Society for Canadian Legal History.

Vanessa Gruben, BScH (Queen's), LLB (Ottawa), LLM (Columbia) is an Assistant Professor at the Faculty of Law, University of Ottawa. Prior to joining the Faculty of Law, she clerked for Justice Michel Bastarache at the Supreme Court of Canada and practiced in the litigation department of a national law firm. Professor Gruben teaches in the areas of property law, family law, and health law and policy. Her research interests include: the intersection between family law and health law, women's health, reproductive health law, feminist legal theory and the protection of language rights in Canada.

Douglas C. Harris (PhD) is the Nathan T. Nemetz Chair in Legal History and the Associate Dean Graduate Studies & Research in the Faculty of Law at the University of British Columbia. He writes and teaches in the areas of property law, legal history, fisheries law, and Aboriginal law. Professor Harris is the author of *Fish, Law, and Colonialism: The Legal Capture of Salmon in British Columbia* (University of Toronto Press, 2001) and *Land-*

ing Native Fisheries: Indian Reserves and Fishing Rights in British Columbia, 1849-1925 (University of British Columbia Press, 2008), which received the John T. Saywell Prize for Canadian Constitutional Legal History in 2011. He is also a co-author of the leading property law casebook in Canada, *A Property Law Reader: Cases, Questions, Commentary* (Carswell, 2012), now in its third edition.

Eran Kaplinsky teaches in the areas of property law and planning law. He holds a Bachelor of Laws from Tel Aviv University, a Master of Laws from the University of Toronto, and a Doctor of Juridical Science from the University of Toronto. Professor Kaplinsky is also a research affiliate of the City-Region Studies Centre. His teaching and research interests include land use planning and regulation, law and economics, municipal law, and property law.

C. Ian Kyer is an historian (PhD in Medieval History from the University of Toronto) turned lawyer. He is counsel to Fasken Martineau, where he formerly headed the Technology & Intellectual Property group. An expert in information technology law, he has long been listed by Lexpert as one of Canada's top 500 lawyers. He has also written a history of legal education in Ontario, *The Fiercest Debate* (Osgoode Society, 1987), and has recently completed a history of the Faskens firm to be published by Irwin Law in conjunction with the Osgoode Society.

Frank Luce is a labour lawyer who currently teaches in the labour studies programme at York University. As the former coordinator of The Harriet Tubman Institute, he was the main organizer of the Dan Hill Symposium which gave rise to the paper co-authored with Karen Schucher on *Bell v. McKay*. His current research interests are focused on contemporary labour history in Brazil and Angola.

Jeremy Martin studied English literature and history prior to entering law, receiving both his MA (English) and JD from the University of Toronto. He currently carries on a litigation practice at Cassels Brock & Blackwell, LLP in Toronto. In 2011 he was awarded the Osgoode Society Book Prize for his work in Anglo-Canadian legal history. He is a co-author of the *Ontario Annual Review of Civil Practice* (Carswell) and publishes primarily in the areas of legal history and civil procedure.

Margaret E. McCallum is a Professor in the Faculty of Law at the University of New Brunswick. She currently teaches property law, natural resources law, law and social justice, trusts, and fiduciary obligations. Her publications include *Lady Landlords of Prince Edward Island: Imperial Dreams and the Defence of Property* (McGill-Queen's University Press, 2008), co-authored with Dr. Rusty Bittermann; *Synthesis: Legal Reading, Reasoning, and Writing in Canada* (CCH, 2012), the 3rd Canadian edition of a text originally written by Deborah Schmedemann and Christina L. Kunz; and *Introduction to Real Property Law* (LexisNexis, 2012), the 6th edition of a text originally written by the late Alan Sinclair.

Mary Jane Mossman is Professor of Law at Osgoode Hall Law School and a University Professor at York University. She teaches Property Law and Family Law, and writes in these areas, as well as in relation to access to justice and the history of women in law. She is co-author of *Property Law: Cases and Materials* 2nd ed. (Emond-Montgomery, 2004); *Families and the Law* (Captus Press, 2012), and *The First Women Lawyers: A Comparative Study of Gender, Law and the Legal Professions* (Hart Publishing, 2006). She is currently researching the history of women lawyers in Ontario 1890s to 1970s for the Osgoode Society.

James Muir is an assistant professor of History and Law at the University of Alberta. He works on Canadian legal and labour history, with publications on 18th- and 19th-century Nova Scotia, 20th-century Manitoba and Alberta and the practice of teaching legal history.

Jim Phillips is Professor of Law, History and Criminology at the University of Toronto, and editor-in-chief of the Osgoode Society for Canadian Legal History. He has co-edited four volumes of the Osgoode Society for Canadian Legal History's Essays in the History of Canadian Law and, with Philip Girard, a volume on the history of Canada's oldest surviving superior common law court, *The Supreme Court of Nova Scotia 1754-2004: From Imperial Bastion to Provincial Oracle* (Osgoode Society, 2004). He has published over fifty articles and book chapters on British imperial history and 18th-century India, on property and charities law, US legal history, and, principally, Canadian legal history. He is also the author, with Rosemary Gartner, of *Murdering Holiness: The Trials of Franz Creffield and George Mitchell* (University of British Columbia Press, 2003).

Eric H. Reiter is Associate Professor in the Department of History, Concordia University, and a member of the Barreau du Québec. His publications have recently appeared in the *Indigenous Law Journal*, the *Canadian Bar Review*, and the *Journal of Civil Law Studies*. He is currently working on a book on social and legal ideas of honour and other intangible interests in 19th- and 20th-century Quebec.

Karen Schucher is a former Toronto labour and human rights lawyer, now teaching in the Paralegal and Law Clerk Programmes at Humber College. She is also a PhD candidate at Osgoode Hall Law School, working on Canadian human rights legal history. Karen has been involved in pro bono human rights litigation and social activism, and has published several articles on Canadian human rights law.

Eric Tucker is a Professor of Law at Osgoode Hall Law School, York University. He is the author of *Administering Danger in the Workplace: The Law and Politics of Occupational Health and Safety Regulation in Ontario, 1850-1914* (University of Toronto Press, 1990) and co-author of *Labour Before the Law: Workers' Collective Action and the Canadian State, 1900-1948* (Oxford University Press, 2001) and *Self-Employed Workers Organize: Law, Policy and Unions* (McGill-Queen's University Press, 2005). He has also edited or co-edited *Working Disasters: The Politics of Recognition and Response* (Baywood, 2006); *Work on Trial: Canadian Labour Law Struggles* (Irwin Law, 2010) and *Constitutional Labour Rights in Canada: Farm Workers and the Fraser Case* (Irwin Law, 2012). He is currently working on a history of regulatory dilemmas in Canadian labour and employment law.

Bruce Ziff is a professor of law at the University of Alberta. He has also taught at the University of Wollongong in Australia, and Osgoode Hall Law School. Professor Ziff has served as a Special Counsel for the Alberta Law Reform Institute and as an advisor on land titles reform in Ukraine. He is a recipient of the AC Rutherford Award for Excellence in Undergraduate Teaching. Professor Ziff's research deals mainly with property and legal history. He is the author of *Principles of Property Law*, 5th ed (Carswell, 2010), and *Unforeseen Legacies: Reuben Wells Leonard and the Leonard Foundation Trust* (Osgoode Society, 2000), and he is a co-editor of *A Property Law Reader* 3rd ed. (Carswell, 2012) and *Borrowed Power: Essays on Cultural Appropriation* (Rutgers University Press, 1997).

Index

PUBLICATIONS OF THE OSGOODE SOCIETY FOR CANADIAN LEGAL HISTORY

2012 R. Blake Brown, *Arming & Disarming: A History of Gun Control in Canada*
Eric Tucker, James Muir & Bruce Ziff, eds, *Property on Trial: Canadian Cases in Context*
Shelley Gavigan, *Hunger, Horses & Government Men: Criminal Law on the Aboriginal Plains, 1870–1905*
Barrington Walker, ed, *The African-Canadian Legal Odyssey: Historical Essays*

2011 Robert J. Sharpe, *The Lazier Murder: Prince Edward County, 1884*
Philip Girard, *Lawyers and Legal Culture in British North America: Beamish Murdoch of Halifax*
John McLaren, *Dewigged, Bothered and Bewildered: British Colonial Judges on Trial*
Lesley Erickson, *Westward Bound: Sex, Violence, the Law and the Making of a Settler Society*

2010 Judy Fudge and Eric Tucker, eds, *Work on Trial: Canadian Labour Law Struggles*
Christopher Moore, *The British Columbia Court of Appeal: The First Hundred Years*
Frederick Vaughan, *Viscount Haldane: The Wicked Step-father of the Canadian Constitution*
Barrington Walker, *Race on Trial: Black Defendants in Ontario's Criminal Courts, 1850–1950*

2009 William Kaplan, *Canadian Maverick: The Life and Times of Ivan C. Rand*
R. Blake Brown, *A Trying Question: The Jury in Nineteenth-Century Canada*
Barry Wright and Susan Binnie, eds, *Canadian State Trials, Volume III: Political Trials and Security Measures, 1840–1914*
Robert J. Sharpe, *The Last Day, the Last Hour: The Currie Libel Trial*

2008 Constance Backhouse, *Carnal Crimes: Sexual Assault Law in Canada, 1900–1975*
Jim Phillips, R. Roy McMurtry & John Saywell, eds, *Essays in the History of Canadian Law, Vol. X: A Tribute to Peter N. Oliver*
Gregory Taylor, *The Law of the Land: Canada's Receptions of the Torrens System*
Hamar Foster, Benjamin Berger & AR Buck, eds, *The Grand Experiment: Law and Legal Culture in British Settler Societies*

2007 Robert Sharpe & Patricia McMahon, *The Persons Case: The Origins and Legacy of the Fight for Legal Personhood*
Lori Chambers, *Misconceptions: Unmarried Motherhood and the Ontario Children of Unmarried Parents Act, 1921–1969*
Jonathan Swainger, ed, *The Alberta Supreme Court at 100: History & Authority*
Martin Friedland, *My Life in Crime and Other Academic Adventures*

2006 Donald Fyson, *Magistrates, Police and People: Everyday Criminal Justice in Quebec and Lower Canada, 1764–1837*

Dale Brawn, *The Court of Queen's Bench of Manitoba 1870–1950: A Biographical History*
R.C.B. Risk, *A History of Canadian Legal Thought: Collected Essays*, edited and introduced by G. Blaine Baker & Jim Phillips
2005 Philip Girard, *Bora Laskin: Bringing Law to Life*
Christopher English, ed, *Essays in the History of Canadian Law, Vol. IX: Two Islands, Newfoundland and Prince Edward Island*
Fred Kaufman, *Searching for Justice: An Autobiography*
2004 John D. Honsberger, *Osgoode Hall: An Illustrated History*
Frederick Vaughan, *Aggressive in Pursuit: The Life of Justice Emmett Hall*
Constance Backhouse & Nancy Backhouse, *The Heiress versus the Establishment: Mrs. Campbell's Campaign for Legal Justice*
Philip Girard, Jim Phillips & Barry Cahill, eds, *The Supreme Court of Nova Scotia,1754–2004: From Imperial Bastion to Provincial Oracle*
2003 Robert Sharpe & Kent Roach, *Brian Dickson: A Judge's Journey*
George Finlayson, *John J. Robinette: Peerless Mentor*
Peter Oliver, *The Conventional Man: The Diaries of Ontario Chief Justice Robert A. Harrison, 1856–1878*
Jerry Bannister, *The Rule of the Admirals: Law, Custom and Naval Government in Newfoundland, 1699–1832*
2002 John T. Saywell, *The Law Makers: Judicial Power and the Shaping of Canadian Federalism*
David Murray, *Colonial Justice: Justice, Morality and Crime in the Niagara District, 1791–1849*
F. Murray Greenwood & Barry Wright, eds, *Canadian State Trials, Volume Two: Rebellion and Invasion in the Canadas, 1837–8*
Patrick Brode, *Courted and Abandoned: Seduction in Canadian Law*
2001 Ellen Anderson, *Judging Bertha Wilson: Law as Large as Life*
Judy Fudge & Eric Tucker, *Labour Before the Law: Collective Action in Canada, 1900–1948*
Laurel Sefton MacDowell, *Renegade Lawyer: The Life of J.L. Cohen*
2000 Barry Cahill, *'The Thousandth Man': A Biography of James McGregor Stewart*
A.B. McKillop, *The Spinster and the Prophet: Florence Deeks, H.G.Wells, and the Mystery of the Purloined Past*
Beverley Boissery & F. Murray Greenwood, *Uncertain Justice: Canadian Women and Capital Punishment*
Bruce Ziff, *Unforeseen Legacies: Reuben Wells Leonard and the Leonard Foundation Trust*
1999 Constance Backhouse, *Colour-Coded: A Legal History of Racism in Canada, 1900 – 1950*
G. Blaine Baker & Jim Phillips, eds, *Essays in the History of Canadian Law, Vol. VIII: In Honour of* R.C.B. *Risk*
Richard W. Pound, *Chief Justice W.R. Jackett: By the Law of the Land*
David Vanek, *Fulfilment: Memoirs of a Criminal Court Judge*

1998 Sidney Harring, *White Man's Law: Native People in Nineteenth-Century Canadian Jurisprudence*
Peter Oliver, *"Terror to Evil-Doers": Prisons and Punishments in Nineteenth-Century Ontario*
1997 James W. St.G. Walker, *"Race", Rights and the Law in the Supreme Court of Canada: Historical Case Studies*
Lori Chambers, *Married Women and Property Law in Victorian Ontario*
Patrick Brode, *Casual Slaughters and Accidental Judgments: Canadian War Crimes and Prosecutions, 1944–1948*
Ian Bushnell, *The Federal Court of Canada: A History, 1875 – 1992*
1996 Carol Wilton, ed, *Essays in the History of Canadian Law, Vol. VII: Inside the Law – Canadian Law Firms in Historical Perspective*
William Kaplan, *Bad Judgment: The Case of Mr. Justice Leo A. Landreville*
Murray Greenwood & Barry Wright, eds, *Canadian State Trials, Volume I: Law, Politics and Security Measures, 1608–1837*
1995 David Williams, *Just Lawyers: Seven Portraits*
Hamar Foster & John McLaren, eds, *Essays in the History of Canadian Law, Vol. VI: British Columbia and the Yukon*
W.H. Morrow, ed, *Northern Justice: The Memoirs of Mr.Justice William G. Morrow*
Beverley Boissery, *A Deep Sense of Wrong: The Treason, Trials and Transportation to New South Wales of Lower Canadian Rebels after the 1838 Rebellion*
1994 Patrick Boyer, *A Passion for Justice: The Legacy of James Chalmers McRuer*
Charles Pullen, *The Life and Times of Arthur Maloney: The Last of the Tribunes*
Jim Phillips, Tina Loo, & Susan Lewthwaite, eds, *Essays in the History of Canadian Law, Vol. V: Crime and Criminal Justice*
Brian Young, *The Politics of Codification: The Lower Canadian Civil Code of 1866*
1993 Greg Marquis, *Policing Canada's Century: A History of the Canadian Association of Chiefs of Police*
Murray Greenwood, *Legacies of Fear: Law and Politics in Quebec in the Era of the French Revolution*
1992 Brendan O'Brien, *Speedy Justice: The Tragic Last Voyage of His Majesty's Vessel Speedy*
Robert Fraser, ed, *Provincial Justice: Upper Canadian Legal Portraits from the Dictionary of Canadian Biography*
1991 Constance Backhouse, *Petticoats and Prejudice: Women and Law in Nineteenth-Century Canada*
1990 Philip Girard & Jim Phillips, eds, *Essays in the History of Canadian Law, Vol. III: Nova Scotia*
Carol Wilton, ed, *Essays in the History of Canadian Law,Vol. IV: Beyond the Law - Lawyers and Business in Canada 1830–1930*
1989 Desmond Brown, *The Genesis of the Canadian Criminal Code of 1892*
Patrick Brode, *The Odyssey of John Anderson*
1988 Robert Sharpe, *The Last Day, the Last Hour: The Currie Libel Trial*
John D. Arnup, *Middleton: The Beloved Judge*

1987 C. Ian Kyer & Jerome Bickenbach, *The Fiercest Debate: Cecil A. Wright, the Benchers and Legal Education in Ontario, 1923–1957*

1986 Paul Romney, *Mr. Attorney: The Attorney General for Ontario in Court, Cabinet and Legislature, 1791–1899*

Martin Friedland, *The Case of Valentine Shortis: A True Story of Crime and Politics in Canada*

1985 James Snell and Frederick Vaughan, *The Supreme Court of Canada: History of the Institution*

1984 Patrick Brode, *Sir John Beverley Robinson: Bone and Sinew of the Compact*

David Williams, *Duff: A Life in the Law*

1983 David H. Flaherty, ed, *Essays in the History of Canadian Law, Vol. II*

1982 Marion MacRae and Anthony Adamson, *Cornerstones of Order: Courthouses and Town Halls of Ontario, 1784–1914*

1981 David H. Flaherty, ed, *Essays in the History of Canadian Law, Vol.I*

Printed and bound by CPI Group (UK) Ltd, Croydon, CR0 4YY

15/09/2026

14962401-0007